JMK in his Treasury office the afternoon before his departure to
negotiate the American Loan: Associated Press

A 'SECOND EDITION' OF *THE GENERAL THEORY*

Volume 1

Keynes had intended to write 'footnotes' to *The General Theory* which would take account of the criticisms made and allow him to develop and refine his ideas further. However, a number of factors combined to prevent him from doing so before his death in 1946.

Just as other composers have 'finished' Schubert's Eighth Symphony, these two volumes of *A 'Second Edition'* contain the work of a representative range of Keynes scholars who have written the 'footnotes' that Keynes never did.

This first volume follows the structure of the original, offers attempts to clarify difficult passages and suggests ways in which Keynes might have revised his theory in the light of his own subsequent work. Some of the contributors have used their own words to outline what they think Keynes would have written in 1938 or 1939. Others have written at least part of their essays in the style of J.M. Keynes, resulting in some fascinating 'messages' from beyond the grave. In addition, the contributors discuss the work they have done in the post-war period on particular issues raised in *The General Theory*.

G.C. Harcourt is Reader in the History of Economic Theory (*ad hominem*) at the University of Cambridge, a Fellow of Jesus College, Cambridge, and Professor Emeritus of the University of Adelaide. He has written and/or edited 16 books and numerous articles on theoretical, applied and policy topics, including specific writings on the economics of Keynes. **P.A. Riach** is Professor and Head of Economics at De Montfort University. His research interests are in the areas of wages, employment and income distribution.

A 'SECOND EDITION' OF
THE GENERAL THEORY

Volume 1

Edited by G.C. Harcourt and P.A. Riach

London and New York

First published 1997
by Routledge
2 Park Square, Milton Park, Abingdon, Oxon, OX14 4RN

Simultaneously published in the USA and Canada
by Routledge
270 Madison Ave, New York NY 10016

Transferred to Digital Printing 2006

Typeset in Garamond by J&L Composition Ltd, Filey, North Yorkshire

British Library Cataloguing in Publication Data
A catalogue record for this book is available from the British Library

Library of Congress Cataloging in Publication Data
A 'second edition' of The general theory/edited by G.C. Harcourt and P.A. Riach.
p.   cm.
Includes bibliographical references and index.
1. Keynesian economics. [1. Keynes, John Maynard, 1883–1946. General theory
of employment, interest and money.] I. Harcourt, Geoffrey Colin. II. Riach,
Peter Andrew. III. Keynes, John Maynard, 1883–1946. General theory of
employment, interest and money.
HB99.7.S43   1996
330.15'6–dc20   96–3293

ISBN 0–415–08215–3 (set)
ISBN10: 0–415–14942–8 (hbk)
ISBN10: 0–415–40699–4 (pbk)

ISBN13: 978–0–415–14942–6 (hbk)
ISBN13: 978–0–415–40699–4 (pbk)

Printed and bound by CPI Antony Rowe, Eastbourne

CONTENTS

CONTENTS

FIGURES AND TABLES

FIGURES

TABLES

CONTRIBUTORS TO VOLUME 1

Ingo Barens, Bergische Universität, Wuppertal, Germany
Wylie Bradford, Fitzwilliam College, Cambridge, UK
J.F. Brothwell, Univerity of Leeds, UK
Volker Caspari, Technische Hochschule, Darmstadt, Germany
Victoria Chick, University College London, UK
Robert W. Clower, University of South Carolina, USA
John Cornwall, Dalhousie University, Halifax, Nova Scotia, Canada
William Darity, Jr, University of North Carolina at Chapel Hill, USA
Robert Eisner, Northwestern University, Illinois, USA
R.M. Goodwin, University of Siena, Italy
G.C. Harcourt, University of Cambridge, UK
Kevin D. Hoover, University of California, Davis, USA
Peter Howitt, Ohio State University, USA
Marc Jarsulic, University of Notre Dame, Indiana, USA
J.E. King, La Trobe University, Victoria, Australia
J.A. Kregel, University of Bologna, Italy
M.S. Lawlor, Wake Forest University, North Carolina, USA
Robin Marris, Lingard House, London/Professor Emeritus, University of
    London, UK
Luigi L. Pasinetti, Universita Cattolica del Sacre Cuore, Milan, Italy
P.A. Riach, De Montfort University, Milton Keynes, UK
Colin Rogers, University of Adelaide, Australia
T.K. Rymes, Carleton University, Ottawa, Canada
Nina Shapiro, Franklin and Marshall College, Lancaster, Pennsylvania,
    USA
Robert Skidelsky, University of Warwick, UK
Jim Thomas, London School of Economics, UK
Christopher Torr, University of South Africa, Pretoria, SA
Warren Young, Bar-Ilan University, Israel

CONTRIBUTORS TO VOLUME 2

A.J. Brown, University of Leeds, UK
John Coates, New York
Paul Davidson, University of Tennessee, Knoxville, USA
John B. Davis, Marquette University, Milwaukee, Wisconsin, USA
Sheila C. Dow, University of Stirling, UK
Bill Gerrard, University of Leeds, UK
Myron J. Gordon, University of Toronto, Canada
Peter Kriesler, University of New South Wales, Australia
Bruce Littleboy, University of Queensland, Australia
Rod O'Donnell, Macquarie University, Australia
Brian Reddaway, University of Cambridge, UK
Jochen Runde, Girton College, Cambridge, UK
Claudio Sardoni, University of Rome, Italy
James Tobin, Yale University, USA
Alessandro Vercelli, University of Siena, Italy

PREFACE

The preparation of this work has involved the willing co-operation and support of a large number of people and we, the editors, are extremely grateful to them all. Obviously, the authors of the chapters must take pride of place. We thank them all for joining us and for making the project an enjoyable and, we hope, rewarding one for them as well as us. In addition, we would like to thank most sincerely Alan Jarvis for his great encouragement, tolerance and enthusiasm for the project since we first approached him about Routledge publishing the volume; Allan Wailoo for his expert preparation of the bibliography; Nacirah Lutton for her unfailing cheerfulness and competence in typing the introduction and handling much of the correspondence which inevitably comes with a far-flung project such as this; Samantha Watson, who also handled a lot of correspondence, and Catherine Carthy for running off copies of the chapters whenever they were needed.

G.C. HARCOURT
Cambridge

P.A. RIACH
Milton Keynes

NOTE ON ABBREVIATIONS

References in the text to the original edition of *The General Theory of Employment, Interest and Money* (1936, London: Macmillan) are abbreviated to *G.T.* plus the relevant page number. Similarly, references to *The Collected Writings of John Maynard Keynes*, ed. D.E. Moggridge, vols I–XXX (1971–89, London: Macmillan), are abbreviated to *C.W.* plus the volume and page numbers.

INTRODUCTION[1]

This project arose from a conversation a few years ago between the two editors (G.C. Harcourt and P.A. Riach). P.A.R. mentioned how musical compositions which are unfinished because of the death of their composers sometimes are 'finished' by other people – he cited the composer Frank Merrick, who attempted to complete Schubert's unfinished Eighth Symphony. Maynard Keynes told Ralph Hawtrey in a letter of 31 August 1936 (*Collected Writings of John Maynard Keynes* (hereafter abbreviated to *C.W.*), XIV: 47) that he was 'thinking of producing in the course of the next year or so what might be called *footnotes* to' *The General Theory*, once he had absorbed the criticisms that had arisen and he himself had become more familiar with his new self.[2] But his severe heart attack in early 1937, the Second World War and his death on Easter Morning 1946 meant that he never did write those footnotes.[3]

So the idea for these volumes materialized: we would ask a wide range of Keynes scholars, varying all the way from some of Keynes's contemporaries to younger scholars beginning to make their mark through their interpretations and extensions of Keynes's ideas, to write essays of 6,000 words or so which would have two broad characteristics:

1 accounts, based on whatever evidence was available and whatever speculation seemed reasonable, of what they thought Keynes would have written in, say, 1938 or 1939; and
2 outlines of what they had done in the post-war period on particular aspects of issues which were first raised in *The General Theory*, and of why they had done what they did.

We have thus assembled here thirty-nine chapters, most of which match the chapters in the original books of *The General Theory*. The remainder relate to extensions and developments since the publication of *The General Theory* which come under the rubric of the economics of Keynes. Some of the contributors interpreted their task as to write the first part of their essays in the form of J.M. Keynes and so we have received some fascinating 'messages' from beyond the grave through such eminent mediums as, in order of appearance, John Brothwell, Bob Clower, Chris Torr, Victoria Chick, Michael Lawlor, Jan Kregel, John King, Robert Skidelsky and James Tobin.

There are some notable absences from the list of contributors. Sometimes this was because the scholars concerned declined (politely, even regretfully) to join in; sometimes because, having initially done so, subsequent unforeseen happenings led to their withdrawal. In particular a chap called Clinton (W.) threw a spanner in our works by putting Alan Blinder and Joe Stiglitz on his Council of Economic Advisors (Blinder subsequently ceased to be a real man and became a money man by going to the Federal Reserve Board). Jim Thomas (consumption) and Myron Gordon (credit rationing) more than ably filled the considerable voids which the withdrawal of Blinder and Stiglitz opened up. Bob Solow thought the project 'a neat idea' but, with his co-author Frank Hahn, declined to contribute because of the pressure of finishing off their joint 'old man of the sea' (Hahn and Solow 1996). Edward Amadeo withdrew at a late stage because of his demanding role in the recent election of a President of Brazil. Alas, the considerable opportunity cost involved brought neither him nor us any corresponding benefit, because his candidate lost. It would probably be invidious to name further obvious omissions. We do, however, want to pay a tribute to two illustrious Keynesian scholars and wonderful human beings who were on the original list. Lorie Tarshis died in October 1993 before his chapter could be written, and his former pupil, Paul Wells, became so tragically and permanently ill that his chapter will never be written either.[4] And, sadly, Richard Goodwin, who was much loved and admired in the profession, died in Siena on 6 August 1996 while the volumes were at proof stage. Thankfully, we have his chapter (10) as a memorial.

As editors we did perhaps show some foresight at the time we planned the project in the early 1990s for it is now clear that we have reached an appropriate conjuncture in history to put Keynes and his contributions back on the agenda, sixty years on from the original publication of *The General Theory*. We have tried to do so, not in a slavish or uncritical manner, but in order to learn again, or possibly for the first time, what his insights and approach to economic theory and policy were, and what the development of his ideas by those who have been influenced by him in a fundamental way has to say about the horrendous economic problems of the world today.

It is true that Keynes said in the original preface that *The General Theory* was primarily a work of theory addressed to his fellow economists; that while the public could eavesdrop, they were not at this stage the primary audience. Nor was the argument of *The General Theory* primarily concerned with policy implications, though Keynes was such an innovative and enthusiastic man of affairs that he could not help peppering the text with ingenious asides and policy suggestions. Now, sixty years on, we hope we may widen the audience so as to include not only economists and students of economics but also that broader public of concerned citizens. Most of the chapters have been written for such an audience. Moreover, because Keynes himself seldom if ever theorized without policy in mind, the same spirit permeates many of the contributions to the present volume.

Edward Amadeo's contribution was to have been on the shifts in Keynes's thought as he moved from the *Tract* to the *Treatise on Money* to *The General Theory*. Though his contribution is dearly missed, we are lucky in that he has written a splendid book on this theme (Amadeo 1989), and, more recently, a succinct account of his interpretations (Amadeo 1994). For most of the 1920s Keynes saw himself as working within the Marshallian tradition and approach, though he found himself rebelling increasingly against certain aspects of it. In this rebellion he was, by the end of the 1920s and especially when writing *The General Theory*, most influenced by Richard Kahn. Kahn's influence was crucial because he had always been sceptical about, indeed hostile to, the quantity theory as a causal explanation of the general price level, and he had done original work on the short period as a subject appropriate for study in its own right in his 1929 fellowship dissertation (Kahn 1929). By contrast, Dennis Robertson near the end of the writing of the *Treatise on Money* was much more accommodating of Marshall's views, an attitude he kept till the end of his life. This is perhaps most clearly seen in his three volumes of *Principles* (Robertson 1957–9) which are based on his lectures while the holder of Marshall's Chair, and were published after he retired from it (see Harcourt 1992).

Keynes's change of heart was associated with a move from emphasis on the long period to emphasis on the short period, and from keeping real and monetary matters separate, at least in a long-period sense, to integrating them from the start of an analysis of a monetary production economy.[5] To reach this second position Keynes needed to liberate himself from the hold which the Quantity Theory of Money and Say's Law (in its neoclassical rather than its classical form) had on the Marshallian system *as Keynes interpreted it* and so on Keynes's own thought.

Not only was there a change of 'vision' involved, there was also a change of method. In Marshall's system the long period was the core and full equilibrium was concerned with both stocks and flows. In Marshallian long-period equilibrium, both the stock of capital goods and the supply of labour were at optimum levels for a given initial situation and set of conditions. Long-period normal equilibrium prices had as components the normal rate of profits and the long-period normal rate of wages for each industry and, by extension, for the economy as a whole. Keynes looked at economic processes in this manner in the *Treatise on Money*, examining the determination of the price of consumption goods, and of the price level of output as a whole, and so, implicitly, of the price of investment goods, both in the short periods on the way to the long period, and in the long-period position itself. This was the role of the fundamental equations which Keynes thought of as a more illuminating way of restating the Quantity Theory. They enabled him to move from the setting of prices in each short period to an analysis of their impact on profits and so on movements in employment, output and accumulation. Kahn, however, interpreted the analysis as an *alternative* theory of sectoral price levels, and the general price level to that of the Quantity Theory.

Because of the Marshallian distinction between the real and the monetary, Keynes felt that there should not be over-much emphasis on the analysis of short-period fluctuations in output and employment in a theory of money. Yet he was at the same time preoccupied with policies directed to the solution of prolonged unemployment, even in the 1920s, and, in order to tackle them, he adapted the system on which he had been brought up. But it was Marshallian analysis, in that inflations and deflations were seen to be associated with gaps between the natural rate of interest determined by the real factors of productivity and thrift and the monetary rate of interest set by the monetary authorities. The other role of the natural rate of interest was to determine the composition of the level of output associated with full employment in the labour market.

As we know, all this was to change radically once Keynes had liberated himself from the Quantity Theory and Say's Law (via the co-operative, neutral and entrepreneur economy models, which sadly did not survive in the final draft of *The General Theory*: see Barens 1990; Tarshis 1989) and had incorporated Kahn's 1931 multiplier concept into his own discussion of the consumption function. Making the money rate of interest rule the roost, defining the marginal efficiency of capital and the investment function, and replacing the Quantity Theory by Marshall's short-period pricing theory, usually with price equal to marginal cost (both suitably aggregated to economy-wide levels) completed the story. His method of analysis was the determination, for the most part, of short-period, flow equilibrium values, with long-period stocks and flows vanishing either into the background (except in Chapter 17) or altogether.[6]

BOOK I INTRODUCTION

Keynes rather disarmingly entitled the first 'book' of his *General Theory* 'Introduction'. It contains three chapters: the one-page Chapter 1, 'The General Theory', Chapter 2, 'The Postulates of the Classical Economics' and Chapter 3, 'The Principle of Effective Demand'. As we know with hindsight, Chapter 2 has been the major chapter most criticized. The received view is that it is unsatisfactory, a view to which Keynes himself was coming. Thus, Keynes wrote: 'Chapter 2 . . . is the portion of my book which most needs to be revised' (1939c: 40, n. 1). In the present volume the chapters by John Brothwell (1), William Darity and Warren Young (2) and Robin Marris (4) all relate to the difficulties and complexities of Chapter 2, some exclusively, the others as part of wide-ranging discussions. Robert Clower's and Luigi Pasinetti's chapters (3, 6) are mainly concerned with the issues of Chapter 3.

Brothwell takes up the basic theme of Keynes's contribution that employment and the real wage are determined in the product market[7] and that Keynes's exposition in Chapter 2 in terms of the classical theory of the labour market – the two classical postulates, one relating to the demand for labour, the other to its supply – obscured the vital role of effective demand. Had Keynes first expounded his theory of effective demand, then the role of expectations about an uncertain future and the crucial role of money in the determination of the rate of interest, and its role, in turn, in the determination of investment, the most vital and volatile component of aggregate demand, the contrast between the old and the new world view would have stood out clearly. In particular, he would have had to bring into his exposition the distinction between the co-operative and neutral economies, on the one hand, and the entrepreneur economy, on the other. He could then have pointed out that the old view used the first two models (implicitly), that he, Keynes, used the third model to provide the second view, and that involuntary (demand deficient) unemployment could be shown not to exist in the first view as it clearly would exist in the second. Finally, Brothwell argues that, while Keynes went a long way towards discarding the old ideas, he did not go far enough. In particular, he was reluctant to take on fully the link between oligopolistic competitive behaviour and his macroeconomic systemic behaviour, as opposed to the complementary link between perfect competition and marginal productivity in the classical real wage economy, so leaving sufficient grounds for a neoclassical revival which jeopardized his revolution – never were truer words spoken. Marris makes the link in his chapter (4) (which both summarizes and expands the work he has been doing for forty years or more, including his 1991 book and his review article in the *Economic Journal* in 1992 of Richard Kahn's 1929 dissertation).

These chapters and the chapter by Darity and Young (2) may prompt the thought: what *is* all the fuss about? If causation runs from the product market to the labour market, if activity in the product market is determined by consumption demand (itself coming from the consumption function) and investment (itself greatly affected by uncertain knowledge about an uncertain future as well by the cost and availability of finance and existing capacity) and if the vital decisions in our sorts of societies are made by people who want to make money profits rather than ensure jobs for their workers, why *should* anyone be surprised that the natural resting places of these economies do not imply full employment of labour, and therefore that involuntary unemployment is a recurring characteristic of them? On this Darity and Young are succinct and to the point. Keynes was not the economist of wage or price inflexibility, or disequilibrium, but of insufficient aggregate demand. Whatever wages were doing when there was unemployment ceased to be of major relevance – it is the elasticity (or not) of aggregate employment with respect to an increase in aggregate demand which is the key point. They document this by reference to *The General Theory* itself and to letters, lectures and articles written after its publication. To them, New Keynesianism is as much a misnomer as the arguments contained under its rubric are not those of Keynes – a point which Peter Howitt, a former New Keynesian, now 'reformed', courageously and convincingly makes in his chapter (15), 'Expectations and Uncertainty in Contemporary Keynesian Models'.

Robin Marris argues that the weakness of *The General Theory* is not to be found in Keynes's analysis of the labour market but in his analysis of the product market. Keynes gives the impression (which was successful in the short run but discouraging to the cause in the long run) that his theory was independent of the particular structure of the product market, though most of his analysis in *The General Theory* itself does imply pure or free competition (of a realistic Marshallian sort rather than the very refined notions of modern economics). Keynes seems to have done this as much for ease of exposition as for any reason of principle. He took the degree of competition as one of his givens (*The General Theory* (hereafter abbreviated to *G.T.*) 245) and cheerfully took on board the findings of Dunlop, Kalecki and Tarshis in his 1939 *Economic Journal* article (Keynes 1939c). Marris argues that this is unacceptable, that Keynes's results cannot, in the main, be obtained when perfect competition in a *general* sense is assumed to hold in the product market. Whereas if we follow Marris's lead and adopt imperfect polipoly – the term Marris uses 'for the type of large-group imperfect or non-perfect competition' – as our microeconomic foundations, we get robust results at the macroeconomic level which are recognizably Keynesian, indeed are truly the economics of Keynes. He makes a most detailed argument for this position, taking us through a number of variations of his model, variations which have to do with the nature of expectations by entrepreneurs, his market-makers in stocks, wage-earners and consumers generally. He contrasts the results from his models with those obtained by assuming perfect competition as the microeconomic foundations. He concludes his chapter by outlining the main changes his approach would make to the structure of a second edition of *The General Theory*.

There is no doubt that Marris makes a strong and, we expect for many, a persuasive case for his point of view, especially for paths for future research. Nevertheless, we should like to enter a mild defence of Keynes's procedure in a pioneering work. It was essential for him to establish that, *however* business people formed expectations as to what their sales would be

— whether they had in mind expected prices with quantity then determined by those prices equalling their marginal costs, or levels of sales at prices for which they were responsible and hoped they got the quantities correct — there would be at any moment of time a determinate *total* of expected sales in the economy which, given the conditions Keynes assumed — a given stock of capital goods, supply of different labour skills and so on — would be translated into a determinate level of employment and production. This production in turn would create an equivalent level of income which through consumption expenditure and predetermined planned investment expenditure would determine whether the expectations of prices or quantities or sales were correct. *If* they were, the economy would be at the point of effective demand, a rest state until the underlying conditions changed (which, because this is a short-period analysis, they soon would). If the expectations were not met, Keynes seems to have thought that plausible stories could be told *for all cases* (here, of course, Marris disagrees with him) whereby the economy would give out signals which would lead it towards the point of effective demand, provided that the underlying determinants of the aggregate demand and aggregate supply (?) schedules were *not* affected by the non-fulfilment of the original expectations. Marris's chapter is a thorough discussion of *all* these possibilities and his imperfect competition model is one of great originality *and* power. Moreover, whatever may be said for Keynes's procedure from an historical point of view, there is no doubt that Marris's approach is the correct way forward *now*, for it captures essential features of the modern world in a particularly illuminating manner.[8]

Thus, in his revision of the structure of *The General Theory*, Marris proposes to scrap Chapter 21, 'The Theory of Prices', and, much earlier on, have his theory of price-setting expounded as the simple, most plausible way of modelling price formation in macroeconomic theory. In doing so, he not only emphasizes his own approach as the proper way forward but reflects his shock and delight, as set out in his 1991 book, at being introduced to the similar approach taken by Kalecki in his 1936 review of *The General Theory* by Ferdinando Targetti and Boguslawa Kinda-Hass, who translated Kalecki's review into English. (The translation was published in the December 1982 issue of *Australian Economic Papers*.)[9]

Nina Shapiro has written a most thoughtful essay (5) on imperfect competition and Keynes. In an unassuming manner she draws mostly on Keynes's own writings to argue the case that it is not perfect or imperfect competition *as such* which is relevant for his results but, rather, the implications of flexibility in prices and wages for the overall workings of the economic system. Hence we have Keynes's assumption that the degree of competition may be taken as given (*G.T.* 245) because, in his view, it is not of great (indeed, of any) relevance for the theory of effective demand. The latter in turn has its roots in the impact of uncertainty on the crucial decisions relating to the accumulation of capital goods and the holding of money, which are the real sources of sustained lapses from full employment in an unregulated capitalist economy. This is especially true of investment decisions which of necessity take in *expectations* of the long term – the expected lives of the assets concerned and, here, flexibility or otherwise of prices – is relevant only in so far as it bears on the subsequent realization or not of the expectations held at the time the investments are undertaken.

This leads Shapiro to contrast the Walrasian view of decision-making, where nothing happens until all decisions have been reconciled by the auctioneer, and the real life *processes* spread out over time which Keynes analyses. They necessarily imply that decisions have to be taken even though in retrospect they may be seen to have been mistaken or misguided. Shapiro ventures the empirical judgement that a world characterized by imperfect competition *may* result in a higher level of activity on average than one characterized by perfect competition because there would be less fluctuations in prices in the first and so less *adverse* feedbacks on two key determinants of the system: the marginal efficiency of capital and liquidity preference functions. But in both worlds it is quite possible, indeed it is inevitable, to have substantial and sustained lapses from full employment. The more flexible prices of a perfect competition world, as seen by Keynes with his emphasis on ongoing processes, and the desire by the key decision-makers to make *money* profits could make the systemic performance even worse than the, admittedly imperfect, performance of a world dominated by imperfectly competitive market structures.

Of course, Nina Shapiro's views are partly at odds with those of Robin Marris, but both are extremely serious attempts to come to grips with the hard problems that have beset Keynes's scholars and analysts of real world behaviour since the publication of *The General Theory*.

We come now to Chapter 3, 'The Principle of Effective Demand'. Robert Clower (3) rewrites it as he thinks Keynes would have (up to 1946) so as to make crystal clear the outlines of the new system as Keynes saw them – in his own words, in fact. Clower next sets the scene by suggesting that Keynes was more preoccupied with problems of existence than with those of stability, in particular, the existence of a rest state with unemployment. He then examines the Marshallian base of Keynes's system. He argues that it grew straight out of Marshall's partial equilibrium demand and supply analysis with quantity leading to price rather than price leading to quantity, as in Walras, whom Clower nevertheless identifies as belonging, when Keynes was learning his trade, to the same tradition as Marshall. Clower then works through various ways in which Keynes has been interpreted, for example by Hansen, Samuelson (and, implicitly, Harcourt, Karmel and Wallace 1967), usually in terms of the Keynesian cross, relating their analyses back to Marshall's models. In the process Clower rather 'does a Marshall on Keynes', that is to say, not so much taking literally what exactly

Keynes wrote but instead interpreting him so as to mean what Clower argues he needed to say and mean: for example, about Say's Law, product market clearing and labour market clearing. Finally, Clower quotes from Chapter 18 the passage which other commentators have taken to be evidence for a long-period interpretation of *The General Theory*:

> In particular, it is an outstanding characteristic of the economic system in which we live that, whilst it is subject to severe fluctuations in respect of output and employment, it is not violently unstable. Indeed it seems capable of remaining in a chronic condition of sub-normal activity for a considerable period without any marked tendency either towards recovery or towards complete collapse.
>
> (*C.W.* VII: 249)

Clower, though, argues that Keynes's vision – as set out by Clower – is the basis for a research programme which, if successful, will constitute a second Keynesian revolution that actually does for economics what Keynes intended to do by publishing the 'first edition' in February 1936. While this is surely inspiring for the present and coming generations, we ought also to examine James Tobin's chapter (25) where he sums up a working lifetime of thinking about and contributing to Keynesian economics following his introduction to (and becoming hooked on) *The General Theory* as a freshman at Harvard in 1936. We ought also to remember Tobin's article on 'Keynesian Models of Recession and Depression' in the May 1975 *American Economic Review*. There, he pointed out that Marshall and Walras differed on the dynamics of adjustment to single-market disequilibrium: Walras assumed that prices responded, by either rising or falling, to excess demand or supply respectively at a given price while Marshall had quantitites responding when demand prices exceeded or fell short of supply prices at a given quantity. Tobin argued that in *The General Theory* Keynes was Walrasian at this juncture and the Walrasian view leads to instability of equilibrium – a point which Tobin gives Friedman credit for perceiving.

Keynes entitled Chapter 3 'The *Principle* of Effective Demand' (emphasis added), not the *theory*. Luigi Pasinetti has written a chapter (6) of sublime simplicity and fundamental insight about this distinction. As is well known, he has devoted his working life to the creation of a multi-sector growth model which could be used to analyse the major issues with which political economy has been concerned since its outset. In doing so he has distinguished between the fundamental or 'natural' relations of his system, free of specific institutions, and the consequent analysis which may operate on a lower level of abstraction, taking account of institutions, in order to get 'closer' to real world observations and behaviour. Each set of arguments is, of course, complementary to the other.

Pasinetti uses this procedure to discuss the principle of effective demand in *The General Theory*. He argues that Keynes never made completely explicit the first, institution-free account of the principle, though he gave us many hints and clues and with his adaptation of Marshallian tools to take in the concepts of aggregate demand and supply he explicitly determined the *point* of effective demand.[10]

To get to the most fundamental level of analysis, Pasinetti explains how the 45° line, which, he argues, did so much damage to the development of Keynesian analysis, is nevertheless the appropriate tool for this particular task. Pasinetti therefore banishes the time-honoured aggregate demand function from his analysis and makes the causal relationship run from expected levels of aggregate demand to corresponding levels of produc- tion. The 45° line thus ceases to be a construction line devoid of economic meaning and becomes instead a simple way of expressing the relationship between all *expected* sales in the economy at a moment of time (whether they be sales of consumption goods or investment goods *including* own sales to inventory) and the production of commodities which is generated by and corresponds to them. Provided we assume that business people never produce unless expected sales fit into one of these three categories (and we measure in the same units on both the horizontal and vertical axis), we must end up with a 45° line. Pasinetti's construction is thus the reverse of Say's Law. Finally, Pasinetti extends these ideas to the long-period devel- opment of the economy, pointing out that, for all the added complexities of technical change, relative price changes, international trade, the ultimate saturation of demand for individual products and so on in any industrial system, any institutional mechanism that may be invented for the matching of production to demand will have to rely on the same basic principle of effective demand.

BOOK II DEFINITIONS AND UNITS

As we know from Volume XIII of Keynes's *Collected Writings*, Lorie Tar- shis's memories of Keynes's lectures in the early 1930s (see Harcourt 1993: 73) and from Tom Rymes's notes of a representative student (Rymes 1989a), definitions and discussion of units took up much of the exposition. The discussions themselves are mainly in Book 2 of *The General Theory.* Keynes's decision to change his definitions of saving and investment so as to make them always equal instead of only so in the long-period, full stock- and-flow-equilibrium of the *Treatise on Money,* initially caused much confu- sion. This was especially so because Keynes himself was not clear in his own mind, or at least exposition, about the difference between the equili- brium condition, which requires planned saving and planned investment to match (more generally, desired leakages to match planned injections) and the national accounting identities which hold good for all time but have no causal or even analytical significance. In this section of the 'second edition' there are two chapters, by Wylie Bradford and G.C. Harcourt on units and definitions (7) and Christopher Torr on user cost (8). Torr divides his chapter into two parts; in the first, the authoritative voice of Keynes is to be discerned reacting to his critics and supporters. In Part II the voice of Torr sets out some wise words on the subject.

Bradford and Harcourt argue that from his earliest times Keynes was preoccupied with philosophical questions relating to definitions, units and measurement. He also always had an aversion to the concept of the general price level as used by Cournot and Jevons and increasingly tried to develop analyses which avoided its use. He distinguished between quantities which were and quantities which were not measurable, even in principle, and put the general price level (and subsequently national output and the capital stock) in the second category. Very early on, too, he identified the puzzles that arose from the fact that definitions of things were not independent of the purpose of the particular inquiry in which they played a part.

As far as the general price level was concerned, Keynes argued that shocks to the system must of necessity have different effects on the prices of different commodities and this occurrence vitiates any attempt to give precision to the notion of the general price level and of changes in it. Moreover, he found it impossible to conceive of weights which were independent of the prices to which they were attached in the construction of index numbers.

In *The General Theory* itself he identified three precise units: money, labour and time, for the specific analytical purposes he had in hand. Yet when we go into details we find that neither labour nor time unambiguously meets his own criteria. For example, time is defeated by his own concept of 'funnels' of process; labour depends upon an assumption of the exogeneity of relativities (probably reasonable, it is true, for the short run Keynes had in mind for most of the analysis of *The General Theory*).

Nevertheless, Keynes's emphasis on definitions and precision was taken up by his younger contemporaries. We have Piero Sraffa's stringent criteria for exact theory at Corfu (Sraffa 1961: 305–6). (Sraffa was probably ahead of Keynes, or at least independently arrived at the same views as Keynes on these issues.) Also Joan Robinson's discussion of the measurement and meaning of capital and profits and the conditions under which they could be precisely defined. Again, the distinction between net and gross concepts was vital for the emerging theory of growth in the post-war period – Keynes was able to use the latter for a theory of employment in the short period. Joan Robinson was not always consistent (neither was Keynes!). Nevertheless, her distinction between precision and making do with what we have, roughly matched her distinction between the analysis of differences and of changes, as well as that between levels of abstraction at which doctrinal debates could be carried out, as opposed to descriptive analyses of processes in historical time. These issues determined the units to be used and sometimes there were neither units nor answers to be found. No one ever discussed these issues with greater clarity or simplicity than Richard Kahn.

Torr (8) has written one of the clearest accounts of user cost *ever*. As we noted, in the first part of his chapter he writes as J.M.K.; he explains the price-setting role that user cost has both in individual firms (where it is an essential component of marginal cost) and at the macroeconomic level where, because user costs have affected the level of individual prices, *any* consequent measure of the general price level must also be affected by them, that is, must continue to reflect their influence even though they have been netted out at the level of the economy as a whole. Torr also brings out the important points that we must always distinguish between *measurement* and *determination*, and that some of the worst confusions in the literature on user cost, as well as on saving and investment, arise because this distinction has not been kept clearly in mind.

In the second part of the chapter, Torr points out that, although Keynes's concept of user cost (which in turn came to Keynes from Marshall) is rarely discussed explicitly, the modern work on national accounting in all the macroeconomic texts of the last fifty years or so has taken on board the essential message about the need to avoid double-counting. Unfortunately, the role of user cost in the formation and determination of individual prices and the general price level itself has not received similar treatment.[11]

BOOK III   THE PROPENSITY TO CONSUME

Historically, Keynes's own discovery of the consumption function together with Richard Kahn's conception of the multiplier were crucial events in the development of Keynes's new system (see Barens 1989; Harcourt 1994a). The two together allowed him to make endogenous the process he first set out in the parable of the banana plantation in the *Treatise on Money*. The parable was inadequate because it was only through *ad hoc* exogenous events that the process of decline (or rise) in prices, profits and activity could come to an end. Making precise the notion of the Propensity to Consume schedule also allowed Keynes to clinch (or at least make plausible) the argument that investment led and saving responded in monetary production economies.[12] Finally, the consumption function was probably the most obvious hostage to fortune in the simultaneously dawning age of econometrics.

In his chapter (9), Jim Thomas mentions how relatively unscathed the consumption function emerged from the early reviews of *The General Theory* before he discusses the criticisms of two particular authors, Hans Staehle (1937, 1938, 1939) and Elizabeth Gilboy (1938a, 1938b). The former critic wanted Keynes to put more emphasis on the distribution of income (both personal and functional); the latter looked at cross-section microeconomic studies and challenged Keynes's views on the simplicity and stability of the function. Keynes's response is presented by Thomas in terms of Keynes's views on models as a way of thinking. Keynes especially emphasized the *object* of a model as the segregation of 'the semi-permanent or relatively constant factors from those which are transitory or fluctuating so as to develop a logical way of thinking about the *latter*, and of understanding the time sequences to which they give rise in particular cases' (*C.W.* XIV: 297, emphasis added). This quotation always catches readers (the present editors, anyway) by surprise because, running ahead in their own thoughts, it could be supposed that the segregation of 'the permanent or relatively constant factors' was done in order to enable the analyst to say things about *their* relationships, having set the factors and their relationships free from effects of 'those which are transitory or fluctuating', about which theoretical generalizations were by their very nature not possible. This is of course a very neo-Ricardian response. In fact, what Keynes had done was to set out simply and succinctly the method which Kalecki and Joan Robinson ultimately were to champion in their mature work. (It is not a bad description of path dependence either.)

Thomas reviews the empirical work on the consumption function in the postwar era. He concludes that Keynes would have been out of tune with postwar developments in the discipline, especially in econometrics, even though they have proved to be more robust in the face of his criticisms of Tinbergen (on investment) than Tinbergen's own early work was thought to be (on this, see Chapter 31 by Rod O'Donnell). He points out that Keynes would have welcomed the permanent income and life-cycle hypotheses, not least because he had anticipated them in his own work in *The General Theory*. Thomas also argues that it is unlikely that these two developments will dominate all others because empirical specifications of the consumption function are usually compatible with a number of alternative theories. Hence he is able to conclude that, with broad enough specification, the consumption function remains alive and kicking sixty years on from its introduction to the world in Book III. Whether its own stability and therefore the usefulness of the multiplier for the purposes of forecasting and policy are as robust is a more vexed question. It is at this juncture that Richard Goodwin's contribution is of great relevance.

Goodwin was always lucid and succinct, and his chapter (10) is vintage Goodwin. Not wasting a word, he emphasizes why Keynes's adaptation of Kahn's multiplier was suitable for a decade in which growth and technical progress were virtually absent. Nevertheless, it was a concept less rich than Kahn's – a retrogression – and, in the more dynamic setting of the post-war world, inadequate. Goodwin draws attention to the complicated overlaps of different processes which start at different times and which take different lengths of time to complete. Such overlaps are reflected in the actual levels and rates of change of output and so on at any moment of time; they interrelate with one another in most complicated ways. Goodwin sketches the difficulties which they cause for both policy-makers and econometricians. He then discusses the application of chaos theory to economic explanation, which, he argues, allows us to forgive forecasters and econometricians their past mistakes and, at the same time, make the present generation of 'economists' more modest in their aims. That is to say, they should be glad to explain and so to illuminate and should be more careful about offering policy recommendations.

What is happening on the monetary side of the economy when the multiplier is doing its thing on the real side has long puzzled students and their teachers. Victoria Chick (11) takes us systematically through this issue, emphasizing the importance of considering existing stocks as well as new flows. First, she writes as Keynes; she brings the finance motive into the argument and responds, principally, to Dennis Robertson in stoutly defending liquidity preference against loanable funds, as well as the logical theory of the multiplier. Then she takes an independent approach, not only to make explicit the achievements as well as the muddles in the original debates, but also to throw much light on the modern debates on the same issues. (A series of exchanges on the issues started with the late Tom Asimakopulos's contribution (1983b) to the Memorial Issue for Joan Robinson in the *Cambridge Journal of Economics* of 1983.) As she had already done so (in Chick 1983), Chick makes good use of Robertsonian process analysis in order to bring out what happens to investment and saving (planned, intended and actual), and to the money supply and the banking system as the multiplier process unfolds, and to challenge effectively Asimakopulos's claim that saving may, after all, sometimes help to determine investment.

BOOK IV THE INDUCEMENT TO INVEST

Just as Book V was the core of Marshall's *Principles* so many economists regard Book IV of *The General Theory*, with its chapters on investment, long-term expectation, the rate of interest, sundry observations on capital and the peculiar properties of money as the core of *The General Theory*. Over the decades since its publication, first one and then another chapter from *The General Theory* has been in fashion. At one stage we all claimed to be Chapter 12 Keynesians; at another, Chapter 17 Keynesians. Often, of course, there were overlaps of periods and thus strong disagreements. Moreover, many would argue that while Keynes certainly identified in Book IV the right ingredients for a theory of investment, the actual recipe in which he put them together was unsatisfactory. The most cogent statements of this critique are by Kalecki (1936), Joan Robinson (1964) and Asimakopulos (1971). The interesting point about two of the contributions to a 'second edition', those by Robert Eisner and Luigi Pasinetti (12, 13) respectively, is that their authors are on the whole Chapter 11 Keynesians – and make excellent fists of explaining why.

Indeed, Eisner remains an unreconstructed Keynesian as far as the theory of investment is concerned. He sets out succinctly Keynes's own theory, the critical role which the marginal efficiency of capital (actually the marginal efficiency of investment) plays; he then examines its main determinants and what government policy can best do to bring about the optimum rate of investment (at the most fundamental level, the rate which creates and absorbs full employment saving). For Eisner, a key relationship is that growth determines investment, *not* the other way about, and therefore governments should look to the creation and preservation of high levels of effective demand – and let investment follow. Such a rate of investment would tend to be socially optimal rather than being 'too much', as it may be because of the sustained use of investment subsidies when employment and output are sub-optimal.

Eisner reviews the econometric literature on Keynesian and neoclassical theories of investment and comes down on Keynes's side. (He does have some qualms about Tobin's q which, he feels, is good in principle but disappointing in practice, for a number of reasons which he sets out.) Eisner argues that many of Keynes's empirical hunches concerning the elasticity of investment with respect to the rate of interest and other variables have been confirmed. In particular, he argues that modern econometric evidence confirms the low elasticity of investment demand to the rate of interest that led Keynes to 'see insufficient variation in the rate of interest and insufficient response to what variation occurred to offer hope that the economy could be self-adjusting to full employment "along these lines"'. Eisner points out that business tangible investment is only a small proportion of total investment, which includes, in addition to household and public tangible investment, vast amounts of investment, public and private, in intangible capital. It follows that policies which affect these other components of investment, particularly public investment and investment in human and intangible capital, may bring about the sort of growth which in turn may help to maintain or even increase investment. These are all down-to-earth, sensible, plausible arguments which are only to be expected from a person who has always kept his eye on the ball, regardless of what the opponents were up to.

Pasinetti (13) contributes an incisive analysis of Keynes's concept of the marginal efficiency of capital (mec) and its role in the theory of investment. He takes serious note of what Keynes himself wrote about the development of the concept – the many drafts and the much clearing up of 'immense' muddles in order to create the mec. He stresses how truly revolutionary a concept it was and, therefore, how seriously illogical a mistake it was for it soon to have been identified with the marginal product of capital and the 'process' of deepening. He relates Keynes's development of the concept to his critique of the rate of interest as being determined by the interaction of saving and investment in the 'classical' theory he was attacking. He argues that Keynes made a more successful critique of the theory of the supply of saving than of the theory of the demand for investment because he was writing before Joan Robinson's and Piero Sraffa's critique of the downward-sloping relationship between 'capital', investment and the rate of interest. Perhaps Pasinetti's most telling analogy is that Keynes's theory is akin to the theory of extensive rent in Ricardo while the 'classical' theory is akin to the theory of intensive rent. Thus, the reason why more investment may be done in a given short-period situation at lower levels of the rate of interest has nothing to do with increasing capital intensity but much to do with lower expected profitability of individual projects and higher *overall* expected profitability. In a given situation, the lower is the rate of interest, the lower is the cost of borrowing and so the greater will be the number of already existing projects thought worth doing, regardless of their capital-intensity – period. Keynes's critique of the 'classical' theories of demand and supply of investment and saving may now at least be completed, he argues, by applying the reswitching and capital-reversing results.

Some commentators have expressed reservations about Pasinetti's argument. When analysing the economy as a whole, is it legitimate, when different values of the rate of interest are considered, to suppose that nothing else will be different, *except* planned levels of investment? In particular, is it legitimate to suppose that expected prices remain unaffected? The simplest answer is 'yes' – *in a given, short-period situation*, such as the one which Keynes assumed and Pasinetti accepted.

Pasinetti also has some wise things to say about the causal nature of Keynes's own analysis as opposed to the mutually determined, general equilibrium interpretations of Keynes's system that soon followed the publication of *The General Theory*. In particular, at one level of abstraction at least, and consistently with Keynes's own method that it is necessary for each purpose in hand to regard some variables as independent, others as dependent, the rate of interest may be argued to be given *before* we determine the amount of investment in a given short-period situation. The rate of interest definitely does rule the roost, and investment, thus determined, determines income and so consumption and saving. By extensive quotation from Keynes's writings, Pasinetti sweeps aside virtually all other interpretations, especially those in the textbooks, and even that associated with Abba Lerner and the distinction between the mec and the mei. Pasinetti accepts the distinction but not the neoclassical construction of 'deepening' which went with it in Lerner's interpretation.

While the themes of Chapter 12 on the state of long-term expectation permeate virtually all of the *The General Theory* and many of the chapters of our 'second edition', it is Kevin Hoover's and Peter Howitt's chapters (14, 15) which bear most directly on them and subsequent developments in the postwar years. In Chapter 12 and the 1937 *Quarterly Journal of Economics* article especially, Keynes highlighted the importance of the effects of uncertainty on systemic behaviour. He analysed how sensible people did the best they could in necessarily uncertain environments, adopting certain conventions in the process. These had the effect of securing, if not satisfactory, then at least stable conditions for much of the time. But because of the fragile nature of the conventions, if they ceased to hold then instability and crisis could quickly emerge. In addition, behaviour within capitalist institutions such as the stock exchange in his day, and in our day the markets for property and the foreign exchanges as well, could be dominated by destabilizing speculative behaviour rather than legitimate and socially beneficial 'enterprise'. As Keynes memorably put it: 'Speculators may do no harm as bubbles on a steady stream of enterprise. But the position is serious when enterprise becomes the bubble on a whirlpool of speculation' (*C.W.* VII: 159).

Against this background Hoover has written a dispassionate and balanced account of the relationship of Keynes's own economics (as well as Keynesian economics) to the rational expectations innovations, especially those associated with Lucas and Sargent. He argues that Keynes anticipated rational expectations as far as *short-term* expectations were concerned (in the sense that he thought that *short-term* expectations were usually quickly realized and so it did no harm to assume in analysis that they were *always* realized) but never thought they were applicable to the long-term expectations which are a major determinant of the process of accumulation. This distinction has been either blurred or scrapped in the writings of the rational expectations new classical macroeconomists. While they recognize the distinction between risk and uncertainty which plays a crucial role in Keynes's analysis, they, unlike Keynes, think uncertainty cannot be modelled, and so it is left out of their models – 'Apart from that, Mrs Lincoln, how did you enjoy the play?' This makes them subject to Keynes's criticism, quoted by Hoover, regarding pretty polite techniques which treat our lack of knowledge of the future as if neither it nor the future existed.

Hoover also argues that Keynes, in his critique of Tinbergen's work on investment in the late 1930s, anticipated the Lucas critique of policy associated with the lack of stability of parameters in empirical relationships – but came to quite different conclusions. For Keynes, judgement and feel allowed policy to be effective. For Lucas, there should be abdication from policy, except perhaps on rules.

As with Keynes, so with Peter Howitt: when he is persuaded that he is wrong he changes his mind (Keynes used to add to his critics: 'What do *you* do?'). Howitt's essay (15) is a splendid account of his intellectual pilgrim's progress from his contributions in the 1970s and 1980s to the literature on co-ordination failures and sunspot equilibria (which were argued to provide rigorous demonstrations of some of Keynes's conjectures) to a plea to move outside the dominant neo-Walrasian code altogether. Instead, we should learn from Keynes's insights by taking direct account of the role of conventions and rules of thumb in coping with uncertainty and expectations. Howitt comments that even Keynes did not depart from using equilibrium analysis – in fact, he used rational expectations in the short term when doing so – but *we* should. He illustrates his new point of view with examples from the analysis of Harrodian instability and dynamic adjustments, depression and inflation. With the last topic he has fascinating things to say about the roles of historical cost accounting and the convention that the long-term value of money is constant.

The issues discussed in the chapters in Book IV – Keynes's liquidity preference theory, his account and critique of the classical theory of interest, observations on the nature of capital and the peculiar and essential properties of money – provide the background for the contributions by Jan Kregel (16), Ingo Barens and Volker Caspari (17), Colin Rogers and Tom Rymes (18), Colin Rogers solo (19) and Michael Lawlor (20). Keynes often said that the relationship between the *Treatise on Money* (he should have added the *Tract* (1923) as well) and *The General Theory* was probably clearer to him than to others (see, for example, his statement in the Preface to *G.T.*: xxi–xxii). Nowhere was this more evident than in Chapter 17, where his difficult but fundamental chapter on the theory of the forward exchanges in the *Tract* is also highly relevant. In his lectures in the early 1930s on the way to *The General Theory*, Keynes came close to praising Marx for the insights contained in his concept of the circuits of capital, for recognizing that the objective of business people was to end up with more *money* at the end of the period of production than they started with at the beginning ($M' > M$; see Sardoni's chapter (36) and the comments on it below). To do so was as important for offering employment and creating production as it was for carrying out accumulation; it was also the means by which the expectations of future prices affected present actions.

According to Kregel (16), Keynes himself combined these insights with his own theory of short-period prices, which were cut loose from the conditions of production in normal conditions. Keynes analysed the latter in the *Treatise on Money* by use of his 'fundamental equations'. Citing chapters and verse and setting out detailed arguments, Kregel makes explicit the role of these ingredients, together with the definitions of user cost and the sharp distinction between the rate of interest as determined by liquidity preference, and the mec, in Keynes's analysis in Chapter 17. He lays bare Keynes's view as to *why* the peculiar properties of money may be such as to prevent full employment of labour (and capital) *even as long-period propositions*. In this way the subtle break with Keynes's former selves (despite his own view that he was naturally evolving: *C.W.* VII: xxii) and the classics, and hence the claim for a revolution in thought, are made explicit, together with Kregel's argument that Chapter 12 is not only an integral part of the book, but is as well 'the *G.T.* in a nutshell' (see n. 6).

As we have already remarked, Chapter 17 has always been something of a mystery to Keynes observers and, indeed, even to some of his closest followers and/or admirers. Barens and Caspari trace the origins of this to the different purposes which Sraffa and Keynes had in mind in their use of the concept of own rates of interest. On the one hand, Sraffa used them essentially for an internal critique of Hayek's theoretical analysis in *Prices and Production* (1931). Keynes, on the other hand, used them as essential ingredients of a theory of the rate of interest, the essential properties of money, and the role of the money rate of interest as the ultimate barrier to attaining full employment in a world *characterized by an environment of uncertainty and missing markets*. Our authors argue that Keynes failed in this regard because own rates of interest are redundant concepts once we have spot and future (or forward) prices in the analysis, which Keynes clearly had. But, they argue, Keynes's central argument about money's role in causing unemployment does not have to be discarded just because own rates are a cul-de-sac rather than a detour.

Colin Rogers and Tom Rymes (18) have written a thoughtful account of the relationship of Keynes's arguments in Chapter 17 to recent attempts to argue that the disappearance of cash in the modern world restores the classical dichotomy and the applicability of the workings of a barter world (with an auctioneer) to the happenings of the contemporary world. Rogers and Rymes show that it is not necessary to have an *actual* commodity money in order to have a monetary economy – that money is a *convention* which is related to the fact that intertemporal decisions *have* to be made in an uncertain environment. (Rogers emphasizes this in his chapter 19 too.) There is therefore always both a need for liquidity and the inescapable fact that the resting place (*if* there is one) of a monetary production economy will always have some different determinants, and therefore different values of the relevant economic variables, than a barter world without money.

They make their argument through a reworking of Keynes–Sraffa own-rates analysis and show that liquidity and the liquidity preference function are respectively an essential variable and an essential relationship in any model, no matter how abstract, that purports to illuminate the workings of a modern economy. They argue that Keynes had already sensed this in the *Tract*, developed it much further in the *Treatise on Money* and brought it to fruition in *The General Theory*, especially in Chapter 17. Rogers and Rymes extend Keynes's analysis in the *Treatise on Money* and the concepts of own rates of interest to banking theory. They argue that the existence and conventional policies of central banks always have effects on the outputs of banks which in turn affect the output and prices in monetary economies, even in economies in which there is no fiat monetary base. They suggest on the evidence of the *Tract* that Keynes *may* have preceded Sraffa, who made explicit the own-rates analysis when he tore into Hayek in 1932, even though in Chapter 17 Keynes acknowledged Sraffa as his source for the concept. We suggest that reading the English translation of Sraffa's 1920 undergraduate dissertation (Wendy Harcourt and Sardoni 1993) could push the argument about who was first back even further![13]

Neither Joan Robinson nor Richard Kahn was happy with the arguments of Chapter 17, not least because of its long-period context and content. Increasingly over the years they were to resist the long-period interpretation of *The General Theory*. Colin Rogers (19) therefore has done us a great service by setting out, as succinctly and clearly as is to be found in the literature, the ingredients of the analysis of *long-period* under-employment equilibrium in Keynes's thought. To do this he has drawn on the work of those Keynesians who have argued for the long-period interpretation of *The General Theory*, who have stressed the role of conventions as a response to an inescapable environment of uncertainty and who, for example, the late Tom Asimako-pulos (1991), have spelt out the essential Marshallian, not Walrasian, nature of Keynes's analysis in *The General Theory*: crucially, that static analysis at a high level of abstraction *necessarily* precedes dynamic analysis and that uncertainty is not a bar to determinate analysis at *this* level of abstraction.

The starting point is the claim by Harrod in his contribution to the Seymour Harris collection (1947) and in his life (1951) of Keynes (and Harrod) that the central contribution of *The General Theory* is the liquidity theory of the rate of interest and especially the notion of a 'normal' rate of interest. The latter may for decades be too high to allow full employment to be sustained, so setting an underlying level around which actual activity fluctuates with its accompanying, never disappearing, involuntary unemployment. Rogers finds this argument attractive, for he argues, correctly, that Say's Law and the Quantity Theory of Money *are* long-period propositions set at a higher level of abstraction than analysis of the trade cycle. Therefore, in order to show that classical theory is a special case of a general theory, Keynes had to set out his system at the same level of abstraction and for the long period too.

Rogers gives a careful exposition of Marshall's methods and of Keynes's description of them and of how to use them in the analysis of *The General Theory*. He then proceeds, again via modern work on the use of conventions as the means to handle inescapable uncertainty, a means which, as we have seen, sometimes works but which sometimes because of their fragility is the cause of crisis, to a Marshallian analysis of the determination of the point of effective demand in the long period. This requires identifying a long-period aggregate supply function (one with normal profits as a component of the proceeds needed to justify the various levels of employment), a long-period aggregate demand function, and their intersection. One of the determining variables is the 'normal' rate of interest, which is itself related to an assumption of *given* long-term expectations and the analysis of Chapter 17. Having thus established existence, Rogers sketches in stability in terms of sticky money-wages and inelastic expectations.

BOOK V MONEY-WAGES AND PRICES

In the first edition, Keynes concluded Book IV by summarizing his findings to date and restating his theory. Then, in Book V, 'Money-Wages and Prices', he dropped his provisional assumption of a given money-wage in order to argue in Chapter 19 that the consequences of *changes* in money-wages (he did not think that economic theory as such could ever say anything systematic or general about their *causes*) made no essential difference to his arguments or findings. He tried to establish this by asking what effect a fall (usually) in money-wages could be expected to have on the principal relations of the system – the consumption and investment functions, the liquidity preference function and the aggregate supply function.

The analysis was a verbal account of various feedback mechanisms on to the underlying relationships. It was an application of the most complicated of the three models of reality which Kregel (1976) discerned in *The General Theory* and related writings, the model of shifting equilibrium.[14] In the light of Chapter 19 and his explicit statements about his attitude to money-wages, it must never cease to amaze that so many subsequent commentators thought that Keynes's system was crucially dependent on the assumption of constant money-wages, that this was to Keynes what many commentators thought a constant capital–output ratio was to Harrod – and they were wrong on Harrod too (see, for example, Eisner 1958). That is not to say that Keynes's own arguments were entirely satisfactory, nor that there was not practical sense in a search for systemic stability to exploit any tendency in the system towards stickiness in money-wages so that a rise in real wages and the maintenance of high levels of employment could be achieved. Arthur Brown and Brian Reddaway have eminently sensible remarks to make on these themes in their chapters (26, 27); and, in his chapter (1), John Brothwell suggests that Keynes could have emphasized that his theory explained unemployment to be the result of a lack of aggregate demand (rather than money-wage rigidity) by including a preliminary discussion of the effects of changes in money-wages in the opening chapters of the second edition.

In *The General Theory* itself, Chapter 19 on changes in money-wages is followed by the rather obscure Chapter 20 on the employment function, where Keynes makes a tentative attempt to tackle aggregation problems when we consider different levels of aggregate demand. Chapter 21 is on 'The Theory of Prices'. Having scrapped the Quantity Theory Keynes, needing a theory of the general price level, transformed Marshall's short-period theory of prices in competitive industries into an economy-wide theory; he explained in the process what he now thought was the appropriate division (or divisions) of economic theory to replace the classical dichotomy (*C.W.* VII: 293–4). In both suggested divisions, uncertainty and the role and function of money were the key determinants.

It is still something of a mystery why Keynes ignored the development of the theories of imperfect competition in his explanation of prices, for he was familiar with Kahn's pioneering work in his fellowship dissertation for King's (1929), Joan Robinson's 1933 book and probably Gerald Shove's views. This issue has been extensively discussed recently in the literature (see, for example, Darity 1985; Harcourt 1987a; Kregel 1985b; and Marris 1992). Here we refer readers to Robin Marris's chapter (4), which provides a most detailed and cogent argument as to how we should proceed now in a second edition directed towards contemporary problems and their explanation.[15]

Michael Lawlor (20) has given sterling service to the volume through his examination of the fundamental theoretical issues associated with the differences, as Keynes saw them, between the classical, then neoclassical, theory of the rate of interest and his own theory. First, writing as J.M. Keynes, Lawlor rewrites the original Chapter 14, 'The Classical Theory of the Rate of Interest', in order to incorporate Keynes's subsequent writings on the rate of interest up to 1939. An implication of the revision is to make Chapter 14 into Chapter 18,[16] so as to allow the arguments on the essential properties of money and own rates of interest in the original Chapter 17 to be included. What comes out clearly is Keynes's insistence that only his theory can take in the implications of behaviour in an uncertain environment, that is, in the world as we know it, and its relevance for systemic behaviour, especially the possibility of sustained lapses from full employment. His objection to the alternative theories is that they are a hybrid of the classical theory of a barter economy and the disequilibrium analysis of transitional states between equilibria.

Lawlor then reviews in more detail the nature of Keynes's reply to his critics and the sources of his interpretation of the classical theory. He argues that Marshall is the real culprit, Marshall of his writings and lectures outside the *Principles*, despite the fact that Keynes only quoted from the *Principles* in *The General Theory* itself. Lawlor argues that Keynes neglected Irving Fisher's great contributions (especially his emphasis on the real factors of productivity and thrift as the principal determinants of the rate of interest, and on the real nature of interest), having persuaded himself that they were 'all in Marshall' anyway. Perhaps Keynes was here a victim of his extraordinary powers of identifying what the assumptions must be for a viewpoint to be valid? He then imposed them on Marshall, having learnt them from him in the first place. Whatever the reasons, while it reflects poorly on Keynes as an historian of thought, it also serves to show anew what a deep and penetratingly original theorist Keynes was, and how great was his grasp of the workings of the entire system.

VI   SHORT NOTES SIXTY YEARS ON

In the last book of the first edition Keynes ranged far and wide through his 'short notes'. Here we take up specifically the trade cycle (Marc Jarsulic, 21), underconsumption (John King, 22) and social philosophy (John Cornwall, 23 and Robert Skidelsky, 24). In his chapter (21), Jarsulic describes the characteristics of Keynes's theory of the trade cycle in Chapter 22 of *The General Theory*. He compares them more than favourably with those of modern theories of real business cycles. (The latter date back at least to the writings of Keynes's greatest chum in the 1920s, D.H. Robertson, as Charles Goodhart made eloquently clear in his 1990 paper celebrating the centenary of Robertson's birth.)

After setting out Keynes's arguments, and especially his explanations of turning points, Jarsulic moves to the modern age through Goodwin's contributions in particular: he asks what the modern theories of non-linear systems and chaotic behaviour have to offer as a way forward to explain the cycle and capture in a more formal manner most of Keynes's insights.

What strikes the editors of this volume is the small to zero part played by technical progress and innovations in Keynes's story and those of most of his successors. Within this constraint Jarsulic tells a clear and lucid story, directing us to deeper explanations and suitable policy measures. Simultaneously, he reveals the basic shallowness of the structure of real business cycle theory; in particular, its failure to tell any *economic* story about the origin of cyclical fluctuations in changes in productivity and other key variables in its account of the cycle.

John Cornwall (23) eagerly took on the tasks of writing about the nature of the trade cycle and of the social philosophy which a second edition of *The General Theory* might supply. He provides a masterly account of the underlying conditions and of the institutions which made possible the Golden Age of Capitalism and Keynesianism in the post-war world. He identifies the cumulative changes that brought them to their end, as well as the immediate shocks that were also responsible. He names two types of labour market and the corresponding wage-setting institutions – adversarial, decentralized go-it-alone markets and socially conscious, relatively co-operative ones. During the Golden Age the first set currently was associated with the worse record of inflation and unemployment.

Cornwall also points to the value of the fixed exchange rate system of the Bretton Woods era. It served to reinforce employer and employee discipline regarding the setting of *money*-wages, thus helping to allow full employment, healthy rates of growth of economies and satisfactory increases in *real* wages. The disappearance of fixed exchange rates and of controls over capital movements (the maintenance of both of which is needed to keep speculation in bounds) have played a key role in the creation of what Cornwall identifies as the high unemployment equilibrium traps of many advanced countries of the last twenty years or more.

To overcome rising unemployment levels and control inflation requires co-ordination as far as fiscal and monetary policies are concerned and labour market institutions which reproduce the results of the socially co-operative regimes of the Golden Age. (It may be thought that so much damage has been done to the social and industrial relations fabric in some countries, such as the United Kingdom, that we may never get back to or be able to create appropriate labour market institutions. By upsetting pragmatic equilibria in the first place any prospect of returning to them may have been destroyed.) We also need international schemes to curb the destabilizing effects of the massive speculation associated with the deregulation of financial markets. As Cornwall says, we can only hope – the difficulties are enormous and the consequences of failure for social cohesion and reasonable life-styles for ordinary men and women are even worse.

When John King (23) rewrites as Keynes the chapter on mercantilism *et al.*, he makes Keynes much more generous than formerly to Marx and Hobson. Moreover, King very sensibly integrates the 'lost pages' found in the laundry basket at Tilton (see *C.W.* XXIX) on the co-operative, neutral and entrepreneur economies, into this section. He relates them to Marx's distinction between $C-M-C'$ and $M - C - M'$ and to how the latter sequence is the better description of the processes at work in modern capitalism. Lorie Tarshis for one had always been puzzled by the omission of the co-operative, neutral and entrepreneur economy models from the first edition. He thought they provided a much better vehicle for the explanation of the central issue of Keynes's book than his ultimately incoherent argument (in *G.T.* 25–6) that the highest Say's Law position was reached by competition between entrepreneurs.

As an interesting connection to the coming discussions by John Coates (35), John Davis (33), Bill Gerrard (32), Rod O'Donnell (31) and Jochen Runde (34) on method in *The General Theory* and in Keynes's writings generally, King refers to Harrod's and Joan Robinson's comments on the method of common sense which Keynes discovered in Malthus and others but to which Ricardo and other classicals were 'blind'. Joan Robinson was as usual more supportive than Harrod who, while he admitted the justice of the emphasis, was nevertheless reluctant to give the older pioneers any more credit than that.

Next, King does us all a service by setting out the history of underconsumption theory since 1936, starting with Otto Bauer, who was publishing at the time when Keynes was finishing *The General Theory*, and ending with the writings of Paul Baran and Paul Sweezy and of Josef Steindl. In the process he rehabilitates poor J.A. Hobson and points out that Baran's *Political Economy of Growth* (1957) was as important a contribution for the developing countries as Baran and Sweezy's *Monopoly Capital* (1966) was for modern capitalism. He shows the relationship of underconsumption to the issues tackled by Harrod (who was unsympathetic to the pioneers of underconsumption) and Domar (who recognized and was pleasant about their contributions).[17]

Following up Joan Robinson's learning curve on Marx, from her 1936 review of Strachey (1935) to her 1942 *Essay* and beyond, King argues that underconsumption theory played a vital and sensible part in Marx's theory of crisis. Finally, he recognizes the role of the profit squeeze associated with the writings of Andrew Glyn and Robert Sutcliffe in the United Kingdom, the French Regulation school, and Tom Weisskopf and others in the USA.

Finally, Robert Skidelsky (24), as befits the eminent author of the ongoing outstanding biography of Keynes, writes as though he were Keynes, looking back (from beyond the grave) at the concluding chapter of *The General Theory* in the light of both wrong interpretations and subsequent events. Inequality, the saturation of wants, the abundance of capital, the euthanasia of the rentier, the 'comprehensive socialisation of investment', state socialism and the benefits of the market mechanism – all these topics are commented upon from this vantage point. He also has Keynes critical of the excessive expansion of the welfare state, especially in the form of state consumption and transfer payments, because it serves to retard the fall in the rate of interest. Skidelsky even has Keynes making common cause with the themes of his natural opponents, the modern proponents of public-choice theory – natural opponents because their central thesis involves the denial that policy-makers ever accepted 'the presuppositions of Harvey Road'.

AN OVERVIEW: JAMES TOBIN

From the start of his undergraduate studies at Harvard, James Tobin has been an ardent Keynesian (see Harcourt 1984: 495). In his chapter (25) at the start of volume 2 he sums up a lifetime of reflecting on the messages of *The General Theory* and presents his considered judgements, many of them, of course, based on his own outstanding contributions to the development of Keynesian economics.

First, in the guise of John Maynard Keynes, he amends the original definition in Chapter 2 of involuntary unemployment in order to make it more simple, operational – and convincing. Otherwise, as both Keynes *and* himself, he remains unrepentant. Demand deficiencies rather than supply constraints bite most of the time in capitalist economies. Policy can do something about this without having radically to change either institutions or political systems. Money is integrated in the workings of the system as a whole; it is *not* a veil. Price and wage flexibility are beside the point theoretically as far as determining the levels of activity and unemployment are concerned, though there is much to be said for relative money-wage stability if we want a stable economy overall. Wage-earners do not, and do not have to, 'suffer' from money illusion to make Keynes's system 'work': their behaviour is perfectly consistent with sensible behaviour, with the balancing of pros and cons, so that it is sensible for wage-earners to resist cuts in money-wages in order to protect relative positions but not to go in for industrial unrest every time the prices of wage goods rise a little.

When we come to the mid-1990s and Tobin writes as Tobin, he argues that we have to come to grips with what we mean by equilibrium when there is unemployment. He tells us that he prefers to use the phrase 'rest state' because, clearly, the labour market is *not* clearing at the given price if, as is usually the case, there is involuntary unemployment present. He then tackles head-on the disequilibrium interpretation of Keynes. Keynesian rest states are centres of gravitation for short-period flow equilibria, given inherited stocks of capital goods, labour supplies and technical knowledge. But clearly all these change over time, some from the very attainment of short-period flow equilibrium. So we must consider the characteristics of the next period's centre of gravitation, taking into account what has happened in the previous period(s) and the implications for stocks, short- *and* long-term expectations and so on, for this period. It is an open question whether, either in fact or in theory, the disequilibrium dynamics so released will produce a succession of short-period equilibria which, left to themselves, will converge on a long-period, full stock and flow equilibrium. Tobin, like Keynes, is not sure that this is a very interesting or relevant question anyway.

SPECIFIC EXTENSIONS AND/OR MODIFICATIONS

Inflation

Though it is wrong to regard *The General Theory* as the economics of depression, it is true that its emphasis is largely on the causes of unemployment. These are systematically analysed in the book whereas the problem of inflation is mostly treated in brilliant bursts and asides. Brian Reddaway was Keynes's pupil when Keynes was writing and lecturing on the themes which became *The General Theory*. Reddaway wrote one of the most perceptive reviews of Keynes's book (Reddaway 1936). (He even 'invented' IS–LM: see the argument and the four equations on pp. 34–35, although he did not set out the argument in that form. His exposition is marked by an acute sense of the limitations of the four equations (and by implication of IS–LM) as well as their ability to give us an initial grip on Keynes's system.) Like Keynes, Reddaway is interested in theory only in so far as it bears on policy; he has, moreover, a very real sense of the complexities which characterize modern economies and the modest claims that can be made for theory in illuminating them.

In his chapter (26), 'The Changing Significance of Inflation', he expresses surprise that Keynes did not include 'Prices' in the title of his book. Though Reddaway acknowledges the presence of Chapter 21, he feels that it is not well integrated with the system of the rest of the book.

This he regards as a limitation when thinking about the post-war period in which prices have been rising 'for ever' as, thirty years ago, he himself predicted (in Reddaway 1966). Reddaway discusses how the analysis would be improved, the emphasis changed, if we take in prices and their changes as well as the determination of employment. In doing so he exhibits his robust common sense, criticizing the disgrace of incurring social and economic costs by aiming for zero inflation when there is no evidence *at all* that this is good either for employment or for growth. He explains how institutions and practices have steadily changed to take into account that we now live in inflationary times. He suggests that it is better to accept this and adjust our expectations as well as our policies accordingly, instead of permanently reducing our rates of growth (and bringing back persistent, unacceptable levels of unemployment) by chasing an imaginary will-o'-the-wisp of zero inflation.

Arthur Brown's chapter (29), 'The Inflationary Dimension', is an ideal complement to Reddaway's. Brown understands the theory of inflation and knows its history as well as anyone in the profession. He has written a masterly account of Keynes's views over his lifetime on inflation and its causes. He uses this and his own acute insights to illuminate especially the history of the post-war period, what might have been different, and what policies we needed then and still need now.

Brown shows how in *The Economic Consequences of the Peace* (1919), the *Tract* (1923) and the *Treatise on Money* (1930a, 1930b) Keynes was well ahead of his time in his understanding of the process of inflation. Especially does Brown stress – so did Richard Kahn – the cost-push, demand-pull distinction in the *Treatise on Money*. He also points out that, while Keynes was usually situation-specific in analysis and especially in his policy recommendations, he was essentially a stable prices person right up to the end of his life.

Brown discusses *How to Pay for the War* (1940b) and suggests that its lucid analysis would have been included by Keynes in any revision of Chapter 21 for a second edition. He puts to rest the canard that Keynes made a watertight distinction between rises in the general price level prior to full employment and those associated with full employment.[18] Rather Keynes recognized situations associated with more and more bottlenecks as activity became higher and higher in the short run.

Brown shows that Keynes also had the Phillips curve in an ordinal form (its only defensible form, we would argue), both as $\dot{p}$ and u, and $\dot{p}$ *and* $\dot{u}$. He gives an important role to Keynes's and to his own views on buffer stocks and primary commodity prices and output. Buffer stocks would have been of value, though probably they would not have been completely successful, in helping economies cope with the two oil price rise shocks.

Brown reminds us of the modest levels of statistical unemployment which Keynes thought would have been associated with zero involuntary unemployment. He wonders whether the Golden Age might not have been even more Golden had it been run at Keynes's levels. The great imponderable, of course, is what would have happened to 'animal spirits' in the otherwise situation. Finally, Brown reminds us that in his own researches, money had been treated as more endogenous than Keynes had it in *The General Theory* and that, still, the money-wage bargain is the vital variable to influence in order to attain and sustain full employment and steady, satisfactory growth with modest to no inflation.

Endogenous money

Sheila Dow (28) tackles the crucial issue of endogeneity of the money supply and why Keynes seemingly chose to make it exogenous in *The General Theory*, especially as in most of his other writings before and after *The General Theory* he was closer to a position associated with the money supply being endogenous. She makes the vital point that there is a difference between taking a particular variable as given for a specific purpose, on the one hand, and regarding it as truly exogenous to the economic system overall, on the other. The former, she argues, was Keynes's stance in *The General Theory*. In her own analysis she gives a very subtle interpretation of Keynes's procedure and of where the money supply, which he takes as given in the analysis of *The General Theory*, actually comes from. Another theme she emphasizes, drawing on recent work by Victoria Chick, is the various phases that have occurred in the evolution of modern monetary systems before and after the writing of *The General Theory*. The latter phases have made it more difficult to follow Keynes's procedure in *The General Theory* but have not, in her judgement, destroyed the value of the liquidity preference approach, nor opened the door for the loanable funds approach to enter and take over again. She outlines a rich modern analysis under the Post-Keynesian rubric (or one sub-division of it), which allows the modern phenomena of liability management, non-bank financial intermediaries and the internationalization of financial services to be tackled within the liquidity preference framework. Neither a horizontalist nor a verticalist be, but leave a place for credit-rationing associated with different estimations of risk as between borrowers and lenders, a Keynesian idea developed especially by Minsky. She also advocates including an analysis of the constraints on what value the rate of interest might take, given the ever-widening influence of international financial markets and trade blocs. And she highlights a distinction Keynes had already made in the *Treatise on Money*: that between the behaviour of the banking system as such and the corresponding role of the monetary authorities. This leads her to consider the nature of the liquidity preference of the *banks* as well as that of the public. Here, her discussion joins up with that of Rogers and Rymes in their chapter (18).

Her arguments are a justification for her conclusion that as long as the supply of credit is not fully demand-determined, Keynes's monetary theory retains its essential liquidity preference characteristics. For changes in interest rate expectations and in confidence concerning the predictions of these changes to lead to changes in real behaviour requires only that the money supply is constrained to some degree.

Finance and investment

As we mentioned earlier, a chap called Clinton robbed us of Stiglitz's proposed chapter on credit-rationing which was to complement Sheila Dow's chapter. We are fortunate that a pioneer in this area, Myron Gordon, has written a chapter (29) which ably fills in the gaping hole that otherwise would have been left. Starting his working life well within the orthodox Massachusetts Institute of Technology fold, Gordon soon departed. He wrote a string of articles which began with one of the earliest critiques of the Modigliani–Miller theorem. Their principal objective was to demonstrate the inadequacy of the neoclassical theory of finance and investment at the microeconomic level. Now in his eighth decade, he has written a book (Gordon 1994) that develops an alternative, Keynesian theory, explores some of the macroeconomic implications of the theory and contains the most complete statement of the critique of the neoclassical theory of finance and investment.

The central role of investment in Keynesian theory gave rise to a considerable body of research on what firms actually do. It was found that financial considerations such as internal funds, capital structure objectives, and non-price credit rationing by banks are more important than the interest rate in a firm's investment decision. Gordon's chapter shows how these financial considerations are captured in a theory of investment that recognizes the concern for long-run survival.

Gordon's chapter takes up themes which figure prominently in Keynes's own writings: the finance motive for holding money in the process of accumulation; borrowers' and lenders' risk; and the destabilizing effects of bankruptcy associated with financial structures and deflations. Gordon outlines a dynamic theory of accumulation and its finance which would have gladdened Keynes's heart – not least because in the last sections he paints on a very broad canvas indeed in the manner of Keynes in the later chapters of *The General Theory* and also that of Marx.

Keynes and the open economy

Though most of the analysis of *The General Theory* was concerned with a closed economy, Keynes usually wrote about open economies and international institutions and policy, albeit often with an eye to the interests of the United Kingdom. Paul Davidson's chapter (30) is concerned with the essential features of Keynes's analysis when applied to the world economy, and with the natural set of institutions and policies which flow from it. He starts by contrasting the experiences of inflation, unemployment and growth of, first, the Gold Standard period and, secondly, the post-Bretton Woods, deregulated foreign exchange rates period, on the one hand, with, on the other, the corresponding experiences in the Golden Age of capitalism when Bretton Woods institutions, combined with individual governments' commitments to full employment, prevailed.

Sensing that the political time is not yet ripe for the world economy to have either an international mechanism whereby to finance international trade and capital movements or a World Central Bank, Davidson designs a half-way house instead. The main features are institutional pressures which would serve to make creditor nations behave in a socially responsible manner at a world level, a 'currency' between central banks to provide liquidity and the creation of an environment wherein all countries can aim for full employment without running into external constraints. The overall aim is to reduce the contractionary bias in the world's operations without running into inflationary pressures which spread world-wide. This will allow the economies of the world to advance steadily with each allowing the others 'free lunches'. It is a scheme fittingly in the spirit of Keynes, and only the dark forces of ignorance and self-interested greed stand in the way of discussion of its principles and details – and its implementation. Now read on.

METHOD AND PHILOSOPHY

Over the last fifteen to twenty years or so there has been a welcome development whereby the link between Keynes's contributions to philosophy and his economics has been systematically examined and his views on method within a discipline such as economics have been reappraised. We call this welcome because the researches involved have revealed both a complex and a rewarding story about Keynes's views and achievements and how modern economics may be pursued more satisfactorily and productively. We are fortunate to have chapters by some of the leading pioneers in these endeavours: John Coates, John Davis, Bill Gerrard, Rod O'Donnell and Jochen Runde. We make no apology for having a number of chapters on these themes for we regard these recent developments as not only amongst the most exciting in Keynes scholarship but also as, perhaps, not as well known within the profession as they ought to be. Certainly they are not as well known as some of the other developments represented in this volume.

We start with Rod O'Donnell's contribution (31), not only because he is one of the pioneers, whose 1989 book (which grew out of his 1982 Cambridge PhD dissertation) has been acclaimed, but also because he puts to rest some of the silliest canards in the conventional wisdom concerning Keynes's attitudes to mathematics and econometrics. O'Donnell draws on his vast knowledge of the Keynes papers in order to set out Keynes's views on the use of mathematics and econometrics in our discipline. They make very sensible reading. Keynes was not in general a zealot, and though we might disagree with some of his particular judgements, such as his opinion of Marschak, his stance was both balanced and highly sophisticated. Mathematics and econometric techniques were indispensable and valuable within their own domains in economics, but misleading and dangerous outside them. Discussing logically whether the conditions which allowed their application to particular issues were present was an inescapable responsibility of the economist. Economic reasoning embraces them both – and more, for it takes in cardinal, ordinal and non-measurable concepts. Economic reasoning can by its very nature present only a sample of the full mode of thought of economists. Mathematics is helpful when used appropriately to make intelligible those samples which are presented. Especially illuminating is O'Donnell's discussion of Keynes's views on an actual use of mathematics in *The General Theory* itself. This is contained in a perceptive account of Keynes's mode of theorizing both generally and, especially, in *The General Theory*. At the close of the chapter O'Donnell outlines the modifications which his arguments suggest for the mode of exposition in a 'second edition' of *The General Theory*.

O'Donnell argues that Keynes did not have a sudden, late change of mind on the value of econometrics (as Richard Stone argued), but was always consistent in his views. He disliked inappropriate specific applications, not mathematics and econometrics as such. What could be fairer than that? From O'Donnell's account of the richness and variety of Keynes's own method and thinking on economic issues there is much that we ought to learn, especially today, when formal methods tend completely to dominate, so impoverishing our discipline and deepening its crisis. The rest of the chapters in this section are concerned with aspects of this general lesson.

Gerrard has written a thoughtful chapter (32) which is based on his sustained reading over the years of Keynes's writings, and especially of *The General Theory*, concerning Keynes's methodology. He examines the various meanings which Keynes attached to 'general' in the analysis of *The General Theory* and how they are associated with a break from previous methods. He highlights what recent commentators on Keynes have rather overlooked: Keynes's preoccupation with finding out what exactly were the assumptions, implicit, explicit or tacit, that supported theories and whether they were appropriate. In particular, can they be traced back to recognizable real world phenomena and situations? Though Keynes's own practice was often intuitive, reaching conclusions before the details of the argument were fully set out, or even sketched or known, his whole structure of thought demanded a clear, explicit, coherent chain which ran from appropriate assumptions to defensible conclusions. Gerrard analyses the details of Keynes's method and the changes it heralds when set in this particular context.

John Davis (33) takes up a theme which has become more prominent in recent years and which we have already mentioned in this introduction: the role of conventions in Keynes's thought and analysis, especially the role that conventions play in his analysis of the behaviour of stock exchanges and of the liquidity preference function in the determination of the rate of interest. Davis allies this discussion with his own researches on Keynes's changing philosophical views following Frank Ramsey's criticism of Keynes's understanding of intuition. Central to Davis's argument is the section in Chapter 12 of *The General Theory* on the analogy between the beauty contest and the determination of prices on the stock exchange. Conventions in this context are seen as interactive, as is confidence, individual and collective. An important point is that while we adopt the convention that the future will be like the present unless there are compelling reasons for expecting a change, this very proviso tends to make individuals concentrate on change, and so makes the convention itself more likely to be precarious. Nevertheless, Davis does not consider that Keynes thought reliance on conventions was irrational; rather, it was an example of sensible people doing the best they could in an environment of inescapable uncertainty.

Finally, Davis speculates that the interactive processes which serve to bring about conventions and determine confidence at a social level have contacts with Wittgenstein's later philosophy which emphasized the importance of language games. In the latter, overlaps of meaning were never the same for different people, yet communication and recognition were possible.[19] In his chapter in this volume, John Coates makes a similar point when he suggests that Keynes's ideas could be developed through the use of fuzzy set logic and analysis.

Jochen Runde has written a finely tuned chapter (34) in which he takes Chapter 12 of the *The General Theory* as the subject matter for a discussion of the relationship between Keynes's views on probability and uncertainty, rational behaviour in an uncertain environment, and his concept of economic theory (as contrasted with the dominant axiomatic theorizing of mainstream theorists). Runde examines Keynes's mode of theorizing within this chapter, which Keynes told Gerald Shove was concerned with matters the analysis of which were outside the realm of the 'formally exact' (see *C.W.* XIV: 2). Runde then relates the discussion to the approaches and contributions of two influential Post-Keynesians, the late G.L.S. Shackle and Tony Lawson, who have taken Chapter 12 and the theorizing therein as starting points for their critiques of orthodox economic theory and the positivist outlook that usually accompanies it.

Runde singles out Robert Lucas as a prominent example of a modern economist who combines the axiomatic method with the positivist methodology, and who believes that explanation and prediction are both possible through the use of toy models which are built on the basis of observed empirical regularities. Runde also mentions the more reflective views of Frank Hahn, who wonders whether empirical regularities or 'laws' will ever be found in economics. Hahn does not think prediction is possible or, at least, likely, but does think that economic theory may explain, if only by giving us a reference point (for example, the Arrow–Debreu general equilibrium model) from which to jump off in order to get back to the real world and its falls from grace.

Runde then examines Shackle's somewhat nihilistic views, especially on policy but also on explanation, and Lawson's more optimistic but complex views. Lawson draws on Roy Bhaskar's writings. Runde explains how this leads to a mutual interrelationship between societal structures and individual behaviour with each moulding and changing the other in a situation-specific manner. He concludes that Chapter 12, with its brilliant analysis of the role and the workings of the stock exchange, of confidence, expectations and conventions, is a fine example of what Lawson has in mind.

John Coates (35) draws on his profound researches into the relationship between Keynes and the Cambridge philosophers, especially Wittgenstein, and what he has dubbed 'ordinary language economics'. He discerns in Keynes's philosophy at the time of the writing of *The General Theory* an anticipation of the modern work on fuzzy logic and fuzzy sets. Coates conjectures that these recent developments may allow a bridge to be erected between the complex, multi-dimensional yet often vague concepts of economics and the powerful analytical procedures of mathematics. Fuzzy sets evidently allow us to handle in a precise analytical manner vague concepts such as 'baldness'. This is written about with feeling by both editors of the present volume, who appreciate the notion of membership or non-membership of a category which is gradual rather than abrupt.

Keynes sensed the conflict between precision and relevance due to the omission of crucial factors which was often associated with the former. Keynes also sensed what the recent developments allow. Furthermore, he understood the rich and widely ranging fund of common knowledge on which economists, by using ordinary language as much as possible, could draw. Coates's chapter is both informative about the past and a foretaste of the promise contained in future developments.[20]

Keynes and Marx

In 1987 Claudio Sardoni published a fine book on Marx's and Keynes's theories of effective demand and crisis. It was based on thorough research into what the two authors actually wrote. Reading his account, it could quickly be realized that after allowing for differences in terminology and attitudes to the survival of the capitalist system and its accompanying institutions as such, whenever these two great analysts of capitalism tackled the same questions, they came up with broadly the same answers. Yet it is known that Keynes had a very low opinion of Marx, calling him 'a very poor thinker indeed' (J.M.K. to Joan Robinson, August 1942). We think that this tells us more about Keynes than Marx and Sardoni's chapter (36) in this volume confirms our view.

Sardoni does not think that Keynes would have changed his opinion of Marx, despite Joan Robinson's attempts to make him see that coming at Keynes's puzzles through Marx's approach was a more rewarding way to tackle them. Sardoni shows how, initially, as Keynes moved towards *The General Theory* he found Marx's emphasis on the circuits of capital and the fact that entrepreneurs want to make money profits rather than produce commodities as such were the clues both to understanding how capitalism works (well and poorly) and to the critique of 'classical' economics, especially of Say's Law. These arguments were contained in the sections on the co-operative, neutral and entrepreneur economies which, as we have seen, did not make it to the published version of *The General Theory*.

Why? Because, by the time the final drafts were being written, Keynes was attacking the marginalist version of Say's Law. The latter implied the full employment of labour, and not only of capital as Ricardo and the other classical economists had it and which Marx attacked. In doing so Keynes unfortunately reduced the emphasis on the key role that capitalists played as he discussed the labour market and the role of the rate of interest in a system with exogenous money. After *The General Theory* was published Keynes brought again to the foreground the role of the banks and emphasized the effects of uncertainty on entrepreneurial behaviour. This allowed his and Marx's insight that the capitalists' ability to hoard was the clue to the emergence of overproduction and crisis. Thus, though Keynes may never have revised his opinion of Marx as such, he may have restored some of his emphasis, suggesting that Keynes's birth in the year that Marx died provided a seamless weave of profound economic sense. All those economists born in 1946 therefore ought to look to their laurels, for they have a great tradition to join!

Keynes and Schumpeter – and beyond

Joseph Schumpeter was fond of Keynes but jealous of him as an intellectual rival. In a fascinating chapter (37) on 'Keynes, Schumpeter and Beyond – a Non-reductionist Approach', Alessandro Vercelli argues that, properly understood in the light of modern developments in approaches to dynamic theory and methodology, the contributions of these two great economists may be regarded as illuminating complements to one another – as befits the contributions of two people born in the year that Marx died. In *The General*

Theory, Keynes neglected those matters closest to Schumpeter's heart, the classical problems of accumulation, growth and distribution, in order to concentrate on uncertainty, on the financial and real crises which arose out of the basic structure of monetary production systems, and on the usually unsatisfactory nature of the system's immediate rest states. Schumpeter, in turn, neglected (indeed, never really understood) Keynes's contributions. Instead, he developed his theories of longer-term development associated with the interplay of financial provisions and the innovating entrepreneurs' role of embodying new methods in production processes through the resulting accumulation.

Vercelli reviews the developments over the centuries in dynamic theories of many disciplines (including economics), showing how pre-classical views gave way to classical dynamics, which in turn was superseded by more general theories which could absorb it as a special case. He writes that Keynes's economics in *The General Theory* followed a similar path of generalization with regard to what Keynes dubbed classical theory, as did Schumpeter's economics with regard to Walras's general equilibrium system. Following an incisive critical review of the approaches and methods of different schools of modern macroeconomics, Vercelli suggests that the terrible economic and social problems of the modern world, both current and to come, would best be tackled by applying modern technical dynamic methods to aspects of the complementary contributions of Keynes and Schumpeter.

Keynes, Kalecki and *The General Theory*

Peter Kriesler, Bruce McFarlane and Jan Toporowski are currently writing the official intellectual biography of Michal Kalecki. Kriesler is also the author of the definitive book on Kalecki's microeconomics (Kriesler 1987). So he has prepared himself admirably for the task of comparing and contrasting the '*General Theories*' of Kalecki and Keynes and of comparing them in turn with the system of their classical/neoclassical rivals. Not surprisingly, Kriesler (38) is more partial to Kalecki's solution of the realization problem than to that of Keynes. The only aspect of their respective analyses in which he argues that Keynes is superior concerns the role of expectations, financial matters and especially the determination of the rate of interest. This is not to say that he does not admire Keynes. It is rather that he thinks that Kalecki's approach, which derives from Marx and the classical economists (in the non-Keynes sense), so that Kalecki's version of *The General Theory* emphasizes accumulation and cyclical growth and the role that distribution between classes plays in these processes, is a more natural way to analyse modern capitalism.

Moreover, Kalecki's realistic microeconomic foundations are superior to those of Keynes for both explaining distribution and accumulation. Finally,

Kalecki made finance and its availability the ultimate constraint on accumulation, whereas Keynes rather neglected this in *The General Theory* (though not in the *Treatise on Money*). He made amends in his subsequent work on the finance motive, thus returning to the path he was on in the *Treatise on Money*. Keynes's and Kalecki's systems in Kriesler's view (and ours) dominate that of the neoclassicals both before and after the publication of *The General Theory*. He explains why through lucid arguments and a judicious use of charts.

Littleboy on Leijonhufvud on Keynes

The publication of Axel Leijonhufvud's *Keynesian Economics and the Economics of Keynes* in 1968 had a major impact on how Keynes's message was seen and understood. Since that date a huge literature has emerged and Leijonhufvud himself has backed off from some of his major suggestions, especially on the reversal of quantity versus price movements in Marshall (and Keynes) and Walras. One of the most insightful surveyors of these developments is Bruce Littleboy, whose PhD on the topic was the basis of a well-regarded book published in 1990. In his thoughtful and wide-ranging essay in the present volume (39) he compares and contrasts Leijonhufvud's views on Keynes then and now with those of some leading Post-Keynesians, especially Shackle, whose views are discerned to be at odds with those of Leijonhufvud. Littleboy argues persuasively that in many instances this is *not* the case, and that, when it appears to be so, it is largely because the Post-Keynesians or Leijonhufvud or, most of all, Keynes have themselves been misunderstood.

CONCLUSION

We do not wish to delay further our readers' enjoyment of the chapters that follow. All we wish to say in concluding this introduction is that our authors have reinforced our belief that Keynes did provide the basic wherewithal for understanding the nature of the malfunctioning of our sorts of economies and the ingredients of sensible and effective policies for remedying them, if only the international political good will is also present. They have also set out clearly the new developments since Keynes died which will serve to reinforce these fundamental claims.

NOTES

1 The editors would like to thank the contributors to the volume, Grant Belchamber and Jörg Bibow for their helpful and supportive comments on a draft of the Introduction.
2 Keynes's suggestions for 'Footnotes to "The General Theory"'

Chapter 1 The Four Parts of the Theory:
      (a) Effective demand
      (b) The multiplier
      (c) The theory of investment
      (d) The theory of interest
    2 The analysis of effective demand
    3 The theory of interest regarded as the marginal efficiency of money
    4 The analysis of liquidity preference regarded as constituting the demand for money
    5 The limitations on the demand for capital goods
    6 Statistical notes

(*C.W.* XIV: 133–4)

3 In his chapter (31), Rod O'Donnell deals briefly with Keynes's plans for books after *The General Theory*.

4 Joan Wells and Christopher Torr (whose PhD dissertation was examined by Paul) have allowed us to quote from a letter which Paul wrote to Christopher in 1983. The passage describes beautifully the aim of the volume and it is fitting that Paul's words should play a part in the volume he so enthusiastically supported:

> Keynes presented us with some fundamental and important concepts. Our job is to shape these ideas in [the] light of current conditions and experience. *The General Theory* is not a straight jacket. It is a marvellously loose book with ideas that can be shaped and reshaped as need be. And therein lies, I believe, its great power. Nobody wants to know what Keynes actually meant or wrote, etc. This is impossible. All we need to do is to take his fundamental ideas and reshape them into something sensible.

5 Paul Davidson (28 September 1995) would have us stress that 'Keynes always argued that what he was trying to write in *The General Theory* was that money mattered and was integrated with the real economy in *both* the long period and the short period'. We do not disagree.

6 Jan Kregel (3 October 1995) is·worried that this may be read as implying that Chapter 17 is 'separate or different from the rest of the book'. We do *not* mean to do so; moreover, we argue that Kregel's chapter (16), which conveys the message that Chapter 17 may be interpreted as being 'the *G.T.* in a nutshell', is a profound one. Also, as Paul Davidson (28 September 1995) reminded us, Keynes had a subtle argument involving user costs which played a role in short-period equilibrium.

7 The story is, of course, more complicated than the bald statement in the text. Once quantity has been determined in the product market, the associated value of the marginal product of labour will help to determine (though not *necessarily* equal) the real wage. The schedule of the marginal product of labour is *not* a demand function for labour *but* it is a wage-setting instrument (see Riach 1995: 164–6).

8 Jan Kregel (9 October 1995) made the following qualification: the theoretical construct of effective demand itself should not be confused 'with particular or peculiar conditions of industry, that the latter should never require a special or different interpretation of effective demand' as such.

9 Keynes, of course, never knew of Kalecki's review but he did refer in his 1939 *Economic Journal* article (Keynes 1939a: 49) to '[Dr Kalecki's] brilliant article . . . in *Econometrica* [as] an important piece of pioneering work'.

10 We should mention at this point the writings of the late Sidney Weintraub who,

together with Tarshis, kept close to Keynes's own distinctive approach (see, for example, Weintraub 1957).

11 Jan Kregel has a discussion of user cost in his chapter (16) on the analysis of Chapter 17 of *The General Theory*, in which his interpretation of the concept differs from that of Torr.

12 Donald Moggridge (1992: 535) recounts the fascinating story of Ralph Hawtrey's 'discovery' of the multiplier in his comments on the proofs of the *Treatise on Money*. He rejected his discovery out of hand ever after while Keynes does not seem to have seen its significance until after Kahn's (and James Meade's) version became available.

13 In their chapter in this volume (17), Ingo Barens and Volker Caspari point out that Irving Fisher (1896) preceded them all as far as the concept, if not the name, is concerned.

14 Tom Rymes has pointed out to us that Mabel Timlin, then an assistant professor at the University of Saskatchewan in her fifty-first year (!), and thirty five years before Kregel's article, analysed the 'system of shifting equilibrium which lies at the heart of Keynesian theory' (Timlin 1942: 7).

15 But note the reservation expressed by Kregel (see n. 8 above). Paul Davidson (28 September 1995) also argues that Keynes always wanted to show that whether competition was perfect or not, unemployment equilibrium could occur.

16 Because our trade is not an exact science, to say the least, Lawlor's chapter is in fact Chapter 20.

17 As Tom Rymes commented to us, and we agree, there is 'a huge difference between [the issues tackled by] Harrod and Domar'.

18 In the latter situation, Brown argues that Keynes not only anticipated Kaldor's 'Keynesian' theory of distribution by over twenty years but also that he would not have been as confident about a lack of fightback by wage-earners and others to rises in prices associated with excess demand.

19 Davis (1994a) is an expanded and most thorough exposition of the arguments of his chapter.

20 Rod O'Donnell has drawn our attention to a passage in the final chapter of his book (1989: 331–2) which complements Coates's contribution (though it does not mention fuzzy logic).

Book I

INTRODUCTION

THE RELATION OF *THE GENERAL THEORY* TO THE CLASSICAL THEORY

The opening chapters of a 'second edition' of *The General Theory*

J.F. Brothwell

INTRODUCTION

If Keynes had produced a second edition of *The General Theory*, there is little doubt that Book I (Introduction), particularly Chapter 2 ('The Postulates of the Classical Economics'), would have been changed considerably. By 1939 Keynes had begun to realize that he had accepted too readily the first classical postulate (*The wage is equal to the marginal product of labour*) together with marginal productivity theory and the assumption that prices must rise and real wages fall as output and employment increase:

> If the falling tendency of real wages in periods of rising demand is denied . . . it would be possible to simplify considerably the more complicated version of my fundamental explanation which I have expounded in my *General Theory* – particularly in Chapter 2, which is the portion of my book which most needs to be revised.
>
> (*C.W.* VII: 401)

Instead of setting out his new theory of employment 'simply as a positive doctrine', Keynes, in the first two chapters, chose to discuss his theory in relation to what he took to be the orthodox, classical theory of employment. In Chapter 1, he argued that the two postulates of the classical theory 'are applicable to a special case only and not to the general case', while in Chapter 2, as mentioned above, he accepted the first postulate (subject to the qualifications required if competition and markets were imperfect), concentrating the whole difference between his new theory and the old one on his 'fundamental objection' to the second postulate (*The utility of the wage when a given volume of labour is employed is equal to the marginal disutility of that amount of employment*): '[T]here may exist no expedient by which labour as a whole can reduce its *real* wage to a given figure by making revised *money* bargains with the entrepreneurs.'

Paradoxically, Keynes's attempt in Chapter 2 to differentiate his new theory from the old has resulted in complete misunderstanding of the fundamental difference between *The General Theory* and pre-Keynesian economics and has paved the way for a neoclassical revival. His uncritical acceptance of the first postulate (diminishing marginal productivity of labour in the short period) without emphasizing that in *his* system the postulate does *not* give us the demand schedule for employment, together with his arguments concerning the stickiness of money-wages and the inability of labour as a whole to reduce its *real* wage, led many to believe that all Keynes's theory amounted to was an, admittedly realistic, critique of the imperfect operation of the labour market. The cure for unemployment was to bring about supply-side improvements to increase the (downward) flexibility of money and real wages – the neoclassical solution. Thus, despite Keynes's arguments elsewhere in *The General Theory*, especially in Chapter 19 ('Changes in Money-Wages'), that cuts in wages were not the remedy for the widespread unemployment caused by lack of effective demand (apart from the stimulus which might be expected in an unclosed system), attention still centred on the working of the labour market and the effect on the market of the 'Keynesian case' of sticky money-wages.

If in Book I Keynes had laid out the framework of his new theory of the level of effective demand, output and employment in a monetary production economy (instead of discussing the postulates of the classical economics), it would have been clear that his theory was fundamentally and completely different from the orthodox theory; that employment *and* the real wage were determined in the goods market, rather than the labour market; that the chain of causation ran from employment to the real wage, *not* vice versa as in the classical theory, and that the cure for unemployment was to increase effective demand, not reduce wages. This last, key point could have been reinforced by a preliminary discussion in Book I of the uncertain effects of cutting money-wages on effective demand and employment, instead of postponing it to a full analysis in Chapter 19:

> It would have been an advantage if the effects of a change in money-wages could have been discussed in an earlier chapter. For the classical theory has been accustomed to rest the supposedly self-adjusting character of the economic system on an assumed fluidity of money-wages; and, when there is rigidity, to lay on this rigidity the blame of maladjustment.
>
> (*C.W.* VII: 257)

Further evidence of the way Keynes might have revised the opening chapters of *The General Theory* is provided by the famous 1937 *Quarterly Journal of Economics* article (*C.W.* XIV: 109–23) in which he tried to re-express the basic ideas underlying his theory. He sums up by stating the two main grounds of his departure from the traditional theory:

> 1 The orthodox theory assumes that we have a knowledge of the future of a kind quite different from that which we actually possess. . . . The hypothesis of a calculable future leads to a wrong interpretation of the principles of behaviour which the need for action compels us to adopt, and to an under-estimation of the concealed factors of utter doubt, precariousness, hope and fear. The result has been a mistaken theory of the rate of interest. . . .

> 2 The orthodox theory [has] ignored the need for a theory of output as a whole.

> (Ibid.: 122–3)

Here Keynes is stressing that the crucial difference between his theory and classical economic theory is that the latter is irrelevant for understanding the world of reality because it cannot deal with the consequences of uncertainty.

> [T]he fact that our knowledge of the future is fluctuating, vague and uncertain, renders wealth [and its accumulation for an indefinitely postponed future] a peculiarly unsuitable subject for the methods of the classical economic theory.

> (Ibid.: 113)

Indeed, it is impossible to understand the role of money in the economy and the determination of the rate of interest unless it is realized that

> our desire to hold money as a store of wealth is a barometer of the degree of our distrust of our own calculations and conventions concerning the future. . . . The possession of actual money lulls our disquietude; and the premium which we require to make us part with money [the rate of interest] is the measure of the degree of our disquietude.

> (Ibid.: 116)

It is only in such a monetary, production economy, moving irreversibly through time towards an *unknowable* future, that chronic lack of aggregate effective demand and consequent large-scale, involuntary unemployment can occur, as the desire for liquidity triumphs over enterprise and investment falls short of the saving which would be forthcoming at a level of income consistent with full employment. Money, in the world we live in, is never neutral as it is in the classical equilibrium; consequently the classical system has no theory of the demand and supply of output as a whole. Thus the basic difference between Keynes's theory and orthodox theory is that his theory deals with an economy in which money plays a part of its own and affects motives and decisions and is, in short, one of the operative factors in the situation, so that the course of events cannot be predicted, either in the long period or in the short, without a knowledge of the behaviour of money between the first state and the last. And it is this which we ought to mean when we speak of a *monetary economy.*

(*C.W.* XIII: 408–9)

This was written in late 1932 when Keynes contributed to a *Festschrift* for Professor A. Spiethoff. He developed the distinction between a neutral (real-exchange) economy and a monetary economy in his Cambridge lectures of 1932–3. Then, in an early draft of *The General Theory*, Chapters 2 and 3 examine in considerable detail 'The distinction between a co-operative economy and an entrepreneur economy' and 'The characteristics of an entrepreneur economy' (*C.W.* XXIX: 76–100). Only in a *real-wage* or *co-operative economy* would the classical postulates be satisfied and the system self-adjust to full employment. In a *money-wage* or *entrepreneur economy* (the economy in which we actually live), output which would be produced in a co-operative economy may be 'unprofitable' and not produced because of inadequate effective demand. It is a mystery why Keynes discarded this very clear explanation of the fundamental distinction between his theory and earlier theories of employment from the opening chapters of the published version of *The General Theory*. Book I mentions the importance of money only very briefly (on p. 19), though Keynes had pointed out in the Preface that: 'A monetary economy, we shall find, is essentially one in which changing views about the future are capable of influencing the quantity of employment and not merely its direction.' If Keynes had found the time to revise *The General Theory* it seems very likely that he would have restored much of the material from earlier drafts, explaining the fundamental difference between the orthodox theory of employment in a world 'in which our views concerning the future are fixed and reliable in all respects' and his theory of employment pertaining to the real world 'in which our previous expectations are liable to disappointment and expectations concerning the future affect what we do today' – the complete theory of a monetary production economy. Thus, in what follows, a very close resemblance to Keynes's words in Volume XXIX (pp. 76–102), Volume XIII (pp. 408–11) and Volume XIV (pp. 109–23) of the *Collected Writings*, together with parts of Chapters 1, 2, 3, 10, 16 and 19 of Volume VII (*The General Theory*) is completely intentional.

CHAPTER 1 THE NATURE AND SIGNIFICANCE OF THE CONTRAST BETWEEN A CO-OPERATIVE AND AN ENTREPRENEUR ECONOMY

J.F. Brothwell writing as J.M. Keynes

It may help us to understand the essence of the distinction between the classical theory of employment, as exemplified by Professor Pigou's *Theory of Unemployment,* and the more generalized theory which I shall here try to develop, if we consider in what conditions the two postulates of the classical theory would be satisfied. These postulates are:

1 The real wage is equal to the marginal product of labour, which decreases according to the law of diminishing marginal productivity as employment increases. This gives us the short-period demand schedule for employment, according to classical theory.
2 The utility of the wage when a given volume of labour is employed is equal to the marginal disutility of that amount of employment, which rises as employment increases. This gives us the supply schedule for employment.

Thus, in the classical theory, the amount of employment is fixed by the workings of the labour market at the point where the utility of the marginal product balances the disutility of the marginal employment. It is assumed that labour is always free to increase employment, reducing its real wage until it equals the marginal disutility of work, by accepting a reduction in its money-wage. Thus, in the classical theory, the money-wage adjusts to clear the labour market. This equilibrium in the labour market is compatible with 'frictional' unemployment – in a non-static society there will always exist a proportion of resources unemployed 'between jobs' preventing continuous full employment – and 'voluntary' unemployment, due to the refusal of labour to accept a reward less than its marginal disutility, but these two categories of unemployment are comprehensive. The classical postulates do not admit of the possibility of the third category of unemployment, which I defined in the first edition of my book as 'involuntary' unemployment, but which is better designated 'demand-deficiency' unemployment. This third category formed the bulk of the unemployed in the twenties and thirties.

Now the classical postulates would be satisfied and there would be no problem of demand deficiency in a community in which the factors of production are rewarded by dividing up in agreed proportions the actual output of their co-operative efforts. This is the simplest case of a society in which the presuppositions of the classical theory are fulfilled. It is not necessary that the factors should receive their share of output in kind in the first instance – the position is substantially the same if they are paid in money, provided they all of them accept the money merely as a temporary convenience, with a view to spending the whole of it forthwith on purchasing

7

such part of current output as they choose. This first type of society we will call a *real-wage* or *co-operative economy*.

The second type, in which the factors are hired by entrepreneurs for money but where there is a mechanism of some kind to ensure that the expenditure of £100 in hiring factors of production will yield an output which is expected to sell for at least £100, we will call a *neutral entrepreneur economy*, or a *neutral economy* for short. The third type, of which the second is a limiting case, in which the entrepreneurs hire the factors for money but without such a mechanism as the above, we will call a *money-wage* or *entrepreneur economy*.

It is obvious on these definitions that it is in an entrepreneur economy that we actually live today. The classical theory, as exemplified in the tradition from Ricardo to Marshall and Professor Pigou, appears to me to presume that the conditions for a *neutral economy* are substantially fulfilled in general; that supply creates its own demand; that the whole costs of production must necessarily be spent immediately in the aggregate, directly or indirectly, on purchasing the product. The conviction which runs, for example, through almost all Professor Pigou's work, that money makes no real difference except frictionally and that the theory of production and employment can be worked out as being based on 'real' exchanges, with money introduced perfunctorily in a later chapter, is the modern version of the classical tradition. It is my belief, however, that the far-reaching and in some respects fundamental differences between the conclusions of a monetary economy and those of the more simplified real-exchange economy have been greatly underestimated by the exponents of the traditional economics; with the result that the machinery of thought with which real-exchange economics has equipped the minds of practitioners in the world of affairs, and also of economists themselves, has led in practice to many erroneous conclusions and policies. The idea that it is comparatively easy to adapt the hypothetical conclusions of a real-wage economics to the real world of monetary economics is a mistake. It is extraordinarily difficult to make the adaptation, and perhaps impossible without the aid of a developed theory of monetary production economics such as my *General Theory*.

Contemporary thought is still deeply steeped in the notion that if people do not spend their money in one way they will spend it in another. Similarly, it is natural to suppose that the act of an individual, by which he enriches himself without apparently taking anything from anyone else, must also enrich the community as a whole; so that an act of individual saving inevitably leads to a parallel act of investment. Those who think in this way are deceived, nevertheless, by an optical illusion, which makes two essentially different activities appear to be the same. They are fallaciously supposing that there is a nexus which unites decisions to abstain from present consumption with decisions to provide for future consumption so that a fall in expenditure on consumption goods is matched by a rise in expenditure on investment goods. But, as we shall see in what follows, a fall in expenditure on consumption goods (an act of saving) is likely to lead to a fall in income, output and employment with no compensation from investment. In other words, the conditions for a *neutral economy* are not satisfied in practice; with the result that there is a difference of the most fundamental importance between a co-operative economy and the type of entrepreneur economy in which we actually live. For in an entrepreneur economy, as we shall see, the volume of employment, the marginal disutility of which is equal to the utility of its marginal product, may be 'unprofitable' in terms of money because of lack of *effective demand*; that is, because aggregate expenditure is less than the aggregate cost of production. For the classical proposition that supply creates its own demand, I shall substitute the proposition that expenditure (effective demand) creates its own income, that is, an income just sufficient to meet the expenditure. In a co-operative or in a neutral economy effective demand cannot fluctuate; and it can be neglected in considering the factors which determine the volume of employment. But in an entrepreneur economy the fluctuations of effective demand are likely to be the dominating factor in determining the volume of employment; and in this book, therefore, we shall be mainly concerned with analysing the causes and consequences of such fluctuations. This also means that, in an entrepreneur economy, the aggregate of employment can fluctuate for reasons quite independent of any changes in the labour market in the relation between the marginal utility of a quantity of output and the marginal disutility of the employment required to produce that quantity. Aggregate employment in the real world is determined in the product market rather than in the labour market.

CHAPTER 2   THE CHARACTERISTICS OF AN ENTREPRENEUR ECONOMY
J.F. Brothwell writing as J.M. Keynes

An entrepreneur economy is a monetary economy. Money is *par excellence* the means of remuneration in such an economy and is not neutral – it is used as a store of wealth because our knowledge of the future is fluctuating, vague and uncertain. Our desire to hold money as a store of wealth is a barometer of the degree of our distrust of our own calculations and conventions concerning the future. Even though this feeling about money is itself conventional or instinctive, it operates, so to speak, at a deeper level of our motivation. It takes charge at the moments when the higher, more precarious conventions have weakened. The possession of actual money lulls our disquietude; and the premium which we require to make us part with money is the measure of the degree of our disquietude. This, expressed in a very general way, is my theory of the rate of interest in the real-world, entrepreneur economy. The rate of interest obviously measures – just as the books on arithmetic say it does – the premium which has to be offered to induce people to hold their wealth in some form other than hoarded money. The quantity of money and the amount of it required in the active circulation for the transaction of current business (mainly depending on the level of money income) determine how much is available for inactive balances, that is, for hoards. The rate of interest is the factor which adjusts at the margin the demand for hoards to the supply of hoards; *not*, as the classical theory would have it, the factor which adjusts the rate of saving to the rate of investment. (Saving and investment in my system are brought into equilibrium by movements of income, as we shall see.)

Thus in a monetary, entrepreneur economy operating under conditions of complete uncertainty, the link between saving and investment is easily broken, so that effective demand (total expenditure on consumption and investment) fluctuates. People are free to save part of their money incomes and either accumulate money (when they are particularly worried about the future and do not wish to commit themselves to a specified expenditure at a specified time) or spend it on something which is not current output and to the production of which current output cannot be diverted. An act of individual saving means – so to speak – a decision not to have dinner today. But it does *not* necessitate a decision to have dinner or to buy a pair of boots a week hence or a year hence or to consume any specified thing at any specified date. Thus it depresses the business of preparing today's dinner without stimulating the business of making ready for some future act of consumption. It is not a substitution of future consumption-demand (investment-demand) for present consumption-demand – it is a net diminution of such demand. Thus, if consumption falls, unless there is a rise in investment expenditure to compensate, effective demand, output and employment fall. But such a rise in investment expenditure is unlikely to occur because, as we shall argue in the chapter on 'The State of Long-term Expectation', investment expenditure (given the rate of interest) depends upon estimates of the prospective yield of assets based on extremely flimsy knowledge.

Our knowledge of the factors which will govern the yield of an investment some years hence is usually very slight and often negligible. Hence we assume that the present is a much more serviceable guide to the future than a candid examination of past experience would show it to have been hitherto. Thus a rise in saving, rather than leading to a rise in investment to compensate, is likely to depress expectations of future demand and so lead to a fall in investment; consumption and investment both falling in a cumulative downward spiral. It is not surprising that the volume of investment should fluctuate widely from time to time. For it depends on two sets of judgements about the future, neither of which rests on an adequate or secure foundation – on the propensity to hoard and on the opinions of the future yield of capital assets. Nor is there any reason to suppose that the fluctuations in one of these factors will tend to offset the fluctuations in the other. Indeed, the conditions which aggravate the one factor tend, as a rule, to aggravate the other. For the same circumstances which lead to pessimistic views about future yields are apt to increase the propensity to hoard, the desire for liquidity.

There is always a danger in an entrepreneur economy that the entrepreneurs will prefer financial investment to real investment, with unemployment arising from the consequent lack of effective demand. Moreover, the richer the economy, the wider will tend to be the gap between its actual and its potential production; and therefore the more obvious and outrageous the defects of the economic system. For a poor community will be prone to consume by far the greater part of its output, so that a very modest measure of investment will be sufficient to provide full employment; whereas a wealthy community will have to discover much ampler opportunities for investment if the saving propensities of its wealthier members are to be compatible with the employment of its poorer members. If in a potentially wealthy community the inducement to invest is weak (as it is likely to be since it depends so critically on spontaneous optimism in the face of the dark forces of time and our ignorance of the future), the working of the principle of effective demand will compel the community to reduce its actual output, until, in spite of its potential wealth, it has become so poor that its surplus over its consumption is sufficiently diminished to correspond to the weakness of the inducement to invest.

The general theory of employment

A brief summary of the theory of employment to be worked out in the course of the following chapters may, perhaps, help the reader at this stage, even though it may not be fully intelligible. The terms involved will be more carefully defined in due course. In this summary, for simplicity and to facilitate the exposition, we shall assume that the money-wage and other factor costs are constant per unit of labour employed. But unemployment is the result of lack of demand, *not* sticky money-wages, and the essential character of the argument is precisely the same whether or not money-wages are liable to change, as will be shown below.

The outline of our theory can be expressed as follows. When employment increases, aggregate real income is increased. The psychology of the community is such that when aggregate real income is increased aggregate consumption is increased, but not by so much as income. Hence employers would make a loss if the whole of the increased employment were to be devoted to satisfying the increased demand for immediate consumption. Thus, to justify any given amount of employment there must be an amount of current investment sufficient to absorb the excess of total output over what the community chooses to consume when employment is at the given

11

level. For unless there is this amount of investment, the receipts of the entrepreneurs will be less than is required to induce them to offer the given amount of employment, that is, there will be insufficient aggregate effective demand. It follows, therefore, that, given what we shall call the community's propensity to consume, the equilibrium level of employment, that is, the level at which there is no inducement to employers as a whole either to expand or contract employment, will depend on the amount of current investment. But investment is liable to fluctuate, as explained above. Any equilibrium is likely to be of a very temporary nature. Indeed, I should be prepared to argue that, in a world ruled by uncertainty with an uncertain future linked to an actual present, a final position of equilibrium, such as one deals with in static economics, does not properly exist. If investment falls, income falls and therefore saving falls until a new, lower equilibrium level of income is reached (when again the reduced amount of current investment is just sufficient to absorb the reduced excess of total output over what the community chooses to consume at the lower level of income). Instead of saving determining investment, as in the traditional theory, it is much truer to say that investment determines saving. Thus, given the propensity to consume and the rate of new investment, there will be only one level of employment consistent with equilibrium; since any other level will lead to inequality between the aggregate costs of output as a whole and aggregate expenditure. This level cannot be greater than full employment. But there is no reason in general for expecting it to be *equal* to full employment. Actual experience shows that we oscillate round an intermediate position appreciably below full employment and appreciably above the minimum employment a decline below which would endanger life.

There follows from the simple principle that an increase in income will be divided in some proportion or another between spending and saving a relationship which I have given attention to in this book under the name of the *multiplier*. An increment of investment cannot occur unless the public are prepared to increase their saving. Ordinarily speaking, the public will not do this unless their aggregate income is increasing. Thus their effort to consume a part of their increased incomes will stimulate output until the new level (and distribution) of incomes provides a margin of saving sufficient to correspond to the increased investment. The multiplier tells us by how much their employment has to be increased to yield an increase in real income sufficient to induce them to do the necessary extra saving, and is a function of their psychological propensities. If saving is the pill and consumption is the jam, the extra jam has to be proportional to the size of the additional pill. Unless the psychological propensities of the public are different from what we are supposing, we have here established the law that increased employment for investment must necessarily stimulate the industries producing for consumption and thus lead to a total increase of employment which is a multiple of the primary employment required by the investment itself.

The theory can be summed up by saying that, given the psychology of the public, the level of output and employment as a whole depends on the amount of investment. I put it in this way, not because this is the only factor on which aggregate output depends, but because it is usual in a complex system to regard as the *causa causans* that factor which is most prone to sudden and wide fluctuation. More comprehensively, aggregate output depends on the propensity to hoard, on the policy of the monetary authority as it affects the quantity of money, on the state of confidence concerning the prospective yield of capital assets, on the propensity to spend and on the social factors which influence the level of the money-wage. But of these several factors it is those which determine the rate of investment which are most unreliable, since it is they which are influenced by our views of the future about which we know so little.

My departure from the traditional theory is, therefore, quite fundamental. The orthodox theory assumes that we have a knowledge of the future of a kind quite different from that which we actually possess. The hypothesis of a calculable future leads to a wrong interpretation of the principles of behaviour which the need for action compels us to adopt, in an entrepreneur, monetary economy, and to an under-estimation of the concealed factors of utter doubt, precariousness, hope and fear. Thus orthodox theory cannot explain why investment, output and employment are so liable to fluctuation. Coupled with this, orthodox theory has ignored the need for a theory of the supply and demand of output as a whole. It has accepted Say's Law that supply creates its own demand and the psychological law underlying the principle of effective demand and the multiplier has escaped notice. The traditional theory, therefore, cannot explain *why*, in any circumstances, employment is what it is; it has nothing to offer, when it is applied to the problem of what determines the volume of actual employment as a whole.

The effect of money-wage changes

The fundamental difference between my theory of employment and the orthodox, classical theory may be illustrated further by a preliminary discussion of the effects of money-wage changes in the two systems. The classical theory has been accustomed to rest the supposedly self-adjusting character of the economic system on an assumed fluidity of money-wages; and, when there is rigidity, to lay on this rigidity the blame of maladjustment. Unemployment, according to this analysis, is essentially the result of too high money-wages. The cure is to reduce money-wages, which will *cet. par.* stimulate demand by diminishing the price of the finished product, and will therefore increase output and employment up to the point where the reduction which labour has agreed to accept in its money-wages is just offset by the diminishing marginal efficiency of labour as output (from a given equipment) is increased. In its crudest form, this is tantamount to assuming that the reduction in money-wages will leave demand unaffected. In any given industry it is assumed that there is a demand schedule for labour relating the quantity of employment to different levels of wages, the shape of the curve at any point furnishing the elasticity of demand for labour. This conception is then transferred without substantial modification to industry as a whole; and it is supposed, by a parity of reasoning, that we have a demand schedule for labour in industry as a whole relating the quantity of employment to different levels of wages. It is held that it makes no material difference to this argument whether it is in terms of money-wages or of real wages. If we are thinking in terms of money-wages, we must, of course, correct for changes in the value of money; but this leaves the general tendency of the argument unchanged, since prices certainly do not change in exact proportion to changes in money-wages.

If this is the groundwork of the argument (and, if it is not, I do not know what the groundwork is) surely it is fallacious. For the demand schedules for particular industries can only be constructed on some fixed assumption as to the nature of the demand and supply schedules of other industries and as to the amount of the aggregate effective demand. It is invalid, therefore, to transfer the argument to industry as a whole unless we also transfer our assumption that the aggregate effective demand is fixed. For, whilst no one would wish to deny the proposition that a reduction in money-wages *accompanied by the same aggregate effective demand as before* will be associated with an increase in employment, the precise question at issue is whether the reduction in money-wages will or will not be accompanied by the same aggregate effective demand as before measured in money, or, at any rate, by an aggregate effective demand which is not reduced in full proportion to the reduction in money-wages. But if the classical theory is not allowed to extend by analogy its conclusions in respect of a particular industry to industry as a whole, it is wholly unable to answer the question what effect on employment a reduction in money-wages will have. For it has no method of analysis wherewith to tackle the problem.

The volume of employment is not determined by movements of money (and real) wages in the market for labour as a whole. It is not determined by the marginal disutility of labour measured in terms of real wages, except in so far as the supply of labour available at a given real wage sets a *maximum* level to employment. The propensity to consume and the rate of new investment determine between them the volume of employment and hence the marginal productivity of labour and the real wage. If the propensity to consume and the rate of new investment result in a deficient effective demand, the actual level of employment will fall short of the supply of labour potentially available at the existing real wage, which will be greater than the marginal disutility of employment. Perhaps it will help to rebut the crude conclusion that a reduction in money-wages will increase employment 'because it reduces the cost of production', if we follow up the course of events on the hypothesis most favourable to this view, namely that at the outset entrepreneurs *expect* the reduction in money-wages to have this effect. It is indeed not unlikely that the individual entrepreneur, seeing his own costs reduced, will overlook at the outset the repercussions on the demand for his product and will act on the assumption that he will be able to sell at a profit a larger output than before. If, then, entrepreneurs generally act on this expectation, will they in fact succeed in increasing their profits? Only if the community's increment of income is all consumed; or if there is an increase in investment, corresponding to the gap between the increment of income and the increment of consumption. In other words, there must be an increase in aggregate effective demand or the proceeds realized from the increased output will disappoint the entrepreneurs and employment, *cet. par.*, will fall back to its previous figure. Thus the reduction in money-wages will have no lasting tendency to increase employment except by virtue of its repercussion either on the propensity to consume for the community as a whole or on the rate of investment expenditure. There is no method of analysing the effect of a reduction in money-wages on total employment except by following up its possible effects on aggregate demand.

We shall consider the effects of a change in money-wages in our model in detail in a later chapter. It will be shown that an all-round reduction in money-wages is unlikely to increase demand and employment. Consumption demand is more likely to fall than rise as a result of money-wage reductions and, although some fall in interest rates is likely due to the reduction in the transactions demand for money as incomes fall, the repercussion of wage reductions on entrepreneurs' expectations of the profitability of investment is very uncertain. While wage cuts (if they do not precipitate labour troubles) may produce an optimistic tone in the minds of entrepreneurs, the depressing influence of their greater burden of debt as money prices and profits fall may offset this. Indeed, if the fall of wages and prices goes far, the embarrassment of those entrepreneurs who are heavily indebted may soon reach the point of insolvency, with severely adverse effects on investment.

Thus a moderate reduction in money-wages may prove inadequate, whilst an immoderate reduction might shatter confidence even if it were practicable. Furthermore, such a collapse of confidence would increase liquidity-preference, more than offsetting any favourable effects on the rate of interest brought about by the release of money from the active circulation. This is yet another example of the far-reaching and fundamental differences between the working of an actual complex monetary economy and that of a more simplified real-exchange economy. In a monetary economy, in which our knowledge of the future is fluctuating, vague and uncertain, it is necessary that wages are sticky in terms of money in order to give some stability to the price level. If labour were to respond to conditions of diminishing employment by reducing money-wages, the chief result of such a policy would be to cause a great instability of prices, so violent perhaps as to make business calculations futile in an economic society functioning after the manner of that in which we live. To suppose that a flexible wage policy is a right and proper adjunct of a system which on the whole is one of *laissez-faire* is the opposite of the truth.

To sum up: given the equipment and technique of production (i.e. the supply function), the amount of employment will depend on the *demand*; and, if there is increased demand leading to more output and therefore, after a point, to a lower marginal productivity of labour and lower real wage, this will not, in general, be interfered with by labour withdrawing its services. Therefore, it is essential to discover what determines demand. That is the subject matter of the following chapters. My solution, put in a sentence, is that, given the propensity to spend, demand is a function of the amount of investment.

CONCLUSION
J.F. Brothwell writing as himself

If Keynes had found the time to revise *The General Theory* and had begun the second edition as set out above, it is tempting to think that the neoclassical resurgence of the post-war years might not have happened; the Keynesian revolution in macroeconomic thought might have been completely successful and become part of mainstream economics. By making clear the crucial distinction between an entrepreneur, monetary economy and a classical real-wage, neutral-money economy, the protracted and sterile controversy as to whether pre-Keynesian economics was a special case of Keynesian economics, or vice versa, might not have arisen. We might have been spared the arguments that Keynesian economics was simply 'fixed-price' or 'fixed money-wage' economics with quantity adjusting rather than price; that Keynesian economics was 'disequilibrium economics' because of the absence of the Walrasian auctioneer necessary to ensure general equilibrium. In particular, the disaster of the neoclassical–Keynesian synthesis, in which a neoclassical production function, labour market analysis and real balance effect were combined with the Hicksian IS–LM model, thereby draining the model of its Keynesian content, might never have occurred. We might have been spared the ravages inflicted on the economies of the West by economic policies based on monetarism and the higher lunacies of the New Classical Economics.

If the macroeconomics of Keynes had maintained its influence over policy-making, as it did until the mid-1970s, the miserable performance of the UK economy during the last twenty years could have been averted. Instead, the acceleration of inflation from the late 1960s onwards (especially after the quadrupling of oil prices in 1973–4) led the 'madmen in authority' to adopt the policies of Friedman and the monetarists, based on the classical economics which Keynes had struggled to overthrow. Monetarists assume that the economy self-adjusts to equilibrium, with the labour market clearing at what they term the 'natural' rate of unemployment. Any attempt by the government to reduce unemployment below the natural rate can only result in accelerating inflation. In other words, monetarists assume that the economy behaves like a classical real-wage, neutral-money economy. All that the authorities can (and should) do is to control the rate of growth of the money supply and the economy will follow a steady, non inflationary, growth path. Low inflation takes precedence over high employment as the main objective of economic policy and demand management is abandoned. Government intervention in the operation of the market system should be reduced to a minimum; the budget should be kept as small as possible and balanced (at least on average over the cycle); discretionary budgetary policy is eschewed; the objective becomes a balanced budget rather than a balanced full-employment economy. The 'Treasury View' – that loan-financed public works merely crowd out private expenditure with little impact on employment – the argument that Keynes had laboured so mightily to refute, re-establishes itself. It is not surprising that the last ten years have seen prolonged unemployment reach its highest levels since *The General Theory* was published.

It is doubtful, however, whether a revision by Keynes of his great work along the lines suggested would have been sufficient to prevent a neoclassical revival. As the above hypothetical opening chapters show, Keynes was unlikely, in a second edition, to have made the complete break with classical marginal productivity theory that was probably necessary if his revolution in economic theory were to be entirely successful. He wrote *The General Theory* to overthrow the neoclassical theory of employment but failed to realize that the neoclassical theories of employment, pricing and distribution are inseparable and need to be discarded *in toto*. The marginal productivity model of varying factor proportions and the substitution of one factor for another, changing technique within a given state of technology in response to changing relative factor prices, is extremely artificial and unreal. It reaches its ultimate absurdity in the concepts of an aggregate production function, 'jelly' capital, and the marginal productivity theory of the macro-distribution of income. As his 1939 *Economic Journal* article (*C.W.* VII: 394–412) shows, Keynes was becoming aware of the inadequacy of marginal productivity theory and of theories of the firm and of distribution based upon it:

Indeed, it is rare for anyone but an economist to suppose that price is predominantly governed by marginal cost. Most businessmen are

17

surprised by the suggestion that it is a close calculation of short-period marginal cost or of marginal revenue which should dominate their price policies. . . . It is, beyond doubt, the practical assumption of the producer that his price policy ought to be influenced by the fact that he is normally operating subject to decreasing average cost, even if in the short-period his marginal cost is rising.

(Ibid.: 407)

And,

it is evident that Mr. Dunlop, Mr. Tarshis and Dr. Kalecki have given us much to think about, and have seriously shaken the fundamental assumptions on which the short-period theory of distribution has been based hitherto.

(Ibid.: 411)

But Keynes was reluctant to accept that marginal product could be constant (or even rise) over a considerable range:

Meanwhile I am comforted by the fact that their conclusions tend to confirm the idea that the causes of short-period fluctuation are to be found in changes in the demand for labour, and not changes in its real-supply price; though I complain a little that I in particular should be criticised for conceding a little to the other view by admitting that, when the changes in effective demand to which I myself attach importance have brought about a change in the level of output, the real-supply price for labour would in fact change in the direction assumed by the theory I am opposing – as if I was the first to have entertained the fifty-year-old generalisation that, trend eliminated, increasing output is usually associated with a falling real wage.

(Ibid.: 411–12)

It seems unlikely, then, that Keynes would have entirely discarded marginal productivity theory in a revised edition of *The General Theory*; his 'struggle of escape from habitual modes of thought and expression' was to that extent incomplete. It is unlikely that he would have taken fully into consideration the advances in microeconomics, the theory of the firm and the short-period theory of distribution made by his colleagues in Cambridge (and by Kalecki) when revising *The General Theory*. This is a pity; it is much more convincing to base Keynes's aggregate supply (aggregate income or proceeds) and aggregate demand (aggregate expected sale-proceeds) functions on the micro-foundation of demand-constrained, price-making, oligopolistic firms – as Lorie Tarshis did in his PhD dissertation. There is no doubt that the macroeconomics of Keynes and oligopolistic competition complement each other in explaining the working of an entrepreneur, monetary economy, just as perfect competition and marginal productivity theory are integral with the classical, real-wage economy. Keynes's understandable failure to escape completely from the old ideas, even in a second edition, might still have left sufficient grounds for a neoclassical revival and jeopardized his revolution in economic thought.

ON REWRITING CHAPTER 2 OF
THE GENERAL THEORY

Keynes's concept of involuntary unemployment

William Darity, Jr and Warren Young

> You go on to say that you must confess that you do not understand my doctrine of involuntary unemployment or full employment. But, heavens my doctrine of full employment is what the whole of my book is about! Everything else is a side issue to that. If you do not understand my doctrine of full employment, it is perfectly hopeless for you to attempt to explain the book to anyone.[1]

Maynard Keynes did not tend to look backward. Instead of continuously resurrecting positions he had taken at earlier stages of his intellectual development as an economist, his inclination was to lay out his latest position in an entirely new work. Perhaps the most dramatic instance of this impulse is the transition from the argument in his *Treatise on Money* to the argument in his *General Theory of Employment, Interest and Money*; in the latter, Keynes had little to say about the former work.[2]

But in one specific instance Keynes averred that he would have considered a significant rewrite of a portion of the *General Theory*. Had there been a second edition – had Keynes lived and had he revised the book – this portion of *The General Theory* is the one most likely to have undergone reconstruction. The specific instance concerns Keynes's presentation of the concept of involuntary unemployment, one of the most innovative ideas advanced in the volume, a presentation that occupies Chapter 2 of *The General Theory*.

In response to Jacob Viner's assessment of *The General Theory* in a symposium in the *Quarterly Journal of Economics*, Keynes promptly observed: 'In regard to his [Viner's] criticisms of my definition and treatment of involuntary unemployment, I am ready to agree that this part of my book is particularly open to criticism'. He went on to describe himself as 'already feel[ing] in a position to make improvements'.[3]

Moreover, in a subsequent paper published in 1939 Keynes reacted to the statistical findings of Dunlop and of Tarshis that the evidence is stronger that real wages move procyclically than anticyclically, a finding suggestive of the possible presence of generalized increasing returns and the theory of Kalecki. Keynes made it clear that the entire argument of Chapter 2 was grounded in an attempt to pursue the implications of his concept of involuntary unemployment on classical terrain.[4] Thus, Keynes could then contend that the Dunlop and Tarshis statistical findings are less of a criticism of his own system than conventional theory. Keynes said that if Dunlop and Tarshis are correct, 'it would be possible to simplify considerably the more complicated version of my *General Theory*'. He specifically indicated that the simplification is '[p]articularly' appropriate for 'Chapter 2, the portion of my book most in need of revision'.[5]

The original presentation of the concept of involuntary unemployment, set up by Keynes's brief treatment of the 'postulates' of the classical economists, made it possible for readers of *The General Theory* to conclude that Keynes's primary concern is with so-called 'disequilibrium' or non-market clearing economics. This, despite the fact that Keynes was explicit in contending that he was advancing a theory of unemployment *equilibrium*. When he compared his own work with that of Ralph Hawtrey in his lecture notes of 1937, he wrote: 'The main point is to distinguish the forces determining the position of equilibrium.'[6]

The treatment of involuntary unemployment from the vantage point of the classical 'postulates' led many readers to interpret the fundamental message of *The General Theory* to be the economics of wage stickiness, whether nominal or real, despite Keynes's investigation in Chapter 19 of the irrelevance of wage flexibility for his conclusions. Hence, the New Keynesians today use Keynes's name to give themselves his imprimatur. Keynes's acceptance of the first classical postulate and rejection of the second classical postulate gives his argument the appearance that he viewed workers as being *on* the aggregate demand curve for labour and as being *off* their aggregate supply curve.[7]

Had Keynes revised the book, based upon his post-*General Theory* observations, it is reasonable to argue that he would have eliminated the misleading overture. For Keynes sought to demonstrate that even an ideally functioning capitalist economy – that is, one with no 'leakages' or 'lags' – could settle into a condition of persistent sub-employment in the absence of aggregate demand management, due to an insufficiency of private investment expenditure. His accommodations with the Classicals – apparently prompted, at least in part, by Harrod's conservative influence – pushed the presentation of his message along a path that would lead some interpreters to find its essence in wage inflexibility, money illusion, and/or imperfections in the market for labour.[8]

Indeed, Keynes did *not* argue, to the extent that money-wages are sticky, that such stickiness was attributable to money illusion on the part of labour. While Keynes did say that workers would be unwilling to accept cuts in real wages brought about by reductions in the nominal wage – although he believed they would accept cuts in real wages brought about by price inflation – he did not attribute this to any intrinsic irrationality or lack of information on the part of labour. Keynes's contention was that the piecemeal nature of money-wage reductions would damage the *relative* wage position of those workers who accepted cuts earlier than others.

Concern over *relative* wages led workers to resist nominal wage reductions as the route to real wage cuts, according to Keynes, since matters of comparative living standards and equity in the distribution of income now came into play. This would not be an issue, in his view, if an all-round, simultaneous reduction in nominal wages could be engineered; then, and only then, would labour's response to wage cuts become symmetric with its response to price inflation.

But Keynes went further. Even if money-wages were perfectly flexible downward, the economy would not self-adjust automatically to full employment. The nature of wage bargains precludes labour being able to determine its *real* wage through nominal wage contracts. If labour were to agree to a money-wage reduction, the repercussions on *monetized* effective demand might be negative, leading to downward pressure on the general price level. If the price level chases the money-wage downwards, there might be little change in the real wage rate and little change in the real performance of the economy. Hence, Keynes argued that *variations in the money-wage might be neutral.*[9]

We also expect – again based upon his post-*General Theory* observations – that he would have dispensed altogether with his first, excessively complicated definition of involuntary unemployment. Keynes offered the following definition on page 15 in Chapter 2 of *The General Theory*:

> *Men are involuntarily unemployed if, in the event of a small rise in the price of wage-goods relatively to the money wage, both the aggregate supply of labour willing to work for the current money-wage and the aggregate demand for it at that wage would be greater than the existing volume of employment.*[10]

Using this first definition, Keynes's notion of full employment means a circumstance where involuntary unemployment is absent, a condition that would exist whenever it is possible simultaneously to reduce the real wage measured in terms of labour's commodity bundle, and to increase employment. This definition is identical with the straightforward notion of an excess supply of labour under the following narrow conditions:

1 the aggregate demand schedule for labour is negatively related to the real wage;
2 the aggregate supply schedule for labour is positively related to the real wage;
3 the only endogenous variable that both schedules depend upon is the real wage rate;
4 there is only one sector in the macroeconomy.

As we shall demonstrate below, Keynes definitely did not squeeze his *General Theory* into the straitjacket of these four conditions, particularly with respect to the latter two.

But under these four conditions, there is only a single level of employment that is consistent with labour market clearing; the benchmark for full employment is given unambiguously where labour demand equates with labour supply. Involuntary unemployment, on the basis of the page 15 criterion, only can occur when the labour market does not clear. However, if we relax any one of these four conditions, the page 15 criterion for involuntary unemployment becomes ambiguous. Dropping any one of these four conditions will mean that labour market clearing need not be consistent with the absence of involuntary unemployment.

If the labour supply schedule is downward-sloping and the labour market clears, a reduction in the real wage could lead to an increase in both the supply and demand for labour beyond the level associated with market clearing.[11] If either schedule is sensitive to any endogenous variable besides the real wage, the direct connection between labour market clearing and full employment is broken once again; there could be many positions where the labour market clears but not all of them would meet Keynes's page 15 criterion for the absence of involuntary unemployment. The relevant endogenous variables could include real bond holdings, real cash balances, the rate of interest, expectations of layoffs, changes in the probability of promotion, accretions in overall levels of education and training for the labour force, the state of expectations and the recent history of unemployment and vacancy rates.[12] Finally, the analytical move from one to at least two sectors – say, a wage-goods and a capital-goods producing economy – results in similar ambiguities concerning the full employment position of the economy.[13]

Keynes explicitly proposed that other variables besides the real wage rate could affect the demand and supply of labour, particularly in his critique of Pigou's aggregate labour market in the appendix to Chapter 19, including the rate of interest and the state of confidence.[14] He was adamant that Pigou had made a major error in not exploring the factors that determine the proportions of employment between the economy's *two* sectors – wage-goods and non-wage-goods sectors – by collapsing the distinct sectoral demand schedules for labour into a demand curve for labour as a whole. And, according to Keynes, Pigou's admission that labour typically could bargain directly only over the money-wage, rather than the real wage, was fatal:

> he [Pigou] stipulates that within certain limits labour in fact, often stipulates, not for a given real wage, but for a given money-wage. But in this case the supply function of labour is not a function of . . . [the general real wage rate] alone but also of the money-price of

wage-goods; – with the result that the previous analysis breaks down and an additional factor has to be introduced, without there being an additional equation for this additional unknown.[15]

Keynes's page 15 definition requires a conceptual experiment: a working-out of the effects of a rise in the price of wage-goods to execute a decline in the real wage. A rise in the price of wage-goods is engineered by the inflationary effects of an expansion of aggregate demand, effected either by activist fiscal or by monetary policy. The core policy experiment is the increase in aggregate demand, and Keynes's later definitions preserve the core policy experiment without mentioning the direction of movement of real wages.

On page 26 of *The General Theory*, in Chapter 3, Keynes presented a second definition of full employment that he characterized as the same as the first:

> An alternative, though equivalent criterion [for full employment] is that at which we have now arrived, namely a situation in which aggregate employment is inelastic in response to an increase in effective demand for its output.[16]

Taken literally, this second definition is *not* identical with the first. The movement of real wages does not enter into this definition, nor, strictly speaking, does the market for labour. The definition says the economy is at full employment when no further increase in employment is forthcoming from an increase in aggregate demand.

Keynes may have considered the page 15 and page 26 definitions as 'equivalent' because, at the time, it was inconceivable for him that employment and real wages could rise simultaneously. Prior to the Dunlop and Tarshis findings, the conventional wisdom had it that real wages must move anticyclically. James Tobin has observed that if real wages and employment could move in the same direction it would reinforce the philosophical intent of Keynes's development of the concept of involuntary unemployment:

> When employment could be increased by expansion of aggregate demand, Keynes regarded it as involuntary. He expected expansion to raise prices and lower wages, but this expectation is not crucial to his argument. Indeed, if it is possible to raise employment without reduction in the real wage, his case for calling the employment involuntary is strengthened.[17]

Once the focus on real wages and the labour market is removed, Keynes's definition of full employment compresses simply to identification of the *maximum level of employment that can be reached by increasing aggregate demand*.[18] Labour market clearing is not a sufficient condition for the elasticity of employment with respect to monetized effective demand to become zero; in fact, whether or not the labour market clears is peripheral to this criterion for full employment.

Consistently in Keynes's various post-*General Theory* discussions of his concept of involuntary unemployment it is the page 26/Chapter 3 definition that was replicated. His departure from the classical mode of thought that linked the conceptualization of unemployment to the apparatus of an aggregate labour market became more pronounced. Consider the following examples:

> I am not sure that the following is not the best definition of full employment in my sense: – 'There is less than full employment if the propensity to consume being assumed unchanged, an increase in investment will cause an increase in consumption.'
>
> As against this the normal assumption of the classical theory is that an increase in investment will involve a *decrease* in consumption.[19]

> The only reason why the orthodox theory denies the multiplier is because it is in fact assuming that there is always full employment, so that output as a whole has a zero elasticity.[20]

> [Full employment is defined] as the limiting case in which the supply of output ceases to be elastic . . . [21]

> If I were writing again, I should feel disposed to define full employment as being reached at the same moment at which the supply of output in general becomes inelastic.[22]

> Indeed the condition in which the elasticity for output as a whole is zero is, I now think, the most convenient criterion for defining full employment.[23]

Under what conditions will the elasticity for output as a whole become zero and, hence, no further increases in employment be obtained by increases in aggregate demand? The most obvious is a condition in which the economy simply has reached full capacity, given its prevailing stock of capital equipment and technical know-how. The sheer physical limits to production would have been reached; a rise in *monetized* effective demand will not lead to any further increase in output and employment. In short, Keynes's aggregate supply price schedule would have become vertical and an actual increase in aggregate demand will buy only inflation with no effect on output and employment.

To arrive at such a condition, if there is a shortfall in *monetized* effective demand, the authorities can use government funds to place orders with businesses. Intersectoral linkages will lead to the multiplier effect as long as the aggregate supply price schedule is not yet vertical. For as Keynes pointed out, the multiplier will be operative as long as the economy is not yet at full employment, as long as the elasticity of output is not yet zero.

There is no reason to be agnostic about what Keynes would have done had he proceeded to rewrite Chapter 2 of *The General Theory*. He would have taken two major steps. First and foremost, he would have revised his definition of involuntary unemployment along the lines indicated above. His definition would have been the following: involuntary unemployment exists if the elasticity of employment (and output) is greater than zero with respect to an increase in aggregate demand.

Second, Keynes would have cleared away the oppressive overhang of any conciliatory accommodations to the Classical School. As a result, the revolutionary line between his general theory and the classical theory would have been marked off with greater sharpness. And New Keynesian economics would have to take another nomenclature, since it would now be unequivocally clear that Keynes's economics is *not* the economics of wage or price inflexibility. It *is* the economics of insufficient aggregate demand.

The effect of Keynes's rewrite of Chapter 2 for the direction of macroeconomic theorizing would be profound. It would entail restoration of a genuinely Keynesian research agenda, especially in place of the New Keynesian research agenda:

> The New Keynesians, while investing vast time and effort in explaining why labor markets do not clear, actually sanctify the intersection of labor supply and demand schedules. They then spend all their time trying to establish why such an intersection is not attained. This is, if anything, as Michael Lawlor . . . has suggested a 'New Pigovian' research agenda. Indeed, in Robert Solow's . . . presidential address to the American Economic Association in which he catalogued the various lines of approach to labor market disequilibrium subsequently pursued by the New Keynesian, it was Pigou's work rather than Keynes's that was given pride of place . . . [A] genuinely Keynesian research agenda would focus not on the variegated foibles of the aggregate labor market but on the theory of investment and the rehabilitation of the multiplier. In particular, the Keynesian researcher's deepest concern would be with the effects of expectations and uncertainty and financial and monetary policy on investment. What makes investment activity accelerate? What makes it slow down? What accounts for its volatility? How do business people's perceptions and psychological bent affect fixed capital formation? This, of course, is far from an alien research agenda for economists; this is the passion of Tobin and Brainard . . . among many others. But it is the research agenda that flows naturally from Keynes's inquiry.[24]

NOTES

1 J.M. Keynes in a letter to Ralph Hawtrey dated 15 April 1936, subsequent to Hawtrey's attempt to 'explain' *The General Theory* in a Treasury memorandum; reproduced in *C.W.* XIV: 24.

2 *C.W.* V, VI and VII, respectively. See Jan Kregel (Chapter 16 in this volume) where the connections between *A Treatise on Money* and *The General Theory* are made explicit.

3 See Viner (1936); and Keynes (1937c; reprinted in *C.W.* XIV).

4 See Dunlop (1938); Tarshis (1939); and Keynes (1939c; reprinted as an appendix in *C.W.* VII).

5 Keynes, ibid.: 40.

6 *C.W.* XIV: 182.

7 Also see the discussion in Lawlor *et al.* (1987). Paul Davidson has argued persuasively that Keynes's marginal productivity schedule for labour is *not* an aggregate demand schedule, for labour, in Davidson (1967, 1983).

Following Davidson, Thomas Tuchscherer (1979) has developed a formal model where the marginal product schedule for labour is an *ex post* equilibrium locus of combinations of real wage rates and employment levels. And John Brothwell has observed: 'The labor market is the center of the neoclassical theory of employment. For Keynes it is peripheral; the center of Keynes' theory of employment is the goods market. Indeed, when Keynes summarized his theory in the famous *Quarterly Journal of Economics* (1937) article he nowhere mentioned the workings of the labor market. His theory of employment dispenses with the labor market . . .'(see Brothwell (1986: 537)).

8 See Harrod's letter to Keynes dated August 1935, reproduced in *C.W.* XIII: 533–4.

9 Keynes (1936: 8–15).

10 Ibid: 15, emphasis in original.

11 Robinson (1937: esp. 172 n. 1).

12 Darity and Goldsmith (1995).

13 Darity and Horn (1983).

14 *C.W.* VII: 275.

15 Ibid.: 275.

16 *C.W.* VIII: 26.

17 Tobin (1972: 3). Also see Jan Kregel's examination of Keynes's confrontation with the Dunlop and Tarshis findings (Kregel 1985b).

18 Darity and Horn (1983: 722–4).

19 Letter from J.M. Keynes to Ralph Hawtrey dated 15 April 1936, reproduced in *C.W.* XIV: 26, emphasis in original.

20 Letter from J.M. Keynes to William Beveridge dated 28 July 1936, reproduced in ibid.: 58.

21 Letter from J.M. Keynes to Roy Harrod dated 30 August 1936, reproduced in ibid.: 85–6.

22 Letter from J.M. Keynes to J.R. Hicks dated 31 August 1936, reproduced in ibid.: 71.

23 *C.W.* XIV: 101–8.

24 Darity and Goldsmith (1995: 89–90).

3

EFFECTIVE DEMAND REVISITED

Robert W. Clower

**THE PRINCIPLE OF EFFECTIVE DEMAND – CHAPTER 3
OF *THE GENERAL THEORY* (REVISED)**
Robert W. Clower writing as J.M. Keynes

I

In a given state of technique, resources and costs, the employment of a given volume of labour by an entrepreneur involves him in two kinds of expense: first, the amounts which he pays out to the factors of production (exclusive of other entrepreneurs) for their current services, which we shall call the *factor cost* of the employment in question; second, the amounts which he pays out to other entrepreneurs for raw materials and other supplies that he has to purchase from them together with the sacrifice which he incurs by employing the equipment instead of leaving it idle, the total of which we shall call the *user cost* of the employment in question.[1] The excess of the value of the resulting output over the sum of its factor cost and its user cost is the profit or, as we shall call it, the *income* of the entrepreneur. The entrepreneur's income thus is the quantity which he endeavours to maximize when he is deciding what amount of employment to offer.

It is convenient, when we view the economy from the standpoint of entrepreneurs in the aggregate, to refer to aggregate receipts *net of user cost* from sales of final goods and services as the *proceeds* of the employment associated with that output. The aggregate income resulting from the output associated with a given amount of employment (that is, factor cost *plus* profit) will of course differ from gross aggregate outlay during any given interval of time by the amount of user cost. But as a general rule, we may safely suppose that the endeavour of entrepreneurs to maximize the excess of sales receipts *gross of user cost* over gross aggregate outlay amounts to much the same thing as endeavours to maximize the excess of *proceeds* over *factor cost*. So although the level of employment and output in individual firms will depend on individual entrepreneurial expectations of

28

gross sales receipts, the amount of employment and output for the economy as a whole may be supposed to depend on aggregate expected proceeds. Hence in a given situation of technique, resources and factor cost per unit of employment, we shall assume that the amount of employment and output in the economy as a whole depends on the amount of proceeds which entrepreneurs in the aggregate can expect to receive from the corresponding output.

Let Z, which we may call *aggregate supply price*, be defined as *the expectation of proceeds* that would just make it worth the while of entrepreneurs to offer a given level of employment N, the relationship between Z and N being written $Z = \varnothing(N)$, which we shall call the *aggregate supply function*.[2] Similarly, let D be the proceeds (aggregate sales receipts *net* of user cost) which entrepreneurs can expect to receive from the employment of N men. The relationship between D and N we may write as $D = f(N)$, which we shall call the *aggregate demand function*. Now if for a given value of N the proceeds that entrepreneurs can expect to receive are greater than the aggregate supply price, that is, if D is greater than Z, entrepreneurs will have no difficulty selling additional output at prices that exceed marginal outlays, so entrepreneurs will have an inducement to increase employment beyond N and, if necessary, to raise costs by competing with one another for the factors of production up to the value of N for which Z has become equal to D. Thus the volume of employment is given by the point of intersection between the aggregate demand function and the aggregate supply function. The value of D at the point of the aggregate demand function where it is intersected by the aggregate supply function will be called *the effective demand*. Since this is the substance of the General Theory of Employment, which it will be our object to expound, the succeeding chapters will be largely occupied with examining the various factors upon which these two functions depend.

So far as our discussion is old-fashioned in a literal sense, for we owe to Adam Smith the observation (Book I, Ch. VII) that:

> The quantity of every commodity brought to market naturally suits itself to the effectual demand. It is the interest of all those who employ their land, labour, or stock, in bringing any commodity to market, that the quantity should never exceed the effectual demand; and it is the interest of all other people that it never should fall short of it.

The position adopted by Ricardo and his classical successors reflects a different doctrine, summarized by the epigram 'Supply creates its own Demand', which involves a special assumption as to the relationship between the functions $f(N)$ and $\varnothing(N)$. For 'Supply creates its own Demand' must mean that except when all resources are fully employed, D can fall short of Z only transiently; so that only at full employment can the point of effective demand correspond to equilibrium for the economy as a whole. In effect the classical theory assumes that the machinery of commerce always operates so that aggregate demand automatically accommodates itself to aggregate supply. That is to say, effective demand interposes no obstacle to increases in employment except in so far as the marginal disutility of labour sets an upper limit. If the classical doctrine were true, competition between entrepeneurs would always lead to an expansion of output and employment up to the point at which the supply of output as a whole ceases to be elastic. Evidently this amounts to the same thing as full employment.

In the previous chapter we have given a definition of full employment in terms of the behaviour of labour. An alternative, though equivalent, criterion is that at which we have now arrived, namely a situation in which aggregate employment is inelastic in response to an increase in the effective demand for its output. Thus classical doctrine, that for all levels of N short of full employment, aggregate demand accommodates itself to aggregate supply, is equivalent to the proposition that there is no economic obstacle to full employment. If, however, this is not the way the existing economic system actually works (i.e. if the economic system is *not* self-adjusting), there is a vitally important chapter of economic theory which remains to be written and without which all discussions concerning the volume of aggregate employment are futile.

II

A brief summary of the theory of employment to be worked out in the course of the following chapters may, perhaps, help the reader at this stage, even though it may not be fully intelligible. The terms involved will be more carefully defined in due course. In this summary we shall assume that the money-wage and other factor costs are constant per unit of labour employed. But this simplification, with which we shall dispense later, is introduced solely to facilitate the exposition. The essential character of the argument is precisely the same whether or not money-wages, etc., are liable to change.

The outline of our theory can be expressed as follows. When effective demand and so employment increase, aggregate real income is increased. The psychology of the community is such that when aggregate real income is increased aggregate consumption is increased, but not by so much as income. Hence employers would make a loss if the whole of the increased employment were to be devoted to satisfying the increased demand for immediate consumption. Thus, to justify any given amount of employment there must be an amount of current investment sufficient to absorb the excess of total output over what the community chooses to consume when employment is at the given level. For unless there is this amount of investment, the receipts of entrepreneurs will be less than is required to induce them to offer the given amount of employment. It follows that, given what we shall call the community's propensity to consume, the equilibrium level of employment, that is, the level at which there is no inducement to employers as a whole either to expand or to contract employment, will depend on the amount of current investment. The amount of current investment will depend, in turn, on what we shall call the inducement to invest; and the inducement to invest will be found to depend on the relation between the schedule of the marginal efficiency of capital and the complex of rates of interest on loans of various maturities and risks. Thus, given the propensity to consume and the rate of new investment, there will be only one level of employment consistent with equilibrium, since any other level will lead to inequaltiy between the aggregate supply price of output as a whole and its aggregate demand price. This level cannot be *greater* than full employment, that is, the real wage cannot be less than the marginal disutility of labour. But there is no reason in general for expecting it to be *equal* to full employment. The effective demand associated with full employment is a special case, only realized when the propensity to consume and the inducement to invest stand in a particular relationship to one another. This particular relationship, which corresponds to the assumptions of orthodox doctrine, is in a sense an optimum relationship. But it can only exist when, by accident or design, current investment provides an amount of demand just equal to the excess of the aggregate supply price of the output resulting from full employment over what the community will choose to spend on consumption when it is fully employed.

This theory can be summed up in the following propositions:

1 In a given situation of technique, resources and costs, income (both money-income and real-income) depends on the volume of employment N.

2 The relationship between the community's income and what it can be expected to spend on consumption, designated by D_1, will depend on the psychological characteristic of the community, which we shall call its *propensity to consume*. That is to say, consumption will depend on the level of aggregate income and, therefore, on the level of employment N, except when there is some change in the propensity to consume.

3 The amount of labour N which entrepreneurs decide to employ depends on the sum (D) of *two* quantities, namely D_1, the amount which the community is expected to spend on consumption, and D_2, the amount which it is expected to devote to new investment.

4 Since D_1 is a function of N, which we may write $\chi(N)$, χ representing the propensity to consume, it follows that $D_1(N) + D_2 = \chi(N) + D_2 = f(N)$, where $f(N)$ is what we earlier called the aggregate demand function.

5 For employment equilibrium, N must assume a value such that $\chi(N) + D_2 = f(N) = \emptyset(N)$. Thus the equilibrium volume of employment depends

on (i) the propensity to consume, χ, (ii) the volume of investment, D_2 and (iii) the aggregate supply function, ø. This is the essence of the General Theory of Employment.

6 For every value of N there is a corresponding marginal productivity of labour in the wage-goods industries; and it is this which determines the real wage. (5) is, therefore, subject to the condition that the equilibrium levl of N cannot *exceed* the value which reduces the real wage to equality with the marginal disutility of labour. This means that not all changes in effective demand are compatible with our temporary assumption that money-wages are constant. Thus it will be essential to a full statement of our theory to dispense with this assumption (as is done in Chapter 19).

7 On the classical theory, according to which the volume of employment cannot be in equilibrium for any value of N less than its maximum, the forces of competition between entrepreneurs may be expected to push it to this maximum value.

8 *When employment increases*, D_1 *will increase, but not by so much as* D, since when our income increases our consumption increases also, but not by so much. The key to our practical problem is to be found in this psychological law. For it follows from this that the greater the volume of employment, the greater will be the gap between the aggregate supply price (Z) of the corresponding output and the sum (D_1) which entrepreneurs can expect to get back out of the expenditure of consumers. Hence, if there is no change in the propensity to consume, equilibrium employment cannot increase unless at the same time D_2 is increasing so as to fill the gap between Z and D_1. Thus – except on the special assumptions of the classical theory according to which there is some force in operation which, when employment increases, always causes D_2 to increase sufficiently to fill the widening gap between Z and D^1 – the economic system may find itself in equilibrium with N at a level below full employment, namely at the level given by the intersection of the aggregate demand function with the aggregate supply function.

Thus the equilibrium volume of employment is not determined by the marginal disutility of labour measured in terms of real wages, except in so far as the supply of labour available at a given real wage sets a *maximum* level to employment. The propensity to consume and the rate of new investment determine between them the equilibrium volume of employment, and the level of employment so determined is uniquely related to a given level of real wages – not the other way round. If the propensity to consume and the rate of new investment result in a deficient effective demand, the equilibrium level of employment will fall short of the supply of labour potentially available at the existing real wage, and the equilibrium real wage will be *greater* than the marginal disutility of the equilibrium level of employment.

This analysis supplies us with an explanation of the paradox of poverty in the midst of plenty. For the mere existence of an insufficiency of effective demand may, and often will, bring the increase of employment to a standstill *before* a level of full employment has been reached. The insufficiency of effective demand will inhibit the process of production in spite of the fact that the marginal product of labour exceeds in value the marginal disutility of employment. Moreover, the richer the community, the wider will tend to be the gap between its actual and its potential production; and therefore the more obvious and outrageous the defects of the economic system. For a poor community will be prone to consume by far the greater part of its output, so that a very modest measure of investment will be sufficient to provide full employment; whereas a wealthy community will have to discover ampler opportunities for investment if the saving propensities of its wealthier members are to be compatible with the employment of its poorer members. If in a potentially wealthy community the inducement to invest is weak, then, in spite of its potential wealth, the working of the principle of effective demand will compel the community to reduce its actual output, until, in spite of its potential wealth, it has become so poor that its surplus over its consumption is sufficiently diminished to correspond to the weakness of the inducement to invest. But worse still: not only is the urgency to consume weaker in a wealthy community, but owing to its accumulation of capital being greater, opportunities for new investment may be unattractive unless the rate of interest falls at a sufficiently rapid rate; which bring us to the theory of the rate of interest and to the reason why it does not automatically fall to the appropriate level, which will occupy Book IV.

Thus the analysis of the propensity to consume, the definition of the marginal efficiency of capital and the theory of the rate of interest are the three main gaps in our existing knowledge which it will be necessary to fill. When this has been accomplished, we shall find that the theory of prices falls into its proper place as a matter which is subsidiary to our general theory. We shall discover, however, that money plays an essential part in our theory of the rate of interest; and we shall attempt to disentangle the peculiar characteristics of money which distinguish it from other things.

III

The idea that we can safely neglect the aggregate demand function – that the existing economic system is inherently self-adjusting – is fundamental to the Ricardian economics, which underlie what we have been taught for more than a century. Malthus, indeed, had vehemently opposed Ricardo's doctrine that it was impossible for effective demand to be deficient; but vainly. For since Malthus was unable to explain clearly (apart from an appeal to the facts of common observation) how and why effective demand could be deficient or excessive, he failed to furnish an alternative construction; and Ricardo conquered England as completely as the Holy Inquisition conquered Spain. Not only was his theory accepted by the City, by statesmen and by the academic world; controversy ceased. The other point of view completely disappeared; it ceased to be discussed. The great puzzle of effective demand with which Malthus had wrestled vanished from economic literature. You will not find it mentioned even once in the whole works of Marshall, Edgeworth and Professor Pigou, from whose hands the classical theory has received its most mature embodiment. It could only live on furtively, below the surface, in the underworlds of Karl Marx, Silvio Gesell or Major Douglas.

The completeness of the Ricardian victory is something of a curiosity and a mystery. It must have been due to a complex of suitabilities in the doctrine to the environment into which it was projected. That it reached conclusions quite different from what the ordinary uninstructed person would expect added, I suppose, to its intellectual prestige. That its teaching, translated into practice, was austere and often unpalatable, lent it virtue. That it was adapted to carry a vast and consistent logical superstructure, gave it beauty. That it could explain much social injustice and apparent cruelty as an inevitable incident in the scheme of progress, and the attempt to change such things as likely on the whole to do more harm than good, commended it to authority. That it afforded a measure of justification to the free activities of the individual capitalist, attracted to it the support of the dominant social force behind authority.

But although the doctrine itself has remained unquestioned by orthodox economists up to a late date, its signal failure for purposes of scientific prediction has greatly impaired, in the course of time, the prestige of its practitioners. For professional economists, after Malthus, were apparently unmoved by the lack of correspondence between the results of their theory and the facts of observation – a discrepancy which the ordinary man has not failed to observe, with the result of his growing unwillingness to accord to economists that measure of respect which he gives to other groups of scientists whose theoretical results are confirmed by observation when they are applied to the facts.

The celebrated *optimism* of traditional economic theory, which has led to economists being looked upon as Candides who, having left this world for the cultivation of their gardens, teach that all is for the best in the best of all possible worlds provided we let well alone, is also to be traced, I think, to their having neglected to take account of the drag on prosperity which can be exercised by an insufficiency of effective demand. For there would obviously be a natural tendency towards the optimum employment of resources in a society which was functioning after the manner of the classical postulates. It may well be that the classical theory represents the way in which we should like our economy to behave. But to assume that it actually does so is to assume our difficulties away.

THE PRINCIPLE OF EFFECTIVE DEMAND REVISITED
Robert W. Clower writing as himself

In my 'posthumous' revision of Chapter 3 of *The General Theory* (above) I have made only such changes in the original text as seemed necessary to give it logical coherence within the framework of ideas that Keynes himself might have held before his death in 1946; otherwise, the original wording has been kept. In this sequel, I extend the revision by expressing my present view of 'The Principle of Effective Demand', taking into account all that I have written or read about *The General Theory* since its publication in 1936.

Before the revolution

I have long agreed with Paul Samuelson that the central theme of the Keynesian Revolution lies in Keynes's denial 'that there is an *invisible hand* channeling the self-centered action of each individual to the social optimum'.[3]

Keynes first stated this theme in a 1934 radio address (*C.W.* XIII: 486–9)[4] where he directed attention to the 'gulf' between 'orthodox' believers in the self-adjustment capabilities of market economies and 'heretical' critics who consider the orthodox faith mistaken. Keynes 'ranged' himself 'with the heretics', claimed to see 'a fatal flaw' in orthodox doctrine, and concluded by indicating that he had 'a better hope' (presumably alluding to his nearly completed and soon-to-be-published *General Theory of Employment Interest and Money*).

Although the non-self-adjusting theme is central to 'The Keynesian Revolution', it is by no means central to *The General Theory*. In *The General Theory*, Keynes focused attention not on the stability of equilibrium but on the determinants of the equilibrium level of output and employment, thereby tacitly assuming stability, because an unstable equilibrium, however 'well determined', would be of little practical interest. As for 'the fatal flaw' in classical theory to which Keynes had earlier drawn attention and which he had initially linked to a supposedly mistaken orthodox 'theory of the rate of interest', Keynes in *The General Theory* wrote not about a 'fatal flaw' but rather (p. 21) about 'the classical theory's "axiom of parallells"', which he identified with the phrase 'supply creates its own Demand'. The latter phrase he took to mean, 'in some significant, but not clearly defined, sense that the whole of the costs of production must necessarily be spent in the aggregate . . . on purchasing the product'.[5] Keynes cited no source[6] for his interpretation of Say's Law, causing me to wonder what Keynes would have made of Walras's statement (Jaffe 1956: 89): 'one cannot demand anything without making an offer. Offer is only a consequence of demand.'[7]

Also, how might Keynes have 'translated' Adam Smith's anticipation of Say's Law of Exchanges?[8] 'It is not from the benevolence of the butcher, the brewer, or the baker, that we expect our dinner, but from their regard to their own interest' (Smith 1776: 14).

In pondering Keynes's varied accounts of Say's Law (see the index entries in *C.W.* XIV), I have come to believe that Keynes was baffled as to how one might express the self-adjustment doctrine analytically. More particularly, I conjecture that Keynes confused the almost self-evident notion that 'products are paid for by products' with a problematic idea that I call the Classical Stability Postulate (CSP). The CSP presupposes the 'reality' of the co-ordinating action of the invisible hand (rather like presuppposing the 'truth' of Euclid's Parallel Postulate). In more technical terms, the CSP presumes that time-series representations of market economies lie almost always in the neighbourhood of market-clearing equilibrium points.

As for the evidentiary basis of the CSP, it has none; it derives from anecdote, casual historical knowledge and ideology.[9] Thus it is hard to regard it as anything more than a metaphysical conception of 'reality', perhaps a kind of superstition, as suggested by Mummery and Hobson's characterization of it (1889: 101) as 'confidence in the automatic machinery of commerce'. In any event, the CSP surely is not a well-defined formal statement about economic models. I conclude that Keynes's apparent belief (*C.W.* VII: ch. 2, esp. 21) that Say's Law was the classical theory's 'axiom of parallels' confused a disguised definition of the concept of·a trader (called 'Say's Principle' by Clower and Due 1972: 64–5), with an ineffable cosmological principle (Leijonhufvud 1985).

Classical preliminaries: conceptual background

Keynes did not become an economist in a vacuum; he lived at a time when economics was dominated by the teaching of Alfred Marshall. Keynes was not ignorant of the work of Walras (see Hicks 1982: 296; Edgeworth 1925); but his family background, education and life as a Fellow of King's College added strength to other influences conducive to Marshallian habits of thought. On matters of doctrine and method, there was in any case little reason for Keynes to regard Walras and Marshall as members of different schools; on the contrary, in the period 1900–36 it was natural for knowledgeable economists to treat and regard Walras as 'just another' interpreter of the classical tradition (cf. Phillips 1924: 236–7; Schumpeter 1954; Walker 1987b).

In the *Elements*, Walras wrote (Jaffe 1956: 83–4):

Value in exchange . . . arises spontaneously in the market as the result of competition. As buyers, traders make their *demands* by *outbidding* each other. As sellers, traders make their *offers* by *underbidding* each other. . . . The more perfectly competition functions, the more rigorous is the manner of arriving at value in exchange. . . . City streets with their

36

stores and shops of all kinds – baker's, butcher's, grocer's, tailor's, shoemaker's, etc. – are markets where competition, though poorly organized, nevertheless operates quite adequately. Unquestionably competition is also the primary force in setting the value of the doctor's and lawyer's consultations, of the musician's and the singer's recitals, etc.

Similarly, Marshall (1920: 341) wrote:

the forces of demand and supply have free play . . . there is no . . . combination among dealers . . . , and there is much free competition; that is, buyers generally compete freely with buyers, and sellers compete freely with sellers. But though everyone acts for himself, his knowledge of what others are doing is . . . generally sufficient to prevent him from taking a lower or paying a higher price.

In modern writing, the contrast between so-called Marshallian and Walrasian perspectives is reflected in the treatment by 'Marshallians' of *quantities* as independent variables and demand and supply prices as dependent, whereas 'Walrasians' treat prices as independent variables and quantities demanded and supplied as dependent.[10] So Marshallian models are commonly described as 'quantity-into-price', while Walrasian models are described as 'price-into-quantity'. In this respect, the US literature, macro as well as micro, has a distinctly Walrasian flavour. But there can be no doubt that, in terms of the categories just described, Keynes was a quantity-into-price Marshallian.

By 'classical economist', as he informs us on page 3 of *The General Theory*, Keynes meant the *followers* of Ricardo. In truth, the followers Keynes mentions – Mill, Marshall, Edgeworth, Pigou – did not deviate much from Adam Smith. Indeed, Smith's classic account of 'the natural and market price of commodities' (Book I, Chapter VII of *The Wealth of Nations*) outlines a theory of market price and quantity behaviour on which no later account is a noticeable improvement (cf. Clower and Due 1972: 41ff). Of course, Smith's discussion, like most others before Keynes, refers to markets for particular commodities – or, as Marshall would have styled it, particular industries; but there is no reason why the same line of argument should not be applied to the economy as a whole by supposing that the economy consists of a multitude of firms all of which produce and sell a single commodity, Q, called *output* (of goods and services).[11] On this supposition, let us imagine a world with a large number of independent market-making producers of Q, here called *marketors*,[12] each of whom fixes his output q_j ($j = 1, 2, \ldots, M$) and asking price p^r_j, and offers units of Q for sale to a horde of prospective buyers called *marketees*, in exchange for units of a commodity called 'money'. Imagine also that each marketor is economically contiguous[13] to at least one other marketor, so the set of marketors – also the set of marketees – is economically connected.[14]

On these assumptions, it is plausible to imagine that each marketor acts competitively in the sense that each plans its output (prospective sales) in the expectation that its probable sale price p^e_j, is independent of its output:

$$\partial p^e_j / \partial q_j \equiv 0.$$

Similarly, we may imagine that each marketor operates a market for inputs of factor services and in fixing its planned input of factor services n_j and the associated bid price w^d_j proceeds on the presumption that the probable wage rate required to attract and hold factors is independent of the planned quantity demanded:

$$\partial w^f_j / \partial n_j \equiv 0.$$

Note carefully that we need not suppose that planned sales equal realized sales (i.e. that $q_j \equiv q^R_j$), or that planned purchases equal realized purchases (i.e. that $n_j \equiv n^R_j$); on the contrary we may suppose generally that neither planned sales nor planned purchases are realized. But to stay within the classical tradition, we must suppose that trading in every market is sufficiently brisk, hence markets sufficiently thick,[15] that the subjective price expectation assumptions defining competitive marketor behaviour, namely:

$$\partial pe_j / \partial q_j \equiv 0 \text{ and } \partial we^e_j / \partial n_j \equiv 0$$

are not disconfirmed by experience. In short, marketors not only subjectively believe, but also objectively 'see' their markets as 'thick' or, more colourfully, as *experientially continuous*.

Before turning to Keynes's development of 'the principle of effective demand', I propose to outline a Marshallesque macromodel[16] as a basis for comparison with the analogous construction of Keynes. To that end, I suppose that short-period output, denoted by $Q \equiv Q_S \equiv \Sigma q_j$, is initially at the level Q_0, so that the (unit) supply price of output, P^s, is indicated by P^s_0, as shown by the Aggregate Supply (Price)[17] curve labelled $S(W_0)$ in Figure 3.1. I draw $S(W)$[18] upward-sloping (with a vertical discontinuity at 'capacity' output, Q_{MAX}) on the assumption that short-run marginal cost does not decline with increasing output[19].

Suppose next that when aggregate output is Q_1 the (unit) demand price is P^d_1 as shown by the Aggregate (output-adjusted)[20] Demand (Price) curve $P^d \equiv \bar{D}\{Q, \mathring{A}\}$[21] in Figure 3.1. Given the supply and demand relations illustrated in the figure, we define *equilibrium* price, P^*, and *equilibrium* quantity, Q^*, by the coordinates of the point of intersection of S with $\bar{D}$ (the point X in figure 3.1). As Marshall (1920: 345) argued:

> When . . . the amount produced . . . is such that the demand price is greater than the supply price, then sellers receive more than is sufficient to make it worth their while to bring goods to market to that amount; and there is at work an active force tending to increase the amount

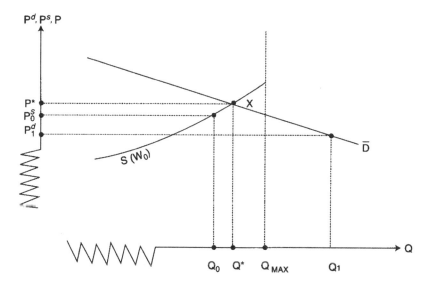

Figure 3.1 The Marshallesque macrocross

brought forward for sale. On the other hand, when the amount produced is such that the demand price is less than the supply price, sellers receive less than is sufficient . . . so that those who were just on the margin of doubt as to whether to go on producing are decided not to do so, and there is an active force . . . tending to diminish the amount brought forward for sale. When the demand price is equal to the supply price, the amount produced has no tendency either to be increased or decreased; it is in equilibrium.

Analogously, in Walras (Jaffe 1956: 224, sec. 187):

in the real world . . . purchases and sales take place according to the mechanism of competitive bidding. When you go to a shoe manufacturer to buy a pair of shoes he acts as an entrepreneur delivering the product and receiving the money. . . . If more products are demanded than supplied, another consumer will outbid you; if more products are supplied than demanded another producer will underbid your shoe manufacturer.

These different views, one quantiity-into-price, the other price-into-quantity, are so similar that a hasty reader might find it hard to decide which writer is Marshall and which Walras.

In both Marshall and Walras, we find hints of the Classical Stability Postulate. But when Marshall (1889: 16) writes:

39

The position of the point of intersection [of S and $\bar{D}$] . . . [represents] approximately the average amount which would be produced and the average price about which the mean price would oscillate

he is presuming merely short-run 'clearance' of commodity markets, which is a far cry from the Classical Stability Postulate. Similarly, when Walras (Jaffe 1956: 188) writes:

Equilibrium in production . . . is an ideal and not a real state. It never happens in the real world that the selling price . . . is absolutely equal to the cost . . . Yet equilibrium is the normal state . . . towards which things spontaneously tend under a regime of free competition

he too seems concerned only with 'clearance' of commodity markets. Belief in the more or less continuous clearance of commodity markets seems long to have been common among economists[22], but we may easily be led into serious confusion if we treat propositions about hypothetically defined equilibrium states as propositions about observable states of the whole or any sector of actual economic systems.[23]

So much for the Marshallesque partial equilibrium macromodel. One could state a comparable *general equilibrium* macromodel (the comparative statics properties of such a system are outlined in Clower 1990: 74–5), but here it is more to the purpose to develop Keynes's partial equilibrium model of aggregate demand and supply.

Aggregate supply and demand

Let us begin by identifying *Aggregate Supply* with the curve $Z(Q) \equiv P'Q(N)$ shown in the two-quadrant diagram, Figure 3.2. This curve shows, for any given level of employment and output, 'the expectation of proceeds [which will] just make it worth the while of entrepreneurs' to maintain the given level of output.[24] This definition mimics Marshall's description of normal supply price for the representative firm, namely, 'the price the expectation of which will just suffice to maintain the existing aggregate amount of production' (Marshall 1920: 342–3). More succinctly, $Z(Q)$ is aptly characterized as 'a reconcoction of our old friend the supply function' (*C.W.* XIII: 513).

Analogously, we identify *Aggregate Demand*[25] with the curve $E(Q,\mathring{A})$ ($\equiv P^d$ $(F(N),\mathring{A})F(N))$ in Figure 3.2; this curve shows for any given level of output (and employment) 'the proceeds which entrepreneurs [can] expect to receive from the employment of N men'.[26] My insertion of the word '[can]' in what is otherwise a direct quote from *C.W.* VII: 25, makes E another 'reconcoction', this time of the Marshallesque demand curve of Figure 3.1. Keynes's original language, if intentional, would pose a puzzle (cf. Patinkin 1982, and Robertson's 3 February 1935 letter to Keynes: *C.W.*

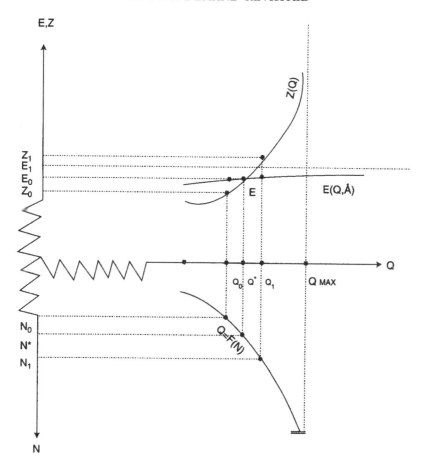

Figure 3.2 A Keynes macrocross

XIII: 497–8); but in my opinion the omission of 'can' at page 25 of *The General Theory* reflects simple inattention in proofreading its various drafts.

Suppose, next, that employment is initially at N_0 and output at Q_0 so that $E(Q_0) > Z(Q_0)$: Aggregate Demand exceeds Aggregate Supply. On standard maximization assumptions[27], some producers will increase employment and output. Dropping further explicit reference to employment, we argue conversely that for Q such that $E(Q) < Z(Q)$, where Aggregate Supply exceeds Aggregate Demand, output will decline. We then conclude that the *equilibrium* level of output (to be faithful to Keynesian terminology we should call this the *effective* level of output) is Q^*, where $E(Q) = P^dQ = P^sQ = Z(Q)$. In general, moreover, and regardless of the manner in which marketors set prices (cf. Walker 1987a), it is concordant with the thought of

41

both Marshall and Keynes to presume that market price, P, typically lies between demand price and supply price, so we conclude that equilibrium price P* in Keynes's system is defined jointly with equilibrium quantity Q* by the point of intersection between Aggregate Demand and Aggregate Supply (the point E in Figure 3.2) and that at E we have $P^d = P* = P^s$.

On this showing, Keynes's theory of effective demand is a straightforward reconcoction of Marshallian short-period demand and supply analysis. *Notice particularly that no individual producer 'feels' sales-constrained at the point of effective demand.*[28] Strictly speaking, therefore, Keynes's excoriation of Ricardian economics for neglecting 'aggregate demand' is a sham; if output equilibrium occurs at a level below capacity (cf. *C.W.* VII: 26), as it certainly may, that should hardly occasion comment on the level of employment of factor services. Whatever the reason factor services remain idle, unemployment in Keynes's *General Theory* does not derive from non-clearance of the market for output. Unemployment equilibrium in Keynes's partial equilibrium macromodel is a consequence of non-clearance of 'the labour market', *not* non-clearance of 'the market for output'.[29] To the extent that Keynes insinuates otherwise (as he surely does) in Chapter 3 and elsewhere, and to the extent that he has been believed (as even more surely he has been), he committed a possible fraud.[30]

If my representation of Keynes's macrocross is valid, then his remark at the bottom of page 25, namely ' "Supply creates its own demand" must mean . . . *f*(N) and ø(N) are equal for *all* values of N', is plain nonsense.[31] If instead Keynes meant what he writes in the next sentence, namely 'the classical theory assumes, in other words, that the aggregate demand price . . . always *accommodates* itself to the aggregate supply price' (my italics), then his text reads sensibly. In all that follows I shall adopt this charitable interpretation of Keynes's several descriptions of Say's Law.

Hansen's hydraulics

I next consider a special case of Keynesian economics that derives not from *The General Theory*, but from the concluding chapter of Alvin Hansen's *Full Recovery or Stagnation* (1938: 321). There Hansen asserts without supporting argument: 'So long as there are unused resources, every increase in demand is matched by an increase in supply.' If we are to call the proposition 'supply creates its own demand' Say's Law, we should with comparable abandon restate Hansen's assertion as 'demand creates its own supply', and call it Hansen's Law.[32]

To convert Hansen's Law into a proposition about aggregate supply, let us suppose that marketors set (full cost)[33] reservation prices, p_{i0}, at levels at or above which they stand ready to sell whatever quantities buyers are willing to purchase. On this special assumption, the Supply (Price) Function S of Figure 3.1 would appear as a horizontal line at the price index P_0 (with vertical discontinuity at Q_{MAX}); so the Aggregate Supply Function, call it Z^H, would be $Z^H \equiv P_0Q$, which would be graphed as shown in Figure 3.3. Combining this revised Aggregate Supply Function with Keynes's Aggregate Demand Function $E = P^dQ$, equilibrium output, Q^*, would be defined by the intersection of Z^H with E (the point $E' = (Q^*, P_0Q^*)$ in (Figure 3.3).

Note that changes in Å shift only equilibrium level of output in Figure 3.3: the 'equilibrium' asking price, P_0, is fixed at a preassigned level 'by the theorist' *outisde* the model (of course the equilibrium value of demand price is affected by changes in Å, but P^d is not 'observable' in the Hansen's Law model). Hence, to all intents and purposes the Hansen hydraulic model eliminates business price-making decisions from the Keynesian model (the term 'hydraulic' is from Coddington (1976: 1263)).

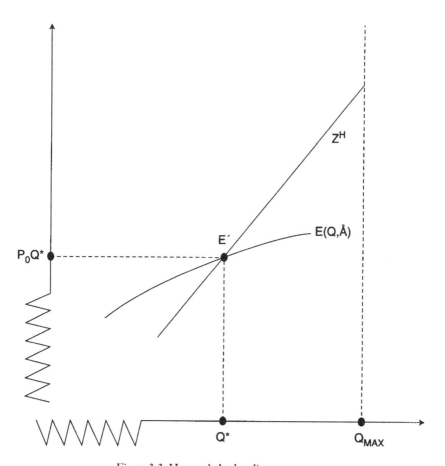

Figure 3.3 Hansen's hydraulic macrocross

The fundamental equation of Keynesian economics

I next restate Keynes's theory of effective demand as a fixed–point (45°-line) proposition. Because Aggregate Demand and Aggregate Supply are both functions of Q, we may for any given value of Å write E as a parametric function, F, of Z:

$$E(Q,\text{Å}) = F(Z\{Q\}). \qquad \text{[H]}$$

Then the point of 'effective demand' (*C.W.* VII: 25), i.e. the point E in Figure 3.2 corresponds exactly to the point A = (Z*,E*) in Figure 3.4,[34] where the curve $F(Z)$ intersects the identity relation E = Y (i.e. the 45°

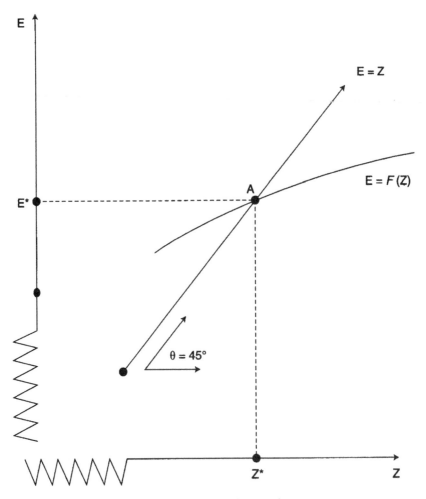

Figure 3.4 Keynes's fixed-point diagram

line).[35] Thus the point A = (Z*,E*) in Figure 3.4 is a *fixed point* of the mapping F[36]; i.e. Z* is a solution to the equation $Z - F(Z) = 0$.

If we confine attention to values Q* of Q that *solve* [H], then for alternative given levels of Å, we obtain the *identity*

$$E\{(Q^*),\mathring{A}\} \equiv F\{Z(Q^*)\}. \tag{K}$$

Hence, for each alternative value of the 'animal sprits' vector Å, the expenditure–income *identity* E* ≡ Z* is seen to hold. Because of the central role that Keynes assigns to this hypothesis (*C.W.* VII: 25), I shall henceforth refer to [K] as *the fundamental equation of Keynesian economics*.[37] This fundamental identity, which defines Keynes's point of effective demand (*C.W.* VII: 25), *holds only for hypothesized equilibrium states* (cf. Samuelson 1947b: 10–11). It is only by supposing that commodity markets are always in equilibrium, so that 'effective demand' is the same thing as 'realized' income and expenditure, that we can make sense of the countless comparative statics multiplier exercises that are found in macroeconomics texts. So-called 'dynamic' multipliers of course make no sense in comparative statics. Keynes himself seems occasionally to treat 'states' and 'equilibrium states' as if they were equivalent. Thus in Chapter 3 of *The General Theory*, Keynes treats 'equilibrium employment' as a synonym for 'employment' (see, for example, *C.W.* VII: 30): 'The propensity to consume and the rate of new investment determine . . . the volume of *employment*' (my italics).

Of course, modern macroeconomic texts are based not on Keynes's theory of effective demand but on the Hansen's Law model from which Paul Samuelson conceived the so-called 'Keynesian Cross' that dominated elemenetary expositions of national income analysis for at least thirty years after it appeared (1948) in Samuelson's *Economics: An Introductory Analysis*. In Figure 3.5, I have drawn the expenditure curve E = E (Q) = H (P₀Q,Å) = H(Y) as a function of income (Y or GNP) as the sole independent variable on the asssumption that aggregate output in the Hansen special case is measured in units such that, at the predetermined reservation price P₀, one unit of money will buy just one unit of output; hence P₀Q ≡ Y (or GNP). Then the intersection of H(Y) with the 45° line (the identity relation E = Y) defines a fixed point (shown as point A′ in Figure 3.5) of the mapping H, corresponding to the point E′ (Y*, P₀Q*) in Figure 3.3.

In his presentation of 'the simple mathematics of income determination' in the Hansen *Festschrift* volume (Metzler *et al.* 1948: 134–5), Paul Samuelson appears to confound the *conditional* equilibrium condition E = F (Z) (equation [H] above) with the national income accounting *identity* Y ≡ C + I, thereby converting a conditional equation in one unknown into an identity that holds for every value of Y (the latter identity asserts that 'the market value of output' is literally a synonym for 'national income'). Perhaps Samuelson had in mind the fundamental equation [K], for then

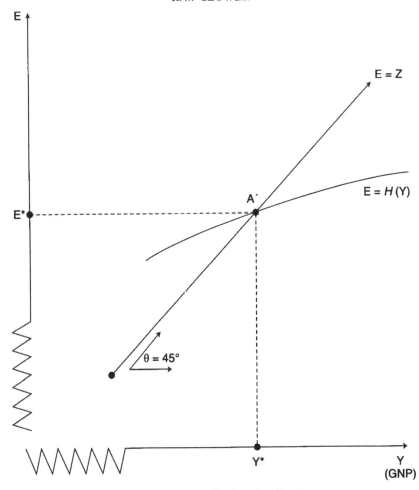

Figure 3.5 Hansen fixed-point diagram

his Keynesian Cross could be regarded as a special case of the fixed-point diagram in Figure 3.4. But as usually described,[38] the Keynesian Cross defines merely a particular solution to the household expenditure function. Because the Hansen hydraulic model dispenses with the business sector of the economy (reducing it to a 'placeholder' for Y, I, Å, and other independent variables and/or parameters), the Keynesian Cross cannot logically be used to determine 'profit-maximizing' business decisions respecting output.[39] Given a solution to the household expenditure equation, aggregate output is trivially determined by Hansen's Law ('Demand creates its own supply'). So when Joan Robinson dubbed the Hansen–Samuelson *et al.* income analysis 'bastard Keynesianism'[40] (Robinson 1962a) she was not being crude; she was just expressing her opinion of the doctrinal legitimacy of the Hicks–Hansen IS–LM model (cf. Harcourt 1987b).

Conclusion

The history of post-*General Theory* macroeconomics is a story of repeated attempts to extract from Keynes's classic more than it actually contains: formally valid arguments that would simultaneously substantiate its disputed revolutionary claims and rationalize its undisputed revolutionary impact. After some sixty years of exegesis and debate, all that appears to have been established is that Keynes's *General Theory* was 'revolution-making' but not 'revolutionary' (I am here paraphrasing T.S. Kuhn 1953: 135). No one disputes the audacity of Keynes's aggregative approach to the economy as a whole, but many have questioned the conventional comparative-statics method that Keynes adopted. But as Patinkin (1982: 88) has hinted, had Keynes not been an already acknowledged economic guru, his choice of method, stripped of extraneous polemical 'dust' (see *C.W.* XIII:

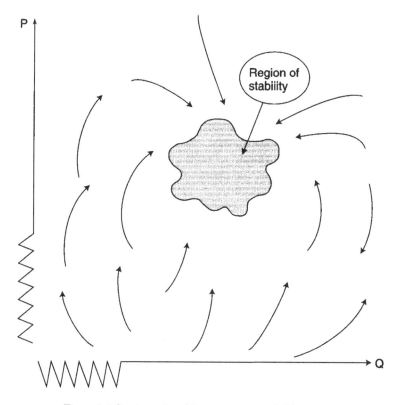

Figure 3.6 Region of stability, non-controllable motions

47

548), might have caused his 'revolution' to founder while *The General Theory* was still warm from the press.

The central issue raised by Keynes's book is: 'How can professional economists best make theoretical sense of contemporary monetary economies?' To this question, Keynes provides no answer; but his book contains myriad insights, one of which merits extensive comment here. Contemporary macroeconomics texts seem uniformly to be obsessed with the idea that every 'reasonable' macromodel must define a full-employment, 'market-clearing' equilibrium. But in Chapter 18 of *The General Theory* Keynes adumbrated a more modern and, I believe, potentially more fruitful 'vision' of contemporary economies.

I have in mind the isolated *General Theory* passage (p. 249) where Keynes outlines a view that dispenses with the equilibrium fixation of contemporary theorists:

> it is an outstanding characteristic of the economic system in which we live that, whilst it is subject to severe fluctuations in . . . output and employment, it is not violently unstable. Indeed, it seems capable of remaining in a chronic condition of sub-normal activity for a considerable period without any marked tendency either towards recovery or towards complete collapse.

More technically, we might restate this passage by saying that, in a Poincaré phase portrait of the economic system, there exists *no* stationary point; but there *does* exist a *region of stability* within which all trajectories are Brownian (dynamic motions that Keynes and Marshall might have called 'neutral' equilibria, and modern systems analysts would call *non-controllable*). Outside the region of stability, all trajectories are governed by attractive forces.

A two-dimensional illustration of such a portrait is shown in Figure 3.6. If we add a time dimension, the region of non-controllable motions might be described as a time 'corridor of stability'.[41] *Inside* the corridor, the economic system is in random motion ('fine tuning' is non-feasible); *outside* the corridor (following the shock, say, of a lost war, a Minskian (Minsky 1975, 1978) financial collapse, or a political revolution) the system 'self-reorganizes' and thereafter tends towards the corridor of non-controllable motion. This 'Keynes Chapter 18' perspective is sufficiently capacious to accommodate a broad spectrum of modern views: Minsky's (1978) financial instability hypothesis; Davidson's (1994) Post-Keynesian and related 'fundamentalist' views; even Shackle's outwardly obscurantist position (cf. Clower, 1975b).

If we insist that every 'reasonable' model economy contain a full employment equilibrium solution then we commit ourselves to preconceptions about the working of economic systems that are purely doctrinaire, supported by neither analysis nor fact; we are then likely to find ourselves embarked (as we have been for the past sixty years) on what amounts to a

Snark-hunting expedition that leads to nothing but confusion. If, instead, we let the equilibrium issue remain moot by adopting the vision adumbrated by Keynes, unemployment equilibrium and other conundrums become topics for subject-matter research rather than semantic debate. If such a change in conceptual perspective is adopted, perhaps we may in future experience a second Keynesian Revolution that *actually* does for economics what Keynes *intended* to accomplish by publishing *The General Theory.*

NOTES

1 A precise definition of user cost will be given in Chapter 6. For the remainder of this chapter, we shall ignore the second component of user cost, which involves subtleties that are best left for later discussion.
2 In Chapter 20 a function closely related to the above will be called the employment function.
3 Samuelson (1966–86: 2. 1317).
4 The transcript of the radio address was published in a slightly revised version in the *New Republic* (20 February 1935: 35–7) under the title 'A Self-adjusting Economic System?'.
5 Cf. Keynes letter to R.F. Kahn of 13 April 1934 (*C.W.* XIII: 422–3).
6 Keynes quotes Mill, but appears to refer specifically to a passage 'from Mill' that he 'lifted' whole from Mummery and Hobson (1889). See Davis and Casey (1977), Patinkin (1978), Kahn (1984), for further comment.
7 This statement seems to owe less to J.B. Say than to the much earlier (1781) French economist, A.N. Isnard; see Hébert (1987).
8 For this translation ('exchanges', not 'markets') of Say's *Loi de Débouchés*, we may thank W.J. Baumol (1977).
9 Cf. Hansen (1953: 3–6).
10 For early comment on the origin of this differentiation, see Edgeworth (1925: III. 169).
11 Marshall used an aggregate output variable called 'gross real income of a country' (*g*), in his 'Notes on the Theory of Economic Growth' (Whitaker 1975: 2. 309).
12 In Clower (1955), I called market makers and operators 'marketees' and called their customers 'marketors'. In keeping with the more familiar meaning of the words 'lessor' (owner of property leased) and 'lessee' (person using property of lessor), the earlier designations are here reversed.
13 By 'economically contiguous', I mean 'has a common geographic border', or 'is electronically connected with (by telephone, direct computer link, etc.)'.
14 My 'definitions' of contiguity and connectedness are meant to be suggestive, not formal.
15 This association of 'brisk' trade with 'thick' markets is impressionistic. Formally, the concept of a 'thick' market requires continuity (or 'effective' continuity, somehow defined) of the marketor's sales function.
16 I write 'Marshallesque' rather than 'Marshallian' because the extension of Marshall's analysis from a single industry to output as a whole entails ideas that are adumbrated only in Marshall's unpublished work (see Whitaker 1975: 2. 305ff).
17 'Price' may be thought of as a scalar index of a distribution of prices, perhaps a distribution over prices at a point in time, possibly a dated distribution of a

single price. It might be a familiar function (mean, median, mode) or index number (CPI, WPI, GNP deflator, etc.). On this, see Clower and Due 1972: 50–1; also Bushaw and Clower 1957: 180.

18 There is a small complication here. We must suppose that, at the fixed money wage rate, W_0, unemployed workers are available for all levels of output less than Q_{MAX}, or we cannot coherently treat the level of the supply price curve as given independently of the volume of aggregate output (cf. Knight 1937: 102).

19 Figure 3.1 and later diagrams represent magnified expansions (not necessarily on the same scale vertically as horizontally) of corresponding full-size diagrams that would be required if units were measured on an absolute scale. Hence in the diagrams as drawn no significance attaches to slopes, curvatures, etc.

20 Elsewhere I have called $\overset{\circ}{D}$ the '*mutatis mutandis*' demand curve (Clower 1989: 136).

21 The symbol $\overset{\circ}{A}$ denotes a 'shift parameter' which, depending on one's model, might refer to a $k \times 1$ row vector representing such imponderables as 'the state of confidence', 'autonomous expenditure', 'uncertainty about future economic conditions', etc. Thus $\overset{\circ}{A}$ is analogous to the 'portmanteau' shift parameter occasionally called 'animal spirits' (cf. Howitt and McAfee 1992: 502–3). On this, see *C.W.* VII: 148–9 (there are numerous implicit shift parameters in Keynes's analysis; see esp. *C.W.* VII: 24, 91–6).

22 Cf. Tobin (1980b: 788–91, 796); Lucas (1972a: 51ff).

23 Given Marshall's views on competition, it seems natural to suppose that actual market (transaction) prices lie generally in the neighbourhood of equilibrium points, and this 'naturalness' is precisely the source of potential confusion. For a definitive non-technical discussion of this issue, see Haavelmo (1958).

24 Cf. Patinkin 1982: 142–50; Clower 1991: 255.

25 I have subsituted the symbol E for Keynes's D to make it clear that Aggregate Demand is an expenditure magnitude, not a quantity or price.

26 As correspondence with Robertson and Hawtrey (*C.W.* XIII) indicates, Keynes's initial description at p. 25 is an inexplicable twist of the later definition (p. 30), where he writes 'which the entrepreneurs *can expect* to get back' (my italics).

27 Compare Keynes's letter to Kahn, *C.W.* XIII: 422–3.

28 The same point arguably is made by Barro (1994: 3); but the paragraph (next to last on p. 3), where he seems to make the point, is too convoluted to admit of unambiguous interpretation.

29 This conclusion supports Amadeo's (1989: 150) remark: 'the price versus quantity dichotomy should not be taken as the basis for a comparison between [the *Treatise on Money* and *The General Theory*]' (cf. Clower 1991: 254–5).

30 I use the word 'fraud' advisedly, because it implies wilful intent. I infer such intent from a 1935 letter to Harrod *C.W.* XIII: 548), where Keynes writes: 'I *want*, so to speak, to raise a dust; because it is only out of the controversy that will arise that what I am saying will get understood.'

31 There is some evidence that the 'nonsense' was suggested by Joan Robinson (see *C.W.* XIII: 639).

32 Hutt has argued (1974: 3 fn.) that the proposition now called Say's Law in macroeconomic texts was first so stated by Keynes (*C.W.* VII: 18).

A purportedly analytical version of Say's Law was proffered by Kalecki, in a 1934 paper (published in English translation as 'Three Systems') in which he assumes that 'all income must be spent immediately on consumer or investment goods'. (Kalecki 1990: 201). What 'immediately' might mean in this context is at least as uncertain as the exact meaning of Keynes's initial statement of Say's Law.

33 See Andrews and Brunner (1975: ch. 2, esp. 29); also Okun (1981: 178–81).

34 In Figure 3.4 I have set the parameter Å to some initial level Å = Å*, to fix the position of the aggregate expenditure curve.

35 Cf. Samuelson (1939: 790; CSP II. 1115).

36 See Arrow and Hahn (1971: 28); Simmons (1963: 337–43).

37 With apologies to Axel Leijonhufvud, whose *On Keynesian Economics and the Economics of Keynes* (1968) distinguishes in a different way between 'Keynesian economics' and 'the economics of J.M. Keynes'.

38 Klein (1947: 51–2) invents an inventory-adjustment 'theory' of output adjustment, thus introducing a business sector of sorts into his 'Keynesian Cross' model; but he omits consideration of such possibilities as prohibitively costly stock-out problems, carrying charges, etc.

39 Ibid.: 114; he, followed by numerous other authors (e.g. Harcourt *et al.* (1967: 54); Parkin (1990: 216, Fig. 26.3), explicitly adopts a mechanical theory of output determination according to which output increases if inventories decline and output declines if inventories increase. On that theory, we can talk about output 'equilibrium' in terms of equality of production and sales alone, without reference to costs or revenues. The problem then is to square such a view with elementary microeconomics.

40 Bruce Littleboy (1990: 308, fn. 113) comments: 'Perhaps a less offensive and more modern term, "love-child Keynesians" could be used instead.'

41 Cf. Leijonhufvud (1981: 109–10).

4

YES, MRS ROBINSON!

The General Theory and imperfect competition

Robin Marris

The purpose of this chapter is to argue that the main weakness of *The General Theory* lay not, as is often suggested, in the labour market, but in the goods market – in the process where changes in nominal demand induce firms to change their physical outputs. We claim that macro theory based on perfect competition is inherently fragile. By contrast, when non-perfect competition is assumed, macro theory becomes robust. Consequently if *The General Theory* had been revised, it *ought* to have been revised accordingly. Of course, the model of profit-maximizing imperfect polipoly[1] is itself a simplification – the real world sees all kinds of oligopoly and non-maximizing procedures, such as mark-up pricing, caused by bounded rationality, which we discuss later. But as with the model of perfect competition, the aim is to generate strong macro theorems from optimizing behaviour by micro agents. Along with an increasing body of support,[2] we believe the one model fails in the task where the other succeeds. Thus the case for imperfect polipoly (that is, large-group non-perfect competition) is at heart theoretical. As a paradigm it is also patently *less* unrealistic.

The General Theory often reads as if it were based on non-perfect competition; but, as is generally agreed, on inspection, apparently it is not.[3] One may say 'apparently' because nowhere does Keynes employ the term 'perfect competition'. There are, however, well-known passages where the wording implies profit-maximization and price-taking. Profit-maximization is indicated on page 24 of Chapter 3 ('entrepreneurs will endeavour to fix the amount of employment at the level which they expect to maximize the excess of proceeds over factor cost'), and price-taking is implied in the use of the Marshallian term 'supply price' on page 25. The definition of full employment (page 23) as a condition where the labour market clears at a real wage equal to the marginal disutility of labour has the same implication. Yet inconsistencies remain. In Chapter 5, page 46, the entrepreneur has to form 'the best expectations he can as to what the consumers will be prepared to pay when he is ready to supply them'. Are consumers 'prepared to pay' for any quantity? In Chapter 18 ('The General Theory Re-stated'), page 245, the list of things taken as given includes 'the degree of competition', implying that it might be other than infinite. Both quotations suggest that the writer believed or, at least desired his readers to believe, that his theory was valid on any microfoundations. If so, it was a trick which, in the short and medium run, was outstandingly successful for the purpose of gaining early acceptance of the theory. In the long run, we shall argue, it left the theory gravely weak against post-1970 reactions.

EXPECTATIONS

Following the recent lead of J.A. Trevithick, we adopt where appropriate assumptions of rational expectations in a Keyensian environment. In his recent excellent contemporary restatement of Keynesian macroeconomics, Trevithick writes: 'The fact that the rational-expectations hypothesis is a free-standing set of criteria which can be applied to a wide variety of macroeconomic models was rarely grasped by early Keynesian critics. A corrective is clearly called for.'[4] As we see it the 'problem' for Keynesians with rational expectations lies not so much in the methodology itself as in the context in which it has mainly been applied, that is, in the context of price-taking. Here, an often overlooked passage from Lucas, originally written in the mid-1970s, is worth quoting:

> From the descriptive point of view it often seems more realistic to think of demand information being conveyed to producers by *quantity* changes: new orders, inventory run-downs and the like. There seems to be no compelling substantive reason to focus exclusively on *prices* as signals to current and future demand. At this verbal level, it seems to me harmless and accurate to use the terms price increase and sales increase interchangeably. Somewhat surprisingly, however, rigorous analysis of income determination when producers set prices is extremely difficult, and no examples relevant to business cycle behavior are at hand.[5]

The quotation reveals (to this writer, at least) a 'fudge' that has become too fashionable. Either we are in a price-taking world or we are not. Between the two, to change the metaphor, there is a sea-change in micro–macro processes. The present writer has attempted elsewhere[6] to show how the analytical difficulties of employing price-setting behaviour in micro–macro models may be reduced by computer simulation. That endeavour was the background to the present chapter. In contrast, we have to say that macroeconomics based on price-*taking* microfoundations seems to us to be essentially non-scientific. That insult applies equally to the price-taking interpretation of Keynes. It is said that Keynes rationalized the interpretation from a desire to 'beat the buggers at their own game'.[7] The result, in our opinion, for reasons we now set out, may not unfairly be described as a buggers' muddle.[8]

TWO GOODS-MARKET MICRO–MACRO MODELS

To frame the argument we provide two models, A and B – textbook micro–macro models with various embellishments. Model A is perfect competition, Model B, imperfect polipoly. Both models concern only the Marshallian–Keynesian short period and play in a Keynesian macro framework. The size and technological structure of the capital stock are fixed and there is no movement of firms or capital between industries. No role is played by long-run profits. In one way or another expenditure may leak from or be injected into the macro system and the labour market is not forced to clear. Both models are aimed at the problem of explaining the micro–macro processes of a Keynesian slump, such as that of 1932–4 or 1937–9, and neither attempts to address the various problems of Keynesian economic management that have arisen since 1950.

In Model A, the employment-giving production sector is divided into industries, each delivering a homogeneous product with a well-defined demand curve. Industries comprise large numbers of small, owner-managed firms with frozen shares of the national capital stock embodied in a regular hierarchy of technical vintages, the older vintages being shut down first if production falls. Consequently, the short-run marginal productivity of labour inclines smoothly downwards – the so-called 'neoclassical' SMPL curve. Firms as goods-sellers and households as goods-consumers are all price-takers, the necessary intermediation being undertaken by stockholding brokers who call going prices at which they undertake to accept all transactions. The firms are also price-takers in the labour market. The pricing role of households as labour suppliers remains for discussion: there are no brokers in the labour market.

The firms' owner-managers pursue short-run profit maximization, always setting output to a point on the SMPL curve where marginal cost (nominal wage/marginal product) equals nominal price. Firms hold no stocks: all output is sold instantly to brokers at the going price. The goods markets clear by brokers adjusting prices. In the labour market, firms' demands for labour are the amounts required to produce the profit-maximizing output given a parametric nominal wage.

This neoclassical model has recently been reconsidered from a Post-Keynesian viewpoint in an interesting way by Amativa Dutt.[9] As compared with the more familiar analysis,[10] he introduces two changes: first, following the actual wording of *The General Theory*[11] he drives producer output choice by reference to expected prices; and second, following Post-Keynesian practice, he assumes that all wages are consumed and all profits saved.[12] The resulting model has the following equations for a Keynesian equilibrium where producers are satisfied that their output levels are profit-maximizing and brokers' stocks are not tending to change:[13]

$$y = f(n) \tag{4.1}$$

$$f'(n) = \left(\frac{w}{p^e}\right) \tag{4.2}$$

$$n = F\left(\frac{p^e}{w}\right) \tag{4.3}$$

$$c = \frac{wn}{p} \tag{4.4}$$

$$y = c + i \tag{4.5}$$

$$f(F(p^e/w)) = \frac{wF(p^e/w)}{p} + i \tag{4.6}$$

where y is real output; n, employment; f, the short-period production function; c, real consumption; i, real investment (exogenous); p^e, expected price; w, nominal wage (predetermined); and p, actual price. Equation (4.1) is the production function; (4.2) the condition that when producers see themselves as expectedly profit-maximizing (marginal cost = price), their employment is such that the marginal productivity of labour equals the ratio of nominal wage to expected price (i.e. to the expected real wage); (4.3) the function derived from (4.2) implying that employment is an increasing function of expected price; (4.4) the condition that real wages are totally consumed; (4.5) that real output equals real consumption plus real investment; and (4.6) the result of combining (4.1), (4.3), (4.4) and (4.5). Stability requires $p^e = p$. In our version, p must also be a price called by brokers if and when their stocks are steady.

In Model B there are no industries. The private production sector is one large imperfect polipoly. Firms remain owner-managed, comparatively small and short-run profit-maximizing, but although price-takers in the labour market, in the goods market they are price-makers. Each makes a distinct product and faces a well-defined demand curve based on the conjecture that all other firms' prices are constant or, at least, are not directly affected by their own price. Firms know their conjectural demand curves over a reasonable range and also know both that the curves are iso-elastic over this range and that the elasticity is cyclically invariant. Firms also know that all other firms are like themselves. (We tiptoe past the question of whether we are assuming that, although the products differ, the demand curves are not only iso-elastic but identical. Implicitly, in some aspects of the discussion we are doing so, but, as we point out later – pp. 71–6,[14] the question has no qualitative effect on our conclusions.)

On the production side, within firms all equipment is equally efficient. Consequently the SMPL curve is, after a certain point, roughly the shape of an inverted letter L – the so-called 'empirical' SMPL curve.[15] Through the cycle the firm is assumed to be on the flat part of this curve, where the marginal productivity curve of labour is constant and equal to the average. In place of the procedure of selling output to brokers, firms choose the profit-maximizing price on their demand curves at that time, and successfully sell the indicated quantity directly to consumers.

The price-setting process can be seen as the choice of a profit-maximizing mark-up of price over marginal (= average) cost, where the latter is nominal wage/marginal (= average) product. Mathematically this mark-up is the reciprocal of the elasticity of demand. *It follows that (with constant MPL) the profit-maximizing price will change only if either the nominal wage changes or the demand-elasticity changes.* It also follows that the price/wage ratio is fully determined by the elasticity of demand for that product and the (constant) MPL. Consequently, if the demand curve shifts, only if the move is also associated with a change in elasticity will profit-maximizing price change. Given our assumption that the elasticity is in fact cyclically invariant, plus the assumption of constant costs, cyclical variation of profit-maximizing price can come about only through cyclical variation of the nominal wage. The latter proposition is not an assumption; it is a theorem.

DEMAND SHOCKS IN THE TWO MODELS

Let us consider what happens if, starting from an initial state where aggregate production is at or below capacity and labour market conditions are such that nominal wages are not tending to change, there is a decline in real investment or other net injections.

In Model A, the decline in nominal aggregate demand causes a leftward shift of the demand curve of each industry. Consequently consumers buy less at the going price, and so brokers find their stocks increasing and call lower prices. Then what happens? As is well known, the answer depends on the dynamics of the resulting wage-price adjustments. To consider these, it is convenient to re-present Dutt's final equation in such a way as to leave open the question of the flexibility of nominal wages. Thus equation (4.6) becomes

$$f(F(p^e/w^f)) = \frac{w\,F\,(p^e/w^f)}{p} + i \qquad (4.7)$$

In place of expected prices alone, the driving indicator for producers is here seen for what it actually is, namely the expected price/wage ratio. Consequently the following three scenarios exhaust the logical possibilities.

In scenario (A/a), although households as labour-suppliers have money-illusion, managers have rational expectations. Managers (correctly) believe that nominal wages are not flexible. The rationally expected price/wage ratio has therefore declined and so, correspondingly (given the neoclassical MPL curve), has profit-maximizing output. Firms reduce their outputs and employment; brokers' excess stocks are reduced and the Kahn–Keynes multiplier does its business: the fall in prices does not restore real aggregate demand because, due to the decline in economic activity, nominal aggregate demand has now fallen further. The real wage has increased because prices have fallen. Real aggregate demand and output stabilize at the new lower Keynesian equilibrium[16] with leakages reduced, by the income process, to equality with the reduced level of injections. The new macro equilibrium is consistent with the new micro equilibrium for the firms.

In scenario (A/b) nominal wages are flexible, and firms know it. Therefore they correctly expect that a fall in prices and aggregate output will be followed by a fall in nominal wages. The expected price/wage ratio is therefore unchanged. Firms do not change output and aggregate excess supply of goods is unchecked. Brokers' stocks of goods continue to rise and wages and prices continue to fall unless and until built-in stabilizers (Pigou-effect or whatever) come into play, or maybe the market breaks down. In the latter case, brokers refuse orders, firms become quantity-constrained and we are no longer in Model A.[17]

In scenario (A/c) nominal wages are also flexible but firms do not know it. Therefore, as in (A/a), they reduce their output and employment, but now, in the event, nominal wages decline. Therefore the actual price/wage ratio and in due course its expected equivalent rise towards their initial levels. Firms therefore restore their original output levels. But for the same reason as in (A/a), real aggregate demand cannot support the aggregate restored output, so the price-and-output decline recurs. Thus the scenario predicts an oscillating output with a downward trend in nominal wages and prices. Successive temporary micro-equilibrium situations in the goods market are associated with persisting Keynesian macro disequilibrium. Eventually, presumably, monetary stabilizers may come into play or firms learn the reality of the situation in the labour market; that is, in contemporary parlance, they become rational. In the latter case, the story shifts back to scenario (A/b).

In Model B, the decline in aggregate demand appears as an iso-elastic leftward shift in the demand curve of each firm, to which the profit-maximizing response, as already noted, is constant price with proportionate reduction in output and employment. Consider scenarios corresponding to (A/a), (A/b) and (A/c).

In scenario (B/a), with constant nominal wages, profit-maximizing firms hold prices constant and reduce output. The end result for aggregate real output is the same as in scenario (A/a) but, unlike the case in that scenario, because we are now assuming constant labour productivity, the real wage is constant.[18]

In scenario (B/b) (where firms correctly expect nominal wages to be flexible), the negative demand-shock appears in the form of the leftward shift in the demand curve, fully rational firms immediately perceive (a) that profit-maximizing output has declined, while profit-maximizing price is constant; (b) that execution of the profit-maximizing change will reduce employment; (c) that reduced employment will be followed by reduced nominal wages; and (d) that the decline in nominal wages will cause a further leftward shift in the demand curve by an amount that will precisely offset the effect of the fall in wages. Therefore fully rational firms permanently reduce output to the lower-level Keynesian equilibrium in a single step.

In scenario (B/c) the end-result of (B/b) will be achieved in stages.

THE MODELS AND *THE GENERAL THEORY*

Scenario (A/a) is neither Hicks's fixprice nor his flexprice story.[19] It is not the former, because prices are flexible, and it is not the latter, because wages are inflexible. For the same or similar reasons it does not correspond to other influential Keynesian interpretations such as 'French Keynesian' or 'New Keynesian'. It is nevertheless an interpretation pervasively implicit in many accounts of macroeconomics, especially in North America where expositors frequently say that the Keynesian slump is caused by inadequate effective demand in association with inflexible nominal wages. Often, however, the reader is left to infer that it is the loss of a potentially stabilizing real-balance effect (or similar monetary stabilizer) that is the cause of the trouble. Here, we emphasize instead what we see as a more important element in the causal chain, namely producer motivation. For it is only in scenario (A/a) – where expectedly inflexible wages combine with flexible prices to create the necessary change in the expected price/wage ratio – that producers faced with a decline in aggregate demand under perfect competition have a clear profit-led incentive to reduce output.

Scenario (A/a) is surely ruled out as a candidate for 'revising' *The General Theory* in accordance with the intentions of the present volume. More precisely, if (A/a) is sustained, Chapter 19 of the book must be excised. Up to that chapter, (A/a) is, as Dutt and others[20] have shown, consistent with the text. But in Chapter 19 Keynes, without too much poetic license can be read as saying: 'Up to now I have been arguing as if nominal wages were constant. Now, with passion, I am going to show you that my theory does not, repeat not, depend on that assumption.' Since scenario (A/a) indeed depends on the inflexible nominal-wage assumption, there is no way it and Chapter 19 can co-exist. Therefore, in *Keynes's* conception of *The*

General Theory we are either not in Model A or we are in another Model A scenario.

But, and it is a very big but indeed, we cannot be in (A/b) because it produces classical rather than Keynesian results. The decline in aggregate demand goes entirely to prices rather than to quantities, and the situation is eventually stabilized by Professors Pigou and Patinkin. So we are left with (A/c): wages are flexible, but firms, suffering 'irrational' expectations, do not expect this. Keynes, it seems, did have something like (A/c) in mind:

> Perhaps it will help to rebut the crude conclusion that a reduction in money-wages will increase employment 'because it reduces the cost of production', if we follow up the course of events on the hypothesis most favourable to this view, namely that at the outset entrepreneurs *expect* the reduction in money-wages to have this effect. It is indeed not unlikely that the individual entrepreneur, seeing his own costs reduced, will overlook at the outset the repercussions on the demand for his product and will act on the assumption that he will be able to sell at a profit a larger output than before. If, then, entrepreneurs generally act on this expectation, will they in fact succeed in increasing their profits? Only if the community's marginal propensity to consume is equal to unity, . . . or if there is an increase in investment . . . [Otherwise] the proceeds realised from the increased output will disappoint the entrepreneurs and employment will fall back again to its previous figure . . . [21]

In this crucial quotation, we are already in a recession which, according to our (and by implication Keynes's) analysis, has occurred because investment fell and producers expected nominal wages to be inflexible. Now, nominal wages in fact decline and Keynes's wording indicates two possible immediate consequences: firms do not change their outputs; or alternatively, they do increase them but are 'disappointed'. Remembering all the time that we are in Model A, not B, let us call these alternatives A/c(i) and A/c(ii) respectively. If we are in A/c(i) we must ask: why do firms not change outputs? The answer must be that the decline in the actual nominal wages fails to stimulate in firms' minds a change in the expected price/ wage ratio. Firms must be expecting that the fall in wages will cause a fall in prices. How could they expect that? Knowing that they live in a regime of perfect competition, they know that prices (as called by brokers) fall when, and only when, brokers' stocks are increasing, that is, they must be anticipating (correctly) that their additional output, after acceptance by brokers, will fail to sell. Thus producers, having previously displayed 'irrational' expectations, now, within the same cycle, display sophisticated rationality. In contrast, A/c(ii) tells a consistent story and 'works' so long as the irrationality is sustained.

It follows that if A/c(i) is dismissed for inconsistency, as surely it must be, we are driven to the conclusion that the Keynesian theory, as expounded in *The General Theory*, can be consistent with perfect competition only on scenario A/c(ii), that is, on the assumption of persistence of what today would be called irrational expectations. In addition, the scenario does not produce an unambiguous 'Keynesian' result for output and employment. In fact, it has some affinities to a Lucas-type model, where cycles are caused by misreading of signals.[22] It is this conclusion, surely, which lies at the heart of the traditional aversion between Keynesians and rational-expectations. Under perfect competition, it is true.

Once we move from Model A to Model B, all the problems are removed. Each of its scenarios produces stable Keynesian results, and none implies inconsistent expectations.

By contrast surely scenario A/c(ii) is a weak foundation for a great new macro theory? Would slumps be impossible if only firms were 'rational'? This critique does not depend on hindsight from rational expectations. It could surely be described in language acceptable to Keynes, Kahn or economists generally in 1937.

DIFFICULTIES WITH IMPERFECT COMPETITION

Numerous economists who agree that, for one reason or another, Model A cannot function as a Keynesian microfoundation, nevertheless query the substitution of Model B. Below, we discuss alternatives. In the meantime we discuss a hopefully exhaustive list of the main difficulties the profession has found with the imperfect-polipoly model as such:

1 No applied economist or econometrician to date has observed conjectural demand-elasticities of individual products of individual firms. Are they in fact observable?
2 If Model B is based on linear, rather than iso-elastic demand curves, it predicts pro-cyclical movements in the profit-maximizing mark-up.
3 Model B is mathematically difficult to analyse according to professionally acceptable standards of rigour.
4 In Model B the average value of the demand elasticity determines the macroeconomic wage–profit distribution, but does not directly influence macroeconomic stability. The model does imply, however, that the elasticity has no strong cyclical association. Therefore, as a concept, it plays a central role in the theory. Many economists express distaste for a theory that assigns a major role to something which they see as emanating 'subjectively' from the minds of mere consumers.
5 Model B fails to take account of the pervasiveness of oligopolistic behaviour. In general, rather than conjecturing that other prices will remain constant, firms conjecture specific reactions. Depending on these, the major macroeconomic predictions may be affected.

6 In assuming that firms profit-maximize on a known but conjectural demand curve, Model B ignores the Herbert Simon bounded-rationality critique of maximizing theory: the assumed calculation is too uncertain and too complex to be feasible. Instead, firms will employ mark-up pricing, which is therefore a much better microfoundation for Keynes.

The last two points are discussed later below. Our rejoinders to the first four are as follows:

1' We would answer that the experiment of measuring individual-product elasticities is perfectly conceivable, although possibly expensive.[23] The fact that it has not yet been carried out is mitigated, in the present writer's view, by the fact that in his previously published computer simulation of Keynesian economics under imperfect competition, it was shown that the main cyclical macro predictions are not sensitive to the value of the elasticity parameter.[24]

2' Because straight lines are easier to draw than curves, most textbook expositions of monopoly fail to notice that a linear shift of the demand curve produces an artificial change in elasticity resulting in correspondingly artificial 'predictions' of profit-maximizing price adjustments. Although consumer demand models, almost without exception, postulate consumer utility functions implying iso-elastic demand curves, the significance of the iso-elastic curve, as a first approximation to reality, is very frequently lost to industrial and theoretical economists. The effect of a change in the general level of demand on an individual consumer of an individual product is to shift the income origin of the price-possibility line in the indifference map. The consumer is moved to a new location on the map, and there is no presumption of any associated qualitative tendency in substitution elasticities. Following standard scientific practice, the first approximation, therefore, is to assume that they are constant; this means, log-linear, rather than linear, demand curves.

3' The market structure of the major employment-giving sector of the twentieth-century capitalist economy represents an interlocking of industrial and consumer forces. Today's catalogue of products, together with the associated consumer demand curves, is partly the result of yesterday's industrial diversification initiatives – society's voracious search for new demand experiences and potential providers' search for new Schumpeterian monopoly opportunities. The end result which, though constantly evolving, we may for convenience regard as fixed in the Keynesian short run, is a matrix of products, suppliers and consumer preferences. The resulting substitution elasticities (fixed in the short run, evolving in the long run) reflect the average competitiveness of the evolved system, which, so long as producers are free to diversify and consumers free to spend, is not easily susceptible to policy manipulation: a policy to eliminate imperfect competition in modern capitalism would be like a chemical that killed all the flowers in the garden. Thus we reply: Model B, rather than representing a 'soft' microfoundation, if not 'hard', is definitely strong.

ALTERNATIVES TO IMPERFECT COMPETITION

There are not a few economists who would agree with our attack on Model A but who, nevertheless, are not convinced that Model B is the right substitute. One or the other will prefer one or another among various alternatives. We briefly discuss (not in historical order) a list of four of these, noting meanwhile that whereas imperfect competition was well developed before 1930 by Richard Kahn[25] (who would surely have been closely involved in any revision of *The General Theory*), and had been fully developed, with some hints of macro implications, by (in alphabetical order) Edward Chamberlin, Mihal Kalecki, Abba Lerner, Richard Kahn and Joan Robinson, before 1940,[26] the best part of another quarter century was required to produce well-developed formal theories in the fields listed below. The items are: the *sticky-price hypothesis, heterogenous oligopoly* and *mark-up pricing*.

The *sticky-price hypothesis* is a shorthand phrase for the substantial literature[27] based in one way or another on the hypothesis that the Keynesian depression is possible only because, for institutional reasons, prices are dynamically constrained by absolute barriers or by the existence of significant private costs for rapid change. In much of this literature there are hints of imperfect competition, but for the present author the end result has always presented problems. Consider the following quotations, the first from Leijonhufvud in 1968, the second two from Hicks in 1965 and 1974, and the fourth from Mankiw and Romer in 1991:

> Under what conditions would a profit-maximizing monopoly respond to a decline in demand by lowering its price? By raising it? By maintaining it constant? How do we predict the speed of price adjustment? We cannot pursue all these questions here. The point is simply that if unemployment is to be blamed on the existence of monopolies, these points should be cleared up.[28]

> On the Temporary Equilibrium method, the system is in equilibrium in every single period; and it is by this equilibrium that prices are determined. If we abandon the demand–supply equation, how are prices to be determined? The answer, which must be faced, is that the new method does not have any way of determining prices. There must be some way by which they are determined, but it is exogenous. The determination of prices is taken right outside the model. . . .

> If prices are fixed exogenously, one will naturally begin by assuming them to be constant. The model becomes a Fixprice model. . . . It is

not implied by the description Fixprice method that prices are never allowed to change – only that they do not necessarily change whenever there is a demand–supply disequilibrium.[29]

In discussing the multiplier theory without attention to prices, I am following a precedent set by a great part of Keynesian literature. It is practically taken for granted, in many expositions, that there are just two causes of changes in prices: changes in real costs and changes in money wages. The former of these, during the time that is taken for the multiplier to work out, is taken to be negligible . . . As for money wages, they may indeed rise from a shortage of labour and they may also rise for what is regarded as an independent and exogenous cause – wage-push by trade unions. The latter is indeed a complication, but (so we are given to understand) it has nothing to do with the multiplier process itself.

I have myself described the analysis which proceeds on these lines as a *fixprice theory* – using the term to mean, not that prices do not vary, but that the causes of their variation are outside the model. So we suspend the rule that price must change whenever there is an excess of supply or excess of demand. I do not deny that this fixprice assumption is a useful assumption, up to a point – but only up to a point. The fact surely is that in modern (capitalist) economies there are, at least, two sorts of markets. There are markets where prices are set by producers; and for those markets, which include a large part of the market for industrial products, the fixprice assumption makes good sense.[30]

A recurrent theme of the new Keynesian economics is that deviations from perfect competition may be crucial for understanding economic fluctuations. In most goods markets, firms are price setters rather than price takers . . . It is almost impossible to comprehend how firms adjust prices in a world in which firms are price takers.[31]

The short answer in 1968 should have been that on the reasonable simplifying assumptions of the iso-elastic demand curve and the empirical short-run cost, the 'monopolist' faced with a change in demand will hold price constant. The short comment on Hicks is: 'did he by "Fixprice" mean non-perfect competition or did he not?' If he did, where was the 'crisis'?[32] Comment on Mankiw and Romer can be more refined. Every word except 'almost' is right, but the fundamental question is: however realistic the costly – hence sticky – price-adjustment hypothesis may be, why is it needed? We cannot have sticky prices without imperfect competition but we can, in principle, have imperfect competition without sticky prices. With the latter alone, we are home and dry. Imperfect, or more precisely (to take in oligopoly, etc.), non-perfect competition is both a necessary and sufficient condition for *The General Theory* to work. Sticky prices are a sufficient condition, but, as Mankiw and Romer say, they depend on the prior condition of price-setting.

Another way of looking at the problem is by relating our Model A to Robert Clower's original idea[33] of a dual-decision hypothesis. We have all the assumptions of a Walrasian world except that, in the absence of an auctioneer, there is quantity constraint. In deciding whether to change current production a firm first asks whether the proposed new quantity could be sold, then whether the change would be profit-maximizing. What is really happening here? In terms of our Model A, the situation must be that the quantity constraint is coming from *brokers*. Faced with rising stocks, rather than marking down price, they call a constant price and ration suppliers.[34] Why do they do that? Patently, brokers are failing in their function; the system has broken down; we are not in Model A at all. Therefore, in logic we are either in Model B or some extension of it such as oligopoly (see pp. 65–7). But in Model B we need no dual-decision hypothesis. The problem is not the absence of the auctioneer but the fact that under non-perfect competition, prices, while continuing to function in a traditional way in microeconomics, have no primary function in macro equilibrium. For example, consider again Leijonhufvud's assertion that if unemployment is to be blamed on monopoly, it is necessary to have a definite theory of how price setters react to a change in demand. To be blunt, that simply is not true. Suppose that rather than the flat empirical cost curve, some firms are on a rising curve, still with an iso-elastic demand curve. Then if demand falls, profit-maximizing price falls somewhat. Whether firms then actually make this adjustment, or whether, owing to price-change costs, they do not, will not have a primary affect on the course of the subsequent slump: in the first case the real wage rises, in the second it does not. The Keynesian low-level equilibrium output and employment (though perhaps not unemployment) will in both cases be approximately the same.

The logic of this matter has been discussed more delicately by Malcolm Sawyer.

> Most theorizing in macroeconomics continued to assume (at least implicitly) atomistic competition, but departing from Keynes by assuming price rigidity. This came to the fore with the reinterpretation of Keynesian economics and the temporary equilibrium school. . . . In the context of atomistic competition, they are correct to argue that there will be elements of trading out of equilibrium (simply because prices cannot adjust instantaneously in an economy without a Walrasian auctioneer), but the general assumption that there is rapid quantity adjustment is unappealing when applied to a production (rather than an exchange) economy. Our argument is that the causes and implications

of price inflexibility are quite different under imperfect competition as compared with perfect competition. Under the latter, price inflexibility is either imposed or arises as an approximation to incomplete price adjustment (cf. Leijonhufvud, 1968), whereas in the former it arises either from the deliberate decisions of producers or from a delay in adjusting prices because of the costs of doing so.[35]

But even Sawyer, in our opinion, here does not go far enough. The term 'price inflexibility' should be abandoned altogether. In Model B we are in a world where firms may change prices as often and as quickly as they wish, and yet is utterly non-Walrasian. If there are also costs associated with adjusting prices, these, interesting though they may be, are to be blunt, irrelevant to the Keynesian theory.[36] It is a hard thing to have to say of thirty years of intellectual fireworks let off by some of the best minds of our profession.

The next alternative is *Oligopoly*. Our question is whether the introduction of oligopolistic behaviour into Model B could significantly qualify the conclusion that faced with cyclical changes in demand, price-setting firms have no first-order motivation to respond with changed prices. Thus, we are mainly concerned with heterogenous oligopoly and only with that aspect of the theory which bears directly on the cyclical effect on prices. There is, of course, a century-and-a-half of literature on homogenous oligopoly,[37] which we cannot directly employ, while, in contrast, much less is available, for application to our problem, on heterogenous oligopoly.[38] We are forced to rely heavily on a slightly embellished version of some previous work of our own.[39]

Oligopoly modifies Model B by allowing for the reality that the pattern of substitution relationships among firms and products is irregular. There are groups of fims which we can call 'industries' among whom product substitution elasticities are sufficiently high that each member, when setting its own price, necessarily takes account of possible reactions of other members. In reality these groups will overlap, but, like all previous analysts, we will simplify by assuming that they do not. We will initially further simplify by assuming that all products are quantitatively commensurate and that all intra-industry demand elasticities are iso-elastic and identical. Short-run average and marginal costs are also constant and the same. We, thus, have a group of identical firms producing different products: when all firms charge the same price they sell the same quantity and earn the same profits.

Initially, we assume that in setting prices, group members ignore the possibility that in the long run high profits could attract 'entry' in the sense of new firms forcing their way into the group by creating, investing-in and marketing a new product with high substitutability for the existing group products and so permanently damage incumbent profits.

In these conditions, as well as the one-firm demand elasticity based on the assumption that all other prices are constant, we can also identify a unique and significantly smaller group elasticity when all group members' prices move together. If, instead of conjecturing that other prices are constant, firms conjecture that any change they make will be followed in either direction by all other firms in the group, a sequential process of profit-maximizing changes will lead the group to a set of equal prices at which marginal revenue determined by group elasticity equals the common marginal (= average) cost. The firms will thus find joint profit-maximization with each firm charging the same price and selling the same quantity with the same mark-up. The mark-up is the reciprocal of the group elasticity. Because the group elasticity is smaller than the one-firm elasticity, the mark-up is higher than in the non-oligopolistic result.

The equal-shares joint-profit-maximizing result can also be seen as the cooperative solution to the group's non-constant-sum game: the 'follow-my-leader' conjecture representing, in fact, a mode of cooperative play. The firms have maximized group benefits and divided the proceeds according to their relative bargaining strengths, which are all equal because each firm perceives an equal, proportionate profit loss should cooperation break down and margins fall to the reciprocal of the one-firm elasticity – the latter situation (in effect, Model B without oligopolistic behaviour) being the predicted result of non-cooperative maximizing.

The simplifications are drastic, but they do enable us to obtain a precise answer to the question of what will happen to the general level of nominal prices set by the group if there is a fall in general demand. The answer (precisely corresponding to the answer for imperfect polipoly) is that so long as the group elasticity does not change, joint-profit-maximizing prices will not change.

If we want to drop the assumption that entry possibilities are ignored, while maintaining the symmetrical homogeneity assumptions, we may assume that, the maroeconomic production sector consisting of a network of these oligopolistic groups, all *group elasticities* are also constant and equal. If long-term production functions are also identical, and all groups are joint-profit-maximizing, all firms in the economy earn the same long-term rates of return. There is therefore no incentive for inter-industry migration. There may, however, be incentive for new entry into the economy as a whole. The effects of the latter on pricing behaviour are elusive,[40] but intuitively unlikely to have a first-order effect on cyclical prices, unless, in some way, a short-term depression causes an expectation of increased danger of long-term entry.

The same goes for the homogeneity assumptions. They are patently unrealistic, but one may surmise with some confidence that dropping them is unlikely to lead to first-order general predictions concerning cyclical prices.[41] There will undoubtedly be second-order effects, for example due to correlations between the micro pattern of a particular macro demand change, on the one hand, and the real-life heterogenous inter-product pattern of elasticities on the other, but the direction could go one way or the other and also differ from one cycle to another.

Thus, we feel we have made our case that the reality of oligopoly does not weaken our argument for basing *The General Theory* on the simpler case of imperfect polipoly.

Finally, we reach *mark-up pricing*. By this is meant a procedure which in some significant way differs from the Model B process of setting prices according to the profit-maximizing mark-up, i.e. according to the reciprocal conjectural elasticity of demand. As is well known, most businesses calculate prices by means of a mark-up on costs; the question at issue is where the mark-up comes from. In effect, we are here concerned with *non-profit-maximizing*, or *npm*, mark-up procedures. Either the firm is maximizing something other than profits or, owing to bounded rationality, it is not maximizing anything. In either case, our essential concern is whether *npm* procedures, as compared with imp-comp *pm* procedures, provide a more robust microfoundation for *The General Theory*.

Consider first the possibility that, in setting current prices, the firm is maximizing something other than short-run profits. The criterion could be total utility of management over time, probably involving the theory of corporate growth, or more simply the security of the firm from threat of entry. In the case of the former example, however, the present author under another hat[42] has surely established that whatever the long-run objectives of management (shareholder-oriented or not as the case may be), it will never pay in terms of utility to pursue a short-run policy that earns less than the maximum available short-run profit: more profit can be used to please shareholders by higher distributions, to please management by higher retentions for faster organizational growth, or to please workers by higher wages. Alternatively, the selected mark-up is merely the outcome of a rational oligopolistic entry-deterrence policy, which, as already discussed, is unlikely to produce significant predictions concerning cyclical prices in a Keynesian context.

In logic, therefore, we are confined to the 'behavioural', 'Simonite', bounded-rationality interpretation. In our view, this powerful school,[43] founded in the 1950s by Herbert Simon, contains the strongest potential source of attack on our Model B. The essence of his well-known argument is that maximizing behaviour is *in practice* impossible because the complexities and data-uncertainties of the typical business problem are too much for the computing capacity of the human brain. Furthermore, some problems are structured in such a way that an optimum solution, even if, which is not necessarily the case, it exists, is inaccessible. For example, the experiment required to discover the conjectural elasticity of demand may be infeasible. Faced with the need to take decisions nevertheless, the decision-taker resorts to bounded rationality, i.e. to simplifying the problem and solving, therefore, only a part of it.[44] These sub-procedures are called rules-of-thumb or, more richly, heuristics.

A rule-of-thumb for imperfectly competitive pricing is to adopt some *reasonable* mark-up and stick to it. If the rule is held through the cycle, we have all we need for *The General Theory*. The 640-million-dollar question, however, is where does the 'heuristic' mark-up come from?[45] If we have no theory concerning the answer to this question we have no presumption that the mark-up will by cyclically stable:[46] why should not a firm adopt a rule-of-thumb that in times of depression the mark-up is sharply reduced? (Indeed, as is known, some do.[47]) One answer is given by the 'satisficing' model published by Herbert Simon[48] in the 1950s. The subject sets an aspiration level of, e.g. profit, and makes a certain effort – e.g. (present writer's interpretation) selects a certain mark-up; then, if in the outcome the aspiration level is under-achieved, search effort is increased, and vice versa for the case of over-achievement. On these assumptions one can write a set of differential equations whose solution represents stable levels of 'effort' (i.e. mark-up?) and result (i.e. profit?) whose values are determined uniquely by the adjustment coefficients of the satisficing model and is completely independent of the economic parameters such as elasticity of demand.

This is a dramatic conclusion but it leaves some very difficult questions.[49] If profits fall below the aspired level, which *way* should mark-up be altered? What happens if the satisficing model predicts higher profits than maximum profits? Where do the adjustment coefficients come from? Suppose two firms with similar costs producing a close substitute have different adjustment coefficients and therefore satisfice at different profit levels, may not the comparison lead to some revisions in the adjustment behaviours? Thus, how do we know that adjustment behaviours may not gradually converge to approximate the results of optimizing behaviours?

Nevertheless, we know that it is not infrequently the case that a diversified firm applies the same mark-up over a range of products that would seem intuitively to be sure to have different demand elasticities. The firm knows the elasticities differ, but has no idea how they differ, so it applies a 'satisfactory' mark-up. Empirically, the question of whether mark-up pricing procedures represent heuristics aimed at *moving towards* maximum profit, or whether they are stand-alone procedures free of any taint of optimization philosophy, remains open. One hypothetical experiment, conceived as undertaken over a wide range of industry, would test the hypothesis that observed mark-ups were independent of actual elasticities. Another would ask business-decision-takers whether they would be interested in changing their rules-of-thumb if it could be shown that they would thereby earn more profit. Sixty years after The *General Theory*, despite the huge advance of applied economics, no such experiments have been attempted.

The essential issue, for the purpose of the present contribution, is whether it would be satisfactory to base a revised *General Theory* on only the microfoundation of stand-alone mark-up pricing. There is no doubt that an affirmative answer to this question underlies most post-Keynesian economics.[50] In effect, one is saying that markets are imperfect but, on account of bounded rationality, maximization is impossible; therefore, stand-alone mark-up pricing is inevitable. Since both maximization and stand-alone mark-up pricing produce the needed result that macro demand changes go to quantities rather than to prices, let us be content with the latter.

But to this writer, that last conclusion contains a major fallacy. If mark-up pricing is seen as a heuristic for imperfect-polipoly profit-maximization or its oligopolistic equivalent, then, since the theory predicts that unless demand elasticity is cyclically correlated, profit-maximizing mark-up is cyclically invariant, the heuristic of holding the mark-up constant in face of fluctuating demand is, clearly, a good first approximation. One is not required to know the elasticity, only to assume that it is cyclically invariant. By contrast, the stand-alone mark-up has no equivalent conclusion. Since it encompasses no economic theory, it has no basis for recommending cyclical stability.

Thus, we re-assert our position that stand-alone mark-up pricing is severely inadequate as a *theoretical* microfoundation for *The General Theory*. By contrast, in the absence of measurements of the relevant demand elasticities, this theory, considered as a profit-seeking heuristic, is, of course, an excellent *applied* microfoundation. As such, as is well known, until quite recently it dominated most applied Keynesian macroeconomics, including the Phillips-curve application.

THE REAL WAGE

In Model B the real wage is the average (= marginal) productivity of labour reduced by the profit-maximizing mark-up, which is governed by the elasticity of demand. Unless one or other of the two elements changes, the real wage must be constant. In order to predict systematic cyclical movement of the real wage one or both of the elements must also have systematic cyclical movement and they must not systematically move in opposing directions. Thus any imperfect-competition micro-macro model, however complex, which ends up predicting cyclical real-wage movement must, somewhere along the line, contain assumptions which have the effect of producing endogenous cyclical variation of labour productivity or demand elasticity. For some reason, a wide range of professional economists, old Keynesian, new Keynesian or Classic, seem to regard this apparently convenient situation with distaste. As one extremely bright young modern theorist once said to the author, 'then the situation is like little more than a value-added tax'. In consequence, there has been a tendency, going way back to the late 1930s, to pursue more complicated scenarios. Keynes, for example, in 1939, now beginning to be apprised, via Kalecki, of the macroeconomic potency of the imp-comp theory, wrote that it would be safest to assume that the short-run marginal cost curve was rising, but real wages were cyclically stabilized by offsetting cyclical movements of the degree of monopoly.[51] The elasticity of demand must move pro-cyclically, or, in an oligopoly story, the degree of collusion, as discussed above, must move counter-cyclically. Alternatively, economists working on imp-comp microfoundations for macro modelling build in formal, but in truth arbitrary, assumptions that have the effect of endo-genizing a cyclical movement of demand elasticity.[52]

But surely, surely, if we want to make the revised *General Theory* as simple and robust as possible, we do not need these complications, especially as, empirically speaking, we do not generally know their direction of effect. If we then assume a constant demand elasticity, constant mark-up, constant marginal and average cost, we have (cyclically) constant real wage. But before leaving the topic, however, two issues must be faced.

The two elements which, in Model B, uniquely determine the real wage (labour productivity and demand elasticity) are themselves exogenous, making the real wage endogenous but independent of the cycle. Therefore, the real wage has no role in the demand side of the labour market. If the supply of labour is influenced by the real wage, it has no link to the demand for labour. Keynesian unemployment is, thus, a highly robust phenomenon being the difference between the labour required to produce Keynesian-equilibrium output and labour supplied according to the real wage. This means that not only is there no cyclical causal connection from real wage to output and employment – a point on which all true Keynesians (but not all neo-Keynesians) agree – but also there is no robust causal connection in the opposite direction, a proposition which leaves some true Keynesians unhappy. Basically, the problem is that Model B seems to say that the real wage is determined in the goods market. Economists do not like the idea of the 'price' of something being determined in a market other than its own. It is not uncommon to hear it said that in theories such as Model B, the real wage is determined, 'partly in the goods market and partly in the labour market'.

The present writer believes this problem is at heart metaphysical. The price of labour is the nominal wage and the price of goods their nominal price level. The real wage is the ratio between the two numbers. Once we confine the discussion to real terms it is apparent that under conditions of price-setting, there are not two 'markets' but only one – the exchange of goods for labour. Correspondingly, the economy contains only one price, the goods/labour exchange rate, which happens to be, in Model B, independent of both the level of output and the demand for labour. The essence of the Keynesian theory is that while that exchange rate may influence the supply side of the labour market, it can do nothing on the demand side.[53]

The second and remaining critical issue is described by posing the question, 'what happens if there is price-setting in the labour market?' For example, suppose, as is commonly and very plausibly assumed, the nominal wage is influenced both by the pressure of demand in the labour market and by the level of nominal prices. In effect, labour suppliers are seeking an *aspired* real wage, and index their nominal-wage requirements accordingly. There is evidently no reason why the aspired real wage should be the same as the wage determined by the mark-up. If they differ, there must be disequilibrium, but it will take the form of continuous change in the nominal wage, and hence prices, in one direction or the other, rather than in output. More precisely the effect will be strictly nominal unless there is a monetary stabilizer such as a strong real-balance effect. If, during the process, the actual price/wage ratio differs from that indicated by the profit-maximizing mark-up, firms at that moment are not profit-maximizing, a condition we assume they will attempt to rectify by price changes. The actual price/wage ratio will therefore oscillate over very short periods. The present writer's previously published[54] simulations showed that in most circumstances the value averaged over several short periods will tend to be constant and equal to the value indicated by the profit-maximizing mark-up. In other words, in the medium (Keynesian 'short') run, firms win. Model B remains a valid paradigm.

REVISING *THE GENERAL THEORY*

Ground rules

We believe we have now made our case that wherever *The General Theory* involved the microfoundations in the goods market, it should have been revised according to Model B, perhaps with some concessions to the potentialities of oligopoly and certainly with recognition for applied purposes of the heuristic of mark-up pricing. We might accordingly suggest some ground-rules:

1 The revision must be in keeping with the spirit of the original *General Theory*. More specifically:

- stable, low-level, open-unemployment equilibrium must be possible;
- the basic Keynesian macro equations (e.g. $Y^* = I/s$) must remain;
- the labour market must not be *forced* to clear – thus unfortunately ruling out the use of the recent interesting work of either Gregory

Mankiw or Richard Startz,[55] both of whom have been otherwise explicitly concerned with imperfect competition as a Keynesian micro-foundation.

2 The deployment of Model B should be 'minimalist' in character. More specifically:

- no macro or micro assumptions should be made that explicitly or implicitly create cyclical variation of conjectural elasticity;
- similarly, as regards cyclical variation of oligopolistic collusiveness;
- similarly, as regards cyclical variation of average or marginal labour productivity (output per person-hour) – there must be no causal relation, in either direction, between real wage and cyclical labour demand; the real wage may affect labour supply but cannot act to clear the labour market.

3 Institutional conditions in the labour market may be somewhat vague. However:

- an assumption of 'fixed' nominal wages, although permissible as a temporary expositional device, may not remain as an essential element in the theory;
- nominal wages may respond to the pressure of demand in the labour market (e.g. as measured by unemployment) and persistent wage-price inflation or deflation, due to persistent non-clearing labour market and/or to real-wage aspirations that are inconsistent with the profit-maximizing mark-up, must be possible;
- models implying some kind of monopsony in the labour market (Hart 1982; Kiyotaki and Blanchard 1987), rich though they may be, would not be suitable for a revision of *The General Theory* in the late 1930s.

Core theory

In one way or another, the revision of the theory would centre on the following equations:

Nominal aggregate demand

$$Y = C + I \tag{4.8}$$

Consumption function

$$C = (1 - s)Y \tag{4.9}$$

Equilibrium nominal demand

$$Y^* = \frac{I}{s} \tag{4.10}$$

Micro profit maximization

$$\bar{e} = \frac{e}{e-1} = \text{profit-maximizing mark-up ratio}$$

$$w = \text{nominal wage}$$
$$\pi = \text{average labour productivity}$$
$$= \text{marginal labour productivity}$$
$$= \text{constant}$$

$$p^* = \frac{\bar{e}w}{\pi} = \text{profit-maximizing price} \tag{4.11}$$

Real macro relationships

$$Y_R = \frac{Y}{p} = \text{real output}$$

$$L_D = \frac{Y^*}{p^*\pi} = \text{effective demand for labour}$$

$$= \frac{I}{p^*\pi s} = \frac{I}{\bar{e}ws} \tag{4.12}$$

Optional labour-market equations

$$L_s = \text{labour supply} = L\left(\frac{w}{p^*}\right) = L\left(\frac{\pi}{\bar{e}}\right)$$

$$U = \text{unemployment} = L\left(\frac{\pi}{\bar{e}}\right) - \frac{I}{w\bar{e}s}$$

$$\text{Full employment: } U = 0; \quad \frac{I}{w\bar{e}} = sL\left(\frac{\pi}{\bar{e}}\right) \tag{4.13}$$

The similarity of some of the foregoing structure to the 'IS' part of the IS–LM model is superficial. In the first place, the above model is not fixprice. Given the nominal wage, the source of the price level is transparent. Second, unlike numerous Keynesian expositions, including some aspects of the original *General Theory*, nominal and real variables and relationships are clearly separated.

Only equation (4.12) needs further comment. It appears to show that the nominal wage has an explicit effect on the demand for labour. This is because investment is defined in nominal terms. If the nominal wage changes while nominal investment is constant, the real weight of injections is, of course, changed and thus the demand for labour. But if, as in the original *General Theory*, investment is defined in wage units (that is to say,

I/w is constant and exogenous) the nominal wage disappears from the equations and, in the absence of real-balance effect, the whole theory, as envisaged in Chapter 19 of the original *General Theory*, becomes true for any nominal wage level. As in Chapter 19,[56] so in the above model, the nominal wage is no stabilizer. Given $\bar{e}$, the same applies to the real wage.

Although not entirely relevant to a revision of *The General Theory* before 1950, the point is worth making that equation (4.12) is also a sound and convenient base on which to erect additional structures, for example Phillips-like structures, Post-Keynesian structures (all one has to do, after the usual modifications of the savings function, is to endogenize $\bar{e}$!) or for that matter neo-Keynesian or 'new' Keynesian structures (tack on a strong real-balance or other stabilizing gimmick).

What is the significance of $\bar{e}$ (remembering that it is the profit-maximizing mark-up ratio derived from the conjectural demand elasticity)? If it were to change, while nominal wage and nominal investment remained constant, assuming that firms continued to maximize, prices would change and so also, therefore, the purchasing power of nominal investment, i.e. real investment. Hence the demand for labour would change. But if we hold real investment, measured in terms of goods rather than wages, constant, then nothing changes. In other words, re-write equation (4.12) as follows:

$$I_R = \frac{I}{w\bar{e}} = \text{real investment}$$

$$L_D = \frac{I_R}{s} = \text{labour demand} \qquad (4.14)$$

Here is the fundamental Keynesian employment-multiplier equation. (The productivity of labour, π, disappears because, if it changes, while the amount of employment created by a given output decreases, the amount of investment created by a given employment increases.) Without anywhere *assuming* inflexible prices or wages, we nevertheless see that neither the nominal wage nor the profit-maximizing mark-up play a direct role in employment determination. The aims of Chapters 3 and 19 of *The General Theory* are thus simultaneously achieved.

Textual revisions

The following is a summary only of the revisions that would need to be made to the affected chapters of the original book.

Book I

Chapter 3 ('The Principle of Effective Demand')

This chapter has to be completely reconstructed in order:

1 to eliminate the concepts of Aggregate Supply and Aggregate Demand Functions, both of which are derived from price-taking micro concepts;[57]
2 to present the concept of effective demand as a nominal equilibrium concept, based on an exposition of the fundamental theory (derived from Kahn's multiplier article[58]), the left-hand side of equation (4.10) above;
3 to redefine full employment so that it is not synonymous with equality of the real wage and the marginal disutility of labour (at some point in the book, after the new microfoundations have been introduced, it has to be further explained that under imperfect competition the labour market clears at a real wage lower than the marginal disutility of labour);
4 to eliminate the implication that *The General Theory* applies only to the male gender.[59]

New chapter (suggested title: 'The Theory of Price')

1 Verbal account of price-setting and imperfect competition in the industrial economy, noting that once agricultural employment has been reduced to a small proportion of the total, the businesses accounting for the greater part of total employment are under this type of regime;
2 Pull back from old Chapter 21[60] the discussion of the shape of the short-run marginal productivity curve of labour and reverse the argument to favour the empirical curve, as discussed in the description of Model B above.[61]
3 Verbal account of profit-maximizing when conjectural marginal cost equals marginal revenue.
4 Intuitive account of the theorem that, when profit-maximizing firms face a change in nominal effective demand, their profit-maximizing price does not necessarily change in either direction and, if unit costs and demand elasticity are constant, must be constant.
5 Theoretical exposition of equation (4.11) above, with appropriate acknowledgement to Abba Lerner (1934).

New chapter (suggested title: 'The Theory of Employment')

This chapter would combine an exposition of equation (4.12) above with a revision of the discussion of the role of wages in the old Chapter 19, which would then become redundant.

Book II

Chapter 4 ('The Choice of Units')

When *The General Theory* first came out some critics believed that the use of wage units was a material factor in the conclusion. As we know, that is obviously a red herring. Sometimes, as in equation (4.12), it is convenient to measure real investment in terms of nominal wages, but essentially, in going from nominal to real values, we must use an appropriate price index.

The original Chapter 4 could usefully be replaced by a brief discussion of the role of index numbers in aggregation from micro to macro, and an explanation of why, both in theory and practice, index number problems do not significantly threaten the step from nominal effective demand to real output and the demand for labour.

Chapter 5 ('Expectations and Employment')

The original chapter is concerned with price-taking under uncertainty. Above, we discussed an expectational critique of *The General Theory* under price-taking. Under price-setting, the uncertainty relates to the demand curve, rather than to price. Thus the original chapter becomes redundant. In its place we can discuss three issues:

1 the need possibly to use a rule-of-thumb mark-up that is only roughly approximate to the 'true' profit-maximizing mark-up;
2 a foretaste of rational expectations. It is not difficult to envisage an intuitive account of the rational power of the conjecture that other prices are constant. In equilibrium, every firm believes the conjecture and, on the conjecture, every firm is correct;
3 a discussion of the role of expectations concerning nominal wages. When price-setting firms experience a fall in demand which they correctly perceive as being of cyclical origin, they reduce output and employment rather than prices, correctly expecting that other firms will do likewise. They can therefore correctly expect that there will be a consequential fall in nominal wages. That expectation does not modify their output decision either way, because they will also correctly perceive that the fall in wages, as well as reducing their costs, will react on their demand curves.

There would be other detailed consequential changes in the text of the book, but the main thrust of the macro chapters in Books II, III and IV should not be affected.

NOTES

1 Imperfect polipoly is the term we use for the type of large-group imperfect or non-perfect competition first described in the books of Edward Chamberlin and Joan Robinson both published in 1933.

2 For excellent studies of these developments, see in particular two papers by Malcolm Sawyer (1992a, 1992b). With some differences of emphasis, we are playing on the same side; if possible, we emphasize more strongly the weakness of perfect competition and the strength of imperfect competition as Keynesian microfoundations.

3 For example, as Geoffrey Harcourt has pointed out, on page 5 of *The General Theory* Keynes (in my opinion most likely at the suggestion of Kahn) remarks that the main postulate of the classical theory of employment – namely simultaneous equality of the real wage with both the marginal product and marginal disutility of labour – is modified 'in accordance with certain principles' when markets are imperfect. But he makes no use of the point in describing his own theory and thus fails to discuss the problem that under imperfect competition, because the real wage is less than the MPL, if the labour market clears it does so where MPL and marginal disutility are not equal, thus creating an ambiguity in the definition of full employment (in later language, the labour market clears at an employment level that is not Pareto optimal; society is consuming 'too much' leisure).

4 Trevithick (1992: 175). The present writer greatly admires this book on macroeconomics from a Keynesian viewpoint for its lucidity, comprehensiveness and, where appropriate, measured polemic. We differ substantially, however, in our respective views on the significance, for Keynesian economics, of imperfect competition. See also note on Trevithick in discussion of 'new Keynesians', p. 79, n. 36.

5 Lucas (1981: 225–6). The quotation was first published in 1977, so may well have been composed as early as 1975. Later, in the 1980s, Lucas wrote to the present author indicating that he could not see a connection between 'monopoly' and Keynesian macroeconomics. For the record, two books based on quantity signalling were published contemporaneously: Barro and Grossman (1976) and Malinvaud (1977). The first book on macroeconomics under imperfect competition was Nikaido (1975). Another pioneer was Negishi (1979). Excellent, comprehensive and rigorous investigation of the field is further found in the work of Ng (1980, 1986). For a discussion of the relevant history of thought, see Marris (1991: ch. 5) with bibliography of the subsequent literature on imp-comp microfoundations of macroeconomics, (ibid.: 214).

6 Marris (1991).

7 The remark is said to have been made to Gardner Means, as reported to Geoffrey Harcourt by Roy Rotheim.

8 Malcolm Sawyer (1992a) prints a nice quotation from James Tobin on this point: 'Why did not Keynes exploit the microeconomic revolution fomented in this very town [Cambridge] . . . in the same years as he was revolutionizing macroeconomics. That is certainly a puzzle . . . But faithful neoclassicals on both sides of the Atlantic have had no compunctions in dismissing imperfect competition . . . as a trivial exception . . . They probably would not have found Keynes's macroeconomics any more appealing if he had based it on imperfect competition.' Catch 22!

9 See Dutt (1987, 1992).

10 See for example, Sargent (1979 ch. 2) or Weintraub (1979: 40–2).

11 See, for example, Keynes (1936: 24).

12 For reasons reviewed in Marris (1991: 205–10), the author has always had grave reservations about this type of model but is happy to concede its convenience and, as it were, harmlessness in the present context.

13 Dutt does not mention brokers, but we believe the story is clearer if their necessary existence is explicitly recognized. Brokers are obviously inevitable in a Walrasian system without an auctioneer; their significance in the present discussion is that they are *not* needed under price-setting.

14 See revisions to Chapter 4 of the *General Theory*, p. 76.

15 See Kahn (1929); Kalecki (1938); Lucas (1981: 146ff); Marris (1991, 1992).

16 Despite objections, we insist on calling a condition where real output is not tending to change an equilibrium.

17 Professor Dutt has written to me that firms cannot expect the money wage to fall equiproportionately with prices, since the final equilibrium ('where expectations are fulfilled') must occur at a higher real wage. But this is true only if the 'final' (i.e. rational) real equilibrium has lower output. My example above presents a rational real equilibrium with unchanged output and employment, consistent with unchanged price/wage ratio. The dispute goes to the nature of the rational-expectations method. *If* past experience links falling prices with falling output, *then* Professor Dutt's scenario will come about, otherwise mine will. Strictly assuming eternal perfect competition, there is no *theoretical* reason for the one case rather than the other.

18 If, still assuming imperfect polipoly, we substitute the neoclassical MPL curve, the real wage will of course rise in proportion to the rise in MPL associated with the output decline.

19 Hicks (1974).

20 For example, Sargent (1979) or Weintraub (1979).

21 Keynes (1936: 261).

22 Lucas (1981: 229–30).

23 Not necessarily more expensive than numerous large economic research projects which have received funding. The most promising method would be a direct enquiry of a non-random but subjectively representative sample of forms in various types of polipolistic markets. Interviewers would attempt to obtain estimates of perceived conjectural elasticities from appropriate decision-makers, and historical cost and pricing data would be studied to compare actual decisions with those predicted from the interviews. The actual mark-up upon which the firms' actual prices were based would be compared with the inter-view-reported elasticity; explanations, consistent or inconsistent with Model B, as the case might be, investigated, the theory refined, and so on. Hall and Hitch (1939) and Dirlam *et al.* (1958) started down the road, though from a less clear theoretical starting point. Since then, to the best of the author's knowledge, there has been silence, a point that may give food for thought to the profession, including himself.

24 Marris (1991: 279–80).

25 For an outstanding exposition of Kahn's work on the subject, see the recent essay by Cristina Marcuzzo (1994).

26 Kahn (1929); Chamberlin (1933); Kalecki (1936, 1938); Lerner (1934); Robinson (1933). Kalecki (1936) is Kalecki's review of *The General Theory* in the Polish *Economic Journal* which was lost to non-Polish-reading economists until redis-covered and translated by Ferdinando Targetti and 'Bogna' Kinda-Hass specifically. In that remarkable document Kalecki specifically associated *The General Theory* with imperfect competition.

27 In historical order of first publication: Clower (1960, 1965); Leijonhufvud (1968, 1981); Dreze (1975); Barro and Grossman (1976); Malinvaud (1977); Mankiw (1985, 1988); Benassy (1986); Blanchard (1987); Blanchard and Kiyotaki (1987); Gordon (1990); Mankiw and Romer (1991).

28 Leijonhufvud (1968: 103).

29 Hicks (1965: 77–8).

30 Hicks (1974: 22–3).

31 Mankiw and Romer (1991: 7).

32 Hicks first introduced the term 'fixprice' in the first quotation in 1965, in the context of the problems of temporary equilibrium in dynamical analysis, and without any direct reference to price-setting. The latter association does not appear until years later, in the second quotation. What Hicks failed to emphasize was that under price-setting, prices are endogenous to the process of profit maximization, which means that in the product market, provided firms correctly estimate their demand curves, gaps requiring 'correction' between supply and demand do not arise. In the product market, there is always a temporary equilibrium, in which both prices and quantities are endogenous, based on predetermined demand curves, nominal wages, etc. The derived demand for labour may not clear the labour market, nominal wages may change, but, for reasons discussed again below, cannot thereby correct that market. The new nominal wages are passed on to the next temporary-equilibrium period and determine prices therein. I claim to have shown elsewhere (Marris 1991) that there is no need to make heavy weather of the dynamics of all this.

33 Clower (1960, 1965). It must be recognized that Clower was the originator of the whole literature.

34 This way of describing the situation owes debt, of course, to Dreze and Malinvaud (Dreze, 1975: Malinvaud, 1977).

35 Sawyer (1992b: 111).

36 This is a more severe position than that of Trevithick, who on p. 214 (Trevithick, 1992, op. cit.) writes, 'Although this [the "new Keynesian"] research programme could prove to be highly productive, I must express a lingering reservation: why do new Keynesians feel the need to rationalize the prevalence of nominal-price rigidities? It appears that, in new Keynesian models, nominal demand disturbances manifest themselves in the form of changes in real variables *only because* nominal prices are inflexible. But . . . in a closed economy, this conclusion rests principally upon the combined strength of the Keynes effect and the real-balance effect.' We all agree that both effects are weak in practice. But the drive of the argument in the present paper is that, as a matter of theory, if by 'flexible' prices are meant price-taking, perfectly competitive prices, then, without a strong monetary stabilizer such as the real-balance effect, *The General Theory* fails.

37 The literature that begins with Cournot (1838) and has a recent culmination in Sonnenschein (1987).

38 See however Sylos-Labini (1956, 1987).

39 Marris (1991) ch. 3.

40 Elsewhere, the present author wrote on this topic, 'The gain or loss of products due to entry is a change in the structure of the economy. The decisions are made by firms, not quasi-firms, and profits accrue to firms, not quasi-firms. The rate of profit earned by a firm is intimately bound up with its rate of growth, each reacting on the other. In turn, diversification (creating new products, new quasi-firms) is an important means of corporate growth. So the theory of macro entry cannot be separated from the theory of macro

growth.' (Marris, 1991, p. 163). A quasi-firm is either a one-product firm or a product division of a diversified corporation. Quasi-firms make price and output decisions, firms (corporations) make investment, financing and 'entry' decisions. In the present contribution, 'firms' are quasi-firms.

41 A possible qualification to this conclusion would be if there is cyclical variation in the degree of oligopolistic collusion. In the discussion here, in arriving at joint profit-maximization we have assumed perfect collusion. Huw Dixon (Dixon, 1987) in his elegant model of quantity-setting oligopoly, neatly provides for varying degrees of collusion by means of a coefficient indicating the conjectured degree of reaction of others' quantitites to own quantity changes – the greater is the degree of positive reaction (my increase in quantity is followed in the same direction by others' increases) the nearer is the equilibrium result to jpm; the smaller is the reaction, the nearer is the result to perfect competition. We may apply this idea to the price-setting case by imagining that it is possible to conjecture *partial* price-following reactions, e.g. if I raise my price 10 per cent, competitors might raise theirs by only 5 per cent, and so on. Such conjectures will produce prices below jpm nearer to the non-cooperative equilibrium. In order to hypothesize that oligopoly prices move systematically with the cycle due to cyclical variations in collusion we must, therefore, hypothesize that the conjectured reaction-coefficient moves *pro*-cyclically – a perfectly possible idea, once considered by Joe Stiglitz (Stiglitz, 1984), but one on which there is no theory or evidence.

42 See e.g. Marris and Mueller (1980).

43 Baumol (1971), Cyert and March (1963), Dirlam, Kaplan and Lanzillotti (1958), Downward (1994), Hall and Hitch (1939), Simon (1959, 1982), Simon, Egidi, Marris and Viale (1992) represent selections of relevant references. For the present author's personal assessment, see pp. 194–224 of the last-named.

44 In an intriguing book on bounded rationality in macroeconomics, Thomas Sargent has recently given the following interpretation to the concept, 'Herbert Simon and other advocates of "bounded rationality" propose to create theories with behavioural foundations by eliminating the asymmetry that rational expectations build in between the agents in the model and the econometrician who is estimating it. The idea . . . might be implemented by requiring that the agents . . . are sure of their model but unsure of the parameter values; they might be . . . unsure of their models and parameter values but can say how they are unsure; or [neither]' (Sargent, 1993, pp. 21–2). To my mind, this seems to miss a major aspect of the Simon insight. A business person may be sure that there is a demand curve but profoundly unsure of the elasticity. Unlike the 'economist' business person the boundedly-rational business person, rather than applying expected values or game theory, might do something completely different altogether.

45 See e.g. Sylos-Labini (1987) p. 702 col. 2.

46 See e.g. Baumol (1971) p. 119 et seq.

47 This is, for example, a possible implication of the 'mark-down' model described in Cyert and March (1963), pp. 137 et seq.

48 Simon (1957, 1959).

49 The following paragraph is a compression of arguments put forward in Marris (1964: 266–74). Baumol (1971) op. cit. raises similar questions.

50 The Kaldor-Pasinetti type models (Kaldor 1957, 1962, 1966; Pasinetti, 1962, 1974; also Wood, 1975, and Harcourt and Kenyon, 1976) assume that Keynesian full employment is maintained by cyclical variations in the average saving propensity working, via distributional effects, through pro-cyclical

movements of the mark-up. The present writer has long criticised these models (Marris, 1964, p. 309, 1972, 1991, pp. 203–10) for lack of adequate micro-foundations. I claim that, containing no micro theory of the mark-up, these models cannot use it for cyclical equilibrating behaviour.

51 Kalecki (1938). Keynes (1939c: 49): but nowhere in this important, thinking-aloud, article, where Keynes responds to evidence of non-cyclical behaviour of the real wage, does he make clear whether he understands that in the formal imperfect-polypoly theory such as used by Kalecki in 1938 or ourselves in Model B, 'the degree of imperfection of the market' is a numerical quantity equal to the reciprocal demand elasticity.

52 See Snower (1984) and Solow (1986). In Snower the change occurs because cyclical movement is modelled as a linear addition of government expenditure to an otherwise iso-elastic demand curve, so mathematically reducing elasticity at all prices; in Solow, government expenditure is assumed to be empirically less demand elastic than private expenditure. For further discussiuon of these two models see Marris (1991: 221–23).

53 A well-known paper (Nickell and Layard, 1985), which has considerably influenced UK econometric macro models, has been criticized by some, including the present writer, for apparently failing to accept this logic. For example, in an opening statement the authors write, 'First, employment. This depends on the real wage and demand'. But as the model which follows has the basic elements of our Model B, something is wrong somewhere.

54 Marris (1991: 276ff).

55 Mankiw (1988) and Startz (1989).

56 'There is, therefore, no ground for the belief that a flexible wage policy is capable of maintaining continuous full employment . . . The economic system cannot be made self-adjusting on these lines' (*G.T.*: 267).

57 The paradox that these concepts were inserted by Richard Kahn, secret creator of the theory of imperfect polipoly (Kahn 1929), has been discussed in Marris (1992). Luigi Pasinetti and Geoffrey Harcourt have also called my attention to an interesting paper by the late and greatly lamented Laurie Tarshis (1979), where the author presents the case for interpreting *The General Theory* under imperfect competition and in so doing reconstructs the aggregate supply function as an inverse relationship where price depends cyclically on output assuming the neoclassical MPL curve. But, with greatest respect to all concerned, I cannot see the point of this. When the concept (of ASF) is defined under price-taking as a dependency of output on a parametric price, it seems a valid tool, derived from microeconomic analogy, in the determination of equilibrium. Under imperfect competition, however, equilibrium is fully determined by equations such as those in my Model B. If we put back the neoclassical MPL curve, so that productivity varies with output, the real wage varies with output and, hence also, given nominal wage, nominal price. Why do we need more? Tarshis's function is a reduced form of the relationships, possibly useful for empirical work, but surely confusing if somehow interpreted as a blade of a theoretical scissors, the other blade of which is a demand function. As is well understood, under imperfect competition there does not exist an aggregate demand function in which output depends on price.

58 Kahn (1931).

59 'Let Z be the aggregate supply price of the output from employing N men . . .' (Keynes 1936: 25).

60 Ibid: 299–300.

61 Keynes would have had to swallow the conclusion he reached on this subject in

Keynes (1939c: 49). The article in question suggests that he would not have found this too difficult. He was impressed by the evidence on the apparent cyclical invariance, in the twentieth century, of real wages, adduced by Dunlop (1938) and Tarshis (1939). For a survey and critique of the theory and evidence on the short-run marginal labour productivity curve, see Marris (1991: 75–86).

5

IMPERFECT COMPETITION AND KEYNES

Nina Shapiro

While price rigidity has become the hallmark of the Keynesian system, the wage and price rigidities that explain unemployment in the economics of the Keynesians do not explain it in the economics of Keynes. Here, the problem was not the stickiness of prices, but the variability, the uncertainties of markets, not the imperfections. Imperfect competition had nothing to do with the unemployment in the system – Keynes himself could not see 'how on earth' it came into it (*C.W.* XIV: 190) – and it was because it did not that the degree of competition was taken as given, and the analysis conducted under the assumption of perfect competition.[1]

Keynes's view is considered below, where it is distinguished from that of the Keynesians and shown to entail a quite different conception of competition and its macroeconomic outcomes. Whereas in the case of the Keynesians, the perfection of competition optimizes the output and employment of the system, in that of Keynes, it volatilizes prices. It is the imperfection of competition, not the perfection, that stabilizes the system, reducing the uncertainties that make investment volatile and liquidity 'preferable'. Perfect competition is not optimal.

RISK AND UNCERTAINTY

The market 'failures' of *The General Theory* were investment failures. They occurred not when wages and prices were 'too high', but when investment was too low, below the level needed for the full employment output to be profitable. That output could not be produced 'without loss to the entrepreneur' unless investment brought the proceeds from its sale up to the level of its costs. It had to 'fill the gap' between the earnings of the factors and their consumption, yet the 'requisite' investment was 'not necessarily there' (*C.W.* XXIX: 215).[2]

Employment was a problem because investment was; and investment was problematic because of the uncertainty of its returns. These were not given with the physical properties of the investment – the 'productivity' of the capital or its output capabilities. The revenue from its employment depended on the prices of its products and the expenses of their production, and those product prices and factor costs were variable. They could be different than they were at the time the investment was undertaken, and different at various times of its life, and the profitability of an investment depended on the money that could be made on it 'over the whole of its life' (*G.T.*: 138).[3]

Markets changed, and while they might not change much in the short run, the time-frame of investment was the long run. The expectations that decided it could not be 'checked at short intervals' (ibid.: 51), and the capital moved into a new line of production when the profit from its existing one fell off. The equipment invested in was inflexible as well as durable, and the funds invested recoverable only if the product the equipment produced was profitable.

Investment was risky – the 'hopes that prompted it' (ibid.: 150) could be disappointed, and the funds invested lost. Revenue shortfalls and capital losses were possible, and these were as likely to occur as capital gains and profits. They could occur in the case of any investment, and while the risks of investment could be discounted and investment undertaken in spite of the possibility of losses, the 'fear' of these was always there – 'below the surface' (Keynes 1937c: 215). A change 'in the news' could upset confidence, 'dimming' the 'animal spirits' and checking investment.[4]

The risks of investment made it volatile, dependent on the disposition and outlook, the 'nerves' and 'reactions', of those who decided it. And while its level depended on interest rates as well as on business views and moods, these could not check its downturns. They could not maintain asset values and demand, countering the effect of a decline in the marginal efficiency of capital, for when confidence ebbed and spirits flagged, liquidity preference increased as well (Keynes 1937c).[5]

Liquidity preference was as changeable as the marginal efficiency of capital, varying with the same 'hopes and fears'. It also reflected market views and news, rising when those views darkened, and doubt and anxiety heightened, for liquidity 'lulled' that 'disquietude' (Keynes 1937c), 'calming the nerves'. It protected agents, and their properties, from the vagaries of markets, maintaining their wealth holdings and covering their losses.[6] Liquidity was valuable for the same reason that investment was risky – because markets were variable[7] – and since it was desired (and required) because of their downturns, when the fear of these 'surfaced' and investment fell, it was the demand for 'cash', not bonds, that rose.[8]

Interest rates moved in the wrong direction, their changes accentuated rather then averted the falls in investment.[9] And while the fears that brought on those downturns were subjective, the uncertainties that they reflected were not. Markets *were* unpredictable, there was no 'long-run' equilibration of their fluctuations, or long-run 'position' that 'centred' their changes.

The risks and uncertainties of market production are highlighted throughout Keynes's work, as is their relation to the employment problems of the system. Their importance is stressed in the critical writings of the 1920s as well as in those of the 1930s, with 'risk, uncertainty, and ignorance' the 'cause' of unemployment in *The End of Laissez-Faire* (Keynes 1926: 47), and risk assumption the critical requisite of production in *A Tract on Monetary Reform* (Keynes 1923).

The analysis of the *Tract* foreshadows that of *The General Theory*. Monetary changes had 'real' effects; price increases and decreases were not 'indexed'. There were no market contracts or price agreements that could protect the firm from the price changes that occurred after its costs had been incurred, in the time between the 'commencement' of its production and sale of its product (*C.W.* IV: 33).

The production process was 'lengthy', and the expenses of production, monetary. They were paid in *money*, in advance of the proceeds from the product, with the costs incurred, and finance contracted, before the money that could be obtained for the product was known. Production under a 'regime of money contract' forced the firm to carry 'a big speculative position', and while much of the risk it bore was the result of fluctuations in the relative values of products, changes in their absolute values were important also (ibid.).[10]

The injuriousness of those 'nominal' price changes was the 'central message' of the *Tract*: inflation was 'unjust' and deflation 'inexpedient' (ibid.: 36); the former 'discredited' enterprise and the latter 'impoverished' it. Inflation shifted the wealth and income of the system to those in a position to take advantage of its price increases. It rewarded speculation and heightened inequalities, turning the business man into a 'profiteer', and delegitimizing his profit:

> No man of spirit will consent to remain poor if he believes his betters to have gained their goods by lucky gambling. To convert the business man into the profiteer is to strike a blow at capitalism, because it destroys the psychological equilibrium which permits the perpetuance of unequal rewards.
>
> (*C.W.* IV: 24)

There was 'injustice' in deflation also, the injustice of unemployment; for while the rising prices of inflation 'overstimulated' production, the falling prices of deflation depressed it. Deflation devalued stocks of all kinds – the finished and semi-finished product inventories of manufacturers as well as the holdings of merchants. The value of those goods fell with the fall in prices, reducing the profit from their sale, and since the manufacturers and merchants were the 'borrowers' in the system, deflation squeezed their profit through its debt effects also.

Deflation increased the cost of debt as much as it increased the value of 'cash'. It raised the real cost of debt payments and finance charges, shifting the revenues of firms to their creditors and bankrupting their operations.[11] And since the 'fact of falling prices' injured their businesses, the 'fear of falling prices' caused them to 'curtail their operations' (ibid.: 34). Plant closures and lay-offs were the ways in which firms protected themselves from the losses of deflation.

The 'hopes and fears' that affected production in *The General Theory* affected it in the *Tract* also. Profit expectations decided output and employment levels, and the fear of losses depressed them. And it was because those expectations were critical that the 'monetary reform' of the *Tract* was essential, for price instability 'greatly' increased the risk of losses, and it was upon the 'aggregate' of the 'individual estimations' of that risk, and the 'willingness' to run it, that the 'activity of production and of employment mainly depends' (ibid.).

The same view of the employment problem is expressed in *The End of Laissez-faire* (1926), although here the analysis centres on the resource allocations of the system rather than the resource utilizations. Those market allocations could be the 'optimal' ones of the *laissez-faire* doctrine only if a number of 'unreal' conditions held, and one of the most important of these was the 'perfect foresight' condition of the 'classical' economics.

Laissez-faire assumed that the 'ideal' distribution of productive resources could be achieved through the separate actions of independent individuals. These would seek out the most advantageous use of their resources, with the competition of those who made the 'right' resource allocations 'destroying' those who made the 'wrong' ones (Keynes 1926: 28). The costs of that 'Darwinian' struggle were not considered – only the benefits of its final result mattered – and since it selected the 'most efficient' through the 'bankruptcy' of the 'less efficient', there could be no 'mercy' or 'protection' for those who misemployed their resources:

> The object of life being to crop the leaves up to the greatest possible height, the likeliest way of achieving this end is to leave the giraffes with the longest necks to starve out those whose necks are shorter.
>
> (Ibid.: 29)

But the 'less efficient' were not necessarily at fault. Their inefficiencies – like those of the 'short-necked' giraffes – might have been outside their control. They might not have known which product model would be the most useful to consumers, or which technique would be the least costly to operate. They might have 'betted' on the wrong ones, or invested their resources before the 'best' ones were developed. Their losses would have been avoidable, and bankruptcy 'just', only if they could have known what the market required; and while *laissez-faire* assumes that they could have known this, that 'foreknowledge' of conditions and requirements is not, in fact, possible (ibid.: 32).

For self-interest to be 'enlightened' and private and public interests to coincide, individuals have to know what others want and require. They have to know each others' 'demands' as well as 'supplies', and when they can supply and demand different things at different times that market knowledge is not 'public' – given with the product prices. These do not provide the 'foreknowledge' of conditions that market success requires, and individuals can find themselves and their resources in the 'wrong' market at the 'wrong' time (ibid.: 31).

There was an element of 'lucky gambling' in every market reward, and speculation in every enterprise. The 'mixed game of skill and chance' that business men played was played by everyone in the system, and the chance aspects of that game were as important in the case of the workers as they were in that of the investors and entrepreneurs. The coal-miners of *The Economic Consequences of Mr Churchill* (*C.W.*: IX) were as unfortunate as the short-necked giraffes of *The End of Laissez-faire* (1926). They, too, lost out through no fault of their own, because of 'circumstances for which they were in no way responsible and over which they had no control' (*C.W.* IX: 222).[12]

The 'freedoms' of *laissez-faire* had their costs: resources could be misemployed, expectations 'disappointed', and jobs and capital lost. Those risks were at the centre of Keynes's 'vision', and their importance was the distinguishing feature of his system. It was the uncertainties of that system that made its outcomes 'sub-optimal', and what is at issue in the validity of its results is not the 'flexibility' of prices but the predictability.[13]

GENERAL EQUILIBRIUM

The risks that are at the centre of Keynes's system are of little importance in the 'clasical' one. Its analysis centres on the long-period equilibrium,[14] and in the case of the 'new' classical economics, there is no other position of the system. Markets are always in 'general' equilibrium, with their prices 'prereconciling' all supply and demand decisions. No product is ever in excess supply, or product price below (or above) product costs. Profits are always 'normal', expectations realized and capital losses impossible.

But while the prices of markets can 'clear' them, they cannot clear them 'all at once' – at one and the same time – for that simultaneous clearance of markets entails the simultaneous determination of their prices, and the prices of markets are not centrally decided. There is no planning board or public 'auctioneer' that sets and aligns their levels, and while the resource allocations of the Walrasian system might be price allocations, they are not market ones.

The market co-ordination of production is 'unconscious'. It occurs through the separate decisions of independent agents, and that decentralization of decision is the hallmark of the market system. The decisions of its agents are not 'prereconciled', their operations are adjusted after they are effected, *ex post* not *ex ante*, through their market valuation.

It is in the sale of their products that market producers find out whether, and the extent to which, their decisions were the 'right' ones, and it is throught the price effects of their mistakes that their errors are corrected. The 'excess demands' of the system are known through, and only through, its prices – these communicate its imbalances as well as its requirements – and since those excess demands are communicated and eliminated through their price effects, the equilibrium of the system cannot be 'continuous'.

The 'general equilibrium' has to be achieved, it cannot be effected 'instantaneously' without the intervention of 'false trades' and market changes. The excess demands of the system have to be expressed in its prices, and these have to induce the output adjustments and resource allocations that eliminate those shortages and surpluses. The price 'reconciliation' of decisions takes time – it is not an 'event', but a process – and it is instantaneous in the case of the Walrasian system, not because its markets are 'perfect', but because its auctioneer preadjusts its prices.

The prices of the Walrasian system are determined in its auction, where all its transactions are effected. The trade is centralized and the prices consciously decided by the auctioneer, who varies his price 'calls' until the equilibrium prices are uncovered. These are determined through those notional price changes – they mark out the price 'dual' of the optimum resource allocation – and while the price calls of the auctioneer identify the equilibrium prices, the trade rules of his auction ensure their realization. They prohibit any 'out-of-plan' transactions, permitting trade at, and only at, the equilibrium prices.

The Walrasian equilibrium is instantaneous because the Walrasian auctioneer effects it; and when the Walrasian trade is decentralized and the auctioneer eliminated, the system has the same equilibration problems as the Keynesian one (Leijonhufvud 1968). Its markets no longer clear simultaneously at prices that effect their general equilibrium. Their prices depend on their own particular conditions rather than on the agggregate ones of the system, and their 'false trades' not only 'constrain' demand, they also jeopardize investments, making the demand for them problematic.

With the equilibrium prices unknown at the time products are produced and supplied, any good can be in 'excess supply'. Losses are possible in the case of all producers – the expectations of any of them can be disappointed and the investment decisions 'wrong'. Investment returns are uncertain and the funds invested at risk; and with capital losses possible and expectations 'rational', liquidity will be valued and 'real' goods and services will not be the only items demanded.

The 'false trades' of the neo-Walrasian system entail the liquidity preference of Keynes, and that money demand will affect the 'notional' (full employment) demand for products as well as the 'effectual' (actual) one. Money will be 'notionally' demanded also, and its full employment demand can bring the rate of interest above the level needed for the product one to be effective. The interest rate that assuages market fears and induces risk assumption may be too high for investment to 'fill the gap' between the earnings of the factors and their consumption. That full employment investment may require a lower interest rate and, if the marginal efficiency of capital is especially low it may even require a negative one. Investment may have to be 'subsidized' for employment to be full.

When money is demanded as well as products, 'general gluts' are possible; excess demands may not 'sum to zero' at feasible prices (Davidson 1977, 1980). The aggregate demand can be inadequate, and it can be inadequate for precisely the reason Keynes stressed: because 'money enters into motives and decisions', playing a 'part of its own' in the system (Keynes 1973a: 408). The uncertainty that generates ('rationalizes') that liquidity preference is all that is needed for Keynesian 'results', and this is the case regardless of the flexibility of wages and prices.

While a lower price level may have 'real balance' effects, the deflation that lowers prices is 'injurious'. It squeezes profits and bankrupts firms, upsetting confidence and unnerving markets. The marginal efficiency of capital will fall with the fall in prices,[15] and the liquidity demand will increase; and the increase in liquidity preference can nullify the 'Keynes' effect of the price decline. Interest rates may not come down with the factor and product prices, and if the money supply itself depends on wage and price levels, because some or all of the money is 'endogeneous', real balances may not increase either. The money supply will contract with the fall in prices, and the deflation may have no real balance effect.[16]

The demand effects of lower prices look quite different when the fall in prices is considered,[17] and while the prices that the Walrasian auctioneer 'cries out' can be lower without a price decline, the prices that markets generate cannot. Those prices cannot be less without the deflation that increases debt burdens, devalues stocks and heightens fears. Their changes have the demand effects that Keynes emphasized, not those that the 'Keynesians' highlight, and it is because the price changes of the Keynesians are the notional ones of the Walrasian auctioneer that they can make the system self-adjusting.

PERFECT COMPETITION

When the unemployment in the system is Keynesian, its prices cannot cure the ill. They cannot keep employment full or money 'neutral'. Their flexibility will not stabilize the system, and indeed, its instability would be greater if its prices were less 'rigid' and markets more competitive, for this would increase the uncertainty that is at the root of its instability (Kregel 1981).[18]

Markets are unpredictable to the extent that they are variable, and their competition changes them. It alters the supply conditions of their products and shifts their sales, changing their prices and the profits of the firms that supply them. Profits fall with the increase in competition, and sales contract; and if the competition is technological, it will alter the product as well as its supply, changing the requirements of its production and those of its market. Competitive industries are changeable, and were industries perfectly competitive, with their products homogeneous and producible by anyone, their conditions would be so variable, and profit uncertain, that no one would be willing to invest in them (Richardson 1990).

Perfectly competitive industries are too open for investment, the risk of loss is too high. With all firms capable of supplying the industry product, and none more proficient at its production or sale than any other, any firm can enter the industry at any time, and any number could enter at any one time. Investment in the industry cannot be based on the assumption of any given or limited number of industry competitors, and while it might be possible to make a profit on the investment in the 'short run', when the industry entry is 'costless' and knowledge of the industry conditions 'perfect', the short run is very short.

Investment under perfect competition would be a pure gamble, with the profit won by those who happened to undertake the investment first. The profit of the speculator would be possible, but not that of the innovator or industrialist.[19] Firms could make a profit on short-term, liquid investments, but not on 'fixed' capital ones. They could not make a profit on a product long enough to recover the costs of a plant and equipment investment, and without the possibility of making a profit on that investment, few would undertake it. The investment would not be 'rational', and there would be little, if any, investment in production.

For product investment to be profitable, and its level high enough for employment conditions to be tolerable, the product market has to be 'imperfect'. Its competition has to be limited, with product differentiation protecting the sales of firms and special knowledge or skill giving them a 'competitive advantage' in the production or development of their products. That 'imperfection' of competition is needed for investment – markets would otherwise not be safe enough for it. Their 'frictions' and 'restrictions' are what protects the investments in their products.

Investment will be higher under imperfect competition than under perfect competition, and it will also be less variable, for the firms that undertake it will have less to fear. The markets of monopolistic firms are protected and their credit good, they can borrow on their assets and draw on their reserves. Their profits are more certain and assets more secure than those of their perfectly competitive counterparts; and since they have the liquidity needed to weather demand 'shocks' and the security for a long-run view, they need not curtail their investment when the demand for their products falls off. Their investment can be acyclical, with its level based on market and technological developments rather than on short-run demand changes (Eichner 1976).[20]

With the revenue of firms more secure under imperfect competition, so will be the income of their employees. They too will have less to fear; and with their income more secure, they will be able to spend a greater amount of it. The necessity of providing for the future will be less – that saving would be quite high under the uncertainties of perfect competition – and their increased job security need not come at the expense of their real wages, either, for these are not necessarily lower under imperfect competition.

Perfectly competitive firms have 'mark ups' also, and their profit margins can be higher than the margins of monopolistic firms. The differences in their mark-ups and the behaviour of those profit shares over the cycle depends on the pricing practices of the monopolistic enterprises. If these are geared to the future – and they would not be 'rational' if they were not – the prices of those firms will not 'maximize' profit. Instead of short-run profit considerations determining their prices, long-run growth ones will decide them. An 'entry-pre-empting' or market penetrating price will be set (Shapiro 1995), and with the product price constant over the cycle, the increase in the profit share in the upswing will be less than it would be under the marginal cost prices of the perfectly competitive enterprise.

The prices of perfect competition are 'flexible' in both directions: they go up when demand increases as well as down when it falls. Their increase can choke off an expansion, cutting the real wage and marginal propensity to consume ('multiplier'), and their average level over the cycle may entail a lower real wage than the one which would be realized under the 'rigid' prices of imperfect competition. Both consumption and investment may be higher when competition is imperfect, and the stability of the system and security of its members will certainly be greater.

While the 'imperfections' of markets have their costs, so do the uncertainties, and these are the other side of their 'freedoms'. Markets cannot be 'perfected' without intensifying the uncertainty that is at the root of their 'failures', and to 'suppose that a flexible wage policy is a right and proper adjunct of a system which on the whole is one of *laissez-faire*, is the opposite of the truth' (*G.T.*: 269).

NOTES

1 For a similar view of that assumption, see Cottrell (1994).
2 The importance of investment, and its treatment, in the employment results of Keynes's theory is emphasized in Sardoni (1992a).
3 The variability of investment returns was the reason why the marginal efficiency

91

of capital depended on the 'prospective' yield of the capital rather than the 'current' one, while the failure to recognize the variability of those returns was the 'main cause of confusion and misunderstanding' in the existing discussions of the marginal efficiency of capital (*G.T.*: 138).

4 Expectations are emphasized throughout *The General Theory* discussion of investment, not just in that of Chapter 12, while their dependence on the 'state of confidence' is a central theme of the discussion.

5 A fall in the marginal efficiency of capital could itself push up the liquidity preference schedule, for it was 'natural' for the latter to rise in the face of the 'dismay and uncertainty' that accompanied a precipitious decline in the former (*G.T.*: 316).

6 Those 'insurance' properties of liquidity are highlighted in Minsky's (1975) interpretation of the liquidity preference theory.

7 In the absence of variable bond markets, and 'uncertainty' as to the future course of their movements, there could be no 'store-of-value' demand for cash. That uncertainty was the 'necessary condition' for the 'existence of a liquidity-preference for money as a means of holding wealth' (*G.T.*: 168).

8 This is emphasized in Keynes's (1937c) response to his critics.

9 In addition to the discussion of those changes in Keynes's (1937c) *Quarterly Journal of Economics* article, see the one in the trade cycle chapter of *The General Theory*.

10 The importance of that 'money contract regime' is highlighted in Davidson (1978). See also Dillard (1948).

11 These aspects of deflation are emphasized in *The General Theory* also, where the discussion of price changes echoes that of the *Tract*.

12 In discussing the plight of those coal-miners, and the sacrifice that Churchill's policy required of them, Keynes (*C.W. IX*: 223) writes:

> Why should coal-miners suffer a lower standard of life than other classes of labour? They may be lazy, good-for-nothing fellows who do not work so hard or so long as they should. But is there any evidence that they are more lazy or more good-for-nothing than other people?

13 Joan Robinson always emphasized the importance of uncertainty in her discussions of Keynes (see, in particular, her Richard T. Ely Lecture (1971b) on 'The Second Crisis in Economic Theory') Also see Kahn's account (1984) of the development of *The General Theory*, and the interpretations of Chick (1983); Davidson (1978); Dutt and Amadeo (1990b); Hahn (1984), Harcourt (1987a, 1994a); Kregel (1980); Meltzer (1988); Shackle (1967); and Vicarelli (1984).

14 This is emphasized in Keynes's discussions of the limitations of the system (see, in particular, the remarks on the Classical School in his 1937 *Quarterly Journal of Economics* article).

15 That adverse effect of the deflation is highlighted in Gaynor (1992). Also see Dutt (1986/87).

16 The importance of 'outside' money in the operation of the real balance effect is noted in Keynes's discussion of the 'Keynes effect' (*G.T.*: 266).

17 This is noted in Hahn and Solow (1986).

18 That price flexibility may worsen the employment situation is noted in Stiglitz (1993), and the adversity of its effects discussed in Tobin (1993).

19 The impossibility of innovation under perfect competition is the central theme of the Schumpeterian theory (Schumpeter 1942).

20 Keynes also notes the stabilising effects of monopoly (see the discussion of the investment practices of public utilities in *G.T.*: Ch. 12).

6

THE PRINCIPLE OF EFFECTIVE DEMAND*

Luigi L. Pasinetti

A (PRESUMABLY) IMPORTANT PRINCIPLE

'The Principle of Effective Demand' is the title of a crucial chapter – Chapter 3 – of Keynes's *General Theory* (hereafter abbreviated to *G.T.*). It is something of a paradox that, after appearing as the title of the chapter, the 'principle' of effective demand is not stated. The only time the term itself is mentioned in the whole of Chapter 3 is on page 31, in an incidental sentence, where it is taken for granted that the reader knows what it is. It is not mentioned again in the whole book. It is not even mentioned anywhere else in Keynes's writings (as far as I have been able to discover) with two exceptions: in a perfunctory sentence in the centenary allocution on Malthus (*C.W.* X: 107) and in a letter to Sraffa (to be mentioned below, p. 100).

The term 'principle' is normally used for something fundamental. The fact that Keynes put it so prominently as the title of a crucial chapter makes us think that his well-known intuition led him to feel that it is very important. Yet he never came back to it explicitly.

It will be argued in the present chapter that most of Keynes's analysis of Chapter 3 was carried out at a level of investigation that concerns the *behaviour* of a 'monetary production economy', within a given institutional set-up. The principle of effective demand belongs to a more fundamental level of investigation, towards which Keynes was able to go only partially. Perhaps, he never had the time or the necessary calm or the appropriate analytical tools to go back and face it explicitly. After Keynes, those who have tried to re-absorb his analysis into traditional theory have been careful not to mention the principle at all;[1] while those who have endeavoured to carry further Keynes's 'revolution' have been too quick to identify it, thus remaining half-way between his behavioural relations and the deeper level to which the 'principle' of effective demand really belongs.

L.L. PASINETTI

EFFECTIVE DEMAND

Chapter 3 of *The General Theory* is devoted to the definition of the *point*, not the 'principle', of effective demand. Keynes introduces the concepts of an Aggregate Supply Function and an Aggregate Demand Function. Then he defines *effective demand* as the point of intersection, that is the point at which demand becomes effective:

> Let Z be the aggregate supply price of the output from employing N men, the relationship between Z and N being written $Z = \phi(N)$, which can be called the *aggregate supply function*. Similarly, let D be the proceeds which entrepreneurs expect to receive from the employment of N men, the relationship between D and N being written $D = f(N)$, which can be called the *aggregate demand function*. . . .
>
> The value of D at the point of the aggregate demand function, where it is intersected by the aggregate supply function, will be called the *effective demand.*
>
> (*G.T.*: 25)

It is worth stressing that the concepts of Aggregate Supply Function, Aggregate Demand Function and Effective Demand were new: all were introduced by Keynes (though he tries, or pretends, to relate them to previous discussions).

Of course, demand and supply functions were at the basis of orthodox economic analysis, but – as Patinkin (1976a: 83) rightly points out – they were demand and supply functions for single commodities. (Marshall would insist, with his partial equilibrium analysis, that they can only be drawn *ceteris paribus* – everything else remaining constant.) Keynes's aggregate demand and supply functions involve the economic system as a whole – a conception that was outside orthodox economics.

Keynes's aggregate functions are precisely introduced in contrast to tradition in order to discuss, and reject, Say's Law. As he writes in a letter to Harrod:

> To me, the most extraordinary thing regarded historically, is the complete disappearance of the theory of demand and supply for output as a whole, i.e. the theory of employment, *after* it had been for a quarter of a century the most discussed thing in economics.
>
> (*C.W.* XIV: 85)

The theory against which Keynes is complaining is the economic theory 'of Marshall, Edgeworth, and Professor Pigou' (*G.T.*: 33), in which any notion of *aggregate* demand and supply would make no sense.

With his aggregate functions, Keynes could present what, in the dominant classical view, was known as Say's Law as equivalent to assuming that the two aggregate functions always coincide at *all* levels of output and employment, so as always to lead the economic system to the point of full employment. In contrast to tradition, Keynes could claim that the two aggregate functions are quite distinct, so that they usually intersect each other at a single point – the point of effective demand – generally entailing under-employment and under-capacity utilization.

AGGREGATE DEMAND AND AGGREGATE SUPPLY

Keynes's Aggregate Demand Function and Aggregate Supply Function are behavioural relations. They presuppose a well-defined institutional set-up – a market economy in which consumers and entrepreneurs behave in accordance with what they perceive as their self-interest – and they are supposed to incorporate all information concerning the decisions of consumers and entrepreneurs acting in a given framework of a specific market structure.

Chapter 3 is very succinct. Keynes comes back later to the Aggregate Demand Function in greater detail, presenting it as the sum of a consumption function and an investment function. Moreover, while in Chapter 3 the aggregate demand function is formulated in terms of employment, from Chapter 8 onwards, Keynes suggests that 'it is more convenient' to formulate it in terms of income, in wage units. And that is how the Aggregate Demand Function has been dealt with from that point on, both by Keynes and by his followers.

On the other hand, Keynes does not go back to expand in any comparable detail the Aggregate Supply Function. Keynes's analysis of this function remains incomplete. The best account we have of it is that offered to us by Lorie Tarshis (1979), who has used his lecture notes, taken at both Keynes's and Kahn's lectures in the early 1930s. The market structure in terms of which Tarshis presents his account of Keynes's Aggregate Supply Function is that of an imperfectly competitive market, considered in its short-run behaviour, as it emerged from the works of Kahn, Joan Robinson and Shove. Tarshis gives three versions of the Aggregate Supply Function: in terms of employment; in terms of output; and in terms of income. Tarshis mentions Keynes's suggestion in Chapter 8 of *The General Theory* to convert the Aggregate Demand Function in terms of income (from its being originally in terms of employment), and he accepts that this may implicitly be taken as a suggestion to do a similar substitution also for the Aggregate Supply Function. Tarshis rightly shows, however, that replacing employment with income, innocuous as it is for the Aggregate Demand Function, deprives the Aggregate Supply Function of any reference to the behaviour of an economy with a specific market structure. The Aggregate Supply Function is simply turned into a 45° line from the origin – a geometrical device, not a behavioural relation – which conveys no information about either costs or elasticities or the degree of imperfection of competition.

Tarshis therefore concludes that the original formulations in terms of employment is preferable. The two aggregate functions, as originally presented by Keynes, are two relations meant to express the *behaviour* of the economy in the most general conditions of competition. Lorie Tarshis actually shows how useful for economic policy and how rich in information on the behaviour of the economic system is Keynes's theoretical apparatus in which *both* aggregate functions are kept as two symmetric behavioural aggregate relations, with very definite 'microfoundations': on the side of demand, the 'psychological law' of consumers spending less than total income; on the side of supply, imperfect competition behaviour in a short-run context.

At the level of investigation concerning the behaviour of a 'monetary production economy', within a given institutional set-up, Tarshis's framework is probably the most useful and, in any case, the one which is logically coherent.

THE KEYNESIAN ADJUSTMENT MECHANISM

Be that as it may, the version of Keynes's aggregate demand and supply theory found in most textbooks is not that of Keynes's *G.T.* Chapter 3, but the one that has sprung from his suggestion of Chapter 8: to take national income as the argument of the demand function. By extension, the same has been done for the aggregate supply function, with the effect of making this function disappear as a behavioural relation. Its place has been taken by a neutral 45° line from the origin.

The Aggregate Demand Function, however, has continued to keep the character of a behavioural relation, expressing a consumption function, $C = f(Y)$, that is, consumption as a function of income, where $0 < f' < 1$, on the top of which investments (which are not a function of income) are simply added.

The resulting diagram is known to many generations of economists, because it has been popularized by most of the textbooks (see, for example, Hansen 1953; Harcourt *et al.* 1967). Though not a model of elegance and coherence, it has been used — one must admit, very effectively — to show how, in 'a monetary production economy', starting from a situation of under-employment equilibrium, an increment of aggregate demand (for example, an increase of investment, dI) leads the economic system to a new equilibrium situation in which income has increased by $dY = [1 / (1 - f')]dI$, the multiplier relation, and the increment of investment dI has generated an exactly equal amount of saving $dI = dS$ (see Figure 6.1).

There is no need to underline how effective this simple diagrammatic device has been in illustrating one of the basic contributions of *The General Theory*, namely, the proposition that, in a situation of under-employment of

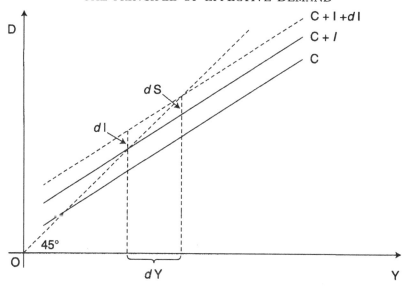

Figure 6.1 The multiplier process

labour and under-utilization of productive capacity, any increase of demand, no matter where it comes from, induces a process of adaptation of *physical* output and employment, at roughly constant prices, to the increased demand (the multiplier mechanism), thus generating exactly the amount of saving required to match the increased investment demand.

It is this physical-quantity adjustment mechanism, operating through the multiplier mechanism up to the point of full-capacity utilization (and full employment), taking place through variations of physical quantities of output (and employment) at roughly constant prices, that has been indicated as representing the central contribution of Keynes's *General Theory*. Some scholars have gone further and have singled out precisely this physical-quantity adjustment mechanism as Keynes's (unstated) 'principle of effective demand'. Edward Amadeo (1989: 1), for example, summarizes beautifully:

> In its most simple and fundamental version, Keynes's principle of effective demand can be enunciated as follows: given a change in investment demand (or any autonomous component of aggregate demand), the level of income (that is, the levels of price and output) will change in such a way that, in equilibrium, the corresponding change in saving will be equal to the initial change in investment.

But this is jumping to the conclusion too hastily. The simple macro-economic scheme is an effective didactical device to show the physical quantity adjustment mechanism operating in a market production economy, and should be presented as such, not as a fundamental principle. It mixes up a behavioural, institutionally based, relation (the sum of a consumption function and an investment function) and a neutral, institutionally free, geometrical device – the 45° line. The two original aggregate functions belonged to the same (behavioural) level of investigation. The textbook macroeconomic model is a hybrid construction. A (one-sided) step towards a more fundamental level of analysis is made on the supply side. The analysis remains at a behavioural level on the demand side. Something fundamental on the one side is mixed up with a remarkable behavioural adjustment mechanism on the other side. It is, in fact, a sort of short cut to achieve didactical effectiveness, without paying too much attention to analytical coherence.

THE PRINCIPLE OF EFFECTIVE DEMAND

In talking of two distinct levels of investigation – one behavioural and the other fundamental, or 'natural', as the early classics called it[2] – I am talking of levels of investigations that are both essential and complementary, though they are distinct and aimed at different purposes. In the present case, these purposes can be shown very clearly.

When the analytical purpose is that of determining effective demand, the appropriate procedure is that adopted by Keynes in Chapter 3 of *The General Theory*, namely the setting up of functions expressing the behaviour of an economy within a specific institutional set-up. In the present case, the construction behind Keynes's aggregate demand function has a solidity beyond question. On the other hand, the incompleteness of Keynes's construction behind the aggregate supply function is so evident as to make it necessary to consider seriously Tarshis's proposal to take advantage of the theory of imperfect competition that was developed in Cambridge roughly at the same time as *The General Theory*. It should be stressed that, in principle, other proposals may legitimately be put forward.[3]

But when the analytical purpose is to single out the basic characteristics of a 'monetary production economy' – as Keynes called it – one must make an effort to descend to a deeper level of investigation.

From this point of view, the replacement of a 45° line for the original aggregate supply function – whatever the intention for which it was originally adopted – has turned out to be a movement towards this more fundamental level. It meant abandoning a level of analysis that was aimed at explaining the actual behaviour of entrepreneurs acting in a specific market structure (imperfect or perfect competition) in order to uncover more fundamental relationships. It meant giving up the details of firms' behaviour in order to gain deeper insights into the more basic – institutionally free – characteristics of the economic system.

98

To move towards fundamentals, it seems logical that we should take a similar step also on the side of demand.

Suppose we give up, for a moment, any pretence to represent the way in which an economy *actually* behaves. In our case, this means no less than leaving aside Keynes's consumption and investment functions. As a simple and crude device, we may keep the same diagram for the time being, but empty it of behavioural relations, thus remaining simply with the two axes and the 45° line. This is not meaningless, if we still keep all the suppositions on which the diagram is built. That is to say: behind the diagram there is the supposition that at any given point in time a *production* economy is characterized by a specific and well-differentiated productive capacity and by a corresponding labour force (with specific skills and training) that are the result of past activity. The productive capacity and labour force are whatever they are: in the short run they cannot be changed. But they only represent *potential* production. *Actual* production will be realized only for that amount for which demand is expected. Actual production will thus turn out to be whatever effective demand is expected to be. In this sense, effective demand generates production.

On Figure 6.2 (emptied of behavioural relations) this process of production-generation by effective demand may simply be represented by a series of alternative arrows, giving the direction of causation. If effective demand is D_1, actual production will be Y_1; if effective demand is D_2, actual production will be Y_2; and so on.

This process is, after all, implied by the graphical step-by-step illustration of the multiplier mechanism that has been given in textbook presentations. Output always turns out to be equal to demand at each single step. And the adaptation mechanism starts all over again, whenever the activation of

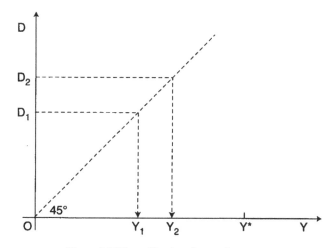

Figure 6.2 The effective demand process

production is not yet at the equilibrium position.[4] The process works up to point Y*, representing full capacity utilization (and full employment). Beyond this point, production becomes physically constrained and the generation of output will no longer be in physical terms, but will take place only in nominal terms (through increases in prices).

Thus, effective demand generates income: as physical output up to point Y*, as income at current (increased) prices beyond point Y*. In other words, fluctuations of demand generate fluctuations of income, in physical terms up to Y*, in nominal terms beyond Y*. This process is a basic characteristic of any production economy. It is quite independent of any behavioural relations and thus of any particular adaptation mechanism. It is independent of market structure, it is even independent of the particular consumption and investment functions introduced by Keynes. Basically, it is independent of institutions, by simply being inherently characteristic of the way in which industrial economies have come to be set up.

It is this basic, non-institutional, or if we like pre-institutional, characteristic, lying at the very foundations of industrial societies, that – I should venture to say – represents the 'principle of effective demand'.

The nearest Keynes came to stating it is in an undated (probably 1935) letter to Piero Sraffa, in which, replying to earlier objections by Sraffa, he describes the way in which entrepreneurs behave, and – quite exceptionally – tries to generalize and reach a sort of 'general principle':

> This is an example of the general principle that *any* expansion of output gluts the market unless there is a *pari passu* increase of investment appropriate to the community's marginal propensity to consume; and any contraction leads to windfall profits to producers unless there is an appropriate *pari passu* contraction of investment.
>
> (*C.W.* XXIX: 159–60)

He would only have needed to turn the same argument the other way round (from a negative approach, focusing on the lack of adaptation of demand to output – which was for him instrumental to reject Say's Law – to a positive approach, focusing on demand requiring no more and no less output than itself) to have stated the principle clearly.

KEYNES VERSUS WALRAS

It is important to realize how inherent and deep a characteristic of industrial economies the principle of effective demand is.

In economies of the earlier, agricultural and artisan type, every farmer and artisan used to produce as much as possible (irrespective of demand). Then they carried whatever was produced to the market, where it fetched the price that the market made. Industrial societies have changed considerably. Any producer must try to estimate the demand that is likely to be effective *before* starting any production at all and quite irrespective of existing productive capacity. Disregarding this simply causes a 'market glut'. In this sense, at any point of time it is expected demand (Keynes's effective demand) that generates production.

On a theoretical level, there can be no doubt that the early classical economists – from Adam Smith to John Stuart Mill (including Marx) – had a clear perception of the *industrial* character of the economies they were investigating. Hence, the crucial role of overall demand, at any given point in time, was bound to come up in their discussions. Analytically, they were not strongly equipped, and they split into two parties, more on instinctive ground than on the strength of their arguments. The enthusiasts of the established institutions – the majority – found in a few pages of Jean-Baptiste Say the clue (or at least the excuse) for affirming, in a rather fideistic way, that demand would be no problem because it would automatically be generated by production itself. The realists (a minority, including Sismondi, Malthus and Marx) acknowledged the facts as they could be observed, and expressed the conviction of the likelihood of periodic market gluts. What is interesting, from our point of view, is that the problem was recognized to exist and needed to be faced.

The intellectual atmosphere changed radically towards the end of the century. Paradoxically, the 'Marginal Revolution', which was characterized by the introduction of more rigorous tools of analysis, adopted an analytical approach that did not draw inspiration from the industrial characteristics of society. It seemed, rather, to have more affinities with the characteristics of earlier, pre-industrial, economic systems. The essential scheme at its basis has by now clearly emerged, especially after the recent refinements that have rendered it so beautiful and transparent. It is what has become known as the Walrasian model of general economic equilibrium. Stripped down to its essentials, this is a model of what has been called a 'pure exchange economy', in which the only problem is that of the optimum allocation of existing, given, resources. Even when such a scheme is enlarged to embrace the phenomenon of production, it does not change its essential analytical features, and inevitably leads to framing the production process itself as a form of exchange.

Now, in a 'pure exchange model', problems of demand for the economic system as a whole do not arise. The theorist is not even induced by such a model to discuss Say's Law, because it makes no sense. Even when attempts have been made deliberately to insert the discussion of Say's Law into the model – in order to investigate the relationships with the previous discussions – the result has been to concentrate attention on a relation that had to be called Walras's Law, which is an identity, that is, a relation that is always, automatically, satisfied.[5]

It can be no surprise, therefore, that, with the advent of marginal economics, discussions of demand and supply for output as a whole, indeed discussions of Say's Law, disappeared from the agenda of economic theorists. They would have been irrelevant. And it is also no surprise that, as soon as Keynes tried to revive interest in the discussion of the characteristics of monetary production economies, so different conceptually from the exchange economies of orthodox economics, he again and inevitably stumbled into the tricky problems of demand and supply for output as a whole.

What is surprising is Keynes's surprise (see his letter to Harrod, quoted on p. 94 above). He had (correctly) developed, at the behavioural level, the consequences of the principle of effective demand, but had not yet been able to penetrate to the deeper level of the foundations, where among other things he would have found immediate links with all earlier classical economists, and not only with Malthus. And he was obviously baffled (as is apparent from the quotation just mentioned). Indeed, he must have been profoundly baffled, to judge from his reaction, which has been to hide his bafflement behind one of the most masterly pieces of rhetoric in the whole of *The General Theory* (on pages 32–3.)

EFFECTIVE DEMAND AND FULL EMPLOYMENT IN THE LONG RUN

A more detailed analysis of the basic characteristics of a production economy, especially with reference to the long run (which Keynes could not go into) reveals even more strongly how important is the role of effective demand.

I have shown elsewhere (Pasinetti 1981, 1986, 1993) that it is possible to develop a very simple theoretical scheme embodying the basic characteristics of a production economy, which appears symmetrical in all its constituent elements to the 'pure exchange model' of orthodox economics. When such a scheme is adopted, we realize that in it the place of Walras's identity is taken by a macroeconomic equilibrium *condition*, in which the relevant components are productivity coefficients and demand coefficients, at a stage of analysis which is independent of institutions and thus precedes any analysis of behavioural relations.

This macroeconomic relation emerges, no longer as an identity but as a *necessary condition* for full employment (in a Leontief-like closed-model formulation, it takes the form of nullity of the determinant of the coefficient matrix – a necessary condition for meaningful equilibrium solutions). A *condition* cannot be satisfied automatically. This means that it becomes the specific task of institutions – that is, of the way a society organizes itself – to make (or to tend to make) that condition satisfied. In fact, it can be shown that, in a dynamic (long-run) context, since productivities are growing unevenly and demand for the various commodities is inevitably bound to tend to saturation, the exogenous basic movements are such that the macroeconomic condition for full employment structurally tends to become *under*-satisfied, precisely due to a lack of effective demand. And this is so, simply as a consequence of the evolution of technology and of the composition of demand, independently of the particular institutions that any economic system may choose to adopt.

In a general dynamic context, therefore, the full-employment condition emerges as a target to be explicitly aimed at, on the background of a series of fundamental dynamic movements that inevitably and continually upset it.

The question that spontaneously arises concerns the major institutional system that has so far been invented in the experience of production economies: the free market institutional system. Can the free market institutional system do the job? This is the question which Keynes explicitly posited to us. And he gave his answer. He invented a very simple macro-economic behavioural scheme (a consumption function plus an investment function) that, in the short-run context of a market economy, showed an adjustment mechanism (through output adaptations) that led the economic system to a (short-run) equilibrium situation, which is not necessarily one of full employment. The same behavioural scheme also suggests what ought to be done to *improve* the market results, if not to actually achieve full employment. It was a very simple scheme, valid within restrictive conditions (that were, however, relevant for the capitalist economies of the 1930s). It is astonishing how slow we have been – and still are – to learn the lesson that Keynes's simple scheme teaches us.

The obvious task bequeathed to us is precisely the same task that he faced, to be carried out, however, in the wider context of a fully fledged monetary *production* economy, considered in its movements through time and in its relation to the outside world. Singling out a 'natural' evolving path along which full employment may be kept is far more complex, structurally, in any multi-sector production economy inserted in an international setting, than could be dreamed of from Keynes's simple scheme focusing on the utilization of full-employment productive capacity. It requires an appro-priate evolution of the relative sizes of the various production branches and an appropriate evolution of the relative prices, jointly with the movement (or rather the near non-movement, or practical 'stability') of the general level of prices. But the overall condition for maintaining full employment remains the same, because it is a single, fundamental, macroeconomic condition. In order to remain satisfied, it must rely on the same basic principle that Keynes's intuition proposed and tried to unveil, a principle which remains behind any adaptation mechanism, indeed behind any insti-tutional mechanism that may be invented for an industrial economy: this is the principle of effective demand.

NOTES

* For useful comments and criticisms on an earlier draft, I should like to thank: Andrea Boitani, Domenico Delli Gatti, Amitava K. Dutt and Geoffrey Harcourt. Financial support is gratefully acknowledged from the Italian Research Council (C.N.R. 95. 0136. CT 10).

1 Patinkin, for example, always talks of the 'theory', not the 'principle', of effective demand (see Patinkin 1976a).
2 For details, see Pasinetti (1981, 1986, 1993).
3 Although the recent literature has favoured the imperfect competition framework as providing the appropriate 'microfoundations' for Keynes's aggregate supply function (see also Marris, Ch. 4 in the present volume), the case of perfect or other types of competition may equally well be advocated. Victoria Chick (1983: ch. 5), for example, provides a set of microfoundations for Keynes's aggregate function, based on perfect competition. For the arguments proposed in the present analysis, the question of how markets are organized is immaterial, as this belongs to the behavioural stage of investigation.
4 See, for example, the presentation given in my own essay on effective demand (Pasinetti 1974: 53.)
5 See Lange (1942). See also Clower (1965), who has perhaps made the bravest effort to reconstruct Keynes's unemployment theory *within* the framework of what he calls 'the pure preference theory of markets', i.e. the orthodox Walrasian model.

Book II

DEFINITIONS AND UNITS

7

UNITS AND DEFINITIONS*

Wylie Bradford and G.C. Harcourt

INTRODUCTION

When Lorie Tarshis went to Keynes's lectures in the early 1930s he expected to hear an exposition and extensions of the arguments of the *Treasise on Money* (1930a, 1930b), in the arguments of which he was thoroughly steeped from his undergraduate days at the University of Toronto. Instead, over the years he attended Keynes's lectures (1932–5), he witnessed the growing embryo of *The General Theory*. He remembers that large parts of the lectures were taken up with definitions and discussions of units and that the really 'new stuff ', that is, the system of *The General Theory*, was rather crammed into the end of each of a course of eight lectures. (Tom Rymes (1989a) has rendered service to us all by setting out the notes of a 'representative student' so that we may now check how accurate Lorie's recollections were.) The important point for this chapter is that Keynes put so much emphasis on the preliminary but necessary task of sorting out definitions of key variables in relationships and discussing what were the appropriate units of measurement for the revolutionary tasks in hand. The emphasis which characterized Keynes's approach was continued in the post-war work of three of his closest colleagues and friends: Richard Kahn, Joan Robinson and Piero Sraffa. (Sraffa, of course, was already independently considering such issues in the 1920s and 1930s as he mapped out his prelude to a critique of economic theory – and devastatingly criticized Dr Hayek on money and capital for good measure.)

Anyone brought up in the post-war world, with its increasing mathematization of economic theory, would be thoroughly familiar with the claims made for the use of mathematics in economic theory and, in particular, how it allows us precisely to define not only the questions but also the answers, setting out clearly what we mean and what we have found out, the better to understand our achievements *and* their limitations, the non-applicability of results as well as their applicability. Economists brought up in this tradition are usually puzzled and irritated by Keynes's mode of discourse, as we post-Modernists say, as well as by those of his disciples, Richard Kahn

107

and Joan Robinson, and by those of Nicholas Kaldor and Piero Sraffa as well. A good example of this puzzled plus irritated reaction is to be found in the work of Avinash Dixit. He read mathematics at Cambridge for his first degree and then did a PhD in economics at MIT. Within the paradigm of *that* eminent place he is perfectly at ease, writing with mastery and clarity (see, for example, Dixit 1976). However, as soon as he has to deal with the conceptual arguments of, say, the capital or growth theory associated with Kaldor, Joan Robinson and Kahn, he loses his cool. Incomprehension and anger take over as he struggles to comprehend their ideas *within an inappropriate setting*. Much the same reaction may be found in Edward Burmeister's response to Sraffa's contributions, especialy the meaning and purpose of the Standard commodity (see, for example, Burmeister 1980: 140–3, esp. 143 fn). Burmeister seems to think it was intended to 'justify' the labour theory of value (as misunderstood by most neoclassical economists), rather than to render visible that which is hidden, namely, a simple inverse relationship between the *rate* of profits and the wage *in the given technical conditions of a heterogeneous commodities model*, a relationship which is obvious in the corn model.

The source of this inability goes back to Keynes's view on method. As we have argued elsewhere (see Bradford 1993; Harcourt 1987a), Keynes argued that there was an entire spectrum of languages which were suitable for discussion in a discipline such as economics, running all the way from poetry and intuition through lawyer-like arguments to formal logic and mathematics. Each point on this continuum could be relevant for certain issues, or aspects of issues, and it was the failure to understand this which made people either misunderstand or miss altogether a large number of insights and illuminations when reading *The General Theory*. Keynes certainly subscribed to the Wildon Carr maxim which was applied by Gerald Shove to Keynes's and Shove's mentor, Alfred Marshall, that 'it is better to be vaguely right than precisely wrong' (Shove 1942: 323). But 'vague' had a particular and definite meaning for Keynes in that it singled out a particular stretch of, or point on, the language spectrum and defined when it was applicable in economic analysis. George Shackle was extremely acute on this issue. His favourite example was Keynes's use of the word 'sentiment', which played a key role in Keynes's analysis of investment and the determination of the rate of interest, yet could not be quantified or even defined in a precise mathematical sense in his theory.

THE ORIGINS OF KEYNES'S VIEWS

In Chapter 21 of *The General Theory*, Keynes criticizes the classical dichotomy whereby short-period relative prices are held to be determined by supply and demand (with emphasis on changes in marginal costs and the elasticity of short-period supply) whilst the general price level is presented as a function of, among other things, the money stock, apparently independently of the determinants of individual prices. He then notes that

> The division of economics between the theory of value and distribution
> on the one hand and the theory of money on the other hand is, I think,
> a false division. The right dichotomy is, I suggest, between the theory
> of the individual industry or firm . . . on the one hand, and the theory
> of output and employment *as a whole* on the other hand . . . as soon as
> we pass to the problem of what determines output and employment as
> a whole, we require the complete theory of a monetary economy.
>
> (*C.W.* VII: 293, emphasis in original)

The first step required for the creation of the complete theory of the monetary economy is to select the units of quantity appropriate to the analysis of the economic system as a whole. It is to this problem which Keynes turns in Chapter 4, 'The Choice of Units'.

Yet this chapter is likely to puzzle the neophyte reader. It seems at first glance to contain little more than a terse discussion of aggregation problems associated with the concepts of real output, the capital stock and the general price level,[1] and a correspondingly brief justification of the use of the wage-unit as a means of avoiding the difficulties outlined. However, the analysis of Chapter 4 represents a summary of various lines of argument which Keynes had pursued throughout his intellectual life and which culminated in a specific motivation with respect to economic theory: the lecture notes compiled in Rymes (1989a) reveal that Keynes informed his students that he felt he could do the whole theory of money[2] without using the concept of the general price level (139). Keynes's rejection of this concept is rooted in his philosophy of measurement, as founded on arguments which he formulated in his earliest academic writings and subsequently developed in the light of his experience as a professional economist.

MEASUREMENT AND THE GENERAL PRICE LEVEL[3]

Keynes first subjected the concept of the general price level to critical enquiry in his Adam Smith prize-winning essay on index numbers (EIN),[4] completed in April 1909 (*C.W.* XI). There he notes that all problems associated with the measurement of aggregate economic quantities revolve around the question of determining a common unit. Further, the source of the difficulties is to be found in the nature of the quantities under investigation. Keynes initially identifies two classes of economic quantities[5] (*C.W.* XI: 53):

i) Those which are, conceptually, perfectly definite and quantitatively measurable, but are incapable of (perfect) measurement *in practice* due to insufficiency of data.

ii) Quantities which are not numerically measurable *even in principle*.

It is crucial to note that just because quantities of the second kind are incapable of measurement, they are by no means vague or imprecise *qua* concepts. Keynes argues (*C.W.* XI: 53–4) that there is a continuum of comparability with respect to quantities. At one extreme there are those quantities which cannot be compared at all (tons and miles). At the other end of the continuum are those quantities which can be directly and numerically compared (distances between points). In between, there are instances of quantities 'between which there is an intermediate degree of intimacy'; comparison is possible, but not numerically. Keynes uses the example of the degree of similarity[6] (*C.W.* XI: 54): 'A green octavo volume is more like a green folio than a red octavo is, but it would be evidently false to say that it is twice or any other number of times as like.' Keynes then refines his definitions of the classes of quantities. He holds that a set of quantities are of the same *kind* when ordinal comparisons are possible between every member of the set, and in the same *unit* when cardinal (numerical) comparisons are likewise possible (ibid.).

As an example, Keynes considers the measurement of total national income. If national income is defined in the manner of the income approach to calcualting GDP (for example, for taxation purposes), then, as a quantity, it is of the first type and measurements for successive years would be in the same unit and thus amenable to numerical comparison. By contrast, if national income is defined as the aggregate of individual utilities, then it is a quantity of the second type. Different aggregates of utilities are not in the same unit due to the impossibility of interpersonal comparisons (a rich man does not enjoy a known multiple of the utility of a beggar). Similarly, such quantities are not of the same kind because ordinal comparisons between them can only be made in special cases, such as the situation where the utility of all individuals is increased. Although the *concept* of the aggregate of utilities is perfectly precise and determinate in itself, it cannot be numerically measured, nor can meaningful ordinal comparisons be made across time or countries.[7] It is not that the answers to such questions of comparison may not exist, but the possibility of obtaining them via measurement and addition is denied. There is an aggregate of utilities, but not a sum (*C.W.* XI: 60).

Clearly, similar reasoning underlies Keynes's concerns about the concepts of real output and the capital stock, as expressed in Chapter 4 of *The General Theory*. He points out that 'the community's output of goods and services is a non-homogeneous complex which cannot be measured, strictly speaking, except in certain special cases' (*C.W.* VII: 38).

In terms of the argument of the EIN, real output is a definite but non-numerical quantity; comparisons cannot generally be made across time as the quantities involved are not of the same kind.[8] The same must be said for the capital stock due to, among other things, the problem of technical progress which results in different vintages.

Turning to prices in the EIN, Keynes notes that problems only arise when we seek to construct *averages* of prices over time and/or space (*C.W.* XI: 56). The selection of any particular measure of central tendency is arbitrary. He illustrates this by comparing European and Indian approaches to the pricing of wheat. In England, the price of wheat is expressed (in 1909) in terms of shillings per quarter, whereas in India it is expressed in seers per rupee. Although neither method is intrinsically superior to the other, it so happens that the average of two prices measured according to one system does not equal the average of the same prices reckoned in the other.[9] In fact, the arithmetic mean of European prices is equal to the harmonic mean of Indian prices, and vice versa (*C.W.* XI: 56–7).

Keynes's explanation of this paradox is central to his rejection of the concept of the general price level and his subsequent advocacy of the wage-unit in Chapter 4. He holds[10] (*C.W.* XI: 57) that price is a *non-numerical quantitative relation* between a currency and a commodity. Different price relations are of the same *kind* in that ordinal comparisons are possible, but are not in the same unit as they are not numerically measurable. However, a suitable system of conventional measurement can easily be constructed (*C.W.* XI: 65). If, in a particular market, x units of money exchanges for y units of a commodity, then it follows that one unit of the commodity exchanges for x/y units of money. Changes in the ratio x/y correspond to changes in the degree of magnitude of the price relation; if the number series is placed in order of magnitude (and high price relations are conventionally defined as those which correspond to a large value of x/y), then the price relations will be ordered accordingly. As a result, the number series can be employed in calculations *as if* the price relation were numerically measurable.

There are, however, serious qualifications to the as-if condition which arise out of the non-numerical character of the price relation and have important implications for the construction of aggregate price indices. Price *ratios* (such as the x/y series) are conventional measures of the price *relation*, but are not fully representative. Particularly important is the fact that 'not all arithmetic operations performed on price ratios have a corresponding economic interpretation' (*C.W.* XI: 69). For most purposes, the use of either the European or the Indian pricing convention will not affect the outcome of calculations. However, as noted above, the results *do* diverge when the same pair of price relations, measured differently, are averaged. Nor would it be meaningful to average the 'Indian' price of one commodity and the 'European' price of another. For Keynes, there is no measure which expresses the average of the two economic facts measured with equal legitimacy by the alternative systems of price ratios. Thus price relations are measurable in some sense (situations where operations on price ratios are economically meaningful) but not universally.[11]

Obviously, such considerations are extremely important when considering the question of the general purchasing power or exchange value of money (*C.W.* XI: 66). The theory of the individual industry or firm must concern itself with the behaviour of particular price relations. However, when considering output as a whole the relevant concept of price (the general price level) is now a complex function of the myriad of distinct particular price relations between commodities and money. The pertinent question is: *Is the aggregation operation involved in the movement from particular price relations to the general exchange value (GEV) of money of the type which is capable of being economically meaningful?*

Keynes indicates that this may not be the case. The GEV of money may be a relation 'quite incapable of measurement and not sharing all the characteristics of the simple price relations of which it is the complex' (ibid). In certain cases it will be possible to make unambiguous comparisons of the GEV of money over time. If relative prices are unaffected by movements in the supply of money, then the general price level can be said to have risen or fallen (depending on the case) and the magnitude may be measured (ibid.). In other words, the two general relations are in the same unit. If there are some disturbances to relative prices, then, so long as they are unidirectional, ordinal comparisons over time will be meaningful. The general relations will be of the same kind and thus unable to be compared numerically.

However, in Chapter 7 of the first volume of the *Treatise on Money* (*C.W.* V) Keynes repudiates the idea that movements in the money stock will affect relative prices in any reliable or stable way. Injections of purchasing power are not typically spread evenly throughout the economy but are instead concentrated in the hands of particular classes of purchasers (*C.W.* V: 82).[12] As a result, the impact in terms of demand, and thus relative price movements, will fall primarily on those commodities principally purchased by the beneficiaries of the monetary stimulus. The resultant diffusion of price changes, and the resolution of the social and economic consequences of the redistribution of purchasing power, will establish a new equilibrium system of relative prices (*C.W.* V: 82).

In addition, the prevalence of contracts fixed in nominal terms means that many prices will not respond to monetary influences even if they would do so if not fixed. The resultant divergences in relative prices will generate redistributional effects which will in turn produce a new array of relative exchange values (*C.W.* V: 82–3). For Keynes, the proper metaphor for the effect of monetary disturbances on price levels is not, as in the classical account, the effect of the movement of the earth through space on the objects on its surface, but the effect of moving a kaleidoscope on the pieces of glass within (*C.W.* V: 81).[13]

As a result, what Keynes labels the Jevons–Edgeworth conception of the general price level (*C.W.* V: 71–7) is untenable. This tradition, which Keynes asserts originated in the work of Cournot, was concerned with measuring the intrinsic value of money; that is, that concept of the price level which retains its value when only relative prices have changed (*C.W.*

V: 77). According to this approach, fluctuations in individual prices result from two distinct influences. On the one hand, there are 'changes on the side of money' which affect all relative prices equally in direction and degree (*C.W.* V: 73), while, on the other hand, there are 'changes on the side of things' which disturb relative prices.

By assumption, only monetary disturbances can affect the intrinsic value of money. Therefore, the task of tracking changes in the value of money involves something of a signal extraction problem; observations of individual price variations need to be 'cleansed' of the influence of 'changes on the side of things', so that the hypothetical movement which *would* have occurred if monetary disturbances were the only ones at work can be identified. The latter corresponds to the change in the value of money as such (*C.W.* V: 74–5). If it may be assumed that relative price movements are statistically independent, the appropriate course of action is to collect a large sample of individual prices and average them. Once the best measure of central tendency (arithmetic mean, geometric mean, harmonic mean, and so on) is decided upon and calulated, the 'noise' represented by 'changes on the side of things' will cancel out and the measure of the residual impact of monetary forces (the intrinsic value of money) will be available subject to known probabilistic error (*C.W.* V: 72–3).

However, as the arguments supporting the 'kaleidoscope' metaphor illustrate, relative price movements cannot be viewed as being statistically independent. As a result the argument is fallacious. Keynes condemns it as 'root-and-branch erroneous' (*C.W.* V: 76) and a 'will-o'-the-wisp, a circle-squaring expedition' (*C.W.* V: 72). He denies the existence of the 'objective mean variation of general prices' (*C.W.* V: 76) and concludes:

> The abstraction . . . is . . . false . . . , because the thing under investigation, namely the price level, is itself a function of relative prices and liable to change its value whenever, and merely because, relative prices have changed. The hypothetical change in the price level, which would have occurred *if* there had been no change in relative prices, is no longer relevant if relative prices have in fact changed – for the change in relative prices has in itself affected the price level.
>
> (*C.W.* V: 77–8)

Hence, the conditions required to render successive GEVs of money even *ordinally* comparable (let alone numerically so) are precluded by the very nature of the economic system itself. As Keynes has it:

> While we have a price corresponding to each *particular* exchange value, it is not true, as it is sometimes assumed, that we have a price corresponding to *general* exchange value. General exchange value is a function of particular exchange values, but it does not possess all of their properties.
>
> (*C.W.* XI: 66–7, emphasis in original)

The measures of the price level which Keynes attacked in the EIN and the *Treatise on Money* were unweighted indices. Due to their conceptual inadequacy, he rejected all such measures and emphasized the importance of weighting. In the EIN Keynes argues that the only way in which the facts which underlie particular price ratios (x_1 units of money have exchanged for y_1 units of A, x_2 units of money for y_2 units of B, and so on) can be combined into a single proposition of the same *kind* is to express the total sum of money expended on goods during a period as the price of that composite commodity represented by the total quantity of goods exchanged during the same period. This price ratio is determinate, unambiguous and numerically measurable in the sense of particular price ratios (*C.W.* XI: 69).

However, as Keynes duly notes, this measure of the general price level is fatally flawed in terms of intertemporal or spatial comparisons:

> The general exchange value of money, conceived of thus, at a given place or period is represented by the power of money to purchase a certain set of things possessing a special economic importance at that place or period. The power of money to purchase this set of things has a perfectly determinate measure at all times and places. But the thing measured is only important at one of them. To use what is partly metaphor, partly example, we wish to compare the price of bread with the price of water – two things which have no common unit of comparison.[14]
>
> (*C.W.* XI: 70)

The only way around this dilemma is to make some allowance for the 'changing importance of commodities' (*C.W.* XI: 71) by introducing weighting. For Keynes, this represents adopting a 'working compromise, something less definite . . . but more useful' (ibid.).

However, the process of weighting is not without pitfalls. Keynes depicts this by using the example of a merchant, with offices in various parts of London, who decides to move his [*sic*] main base of operations. The motive is to move 'nearer to his business' (ibid.). Although the distances between the various offices are definite, numerical quantities, simply comparing the average distance between the present base and the branches with that for the new site is insufficient. What needs to be done, it seems, is to weight the distance to each office by its 'importance' to the business as represented by, say, the normal frequency of visits within a given period. This solution corresponds with the need to produce weighted price indices when trying to measure the general price level.

Yet the frequency with which each office is visited is unlikely to be independent of its distance from the existing base (ibid.). Hence, different sets of weights could be used to produce different conclusions as to whether the existing base or the proposed new site is 'closer' to the network of branches. In other words, there is no definite numerical measure of the 'distance' of either base from the merchant's 'business in general'.

The problem of the interdependence of observations and weighting criteria is particularly acute in the case of price indices. Keynes notes (*C.W.* XI: 62) that comparisons of real wages in London and the Midlands can indicate that either is the higher according to whether the representative consumption bundle (composite commodity) chosen is that appropriate to the former or the latter. With respect to international comparisons, he records that the cost of living is cheaper in England using the English standard, and in France using the standard appropriate to that country (ibid.: 63). More fundamentally, no matter which set of quantity weights is chosen, there remains the problem that relative price changes may (and, in terms of orthodox theory, should) induce corresponding changes in relative quantities.

This difficulty cannot be avoided, 'there is no way out' (ibid.: 72). The only recourse is to 'adopt devices and compromises, which will render it as unimportant as possible and give us an approximate index useful for the matter in hand' (ibid.). The compromises which must be adopted have a special, methodologically significant,[15] character. They will 'depend upon the particular object which [the researcher] has in view' (ibid.) and will always contain some element of convention. The interdependence of the purpose of enquiry and the weighting criterion employed extends beyond the use of quantity weights; it is yet another factor which demonstrates the erroneous nature of the Jevons–Edgeworth conception of the general price level. In the *Treatise on Money* (*C.W.* V: 87), Keynes argues that if the elimination of 'influences on the side of money' is taken to mean that the total volume of monetary transactions remains constant, then the measure of the intrinsic value of money collapses to the cash transactions standard. If, by contrast, it is required that the stock of money remains unchanged, the required index number is the cash balances standard. Hence the *quaesitum* has no existence independently of the definitions employed by, and hence the object of enquiry of, the researcher. For Keynes,

> There is no moving but unique centre, to be called the general price level or the objective mean variation of general prices, round which are scattered the moving price levels of individual things. There are all the various, quite definite, conceptions of price-levels of composite commodities appropriate for various purposes and inquiries . . . There is nothing else. Jevons was pursuing a mirage.
>
> (*C.W.* V: 86)

This is why the concept of the general price level is subject to an 'unavoidable . . . element of vagueness' (*C.W.* VII: 39). The fact that price is a non-numerical quantitative relation means that while particular relations are of the same kind, they are not in the same unit. Even though it is possible to treat price relations (for most purposes) *as if* they were numerically comparable by adopting the convention of price *ratios*, the concept of the general price level conceived of as an *ensemble* of particular prices remains inexact; 'a relation determined by several numerically quantitative relations is not necessarily itself one' (*C.W.* XI: 72). The vagueness can be alleviated somewhat by defining the general price level as the value of some composite commodity. However, the lack of precision remains, due to the fact that the composite will not be representative over time and space, and in any case there is no unique 'best' composite independent of the object of enquiry.

UNITS IN *THE GENERAL THEORY*

In *The General Theory* itself, Keynes was concerned that his complete theory of the monetary production economy should be exact and precise. As such it could not be based on concepts which were quantitatively vague (*C.W.* VII: 39). Unlike the theory of the individual industry or firm, the variables of interest in a theory of output as a whole must, unavoidably, be heterogeneous aggregates. It is just such 'non-homogeneous' (*C.W.* VII: 38) complexes, 'incommensurable collections of miscellaneous objects' (*C.W.* VII: 39) which fall foul of Keynes's philosophy of measurement. As has already been shown, the concept of real output understood in physical terms is inherently non-quantitative and unmeasurable. As such it cannot be utilized in the theory.

The money value of output in a given period is a perfectly precise and determinate quantity, as money values are at all times strictly homogeneous.[16] However, the usual route to a concept of real output, deflation of the nominal value by an index of the price level, is unacceptable. As argued above, the concept of the general price level cannot be articulated or measured without vagueness. Indices suitable for various purposes *can* be constructed and fruitfully employed, but these belong to the realm of broad historical generalizations rather than precise theoretical enquiry. To attempt to employ them as the basis of a quantitative analysis can only lead to 'mock precision' (*C.W.* VII: 40). Thus Keynes remains true to his intention (see p. 109) and eschews the use of the concept of the general price level in his theory of output.[17]

In order to be able to say anything at all about movements in real output, Keynes employs a device which dates from the EIN.[18] There (*C.W.* XI: 55) he asserts that numerical comparisons (of a sort) of non-numerical quantities can be accomplished if a suitable, numerical proxy measure can be identified. For the purposes of tracking movements in output, he chooses the amount of employment associated with a given stock of capital goods (*C.W.* VII: 41).

At first glance there seems to be little reason to believe that the quantity of employment is not just another 'incommensurable [collection] of miscellaneous objects'. Keynes argues that it *can* be made homogeneous if an hour's employment of one grade of labour is chosen as the *numeraire* (the labour-unit), and the employment of all other grades is weighted by the ratio of their money wage to that of the benchmark grade (the wage-unit). Hence an hour's employment of labour at a rate x times the wage-unit will count as x labour-units (*C.W.* VII: 41). Employment measured in labour-units is now a numerical quantity and it follows that the supply functions for individual industries (expressed as functions of employment in the industry in terms of labour-units) can be aggregated to yield the aggregate supply function. Such an operation would be impossible if the analysis were couched in terms of the output of individual industries (*C.W.* VII: 44). Changes in current output are measured by reference to the number of labour-units paid for; it is important to remember, however, that although the two will move together, they will not do so in a definite numerical proportion (*C.W.* VII: 41).

The argument for the use of the labour-unit is based on a number of assumptions which perhaps vary in plausibility. These will be considered in turn:

1 *Relativities are stable* The procedure of weighting grades of labour by their relative renumeration would obviously be extremely difficult in the case where there were no fixed patterns of relativities. Keynes admits this (*C.W.* VII: 43), but holds that the problem could be circumvented by assuming that labour supply and the shape of the aggregate supply function adjust rapidly and accordingly. Although this looks for all the world like the standard neoclassical technique of assuming away features of the world which vitiate theories, it is clear from the context (and from Chapter 2) that Keynes believed that relativities were sufficiently stable.

2 *Diminishing returns due to non-homogeneity of equipment* Clearly, workers are not homogeneous in terms of skill. However, if wages reflect efficiency then the device of weighting by relative renumeration will take account of the variations. Where wages do not fully reflect efficiency, Keynes assumes that the diminishing returns from the capital stock in terms of output as employment is increased are due to the varying efficiency of the equipment rather than labour. With increasing output, capital equipment is regarded as less and less adapted to employing available labour units instead of the converse (*C.W.* VII: 42). He argues that the main reason for viewing the problem in this way is that the increasing surpluses which accompany increasing output accrue typically to the owners of equipment and not to efficient workers (*C.W.* VII: 43n). That is, wages do not typically reflect efficiency.

3 *Unique distribution of effective demand among products* When dealing with aggregate employment, differentials in the demand for particular grades

of labour can be ignored so long as a given volume of effective demand is uniquely associated with a particular distribution of demand among different products (C.W. VII: 42n). The interesting problem noted by Keynes is the possibility that this condition would not be robust to the cause of a change in demand. An increase in effective demand which is caused by an increase in the MPC or APC might yield a different aggregate supply function to an increase associated with a higher propensity to invest. In this case the quantity of employment would no longer serve as a proxy for output as the two could not be guaranteed to move in the same direction. Keynes does not discuss this further in Chapter 4.

4 *Average wage is numerically quantitative* Keynes makes no mention of this assumption in *The General Theory*, but it occurs in the context of a similar discussion (regarding the construction of wage indices) in the EIN. There he states that 'The average wage is a perfectly unambiguous numerically quantitative conception' (C.W. XI: 61). The only justification he offers is that the individual can be regarded 'as a unit of constant importance' and thus the 'principal difficulty' associated with price indices can be avoided (C.W. XI: 61n). What is meant by this is not entirely clear, either in absolute terms or in the context in which it occurs.[19]

It is, however, important to the issue of the labour-unit. If price is a non-numerical relation between a commodity and money, then can the wage be viewed as the price of labour, a similar relation between labour expended and money? If so, then would not the attempt to measure average wages be subject to the same pitfalls associated with attempts to measure average prices? If this were the case, then the measurement of the quantity of employment in terms of labour-units would no longer be precise. The remunerations used to determine the weighting of the employment of different grades of labour are not individual wages, but those appropriate to professions or skill levels or some other collective criterion. As such they *must* be averages, wage indices of some kind. If they are subject to residual vagueness in the same sense as price indices, then the labour-unit device is similarly infected and hence the quantity of employment so measured ceases to function as a precise numerical index for the quantity of total output. In short, Keynes's argument for his choice of units appears to fail.

The alternative possibility[20] is that Keynes did not view the wage as a kind of price. If so, the above difficulties are avoided, but important questions are raised. What is the nature of the wage for Keynes? Why is it not a price? There is a dearth of textual evidence bearing directly on the matter. However, his acceptance in Chapter 2 of the first Classical Postulate (that the wage equals the marginal productivity of labour) *might* suggest that he did view the wage as a price.

The fact remains that the coherence of the labour-unit framework appears to hinge on the resolution of this question. Unfortunately, Keynes further undermines his approach to units in Chapter 21. Here he presents a theory of the general price level which is essentially a generalization from the case of an individual industry or firm. As such, the general price level depends upon the volume of employment and the wage unit – subject to the assumption that the remuneration of all factors which enter into marginal cost change in the same proportion as the wage-unit (*C.W.* VII: 295).

In the case where the latter condition is not fulfilled, Keynes proposes to replace the wage-unit with the *cost-unit*, a weighted average of the payments to factors of production entering into marginal prime-cost (*C.W.* VII: 302). This cost unit is to be regarded as the essential standard of value.

However, the reader who has just finished reading the EIN would surely look aghast at such a construction. If a weighted average of prices of *commodities* is subject to irredeemable imprecision (on the grounds that the weights will be neither uniquely relevant over time nor independent of the object of enquiry) how then can a weighted average of the prices of *factors* be not so? How could comparisons of the price level be made over time if investment results in changes in techniques? Why are past techniques relevant in assessing the general level of prices today?

On balance, it appears that for all the ingenuity and subtlety of Keynes's reasoning on the question of units, he ultimately failed to apply it consistently in *The General Theory*. Given the importance attached to these concerns in Chapter 4, this is a serious defect (although it does not necessarily invalidate the major theoretical insights therein) and may shed further light on the failure of later Keynesians to employ his approach to units.

TIME AS A UNIT

In Chapter 16 (*C.W.* VII: 214) Keynes informs the reader that, apart from money and labour, his economic system is expressed in units of time. This comes as somewhat of a surprise, as the nature of the time units in question is not discussed in Chapter 4. Indeed, it is not taken up in detail anywhere in *The General Theory*. Keynes's failure to do this is puzzling; the elaboration of an appropriate set of units seems to be presented in Chapter 4 as a *sine qua non* for the development of the theory of output and employment as a whole, the complete theory of a monetary production economy. Furthermore, there are inconsistencies in Keynes's approach to the definition of time-units which indicate that it was not until after the publication of *The General Theory* that he systematically applied the reasoning of Chapter 4 to the question of time.

Rymes (1989a: 104, n. 32) records that, in his 1932 lectures, Keynes

119

informed students that units of time 'are in their nature homogeneous'. In the light of the arguments underlying Keynes's treatment of units, first proposed nearly thirty years earlier, this is a surprising claim. Time is surely the example *par excellence* of a non-numerical quantitative relation.[21] Furthermore, it is clear that the only 'units' of time which are in some way homogeneous are those involved in the scales by which time is conventionally 'measured'. Yet these standards of measurement are arbitrary, and display significant variation across cultures and (dare it be said) time.[22] As a result it appears that conventional methods of time measurement resemble price ratios: both are merely proxies for an underlying relation which is quantitative but non-numerical. As such, their homogeneity should not be taken to imply that the underlying relations are in the same *unit*, in the sense defined above, and we must not lose sight of the fact that not all arithmetic operations performed on these measures will be meaningful.

Clearly Keynes's approach to time in 1932 is related to his use of sequence analysis in the *Treatise on Money*. Central to this method is the notion that there exists a definite relationship between aggregate effective demand at one time and aggregate income at a later point in time (*C.W.* XIV: 180). In order for this approach to be viable it is clear that a determinate time unit must be discovered.

Yet Keynes explicitly repudiates this in the draft notes for his 1937 lectures. Rejecting his earlier sequence analysis as nonsensical (*C.W.* XIV: 180), he concludes that there is no definite intertemporal relationship between aggregate effective demand and aggregate income. Rather, all that can be compared is the expected and realized income resulting to an individual enterpreneur from a given decision (*C.W.* XIV: 180–1). Keynes relates that he once referred to the period between expectation and result as 'funnels of process', but he notes that comparisons of aggregate realized results at a given date with aggregate expectations at an earlier date are precluded by the fact that the 'funnels' differ in length and overlap one another (*C.W.* XIV: 185). This conclusion represents the analysis of Chapter 4 (and the EIN) applied to time: the time relationship between effective demand and income cannot be made precise (*C.W.* XIV: 179) because there is no way in which the two can be rendered in the same *unit* with respect to time. From a temporal point of view, they represent yet another example of 'incommensurable collections of miscellaneous objects' (*C.W.* VII: 39).

This is the line of argument which is not explicitly stated in *The General Theory*. Indeed, Keynes's solitary attempt to define the units of time referred to in Chapter 16 seems almost to ignore it. In Chapter 5, after noting that the daily output decisions of individual firms are a product of short-term expectations, he explains[23] that '*Daily* here stands for the shortest interval after which the firm is free to revise its decision as to how much employment to offer. It is, so to speak, the minimum effective unit of economic time' (*C.W.* VII: 47, n. 1).

However, it is clear that this period of time cannot be a 'unit' in the same sense as the wage-unit. The latter can be aggregated and thereby provides a means whereby normally incommensurable quantities may in some way be compared. There is no way in which the former can be meaningfully aggregated, and to label them 'units' is to employ the term to mean simply a standard of measurement irrespective of whether measurement in such terms is capable of being made precise. Yet it was exactly this kind of conventional usage which Keynes rejected in the EIN; the purpose of determining units is to enable precise analysis.[24] Keynes seems, in *The General Theory*, to have failed to have comprehensively applied his own reasoning.

This suspicion is heightened when Keynes later turns to the concept of the period of production. He holds that a product has a period of production *n* if '*n* time-units of notice of changes in the demand for it have to be given if it is to offer its maximum elasticity of employment' (*C.W.* VII: 287). Are we to assume that the time-units in question are those defined in Chapter 5? If so, the definition is a strange one.[25] How can notice of demand changes be given in multiples of the shortest interval after which employment decisions can be revised? What meaning can be attached to such multiples? How could they be aggregated across products, as required in statements like 'consumption goods, taken as a whole . . . have . . . the longest period of production' (*C.W.* VII: 287)?

If, by contrast, the time-units in this context refer to definite periods of calendar time, then Keynes has departed from his Chapter 5 definition. Such inconsistencies may simply be the result of an unfortunate choice of terms, but when considered in conjunction with the ambiguity surrounding the calculation of the wage-unit, and the adoption of the cost-unit in Chapter 21, the impression of an author failing to apply consistently his own methodological prescriptions is considerably strengthened.

How are his views which we have discussed above reconcilable with the Marshallian base for the theory of prices in Chapter 21? Having liberated himself from the hold which the QTM had had on him and the tradition in which he had been brought up, he knew he needed to find an alternative theory of the formation of the level of prices in general and of their rate of change. The simple answer is that they are not. Partly, Keynes's views reflected his understanding of the Pigou–Hayek debates on the meaning of maintaining capital intact;[26] partly, it reflected his distinction between precise analysis and vague but useful qualitative remarks and judgements such as the relative happiness and relative goodness of English queens.[27] But for precise analysis within the explicitly defined framework of *The General Theory*[28] he settled, as we know, on money and employment as the appropriate units. He argued:

It is my belief that much unnecessary perplexity can be avoided if we limit ourselves strictly to the units, money and labour, when we are dealing with the behaviour of the economic system as a whole; reserving the use of units of particular outputs and equipments to the occasions when we are analysing the output of individual firms or industries in isolation; and the use of vague concepts, such as the quantity of capital equipment as a whole and the general level of prices, to the occasions when we are attempting some historical comparison which is within certain (perhaps fairly wide) limits avowedly unprecise and approximate.

(*C.W.* VII: 43)

To use these units he made it clear that he *had* a Marshallian setting and method in mind, modified, of course, to take in analysis of the level of employment as a whole. He gave a number of cogent reasons why he preferred to work in terms of wage units and not in terms of real output, for example, as subsequent expositors of his system (including one of the present authors in his first book, written jointly with Peter Karmel and Bob Wallace – Harcourt *et al.* 1967) were to do.

His concern about wage units is related to his definitions, especially to the distinction between net and gross concepts, an emphasis which is also to be found in the work of Kahn and Joan Robinson in the post-war years. Indeed, it was even more relevant and significant for them; for they were attempting 'to generalise the *General Theory* to the long period', and there, because growth was the centre of attention, the *net* concepts came into their own. In *The General Theory*, because Keynes was primarily concerned with the determination of the overall level of employment in the short period, *gross* investment was the relevant concept because it was directly related to the amount of employment created, while a measure of the net increase or decrease in capacity was of secondary importance. Keynes in fact usually abstracted from it altogether in his analysis – it was one of those factors to be 'kept at the back of our heads'. It follows that gross saving was also important, but Keynes did not discuss it exhaustively or systematically.[29] He did make some wise comments on it in connection with the distinction between depreciation allowances and actual replacement expenditures in the section on financial prudence in the chapter on the consumption function (see *C.W.* VII: 98–106), and in Chapter 4, as we have seen, on what exactly was meant by replacement when new and different machines, for example, were associated with current investment expenditure.

Salter (1960) was to take this up in his seminal work on productivity and technical change, in which he discussed how new ways of doing things were embodied in the existing stock of capital goods. They represented the 'best-practice' ways of producing, given existing knowledge and current expectations, and they took their place alongside existing fossils or vintages because of the different criteria applicable: for new investment, total costs must be expected to be covered, while for existing machines only variable costs need to be covered to make it worthwhile to keep them running (see Chris Torr – Chapter 8 in this volume – for the subtle role which Keynes's concept of user cost plays in this and other aspects of the working of the economy). Keynes foreshadows much of this argument and also some aspects of the capital theory debates (see Harcourt 1972, 1976, 1992), when he says that we shall never be able to measure rigorously the stock of capital goods nor rigorously compare the stock at one moment of time with another at another moment of time unless we assume away technical progress and changes in the composition of demand (and supply), so ruling out the essence of capitalism in the process.

When we move to the post-war period we find, as we have mentioned, Keynes's views influencing (or perhaps he was influenced by) Sraffa (especially), Joan Robinson and Richard Kahn. Thus Sraffa set out at the Corfu conference on capital theory (Lutz and Hague 1961) his views on the nature of theoretical coherence and the criteria which theory must meet to be acceptable. He sharply distinguished the latter from those which were appropriate for statistical analysis:

> *Mr Sraffa* thought one should emphasize the distinction between two types of measurement. First, there was the one in which the statisticians were mainly interested. Second there was measurement in theory. The statisticians' measures were only approximate and provided a suitable field for work in solving index number problems. The theoretical measures required absolute precision. Any imperfections in these theoretical measures were not merely upsetting, but knocked down the whole theoretical basis. One could measure capital in pounds or dollars and introduce this into a production function. The definition in this case must be absolutely water-tight, for with a given quantity of capital one had a certain rate of interest so that the quantity of capital was an essential part of the mechanism. One therefore had to keep the definition of capital separate from the needs of statistical measurement, which were quite different. The work of J.B. Clark, Böhm-Bawerk and others was intended to produce pure definitions of capital, as required by their theories, not as a guide to actual measurement. If we found contradictions, then these pointed to defects in the theory, and an inability to define measures of capital accurately. It was on this – the chief failing of capital theory – that we should concentrate, rather than on problems of measurement.
>
> (Sraffa 1961: 305–6)

Sraffa went on to say that:

the usefulness of any theory lay in its explanatory value . . . [He] took the view that if one could not get the measures required by the theorists' definitions, this was a criticism of theory, which the theorists could not escape by saying that they hoped their theory would not often fail. If a theory failed to explain a situation, it was unsatisfactory.

(Ibid.: 306)

Already in October 1936, in a letter to Joan Robinson,[30] he had signalled why he thought the neoclassical theory of capital did not meet the criteria and in a number of places in *Production of Commodities* . . . he explicitly said why, delivering the knock-down blow in his reply to Harrod in the *Economic Journal* in 1962. Thus Sraffa asked: 'what is the good of a quantity of capital . . . which, since it depends on the rate of interest, cannot be used for its traditional purpose . . . to determine the rate of interest?' (Sraffa 1962: 479).

Joan Robinson applied similar criteria in her discussion of what we mean by capital, and how we may measure it, within the confines of neoclassical long-period theory, and in fact. She drew out the implications of this for the measurement of profits and set out precisely the conditions that have to be met for these concepts to have exact meaning in theory. This allowed her to go on to discuss depreciation in a precise and coherent manner (see Robinson 1965: 209–21). But is there an element of inconsistency in her stance, for she says in the preface to *The Accumulation of Capital* that vagueness, or rather precision, must be defined in relation to the task in hand, which seems to echo Wildon Carr's remark. When referring to a quotation from Popper (to the effect that terms like 'wind', although vague, in the sense that they are difficult to define quantitatively, are sufficiently precise when used in contexts where greater differentiation is not only unnecessary but would be burdensome) Joan Robinson (1956: ix) noted: 'Economic concepts such as wealth, output, income and cost are no easier to define precisely than wind. Nevertheless these concepts are useful, and economic problems can be discussed.'

Joan Robinson also was sceptical of the value of Sraffa's concept of a Standard commodity. He constructed it in order to render visible that which was hidden – the simple inverse relationship under specified conditions between the wage-rate and the rate of profits (*not* share of profits), an idea which has existed in political economy since at least the time of Ricardo and which was, of course, central in Marx's work. Joan Robinson in a number of places tried to get at the essence of the Sraffa result while dodging the use of the Standard commodity as the measuring rod.

Thus Joan Robinson correctly interpreted the use of the Standard commodity by Sraffa to solve, first, Ricardo's problem (actually, only one aspect of it)[31] that the value of the surplus to be distributed varies with changes in the distribution itself between wages and profits and therefore in the pattern of prices corresponding to each level of the rate of profits (or wages), and, secondly, to solve Marx's transformation problem. She, how-ever, preferred to take a short cut which 'Sraffa himself would scruple to do' (Robinson 1975b: 175). She measured everything in terms of labour time by postulating a given money-wage per man (sic) hour of ordinary labour. Corresponding to each value of the rate of profits there is a level of prices in money terms and a pattern of prices such that both wages and profits (reckoned at the given rate on the value of capital required for production) are covered by sales receipts. This allowed her, with further simplifications, to establish that $r = g/s_c$, the Cambridge equation.

Elsewhere (Robinson 1961a, 1975b: 10) she had argued, following a succinct account of what the Standard commodity was for and how it was constructed, that

> assuming that wages are paid at the end of the year . . . here is a linear relationship between the share of wages in the surplus and the rate of profit[s].
>
> This . . . established, the Standard commodity can be left to look after itself and the argument conducted in terms of the rate of profit[s] corresponding to zero wages . . . and the actual rate of profit[s], with the wage rate that it entails.

Of course, Sraffa himself also followed the same procedure.

The impact of these aspects of Keynes's work on Richard Kahn may be found in two of his post-war papers (Kahn 1959, 1971: Essay 10), and in his discussion of the quantity theory of money in *The Making of Keynes's 'General Theory'* (1984). For example, in his 1959 Oxford exercises, Kahn tells us that the 'developments in the last few years of theories of economic growth have introduced new concepts and called on unfamiliar tools'. He intended to 'take out for an airing a few of the concepts to which Mrs Robinson and others have introduced us and try out the edge of a few of the tools. [He was] not attempting to build up a new theory [or] to arrive at any conclusions' (Kahn 1971: 192).

Kahn starts with 'the fundamental identity, based on treating income as divided between capitalists' incomes and wages. At any and every moment of time there is a simple relationship between the rate of growth in the value of the stock of capital and the ratio to that value . . . of the current incomes of the capitalists' (ibid.). The relationship involves the respective saving proportions from the capitalists' incomes and wages. 'What is necessary for the simple relationship to be generally valid is that *income* should be defined in a suitable manner, so that the excess of income over consumption is the same thing as the rate of change in the value of the stock of capital' (ibid.: 193, emphasis in original).

Nothing imbues the relationship with any causal force – 'purely an identity – a glorified version of the identity between savings and investment' (ibid.: 194). Kahn nevertheless claims that it is useful for detecting error as well as implying nothing about directions of causation from the rate of growth to the rate of profits, or the other way around; nor does it require any particular form of technical progress to be occurring for it to be valid. Kahn adds that 'the relationship is not expressed in terms of the *rate of profit[s]* [which] if properly defined' relates to *expected* capitalists' incomes not to the *current* incomes of capitalists. Moreover, if long-period equilibrium conditions prevailed with expectations realized 'in the broad', his basic 'postulate results in a rate of profit[s] constant through time. And indeed it is only when the rate of profit[s] is constant through time that it can be uniquely defined and unambiguously measured' (ibid.: 194–5).

TENTATIVE CONCLUSION

So what is the upshot of all this? Joan Robinson herself was pessimistic, indeed, nihilistic, about the economic theory of the long period, feeling that, in the end, it had come to pieces in her hands. While properly trying to walk, as Kahn had put it, they had taken the wrong track and so were not able, subsequently, to run. We think that she was too hard on herself (and others); that she, with Kalecki's inspiration, *had* provided one of the ways in which developments over historical time could be analysed. In her 1953 Cambridge Lecture in Oxford she had sorted out the crucial distinction and had shown the ways forward:

> Never talk about a system *getting into* equilibrium, for equilibrium has no meaning unless you are in it already . . . think of a system *being* in equilibrium and having been there as far back towards Adam as you find it useful to go . . . so that every *ex ante* expectation about today ever held in the past is being fulfilled today . . . the *ex ante* expectation today is that the future will be like the past . . . Capital goods are selling today at a price which is both their demand price, based on *ex ante* quasi-rents, and their supply price, based on *ex post* costs.
>
> (Robinson 1953: 262; emphasis in the original)

From this insight it followed that there were two vital but different questions in economic analysis: 'What would be different if . . .' and 'What would follow if . . .' (see Robinson 1980: 161).

Kalecki, too, in his last paper on the process of cyclical growth (1968, 1990), defined the approach succinctly but deeply: 'In fact, the long-run trend is only a slowly changing component of a chain of short-period situations; it has no independent entity' (Kalecki 1991: 435). That Joan Robinson recognized this, to some extent, is clear, for example, in her 1980 *Cambridge Journal of Economics* paper with Amit Bhaduri (who recently has given us a most powerful, if brief, insight into her contributions to the theory of distribution and growth). Bhaduri points out that there were 'two distinct, although interrelated, aspects' of Joan Robinson's critique of neoclassical capital theory. The first concerned 'the problem of value . . . and distribution'; the second, 'the structure of production, i.e. the pattern of existing capacities in relation to the composition of aggregate demand in the process of economic growth' (Bhaduri 1996: 200). He adds that 'she became increasingly more concerned with the latter aspect [, that] it was accumulation in "historical time" which lay at the heart of the entire problem [so that] the problem of distribution associated with capital theory [was] a derived problem . . . arising from the evolution of the structure of production in relation to the changing composition of aggregate demand' (ibid.: 200). By using Marx's schemes of reproduction Joan Robinson was able to bring to the surface the connections between the proportions of capacities in various sectors which allowed the achievement of derived rates of growth and the demands and prices which allowed uniform rates of profit as between the sectors.

The key then is that we must try to choose concepts, definitions and units for our models such that they are simple enough to give us both a proper 'feel' for the processes at work and understandable results. The latter in turn are required to be robust when complications – those factors which we kept at the back of our heads, as Keynes told us – are brought into the analysis: robust in the sense that the insights and outlines emerge unscathed from further analysis. What separates good economists from great economists *is* just this ability to extract the crucial factors, to make the appropriate simplifications, so as to pass this essential test of robustness. Keynes and Kalecki, together with Kahn, Kaldor, Joan Robinson and Sraffa (probably in a different sense?) were in the latter category – which is why their work should live on alongside that of Keynes, and is one of the major reasons why this is a chapter in a volume on a 'second edition' of *The General Theory.*

As Kalecki and Joan Robinson were both very much 'horses for courses' people, it is not surprising that when they operated on a very abstract plane they were not interested in immediate applications to the real world as such, but in sorting out exact relationships, often in the context of a doctrinal debate.[32] Furthermore, as great economists and theorists, they were keenly aware of *when* theory *was* applicable and when it might never be. For another mark of a great economist is to know the limitations of the discipline and its methods, to know when there are questions, albeit often vital questions, to which in the nature of the case there can be no answers, or, at least, no full, well-defined and definitive answers.

NOTES

* We thank but in no way implicate Jochen Runde for his comments on a draft of the chapter.
1 Although, as will be argued subsequently, the case for the 'vagueness' associated

with the concept of the general price level is central to Keynes's approach to the choice of units, it is represented in Chapter 4 by a solitary sentence.

2 Which presumably means the complete theory of the monetary economy.

3 The material in this section (unavoidably) overlaps to a large extent with the treatment to be found in Carabelli (1992) which is, to the authors' knowledge, the only other published work on the topic of Keynes's approach to the choice of units.

4 'The Method of Index Numbers with Special Reference to the Measurement of General Exchange Value' (*C.W.* XI: 49–156).

5 Carabelli (1992) presents this material in the 'Essay on Index Numbers' as an extension of similar reasoning applied to probability in the various stages of development of the *Treatise on Probability* (1921). Keynes first wrote on the question of index numbers and general exchange value for Marshall in 1905. This early work reappeared in 1909 as the essay successfully submitted for the Adam Smith prize. Unfortunately, it has not been possible to verify whether the distinction between numerical and non-numerical quantities originated in Keynes's work on index numbers and was extended to his reasoning on probability, or vice versa as is implied by Carabelli.

6 Unfortunately, this example is problematic for two reasons. First, ordinary language usage surely suggests that the 'degree of similarity' is a *qualitative* relation, rather than a quantitative one. As such, it would seem to shed little light on the properties of quantities with respect to measurement. Second, the basis for judgements with respect to the degree of similarity is not objective; a green octavo is more like a green folio for the purposes of colour-coding, but more like a red octavo for the purposes of storing documents of a particular size. The example conflicts with subsequent implications (discussed below, pp. 115–16) which Keynes draws from his overall argument, namely, that the method of defining the purchasing power of money is not independent of the purpose of enquiry.

7 Keynes felt that numerical comparison (of a sort) of non-numerical quantities could be achieved if a numerically measurable proxy could be found. He cites (*C.W.* XI: 55) the example of the degree of closeness of relationship between members of a family group. In itself, it is not open to numerical measurement. However, it may be proxied by the proportion of common ancestors in the previous four generations. This latter index is numerical and may be useful for the purpose of comparisons. This point is important in the context of Chapter 4 and will be discussed further (pp. 116–17).

8 Note that, for quantities, being of the same kind is a necessary condition for being in the same unit.

9 The numerical example provided (*C.W.* XI: 57) runs as follows: the average of 8 seers/rupee and 4 seers/rupee is 6 seers/rupee. In European terms the average of $\frac{1}{8}$ rupee/seer and $\frac{1}{4}$ rupee/seer is $\frac{3}{16}$ rupee/seer. Note this does not equal the 'Indian' average in European terms, i.e. $\frac{1}{6}$ rupee/seer.

10 It must be acknowledged, however, that Keynes offers no supporting argument for this crucial and, admittedly, extremely subtle contention.

11 In order to grasp the subtleties of the argument, it is helpful to remember that Keynes felt that price relations are analogous to certain physical relations such as 'that quality of a substance which is constituted by the relation between its mass and the space it fills' (*C.W.* XI: 57). Although non-numerical, this quantitative relation can be given a conventional measurement by calculating either the specific density ratio or that for specific volume. In this way the non-numerical mass-space relation can be associated with an ascending and descending series

128

of numbers. Calculations based on either measure exclusively will yield the same answers. Yet for two substances, the average specific volume will diverge from the average specific density despite the fact that they measure the *same* physical quantities. In addition, there is no meaning to be attached to the average 'volume-density' of two substances.

12 Although such speculations run the risk of historical inaccuracy, it is probable that helicopters were yet to be invented in 1930.

13 He also argues cogently that the *failure* of monetary disturbances to influence all classes equally (in direction, degree and time) is the *raison d'être* of the study of short-period fluctuations. To assume this failure away is to make the investigative endeavour pointless.

14 It is interesting to note that this criticism appears to have had little impact in terms of index number theory and practice. Both Laspeyres and Paasche indices are still taught and calculated, despite the fact that the former (*qua* a price index) compares the price of the composite commodity in the period to what it would cost in the current period, while the latter compares the cost of the current composite to its value in base year prices.

15 Carabelli (1992: 18) remarks that the 'attempt to match theoretical tools with the object and the material under investigation is one of the main methodological interests in all Keynes's writings'. Interestingly, it is just this kind of reasoning which Keynes fails to display in the 'green octavo–red octavo–green folio' example (see note 6 above).

16 Carabelli (1992: 23) notes that Keynes offers no argument for this point, and proceeds to attempt a justification based on an analogy between the role of money in the economy and that of ordinary language in society. In the present authors' opinion, the analogy is forced and unnecessary. In what circumstances could money values *not* be homogeneous and money continue to fulfil its traditional, and defining, functions? If $10 is not twice $5, then money is not a unit of account. If $10 today is not $10 tomorrow, then money is not a reliable store of value. If money values are actually 'incommensurable collections of miscellaneous objects' then money is not a medium of exchange. Surely it is the properties required for something to be regarded as 'money' which imply that money values will be homogeneous?

17 Chick (1983: 58) argues that Keynes might have rejected the recovery of 'real' values by deflation on the grounds that the use of a *general* price level diminishes the importance of the consumption–investment distinction. The two components of aggregate demand essentially operate in different time frames as consumption expenditure is geared toward the satisfaction of wants in the present, while investment is the provision of *future* productive capacity. As such, the role of expectations (and the rate of interest) is important in determining the demand, and thus price, of investment goods, but not for single-use consumption goods. The real income of households is dependent on the price of consumption goods but not at all (effectively) on that of investment goods. Hence the use of a general price index to recover real values is not appropriate, obscuring, as it does, these important differences.

18 See note 6 above.

19 Carabelli (1992) quotes the remark but also makes no attempt to explain it.

20 Of course, we may conclude that Keynes's assertion that price is a non-numerical quantitative relation is bogus. After all, it does not appear to be supported by argument anywhere. Such a conclusion would effectively leave the arguments of Chapter 4 hanging in Limbo; they could still be put forward

and supported, but not on the basis of exegesis. The resolution of this question is beyond the scope of the current work.

21 For an interesting discussion of the problems associated with the definition of time in theoretical physics, and the relationship thereof to various other conceptions of time, see Coveney and Highfield (1990).

22 Thrift (1990) provides a fascinating account of the historical development of time consciousness in European society.

23 The somewhat nebulous character of these 'units' lends some support – *contra*, for example, Asimakopulos (1991: 5) – to the contention that the Keynesian short period should not be interpreted as some specific interval of calendar time. Rather, as Bhaduri (1986: 90) has it, the Keynesian short period is necessarily open-ended and not a self-contained unit of time. The recognition of this aspect of the short period, and the related conjectural nature of equilibrium, is held by Bhaduri to be of 'fundamental importance in character-ising a monetary economy'.

24 By way of example, consider utility in the cardinal utility framework. Conven-tional textbook discussions would refer to 'utils' as the units in which utility is measured. Although such statements make perfect sense at a superficial level, it is obvious that utils would not qualify as units in terms of the analysis of the EIN. Keynes rejects interpersonal comparisons of utility; the utilities of dif-ferent individuals are not in the same unit, let alone of the same kind.

25 It also contrasts with the treatment found in Keynes's 'Notes on a Measure of Roundaboutness'. There he defines the unit of time as the period of production of that part of current output which has the shortest period of production (*C.W.* XXIX: 156). Substitution of either of these accounts into the other produces circular definitions of either the time-unit or the period of production.

26 In commenting on the measurement of the net addition to the stock of capital equipment, Keynes writes: 'The problem of comparing one real output with another and of then calculating net output by setting off new items of equip-ment against the wastage of old items [when, owing to changes in technique, they are not identical] presents conundrums which permit . . . of no solution' (*C.W.* VII: 39).

27 'To say that net output to-day is greater, but the price-level lower, than ten years ago or one year ago, is a proposition of a similar character to the statement that Queen Victoria was a better queen but not a happier woman than Queen Elizabeth – a proposition not without meaning and not without interest, but unsuitable as material for the differential calculus. Our precision will be a mock precision if we try to use such partly vague and non-quantitative concepts as the basis of a quantitative analysis' (*C.W.* VII: 40).

28 'We take as given the existing skill and quantity of available labour, the existing quality and quantity of available equipment, the existing technique, the degree of competition, the tastes and habits of the consumer, the disutility of different intensities of labour and the activities of supervision and organisation, as well as the social structure including the forces, other than our variables set forth below, which determine the distribution of the national income. This does not mean that we assume these factors to be constant; but merely that, in this place and context, we are not considering or taking into account the effects and consequences of changes in them' (*C.W.* VII: 245).

29 It is significant, we think, that Lorie Tarshis, who was an astute interpreter of Keynes, preferred gross measures (see Tarshis 1948: 263).

30 We cannot resist printing the letter in full:

King's College
King's Parade
Cambridge
27.10.1936

Dear Joan

Many thanks for your letter – it is a valuable addition to my museum and I shall hang it next to an extract from Sidgwick where, after lecturing Ricardo on a quantity of labour, he goes on cheerfully himself to talk of quantities of utility.

If one measures labour and land by heads or acres the result has a definite meaning, subject to a margin of error: the margin is wide, but it is a question of degree. On the other hand if you measure capital in tons the result is purely and simply nonsense. How many tons is, e.g., a railway tunnel?

If you are not convinced, try it on someone who has not been entirely debauched by economics. Tell your gardener that a farmer has 200 acres or employs 10 men – will he not have a pretty accurate idea of the quantities of land & labour? Now tell him that he employs 500 tons of capital, & he will think you are dotty – (not more so, however, than Sidgwick or Marshall).

Yours

P.S.

31 He showed at the same time that there was no unit which could take into account the effects of technical advances over time on the size and composition of the surplus.

32 Following their lead, I (G.C.H.) made most of the arguments in *Some Cambridge Controversies* . . . (Harcourt 1972) in terms of stationary state comparisons. If results could not be shown to be robust in that setting, they were hardly likely to be robust in more complicated situations.

131

8

USER COST*

Christopher Torr

PART I

Christopher Torr writing as J.M. Keynes

I

In my preface to the French edition of *The General Theory* I noted that:

> I am chiefly concerned with the behaviour of the economic system as a whole, – with aggregate incomes, aggregate profits, aggregate output, aggregate employment, aggregate investment, aggregate saving rather than with the incomes, profits, output, employment, investment and saving of particular industries, firms or individuals. And I argue that important mistakes have been made through extending to the system as a whole conclusions which have been correctly arrived at in respect of a part of it taken in isolation.

Prior to the appearance of *The General Theory*, Professor Ragnar Frisch of the University of Oslo made a similar distinction between the behaviour of individual firms and households and the behaviour of the economic system as a whole. When investigating the oscillations of certain sections of an economic system, he speaks of micro-dynamic analysis, whereas his 'macro-dynamic analysis . . . tries to give an account of the fluctuations of the whole economic system taken in its entirety' (Frisch 1933: 172). I shall employ Frisch's felicitous terminology, and take some pains to distinguish between the micro and the macro sides of the story.

Although my approach is concerned largely with macroeconomics, the microeconomic side of the story can hardly be ignored even though I remain convinced that the whole is not simply the sum of the parts. I am, however, not altogether clear in my own mind what the link between microeconomics and macroeconomics is, and I venture to suggest that in time to come someone is bound to regard the missing link as one of the major scandals of our miserable subject.

User cost has one foot resting in microeconomics and the other in macroeconomics. It is concerned with the cost of items that entrepreneurs buy from entrepreneurs, and at the micro level it must be included in the cost subtracted from total sales in order to establish the position of profit maximization. At the macro level, user cost must also be subtracted from total sales, since it is the cost of items used up in the production process and as such must not be included in the total of final consumption and investment goods.

It will be useful in what follows to make a distinction between inter-firm purchases (when an entrepreneur buys goods from another entrepreneur) and intra-firm purchases (when an entrepreneur buys goods from himself). If entrepreneurs use up part of their own equipment, they will be disinvesting and this is an intra-firm transaction.

The user cost for firm i (U^i) can be broken down into inter-firm (U^i_{inter}) and intra-firm (U^i_{intra}) components, i.e.

$$U^i = U^i_{inter} + U^i_{intra}$$

In such a breakdown we shall have to specify what is to be included under U^i_{inter} and U^i_{intra}. U^i_{inter} is not equivalent to the sum of inter-firm transactions, since user cost is defined to include only the cost of items used up in the production process during the period under consideration, and some inter-firm transactions will involve goods that will not be used up in their entirety. Suppose that a baker buys ten bags of flour from a miller and the baker uses all ten bags to bake bread. Suppose that the baker also buys an oven from an oven maker. Both the flour and the oven represent inter-firm transactions, but only the cost of the flour represents the inter-firm component of user cost, since the oven will survive to bake another day.

As far as U^i_{intra} is concerned, it will by definition not include the purchase of the oven, since that is an inter-firm transaction. However, that part of the oven which the baker uses up to bake bread now represents an intra-firm component of user cost (disinvestment).

User cost must be distinguished from the expenses involved when entrepreneurs purchase or hire other factors of production (such as labour). I shall refer to such payments as factor cost.

User cost is not a new idea. Marshall associates it with the 'extra wear-and-tear of plant'. But as I mentioned in my first edition (page 72), Marshall provides little guidance on how to calculate user cost or on how important it is. The fact that Marshall refers to the extra wear-and-tear of plant suggests that he has in mind the intra-firm component of user cost.

Even sympathetic readers of *The General Theory* were puzzled with the way I brought user cost into the picture. Since I chided classical theory for overlooking user cost at the micro level, yet presented my aggregate supply and demand curves as net of user cost, I may in the process have created the impression that user cost should be included at the micro level but excluded at the macro level. That was not my intention. My intention was to emphasize the importance of user cost at both the macro and the micro levels, and to indicate the problems that would arise if it were left out of the analysis. I admit that I subtracted user cost from total sales at the macro level. But in establishing the profit-maximizing position at the micro level, I also subtracted user cost (and factor cost) from the sales of the individual firm.

User cost must always be incorporated in the analysis, at both the micro and macro levels. We incorporate it at the micro level in order to arrive at the profit-maximizing position of the firm, and we take it into account at the macro level to ensure that our measure of total output does not include goods used up in the production process.

If we can identify what final goods are, and paint all such goods red, we shall arrive at a satisfactory measure of total output by measuring the value of all red goods. Let us refer to this method of counting only final (red) goods as the method of addition.

We can also, however, arrive at a measure of total output by subtracting the value of goods used up during the period from the total of all goods. Suppose that we paint the goods that will be used up blue. The total that we are looking for consists of total sales minus the value of the blue items. This approach can be called the method of subtraction. The method of addition amounts to the same thing as the method of subtraction.

There is little doubt that in order to arrive at a satisfactory measure of total output, we need to subtract the value of blue goods from total sales. In my approach the blue goods must include both inter-firm and intra-firm components. If a farmer buys fertilizer to produce wheat and uses up part of his tractor in the process, both the bags of fertilizer (inter-firm user cost) and the part of the tractor used up (intra-firm user cost) must be painted blue. User cost is the value of the blue items.

Although I subtract the value of the blue items in order to arrive at total income, the price of the blue items obviously plays a role in establishing the price of the red items. In order to produce a red good (wheat) a farmer will buy blue goods (fertilizer) and use up part of those blue goods he has already bought (parts of his existing tractor fleet). The price that consumers pay for red goods cannot be seen independently of what producers have to pay for blue items. While user cost netts out at the aggregate level, it will play a role in setting both individual prices and the aggregate price level.

In section II I shall concentrate on the role of user cost at the micro level. In section III the accent shifts to the macro level. The analysis is unavoidably technical, and readers who are happy with the idea that user cost needs to be subtracted from sales at both the micro and the macro levels may wish to proceed to the next chapter.

II

Consider an economy consisting of a firm producing wheat (firm 1), a firm producing fertilizer (firm 2) and a firm producing tractors (firm 3). Wheat is an example of a consumption good, a tractor is an example of an investment item (fixed capital) and fertilizer is an example of an intermediate good used up during the period. Since entrepreneurs will keep on hand stocks of wheat, fertilizer and tractors, we also need to take changes in stocks into account. Once we do so, however, the dividing line between the different categories starts getting a bit messy.

Let A^1 represent the sales of wheat by the wheat firm to the tractor and fertilizer firms, plus sales to consumers. A^2 is the value of fertilizer sales to the wheat and tractor firms and to consumers, and A^3 is the sale of tractors to the wheat and fertilizer firms and to consumers. Some of the A^i entries may be zero. We may assume, for example, that tractor firms do not sell tractors to households and we may also wish to assume that households do not buy fertilizer. The total of all sales (a macro-economic concept) is given by ΣA^i.

Let the inter-firm purchases of firm i be represented by $A_1^i (i = 1, 2, 3)$. For the wheat firm, A_1^i consists of the purchases of tractors and fertilizer. Intra-firm transactions arise when the wheat firm uses up its own equipment (its stock of wheat, tractors and fertilizers). Such disinvestment is equivalent to the intra-firm component of user cost.

At the risk of repetition, I should like to emphasize a few points:

1 The purchases by firm i of output from other entrepreneurs (A_1^i) does not include intra-firm transactions.
2 The purchases by firm i of output from other entrepreneurs (A_1^i) includes the purchase of fixed capital goods (tractors) that will not be entirely used up in the period. The purchases also include items that will be used up in the period (fertilizer).
3 Since user cost is concerned only with the cost of items used up, it follows from 2 that the cost of inter-firm transactions (A_1^i) is not equivalent to the inter-firm component of user cost.
4 The sale of output by firm i to other entrepreneurs and to consumers (A^i) does not include intra-firm transactions.
5 The difference between A^i and A_1^i represents consumption expenditure on the product made by firm i (C^i), i.e. $C^i = A^i - A_1^i$.

In producing wheat, the wheat firm will use up part of its machinery and equipment. Suppose that the wheat firm buys a new tractor for £50,000 (an inter-firm purchase). If the entrepreneur makes use of the tractor, it will normally be worth less at the end of the period than if it had not been used, and such wear and tear is included under the intra-firm part of user cost. If the entrepreneur does not use it, something may have to be spent to keep it in good shape. For example, the entrepreneur might buy some oil and pay somebody to oil it while it is set up on blocks.[1] The intra-firm user cost will be the difference between the value of the tractor at the end of the period (if used) and its value at the end of the period (if not used), taking into account the amount that must be spent to keep it in good shape if it is not used.

Suppose that the tractor would have been worth £40,000 at the end of the season if it had been used, and that it would have been worth £45,000 at the end of the season if it had not been used, provided that the entrepreneur had spent £1,000 on maintenance (oil and labour). The disinvestment in the tractor amounts to £40,000 − (£45,000 − £1,000) = −£4,000. The intra-firm component of user cost is equivalent to +£4,000. By using the tractor instead of letting it lie idle, the farmer is disinvesting.

User cost has an inter-firm and an intra-firm component. For firm i, inter-firm transactions are measured by A_1^i. A_1^1 accordingly includes the purchase of tractors (fixed investment) and the purchase of fertilizer (an item that will be used up during the period) on the part of the wheat firm. Intra-firm transactions are measured by estimating how much of its own equipment firm i uses up. Let G_i be the value of machinery and equipment of firm i at the end of the period, and let G_i' be the value it would have had at the end of the period if it had not been used, with an amount of B_i' having been spent on maintenance. $G_i − (G_i' − B_i')$ is equal to the investment undertaken by firm i (I^i). I define user cost for firm i (U^i) as follows:

$$U^i = A_1^i + (G_i' − B_i') − G_i \qquad (8.1a)$$
$$= A_1^i − [(G_i − (G_i' − B_i'))]$$
i.e. $$U^i = A_1^i − I^i \qquad (8.1b)$$

While the first term on the right-hand side of equation (8.1b) (A_1^i) consists of inter-firm transactions, the second term (I^i) is a mixture of inter-firm and intra-firm purchases, for the investment undertaken by firm i consists of the items that it buys from other firms plus that part of its equipment that it uses up. Equation (8.1b) does not, therefore, present a breakdown of user cost into its inter-firm and intra-firm components. We can, however, break it down further.

I^i includes the purchase of investment items from other firms (inter-firm transactions) which will be called I^i_{inter}. It also includes intra-firm transactions (disinvestment) which will be termed I^i_{intra}. $I^i = I^i_{inter} + I^i_{intra}$.

A_1^i in equation (8.1b) can be broken down into inter-firm transactions involving fixed capital (I^i_{inter}) plus inter-firm transactions involving items used up during the period (fertilizer), indicated as X^i_{inter}. $A_1^i = X^i_{inter} + I^i_{inter}$.

As we saw in equation (8.1b), user cost for firm i is:

$$U^i = A_1{}^i - I_i$$
$$= X^i_{inter} + I'_{inter} - (I^i_{inter} + I'_{intra}) \qquad (8.1c)$$
i.e. $\qquad U^i = X^i_{inter} - I'_{intra} \qquad (8.1d)$

Equation (8.1d) presents user cost in terms of its inter- and intra-firm components. In the three-sector example, X^1_{inter} consists of the fertilizer that the wheat farmer buys from firm 2. Suppose this came to £1,500. I^1_{intra} is that part of the farmer's tractor used up in the period. It amounted to £40,000 − (£45,000 − £1,000) = −£4,000 in the above example. Total user cost for the wheat firm comes to £1,500 − (−£4,000) = £5,500. The original cost of the tractor, £50,000, an inter-firm purchase of fixed capital, (I^1_{inter}) fell out of the proceedings in equation (8.1c).

User cost has to do with the cost of goods that entrepreneurs use up to produce other goods. Part of such cost is the amount that the entrepreneur pays to other entrepreneurs (inter-firm transactions) for goods used up and part is the amount of the entrepreneur's own equipment used up (intra-firm transactions). Inter-firm transactions consist of items completely used up during the period (fertilizer) but they also include items that will live to fight another day (tractors). The rationale behind my definition contained in:

$$U^i = A_1{}^i - I^i \qquad (8.1b)$$

which has been reduced to:

$$U^i = X^i_{inter} - I'_{intra} \qquad (8.1d)$$

is that we must subtract from total inter-firm purchases all those items that will live to fight another day (I^i). One part of inter-firm transactions ($A_1{}'$) is I'_{inter}. One part of I^i is also I'_{inter}. So when I^i is subtracted in equation (8.1b) I'_{inter} falls away, and we are left with the cost of those goods bought from other firms that will be used up during the period minus the amount of a firm's own equipment that will be used up.

From equation (8.1a) we can deduce that total user cost for all firms is given by:

$$\Sigma U^i = \Sigma A_i{}' + \Sigma(G_i' - B_i') - \Sigma G_i$$

which for simplicity we may write as:

$$U = A_1 + (G' - B') - G \qquad (8.1e)$$

Since $G - (G' - B')$ is equal to aggregate investment, total user cost at the macroeconomic level is given by:

$$U = A_1 - I \qquad (8.1f)$$

Apart from user cost, a firm will also make payments to other factors of production. Of these factor costs, labour costs are the most obvious example. While these factor payments constitute a cost to the firm, they represent income to the factors receiving them.

Prime cost is the sum of user cost and factor cost. To find the profit-maximizing position for firm 1, we must find the level of output that maximizes the difference between total sales for firm 1 (A^1) and total prime cost for firm 1. To simplify matters, suppose that labour is the only other factor of production. Prime cost then consists of user cost plus labour cost.

Let P^1 be the price of wheat and q^1 the number of bushels of wheat sold to consumers and other firms by firm 1. Let W^1 be the wage bill for firm 1, and let N^1 be the amount of labour it hires with w being the money wage-rate. U^1 is the user cost for firm 1. Profits for firm 1 are given by:

$$\begin{aligned}
\pi^1 &= \text{Total sales of wheat } - \text{ prime cost} \\
&= \text{Total sales of wheat } - \text{ wage cost } - \text{ user cost} \\
&= P^1.q^1 - W^1 - U^1 \\
&= P^1.q^1 - w.N^1 - U^1
\end{aligned}$$

The firm must select that level of output (q^1) that maximizes profits. This level is found by setting $\delta\pi^1/\delta q^1 = 0$ and solving for P^1. We can then express the profit-maximizing position in three ways:

$$P^1 = MPC^1 \tag{8.2a}$$
$$P^1 = MFC^1 + MUC^1 \tag{8.2b}$$
$$P^1 = w/MPL + MUC^1 \tag{8.2c}$$

MPC^1 is the marginal prime cost for firm 1. MFC^1 is its marginal factor cost and MUC^1 its marginal user cost. MPL is the marginal physical product of labour. Firm 1 will maximize profits at the point where price is equal to marginal prime cost (8.2a) where marginal prime cost consists of marginal factor cost (the marginal product of labour) plus marginal user cost (8.2b and 8.2c).

An examination of equation (8.2b) will reveal my complaint against traditional microeconomic theory. Traditional theory maintains that the profit-maximizing position is obtained at the point where marginal revenue is equal to marginal factor cost (in this case the marginal product of labour). In equations (8.2b) and (8.2c) this is equivalent to the assumption that marginal user cost is zero. As I pointed out in my first edition (pages 67, 69–70):

the short-period supply price is the sum of the marginal factor cost and the marginal user cost [see equation (8.2b)].

Now in the modern theory of value it has been a usual practice to equate the short-period supply price to the marginal factor cost alone [i.e. $MUC^1 = 0$ in equation (8.2b)].

User cost constitutes one of the links between the present and the future. For in deciding his scale of production an entrepreneur has to exercise a choice between using up his equipment now and preserving it to be used later on. It is the expected sacrifice of future benefit involved in present use which determines the amount of the user cost, and it is the marginal amount of this sacrifice [MUC^1] which, together with the marginal factor cost [MFC^1] and the expectation of the marginal proceeds [P^1], determines his scale of production.

In Chapter 2 of my first edition I presented what I termed the first classical postulate, namely that the (real) wage is equal to the marginal product of labour (w/MPL in equation (8.2c)). Examination of equation (8.2c) reveals that implicit in the first classical postulate is the assumption that MUC^1 is equal to zero. Classical theory is flawed at the micro level.

Although equation (8.2b) incorporates, I believe, the correct analytical approach with which to establish the optimum level of output for the firm, I am fully aware that it is not an easy matter to measure user cost. Mr Hugh Townshend has been kind enough to point out some of the practical problems involved. Mr Townshend works at the Post Office, and he has indicated just how difficult it is to estimate what the value of capital might be if it is not used and kept in good running order. He has also pointed out that accountants will measure the cost of using up capital in ways that are different from those of economists. While I do not wish to gloss over these difficulties, I believe it important that we start off with the correct analytical apparatus before we start dirtying our hands.

III

At the macro level we need to subtract user cost to arrive at a measure of the aggregate level of output and income. In my first edition (page 24, footnote 2) I noted, therefore, that I was subtracting user cost from the aggregate supply and demand schedules. If we do not do so, national income will include those goods used up in the production process.

To arrive at the income for the whole economy, we need to take the total sales of all firms and subtract certain intermediate sales. User cost identifies which inter- and intra-firm transactions must be subtracted. I have defined user cost in such a way that when I subtract it from total sales, I will be left with the value of consumption and investment goods.

The total sales of firm i to consumers and other firms is given by A^i. Total sales of all firms is given by $A = \Sigma A^i$. User cost for firm i is given by U^i and total user cost is given by $U = \Sigma U^i$. Total income for the economy is given by:

$$Y = A - U \tag{8.3a}$$

The purchases of firm i from all other firms is A_1^i. The total purchases of all firms from other firms is $A_1 = \Sigma A_1^i$. Since A is total sales to consumers and other firms, and A_1 is total purchases from other firms, it follows that aggregate sales to consumers is given by $C = A - A_1$. Since

139

$$Y = A - U$$

it follows (from equation (8.1f) that $Y = A - (A_1 - I)$
$$= A - A_1 + I$$
i.e. $Y = C + I$ (8.3b)

National income can be measured either by the method of subtraction (equation (8.3a) or by the method of addition (equation (8.3b).

Since aggregate saving (S) is that part of income not spent on consumption, it is given by:

$$S = Y - C$$
$$= (A - U) - (A - A_1)$$
$$= A_1 - U$$
$$= I \quad \text{(see equation 8.1f)}.$$

Because of the way in which I have defined my terms, saving is equal to investment. It has been suggested to me that the way in which I have defined my terms implies that actual investment will always be equal to actual saving, but that it is only when the economy is in a state of rest that planned investment will be equal to planned saving. I hope to pursue this matter in a forthcoming article, since Hawtrey (1937a: 176–80) has argued that I ought to have made something more of the distinction between active and passive investment. He points out that the unintended accumulation (or running down) of stocks of goods is counted as investment in my system, and that such passive investment should be distinguished from 'designed' or 'active' investment such as the willing purchase of a new tractor (see Keynes 1973d: 599, and *The General Theory*: 75–6).

Intra-firm user cost is concerned with what it costs to use a machine as opposed to leaving it idle. This might lead the reader to suspect that the notion of user cost is bound up with the question of depreciation. In my approach, however, user cost does not amount to depreciation. Whether a tractor is used or not, it will depreciate in value, and such depreciation (which I prefer to call supplementary cost, V) is something that I regard as distinct from user cost. The total income for the community is given by total sales minus user cost. This can be expressed as a gross figure (in which V is not subtracted) or as a net figure (in which V is subtracted). If, in the Y = C + I equation, investment is regarded as gross investment, the equation gives gross income. If investment is interpreted as net investment the equation gives us net income.

At the macro level, total profits accruing to the entrepreneurs (π) are obtained by taking total sales (A) and subtracting total factor cost (F) and the total wage bill (W), i.e. $\pi = A - F - U$, which we can rearrange as $\pi + F = A - U$.

I have, therefore, developed three methods of measuring national income. The method of addition gives us:

$$C + I = Y,$$

the method of subtraction gives us:

$$A - U = Y,$$

and the method of adding profits and the wage bill gives us:

$$A - U = \pi + W$$

When, in my first edition, I introduced my aggregate supply and demand curves, I noted that they were to be interpreted as net of user cost. I did so to ensure that the goods embedded in my aggregate supply and demand curves are consumption and investment goods.

IV

Throughout the chapter I have emphasized the inter- and intra-firm components of user cost. In conclusion I should like to emphasize the inter-temporal aspect of user cost.

The inter-temporal aspect of user cost is tied up with the role of expectation. In my 1937 article in the *Quarterly Journal of Economics* I stressed that we set ourselves too easy a task if we ignore the role of uncertainty (and hence expectation) in our analysis. There I referred to the general problems associated with uncertainty, but did not spell out the implications for user cost.

Anybody who examines my definition of user cost (see equations (8.1a) and (8.1d)) will find that they are suffused with expectations. At first sight, the inter-firm component of user cost seems to present less of a measurement problem than the intra-firm component. It seems easier to measure how many bags of fertilizer I use up in producing wheat than to measure how much of my tractor I use up. My definition of user cost requires me to imagine what my tractor would be worth at the end of the period if I were to use it, and what it would be worth were I not to use it. Such requirements bring expectation into the picture and user cost can change overnight if my expectations change. Moreover, although intermediate goods (fertilizer) have one foot in inter-firm transactions, they have another in intra-firm transactions, since I can invest or disinvest in stocks of fertilizer. The neat analytical distinction between inter-firm and intra-firm transactions starts breaking down when we start peering into the future.

In this chapter I have shown how income might be measured in one particular period. Once we bring uncertainty and expectation into the picture, our measurement of income in one period is not independent of what we think happens in future periods.

I measure my height with a yardstick, but whatever my height is, it is not determined by the yardstick. We need to distinguish *measurement* from *determination*. I consider my main theoretical innovation to be the principle of effective demand which suggests that the level of income is *determined* by the level of investment. I introduce user cost in order to facilitate the measurement of income. When I measure income, I run into investment again, since user cost is equal to total sales minus investment.

Investment, therefore, plays a crucial role in both the measurement and determination of national income. Investment, however, depends on expectation which I know neither how to measure nor how to determine. Perhaps in time to come somebody will put forward a rational way of measuring expectations in order to render them determinate. I doubt, however, whether they will then still be expectations.

Although I do not know how to measure or how to determine expectations, I refuse to conclude that they should be left out of the picture. Other academic scribblers who believe in the inexorable forces of history might draw a different conclusion.

PART II
Christopher Torr writing as himself

Keynes's notion of user cost has had a chequered career. It has achieved a limited amount of success at the micro level, and at the macro level its success can be regarded as either overwhelming or non-existent, depending on whether you take a charitable or non-charitable view of certain post-1936 developments.

Because user cost is concerned with the cost of using capital as opposed to not using it, it has been applied at the micro level in the study of exhaustible resources. Bauer (1945), for example, examines the implications of user cost in the gold mining industry and Davidson (1963) draws implications for oil extraction. (See also Lewis 1949; Lutz and Lutz 1951; and Scott 1953.) These few references give a flavour of the type of literature involved, but because *The General Theory* is largely a book about macroeconomics, this part of the user cost legacy is not pursued here.

The current status of user cost in the macroeconomic league is bizarre. The non-charitable view is that it represents one of Keynes's least successful innovations. Even an interpreter as sympathetic as Hansen (1953) has adopted such a view, and if we wanted to add insult to injury we could argue that user cost was hardly a new idea, since Keynes, on his own admission, simply borrowed the idea from Marshall (*C.W.* VII: 72).

Forty years ago Scott (1953: 369) pointed out that: 'User cost is a concept widely known, little understood and almost never used.' The charitable view is that user cost is the most widely used of all Keynes's innovations and that it represents a principle about which there exists little or no controversy. If you open any textbook on macroeconomic theory written over the last fifty years, you will come across user cost, albeit in disguise.

For macro textbooks invariably devote a chapter to national income concepts, in which undergraduate students are warned that when we measure national income, we must beware of the sin of double counting. The intermediate transactions of the farmer, the miller and the baker must not be included in total income – we must measure only the value of the final product, bread. The student will inevitably be warned that even bread might not be a final product because we can buy sandwiches at a restaurant and sandwiches require an intermediate product, bread. But if we know how to recognize a final product when we see one, total income will consist of the sum of all final products.

Although our macroeconomic students might very well complete their studies without ever having heard of user cost, they will probably remember that a key feature of national income accounting theory is that we mustn't count goods used up in the production process, because that would involve double counting. This is the idea upon which user cost is based and the charitable view on the current status of user cost is that it is a concept which has remained unscathed since 1936.

The idea behind Keynes's exclusion of user cost from total sales and the idea behind the exclusion of intermediate sales from total sales in the textbook approach amount to the same thing, although there are differences in emphasis. While Keynes did not ignore the role of stocks or inventories (*C.W.* VII: 70–1) he tended to suppress them under the intra-firm component of user cost. In the conventional treatment, changes in inventories are given a separate heading, and such changes bear the brunt of ensuring that investment is always equal to saving.

Another difference between Keynes's system of national accounts and the conventional system is that Keynes did not want to associate user cost with depreciation. In attempting to isolate the cost that would be involved in the decision to use machinery and equipment, he did not wish to include under user cost the loss in value (which he called supplementary cost) which would occur whether or not the machinery were used. The conventional treatment implies that depreciation includes both the loss in value that occurs whether or not the machinery is used, and the loss that occurs through use.

The charitable view on the macroeconomic status of user cost in the post-1936 literature is that its spirit has conquered the measurement part of the macro field without a shot being fired. After all, the economics profession is at one that blue goods must be subtracted from total sales. There may be disagreement on when and where to wield the blue brush, but such disagreement hardly invalidates Keynes's claim that the blue brush must be wielded. Some have gone so far as to suggest that Keynes

> took the process further than the modern national income statistician is prepared to go, because Keynes, unlike the modern statistician, saw no reason to distinguish between the costs of raw materials and components

that are used up in the production process and that part of the cost that corresponded to the using-up of tools, equipment, and plant directly resulting from their use in production. The national income statistician today makes no such allowance. Thus, there is an element of double counting in his estimates.

(Tarshis 1979: 371)

While it is rare to find a comprehensive discussion of user cost in the post-1936 macroeconomic literature, it seems fair to say that those expositions that have appeared have tended to concentrate on clarification of what Keynes meant by user cost rather than on development of the concept. The contribution in this chapter is simply another example of this genre. That the existing literature on the macroeconomic role of user cost tends to be elucidatory is not a coincidence. Keynes's presentation of user cost is not user-friendly.

Keynes's reasons for incorporating user cost at the micro stage seem at first sight to be different from his reasons for wishing to view national income as net of user cost, but there is a unifying principle at work. At both the micro and macro levels, we find Keynes attempting to measure the income accruing to the entrepreneur(s) and to the other factors of production. At the micro level, entrepreneurial profit is given by entrepreneur's total sales minus factor cost (income to the factors of production concerned) minus user cost. The income accruing to the entrepreneur plus other factors of production is given by:

entrepreneural income + factor income = total sales − user cost

The left-hand side of the equation gives the income going to the factors of production, including entrepreneurs. If we sum this equation over all firms and indicate the summation process by rewriting the equation in capitals, we obtain:

ENTREPRENEURIAL INCOME + FACTOR INCOME = TOTAL SALES − USER COST

This might appear as a rather elaborate way of stating the obvious. It suggests, however, that at both the micro and the macro levels, Keynes's intention in subtracting user cost is to arrive at a measurement of income. User cost is an analytical device employed to measure income.

NOTES

* I should like to thank Geoff Harcourt and Jochen Runde for the useful comments they made on earlier drafts.
1 Although I have tried to keep a watertight distinction between user cost and factor cost, Professor Lerner has pointed out that user cost will include some factor cost if people are paid to oil a machine (see Lerner 1943).

Part III

THE PROPENSITY TO CONSUME

9

THE PROPENSITY TO CONSUME AND THE MULTIPLIER*

Jim Thomas

INTRODUCTION

While it is fun to play the game of guessing what Keynes might have written had he published a second edition of *The General Theory* (*G.T.*)[1] in the late 1930s, it is sensible (as far as possible) to base the speculation on writings that Keynes produced to counter critical reactions to and misunderstandings of *G.T.*; it seems reasonable to assume that Keynes would have taken the opportunity offered by a second edition to clarify some of the concepts that had caused problems to readers of the first edition and to deal with substantive criticisms.

Critical reviewers of *G.T.*, such as Cassel (1937), Hawtrey (1937a), Knight (1937), Pigou (1936) and Viner (1936), had little to say in connection with the Propensity to Consume and the Multiplier.[2] However, Keynes was involved in several exchanges of notes in academic journals in the years immediately following the publication of *G.T.* concerning the propensity to consume and the substance of these disagreements is summarized in the next section. These criticisms had implications for the Multiplier and they are discussed on pp. 151–2, together with the theoretical efforts of early empirical researchers to deal with the implications for the aggregate Multiplier of a variable Propensity to Consume in cross-sectional data. Several principles emerge about Keynes's priorities in these early debates and these are used to speculate on Keynes's probable reaction to later developments in the theory and estimation of the Consumption Function, which are discussed on pp. 152–4. Developments of the Propensity to Consume and the Multiplier after Keynes are discussed on pp. 154–9, while some conclusions are presented on pp. 159–60.

KEYNES'S REACTIONS TO CRITICISMS OF THE PROPENSITY TO CONSUME

'The Propensity to Consume' is the subject of Book III of the *G.T.* which consists of three chapters: Chapter 8, 'The Propensity to Consume: I. The

147

Objective Factors'; Chapter 9, 'The Propensity to Consume: II. The Subjective Factors'; and Chapter 10, 'The Marginal Propensity to Consume and the Multiplier'. Despite devoting forty-three pages to the topic (out of a total of 403 pages in *G.T.*), Keynes's reluctance to specify any particular parametric form to the propensity to consume left considerable scope for different interpretations and misinterpretations.

In Chapter 8, Keynes wrote:

> We will therefore define what we shall call *the propensity to consume* as the functional relationship χ between Y_w, a given level of income in terms of wage-units, and C_w, the expenditure on consumption out of that level of income, so that
>
> $$C_w = \chi(Y_w) \text{ or } C = W.\chi(Y_w). \qquad [9.1]^3$$
>
> The amount that the community spends on consumption obviously depends (i) partly on the amount of its income, (ii) partly on the other objective attendant circumstances, and (iii) partly on the subjective needs and the psychological propensities and habits of the individuals composing it and the principles on which the income is divided between them (which may suffer modification as output is increased).
>
> (*G.T.*: 90–1)

The rest of the chapter lists and discusses six objective factors:

1 a change in the wage-unit;
2 a change in the difference between income and net income;
3 windfall changes in capital values not allowed for in calculating net income;
4 changes in the rate of time-discounting, i.e. in the ratio of exchange between present goods and future goods;
5 changes in fiscal policy;
6 changes in expectations of the relation between the present and the future level of income.

The way in which these objective factors affect the propensity to consume is not explained precisely; Keynes wrote:

> Granted then, that the propensity to consume is a fairly stable function so that, as a rule, the amount of aggregate consumption mainly depends on the amount of aggregate income (both measured in wage-units), changes in the propensity itself being treated as a secondary influence, what is the normal shape of this function?
>
> The fundamental psychological law, upon which we are entitled to depend with great confidence both *a priori* from our knowledge of human nature and from the detailed facts of experience, is that men are disposed, as a rule and on average, to increase their consumption as

their income increases, but not by as much as the increase in their income. That is to say, if C_w is the amount of consumption and Y_w is income (both measured in wage-units) ΔC_w has the same sign as ΔY_w but is smaller in amount, i.e. dC_w/dY_w is positive and less than unity.

(G.T.: 96)

This is consistent with the relationship between C_w and Y_w proposed by Keynes in equation [9.1], with changes in the objective factors causing temporary shifts in a stable relationship, rather than these factors appearing directly in the propensity to consume.

Keynes continued, in a passage that seems to predate the permanent income hypothesis:

> This is especially the case where we have short periods in view, as in the case of the so-called cyclical fluctuations of employment during which habits, as distinct from more permanent psychological propensities, are not given time enough to adapt themselves to changed objective circumstances. For a man's habitual standard of life usually has the first claim on his income, and he is apt to save the difference which discovers itself between his actual income and the expenses of his habitual standard; or, if he does adjust his expenditure to changes in his income, he will over short periods do so imperfectly. Thus a rising income will often be accompanied by increased saving, and a falling income by decreased saving, on a greater scale at first than subsequently.
>
> But, apart from short-period *changes* in the level of income, it is also obvious that a higher absolute level of income will tend, as a rule, to widen the gap between income and consumption. For the satisfaction of the immediate primary needs of a man and his family is usually a stronger motive than the motives towards accumulation, which only acquire effective sway when a margin of comfort has been attained. These reasons will lead, as a rule, to a greater *proportion* of income being saved as real income increases.

(G.T.: 97)

The lack of clarity in these passages led to criticisms of Keynes's propensity to consume from two sources: Geneva (Staehle 1937) and Cambridge, Mass. (Gilboy 1938).[4] Staehle (1937) had two objectives: (a) to test Keynes's 'fundamental psychological law', which he interpreted as saying that as income increased, consumption fell as a *proportion* of income, rather than that the gap between consumption and income grew in absolute terms; and (b) to criticize Keynes for failing to take sufficient account of the effects of income distribution on the propensity to consume. In response to a note from Keynes (see Keynes (1939a), Staehle accepted with profuse apologies the rebuke that he had misrepresented what Keynes had written, but as his income distribution variable was statistically significant, he did not yield the field to Keynes. In a rearguard action, he suggested that Keynes did not always distinguish between the size distribution of income (i.e. the distribution of individual incomes) and the share distribution (i.e. the functional shares going to labour, entrepreneurs and rentiers) and urged the need 'to insert some variable characterizing the distribution of incomes in the fundamental formula printed on page 90 of *The General Theory*' (Staehle 1939: 130).[5]

Gilboy (1938), working with cross-sectional data on household expenditure and income and using graphical analysis and free-hand methods to find the best-fitting relationship between these variables, argued that the elasticity of expenditure with respect to income varied both across different occupational groups and with different levels of income. She concluded that

> it appears that the relation between income, consumption, and savings is neither as simple nor as stable as Mr Keynes assumes in his statement of the propensity to consume. Statistical evidence indicates a great diversity in these relationships and a marked increase in income–expenditure elasticity in certain income ranges. It also shows that the elasticity of savings tends to decline as income increases.
>
> (Gilboy 1938: 140)

Gilboy (1939) contains a letter from Keynes claiming that all the fundamental psychological law needs is a marginal propensity to consume less than one, a claim that she accepts with reservations. His response illustrates his preference for trusting his feel for the numbers rather than formal statistical results:

> My argument does not require, of course, that this rule holds good of every individual or even of every class, but only of the community as a whole; and it is subject to the usual ceteris paribus clause; though I should distrust any statistics which seemed to show the contrary as applying to a whole class.
>
> (Keynes, quoted in Gilboy 1939: 633)

Gilboy interpreted Keynes as believing that a number of institutional factors (including the distribution of income) changed relatively slowly and could therefore be disregarded in the short run. She remained sceptical and argued that there was statistical evidence that the distribution of income 'does change over short periods of time, perhaps cyclically. If so, the propensity to consume will change, and the situation becomes more complicated than Mr Keynes assumes' (Gilboy 1939: 636).

IMPLICATIONS FOR THE MULTIPLIER

The multiplier received much less attention from early critics of the *G.T.* than did the Propensity to Consume. One exception was Sir William Beveridge, who presented a paper (Beveridge 1936a) to Hayek's seminar at the London School of Economics in May 1936 that was critical of the *G.T.* and singled out the multiplier for particular criticism. Beveridge's criticisms seem to have been based on a complete misunderstanding of what Keynes had in mind; he was particularly unhappy with the idea of paying workers to dig holes in the ground:

> Surely this ridicule recoils on the reasoning that leads to it, as a *reductio ad absurdum*! If the General Theory of Employment leads to this – so much the worse for the theory. For if, on the General Theory of Employment the community is enriched by paying people to dig holes in the ground under the name of investment, why not take a leaf from President Roosevelt's book and pay them – under the name of investment – for not digging holes? If investment enriches, irrespective of the object of expenditure, why not trump Roosevelt by Townsend and pay people – under the name of investment – for going on living after sixty? The effects of such a process are simply those of inflation. . . .
>
> Nor, finally, does Mr. Keynes make any attempt to show how the benefits of investment in digging holes would spread, through distribution of purchasing power or otherwise; he merely recites like an incantation the magic virtues of the Multiplier. His argument must be more sensible than saying that because a man who jumps from a fourth floor window is almost certain to break his legs, therefore a man who has broken his legs in a railway accident is almost certain soon after to jump out of a window. But it is hard to see where the difference between the two arguments lies.
>
> (Beveridge 1936a: pp. 7–8)

Beveridge's central criticism of the *G.T.* was that Keynes did not base his analysis on a foundation of facts and, in Beveridge's view, 'economic theorising divorced from facts undoubtedly will lead nowhere' (ibid.: 31). This criticism was not confined to Keynes, since Beveridge was also unhappy about the increasing theoretical nature of economics at the London School of Economics under Robbins and Hayek (see Darhendorf 1995: 216–17). This seems to be reflected in another comment of Beveridge on *G.T.*:

> My fundamental difference from Mr. Keynes (and I fear many other economists) is one of method.
> (1) Mr. Keynes aims at making a revolution in economics, comparable to that made by Einstein in physics. Unlike Einstein he neither starts

from facts nor returns to them for verification, nor suggests where verification should be sought.

(Beveridge 1936b: 1)

Keynes responded to Beveridge's paper in a letter of 28 July 1936 in which he confessed that 'the general nature of your points is such as to convince me that I have really had a total failure in my attempt to convey to you what I am driving at' (*C.W.* XIV: 56). Keynes countered Beveridge's apparent disbelief in the existence of the multiplier with a simple example spelling out the secondary and subsequent stages in the multiplier process. Beveridge remained unconvinced, but the correspondence ended.

The argument of Staehle and Gilboy, that changes in the distribution of income would affect the aggregate propensity to consume, had obvious implications for the multiplier. Given cross-sectional data on incomes and expenditures, the aggregate marginal propensity to consume would be a weighted average of the marginal propensities to consume of the different income groups. Stone and Stone (1938) showed that, given a cross-sectional relationship between average consumption ($\bar{c}$) and average income ($\bar{y}$) for each income group, then the aggregate marginal propensity to consume (K) is

$$K = \Sigma y. \ (d\bar{c}/d\bar{y})/\Sigma y \qquad (9.2)$$

where y is the aggregate income in a particular income group. Since their empirical work suggested that a variable which measures changes in income distribution was not statistically significant in the consumption function, they concluded that the weights in equation (9.2) were constant and that the aggregate marginal propensity to consume (and hence the multiplier) was well defined.

Later, other investigators analysed the effects on the multiplier of redistributing income from those with a low to those with a high marginal propensity to consume. The general conclusion was that this would have relatively little effect and that the multiplier was robust with respect to such changes.[6] These issues will be discussed further on pp. 154–9 below.

POSSIBLE CHANGES IN BOOK III FOR A NEW EDITION OF *THE GENERAL THEORY*

In the exchanges summarised above, Keynes concentrated on conceptual and textual matters and ignored the statistical arguments put forward by his critics. This is consistent with a view of the role of models that he expressed in a letter to Roy Harrod (6 July 1938):

> But it is of the essence of a model that one does *not* fill in real values for the variable functions. To do so would make it useless as a model. For as soon as this is done, the model loses its generality and its value as a mode of thought.

152

Economics is a science of thinking in terms of models joined to the art of choosing models which are relevant to the contemporary world. It is compelled to be this, because, unlike the typical natural science, the material to which it is applied is, in too many respects, not homogeneous through time. The object of a model is to segregate the semi-permanent or relatively constant factors from those which are transitory or fluctuating so as to develop a logical way of thinking about the latter, and of understanding the time sequences to which they give rise in particular cases.

(C.W. XIV: 296–7, italics in the original)

On statistics and statisticians, he wrote (in a letter to Roy Harrod, 16 July 1938):

Tinbergen endeavours to work out the variable quantities in a particular case, or perhaps in the average of several particular cases, and he then suggests that the quantitative formula so obtained has general validity. Yet in fact, by filling in figures, which one can be quite sure will not apply next time, so far from increasing the value of his instrument, he has destroyed it. All the statisticians tend that way. Colin [Clark], for example, has recently persuaded himself that the propensity to consume in terms of money is constant at all phases of the credit cycle. He works out a figure for it and proposes to predict by using the result, regardless of the fact that his own investigations clearly show that it is not constant, in addition to the strong *a priori* reasons for regarding it as most unlikely that it can be so.

(C.W. XIV: 298–300)

In the light of his view of models and statisticians and the fact that Keynes had published rebuttals of the criticisms, it seems unlikely that he would have undertaken a major revision of the chapters in Book III in 1939; other chapters in the first edition of *G.T.* had raised more controversy and were more in need of rewriting and editing. The most important revisions he might have made would have been to clarify (a) the proposition that the particular functional form of the propensity to consume was unimportant, provided that the marginal propensity to consume was a positive fraction between zero and one; and (b) to emphasize the extent to which his analysis might be affected by changes in the distribution of income, both between individuals and between groups.

In Chapter 10, Keynes had used some back-of-envelope calculations based on Kuznets's US data (even though they were 'very precarious' (*G.T.*: 127) to estimate the multiplier, from which he reported indirect estimates of the marginal propensity to consume. In the second edition of *G.T.*, he might have had some interesting comments to make on the direct estimates of the marginal propensity to consume based on regression analysis that were presented in Stone and Stone (1938).

So far the discussion of what Keynes might have revised in Book III of *G.T.* has been based on actual exchanges between Keynes and his critics in the late 1930s. To speculate further, we might consider a scenario in which Keynes did not suffer a fatal heart attack in 1946, but devoted his entire energies after 1946 to active service as a policy adviser until he returned to academic life as a Fellow at King's College in the 1950s.[7] Suppose an enterprising representative from Macmillan had approached Keynes and invited him to provide a third and definitive edition of *G.T.*

The most likely outcome seems to be that the offer would be declined, as the economic scene had changed dramatically since 1939. Whereas in the 1930s Keynes was in a powerful position to control the development of what became macroeconomics, this was no longer the case by the 1950s. First, following the development of the IS–LL model in Hicks (1937), a number of studies appeared in the late 1940s and 1950s that attempted to translate *G.T.* into 'Keynesian economics' – for example, Modigliani (1944); Klein (1947); Dillard (1948); Hansen (1953); and Kurihara (1956). Second, Klein (1950) and Klein and Goldberger (1955) had estimated macroeconomic models whose post-Cowles Commission results could not lightly be dismissed by the arguments that Keynes had used against Tinbergen (see Keynes 1939b, 1940a; Tinbergen 1940).[8]

Keynes might not have wished to devote much time to addressing an audience that was (a) being taught to reduce *G.T.* to a set of equations; (b) treat their parameters as constants; and (c) estimate them by methods that he regarded with deep scepticism. Yet, without accepting these constraints, Keynes would have had difficulty in communicating with a younger generation of economists who were being trained as 'Keynesians', with the result that a third edition of *G.T.* might have been no more than the coda to a great work from an earlier era.

THE PROPENSITY TO CONSUME AND THE MULTIPLIER SINCE KEYNES

Rather than providing a detailed discussion of developments in consumer theory and the estimation of consumption functions since Keynes, this section will concentrate on patterns and trends in this area.[9] During the period from 1946 to the late 1950s, two important strands in the development of the consumption function may be identified.

First, there was the accumulation of evidence (both microeconomic cross-sectional and aggregate macroeconomic time series data) that encouraged the development of new theories of consumer behaviour, such as the Life-Cycle Hypothesis (Modigliani 1949; Modigliani and Ando 1957; and

Modigliani and Brumberg 1954) and the Permanent Income Hypothesis (PIH) (Friedman 1956).

Second, econometricians were building simultaneous-equation macro-economic models, estimating the parameters and using the estimates for policy analysis and forecasting. The early models were small, being limited in size by the short length of many economic time series and serious computational constraints in this period before mainframe computers became more widely available.

Had there been a third edition of *G.T.* in the 1950s, Keynes would have had little trouble in reconciling the Life-Cycle Hypothesis and the Permanent Income Hypothesis to his treatment of the propensity to consume in the first two editions, as he could have pointed to the discussion in Chapter 8 of the importance of 'a man's habitual standard of life' (quoted above) as predating these ideas. Given his own penchant for back-of-envelope calculations rather than formal econometrics, he would probably have applauded Milton Friedman's ingenuity in presenting cross-sectional evidence in favour of the PIH. However, Keynes's comments on the quality of much of the empirical work on the consumption function during the 1940s might well have been caustic and one suspects that Tinbergen would have agreed with him.[10]

The 1960s saw the opening of the battle between Keynesians and monetarists, although Friedman's Permanent Income Hypothesis may be seen as an early salvo in that war. Events were not kind to the Keynesians, since in the late 1960s and early 1970s, some key Keynesian relationships (such as the Phillips curve) were misbehaving and the builders of econometric models (now often considerably larger than those built during the 1950s) were having problems in obtaining plausible parameter estimates and making accurate forecasts.

Whilst consumption functions were reasonably well behaved and did not produce particular problems in forecasting during this period, there were many developments in the specification of the function during the 1970s, in response to a number of theoretical questions.[11]

For example, following the early work by Zellner *et al.* (1965), which showed the importance of wealth in the consumption function (in the form of liquid assets), there were further studies by Mishkin (1976, 1977), which investigated the effect of the structure of an individual's asset portfolio on the demand for durables and suggested that this variable played an important role in the decline in consumer spending in the US in the 1973–5 recession; and Townend (1976), whose results for the UK suggested that real liquid assets were important in explaining consumption of non-durables and services.

The question of whether consumers are liquidity-constrained was studied by Blinder (1976), who found evidence of this problem for households that could expect large cash inflows in the future, but could not borrow on them now; Pissarides (1978), who explored the effect of market imperfections on the liquidity of different assets in an individual's portfolio; and Heller and Starr (1979), who examined a consumer's optimal consumption plan when there are severe borrowing constraints.

The discovery of money illusion in the consumption function by Branson and Klevorick (1969) was followed by studies of the effects of inflation on consumer behaviour by Juster and Wachtel (1972), who suggested that unanticipated inflation had a strong effect on saving, whereas anticipated inflation encouraged spending on non-durables and services; Burch and Werneke (1975), who reported mixed results on the findings of earlier studies with respect to money illusion and the role of inflation; Springer (1977), who examined the income and substitution effects of expected inflation on expenditure on durables and non-durables; and Deaton (1978), whose results suggested that it was changes in the rate of inflation that affect consumption.

The effect of unemployment on consumer behaviour was studied by Westin (1975), with results suggesting that a rise in unemployment led to delays in the replacement of cars in the US; Juster and Taylor (1975), whose results suggested a positive correlation between rising unemployment and US personal saving during the period 1953 to 1973; Modigliani and Steindel (1977), who in contrast found a positive relationship between unemployment and consumption, as did Barro (1978b).

The effect of the rate of interest on consumption had been the subject of an exchange of notes between Holden and Keynes in which Keynes wrote that while the rate of interest was one of the factors which influence the propensity to consume, he concluded 'that it is difficult to generalize as to the nature of this influence' (Keynes 1938a: 708).[12] Later studies produced mixed results, with Modigliani (1977) finding evidence that the rate of interest does affect consumption, while other studies, such as Howard (1978) and Howrey and Hymans (1978) failed to find this effect.

The adoption of 'rational expectations' by monetarists provided them with a powerful weapon in the war against Keynesians, for example, with the Lucas critique of traditional policy analysis in the context of rational expectations raising questions about the effectiveness of a government's economic policies if they are fully anticipated by economic agents (see Lucas 1976).

The implications of rational expectations for the consumption function were explored by Hall (1978), under the assumptions that consumers with rational expectations maximized a quadratic utility function in an environment in which there were no credit restrictions, no habits or adjustment costs, and a constant real interest rate. Given rational expectations, the consumer will have incorporated all the relevant information available at time $t - 1$ that determines consumption into the decision on what to consume, C_{t-1}. Since C_{t-1} already contains this information, none of the variables contained in this information set (such as lagged income, Y_{t-1}) should make a significant statistical contribution to a model explaining current consumption, C_t. Hall argued that current consumption could be explained by last period's consumption plus a random term, an unanticipated component that could not be predicted from past information. Mathematically, changes in consumption would be a random walk, that is:

$$C_{t+1} - C_t = \varepsilon_t \tag{9.3}$$

where ε_t is an unpredictable consumer's forecasting error.

Hall's findings were challenged by Flavin (1981), Mankiw and Shapiro (1985) and Campbell and Mankiw (1989). The evidence for the UK is largely against Hall's hypothesis (see Daly and Hadjimatheou 1981; Muellbauer 1983; Bean 1984; and Wickens and Molana 1984).[13]

A detailed specification of the relationships estimated in the studies referenced above would show that, in some cases, the same equation could be claimed by different theories of consumer behaviour. For example, Modigliani (1975) noted that under certain assumptions, the equation

$$C_t = \alpha Y_t + \beta C_{t-1} + u_t \tag{9.4}$$

could represent the permanent income hypothesis, the life-cycle hypothesis or the relative income hypothesis.

This failure of economic theories to produce clearly differentiated representations is highlighted in work carried out by a group of econometricians associated with J.D. Sargan of the London School of Economics and Political Science. While economic theories are used to specify the likely variables to appear in a relationship, the objective is to find a specification of the model that explains the data and is satisfactory from a statistical viewpoint, in terms of passing a battery of diagnostic tests and having stable parameters over time.

The first application of this approach to the consumption function in the UK was the study by Davidson, Hendry, Srba and Yeo (1978), usually abbreviated to DHSY. Working with quarterly data for the UK from 1958Q2 to 1970Q4 on real personal disposable income (Y), real consumers' expenditure on non-durable goods and services (C) and the implicit price deflator of that variable (P), their chosen specification was:

$$\Delta_4 c_t = \beta_0 + \beta_1 \Delta_4 y_t + \beta_2 \Delta_1 \Delta_4 y_t + \beta_3 \Delta_4 p_t + \beta_4 \Delta_1 \Delta_4 y_t + \beta_5 (c - y)_{t-1} + u_t \tag{9.5}$$

where lower-case letters indicate that variables are measured in natural logarithms, $\Delta_4 c_t = c_t - c_{t-4}$, $\Delta_1 c_t = c_t - c_{t-1}$ and $(c - y)_{t-1}$ is the 'error-correction' term that characterizes the work of this school of applied econometrics.[14]

While the DHSY model does not correspond specifically to any one of the alternative theoretical models summarized above, it is able to encompass most of them. In addition, it passes a large range of diagnostic tests for correct specification, has stable parameters and allows both short-run and long-run effects to be analysed. Further studies have shown that equation (9.5), or variants of it, retains these properties when applied to different data sets (see Hendry and von Ungern-Sternberg 1980; Hendry 1983; and Hendry *et al.* 1990).

Summary

The development of the consumption function since Keynes has the following characteristics:

1 In terms of theoretical development, the trend has been to incorporate explicitly into the model of the consumption function many of the factors that Keynes listed in Chapters 8 and 9 of *G.T.* as having implicit effects on the propensity to consume, such as unemployment, rates of interest, windfalls and changes in expectations.
2 Econometric analysis has played an increasingly important role both in testing hypotheses that attempt to discriminate between rival theories and in providing theoretically agnostic models with satisfactory statistical and economic properties, such as the DHSY model.
3 It seems unlikely that any one theory will dominate all others, since any particular specification of a consumption function is usually compatable with a number of alternative theories. However, a recent survey of the consumption functions in eight econometric models of the UK noted that the 'models under consideration have their roots in life-cycle theory which, as Deaton (1992) says "is the basis for essentially all modern research on consumption and saving"' (Church *et al.* 1994: 71).

The multiplier

The multiplier has played an important role in the use of macroeconomic models for the analysis of policy issues from the early days of the construction of such models.[15] The *structural form* of a typical macroeconomic model consists of a set of equations, a mixture of behavioural equations, identities and equilibrium conditions that provide an economic explanation of the behaviour of the endogenous variables in the model in terms of the behaviour of the exogenous variables in the model.

Having estimated the parameters in the structural equations, these numerical values may be used to 'solve' for the endogenous variables, that is to obtain a new set of equations in which each of the endogenous variables is expressed as a function of the exogenous variables in the model. This new set of equations is the *reduced form* of the model and may be used for policy analysis, using so-called 'multiplier analysis'. For example, starting from the current set of values for the exogenous variables and the esti-mated structural parameters, the reduced form may be used to give a benchmark set of values for the endogenous variables. The effects of policy changes may now be analysed by changing the values of one or more exogenous variables and resolving the model to find the new values of the endogenous variables.[16]

This kind of analysis is of great importance, both to model builders in analysing policy changes and in making forecasts and for economists interested in analysing differences in the performances of competing macroeconomic models (see Wallis *et al.* 1984, 1986, 1987; and Whitley 1994).

CONCLUSIONS

Providing the consumption function is defined broadly enough, for exam-ple as a relationship to explain consumers' behaviour that will involve income among other variables, this relationship may be said to have survived and to be flourishing. It has been the subject of considerable theoretical and econometric attention in recent years as economists have tried to explain the large swings in the value of the marginal propensity to consume in many countries in the wake of financial deregulation (see, for example, Berg 1994; Hendry 1994).

The developments in the consumption function summarized in the previous section concentrated on research on consumers' behaviour at the aggregate level, but recently the trend in theoretical analysis has tended towards analysing the microeconomic foundations of aggregate consumers' behaviour, while empirical analysis has made increasing use of data from large household surveys and panels of consumers that allow investigation of behaviour over time (see Blundell 1991; Deaton 1992). These develop-ments are producing interesting theoretical advances and data that allow for more discrimination between alternative hypotheses than is possible when working with aggregate time series data.

As a pedagogic device, the consumption function still plays an important role in the teaching of macroeconomics, though the version used and its prominence varies considerably.[17] Certainly, the simple 'Keynesian' model

$$C_t = \alpha + \beta Y_t + u_t \tag{9.5}$$
$$Y_t = C_t + I_t \tag{9.6}$$

remains in the toolkit of most econometricians as a useful model for illustrating the perils of bias and inconsistency when using ordinary least squares in simultaneous-equation estimation.

Keynes might well have approved of some of the theoretical develop-ments relating to the propensity to consume, though it is doubtful that he would have embraced rational expectations with any great enthusiasm. He would probably retain much of his scepticism concerning econometric techniques and their results and point to the spectacular forecasting failures of most large-scale econometric models in recent years, as well as major differences in the assumptions underlying the models. In his criticisms of Tinbergen's work he wrote:

> It will be remembered that the seventy translators of the Septuagint were shut up in seventy separate rooms with the Hebrew text and brought out with them, when they emerged, seventy identical translation. Would the same miracle be vouchsafed if seventy multiple correlators were shut up with the same statistical material? And anyhow, I suppose, if each had a different economist perched on his *a priori*, that it would made a difference to the outcome.
>
> (Keynes 1940a: 155–6)

NOTES

* I am very grateful to Geoff Harcourt for helpful comments on and constructive criticisms of the first draft of this chapter. Conversations with Charlie Bean and Ken Wallis were also very helpful. The usual disclaimer applies.
1 *The General Theory* (Keynes 1936) will be abbreviated to *G.T.* in the remainder of this chapter.
2 An interesting collection of some of the early reviews of *G.T.*, together with afterthoughts of the reviewers from the 1960s, is Lekachman (1964a). A critical evaluation of early reviews of *G.T.* is presented in Klein (1947: ch. 4).
3 Equations are not numbered in *G.T.*, but are numbered here to facilitate cross-referencing.
4 There was an additional exchange of notes between Keynes and G.R. Holden of Harvard University (Holden 1938a, b; and Keynes 1938a, b). Since Keynes was able to demonstrate that Holden's criticisms were based on a misinterpretation of a particular passage (which the latter admitted), the details of this exchange are ignored here.
5 Staehle (1937) used multiple regression to evaluate the evidence concerning his two objectives and, given the econometric standards of the time, his methods were sophisticated and his measure of income inequality was statistically significant. See Thomas (1992: 165–70) for a detailed analysis of his results.
6 See Marschak (1939)) Metzler (1943); and Lubell (1947). Their arguments are summarized in Thomas (1992: 174–6).
7 The simplifying assumption that Keynes survived but was not engaged in economic analysis is made to avoid the obvious problem that, if Keynes had continued to publish articles and books on economic theory, the work of other authors (who are cited in the text) would have been different.
8 For later generations of econometricians, the appeal of Tinbergen's work is his great intuitive ability to deal with problems that were still unexplored theoretically. By the 1950s, the Cowles Commission had provided the basic foundations for the development of econometric theory. These developments explored areas where Keynes had doubts and clarified issues where Keynes was wrong (such as the need for explanatory variables to be independent of each other).
9 The treatment of this topic will be relatively brief, as the story is well known.

The consumption function has been the subject of periodic surveys; see, for example, Orcutt and Roy (1949); Ferber (1953); Suits (1963); Ferber (1966, 1973). Recent developments in the theory of the consumption function and empirical applications are discussed in Hadjimatheou (1987); Speight (1990); and Muellbauer (1994).

10 See Thomas (1989: 145–9, Table A1) for references and a summary of the regression equations.

11 The references given below are intended to give a flavour of some of the debates surrounding the consumption function that were going on in the 1970s. For a more extensive exploration of these debates and how they progressed, see Hadjimatheou (1987).

12 See note 5 above.

13 Speight (1990) contains a very extensive discussion of rational expectations and the consumption function.

14 This term is interpreted as capturing any disequilibrium in the *levels* of consumption and income in the previous period. For a general introduction to error correction models, see Thomas (1993: ch. 7). For a discussion of their use in modelling the consumption function, see Hadjimatheou (1987: ch. 8).

15 For example, see Klein (1950); and Klein and Goldberger (1955).

16 Fair (1994: 262) points out a semantic inconsistency in the labelling of this kind of exercise: 'This exercise is usually called multiplier analysis, although the word "multiplier" is somewhat misleading. The output that one examines from this exercise does not have to be the change in the endogenous variables *divided* by the change in the exogenous variable; it can merely be, for example, the change or percentage change in the endogenous variable itself. . . . The form of the output that is examined depends on the nature of the problem, and thus the word "multiplier" should be interpreted in a very general way.' Despite this caveat, the term 'multiplier analysis' has an intuitive appeal.

17 For example, in Burda and Wyplosz (1993) – a recent macroeconomic textbook that was well received by the critics – the discussion of Consumption occupies nine pages (out of 486), concentrates on a microeconomic exposition of the Life-Cycle and Permanent Income hypotheses, and the book contains no reference to the multiplier. Another 'European' text (Barro and Grilli 1994) takes a more balanced view by presenting one chapter on the Permanent Income Hypothesis and a later chapter discussing earlier theoretical issues under the heading 'The Keynesian Theory of Business Fluctuations'.

10

KEYNES AND DYNAMICS

R.M. Goodwin

Writing in the 1930s Keynes was understandably not much concerned with change and growth in discussing the short- or medium-run behaviour of the economy. It is difficult for people now to realize how different the economy was in that period. The economy was so depressed that for a decade it showed little technological progress and growth. Hence it was not unnatural for Keynes to tend to use a statical view of analysis.

He adopted as a central conception the multiplier from his pupil and friend Richard Kahn. In Keynes this became a single number which could be used to estimate the effect of a change in the public budget. But in fact, as formulated by Kahn, it was a dynamic, temporal sequence asymptotic to a final equilibrium, approached only after a considerable time lag. The consequences for dynamics are serious. If, as is common, there is a continuing variation in the government deficits or surpluses, then each time period initiates a different magnitude of successive multiplier effects on incomes and demand. Hence at any one time the economy is subject to a large number of different stimuli in various stages of decay. The sum of all these coexisting, diminishing effects will be, for any particular historical stretch, a highly complicated, irregular time series.

This aspect of the theory becomes crucial in trade cycle and policy analysis. Keynes tended to treat the problem in terms of the demand for capital as a function of the rate of interest, i.e. supply and demand for durable goods (and stocks). This was unduly traditional and neoclassical in flavour. It is true that in the 1930s, with little technological change and growth, the long-term analysis was limited and flawed. He did discuss stocks of non-durables, but too roughly, and it was left to Metzler to provide a proper Keynesian theory of the shorter waves. His discussion of the major cycle was inadequate and the theory of long-term growth was left for post-war analysis.

The prime aim of Keynes was to persuade economists that demand, not supply, determined output and employment, thus setting the central problem for applied analysis, public policy and control; in that he was dramatically successful. But when one considers more closely the possible dynamical sequences, problems arise. From any continuing alteration in public spending and taxing there will occur first acceleration, then to be followed by deceleration. This is bound to initiate complicated changes in individual and company expenditures. Harrod, who had followed the development of *The General Theory*, saw clearly that its basic shortcoming lay in the dynamical problem (though he was not quite equipped to develop a helpful solution). If the aim is to cure the depression by reducing or eliminating unemployment, then as full employment is gradually approached there must be a careful reduction in the income-generating budget. As and if such a policy is successful, demand and output level off (or grow very much less), so that private investment falls and hence also demand and output, with the result that the policy is bound to be unsuccessful.

To lift employment to any desired degree of fulness and maintain it, then requires a very ambitious, dynamically variable policy. What in principle is required is correct forecasting of demands in the near future, so that a public policy can be agreed and carried out in time to have its variable consequences fitting appropriately the timing of the problem. This involves handing over control of public spending and taxing to competent experts. But spending and taxing are ultra-sensitive political things and no sane politician in a democratic society is going to surrender control over them to bureaucrats.

The problem is further exacerbated by the difficulty of making reliable forecasts for longer than quite short periods. Not only has this been found to be inaccurate, but we now have some rational explanation for the difficulties of longer-term forecasting: the discovery of chaotic theory in the 1960s has opened up a new vision. Who can predict the weather for next summer, or next winter, in spite of the fact that weather is a deterministic system? In this sense chaos is plausibly applicable to the economic weather. Who can predict next year's output or next decade's output? Chaotic analysis gives a clear explanation of how and why a completely deterministic system can be unpredictable, *in principle*. Who could have predicted that the economy would behave quite differently in the aftermath of the Second World War as compared with the First World War; or who could have foreseen how different the 1970s and the 1980s would be from the 1950s and 1960s? So now we know that it is not only exogenous events which make economies behave so unpredictably erratically: this puts severe limits on the usefulness of econometric expertise and excuses some past errors.

Keynes lucidly and correctly explained what should have been done in the 1930s (though with little influence on policy), but he left a more difficult problem than he foresaw for future generations of aspirant economic advisers.

163

11

THE MULTIPLIER AND FINANCE*

Victoria Chick

I have written the first part of this chapter as if by Keynes, projecting what he might have been aware of as a result of either internal critique or comments made before his death. There are of course anachronisms: the Harvard reference system and references to the *Collected Writings*. Where I wish to refer to work which could not have been known by Keynes, I put the comment in endnotes and use square brackets.

PART I
Victoria Chick writing as J.M. Keynes

Two of the most important propositions made in earlier chapters are the distinction between expenditures which are independent of current income and those which are income-sensitive, and by way of developing the second of these, the 'psychological law' that consumption rises with income but not to the full extent of any increase in income. The first of these propositions puts investment in the role of *causa causans*, responsible for initiating changes in income, consumption expanding in response. In Chapter 3 I demonstrated that short-period equilibrium, defined as equality between correctly expected aggregate demand and aggregate supply, was compatible with either unemployment or full employment. Using the hypothesis that the marginal propensity to consume (MPC) is less than 1, it was possible to show that the equilibrium was stable: the self-correcting mechanism which had been so long believed was disproved by my theory.

On this demonstration rests my claim to generality, for my theory encompasses the classical theory, which only admits of equilibrium at full employment and explains equally well the phenomenon of persistent (equilibrium) unemployment. Such a more general theory is clearly required, in the face of the observation of unemployment levels of 10 per cent and more in Britain persevering over the fifteen years 1922–37; this the classical theory would be powerless to explain.

164

The disaggregation of income into autonomous and induced types of expenditure – broadly identified (in a closed economy with no government) with investment (I) and consumption (C) respectively – yields as a matter of definition a relation between changes in investment and changes in income (Y):

$$\Delta Y = 1/(1 - c). \; \Delta I$$

where c is defined as the ratio of the actual change in consumption to the actual change in income. This is not a theory but a truism, a relation between realized (or, as the Swedes would say, *ex post*) values. It serves to make the point that with the exception of the case – which we would argue was so rare as not to deserve consideration – that C does not respond to changes in Y at all, changes in I will have a magnified or *multiplied* effect on income.

Some history of the multiplier

Though the multiplier, in the causal form which I shall shortly explain, is now associated with Mr. R.F. Kahn's 1931 article and with the first edition of this book, it has a longer, and rather curious, history.[1] It had long been understood that a rise in employment in one part of the economy would have favourable repercussions elsewhere. This had been discussed in terms of primary and secondary employment, which referred to employment in one industry giving rise to employment in the industries which supplied it with parts and raw materials. These favourable repercussions, known as secondary employment, were part of the mechanism by which an economy disturbed from full employment would be led back to it (the orthodox doctrine of the self-righting economy).

While in the case of the private sector secondary employment was viewed entirely favourably, it was feared by some that stimulation by government loan expenditure, not constrained by the need to make sufficient profit, would lead to an infinite expansion, and hence inevitably to inflation.

Mr Kahn's employment multiplier alters this debate: first, by broadening the source of secondary employment to stress the increased consumption of the newly employed workers; and second, showing, by the simple device of a convergent series, that while the number of induced expansion terms was indeed infinite, their sum was finite so long as there were 'leakages' from the industrial circulation. Mr Kahn noted especially the diversion of expenditure to imports, which would stimulate employment abroad, not at home. A considerable literature on the foreign trade multiplier now makes use of this contribution.[2]

The multiplier was just what was needed to complete the case, begun in *Can Lloyd George Do It?* (with H.D. Henderson, *C.W.* IX: 86–125), for public works in time of deep depressions. I first presented it in a memorandum to the Committee of Economists of the Economic Advisory Council in

September 1930, having seen a draft of Mr Kahn's article (*C.W.* XIII: 178–200). I then wrote on it for the *New Statesman* in 1933 and included that material in the American version of *The Means to Prosperity* (*C.W.* IX: 335–66).

From truism to theory

In order to adapt Mr Kahn's theory to a closed economy and simultaneously to turn the truism with which the chapter began into a theory, it suffices to reinterpret *c*. It is also convenient to change the focus from employment to income. In Chapters 8 and 9 of the first edition, the concept of the propensity to consume was developed, based on a variety of subjective and objective factors, most of which relate the propensity to consume ultimately to income. Consumption and income are defined in wage-units, as the relation between them is more stable than between money-values of the same variables. The marginal propensity to consume, *c*, is the first derivative of this function and, as argued in the earlier chapters, is assumed to take a value between 0 and 1.[3] It differs from *c* in the above equation in indicating people's consumption plans, or their behaviour when fully appraised of and adjusted to the level of income. As explained in Chapter 3 of the first edition, consumption expenditure is well anticipated by firms, so that production of C-goods normally adjusts quickly to demand. In equilibrium, of course, it is fully adjusted. Under these assumptions the relation

$$\Delta Y_w = 1/(1 - c).\Delta I_w$$

'holds good continuously, without time-lag, at all moments of time' (*C.W.* VII: 111). It is a *logical* relation between variables when the effects of a change in investment expenditure on the economy as a whole are foreseen. It represents a state of continuous equilibrium, though that equilibrium may move as I_w changes. I have called it the logical theory of the multiplier.[4]

It can be seen that the difference in equilibrium income consequent on a higher level of investment is, when the effects are fully worked through, larger by the amount $1/(1 - c)$ than the alteration in investment itself. Let us call the multiplier, $1/(1 - c)$, the investment multiplier, to distinguish it from Mr Kahn's employment multiplier. It is obvious that the multiplier is the larger the greater is the MPC. Thus one can say that in poorer countries, where almost all income is consumed, a small amount of investment can have an effect on income much larger than in richer countries.

A dynamic multiplier

Equilibrium relations are the culmination of causal forces, though in concentrating on equilibrium the causal forces are not revealed. This causal relation can only really come into play, however, when the multiplier takes its dynamic form. Let the story begin with an increase in investment of 1, which immediately raises income by the same amount. This will cause consumption to rise by c, which in turn raises income Y_w by the amount c. Consumption responds further (by c^2) and so on. The sum of the series $1 + c + c^2 + \ldots + c^n$ is the multiplier, $1/(1 - c)$. It is only the final outcome which corresponds to the 'logical theory'.

The system is complicated in the more usual case in which an investment decision takes several periods to complete. This can be described by overlapping multipliers of this type. The system of a permanently elevated level of new investment will occupy us later in discussing the finance of this process.

A digression on saving and investment

It follows from the fact that saving and consumption are mutually exclusive and exhaustive dispositions of income that $1 - c$ is the marginal propensity to save (s). Yet I have not used the simpler formulation $1/s$ in the multiplier. Both the logical theory and the dynamic multiplier assume that the aggregate of consumption choices have been met, in the first with full foresight and in the second with knowledge of the immediate past. It is aggregate saving which is systematically surprised in the transition phase of the dynamic multiplier. This conforms to the following statement, which I made about aggregates in Chapter 4 on the definition of income:

> Clearness of mind . . . is best reached, perhaps, by thinking in terms of decisions to consume (or to refrain from consuming) rather than of decisions to save. A decision to consume or not to consume truly lies within the power of the individual; . . . [but the] amounts of aggregate income and of aggregate saving are the *results* of the free choices of individuals whether or not to consume and whether or not to invest; but they are neither of them capable of assuming an independent value resulting from a separate set of decisions taken irrespective of the decisions concerning consumption and investment. In accordance with this principle, the conception of the *propensity to consume* will, in what follows, take the place of the propensity or disposition to save.
>
> (*C.W.* VII: 64–5, emphasis in original)

Yet it is still true that at every stage of the multiplier actual saving equals actual investment. And of course in equilibrium planned consumption plus investment equals income; this could be phrased as planned saving (in the sense of sY_w) being equal to investment, though for the reasons stated above this is not recommended. But in the transition expressed by the dynamic multiplier saving may bear little relation to people's intentions because changes in income are not fully foreseen.

V. CHICK

Practical significance of the multiplier

The importance of the multiplier for my theory is to show the mechanism by which a change in an autonomous variable is amplified by induced changes in income (I shall consider rises, as the story is less depressing). It is all very well to derive the properties of the equilibrium of a system, but if there is no mechanism which shows how the system moves from one equilibrium to another, the result is of little practical value. We needed to show that unemployment equilibrium was possible and stable, and also that there was a finite stop to expansion; the multiplier serves that latter purpose.

If the rise in income is significant, the marginal propensity to consume may fall in the later stages of the multiplier process. Furthermore, as production increases in the short period (i.e. with capital fixed) the share of profits increases at the expense of the share of wages. This too may cause the aggregate MPC to fall.

A lagged response to an increase in investment must be regarded as the normal case, but it brings with it complications, such as changes in the relative prices of consumption and investment goods beyond the changes necessitated by different degrees of diminishing returns in the two groups of industries. If the rise in income occasioned by investment is not foreseen, so that consumption demand lags behind the change in income[5] and production of consumption goods lags behind demand, prices of wage-goods will rise above their equilibrium level for a time. This is reflected in a temporary departure of the marginal propensity to consume from its normal value, followed by a gradual return to it. (This case is analysed in the first edition, C.W. VII: 124.) I have assumed rather than proved that the end result of such an expansion would be the same whether the initial rise was anticipated or not, though the paths would of course be different.

The multiplier has been one of the most successful features of *The General Theory*, in that the basic idea has been widely and quickly accepted. This is not surprising, for it has important policy conclusions. I emphasize investment, but if one substitutes government expenditure one has the proposition that a small stimulus will provoke the private sector into the expansion one needs. Fiscal policy becomes quite powerful. However, even in the first edition I issued several caveats.

Reservations

My theory is based on the interaction of investment, which is subject to unpredictable variation, and a stable relation between consumption and investment. Yet if investment were completely unstable there would be no point to the multiplier – or indeed my theory. In real life perhaps only the first few rounds would be observed. The multiplier remains, however, an important part of my theory, for it concerns the transition from one equilibrium to another. Thus while I have concentrated much attention on the properties of equilibrium, my theory is not equilibrium theory: it pertains to disequilibrium too.

A stable relation between consumption and income (in wage units) is a fundamental assumption. But as I have already indicated, changes in the distribution of income, either as between rich and poor *per se* or as between wage-earners and profit-earners (related to the first point but not the same) will tend to lower the MPC as income rises. Then there is the fact that I have assumed a closed economy, ignoring the matter of spending abroad which was the main subject of Mr Kahn's article. In so far as consumption demand is for imported goods, the MPC overestimates the multiplier.

Other caveats affect the multiplicand. The multiplicand in the exposition so far has been net investment – net to allow for the fact that some of the unanticipated rise in consumption may be met out of stocks, a disinvestment to be set against the original investment.

The offsetting influence of changes in stocks has been included (*C.W.* VII: 124)[6] but other possible offsets were not. Two were mentioned in the first edition. First, 'with the confused psychology which often prevails, [a] Government programme may, through its effect on "confidence", increase liquidity-preference or diminish the marginal efficiency of capital' (page 120), a factor which I consider irrational but particularly potent in times of strong 'free market' sentiment.

The second factor concerns finance: the means of financing the policy and the increased need for working capital which accompanies expansion may increase the rate of interest unless the monetary authorities take countervailing action. This may cause an offsetting reduction in the rate of private investment. This factor, of course, can be equally potent in the case of private investment; I am not sure why I chose to mention it only in the case of public works.[7]

However, the dynamic multiplier, which is the expression of the multiplier in historical time, is intimately involved with the question of the finance of the initial investment or government expenditure. Amongst my colleagues there are opposing views on how to handle this matter: those of Mr Kahn[8] and of Mr D.H. Robertson (1936, 1937 and 1938a, b). I also had the benefit of the views of Mr Hicks (1936), Mr Hawtrey (1937b) and Professor Ohlin (1937b).

Finance and the multiplier

One of the features of the multiplier which so excited readers at *The General Theory*'s first publication was the implication that, at the end of the multiplier, sufficient saving is generated to 'finance' the investment which began the process. Mr Kahn remained of this view,[9] attacking particularly the attempt, as he saw it, to co-opt the theory of the multiplier into the framework of the quantity theory of money. Though he does not say so, this clearly refers to the period construction of Mr Robertson, of which I shall have more to say below. In emphasizing as strongly as I did the perpetual equality of saving and investment I further contributed to this conclusion. Responses to the critics listed above (Keynes 1937a, b, 1938c; see also 1939d), after the publication of the first edition, have taken these points further.

I was perhaps too anxious not to give any quarter to the loanable funds theory to pursue the question of the finance of investment very far. In particular I rejected the proposition, to which Professor Ohlin subscribed, that the rate of interest depends on the supply of new credit, which he relates to *ex ante* saving, and the demand for credit arising out of *ex ante* investment (*C.W.* XIV: 216). In Chapter 13 of the first edition I simply assumed that the current rate of interest as determined by liquidity preference would hold in the face of whatever demands investment placed upon credit markets.

Although I mentioned the possibility that loan-financed government expenditure might cause interest rates to rise unless the monetary authorities took countervailing action (page 119), or unless the conditions of credit are relaxed (page 201), I did not develop this point. In fact, I paid scant attention to the source of funds for investment, only to the terms: 'The schedule of the marginal efficiency of capital may be said to govern the terms on which loanable funds are demanded for the purpose of investment; whilst the rate of interest governs the terms on which funds are being currently supplied' (page 165). This strategy followed my practice, in the first edition, of dealing explicitly with money only after it had been created, not discussing how it came into being.

I continued that strategy in developing the idea of the 'finance motive', for I treated this as a motive for holding money in preparation for investment expenditure. In Keynes (1937b) I defined 'finance' as the 'credit required in the interval between planning and execution' (*C.W.* XIV: 216, n. 1). It is clear that this finance cannot be supplied by *ex ante* saving. It must be found by a release of cash on the part of the entrepreneur (internal finance) or of the rest of the public; the terms of that finance are determined by the existing state of liquidity preference and the policy of the banking system regarding the money supply (*C.W.* XIV: 217).

During the period between arranging finance and spending it, someone, the entrepreneur, a bank or a direct lender, must accept to become less liquid to satisfy this 'finance motive'. Once spent, the money returns to the banking system and the bank's liquidity is restored. The money can, as it were, be used again; this is the 'revolving fund' of finance (*C.W.* XIV: 219). In an overdraft system, if the banks do not count a rise in unused overdrafts as a diminution of liquidity, the position is exactly as I described it in my first edition.

Later (1939d) I distinguished two aspects of the financial background to investment expenditure: the funds needed to get an investment project started, and longer-term means of funding that investment, which ideally should last for as long as the investment is on the firm's books as a capital asset. It is only the first of these which is properly called finance. It is quite clear that finance in the sense of funds used to start a project cannot be forthcoming at the *end* of a process which runs through real time; it is necessary to have them at the beginning. Therefore it is impossible for saving to finance investment except in a steady-state equilibrium which has been going on for some time.

In my *Economic Journal* article of 1939 I introduced

> a conception . . . of 'funds available for investment' under the name of 'finance' which . . . covers equally the use of the revolving pool of funds to finance the production of capital goods or the production of consumption goods or (e.g.) an increased turnover on the stock exchange. In the same way the conception of the rate of interest as being determined by liquidity preference emphasises the fact that *all* demands for liquid funds compete on an equal basis for the available supply . . . [W]hilst saving takes place concurrently with investment . . . the flow of funds . . . available for investment (in the sense of the first acquisition of this capital good by a permanent holder) takes place subsequently; the bridging of this time-lag by 'finance' (i.e. by the supply of money) being the function of the credit system (which is solely concerned with finance and never with saving).
>
> (*C.W.* XIV: 283–4)

PART II
Victoria Chick writing as herself

There are three issues in the material presented above which were widely debated: the nature of the multiplier from the point of view of method, the related issue of the equality or identity of saving and investment, and the role of finance.

The nature of the multiplier

The multiplier appears in several versions which are methodologically distinct: a definition, a moving rational expectations equilibrium, a comparative statics equilibrium and a process. On the interpretation of the logical theory of the multiplier, I believe the jury is still out, and what I have put in Keynes's mouth in the first part of this chapter is controversial.[10]

Some would say that the multiplier is a 'fifth wheel', offering nothing new; I believe these are people to whom equilibrium is the only interesting part of theory and I have had Keynes argue against this view (thus siding with Robertson against Kahn!), although he was certainly in two minds in the first edition (documented in Chick 1983: 253–4, 269–70).

Much textbook discussion has been devoted to developing the implications of a once-for-all investment as opposed to a new level of continuous investment. The point, I suppose, was to choose between the two interpretations, but no conclusion was ever reached. The only interesting point to note in the textbook treatment is the transformation of a theory of income (production) into a theory of expenditure and from wage-units into output-units ('real terms').

The transformation of the multiplier into a theory of expenditure is a victory for Hawtrey's expenditure interpretation over Keynes's production multiplier and is part of the neoclassical project to return Keynes's model of a monetary production economy to the real exchange economy which he had set out to overturn. To embrace the expenditure version fully we must accept the most difficult aspect of the 'logical theory': that production, not only of consumption goods but also of capital goods, always correctly anticipates demand (an early example of strong rational expectations!). If understood consciously, this assumption would rob *The General Theory* of its central novelty: the insistence on uncertainty as the central fact of market capitalism. But this implication was not recognized: the production side of the multiplier was simply forgotten altogether and *The General Theory* became a theory of aggregate demand (exchange) to which the 'missing' supply side (production, in the shape of exchange of inputs for outputs) was later added.

The transformation from wage units to 'real terms' was the second part of the project. Embedded in it is the idea that Keynes assumed fixed prices – a belief which flies in the face of all the evidence. The evidence in the context of the multiplier comes from the opening of section iv, Chapter 10:

> The discussion has been carried on, so far, on the basis of a change in aggregate investment which has been foreseen sufficiently in advance for the consumption industries to advance *pari passu* with the capital-goods industries without more disturbance to the price of consumption-goods than is consequential, in conditions of decreasing returns, on an increase in the quantity which is produced.
>
> (*C.W.* VII: 122)

Belief in diminishing returns is not the issue, only that prices alter systematically with output – and even a hardened Kaleckian must see that there are limits to constant returns. If prices are allowed to alter, the multiplier can be used as a theory of inflation[11] as the economy approaches, and when it reaches, full capacity and/or full employment.

Finally, there is the matter of the multiplier as an equilibrium condition or something true by definition. This is related to the vexed question of the identity or equality of saving and investment. One is struck with how muddled the issues were in that debate,[12] and recent contributions still confuse identities with statements about volition (e.g. Moore 1994; Dalziel 1996). I have tried in the first part of the chapter to set out the matter as I think Keynes might have understood it, but it will do no harm to rehearse some of the arguments.

Saving and investment

Lange (1938b: 620) has written that

> The recent discussion of the question whether saving and investment are identically equal or equal only in equilibrium reveals among economists an astonishing attachment to words. For many an economist it seems easier to shift from German or French to English, or *vice versa*, than to change his pet definition of the word 'saving'. Such tenacity really deserves to be applied to a better cause . . .

Lange goes on to establish, at least to his own satisfaction, that the conflict between Keynes's, Robertson's and the Swedish concepts of saving are reducible to definitional differences and that none of them have pride of place in causal analysis.

But surely the resolution of the dilemma in terms of *ex ante* and *ex post* magnitudes is exactly about what is definitional and what is causal.[13] The causal element is the propensity to consume, but in aggregate there can be no presumption that the aggregate of individual decisions will result in the expected outcomes. This is the fallacy of composition. There is, however, an asymmetry in the treatment of consumption and saving by Keynes; recall the passage cited on p. 167 above. 'A decision to consume or not to consume truly lies within the power of the individual', but not so with saving.

Myra Curtis (1938: 623) makes perhaps the central point in the debate: that

> 'the difference between income and consumption-expenditure' covers two different concepts:
>
> (a) the extent to which the income of a period is disposed of in the period otherwise than by consumption-expenditure,
> (b) the increase in the assets of which the savers find themselves in possession at the end of the period,
>
> and that the theorem $S = I$ is consequently a portmanteau presentation of two statements, one being a mere identity and the other a proposition which cannot be substantiated.

Saving in sense (a) is determined by savers; saving in sense (b) is determined by investors. Had she added that saving in sense (a) concerns individual behaviour, albeit aggregated, and saving in sense (b) pertains directly to aggregates, we would be home and dry. Here is Keynes, replying to Hawtrey:

> In spite of my best efforts to explain the contrary to him, Mr Hawtrey is convinced that I have so defined saving and investment that they are not merely *equal* but *identical* . . . [I]t is only aggregate saving and aggregate investment which are . . . necessarily equal in the same way in which aggregate purchases . . . are equal to aggregate sales. But this does not mean that 'buying' and 'selling' are identical terms, and that the laws of supply and demand are meaningless.
>
> (*C.W.* XIV: 211–12)

To restate the proposition made in the first part of this chapter, aggregate saving is determined by income, according, at the individual level, to the propensity to consume. Aggregate income, however, is determined not by savers but by investors.[14] Only in equilibrium is the income expected by savers equal to actual income, and therefore only in equilibrium are saving intentions realized. Thus Keynes was correct to say that income is the factor in his theory that brings saving and investment into equality; the accusation that he had proposed a mechanism to preserve an identity (see, for example, the references cited in Lipsey 1972) is false.

Finance

The impression has been hard to dislodge that saving finances investment, if not at the beginning then certainly at the end of the multiplier process. As pointed out at the beginning of this chapter, this can only be the case in the stationary state. Robertson was surely right when he complained that the multiplier theory which gave this result paid attention only to the final equilibrium and not to the process.[15]

Very quickly after the publication of *The General Theory* Keynes acknowledged the role of bank finance in the initial investment but only in the most implausible context: that entrepreneurs required *cash* (as opposed to bank deposits) in the interval between the decision to invest and the execution of that decision.[16] He even admitted that it was implausible by bringing in the overdraft, which after all has always been the credit instrument of British banking. No cash is then required, only a line of credit. The question thus shifts to the willingness of the banks to become less liquid.

This line of reasoning Keynes denied, on the grounds that once the money is returned to the banking system liquidity is restored. This position is explained by Richardson (1986): when the money is spent (assuming, with Keynes, that the money was withdrawn in the first place), it returns to the banking system and restores the reserves lost when the cash is with-drawn. This restores $(100 - x)$ per cent of liquidity, where x is the (percentage) reserve ratio, but does not restore it 100 per cent, because the loan portfolio and the level of deposits have risen. In an overdraft system, the same point can be made, provided, as seems reasonable, that banks can be described as less liquid when an overdraft arrangement is actually used.

Robertson, however, would not accept this: he accused Keynes of

confusion as to what is the process by which, and the moment at which, the illiquidity taken on itself by the banking system in the provision of 'finance' is cancelled . . . [–] as soon as the bank loan is *used*, [or is] the liquidity of the bank . . . only restored by the *repayment* of the loan out of the proceeds of the sale of the goods (whether consumption goods or capital goods) in furthering the production of which it has been used.

(*C.W.* XIV: 228)

In reply, Keynes accused Robertson of 'thinking of "finance" as con-sisting in bank loans, whereas in the article under discussion I introduced the term to mean the *cash* temporarily held' (ibid.: 229). Keynes favours this formulation as preserving intact his liquidity preference, although in emphasizing cash he rather goes back on his choice, in the first edition (page 167, note 1), to treat money as 'co-extensive with bank deposits'.

As Graziani (1984) pointed out, in effect Keynes was trying to deal with an increase in the money supply by a construction devised to deal with money demand. The general consensus amongst Post-Keynesians is that Keynes's finance motive really has posed the problem in too trivial a way.

The second debate on finance[17] went over the same ground again; Asimakopulos (1983b) was of Robertson's persuasion that full liquidity is only restored by repayment, and that repayment will only come about at the end of the multiplier process; therefore saving finances investment.

On the matter of liquidity I cannot side with either Keynes/Richardson or Robertson/Asimakopulos. Strictly speaking, when banks expand their lending they always become less liquid, as the ratio of their reserves to deposits will fall, but it is also true that the *bulk* of liquidity is restored when the loan is spent – if money leaves the banking system at all. It would seem that, if the reserve requirement is 10 per cent, Keynes was 90 per cent correct, Robertson 10 per cent. Average reserve holdings of British banks are now about 3 per cent; Keynes is getting more right all the time – but not 100 per cent.

To assume that bank loans are the main source of finance for investment *at the margin* (i.e. for that investment which represents a rise above the previous equilibrium level),[18] is not only sensible and once espoused even by Keynes,[19] it also explains how it is that investment is independent of current income and why investment is, with a modern banking system, independent of saving. Let us take these points in turn.

Current income, for individual agents, is a cash flow. For households it can be expected to pay for recurrent expenditures (consumption); for firms it should cover the wage bill and possibly some working capital. It is large, lumpy expenditures which are usually financed by borrowing. Thus investment is both independent of current income for its motivation (which is long-term expectations of profit) and for its finance.

Bank lending, like the asset side of any company balance sheet, needs to be balanced by liabilities (funded). Retail banks are mainly funded by deposits. Banks first attracted deposits as a means of holding savings, but once bank deposits are used widely as means of payment, deposits are transactions balances as well as savings: the funds used to pay for consumption as well as to 'hold savings' flow through the banking system and fund lending. Thus 'saving has no special efficacy, as compared with consumption, in releasing cash and restoring liquidity' (*C.W.* XIV: 229; see also 233). The fact that the result of bank lending – new deposits – are willingly accepted means that banks *create* (money-)income when they increase their lending. If the loan is used to finance real output, real income rises as well.

To see this, Robertson's process analysis is instructive. Robertson used a lagged consumption function,

$$C_t = cY_{t-1}$$

and from the fact that $C_t + S_t = 1$ we have that

$$S_t = (1 - c)Y_{t-1}$$

(Since we are dealing with changes we ignore the constant.) In Table 11.1 we represent the consumption and saving derived from this formulation as C_R and S_R (for Robertson). We shall for the moment impose Robertson's consumption hypothesis on Keynes, but allow him to keep his own definition of saving:

$$S_t = Y_t - C_t$$

We shall call this S_K. Taking Robertson's assumption of bank-financed investment and a one-off rise in investment of 1 unit gives the results of Table 11.1. Values are differences from the previous period.

The first two periods are enough to make the point that the two definitions of saving (Curtis's saving types (a) and (b) respectively) give different results. Since Robertson's definition specifies *ex ante* intention and Keynes's definition is the difference between two *ex post* values, the difference must be something which savers did not expect: namely, the increase in investment (and hence income). The difference between S_K and S_R in any time period is unintended saving.[20]

Table 11.1 Two definitions of saving

Period	I_t	Y_{t-1}	C_{Rt}	S_{Rt}	ΔM_t	Y_t	S_{Kt}
0	1	0	0	0	1	1	1
1	0	1	c	$1-c$	0	c	0
2	0	c	c^2	$c(1-c)$	0	c^2	0
.	.	.	.	.	.	.	.
.	.	.	.	.	.	.	.
.	.	.	.	.	.	.	.
n	0	c^{n-1}	c^n	$c^{n-2}(1-c)$	0	0	0
Σ_0^n	1	$1/(1-c)$	$c/(1-c)$	1	1	$1/(1-c)$	1

What *form* does the unexpected saving take? Not, *pace* hundreds of textbooks, inventories. Rather, from the discussion of the banking system, it is clear that unexpected saving is the new deposits which arose from the lending that financed the investment.[21]

The unintended acquisition of bank deposits is a truly macroeconomic outcome; it is not the sum of individual decisions anywhere in the economy, but rather a consequence of the money-creating property of bank lending, which in turn rests on the general acceptability of bank liabilities.[22]

Here Keynes picks up the story (in the context of government expenditure) of what happens to the new money:

> The new level of income . . . will not continue sufficiently high for the requirements of M_1 to absorb the whole of the increase in M; and some portion of the money will seek an outlet in buying securities or other assets until r has fallen . . . to the extent that the new money is absorbed either in M_2 or in the M_1 which corresponds to the rise in Y caused by the fall in r.
>
> (*C.W.* VII: 200)

The saving which in the first period is an unintended increase in money balances is subsequently allocated to transactions balances, securities and idle balances – intentionally. Naturally, the change in the rate of interest is another disturbing influence on the multiplier, from which Keynes abstracts. There is one circumstance in which no such changes will take place: that is if all (intended) saving which is directed to securities is matched, period by period, by new issues,[23] while all the other influences on liquidity preference remain unchanged.

This condition (though wildly implausible) is worth discussing, as the counterpart to this condition is that all saving directed to new securities presents firms with 'new money' (borrowed funds). By contrast, if exact matching of flow supplies and demands is not maintained and some savers buy from existing holders, the previous holders get a capital gain; but this is merely a transfer of assets, not new lending.

Our condition, though implausible, is mild compared to the assumption made by loanable-funds theorists: for them, saving was defined to exclude 'hoarding', and was equivalent to lending. This was perhaps a plausible assumption when markets for secondhand securities were undeveloped and a loan to business enterprise really was more or less 'permanent and indissoluble, like marriage' (*C.W.* VII: 160); but it is obviously quite unsuited to a country with developed capital markets, for it implies not only that *all* saving goes into securities but also that this flow of funds is exactly matched by new issues. The recognition of the importance of markets for seasoned securities opens up a position which conforms neither to strict liquidity preference, where flows can have no influence on the rate of interest, nor to loanable funds, where stocks do not matter at all. This is the position we are adopting here.[24]

When firms capture saving by making new issues, firms are increasing their long-term liabilities and *funding* their investment.[25] They may use the funds so acquired to repay the bank loans which initiated the investment. Since this will diminish the money supply, there will be further repercussions on the rate of interest, which we here ignore.

In the last line of the multiplier process of Table 11.1 we have the cumulative result: all saving is 'intended' and the cumulative total is equal to investment. In a loanable funds story the column S_R gives also the purchase and new supply of securities. We should expect to see some negative terms in the ΔM column, as banks are repaid and deposits are thereby extinguished. The final result according to loanable-funds theory should be a money supply restored to its original level and the entire investment funded.[26]

On these assumptions, Asimakopulos (1983b) would be right on one point: at the end of the multiplier, the banks are repaid out of savings. However, although the bank's liquidity has been fully restored (repayment restores the reserve ratio by reducing the size of the balance sheet), overall liquidity is even less than before, according to ordinary reckoning, for short-term loans have given way to long loans and the increased liquidity represented by new money has been extinguished. And the repayment has come, not from sales and profit, where Asimakopulos expected it, but from funding.[27]

Repayment from sales is the culmination, not of a short-period process like the multiplier, where the criterion of equilibrium is whether production is sold at the prices firms expected, but rather of a long-period process by which it is discovered whether the investment was a good idea or not – that is, whether the marginal efficiency of capital turned out to be adequate to repay the loan which supported the investment throughout its productive life (the funding). This is the province of the long run – not an area Keynes thought it fruitful to explore: it was too far away and too much could happen in the meantime. The question of final repayment is well outside the purview of the multiplier.

Once we break with loanable-funds theory and allow saving to be allocated not only to the purchase of new issues but also to seasoned issues, idle balances and larger transactions balances, it is clear that the whole of the original bank loan will not be extinguished by the end of the process. Some of the repayment must come from gross profit: that is, from sales – in other words, consumption. How much, the multiplier analysis does not allow us to say, but the principle is important, for it illustrates the central point on which Keynes consistently insisted: that not only bank lending but also repayment depends on consumption every bit as much as it depends on saving.

For completeness, consider a multiplier scheme based on continuous investment (Table 11.2; its form is taken from Studart 1995: 52, Table 4.2). The table gives the succession of intended or Robertsonian saving flows with investment increasing each period by 1. Studart makes the point that textbook treatments of the multiplier concentrate on the horizontal sum and not on the vertical. The latter shows that once the steady state is reached for the first round of investment (at N) the whole of next period's investment could in principle be financed by saving – provided, as before, that all saving goes into new issues.

Thus while in the case of the once-for-all investment, saving funds investment, in the continuous case concurrent, intentional saving is sufficient to *finance* new investment once the new steady-state equilibrium is reached. This leaves no saving left over for any funding to take place.

The implications of the continuous-investment case are clear: at the end of the multiplier there is a considerable accumulation of debt (bank loans) and the money supply has risen by at least[28] $1/(1 - c)$. No bank debt is even funded, let alone paid back.

Table 11.2 Overlapping multipliers

Period	1	2	3	...	N	N + 1	S_R
1	$1 - c$	$c(1 - c)$	$c^2(1 - c)$	...	$c^N(1 - c)$		1
2		$1 - c$	$c(1 - c)$	...	$c^{N-1}(1 - c)$	$c^N(1 - c)$	1
3			$1 - c$	...	$c^{N-2}(1 - c)$	$c^{N-1}(1 - c)$	< 1
.	.	.	.	.	.	.	.
.	.	.	.	.	.	.	.
N					$1 - c$	$c(1 - c)$	< 1
N + 1						$(1 - c)$	< 1
S_R	$1 - c$	$1 - c^2$	$1 - c^3$	...	$1 - c^N$	$1 - c^{N+1}$	

NOTES

* I am grateful for the helpful comments of Adriana Moreira Amado, Geoff Harcourt and Maria Cristina Marcuzzo. Adriana very kindly compiled the bibliography. I am solely responsible for any remaining errors.

1 See also my correspondence with Mr Colin Clark (*C.W.* XII: 804–7). [Keynes's history was perhaps an example of that selective attention for which Cambridge has an unfortunate reputation. As Clarke (1988), Davis (1980), Dimand (1988) and Moggridge (1992) remind us, Hawtrey and Giblin also are important in the history of the multiplier. Giblin's was an independent discovery (1930) in Australia and would have been communicated to Keynes after he had absorbed the message from Kahn. The Hawtrey story is more mysterious. Although Hawtrey prepared a critique of the *Treatise on Money* for the Macmillan Committee which includes a section on the multiplier (Davis 1980) as a 'last-minute addition in December 1930' (Clarke 1988: 242), and they naturally corresponded about it, Keynes omits to mention his contribution.]

   The role of Meade in developing his 'Relation' (Kahn 1931: 187n) is probably to shift attention – disastrously in my view – from the role of consumption to the role of saving, and to reinforce Kahn in his determination to look only at the end-point of the analysis. Shackle (1951: 242n) states quite categorically: 'Mr. Meade's contribution was the equality, *ex post*, of saving and investment.' This is not Meade's own interpretation (1993). I would characterize his approach as Robertsonian.

   [The contribution of Warming 'around the 1930s' includes two articles in Danish (1931 and 1932, not cited here) and one in English in the *Economic Journal* (1932) (Hegeland 1954: 5, 39n). He is first rehabilitated by Shackle (1951). See also Boserup (1969).]

2 See Haberler (1941: 461–73) and references cited there.

3 Since my theory has been devised to hold for a closed economy, I could not rely on a foreign 'leakage'. The full theory must include an explanation of 'leakages' in a closed economy; this involves a confrontation with the classical assertion that all money not consumed is automatically invested. This will be the subject of subsequent chapters.

4 [There are resonances here with Joan Robinson's 'logical time', though as far as the present author knows, she did not use the term – at least in print – until 1962 (see Robinson 1962b: 23–9; 1974).]

5 This point is emphasized by Mr D.H. Robertson. His perspective is essentially that of the individual's behaviour, such that consumption only occurs after income has been earned. I, on the other hand, have taken the view that consumption in aggregate is determined as much by current and even expected income as by past income. This reflects that fact that my basic time-unit is 'the shortest interval after which the firm is free to revise its decision as to how much employment to offer' (*C.W.* VII: 47n). It is only at the end of such a period (let us call it a 'production period') that aggregate income, the wage bill *plus* profits, is determined. Wages are paid more frequently and consumption takes place not only on receipt of wages but also, to some extent, in their anticipation. Even more reasonable is the idea of consumption out of anticipated profits. Thus when consumption lags behind income in my theory this represents a lag in adjustment, where for Mr Robertson this lag is structural and systematic.

6 [This would surprise the writers of 'Keynesian' textbooks. The textbook resolution of actual and intended investment rests on unintended changes in

inventories. Somewhat ironically (see note 1), this is Hawtrey, not Keynes. Hawtrey worked within the production period, when output was already determined, so this was the only adjustment possible. Keynes's short period, encompassing as it does several production periods, allows for adjustment of current output and price. See also note 13 below.]

7 See also first edition [*C.W.* VII: 200].

8 [Although these views were expressed most clearly in print after Keynes's lifetime (Kahn 1984), the present author assumes they were the same during Keynes's lifetime and that he knew of them.]

9 [Throughout his life (see Kahn 1984: 103–4). 'Kahn's very early quantity theory stance had the flavour of pre-analytic intuition or even – as he himself was ready to admit – prejudice' (Dardi 1994: 92; he cites Kahn 1984: 52).]

10 I have changed my own position as compared to my interpretation in 1983 (Chick 1983: 267, n. 2). There, the logical theory is represented as an *ex post* relationship. Somewhat to my surprise, on reviewing Hansen (1953) for this piece, I found his argument convincing.

   Shackle's interpretation (1965: 64) differs yet again: he supposes that what 'holds good continuously' is the MPC, not the multiplier at all.

11 In the draft Table of Contents of *The General Theory* from 1933, the chapter on 'The Multiplier' was part of Book IV: 'The Theory of Prices' (*C.W.* XIV: 422).

12 Harcourt (1994b: 10) has argued that Keynes was 'not clear in his own mind' about the distinction between the identity and equality of saving and investment. The quotations offered below (p. 174 and note 21) should demonstrate that he was perfectly clear. It is his successors who have not distinguished between the aggregate of intended saving and aggregate saving which includes unanticipated (but in some sense not involuntary – see the discussion of forced saving in Chick 1983) acquisitions of bank deposits.

13 That this resolution in Keynesian textbooks depends on unintended investment (positive or negative) is, however, completely unsatisfactory, since it refers to the immediate response, within the production period, to falsified sales expectations. Zero unintended investment only indicates that expectations are met for that period, but to establish short-period equilibrium one needs a succession of production periods.

14 This is the point of which it is hardest to convince neoclassical economists. For them, saving is the result of inter-temporal choice and those microeconomic decisions are simply aggregated to obtain an aggregate saving function which is on a par with aggregate investment. Their whole ideology is that at least all parties should have equal power; at best, households direct the operations of firms. Keynes's system is uncomfortable, for it speaks loudly of the powerlessness of households, both as suppliers of labour and as savers.

15 Kahn did not only accept this: he stuck doggedly to consideration only of the equilibrium position (1931: 183n; 1984: 102–4). There was a political point to arguing that saving financed investment: it allays the Ricardian fears of inflation, which according to that system must occur when investment is not financed by 'genuine' saving. The Bundesbank holds this view today.

16 This assumption is even less acceptable than that made in Shaw–McKinnon financial liberalization models, where entrepreneurs are portrayed as accumulating bank deposits before investing. Studart (1995) has aptly described this as treating banks as if they were safes. Keynes puts the safe, as it were, in the manager's office.

17 A full bibliography can be found in Dalziel (1996).

18 See Chick (1988) for an explanation of the significance of marginal investment here.

19 Trevithick (1994) points out that this had been Keynes's assumption in *Lloyd George* and *Prosperity*. In *The General Theory* and after, despite the obvious acknowledgements of the need to relax credit in expansions, he resisted it.

20 Wonderful! Keynes and Robertson reconciled (the subject of a paper I gave at the annual meeting of economists in Brazil in 1986 and never published). But this neat resolution does not work if new credit finances a rise in autonomous consumption instead of investment.

21 See Chick (1983: 236–8); I place the discussion in the context of the earlier 'forced saving' debate. Moore (1988) calls this unintended saving 'convenience lending', which is too volitional for my taste – but then, he does not distinguish between acceptance of money and demand for it.

Shackle (1951) struggled with the question of why saving, and not consumption, should be a residual. This point would have clinched the matter. It also makes clear why Keynes says, in the context of saving always exactly keeping pace with investment, that '[a]s for the concept of *ex ante* saving, I can attach no sound sense to it' (*C.W.* XIV: 210 and n.). He clearly means aggregate saving, for on the next page we have: 'it is only aggregate saving and aggregate investment which are equal'. Thus also, Hegeland (1954: 58) is wrong when he criticizes Keynes for adopting 'Marshallian thinking in terms of aggregates, where [Sigma] micro = macro'. Clearly that applies to saving, and the multiplier, only in equilibrium.

22 Chick (1983: 189–91; 1986).

23 Davidson's (1972) marginal propensity to buy 'placements' (technically, a term for securities placed privately rather than through the open market, but here simply meaning securities) is not sufficient for our needs, for only new issues allow funding to take place.

24 Terzi (1986–7) has called me a loanable-funds theorist for daring to look sympathetically at Robertson (Chick 1983: ch. 14). J.C. Gilbert, a most sophisticated student of these matters, has expressed the opinion that a theory of finance must be either one or the other. They are mistaken.

25 This role for saving was first sketched in Chick (1983: 262–3) and developed in Chick (1984). See also Davidson (1986). The best-developed exposition is in Studart (1995).

26 Kaldor (1939–40) made quite the opposite assumption – and was worried about a different problem. For him the problem was how to get the multiplier to work without a change in the rate of interest. His solution was to have speculators play the role of the residual suppliers of securities; the increasing saving would put the speculators under pressure but their stocks might be adequate to meet it.

This solution in effect prevents saving from reaching the firms and prevents funding. So while it solves the interest rate conundrum which we have, in this chapter, merely assumed away, it creates other problems. In particular, the growing economy would become financially fragile to a much greater extent than under the regimes which we have spelt out in the text.

27 Kregel's (1994) analysis of the origins of Asimakopulos's construction in terms of Kaleckian influences is quite brilliant and deserves close study.

28 This minimum assumes that all voluntary saving goes into new issues, as before.

Part IV

THE INDUCEMENT TO INVEST

12

THE MARGINAL EFFICIENCY OF CAPITAL AND INVESTMENT

Robert Eisner

> I expect to see the State, which is in a position to calculate the marginal efficiency of capital-goods on long views and on the basis of the general social advantage, taking an ever greater responsibility for directly organizing investment; since it seems likely that the fluctuations in the market estimation of the marginal efficiency of different types of capital . . . will be too great to be offset by any practicable changes in the rate of interest.
>
> (*The General Theory*, p. 164)

Can we rely on the economy, without appropriate public intervention, to attain an optimum rate of investment? Keynes's answer in 1936 was a clear 'No'. He was right then and that answer would be equally correct today. Why he was right then and why he would be right today is not, however, for some of the reasons often enunciated.

The fundamental problem then and now – and investment is central to the issue – is the varying but chronic inability of reasonably free, market economies to attain full employment. They do in war-time and they come close in major booms, as in Japan until recently. But in the United States we have not come really close since the Vietnam War, when unemployment was under 4 per cent, and most of western Europe is now suffering double-digit unemployment rates that none dares call 'natural'.

In Keynes's formulation – and I know of none better – the rate of investment necessary to fill the gap between full employment output and consumption might be and generally had been unattainable. In his terms, a full-employment rate of investment would imply a marginal efficiency of capital[1] below the lowest attainable rate of interest; investment demand could equal the rate of saving forthcoming at full employment only if the rate of interest were below the level that liquidity preference would permit. And this, it may be pointed out, did not depend upon the existence of a positive 'liquidity trap'. Business expectations of the marginal rate of *net* profit on investment at the rate necessary to attain full employment might after all be negative. In that situation, clearly, there was no practicable

185

action by the central bank that could bring investment to a level consistent with full employment – and full employment could not be reached through monetary policy alone.

A major contribution of Keynes was to point out that, while this situation might clearly exist in cyclical downturns where expectations and the investment demand schedule were low and the cost of inevitably risky credit was high, the problem was not necessarily short-run. It might last for years and years, as experienced in Europe today; it might prove permanent.

Keynes did not eschew efforts to ease credit and lower interest rates to promote investment and higher output and employment. Indeed, he lamented the lack of sufficiently aggressive action by the monetary authority to do so. He was right then and he would be right now. Monetary authorities, at least throughout the developed western world, perhaps because of their generally close ties with the banking community, are frequently obsessed with fears of inflation. They are ready to relax credit, at most briefly, during economic downturns. But this will not sufficiently drive down the long-term rates of interest critical to most investment, if financial markets understand that at the first signs of economic upturn the monetary authority will tighten again.

Keynes saw investment impeded by risk, borrower's risk and lender's risk. Borrower's risk that unfulfilled expectations might contribute to bankruptcy would raise the expectations of profit – marginal efficiency – necessary to justify investment at any given interest rate. Lender's risk of default would raise that given rate of interest. To the extent that these risks were individual rather than social they would keep investment below its socially optimum rate – and make more difficult the attainment of full employment.

But Keynes also pointed out that much investment is based on 'animal spirits' and does not prove justified by its eventual returns. This suggests that aggregate investment may in fact be not less than its optimum amount but, rather, excessive – for the existing level of employment and output. The way to get investment nearer an optimum is not necessarily, then, to look for long-term tax incentives or subsidies for private investment at the existing level of employment but rather to take measures to increase that employment and output and let investment rise in their wake.

This perception, clear for those who would look for it in *The General Theory*, seems to have been lost by many – including leading Keynesians in the United States. They and others have been persistent advocates of various special tax benefits – investment tax credits, accelerated tax depreciation and lower taxes on capital gains, in particular – to stimulate business investment. Measures to provide these benefits have been adopted and expanded, contracted, repealed and reinstated but have had limited effect[2] and, it may be argued, what positive effect they have had on investment may not have been desirable.

The investment 'incentives' have of course been supported not only for

Keynesian demand reasons but on the grounds that more business investment contributes to productivity and growth. That more investment
brought on by means of these incentives may not be desirable is implicit
in Keynes's view that the net return from private investment under existing
conditions may well be zero or negative. Making the after-tax return
positive by tax concessions will then hardly add to social productivity.
Ten-dollar investment tax credits to persuade firms to buy $100 pieces
of machinery that will return $95 of proceeds over their lifetimes is the way
not to growth but to economic decline.

This is not to say that Keynes ruled out fiscal policy as a means of
securing an optimal rate of investment. And neither should we today. But
the optimal investment is that which would come with full employment.
This could be reached by a combination of tax cuts and government
spending that would raise aggregate demand and increase both consumption and private investment, and public investment as well. Keynes was
happy to rely on the workings of free markets to allocate resources,
including the choice in the Euclidian world as between consumption and
investment. That free market choice lost its optimality properties if under-
employment brought in a third variable or dimension: the extent to which
resources were actually utilized.

There is certainly ample contemporary evidence of the wisdom of this
restraint, from the vast waste of misguided investment in largely planned or
controlled economies such as those of the old Soviet Union and India, to
over-built office buildings, shopping centres and steel mills in the United
States over recent decades. A widespread misunderstanding as to the nature
of the relation between investment and growth has contributed to all this
colossal waste.

In a free economy we do not expect business to add to its capital (invest)
unless it expects such investment to be profitable. Returns must exceed
costs. If business generally guesses correctly and expectations are fulfilled,
investment will thus add to total output. But it is not that investment
inherently adds to productivity. As Keynes pointed out, the marginal
efficiency of particular capital assets will decline as more of them are
acquired. And Keynes foresaw the possibility that at some time in the
future mature economies would have accumulated all of the capital that
could profitably be employed; the aggregate marginal efficiency might even
be zero. At that point net investment – and net saving – would be zero.
With a stable, equilibrium rate of output there would be no need for more
capital, and investment would consist only of the production of capital
goods to replace those wearing out.

Keynes was at pains to indicate that he did not believe that time had been
reached in 1936, although he suggested it might be reached in twenty-five
years. Most of us would argue that it has still not been reached (in 1996).
New technologies and vast expansions in services and in new industries

such as aviation and telecommunications have delayed the day of capital saturation. Population growth and continued technological development are apparently delaying that day indefinitely. But more investment, guided not by the pursuit of profits but of tax advantage, will not necessarily contribute to growth. What is most relevant is the inverse: without growth there is likely to be little incentive for new investment. Investment may not bring growth but growth almost certainly brings investment.

It is widely lamented in the United States today that 'national saving' is too low. Gross national saving of course equals gross investment, which is the sum of gross private domestic investment and net foreign investment. The major component of the former is fixed investment, now running at a gross figure of about $800 billion in 1987 dollars but a net rate of only some $200 billion. With a capital–output ratio of approximately two, the net fixed capital stock, also in 1987 dollars, is about $10,000 billion. A constant capital–output ratio and a rate of growth of output of 2 per cent per annum will then imply a growth of capital stock or net investment of $200 billion. That is in fact just about the average per annum rate of growth of real output in the United States over the last five or six years. Each percentage point of growth in GDP has been associated with net investment equal to two percentage points of output, and net investment has been about 4 per cent of GDP. We may expect then that a rate of growth just one percentage point more would increase net investment from 4 per cent of GDP to 6 per cent of GDP, an increase of $100 billion 1987 dollars, or 50 per cent.

It is common to compare the large proportion of GDP going to investment in Japan with the presumably small proportion in the United States. It is then said that slower US growth is due to lesser US investment. But is it not rather that faster growth in Japan has generated more investment? To make the point more sharply, suppose there were no growth at all in an economy. There would then be no net investment unless capital-intensive technological change and/or perpetually falling costs of capital brought about a continually increasing capital–output ratio.

The most obvious way to generate more investment is to increase the rate of growth of output.[3] In the short run, this may be accomplished by bringing the economy up to full – or at least fuller – employment. This would spark a burst of gross and net investment. Once the economy reached (and became fully adjusted to) its full-employment path (or constant employment-to-labour-force ratio), net investment as a ratio of GDP would decline to a figure equal to the product of the rate of growth of output and the capital–output ratio. An increase in the investment ratio would then require either an increase in the rate of growth or of the capital–output ratio.[4]

All this is remarkably consistent with most of the volumes of empirical research on the investment function since *The General Theory* revolutionized, indeed created, macroeconomics. Liquidity – difficult to measure – and related but not identical profits (or 'cash flow', the sum of profits and depreciation charges) were found to be associated with investment.[5] Keynes would argue, though, that firms might invest more when they had more cash but, in the long run, not current profits but the expected profitability of investment would determine the level of investment. And this in turn would depend heavily on the expected demand for output for which additional productive capacity and capital would be needed. This has been confirmed in cross-section studies of individual firms, where profits or 'liquidity' variables were generally shown to be proxies for changes in sales and measures of the pressure of output on capacity.[6]

Sophisticated or flexible versions of the acceleration principle took pride of place in the explanation of investment. Investment was viewed largely as a distributed lag function of past changes in sales or output. The lag function was related to costs of adjustment, which were a rising function of the rate of acquisition of capital, and to delays in the modification of expectations of future sales to reflect past changes, and might also be affected by liquidity considerations.[7] A 'permanent income theory of investment', analogous to that for consumption, suggested that investment would be slow to respond to temporary or short-run changes in sales. It would rather await confirmation that the changes were in at least considerable part 'permanent' rather than 'transitory'. Empirical studies appeared to support these views of the investment process.

A 'neoclassical' theory of investment came to dominate the field and much empirical work in the 1960s. Investment was then seen as dependent on both changes in sales, output or demand and the user cost or 'rental price' of capital. The latter determined the capital–output ratio, and hence the net investment that would be generated by changes in aggregate demand or output as well as longevity and the needs for annual replacement of existing capital. Gross investment was of course the total of net investment and replacement investment.

The rental price or cost of capital was the sum of real interest or borrowing costs of capital and depreciation, all adjusted to reflect tax considerations which bore on the tax deductibility of interest and borrowing costs, the taxation of capital gains, and the present value of tax depreciation deductions and investment tax credits or subsidies. This formulation left the rate of taxation of business income (corporate profits tax rates) with little or no clear role in investment. Whether lower business income tax rates would – aside from their ultimate effect on aggregate demand – increase business investment came to depend upon their interaction with the other components of the rental costs of capital.

A critical question in the neoclassical formulation was the extent to which the rental cost of capital varied over time and the response of investment to such variation. Keynes saw insufficient variation in the rate of interest and insufficient response of investment to what variation occurred to offer hope that the economy could be self-adjusting to full employment 'along these lines'. It appears that recognizing the rate of interest as only one component of a rental cost of capital, the other components of which were not self-adjusting, would only aggravate the difficulty.

Initial estimates by Dale Jorgenson and his associates seemed to suggest that investment was highly responsive to changes in the rental price of capital.[8] But then it was noted that estimates with these results were based upon constraints that imposed long-run unitary elasticity of the response of capital to a composite variable, Q/c, where Q was output and c that rental cost of capital. All that was freely estimated was the lag structure and that was dominated by the responses to output.

Unconstrained estimates suggested that while the elasticity of capital stock to output was indeed close to unity, perhaps somewhat less, reflecting increasing returns to scale, its elasticity with respect to its rental cost was much less. Some estimates suggested it was close to zero.[9] This would strongly confirm Keynes's view of an inelastic investment demand function.[10] Increases in the quantity of money that would lower the rate of interest could not be expected to have a major impact on investment, certainly not enough to counter the overwhelming changes associated with shifts of the marginal efficiency of capital schedule. This would preclude a dominant role for the monetary authority. It would rule out, all the more, increases in the real quantity of money that would come from falls in wages and prices in response to unemployment. Here the economy would suffer from the depressed marginal efficiency of capital schedule caused by expectations of falling prices and from increases in borrower's and lender's risk and associated bankruptcies generated by falling nominal revenues in the face of fixed nominal debt.

It will be recalled and should be emphasized that the marginal efficiency of capital schedule relates to the *expectations* of future net returns on investment, not to past returns. Investment will be undertaken to the extent that the marginal efficiency or expected rate of return over cost exceeds the rate of interest. A parallel formulation indicates that investment will be undertaken as long as the present value of expected future returns, discounted at the rates of interest of the current term structure, exceeds its supply price. The latter is the cost of the new physical assets, installed.

The various investment studies I have cited thus far relate generally, however, to past data.[11] Expectations enter only implicitly as some unknown function of past and current variables. Estimated equations involving these *ex post* variables may be thought of as reduced forms of systems in which investment is a function of expectational variables and the expectational variables are functions of the *ex post* variables. A difficulty with this is that the relation between the expectational and *ex post* variables is hardly fixed. It may be quite unstable because it ignores all the information going into expectations that is not found in the *ex post* variables available to the inquiring econometrician.[12]

James Tobin came up with a formulation, labelled 'Tobin's *q*', that at first glance seemed a direct rendition of Keynes's view of investment as related to uncertain expectations of the future.[13] Tobin's *q* was the ratio of the market valuation of firms to the replacement cost of its assets ($q = $ MV/RC). The numerator, the demand price, was thus the present value of expected future returns as measured by the sum of the value of equity and firm liabilities and the denominator was the supply price. In principle, a value of *q* greater than unity indicated that there were gains to be made by acquiring new assets, since the market was valuing such assets in a firm at more than their cost. Values of *q* less than unity implied that it would be better to take over existing firms (in whole or in part, by investing in their stock) and to acquire physical assets that way rather than by investing in new plant and equipment. The expectations that are key to investment would be reflected in the stock market evaluation of firms' equity.

Alas, Tobin's *q*, so promising in principle, has not proved of much use in its empirical formulations. For many years, *q* was well below unity in the United States while investment proceeded reasonably briskly. Then, as the US stock market went into a long bull period and *q* rose, investment lagged. Part of the problem no doubt related to differences between the relevant marginal *q* and the observed average *q*, although under certain assumptions they could be shown to be the same. A further problem may well relate to the fact that share prices on stock exchanges are only the prices at which relatively small proportions of total outstanding stock are traded. It may be quite inaccurate to infer that, if a stock is selling for $10 a share and there are one billion shares outstanding, the company can be bought for $10 billion. The history of corporate takeovers sugests, indeed, that this is far from true. Companies have usually been valued in these efforts at prices well above their market valuation based on prices of shares traded before the efforts began.

There may well be further difficulties in correcting *q* for taxes, that is, calculating an after-tax *q*. However, the most formidable problem, I believe, involves the fact that the value of a firm reflects much more than its physical assets, and the value of all the companies with shares listed on the exchanges reflects more than the returns that can be ascribed to their physical assets. For one thing, monopoly rents – or the rents of imperfect competition – may be a significant element in expected returns and the valuation of firms. Additional physical capital may reduce as well as increase these returns. Returns may relate to advertising budgets and customer loyalties. They may relate to management skills, from the chief executive officer down, and efficiency in curbing costs. They may relate to the skills and dedication of the labour force. And they may relate to R&D expenditures and the ability of firms and economies to keep ahead in the fast pace of developing new products and technological change.

This leads me to probably the most significant modifcations and additions that I would embody in a new edition of *The General Theory*. These would involve attention to the totality of a nation's invesement, public as well as private, by households as well as business and non-profit institutions, and in intangible and human capital as well as tangible. I have estimated investment in intangible capital in the United States in 1981 at $415 billion 1972 dollars, of which $34 billion was in R&D, $318 billion in education and training, and $63 billion in investment in health. Total investment in tangible capital was $522 billion, but of this only $166 billion was in business structures and equipment and housing not owner-occupied. Tangible investment by government was close to $50 billion and household investment totalled $264 billion: $35 billion for owner-occupied dwellings, $141 billion for consumer durables and $88 billion for 'semi-durables'.[14] Business fixed investment was thus only 18 per cent of total investment.

Not only are intangible and non-business investment large in magnitude. Robert Solow's seminal work, indicating that the 'residual' was the major component in regressions seeking to explain the factors in economic growth, suggested that business investment was only a relatively minor factor in that explanation. Considerable evidence to confirm this has been developed since. There are at least two major implications. First, the 'investment' necessary to bring aggregate demand up to full-employment aggregate supply will go well beyond business investment. Second, if private business investment depends upon growth, perhaps more than growth depends upon private business investment, the support of all other investment may be the best way of encouraging private business investment. Going back to our earlier example, suppose massive expenditures on education and training and on research and development along with public infrastructure could both raise current aggregate demand to full-employment levels and increase the long-run rate of growth of the economy from 2 per cent to 4 per cent per annum. This would offer that initial burst of investment to match the increase to full-employment GDP. It would then double the equilibrium rate of net investment in tangible business capital — as well as all other kinds of capital.

What then are we to say now about 'the State . . . taking an ever greater responsibility for directly organizing investment'? First, government must see to it that aggregate demand is sufficient to maintain full employment. As unemployment rose by two percentage points in the United States from 1989 to 1992, gross private fixed investment fell by 10 per cent.

Second, the monetary authority should get and keep real interest rates, short and long, as low as it can. No shortage of liquidity or excess of borrower's or lender's risk or interest rate higher than the minimum attainable should be allowed to reduce the demand price or reduce the rate of investment, public[15] or private.

Third, government must provide all the public investment appropriate for maximizing productivity and pursue actively adequate investment in human capital.[16] Much investment in basic research and in education and training involves externalities or moral hazard such that private firms are unlikely to undertake it in adequate amounts. Basic research by its nature must be largely a public good and individual firms are able to keep to themselves only a small proportion of its eventual fruits. Further, in a non-slave economy it is difficult, if not impossible, for individual employers to keep all the benefits of investment in human capital, and individuals usually cannot obtain the private financing for investment in themselves. Government must provide, or at least finance, the great bulk of investment in education and training.

Fourth, government must recognize its role in the determination of household investment in tangible capital as well. Conventional national income accounting can mislead in its inclusion of household expenditures on durable goods as 'consumption'. A household purchase of an automobile is just as much investment as its purchase by a leasing agency which then rents it to households. But arguments frequently heard in the United States that saving and investment have been depressed because Americans are on a 'consumption binge' have quite ignored the investment component of much of what is counted as consumption. Taxes on 'consumption' or higher income taxes have consequently been advocated as a means of increasing investment. Whatever the actual effect on business investment of curbing household expenditures, it almost certainly entails a reduction in household investment.

And fifth, government should generally follow policies that permit and, where this is optimal, promote maximum growth. These policies will be not only fiscal and monetary but also those that provide an environment of competition, domestic and international, that will promote the optimal allocation of resources. Business investment in tangible capital will follow from growth – in aggregate demand and output, in employment, and in all the other, generally complementary factors of production.

Much contemporary attention has been devoted to saving rates. Net 'national saving' has been viewed in the United States as inordinately low by historical and by international standards. This has led to a plethora of laws and proposals to stimulate private saving and major efforts to decrease public dis-saving, defined as government budget deficits. *The General Theory* would suggest that these laws and proposals are generally misguided.

Confusion stems in part from a misunderstanding of the implications of the saving–investment identity. As pointed out above, gross saving in the national income and product accounts is identically equal (aside from the statistical discrepancy) to gross investment. Gross saving is the sum of public saving (government budget surpluses) and private saving (personal saving and business saving). Gross investment is the sum of gross private domestic investment and net foreign investment. Clearly, if one side of the account – saving – rises, the other side – investment – must rise as well. That does not mean, though, that efforts to increase some component of saving will necessarily – by some combination of changes in the rate of interest and the marginal efficiency of capital schedule – raise investment. The effects on investment may well be perverse, with corresponding perverse effects on aggregate saving itself.

Take tax incentives for personal saving or increased taxes on consumption, for example. Both are likely to lower consumption. With given income, that must increase saving and hence investment. But can income be taken as given? In a famous review article on *The General Theory*, Oscar Lange (1938a) pointed out that there was an 'optimal propensity to consume'. Increasing consumption, in Lange's rendition of Keynes, had two effects. On the one hand, it raised the rate of interest, thus depressing investment. But on the other hand, by increasing the demand for output and the need for capital with which to produce it, more consumption raised the marginal efficiency of capital and investment demand. Initially, at low levels of employment, output, consumption and investment, the output or demand effect of increases in consumption would be dominant and more consumption would bring more investment. At some point, consumption would begin to crowd out investment; the higher interest effect would become dominant. It may be presumed that this would be so as the economy approached full employment. Where no more free resources were available, more consumption clearly would have to imply less investment.

My own empirical work indicates that the US economy in peacetime has generally been on the low side of this optimal propensity to consume. Unemployment has been such that more consumption has brought more, not less, investment. In this situation higher taxes to discourage household purchase of new automobiles, for example, are likely to bring less, not more, investment by automobile manufacturers. And multiplier and ultimately accelerator effects are likely to reduce investment elsewhere as well.

The chief culprit in the investment scenario, according to many, has been high government budget deficits. Some may use the saving–investment identity to infer that less public dis-saving would raise total saving and hence raise investment. Such simplistic reasoning, however, is clearly inadmissible. Reduction of government deficits, whether by raising taxes or reducing outlays, may clearly lower aggregate demand and output and perhaps lower gross private domestic investment. Again, we come up against Lange's analysis. Of course, if the reductions in deficits entail or bring on less public and household investment, total investment, appropriately measured, may be reduced all the more. It should be acknowledged, though, that while reduced government and household spending may lower domestic investment, they will very likely raise net foreign investment. Lower expenditures will mean not only less spending on domestic output but also less spending in imported goods. Net exports will thus rise and, with them, net foreign investment of which net exports is the major component.

It may be argued that all this has abstracted improperly from monetary policy. Lower consumption and non-investment government spending may be offset by expansionary monetary policy. This would ease credit and lower interest rates sufficiently for domestic investment to increase. (Lower interest rates would also contribute to lower exchange rates and hence increased net exports and net foreign investment.) But this comes up against Keynes's view of the investment function as being of low interest elasticity. Expansionary monetary policy may not therefore be sufficiently potent to hold up investment in the face of contractionary fiscal policy.

We may turn again to econometric examination of the data to offer some answers to these questions. They indicate that higher real structural deficits have been associated with more subsequent output, consumption and investment.[17] While they have also been associated with less subsequent net exports and net foreign investment, as has been anticipated, their effect on total national saving has been positive. This has been true for conventional measures of national saving. It has been true *a fortiori* for more comprehensive measures including public and household investment in tangible capital.[18]

For those concerned with investment, I would then find little to rewrite in a new edition of *The General Theory*.[19] Business investment may usefully be viewed as jointly determined by the rate of interest or, more broadly, the cost of capital, and the marginal efficiency or expected profitability of investment. Insufficient business investment is associated with inadequate aggregate demand and economic growth but the major causal relation is not so much from investment to demand and growth as the other way around. Lower interest rates may increase investment and they should be encouraged, but their effects are generally modest. Prime place must be given to fiscal policy to contribute to full employment aggregate effective demand. And along with that there should be adequate public and household investment and investment in human and intangible capital to promote maximum productivity and economic growth.

NOTES

1 If we take C to be the cost or supply price of an asset and Y_j to be the return (net of other costs) to be expected from the asset in the year j, then the rate of return on that asset, r, is the rate of discount which will equate its expected future returns to its supply price, as indicated in the following equation:

$$C_t = \sum_{j=t}^{\infty} Y_j/(1 + r)^{j-t}.$$

When a firm contemplates adding another unit of a particular type of asset, the 'marginal efficiency' of that asset is the rate of return to be expected on that additional unit. There can thus be a marginal efficiency schedule for that particular asset, indicating the return to be expected on each additional dollar spent in acquiring the asset as a function of the total amount spent. Keynes indicates that these schedules can be aggregated for all firms and all assets to derive a marginal efficiency of capital schedule for investment as a whole, or an investment demand function.

Keynes points out that the marginal efficiency of capital schedules will decline as a function of investment, both because of diminishing marginal returns from particular assets or from capital as a whole and because the supply curves for assets or for capital goods will tend to slope upward. The more capital is being acquired, the greater will be the supply price. The supply, however, represents a flow of output and it would rise as a function of the rate of that flow. It is clear, therefore, as Abba Lerner pointed out, that what Keynes really had in mind was a marginal efficiency of *investment* schedule. Where I, faithful to Keynes's original terminology, have used the phrase 'marginal efficiency of capital', I have had in mind, as did he, the 'marginal efficiency of investment'.

2 See Eisner and Chirinko (1983).

3 See Domar (1946) and Eisner (1953) for some early formal development of this Keynesian idea.

4 See Solow (1956). See Eisner (1958) for a comment on Solow's work setting forth the underlying difficulty, in the Keynesian framework, of getting sufficient increase in the capital–labour or capital–output ratios to generate enough investment demand, at any given rate of growth, to attain and sustain full employment. This difficulty relates, again, to the unprofitability of investment by firms beyond the point at which the declining marginal efficiency of capital equals the rate of interest.

5 Meyer and Kuh (1957).

6 See Eisner (1960, 1978), in particular.

7 See Eisner and Strotz (1963) and Coen (1971).

8 See Jorgenson (1963) and Jorgenson and Stephenson (1967), in particular.

9 See Eisner and Nadiri (1968).

10 Set forth in a number of places in *The General Theory*, for example: '[m]oderate changes . . . in the rate of interest will not be associated with very great changes in the rate of investment' (*G.T.*: 250); 'the marginal efficiency of capital may suffer such enormously wide fluctuations that it cannot be sufficiently offset by corresponding fluctuations in the rate of interest' (p. 320); and on p. 164, as set forth in the quotation at the beginning of this chapter.

11 There have been some studies that made use of data on sales expectation and investment plans but these too did not bear directly on the expected profitability of investment.

12 It may be noted that this is a more general formulation of the famous 'Lucas Critique' (1976) of the use of conventional econometric models for policy simulations. Lucas pointed that a change in the policy regime may change the relation between *ex ante* and *ex post* variables that underlay the parameters estimated in the reduced form model involving only *ex post* variables. I am suggesting that this relation may be altered by many more factors than changes in policy regimes. If an economy becomes more stable, for example, changes in demand that do occur may be looked upon as in greater part permanent and hence yield greater accelerator coefficients than were estimated in a less stable economy. Similarly, responses to interest rate changes or price changes will vary with changes in the elasticity of expectations, whatever the reason. In these cases and those of investment tax credits or subsidies, though, changes which are expected to be temporary will have greater impact. They may be expected to induce investment during the periods when the interest rates, prices and tax treatment are favourable.

13 See Brainard and Tobin (1968) and Tobin (1969).

14 See Eisner (1989: 233, 234).

15 Much investment by state and local governments, in the United States at least, is heavily influenced by interest costs of borrowing.

16 Aschauer (1989) sparked some lively discussion on the role of public infrastructure investment in increasing productivity and in stimulating private investment. Probably offering even greater returns is investment in intangible and human capital, as suggested in Eisner (1989: appendix D, and 1994c), and in numerous works on the return to R&D by Zvi Griliches, Edwin Mansfield and others. Few question the returns to education in a world of more and more sophisticated technology.

17 See Eisner (1986, 1994b, 1996). In my formulations developed jointly with Paul J. Pieper (Eisner and Pieper 1984), I have worked with a 'price-adjusted, high-employment deficit' (PAHED). This is the structural or cyclically adjusted deficit defined as the deficit that would occur at fixed unemployment levels, usually of 6 per cent, adjusted for the 'inflation tax', or loss in the real value of existing federal debt (held by the public) due to inflation.

18 See Eisner (1993a, b, 1994a, b and 1996).

19 An admirable new survey of work on business fixed investment is to be found in Chirinko (1993).

13

THE MARGINAL EFFICIENCY OF INVESTMENT*

Luigi L. Pasinetti

THE INDUCEMENT TO INVEST

Book IV of *The General Theory* (*G.T.*) contains eight chapters (from 11 to 18) which are meant to analyse the factors determining 'The Inducement to Invest'. Keynes singles out two major sources of inducement: one – which is brought to the surface in Chapter 12, on 'the state of long-term expectations' – is the result of entrepreneurs' 'animal spirits – a spontaneous urge to action rather than inaction' (*G.T.*: 161). It is 'autonomous', with respect to formal economic analysis. The other comes from careful economic calculus. Let us call it 'endogenous' investment.

It is with reference to the endogenous source of investment that Keynes coins the analytical concept of the 'marginal efficiency of capital'.

A CURIOUS FATE

The 'marginal efficiency of capital' was meant to be a major ingredient of *The General Theory*. In a widely quoted letter to Roy Harrod on 30 August 1936, which has been taken as Keynes's own account of the steps which the making of *The General Theory* went through, Keynes lists the marginal efficiency of capital as one of four basic ingredients of his major work, the others being effective demand, the psychological law behind the consumption function (and thus the multiplier), and liquidity preference. In Keynes's words, 'the proper definition of the marginal efficiency of capital . . . [came] last of all, after an immense lot of muddling and many drafts' (*C.W.* XIV: 85). The notion of the marginal efficiency of capital was therefore the outcome of a laborious, painstaking process.

Paradoxically, Keynes's notion was destroyed almost immediately after the publication of *The General Theory* by being reduced to, and confused with, the orthodox notion of the 'marginal productivity of capital'. In his famous *Econometrica* article, presenting his IS–LM interpretation of *The General Theory*, J.R. Hicks (1937) formulated an investment function (investment as a downward-sloping function of the rate of interest), which is *exactly the same* both in the orthodox model and in Keynes's model. Keynes had abstained from giving his notion any formal representation. Through Hicks's formalization, Keynes's notion of the 'marginal efficiency of capital' and the orthodox notion of the 'marginal productivity of capital' were taken *as if* they were exactly the same thing.

A curious fate: all Keynes's laborious process, all 'the immense muddling and many drafts' which had gone into a 'proper definition' of 'the marginal efficiency of capital' were thereby reduced to nothing.

But why did Keynes not react? This question has been raised by many scholars. We know that Keynes was very uneasy about Hicks's article.[1] We also know that he was tired, weak and ill. But the point was important. Forty years later, Richard Kahn was to call that lack of reaction 'tragic' (Kahn 1984: 160). But we can see much better today that, though Keynes's intuition was right, his theoretical position was weak. On analytical grounds, he was not well equipped to rebut the orthodox interpretation and correct the distortion that was taking place.

THE ORTHODOX THEORY

The 'marginal efficiency of capital' is a rather wide and comprehensive notion, conceived by Keynes in order to arrive at the determination of the size of demand for investments, and thus of effective demand for the economic system as a whole.

The orthodox 'marginal productivity of capital' is, on the other hand, a very restrictive notion; it is simple, in fact simplistic – conceived for the purpose of building up the demand side of the orthodox theory of the rate of interest. It presupposes the existence of an aggregate production function of the neoclassical type, i.e. of a relation expressing output as a convex, smooth, differentiable function of 'capital' and 'labour', in such a way as to allow substitution of one factor for the other, at decreasing returns to changing proportions. In this way, the demand side of the orthodox theory of the rate of interest is expressed by an inverse monotonic relation between capital per worker (and thus investment) and the rate of interest.

The other (supply) side of the orthodox theory takes the form of a symmetric, increasing relation between saving and the rate of interest. This orthodox theory, surprisingly, continues to be presented today in most macroeconomics textbooks. It has been resuscitated by providing it with 'microfoundations', consisting of the assumption of a 'representative' individual, who – in a one-commodity world – maximizes over time the utility of consuming various quantities of a certain commodity, available at various points in time, either in the form of an original endowment or obtainable as a result of exchange. The inter-temporal utility function is supposed to be convex, smooth, differentiable (just like the production function), and such as to allow the representative individual to exert his or her time preference, through substitution of consumption of the same commodity at various points in time, in response to changes of the rate of interest.

Overall, therefore, in a scheme in which there is a downward-sloping demand schedule for investments and an upward-sloping supply schedule for saving, both as functions of the rate of interest, the latter is shown to be determined, as any other market price, at the point of equilibrium between demand and supply.

Whatever interpretation we may give of *The General Theory*, surely we must say that Keynes emphatically rejected this theory.[2] He rejected *both* sides of it: the supply side as well as the demand side, proposing an alternative (new) theory of the rate of interest of his own.

KEYNES'S CRITIQUE OF THE ORTHODOX SAVING-SUPPLY FUNCTION

The critique of the orthodox supply-side function of the theory is the clearer part of Keynes's elaboration. First of all, Keynes provides a truly alternative, remarkably novel theory of saving as a function of income, which is at the basis of the multiplier relation, and which need not detain us here. At the same time, he provides a brilliant critique of the orthodox theory of saving. His words are worth reproducing at length:

An act of individual saving means – so to speak – a decision not to have dinner to-day. But it does *not* necessitate a decision to have dinner or to buy a pair of boots a week hence or a year hence or to consume any specified thing at any specified date. Thus it depresses the business of preparing to-day's dinner without stimulating the business of making ready for some future act of consumption. It is not a substitution of future consumption-demand for present consumption-demand, – it is a net diminution of such demand.

.   .   .

If saving consisted not merely in abstaining from present consumption but in placing simultaneously a specific order for future consumption, the effect might indeed be different. For in that case the expectation of some future yield from investment would be improved, and the resources released from preparing for present consumption could be turned over to preparing for the future consumption.

. . . In any case, however, an individual decision to save does not, in actual fact, involve the placing of any specific forward order for consumption, but merely the cancellation of a present order. Thus, since the expectation of consumption is the only *raison d'être* of employment, there should be nothing paradoxical in the conclusion that a diminished propensity to consume has *cet.par.* a depressing effect on employment.

200

The trouble arises, therefore, because the act of saving implies, not a substitution for present consumption of some specific additional consumption which requires for its preparation just as much immediate economic activity as would have been required by present consumption equal in value to the sum saved, but a desire for 'wealth' as such, that is for a potentiality of consuming an unspecified article at an unspecified time. The absurd, though almost universal, idea that an act of individual saving is just as good for effective demand as an act of individual consumption, has been fostered by the fallacy, much more specious than the conclusion derived from it, that an increased desire to hold wealth, being much the same thing as an increased desire to hold investments, must, by increasing the demand for investments, provide a stimulus to their production; so that current investment is promoted by individual saving to the same extent as present consumption is diminished.

It is of this fallacy that it is most difficult to disabuse men's minds.

. . . The prospective yield of the marginal new investment is not increased by the fact that someone wishes to increase his wealth, since the prospective yield of the marginal new investment depends on the expectation of a demand for a specific article at a specific date.

Nor do we avoid this conclusion by arguing that what the owner of wealth desires is not a given prospective yield but the best available prospective yield, so that an increased desire to own wealth reduces the prospective yield with which the producers of new investment have to be content. For this overlooks the fact that there is always an alternative to the ownership of real capital-assets, namely the ownership of money and debts.

(*G.T.*: 210–12)

As may be realized, the critique of the orthodox saving function springs from the theoretical core of *The General Theory*. Orthodox theory always tended to develop its arguments on the basis of what may be called an 'exchange economy', which is treated as a barter economy. In a barter economy, any decision to save today is *ipso facto* a decision to consume a specific good at a specific later date. There can never be any problem of lack of effective demand.

Keynes's point of departure is that we do not live in a barter economy (and not even, as he explicitly points out, in a co-operative economy). The economies in which we live are 'monetary economies of production'.

In monetary production economies, decisions to save and decisions to invest are carried out independently, by different people. Any decision to save is simply a decision *not to spend*, with the desire to hold a corresponding amount of abstract purchasing power to be exerted in the future, without, however, any commitment either to demand any specific commodity or to demand it at any specific time. An organization of this type carries enormous advantages, with respect to barter economies, but it also carries systemic consequences of crucial importance. Decisions to save come to play a sort of passive role, with respect to the active role played by investment decisions. As has also been said, it is investment that 'rules the roost'. Saving will not even materialize; it will simply be frustrated if, quite independently, a corresponding demand to invest is not being exerted. The Keynesian mechanism of the determination of the levels of income, production and employment emerges in this way very clearly, and in striking contrast to orthodox theory.

A CRITIQUE OF THE ORTHODOX INVESTMENT-DEMAND FUNCTION

The critique of the other part of the orthodox theory – the investment-demand function – was a much harder task. A sound critique of such a function would have needed a preliminary critique of the neoclassical theory of capital. But at the time of publication of *The General Theory*, Keynes was not in a position to do that. It is only since the appearance of Piero Sraffa's 1960 book that a radical critique of the orthodox theory of capital has become possible.

It is interesting to notice, however, that many hints may be found in *The General Theory*. Consider, for example, the following excerpts taken from Chapter 16 ('Sundry Observations on the Nature of Capital'):

> It is much preferable to speak of capital as having a yield over the course of its life in excess of its original cost, than as being *productive*.
>
> . . .
>
> . . . I sympathise . . . with the pre-classical doctrine that everything is *produced by labour*, aided by what used to be called art and is now called technique, by natural resources which are free or cost a rent according to their scarcity or abundance, and by the results of past labour, embodied in assets, which also command a price according to their scarcity or abundance. It is preferable to regard labour, including, of course, the personal services of the entrepreneur and his assistants, as the sole factor of production, operating in a given environment of technique, natural resources, capital equipment and effective demand. This partly explains why we have been able to take the unit of labour as the sole physical unit which we require in our economic system, apart from units of money and of time.
>
> It is true that some lengthy or roundabout processes are physically efficient. But so are some short processes. Lengthy processes are not physically efficient because they are long. Some, probably most, lengthy processes would be physically very inefficient, for there are such things

as spoiling or wasting with time. With a given labour force there is a definite limit to the quantity of labour embodied in roundabout processes which can be used to advantage.

(*G.T.*: 213–14)

Given the optimum amount of roundaboutness, we shall, of course, select the most efficient roundabout processes which we can find up to required aggregate. But the optimum amount itself should be such as to provide at the appropriate dates for that part of consumers' demand which it is to defer. In optimum conditions, that is to say, production should be so organised as to produce in the most efficient manner compatible with delivery at the dates at which consumer's demand is expected to become effective.

(*G.T.*: 215)

Consider, moreover, the following comments on the orthodox use of the concept of capital:

There is, to begin with, the ambiguity whether we are concerned with the increment of physical product per unit of time due to the employment of one more physical unit of capital, or with the increment of value due to the employment of one more value unit of capital. The former involves difficulties as to the definition of the physical unit of capital, which I believe to be both insoluble and unnecessary.

(*G.T.*: 138)

It is evident from the above that Marshall was well aware that we are involved in a circular argument if we try to determine along these lines what the rate of interest actually is.

(*G.T.*: 140)

These hints seem to indicate that discussions must have been going on in Cambridge with reference to a theoretical framework which was to become explicit only later on, in the 1950s and 1960s, from the works of Joan Robinson (1956) and Piero Sraffa (1960).

Keynes was not able, or was not in time, to take advantage of Sraffa's ongoing critical elaborations. But we are in a position now to state the results of the critique of the neoclassical production function, which would have been needed to debunk the demand-for-investment side of the orthodox theory.

The reswitching-of-technique controversy in capital theory that took place in the 1960s has by now conclusively demonstrated that, in general, with given techniques of production, an inverse monotonic relation between capital per worker and rate of interest or, for that matter, between capital per unit of output and rate of interest, does not exist.[3] This means that a 'well-behaved' aggregate neoclassical production function, in general, does not exist. It also means that an investment-demand function, to the extent that it is based on the neoclassical postulates – i.e. such as to entail the demand for more and more capital, because of the coming into operation of more and more capital-intensive techniques, as the rate of interest falls – in general does not exist. The conclusions are strictly logical and devastating. The downward-sloping investment-demand function, *to the extent* that it relies on a continuous process of substitution of capital for labour, as the rate of interest falls, is theoretically unsound; it has no logical foundations.

It will now be realized how tricky the implications of these conclusions are for the problem we are here investigating. We cannot deduce from them a general proposition such that a downward-sloping demand function for investment, as the rate of interest falls, does not exist. The 'reswitching' results only means that, if such a downward-sloping relation exists, it cannot be explained by a process of substitution of capital for labour (i.e. by a neoclassical production function); it cannot be explained by more and more capital-intensive techniques as the rate of interest falls. Such a relation, if it exists, must be explained by something else – by some *other* theory or circumstance.

It is to this effect that we must logically search for a meaning (a non-orthodox meaning) of Keynes's notion of the 'marginal efficiency of capital'.

KEYNES'S VERSION OF THE 'MARGINAL EFFICIENCY OF CAPITAL'

It is worthwhile reproducing the whole section in which Keynes gives the 'proper definition' of the notion of the 'marginal efficiency of capital':

> When a man buys an investment or capital-asset, he purchases the right to the series of prospective returns, which he expects to obtain from selling its ouput, after deducting the running expenses of obtaining that output, during the life of the asset. This series of annuities $Q_1, Q_2 \ldots Q_n$ it is convenient to call the *prospective yield* of the investment.
>
> Over against the prospective yield of the investment we have the *supply price* of the capital-asset, meaning by this, not the market-price at which an asset of the type in question can actually be purchased in the market, but the price which would just induce a manufacturer newly to produce an additional unit of such assets, i.e. what is sometimes called its *replacement cost*. The relation between the prospective yield of a capital-asset and its supply price or replacement cost, i.e. the relation between the prospective yield of one more unit of that type of capital and the cost of producing that unit, furnishes us with the *marginal efficiency of capital* of that type. More precisely, I define the marginal efficiency of capital as being equal to that rate of discount which would

make the present value of the series of annuities given by the returns expected from the capital-asset during its life just equal to its supply price. This gives us the marginal efficiencies of particular types of capital-assets. The greatest of these marginal efficiencies can then be regarded as the marginal efficiency of capital in general.

The reader should note that the marginal efficiency of capital is here defined in terms of the *expectation* of yield and of the *current* supply price of the capital-asset. It depends on the rate of return expected to be obtainable on money if it were invested in a *newly* produced asset; not on the historical result of what an investment has yielded on its original cost if we look back on its record after its life is over.

If there is an increased investment in any given type of capital during any period of time, the marginal efficiency of that type of capital will diminish as the investment in it is increased, partly because the prospective yield will fall as the supply of that type of capital is increased, and partly because, as a rule, pressure on the facilities for producing that type of capital will cause its supply price to increase; the second of these factors being usually the more important in producing equilibrium in the short run, but the longer the period in view the more does the first factor take its place. Thus for each type of capital we can build up a schedule, showing by how much investment in it will have to increase within the period, in order that its marginal efficiency should fall to any given figure. We can then aggregate these schedules for all the different types of capital, so as to provide a schedule relating the rate of aggregate investment to the corresponding marginal efficiency of capital in general which that rate of investment will establish. We shall call this the investment demand-schedule; or, alternatively, the schedule of the marginal efficiency of capital.

Now it is obvious that the actual rate of current investment will be pushed to the point where there is no longer any class of capital-asset of which the marginal efficiency exceeds the current rate of interest. In other words, the rate of investment will be pushed to the point on the investment demand-schedule where the marginal efficiency of capital in general is equal to the market rate of interest.

(*G.T.*: 135–7)

Keynes goes on to give an alternative definition of the same concept:

The same thing can also be expressed as follows. If Q_r is the prospective yield from an asset at time r, and d_r is the present value of £1 deferred r years *at the current rate of interest*, $\Sigma Q_r d_r$ is the demand price of the investment; and investment will be carried to the point where $\Sigma Q_r d_r$ becomes equal to the supply price of the investment as defined above. If, on the other hand, $\Sigma Q_r d_r$ falls short of the supply price, there will be no current investment in the asset in question.

It follows that the inducement to invest depends partly on the investment demand-schedule and partly on the rate of interest. Only at the conclusion of Book IV, will it be possible to take a comprehensive view of the factors determining the rate of investment in their actual complexity. I would, however, ask the reader to note at once that neither the knowledge of an asset's prospective yield nor the knowledge of the marginal efficiency of the asset enables us to deduce either the rate of interest or the present value of the asset. We must ascertain the rate of interest from some other source, and only then can we value the asset by 'capitalising' its prospective yield.

(*G.T.*: 137)

This second definition is useful for the purpose of bringing clearly to the fore that in the very process of constructing the concept of the 'marginal efficiency of capital', we need first to know the rate of interest, which must therefore be known in advance. The rate of interest (contrary to what orthodox theory was claiming) has to be determined elsewhere, by a mechanism that is working (and must be investigated) independently.

THE MARGINAL EFFICIENCY OF 'INVESTMENT'

If we read the foregoing excerpts carefully, we realize that Keynes's notion of the marginal efficiency of capital is not an easy concept to grasp. No wonder it emerged after 'an immense lot of muddling and many drafts'. At least three aspects of this complex concept will here be highlighted:

First, Keynes's notion is a short-run sectoral, or even a single-enterprise or microeconomic notion. Each entrepreneur is assumed to have expectations about the future. On the basis of these expectations, each entrepreneur will normally consider many prospective investment projects. (They may entail enlargements of previous plants, or entirely new plants, or entirely new products.) Notice that the concept itself of an investment project is a composite one. It is not merely a technical notion. It involves not only existing techniques, such as may be provided by engineers, but also expectations about possible innovations and about how the techniques may evolve. It involves expectations about new market developments, and new goods. In other words, it involves expectations about any factor that may influence future returns and thus the profitability of the investment project to be undertaken. Then, provided that finance is available, it appears to be rational for each entrepreneur to carry out all the investment projects that yield a rate of return higher than, or at least equal to, the prevailing rate of interest at which finance is available. Total investments will result from the sum of all entrepreneurs' decisions.

This means that, starting from any given situation, a fall in the rate of interest will indeed cause an increase in total investments – not because of any substitution of capital for labour, i.e. *not* by causing a change of technique in favour of more capital-intensive processes of production; but simply because (all other profitable investment projects remaining in place) some extra investment projects will become profitable and thus be added – those projects whose profitability has become *infra*-marginal, because of the fall in the rate of interest. Notice that nothing is implied about the capital-intensity of these projects; the capital-intensity of these extra investment projects might well be the lowest of all.

There is therefore no relation between the 'marginal efficiency' of the last investment project and the *capital-intensity* of the production processes. This is precisely where the confusion has crept in. It would clearly have been much more appropriate if Keynes had called his notion, not the 'marginal efficiency of capital', but, as has been pointed out by many economists though with different reasons (for example, Lerner 1944), the 'marginal efficiency of investment'. This is in fact what it is. We may as well call it so, from now on.

Second, the distinction we have just sketched between Keynes's notion of the marginal efficiency of investments, in terms of the last investment project that becomes profitable, and the orthodox notion of the marginal productivity of capital, in terms of production processes that become more capital-intensive, may bring to mind an analogy with the classical (especially Ricardian) distinction between 'extensive' rent and 'intensive' rent. Keynes's notion of the marginal efficiency of investment might appear to have some analogy with Ricardo's notion of extensive rent. By the same token, therefore, we might think of an extension of Keynes's notion to the case of an 'intensive' concept of marginal efficiency, and this would lead precisely to the orthodox concept of the marginal productivity of capital.

It must be admitted that, at the time of publication of *The General Theory*, this interpretation could not be excluded, at a purely theoretical level. In other words, Keynes's marginal efficiency of investment schedule could have been thought of, *both* in terms of extra investment projects becoming profitable as the rate of interest falls *and* in terms of the same investment projects being rearranged and becoming more capital-intensive as the rate of interest falls. This theoretical possibility may have contributed to confusing the discussions that have led to the textbook formalizaton of *The General Theory*. No doubt, the more traditionally minded Keynesians themselves were prone to interpret the marginal efficiency of investment schedule in the 'intensive' version, and thus to take it *as if* it were based on the orthodox concept of the marginal productivity of capital. This is what Hicks, and most probably also Harrod, did. At the same time, it must be admitted that it was difficult to resist such an interpretation, even for those who intuitively felt opposed to it. The 'reswitching' controversy on capital had not yet taken place. Keynes himself – though being on the right track with his intuition, as the above quotations from his Chapter 16 indicate –

may not always have had a clear mind on the point. Sometimes, he too easily conceded propositions that led to the confusion of his notion with the demand-side schedule of orthodox theory.[4]

But now, after the reswitching controversy in capital theory, we definitely know that the 'intensive' interpretation of the marginal-efficiency-of-investment schedule is invalid. The concept of factor intensity could indeed be used by Ricardo with reference to land, for which a physical measure is logically admissible; but it cannot be used for capital, for which, as the reswitching controversy has demonstrated, an aggregate physical measure, independent of the rate of interest, is not possible.

All this shows, therefore, how important it is to draw a sharp distinction between Keynes's marginal-efficiency-of-investment schedule and the orthodox investment-demand function. When reduced to simple aggregate functions, they may both appear as downward-sloping curves, with respect to the expected rate of profits. But they have a completely *different* foundation; they have a completely different meaning; and they must therefore be given a completely different interpretation. One might suggest that, by appearing to have exactly the same shape, they are not incompatible with each other. Yet the orthodox schedule relies on very restrictive assumptions indeed – so restrictive as to make it, in general, non-existent; or rather, so as to make it refer to a purely imaginary world. It is Keynes's schedule that is relevant. The limitations of a simple mathematical representation of the marginal-efficiency-of-investment schedule here emerge strikingly. They lead to confusion. By not perceiving, or by being induced to forget, their analytical foundations, we may be led to attribute the practical strength and thus the analytical powerfulness of Keynes's schedule to an orthodoxly based schedule, which may not even exist at all.

A third aspect to be considered refers to the construction of the marginal-efficiency-of-investment schedule itself. Clearly, if we list the sizes of the various investment projects in order of decreasing expected profitability, we obtain a downward-sloping schedule, which at a certain point is cut off by the line representing the rate of interest. Keynes took care to stress the meaning of this. The rate of interest *determines* what the marginal efficiency of the last investment project is going to be. Hence, the rate of interest does influence the total amount of investment to be carried out (it may also influence the expected flow of future yields of the various projects), according to a relation which has the appearance of the orthodox schedule (but a different analytical foundation, because it has no determinate relation with the capital-intensity of the investment projects). Yet, although the rate of interest influences the size of investments, the opposite is not true.

The rate of interest determines what the marginal efficiency of the last investment project is going to be. But the marginal efficiency of investment does *not* determine, it does not even contribute to determining, the rate of interest. In other words, the relation between the marginal efficiency of investment and the rate of interest is not one of interdependence; it is one of causality. The causal chain goes from the rate of interest to the marginal efficiency of the last investment project that is put into operation; *not* the other way round.

This implies that the rate of interest must be determined by a separate institutional mechanism which is *independent* of the marginal efficiency of investment.

This is one of the major characteristic features of *The General Theory*. It is essential to the significance of the notion of the marginal efficiency of investment itself. At this point, it becomes necessary to open a parenthesis and discuss the rate of interest.

KEYNES'S THEORY OF THE RATE OF INTEREST

The choice of the middle of Book IV of *The General Theory* to present a new theory of the rate of interest may superficially look like a digression. Yet that is precisely where Keynes's new theory becomes appropriate. Again it is worth reproducing his words:

> The rate of interest . . . is the 'price' which equilibrates the desire to hold wealth in the form of cash with the available quantity of cash: – which implies that if the rate of interest were lower, i.e. if the reward for parting with cash were diminished, the aggregate amount of cash which the public would wish to hold would exceed the available supply, and that if the rate of interest were raised, there would be a surplus of cash which no one would be willing to hold. If this explanation is correct, the quantity of money is the other factor, which, in conjunction with liquidity preference, determines the actual rate of interest in given circumstances.
>
> (*G.T.*: 167–8)

> The three divisions of liquidity-preference which we have distinguished above may be defined as depending on (i) the transactions-motive, i.e. the need of cash for the current transaction of personal and business exchanges; (ii) the precautionary-motive, i.e. the desire for security as to the future cash equivalent of a certain proportion of total resources; and (iii) the speculative-motive, i.e. the object of securing profit from knowing better than the market what the future will bring forth.
>
> (Ibid.: 170)

> the liquidity-preference due to the transactions-motive and the precautionary-motive are assumed to absorb a quantity of cash which is not very sensitive to changes in the rate of interest as such and apart from its reactions on the level of income, so that the total quantity of money,

less this quantity, is available for satisfying liquidity-preferences due to the speculative-motive. . . .

As a rule, we can suppose that the schedule of liquidity-preference relating the quantity of money to the rate of interest is given by a smooth curve which shows the rate of interest falling as the quantity of money is increased.

(Ibid.: 171)

after the rate of interest has fallen, to a certain level, liquidity-preference may become virtually absolute in the sense that almost everyone prefers cash to holding a debt which yields so low a rate of interest. In this event the monetary authority would have lost effective control over the rate of interest.

(Ibid.: 207)

Keynes elaborates further:

Whilst the amount of cash which an individual decides to hold to satisfy the transactions-motive and the precautionary-motive is not entirely independent of what he is holding to satisfy the speculative-motive, it is a safe first approximation to regard the amounts of these two sets of cash-holdings as being largely independent of one another. Let us, therefore, for the purposes of our further analysis, break up our problem in this way.

Let the amount of cash held to satisfy the transactions- and precautionary-motives be M_1, and the amount held to satisfy the speculative-motive be M_2. Corresponding to these two compartments of cash, we then have two liquidity functions L_1 and L_2. L_1 mainly depends on the level of income, whilst L_2 mainly depends on the relation between the current rate of interest and the state of expectation. Thus

$$M = M_1 + M_2 = L_1\ (Y) + L_2\ (r),$$

where L_1 is the liquidity function corresponding to an income Y, which determines M_1, and L_2 is the liquidity function of the rate of interest r, which determines M_2.

. . . A change in M can be assumed to operate by changing r, and a change in r will lead to a new equilibrium partly by changing M_2 and partly by changing Y and therefore M_1. The division of the increment of cash between M_1 and M_2 in the new position of equilibrium will depend on the responses of investment to a reduction in the rate of interest and of income to an increase in investment.

. . . It is not always made clear whether the income-velocity of money is defined as the ratio of Y to M or as the ratio of Y to M_1. I propose, however, to take it in the latter sense. Thus if V is the income-velocity of money,

$$L_1(Y) = \frac{Y}{V} = M_1.$$

There is, of course, no reason for supposing that V is constant.

(Ibid.: 199–201)

Notice how Keynes is never committing himself to any particular simple relation. He talks quite easily and indifferently about what to the reader might appear a *movement* along the liquidity preference schedule and what might appear as a *shift* of the schedule:

> *uncertainty* as to the future course of the rate of interest is the sole intelligible explanation of the type of liquidity-preference L_2 which leads to the holding of cash M_2. It follows that a given M_2 will not have a definite quantitative relation to a given rate of interest of r; – what matters is not the *absolute* level of r but the degree of its divergence from what is considered a fairly *safe* level of r, having regard to those calculations of probability which are being relied on. Nevertheless, there are two reasons for expecting that, in any given state of expectation, a fall in r will be associated with an increase in M_2.
>
> . . .
>
> It is evident, then, that the rate of interest is a highly psychological phenomenon.

(Ibid.: 201–2)

> It might be more accurate, perhaps, to say that the rate of interest is a highly conventional, rather than a highly psychological, phenomenon. For its actual value is largely governed by the prevailing view as to what its value is expected to be. *Any* level of interest which if accepted with sufficient conviction as *likely* to be durable *will* be durable; subject, of course, in a changing society to fluctuations for all kinds of reasons round the expected normal. In particular, when M_1 is increasing faster than M, the rate of interest will rise, and *vice versa*.

(Ibid.: 203–4)

These lengthy quotations are necessary to give a comprehensive view of Keynes's remarkable claim. He has stated nothing less than a completely *new* theory of the rate of interest.

THE RATIONALE OF KEYNES'S DECISION TO CRITICIZE THE SUPPOSED ROLE OF 'WAITING' AND 'PRODUCTIVITY'

Two aspects of Keynes's analysis are worth stressing at this point: one theoretical, the other methodological.

The theoretical aspect concerns the importance of Keynes's decision to carry out a critique of the orthodox theory of the rate of interest. Keynes claimed that *any* level of the rate of interest is durable, if accepted with sufficient conviction – the rate of interest, in our societies, is a 'conventional' phenomenon.

But how could he claim that? The immediate orthodox objection is quite revealing: Keynes's theory of the rate of interest is 'hanging by its own bootstraps'. But that is precisely what Keynes's theory in fact is. Obviously, Keynes could make such a claim only if he could prove that the rate of interest is, so to speak, a 'free variable', or, as Keynes put it, a truly *independent* variable, i.e. a variable that is independent of both basic forces – technology and utility – that are traditionally considered to be at the foundation of economic variables.

Only by getting rid of the orthodox pillars of 'productivity' and 'waiting' as determinants of the rate of interest, could Keynes in fact claim *independence* of the determination of the rate of interest. This also explains his particularly aggressive stand in the critique of the traditional theory, even though he did not have all the elements necessary to carry it out in a complete way. As we have seen, he was on safe ground as far as the critique of the saving-supply side is concerned (i.e. with reference to 'waiting'). He was not yet in possession of sufficiently sound analytical arguments for a critique of the investment-demand side (i.e. with reference to 'productivity'). Yet he boldly decided to propose his 'marginal efficiency of investment' as an alternative, though it became for him difficult to prevent a confusion with the orthodox concepts. The reswitching discovery has by now vindicated his critical stand, by completing the investment-demand side of his critique.

KEYNES'S USE OF LOGIC AND MATHEMATICS

The methodological aspect of Keynes's analysis, in striking contrast with orthodox economics, concerns the way in which he sets up his logical schemes and uses mathematics.

There is a sort of idolatry of mathematics, even more today than at the time of *The General Theory*, among economists. In fact, it is a sort of idolatry of particular mathematical schemes that are uniquely congenial to orthodox economics. In the attempts at representing Keynes's relations in simple mathematical terms, the schemes that have found favour in the textbooks are those that are nearest the traditional scheme of simultaneous equations, representing a Walrasian general equilibrium of the economic system. This scheme has two peculiar characteristics: (a) it makes a sharp distinction between the variables that are considered and the variables that are not considered and are ignored; (b) those variables that are considered are all treated in the same way; normally they are framed in a system of simultaneous equations, as if they were all equally important.

Keynes's way of thinking goes quite sharply against this methodology. Towards the end of *The General Theory*, Keynes finds it expedient to give an explicit account of his method of using logic and mathematics:

> The object of our analysis is, not to provide a machine, or method of blind manipulation, which will furnish an infallible answer, but to provide ourselves with an organised and orderly method of thinking out particular problems; and, after we have reached a provisional conclusion by isolating the complicating factors one by one, we then have to go back on ourselves and allow, as well as we can, for the probable interactions of the factors amongst themselves. This is the nature of economic thinking. Any other way of applying our formal principles of thought (without which, however, we shall be lost in the wood) will lead us into error. It is a great fault of symbolic pseudo-mathematical methods of formalising a system of economic analysis, such as we shall set down in section VI of this chapter, that they expressly assume strict independence between the factors involved and lose all their cogency and authority if this hypothesis is disallowed; whereas, in ordinary discourse, where we are not blindly manipulating but know all the time what we are doing and what the words mean, we can keep 'at the back of our heads' the necessary reserves and qualifications and the adjustments which we shall have to make later on, in a way in which we cannot keep complicated partial differentials 'at the back' of several pages of algebra which assume that they all vanish. Too large a proportion of recent 'mathematical' economics are mere concoctions, as imprecise as the initial assumptions they rest on, which allow the author to lose sight of the complexities and interdependencies of the real world in a maze of pretentious and unhelpful symbols.
>
> (*G.T.*: 297–8)

It must be pointed out that Keynes himself is making ample use a few pages later – as he himself states – of derivatives and calculus. Thus his statements cannot be interpreted as having an anti-mathematical bias. Keynes is simply making a strong plea for a use of mathematics that is appropriate to economic analysis. In economics, this means using mathematics not in a mechnical way. Any mathematical expression of any economic relation, as it inevitably simplifies, must never be taken as definitive but always as a first approximation, to be qualified, completed, revisited at a second or even higher stage of approximation. Most fundamentally, it is necessary to bring out, first of all, the relations that are most important. One must then reconsider also the others. Moreover, even the factors at the foundations of any relation and the variables in the relation itself are never contrasted in an absolutely clear-cut way.

As a corollary, it becomes evident that in Keynes's mind there always is a typical preoccupation to figure out and specify the *direction* in which each variable influences the others. (The relation between the rate of interest and the marginal efficiency of investment is only one of the most striking examples.) There may well be interdependence and mutual influences, but also there certainly are very definite directions of causality. Keynes is convinced that when the latter are singled out, the relations which are specified become richer, in the sense that they contain more information than if the directions of causation were not specified. Even the distinction between interdependence and one-way causality is by Keynes never juxtaposed in a completely rigid form. A one-way causal relation, stated as a first approximation, may well be qualified for interdependence of minor importance at a second or higher stage of approximation. Significant examples are the excerpts given on pp. 210–11 above, with reference to liquidity preference.

'THE GENERAL THEORY OF EMPLOYMENT RE-STATED'

With this title, given to Chapter 18, Keynes concludes Book IV ('The Inducement to Invest'). He gives a synthesis of *The General Theory*:

it may be useful to make clear which elements in the economic system we usually take as given, which are the independent variables of our system and which are the dependent variables.

We take as given the existing skill and quantity of available labour, the existing quality and quantity of available equipment, the existing technique, the degree of competition, the tastes and habits of the consumer, the disutility of different intensities of labour and of the activities of supervision and organization, as well as the social structure . . .

. . .

Our independent variables are, in the first instance, the propensity to consume, the schedule of the marginal efficiency of capital and the rate of interest, though, as we have already seen, these are capable of further analysis.

Our dependent variables are the volume of employment and the national income (or national dividend) measured in wage-units.

(*G.T.*: 245)

From a tri-partition of this type, it is quite clear that Keynes is *not* thinking in terms of a logical scheme of simultaneous equations. Against the background of what is taken as given (but not necessarily as constant, as he hastens to specify on the same page), he distinguishes between *independent* and *dependent* variables. Definitely more appropriate to this way of arguing is the logical scheme of the causal type. So convinced is he of the necessity of characterizing the independent variables that he goes on trying to deepen their relation with the given factors, which however 'do not completely determine them' (ibid.: 246). At the end, he concludes:

> Thus we can sometimes regard our ultimate independent variables as consisting of (1) the three fundamental psychological factors, namely, the psychological propensity to consume, the psychological attitude to liquidity and the psychological expectation of future yield from capital-assets, (2) the wage-unit as determined by the bargains reached between employers and employed, and (3) the quantity of money as determined by the action of the central bank.
>
> (Ibid.: 246–7)

It is not easy to frame all these elements within a synthetically neat scheme of equations, but we can at least try a first-approximation logical scheme of the causal type.

After specifying the 'given' elements as those listed at the beginning, we must place at the top of the logical scheme the rate of interest, determined by liquidity preference and by that amount of money that is left over for speculative purposes (M_2), after deducting the amount of money that is retained for transactions and precautionary purposes (i.e. $M_2 = M - M_1$). Then the rate of interest determines the marginal efficiency of the last investment project; this determines the amount of endogenous investments, which – added to the amount of autonomous investments (determined independently) – sets into motion the multiplier process through the 'psychological law' behind the consumption function. This finally determines the level of national income and employment (the dependent variables).

There remains a feed-back relation that has haunted some of Keynes's interpreters.[5] It goes from the level of the national income to that quantity of money which is demanded for transaction and precautionary motives, i.e. M_1. This quantity of money 'is not very sensitive to changes in the rate of interest' (*G.T.*: 161), and may be taken as roughly proportional to the level of income, with the causal relation going from Y to M_1.[6] It seems to me reasonable, therefore – at least as a first approximation – to take M_1 as endogenously determined – call it 'endogenous' money; in the sense that the central bank will automatically issue it in proportion to Y, in order to satisfy transaction and precautionary needs. This means that the discretionary decisions of the central bank will manifest themselves with reference to $M_2 = L_2(r)$. It is M_2 that, jointly with the liquidity function L_2, determines the rate of interest. In other words, the relevant liquidity preference schedule is $L_2(r)$. It is this function that is relevant for the determination of the rate of interest. And it is the decision about M_2 (the amount of money that the central bank decides to issue, after satisfying the needs for transaction and precautionary motives) that becomes a crucial 'independent' variable of monetary policy. For, through the determination of the rate of interest, it will also determine the point at which the marginal efficiency of investment schedule is cut off. It will determine the marginal efficiency of the last investment project to be carried out, and hence the amount of total 'endogenous' investments.

'ANIMAL SPIRITS' AND MONETARY POLICY – BUT ARE THEY ENOUGH?

It is of course the size of *total* investments that is playing the crucial role in the whole *General Theory*. Whenever it turns out to be below that level which, added to consumption, would ensure full-employment effective demand, the economic system falls short of its production potential. This is for two reasons: because it fails to achieve the full utilization of its resources (under-employment of both existing capital and existing labour), and because it fails to achieve the highest achievable productivity (which would correspond to an ideal world 'saturated' with capital). It is difficult not to agree with Keynes's diagnosis on the first reason. Keynes's second reason still reveals some remnants of orthodox theory on the role of capital in the production process.

In any case, Keynes's conviction of the importance of investigating the factors that determine the size of investments is not in question. This is precisely what he does with his analysis of the effect of the rate of interest on the marginal efficiency of investment. But his conclusion is that such an effect might not be sufficient, because of the practically infinite elasticity of liquidity preference below a certain level of the rate of interest.

At this point the other – the 'autonomous' – part of investments, which cannot be analytically investigated, becomes relevant. In one of the most brilliant passages of *The General Theory*, Keynes claims that:

> there is the instability due to the characteristic of human nature that a large proportion of our positive activities depend on spontaneous optimism rather than on a mathematical expectation, whether moral or hedonistic or economic. Most, probably, of our decisions to do something positive, the full consequences of which will be drawn out over many days to come, can only be taken as a result of animal spirits – of a spontaneous urge to action rather than inaction, and not as the outcome of a weighted average of quantitative benefits multiplied by quantitative probabilities. Enterprise only pretends to itself to be mainly actuated by the statements in its own prospectus, however candid and sincere. Only a little more than an expedition to the South Pole, is it based on an exact calculation of benefits to come. Thus if the animal

spirits are dimmed and the spontaneous optimism falters, leaving us to depend on nothing but a mathematical expectation, enterprise will fade and die; – though fears of loss may have a basis no more reasonable than hopes of profit had before.

It is safe to say that enterprise which depends on hopes stretching into the future benefits the community as a whole. But individual initiative will only be adequate when reasonable calculation is supplemented and supported by animal spirits, so that the thought of ultimate loss which often overtakes pioneers, as experience undoubtedly tells us and them, is put aside as a healthy man puts aside the expectation of death.

This means, unfortunately, not only that slumps and depressions are exaggerated in degree, but that economic prosperity is excessively dependent on a political and social atmosphere which is congenial to the average business man. If the fear of a Labour Government, or a New Deal depresses enterprise, this need not be the result either of a reasonable calculation or of a plot with political intent; – it is the mere consequence of upsetting the delicate balance of spontaneous optimism. In estimating the prospects of investment, we must have regard, therefore, to the nerves and hysteria and even the digestions and reactions to the weather of those upon whose spontaneous activity it largely depends.

(*G.T.*: 161–2)

This is one of the passages – in spite of Keynes's dislike of Ricardo – that bring to the fore the profound affinities between these two great economists in their conviction concerning the social function of the capitalist class. But 'animal spirits' cannot be engineered. They must be accepted for what they are, while at the same time strongly pursuing strict economic calculus as a rational basis for shaping socially effective economic policies. Keynes returns to the importance of monetary policy:

we are still entitled to return to the rate of interest as exercising, at any rate, in normal circumstances, a great, though not a decisive, influence on the rate of investment. Only experience, however, can show how far management of the rate of interest is capable of continuously stimulating the appropriate volume of investment.

(*G.T.*: 164)

Yet, if monetary policy plus 'animal spirits' are still not enough, one cannot stand and wait. Keynes goes straight to the logical conclusion:

For my own part I am now somewhat sceptical of the success of a merely monetary policy directed towards influencing the rate of interest. I expect to see the State, which is in a position to calculate the marginal efficiency of capital-goods on long views and on the basis of

217

the general social advantage, taking an ever greater responsibility for directly organizing investment; since it seems likely that the fluctuations in the market estimation of the marginal efficiency of different types of capital, calculated on the principle I have described above, will be too great to be offset by any practicable change in the rate of interest.

$(G.T.: 164)$

This is where Keynes's analysis ends. Government investment policy enters the scene: not to replace (or 'crowd out') private investments but to complement them because of their insufficiency, if the task to be pursued is that of achieving, and maintaining, full employment.

NOTES

* For useful comments and criticisms on an earlier draft, I should like to thank Enrico Bellino, Andrea Boitani, Domenico Delli Gatti and Geoffrey Harcourt. Financial support is gratefully acknowledged from the Italian Ministry of University (MURST 40 per cent).
1 See the account given by Skidelsky (1992: end of ch. XVI, and also end of ch. XVII relating to Keynes's health).
2 To give just one of many quotations: 'the rate of interest is not the "price" which brings into equilibrium the demand for resources to invest with the readiness to abstain from present consumption' $(G.T.(167)$.
3 See Pasinetti et al. (1966); also Harcourt (1972).
4 Pierangelo Garegnani (1978–9) is referring to these concessions when he himself claims that Keynes's notion is no different from the orthodox one. To realize that it is not so, it is enough to do a mental experiment. Suppose that, for all commodities, only one method of production is known. Then all traditional elements are eliminated *ex hypothesi*: there is no neoclassical production function, no possibility of factor substitution. Yet, Keynes's 'marginal efficiency' of investment maintains all its characteristics. Starting from any initial position, a cut in the rate of interest will make some extra investment projects potentially profitable and be undertaken.

What may be misleading is that Garegnani's arguments are set within a context of long-run equilibrium positions, with rate of interest and rate of profits being considered as one and the same thing, and thus inversely related to the wage rate. Keynes's context is quite different: it is a short-run context with entrepreneurial expectations about the future. In this Keynesian context, a cut in the rate of interest simply reduces the financial costs, leaving the wage rate unaffected and increasing profits expectations.
5 See, for example, Patinkin (1990: 222–3), who has used it as his main objection to my own (Pasinetti 1974: 31–42) simplified presentation of Keynes's scheme.
6 See the quotation, given on pp. 210–11 above, from $G.T.: 199–201$.

14

IS THERE A PLACE FOR RATIONAL EXPECTATIONS IN KEYNES'S *GENERAL THEORY*?*

Kevin D. Hoover

EXPECTATIONS IN *THE GENERAL THEORY*

It is a commonplace that what is widely known as 'Keynesian' economics is not the economics that John Maynard Keynes develops in *The General Theory of Employment, Interest and Money*. In one of the many ironies of the history of economic thought, the new classical macroeconomics attacked 'Keynesian' economics – and is widely regarded as having dealt both it and the economics of *The General Theory* a body blow – over its treatment of expectations (see, for example, Lucas and Sargent 1979). Yet nowhere do hydraulic Keynesian models and their econometric successors differ from *The General Theory* more than in their treatment of expectations.[1]

Where expectations are either ignored or modelled by simple extrapolative devices in the macroeconometric models of the 1940s to 1970s, they command centre-stage in *The General Theory*. Of the three principal functions of Keynes's analysis of aggregate demand, two depend essentially on expectations. Keynes's investment schedule depends upon the comparison of the market rate of interest with the marginal efficiency of capital – that is, of the discount rate that makes the *expected* stream of future revenues equal to the current supply price of capital goods (Keynes 1936: ch. 11; hereafter abbreviated to *G.T.*). His liquidity preference function is the aggregation of individual liquidity preferences, which depend, in turn, after accounting for money required for transactions purposes, on whether individuals *expect* interest rates to fall, producing *expected* capital gains and a preference for bonds, or to rise, producing *expected* capital losses and a preference for money (*G.T.*: ch. 13). The consumption function, the third member of the Keynesian triumvirate, is usually – and not incorrectly – thought to depend principally on current income. Even so, Keynes carefully analyses the importance of *expected* future incomes and *expected* capital gains on current consumption (*G.T.*: ch. 8). It would not be misleading to say that he anticipated the permanent-income and life-cycle hypotheses. Expectations are important elsewhere in *The General Theory*. For example, Keynes argues that flexible money wages will not necessarily clear the labour market

219

because of perverse expectations in which cuts in the market wage generate a belief that further cuts are likely (*G.T.*: ch. 19, esp. p. 263).

Keynes distinguishes between *long-term* and *short-term* expectations (*G.T.*: 46–7). The distinction mirrors Marshall's distinction between the long run, in which factors of production are all variable, and the short run, in which the firm's capital equipment is fixed. Keynes argues that an entrepreneur consults his long-term expectations in determining the amount of his investment in plant and machinery, and consults his short-term expectations in determining the scale of his current output.

Macroeconomic equilibrium for Keynes is defined using short-term expectations: '[T]he aggregate supply price of the output of a given amount of employment is the *expectation* of proceeds which will just make it worth the while of the entrepreneurs to give that employment' (*G.T.*: 24, emphasis added). Similarly, the aggregate demand function relates the number of men employed to the proceeds entrepreneurs *expect* to receive from their employment (*G.T.*: 25). The intersection of the aggregate supply function and the aggregate demand function determines the point of effective demand, which is the 'point [at which] the entrepreneur's *expectations* of profits will be maximised' (*G.T.*: 25, emphasis added). The point of effective demand is an equilibrium since firms have no incentive to alter the scale of their output or employment.

Although the point of effective demand is a short-run equilibrium, it is long-term expectations that do the work in determining aggregate demand. It is the long-term expectations of other people that determine what demands entrepreneurs should expect in the short run. Changes in long-term expectations govern changing levels of investment through the marginal efficiency of capital and the interest rate through liquidity preference, and may even affect consumption. Investment and consumption together form the largest component of aggregate demand. Thus, far from dismissing long-term considerations as in the common misconstrual of his famous remark, 'in the long run we are all dead', Keynes's position is in fact that the long run is always with us (*G.T.*: 50, 51).[2]

If it were founded only in Marshall's distinction between different variabilities of factors of production, the distinction between long-term and short-term expectations would be one of degree, not of kind. In Keynes's usage, however, the distinction is more fundamentally between quantifiable and unquantifiable (or partially quantifiable) expectations or probabilities. On the one hand, Keynes believed that short-term expectations could be quantified relatively accurately; on the other hand, long-term expectations were founded on a precarious basis. In *The General Theory* (*G.T.*: 149, 150) he writes:

> Our knowledge of the factors which will govern the yield of an investment some years hence is usually very slight and often negligible. If we speak frankly, we have to admit that our basis of knowledge for

estimating the yield ten years hence of a railway, a copper mine, a textile factory, the goodwill of a patent medicine, an Atlantic liner, a building in the City of London amounts to little and sometimes to nothing; or even five years hence.

While in the short term, quantifiable risk and the calculus of probabilities may be of some use, Keynes, in his 1937 précis of *The General Theory* in the *Quarterly Journal of Economics*, emphasizes the 'uncertainty' of long-term expectations:

> By 'uncertain' knowledge . . . I do not mean merely to distinguish what is known for certain from what is only probable. The game of roulette is not subject, in this sense, to uncertainty; . . . the expectation of life is only slightly uncertain. Even the weather is only moderately uncertain. The sense in which I am using the term is that in which the prospect of a European war is uncertain, or the price of copper and the rate of interest twenty years hence, or the obsolescence of a new invention, or the position of private wealth owners in the social system in 1970. About these matters there is no scientific basis on which to form any calculable probability whatever. We simply do not know. Nevertheless, the necessity for action and for decision compels us as practical men to do our best to overlook this awkward fact and to behave exactly as we should if we had behind us a good Benthamite calculation of a series of prospective advantages and disadvantages, each multiplied by its appropriate probability, waiting to be summed
>
> (*C.W.* XIV: 113, 114)[3]

Beyond the issue of whether it is possible to attach numerical probabilities to expectations, the quotation refers to another dimension of expectations crucial to Keynes's analysis: *confidence.* Keynes argues that the marginal efficiency of capital depends separately on the probabilies of various prospective yields and the confidence with which those probabilities are held. He relates confidence to the intuitively appealing, but difficult to explicate, notion of the 'weight of argument' borrowed from his *Treatise on Probability* (1921/*C.W.* VIII: ch. 6; see *G.T.*: 148).

Expectations for Keynes are not single-valued. In the short term, an entrepreneur may consider a range of possibilities, each with a probability attached. Keynes suggests that this is easily dealt with through the idea of a certainty equivalent: that expectation which if held with certainty would yield the equivalent behaviour to the range of actual expectations with their associated probabilities (*G.T.*: 24, fn. 3).

It is not clear in *The General Theory* whether Keynes believes that long-term expectations can be dealt with in the same way. He does suggest in later writings that there is an equivalent expectation that would rationalize any action *ex post*, although he does not seem to suggest that such expectations play any role in decisions to act (*C.W.* XIV: 289).[4] What is clear in *The General Theory* is that even if long-term expectations were certainty equivalents, they would not be certain, because of the low weight of evidence on which they are formed. Entrepreneurs are faced with the necessity of choice. And Keynes argues that, in the absence of weighty evidence, conventions or arbitrary rules or psychological factors govern expectations and choice. Long-term expectations and, consequently, investment is, on Keynes's view, extremely precarious. The accumulation of capital can be explained only by confidence of entrepreneurs in excess of the weight of available evidence. Thus:

> In former times, . . . investment depended on a sufficient supply of individuals of sanguine temperament and constructive impulses who embarked on business as a way of life, not really relying on a precise calculation of prospective profit . . . Business men play a mixed game of skill and chance, the average results of which to the players are not known by those who take a hand. If human nature felt no temptation to take a chance, no satisfaction (profit apart) in constructing a factory, a railway, a mine or a farm, there might not be much investment merely as a result of cold calculation.
>
> (*G.T.*: 150)

In a similar vein, Keynes writes:

> Most, probably, of our decisions to do something positive, the full consequences of which will be drawn out over many days to come, can only be taken as a result of animal spirits – of a spontaneous urge to action rather than inaction, and not as the outcome of a weighted average of quantitative benefits multiplied by quantitative probabilities . . . [I]f the animal spirits are dimmed and the spontaneous optimism falters, leaving us nothing but mathematical expectation, enterprise will fade and die; – though fears of loss may have a basis no more reasonable than hopes of profit had before.
>
> (*G.T.*: 161–2)

It has been argued by Patinkin (1976a: 142), among others, that Keynes does not have a theory of expectation formation. If what this means is that Keynes does not have a single mechanical algorithm for the generation of expectations, this is no doubt true. In the *Treatise on Probability* (*C.W.* VIII: 413–18), Keynes rejects the foundations of the Bayesian argument. He does not recant in *The General Theory* nor does he offer any alternative formulaic approach.[5] Instead, Keynes subsumes the formation of short-term expectations to his general views on induction. In the *Treatise on Probability* (ibid.: ch. 27), Keynes argues that in sufficiently stable, homogeneous environments statistical methods unveil recurrent facts about populations. Extrapolations of such facts, something like the weighted averages of adaptive expectations in common use before the rise of rational expectations, are, in Keynes's view, a perfectly adequate basis for forming short-term expectations. In *The General Theory*, Keynes regards the formation of short-term expectations as a second-order concern, and assumes, for purposes of exposition, that short-term expectations are always fulfilled.[6]

Again, long-term expectations are a different matter. Because the evidential basis on which we might form long-term expectations is so slender, while the necessity for choice in questions that inextricably involve long-term expectations is so compelling, Keynes argues that we fall back on conventions. In particular, Keynes argues that we adopt the convention that expectations are held constant until we have a positive reason to alter them. Keynes specifically rejects the interpretation that an expectation is constant because there is an equal probability of a rise or fall in its value (*G.T.*: 152). This rules out the modern interpretation that expectations follow a random walk. In the *Treatise on Probability* (1921/C.W. XIV: ch. 4), Keynes had argued that equiprobability arguments could succeed only with specific causal knowledge, say, knowledge of the uniform construction of a die. The appeal to convention in *The General Theory* can be seen as appealing to the same insight.

Long-term expectations are held constant because there is little weight of evidence supporting a change. But, because this weight is so little, small but positive reasons, reasons which provide a causal case, justify changes in expectations. Long-term expectations are precarious in that they may change a great deal for relatively slight reasons. Still, Keynes denies that long-term expectations are the result of nothing but irrational psychology:

> On the contrary, the state of long-term expectation is often steady . . .
> We are merely reminding ourselves that human decisions affecting the future, whether personal or political or economic, cannot depend on strict mathematical expectation, since the basis for making such calculations does not exist; and that it is our innate urge to activity which makes the wheels go round, our rational selves choosing between the alternatives as best we are able, calculating where we can, but often falling back for our motive on whim or sentiment or chance.
>
> (*G.T.*: 102, 103)

One final feature of Keynes's treatment of expectations in *The General Theory* deserves emphasis. While Keynes recognizes the aggregate consequences of expectations for interest rates or national income, he does not aggregate expectations themselves. The expectations of individuals are heterogeneous – and fundamentally so.[7] Thus, Keynes recognizes that it is only diversity of opinion about expected values of financial assets that permits trades without massive swings in asset prices (*G.T.*: 172). Similarly, an aggregate liquidity preference function requires diverse expectations

(*G.T.*: 197–9). People will either hold speculative money balances or bonds, depending on whether they expect interest rates to rise or fall. To turn this individual analysis into an aggregate function that smoothly maps the holdings of money against the interest rate, requires that different individuals expect different interest rates to prevail.[8]

A SECOND EDITION?

Had Keynes written a second edition of *The General Theory* in 1938, how might his treatment of expectations have changed? I will suggest two changes. Keynes himself suggests the first change; the second is implicit in some of Keynes's writings.

In a set of rough notes from his 1937 lectures, Keynes (*C.W.* XIV: 181) writes:

> I now feel that if I were writing the book again I should begin by setting forth my theory on the assumption that short-period expectations were always fulfilled; and then have a subsequent chapter showing the difference it makes when short period expectations are disappointed.

As observed on p. 223, short-term expectations are typically assumed to be correct in *The General Theory*. Keynes saw a need for a subsequent chapter because he wanted to clarify the proper role of expectations in his analysis, and because he wanted to relate his analysis more closely to alternative views.

For Keynes (*C.W.* XIV: 179–81), effective demand is a matter of expectations; it is not on a par with realized income. Realized or actual income and, in particular, the disparity between it and previously expected income is important only to the degree that it is useful information in the formation of short-term expectations of future income.

Keynes (*C.W.* XIV: 181–3) faults Robertson for regarding the income of the previous period as *the* constraint on the expenditure of today:

> Expenditure is determined partly by yesterday's income, partly by today's, partly by expectations of tomorrow's and by many other things too. What primarily matters is the expectation of expenditure formed by the entrepreneur beforehand and secondarily by the gradual revisions of this expectation in the light of experience.
>
> (*C.W.* XIV: 181, 182)

While acknowledging the desirability of discussing economic behaviour under disappointed short-term expectations, Keynes nevertheless believes that the issue is secondary. He does not repent of his tactic of treating short-term expectations as fulfilled. Hawtrey, he argues, disregards the fundamental factors in dynamic change – presumably the state of long-term expectations – in order to concentrate on the ephemera that 'is better described as the higgling of the market' (*C.W.* XIV: 182).

More speculatively, I suggest that Keynes might have used his notion of weight to clarify and extend the role of liquidity preference in a second edition of *The General Theory*. Money is the most liquid of assets. 'Money', Keynes writes, ' . . . is, above all, a subtle device for linking the present to the future' (*G.T.*: 294). And the most salient feature of the future is that it is unknown; our long-term expectations of the future are for Keynes, as we have seen, hardly quantifiable and rest on evidence of low weight. Financial assets in a monetary economy, to varying degrees, allow us to keep our options open in the face of the dark future.

Surprisingly, Keynes treats liquidity preference as a matter of risk and certainty-equivalence. As a result, we would seem justified in carrying away from *The General Theory* a notion of the liquidity-preference function as smoothly mapping interest rates on to the demand for money, and as supporting the simple manipulations of the supply of money that are the standard fare of the IS–LM model of the 'Keynesian' textbook. Yet, even in *The General Theory*, Keynes acknowledges that risk and liquidity have been conflated, and notes 'the difference [corresponds] to the difference between the best estimates we can make of probabilities and the confidence with which we make them' (*G.T.*: 240). Still, the distinction affects the substance of *The General Theory* relatively little.[9]

Keynes, however, continued to think about the question of weight and confidence. In a letter to Hugh Townshend in 1938 (*C.W.* XIV: 293–4), he again distinguished the risk premium, the higher-than-average return one expected to receive as a compensation for bearing risk, from the liquidity premium, a payment that does not on average produce a greater return, but provides comfort and confidence in the face of the unknown. I speculate that Keynes would, given an opportunity, have made better use of the fundamental notion of the liquidity premium in a manner similar to that developed more recently by Hicks (1974: ch. 2), Bernanke (1983) and Makowski (1989). The central point in these treatments is that liquidity is about keeping options open in the face of ignorance. Waiting produces information that will permit a better choice when long-term expectations do not possess a firm evidential base. Thus, when confidence collapses and animal spirits can no longer outweigh uncertainty, the psychic reward to waiting rises. Entrepreneurs hold back on investment, not because their cold calculations of return have altered, but because they would be more comfortable with a less cloudy view of the future and choose to wait for it.[10] Simultaneously, they keep their options open by shifting to more liquid assets – money being the extreme. The conclusions of the modern litera-ture are, first, that the IS curve (marginal efficiency of capital) and the LM curve (liquidity preference) are not independent; and, second, that there might be a liquidity trap, operating not because the demand for money routinely becomes elastic at low interest rates (a situation of which Keynes – *G.T.*: 207 – denied knowing any practical examples), but because money is the most flexible form in which to lodge purchasing power – whatever the interest rate – when entrepreneurs are waiting for the evidence that would restore confidence in particular capital projects. Given his concern with the notion of confidence, I fancy that Keynes would have wanted to clarify its role in something like this way in a second edition.

RATIONAL EXPECTATIONS

Keynes, of course, did not write a second edition of *The General Theory*. Expectations were ignored in the early development of 'Keynesian' economics. Gradually, they were reintroduced – for example, into the analysis of consumption with the permanent income hypothesis (Friedman 1957) and into the analysis of money demand (Cagan 1956). And although in the recent work cited above (p. 225) ideas congenial to Keynes's concern with confidence and weight of evidence have been developed, they are out of the mainstream. Instead, the single most important development with respect to expectations in modern macroeconomics is the introduction around 1970 by Robert Lucas, Thomas Sargent and others of John Muth's idea of rational expectations.

Muth's (1961: 4–5) formulation runs: 'Expectations . . . tend to be distributed, for the same information set, about the prediction of the theory (or the "objective" probability distribution of outcomes).' If an expectation differed from what the theory suggests, then either the theory is incorrect or one's expecation is failing to use the information contained in the correct theory. Rational expecations are thus sometimes viewed as 'model-consistent' expectations.

Rational expectations are usually noted with a formulation such as

$$_{t-1} X_t^e = E_{t-1} (X_t | \Omega_{t-1}), \qquad (14.1)$$

which says that the expectation of X formed at time $t{-}1$ is the mathematical expectation of X conditional on all the information available at time $t{-}1$. The information set Ω_{t-1} in any theoretical account includes the model postulated by the theory. In empirical applications, equation (14.1) is sometimes treated – independently of a particular model – as a regression of X_t on the variables in Ω_{t-1}. The residuals from such a regression are definitionally uncorrelated with X_t; the fitted values can then be treated as the expected values, provided that no information omitted from the regression is correlated with the residuals.

In the interpretation of rational expectations as model-consistent expectations, equation (14.1) is embedded into the model and Ω_{t-1} consists of the model itself and its variables. In this form, as in the empirical interpretation, expectations cannot systematically differ from realizations: in stochastic models rational expectations are not always correct, but they can differ from the actual values only by a serially uncorrelated error. In either interpretation, the rational expectations hypothesis is usually justified heuristically by the observation that any reasonable person would not persist in identifiably systematic mistakes, so that actual expectations should closely approximate rational expectations.

The rational expectations hypothesis was introduced into macroeconomics by the new classical school (see Hoover 1988). In the past quarter century, however, it has become the common property of all macroeconomists – valued by some more than others. Within the new classical school, the rational expectations hypothesis was centrally identified with three important theoretical developments.[11]

First was the *policy-ineffectiveness proposition*. Milton Friedman (1968) and Edmund Phelps (1967) argued that there was a natural rate of unemployment unaffected by aggregate demand policies. This was equivalent to claiming that the Phillips curve and the aggregate supply curves were vertical in the long-run. Friedman and Phelps maintained that inflationary policies might stimulate output and employment in the short run as workers, misperceiving the price level, would regard an increase in their nominal wage as an increase in their real wages when it was, in fact, a fall. This stimulus could not last, in Friedman's and Phelp's view, because workers' expectations would adapt.

Lucas (1972a) and Sargent and Wallace (1975, 1976) used the rational expectations hypothesis to argue that workers' misperceptions and the resulting stimulus could be, at most, random and could not be systematically exploited by monetary and fiscal authorities. Fischer (1977) and Phelps and Taylor (1977) demonstrated that rational expectations were necessary but not sufficient for policy ineffectiveness. The vertical long-run Phillips curve (or natural rate hypothesis) was also needed. They demonstrated in models of staggered contracts that rational expectations and policy effectiveness were in fact compatible.

The second important development was the *policy non-invariance proposition* or 'Lucas critique' (Lucas 1972a, 1976). Lucas argued that estimated macroeconometric models do not represent the true structure of the economy. Instead, their equations relate aggregates that are composites of the microeconomic behaviour of firms, consumers and policy-makers. In a rich description of such agents, each would form expectations using something like equation (14.1). Solving the model would generate some rule for forming expectations from available data. Among the information in Ω_{t-1} would be the perceived policy rules of the government. If the government adopted new policy rules, then the rules for forming expectations would themselves change. Aggregating up to the level of the macroeconometric model, its equations too would show 'structural breaks'. Lucas argued that 'Keynesian' macroeconometric models, because they failed to incorporate rational expectatons, could not reasonably be used for policy analysis because their equations – however well they appeared to fit the data – would not be stable in the face of the very policy regime they were used to analyse.

The third important development tied rational expectations to game theory. Barro and Gordon (1983a, 1983b), following Kydland and Prescott (1977), argued that policy under rational expectations must be 'dynamically consistent': that is, what appears optimal today must turn out to be optimal tomorrow. In their illustration, the monetary authorities dislike inflation, but are willing to trade some inflation for lower unemployment. With a vertical long-run Phillips curve, unemployment can be reduced only if inflation is unexpected. If the authorities announce that they will pursue a zero inflation policy, and if people believe them, then they will be tempted to renege on their announcement and lower unemployment through higher inflation. To do so would be to lose credibility; but, under rational expectations, people understand that the temptation is too great for them to resist. Only at a higher rate of inflation, at which the loss to further inflation exactly balances the gain to unemployment, will there be no temptation to cheat. People with rational expectations will treat only this higher inflation policy as credible, and policy will inevitably converge on it. Unfortunately, since there is a natural rate of unemployment and no permanent gains to inflation, this high-inflation equilibrium is inferior to one with zero inflation and the same level of unemployment.

ANTICIPATIONS OF RATIONAL EXPECTATIONS

Rational expectations was such a striking feature of the new classical revolt against 'Keynesian' economics that for a long time economists such as Lucas, Sargent, Wallace, Barro, Kydland and Prescott were commonly referred to as 'rational expectationists'. The misleading belief that their main results derive principally from the rational expectations hypothesis persists in some quarters even today. This belief is misleading because the most characteristic feature of the new classical school is its adherence to the assumption of continually clearing, perfectly competitive markets as a basis for macroeconomics. Policy is ineffective in the long run because the economy is assumed to be fully employed. Rational expectations extends that result to the short run, because it rules out over-employment due to systematically mistaken perceptions about real wages and prices. There is no doubt that, were Keynes alive today, he would still reject the assumption of continuous full employment as a basis for macroeconomics. Keynes would then have no truck with the policy-ineffectiveness proposition. The general principle of dynamic consistency would be more congenial and would fit in with his move toward rules in the conduct of policy.[12] He would none the less not have been able to accept the underlying economic assumptions of Barro and Gordon and the related natural-rate models.

This leaves policy non-invariance (the Lucas critique) and, of course, rational expectations itself. Surprisingly perhaps, Keynes anticipated rational expectations, and may well have embraced it in limited circumstances. As early as 1923 in the *Tract on Monetary Reform*, Keynes wrote of 'intelligent anticipations'. He argued that people, especially those engaged in business, use their intimate knowledge to form expectations in such a way that, although they make errors, their errors are not pervasive and are insufficient to explain cyclical fluctuations (*C.W.* IV: 18). Bradley Bateman (1994: ch. 4) argues that Keynes abandoned 'intelligent anticipations' by 1930 as part of a sea-change in his views on probability and confidence. According to Bateman, Keynes abandoned his notions of probabilities as Platonic entities expressing the objective logical relationship between evidence and conclusions in favour of Frank Ramsey's thorough-going subjectivism. Whether and to what degree Keynes's views changed are hotly debated among Keynes scholars (see O'Donnell 1989: esp. 138–48; Carabelli 1988: ch. 6). It is enough here to observe that, in his analysis of Hawtrey's theory of the cycle (cited on pp. 224–5 above), as late as 1937 Keynes continued to deny that pervasive expectational errors were the cause of cyclical fluctuations. Furthermore, as noted earlier, in *The General Theory* itself, Keynes assumes that short-term expectation are fulfilled. How he might have analysed the effects of expectational errors and whether that analysis would have been consistent with rational expectations is impossible to say, given the sparse details in his lecture notes. That he regarded the issue of short-term expectational errors as second-order is none the less clear.

One of the more surprising results in the history of the rational expectations hypothesis was the realization, first by Muth (1960) and then in other contexts by Lucas (1972a) and Sargent and Wallace (1973), that schemes in which expectations are formed by fixed weights on lagged variables could be fully consistent with rational expectations. Many people thought, for example, that a test of the natural-rate hypothesis would be to regress real output on the current and numerous lagged values of the money stock. If all the coefficients summed to a value insignificantly different from zero, then it could be presumed that the natural-rate hypothesis was true, because the effect for output of an increase in the stock of money would be zero in the long run. If the sum of coefficients was not zero, then it could be presumed that the natural rate hypothesis was false. Lucas (1972a) showed that this conclusion was false: if the natural-rate hypothesis were true by assumption, and the monetary authority created money according to a constant percentage growth rule, then the coefficients on lagged values of money in an output regression would not sum to zero. Lucas's conclusion is related to the policy non-invariance proposition. A regression of output on lags of money is not a deep structural equation. Rather, it conflates the *ex hypothesi* true (natural-rate) aggregate-supply curve, the aggregate-demand curve and – through rational expectations – the rule for money creation, which governs the development of the price level over time. Lagged money appears in the regression equation because expected prices help to determine deviations of output from the natural rate, and the rational expectation of prices depends on the rational expectation of the money stock, which in turn depends on lagged money because the authorities set tomorrow's money stock as a fixed percentage increase over today's money stock.

Keynes does not offer Muth's or Lucas's argument in any detail. Nevertheless, he clearly understands the main point. For example, in his 1940 rejoinder to Tinbergen's reply to his review of Tinbergen's book on the statistical testing of theories of the business cycle, Keynes (*C.W.* XIV: 319) remarks: 'I understand well enough that his method can deal with time lags with expectations of the type that the future will resemble the very recent past.' This is of a piece with Keynes's general approach that, as we saw above (pp. 222–3), subsumes the formation of short-term expectations to his general views on statistical induction, and imagines that short-term expectations are correct to a first approximation.

A consequence of Lucas's analysis is that adaptive expectations may sometimes coincide with rational expectations. Keynes understood the essence of this point. But, like Lucas, Keynes also understood that this is a special case that requires a constant policy regime. Keynes (*C.W.* XIV: 319) follows up his concession to Tinbergen on the approximation of expectations with a question: 'How does [Tinbergen] deal with expectations of change?' In his review, Keynes (*C.W.* XIV: 306–18) had questioned among other things whether Tinbergen's equations represented the 'deep structure' of the economy, and whether they were stable in the face of a changing economic environment. In posing this new question, Keynes suggests what is essentially the narrow version of the Lucas critique – that is, that estimated aggregate econometric relationships will not be stable because expectations of changing economic environment cannot be accounted for adequately using a set of fixed weights on lagged variables.

Demonstrating not only a general understanding of policy invariance but also the specific context of many new classical analyses, Keynes argued in *The General Theory* (*G.T.*: 198–99) that open-market operations would alter not only the money supply directly but also the demand for money, because people's expectations would change with their changing understanding of the policies of the central bank and the government. In general, the liquidity preference function, he believed, would be discontinuous, shifting with the 'news' – changing expectations of policy or the economic environment. Keynes's understanding of policy non-invariance was, like his understanding of the formation of short-term expectations, of a piece with his general views on induction established long before *The General Theory*. He wrote in 1925:

> It is dangerous . . . to apply to the future inductive arguments based on past experience, unless one can distinguish the broad reasons why past experience was what it was. Otherwise there is a danger of expecting results in the future which could only follow from the special conditions which have existed in the . . . past.
>
> *(C.W.* XII: 248)

Lucas could not have put the point more lucidly. Taken in conjunction with Keynes's general dissent from econometric modelling expressed most clearly in his review of Tinbergen, that Keynes was not a 'Keynesian' in the sense of Lucas and Sargent (1979) is manifest.

Keynes was not a 'Lucasian' either. Lucas (1976: 108–9) points out that giving a large weight to the most recent data is a way of improving economic forecasts. Similarly, Keynes *(G.T.:* 51, 148, *passim)* observes that people typically give undue weight to the most recent data or to the *status quo*. Lucas and Keynes observe the same phenomenon; but, for Lucas, it is an *ad hoc* response to the problem of policy non-invariance, revealing a deep flaw in formal modelling; whereas for Keynes, it is a conventional stratagem used to short-circuit our inevitable ignorance of the long term.

THE LIMITS OF RATIONAL EXPECTATIONS

Keynes understood the essential message of the rational expectations hypothesis long before it was formulated by Muth, and he clearly would have approved of its use in demonstrating the policy non-invariance proposition. He would nevertheless not have been a 'rational expectation-ist'. The most important reason is that rational expectations – as it is understood in modern macroeconomics – cannot accommodate Keynes's fundamental distinction between short-term and long-term expectations.[13]

Although Keynes understood the basis and some of the implications of the rational expectations hypothesis long before it bore that name, he would not have used it in the way that the new classicals typically have themselves done. Early new classical models of the business cycle had sought to explain fluctuations in output as the product of expectational errors.[14] It soon became apparent that these fluctuations were too serially correlated or persistent to be simple random deviations from a natural rate of output. The new classicals then proposed a series of models with the common feature that random expectational errors were propagated by long-lived capital: an unanticipated shock to the money supply not only increases output but also shifts the natural rate of output temporarily higher; re-adjustment to equilibrium occurs immediately if there are no futher random shocks; but the natural rate itself adjusts only slowly back to its steady-state level as a sub-optimal stock of capital is optimally depreciated.[15] Essentially, to explain persistence, the new classicals graft rational expectations on to the neoclassical growth model of Robert Solow (1956).

We know that Keynes would not himself have adopted the new classical modelling strategy because he clearly sketched out and criticized the argument in his 1937 article in the *Quarterly Journal of Economics*. Keynes (*C.W.* XIV: 112) argued that Marshall, Pigou, Edgeworth and other 'classicals' followed Ricardo and, fundamentally, analysed only long-period equilibrium. Nevertheless,

> [t]his does not mean that [the classicals] were dealing with a system in which change was ruled out, or even one in which disappointment of expectations was ruled out. But at any given time facts and expectations were assumed to be given in a definite and calculable form; and risks, of which, though admitted, not much notice was taken, were supposed to be capable of an exact actuarial computation. The calculus of probability, though mention of it was kept in the background, was supposed to be capable of reducing uncertainty to the same calculable status as that of certainty itself; just as in the Benthamite calculus of pains and pleasures or of advantage or of disadvantage . . .
>
> (*C.W.* XIV: 113)

As we have already seen, Keynes had no objection to applying the calculus of probabilities to expectations in the short term; but what the classicals have done is to attach short-term methods for forming expectations to otherwise long-run models. On Keynes's analysis, the new classicals, joining the rational expectations hypothesis – the quintessence of the calculus of probabilities applied to expectations – to the neoclassical model of long-run growth, adopt the same strategy. Keynes (*C.W.* XIV: 115) believes that the classicals, however, have fallen into a trap: 'I accuse the classical economic theory of being itself one of those pretty, polite techniques which tries to deal with the present by abstracting from the fact that we know very little about the future.' He would no doubt believe that the new classicals – as in so much else – had repeated their forebears' error.

One of the prettiest of the polite techniques employed by the new classical macroeconomics is the representative agent. The economy is assumed to be governed by the microeconomic optimization problem of a single agent who treats national income as his own budget constraint. Representative-agent models could represent the economy accurately only if the conditions of exact aggregation were fulfilled. Essentially, all agents would have to be identical with homothetic preferences, so that the poor were effectively scale models of the rich. Such conditions are absurd. They produce puzzles that highlight the limits of representative-agent models. For example, if all agents have identical preferences, constraints and expectations, how can we explain asset trading? Keynes (*G.T.*: 199) clearly understood that the assumption of identical information, much less identical preferences or constraints, would be enough to inhibit trade in financial assets. In this, he anticipated the recent interest in 'noise trading', which seeks to avoid the odd consequence of rational expectations applied to financial markets (for example, Black 1987: ch. 14).

The appeal of the representative-agent model is that it is analytically tractable. To maintain tractability such models typically assume a single good with a single production function (or at the most a few goods). Keynes, on the other hand, argued for heterogeneity on this dimension as well. In a representative-agent model, rational expectations (the calculus of probabilities) is easily joined with the production constraint to cast the investment problem in a present-value framework. Keynes (*G.T.*: 137–41) recognizes the equivalence of his preferred concept of the marginal efficiency of capital with the expected discounted present value of the marginal product of capital in a world in which capital is physically homogeneous. Recognition that capital is not, in fact, physically homogeneous is one of the features that undermines mathematical tractability and closure of formal economic models. The necessary complexity and intractability of an adequate economic model is one of the elements that undermines the evidential base necessary to form long-term expectations; and, in turn, the difficulty of forming long-term expectations in a numerical manner subject to the calculus of probability undermines the formation of tractable formal models. Precision about expectations or economic structure is for Keynes impossible. In a letter to G.F. Shove in 1936, Keynes (*C.W.* XIV: 2) writes: 'But you ought not to feel inhibited by a difficulty in making the solution precise. It may be that part of the error in the classical analysis is due to that attempt. As soon as one is dealing with the influence of expectations and of transitory experience, one is, in the nature of things, outside the realm of the formally exact.'

Keynes argues that in the face of difficulties in forming long-term expectations people typically apply different techniques than the inductive extrapolations used in forming short-term expectations. In the 1937 *Quarterly Journal of Economics* article (*C.W.* XIV: 14), he mentions three techniques. First,

> we assume that the present is a much more serviceable guide to the future than a candid examination of past experience would show it to have been hitherto. In other words we largely ignore the prospect of future changes about the actual character of which we know nothing.

Second, we use market information – prices and output – as correct summary statistics for future prospects based on currently available information. Third, we suppress our individual judgements in favour 'of those of the rest of the world which is perhaps better informed'. Adherence to conventions replaces any attempt to form individual assessments. In *The General Theory*

(158) Keynes puts it thus: 'Worldly wisdom teaches that it is better for reputation to fail conventionally than to succeed unconventionally.'

Considering these strategies in relation to the rational expectations hypothesis provides at once a view on Keynes's probable attitude towards modern developments in the treatment of expectations and a deeper understanding of the differences between three strands of new classical thinking. The second technique is the closest to typical modern applications of rational expectations. Indeed, it is essentially the basis for the efficient-markets view of financial markets. Prices fully reflect available information so that there are no residual arbitrage opportunities.

The first technique is related to the second. Were it not for Keynes's insistence on non-numerical probability, the first technique would suggest that the development of expectations, because they fully incorporate available information (second technique), followed a random walk. Such a hypothesis has proved important, not only in the analysis of efficient financial markets, but also in, for example, Hall's (1978) work on consumption functions with rational expectations.

Interpreted in this way, the first technique is essential to the sort of rational expectations modelling associated with Sargent (1978, 1981; also see Hansen and Sargent 1980). Sargent seeks to solve the policy non-invariance problem by formulating explicit structural models that account for rational expectations. The evidential base for expectations formation in such models is extremely narrow. Some variables are described as governed by exogenous processes. Expectations are formed conditional on these variables and the hypothesized structure of the model. That this is a narrow base is evident if one contrasts such modelling to so-called 'strong' tests of the efficient-markets hypothesis in which one asks if changes in the price of a financial asset are predictable using *any* variable – not just those singled out as key in a formal model. Modelling on the narrow evidential basis of a formal econometric model amounts to adopting Keynes's convention of ignoring changes that cannot be processed easily through the calculus of probabilities. And Sargent (1984) is explicit on this point: policy analysis proceeds on the assumption that a policy change once made is in place forever, even though there may be further regime changes in the future.

Just as Ramsey rejected Keynes's notion of non-numerical probabilities, a second strand of new classical analysis associated with LeRoy argues that there is no reason to treat policy changes as beyond probabilistic analysis.[16] LeRoy accepts the subjectivist view (essentially Ramsey's view) that probabilities can always be assigned to any future event. He argues that the fact that a policy regime has changed in the past means that a rational person would not place a zero probability on another change of regime, and that these probabilities should be incorporated into the rational expectations within a formal model. What Keynes stigmatizes as a 'pretty, polite technique', LeRoy holds up as a requirement of logical consistency.[17]

The third strand associated with Lucas is diametrically opposed to LeRoy's 'fundamentalist' interpretation of the rational expectations hypothesis, and is ultimately the closest to Keynes. Like Keynes, Lucas distinguishes between quantifiable risk and unquantifiable uncertainty.[18] Rational expectations can deal with risk, but not with uncertainty. Where Keynes and Lucas differ is in their assessments of the limits that this distinction places on economic analysis. Lucas (1977: 15) expresses a view that Keynes would never concede: 'In cases of uncertainty, economic reasoning will be of no value.' Lucas, however, is true to his word. Unlike Sargent, Lucas does not estimate structural models subject to rational expectations. Instead, in his empirical analyses he concentrates on long-run or steady-state properties and uses techniques such as cross-section regressions on temporally averaged data, two-sided moving averages and calibration methods that might transcend particular structural models and the exact transition dynamics implied by rational-expectations models.[19] Essentially, Lucas accepts that rational expectations cannot cope with the sort of changes that generate policy non-invariance, and he wants to let the economy settle down after any such change before again applying analysis based on the rational expectations hypothesis.[20]

Why, then, is Lucas so insistent upon the rational expectations hypothesis in formal economic models? Perhaps it is simply a taste for the formal and precise. Perhaps it also a matter of convention: Lucas (1987: 13, fn. 4) defends the rational expectations hypothesis not on grounds of realism or even because the economy behaves 'as if' it were true, but as a consistency criterion for economic models. In contrast, Keynes's conventions are about the substance of the economy and not about the form of models. Keynes was always willing to give up the possibility of a formal, tractable model if he could replace it with a – perhaps imprecise – causal account that would permit him to say something about economic policy. While understanding the intellectual basis for what eventually became the rational expectations hypothesis, Keynes would dissent from most versions of it. Surprisingly, his analysis of expectations is remarkably close to Lucas's. Where they differ most is in Lucas's willingness to allow our ignorance of the future to set a limit to policy action. In contrast, Keynes is, to paraphrase his own description of the entrepreneur, of a more sanguine temperament; imbued, in matters of economic policy, with a spontaneous urge to action, unimpeded by the fragile calculations of rational expectations.

NOTES

* I thank Geoffrey Harcourt, Bradley Bateman and Kevin Salyer for comments on an earlier draft.
1 The term 'hydraulic Keynesianism' is due to Coddington (1983: ch. 6).
2 Keynes's comment, which long predates *The General Theory*, is directed at

Marshall and aims, not to deny the importance of the long run, but to under-score how easy it is to say something sensible about the long run that ignores vital immediate concerns. Although perpetuating the misconstrual of Keynes's remark, Rostow (1980: esp. Preface) notes the Marshallian roots of the idea that the long run is always with us.

3 The distinction here is not between insurable and uninsurable risk – that is Knight's distinction (see LeRoy and Singell 1987). So long as risks can be ordered, even if not all of them can be given a numerical probability, insurance may be rationally extended (see *C.W.* VIII: 23).

4 Bateman (1994: ch. 5) acknowledges that many such rationalizations are *ex post*. He also argues that Keynes is clearly committed to treating long-term expecta-tions on the basis of certainty equivalents. The evidence seems much less decisive to me.

5 Cf. Bateman (1994: ch. 5).

6 Kregel (1976) argues that in different parts of *The General Theory* Keynes employs three of the twenty-seven possible analytical strategies that differ as to whether long-period expectations are constant or shifting, whether short-period expectations are realized or may be disappointed, and whether long-period and short-period expectations are independent or interdependent.

7 By the time of *The General Theory*, Keynes may or may not have abandoned his view that probabilistic relations were objective in favour of Ramsey's subjecti-vism (see p. 229). If he did, expectations are obviously radically heterogeneous; and, even if he did not, no two people will have the same information set and therefore have the same 'objective' assessment of the probabilities.

8 See the discussion of representative agent models on pp. 232–3.

9 Keynes's failure to use this distinction to great effect may explain the manner in which later economists interpreted *The General Theory* and sought to develop a Keynesian position. Tobin's (1958) analysis of liquidity preference in terms of risk and return provides but one example.

10 Pindyck (1991) provides a survey of some modern attempts to model invest-ment under uncertainty, in which keeping options open is an important consideration.

11 These three developments are essentially the new classical agenda of the 1970s. While the new classical macroeconomics has continued to flourish since then, and its subsequent developments (e.g. real-business-cycle models or growth models with increasing returns) have continued to use rational expectations, the rational expectations hypothesis itself is not seen as the central feature of these developments.

12 Keynes (*G.T.*: 203) provides an instance of this preference with respect to monetary policy. See also Bateman (1994: ch. 6) and Meltzer (1988).

13 O'Donnell (1989: 45, 265–6) and Darity and Horn (1993) claim that Keynes has a wider theory of rational expectations of which the new classicals theory is a special case. This is within the spirit of my interpretation in this paper.

14 Lucas (1972b, 1973); see also Hoover (1988: ch. 3).

15 See, for example, Lucas's (1975) monetary model or the non-monetary or real-business-cycle models of Kydland and Prescott (1982) and their followers.

16 Cooley *et al.* (1984) and LeRoy (1994); also see Sims (1982, 1986a, b).

17 Sims (1982, 1986a, b) agrees with the essence of this point and finds in it a defence of his use of vector autoregression techniques in the face of the Lucas critique.

18 Lucas attributes the distinction to Frank Knight, explicitly denying that it is Keynes's (see interview with Lucas, in Klamer 1984: 44). LeRoy and Singell

(1987), however, argue persuasively that Knight's distinction is between insurable and uninsurable risks and is fundamentally different from Lucas's distinction which is in fact attributable to Keynes (cf. note 4 above).

19 See, for example, Lucas (1973, 1980, 1986, 1988a).
20 Lucas thus concentrates on what LeRoy (1994) calls 'stationary expectations' rather than rational expectations.

15

EXPECTATIONS AND UNCERTAINTY IN CONTEMPORARY KEYNESIAN MODELS*

Peter Howitt

INTRODUCTION

The distinction between Keynesian economics and the economics of Keynes (see Leijonhufvud 1968) is nowhere clearer than in the treatment of expectations and uncertainty. Although Keynes invoked what we would now call rational expectations in the short-run theory of effective demand in Chapter 3 of *The General Theory* (see Hoover, Chapter 14 in this volume), nevertheless in Chapter 12, and again in his 1937 *Quarterly Journal of Economics* reply to the critics, he maintained that the knowledge underlying most long-term investment decisions is too fragmentary and incomplete to allow numerical probabilities to be assigned to the possible outcomes.[1] Such unquantifiable uncertainty would *a fortiori* make rational expectations impossible. Yet the modern mainstream of Keynesian economics, as exemplified by the Mankiw–Romer (1991) collection, or by the Blanchard and Fischer (1989) graduate text, has adopted rational expectations as an almost universal standard for modelling long-run as well as short-run beliefs.

Breaking faith with one's intellectual ancestors is normally a sign of progress, and the present case is no exception. The Mankiw–Romer collection and the Blanchard and Fischer text contain rational expectations models that shed new light on depressions, unemployment, money, speculative bubbles, financial panics, animal spirits, wage-flexibility and much else. Even though the universal assumption of rational expectations flies in the face of Keynes's views on uncertainty, much of this work has advanced the cause of Keynesian economics by showing that results with a distinctly Keynesian flavour would not be undermined, and in many cases would even be enhanced, if people had unlimited cognitive abilities.

Progress, however, is a slippery concept. Progress in one direction often goes along with regress in others. And the worth of a theoretical contribution depends very much upon the research programme to which it is

238

contributing. What I argue in this chapter is that rational expectations models have rationalized Keynesian economics in terms of a research programme that has only a limited ability to sustain its development, and that the compromises needed to make Keynesian ideas fit into this alien programme have resulted in models that are incomplete and misleading in important respects. In particular, they pay too little attention to two phenomena to which Keynes devoted much thought: the problem of decision-making in ill-structured situations where conclusive reasoning is impossible; and the role of custom, convention and institutions in economic life. In an attempt to be constructive, I also sketch a behavioural approach to dealing with expectations and uncertainty that I argue is better suited than rational expectations to analysing the basic questions of Keynesian economics. I present three specific examples to illustrate how this behavioural approach might overcome some of the limitations of mainstream Keynesianism.

BEYOND THE NEO-WALRASIAN CODE

The adoption by mainstream Keynesians of rational expectations reflects a commitment to what I call the neo-Walrasian code: the elaborate formal system for describing the set of actions undertaken in an economy as the solutions to a mutually consistent set of rationally conceived plans.[2] Almost all the theoretical work found in the Mankiw–Romer collection and the Blanchard and Fischer text conforms to this code; thus the explanation of sticky prices is not that it takes time for buyers and sellers to grope, but that the menu-cost of adjustment exceeds the private gain that sellers have rationally calculated, taking correctly into account the buyers' reactions to any hypothetical changes; and the account of persistent depression involves not the instability of disequilibrium adjustment mechanisms but the multiplicity of rational-expectations equilibria. To invoke adaptive or other non-rational expectations would be an *ad hoc* violation of the code, and is almost never done except perhaps as a way of selecting among multiple equilibria, in which case the dynamics of adaptation are assumed to take place in non-observable metatime.

In one form or another, the neo-Walrasian code has always played a major role in the development of Keynesian economics. The conventional IS–LM apparatus was an attempt to formalize Keynes's ideas with concepts imported from neo-Walrasian equilibrium analysis.[3] Modigliani's life-cycle hypothesis and Tobin's theories of the demand for money were both attempts to ground the behavioural equations of Keynesian economics in the logic of rational choice. Phelps's island parable and Clower's dual-decision hypothesis were aimed at reconciling systemic Keynesian behaviour with the notion that transactors act rationally in the light of perceived constraints. In adopting rational expectations the current mainstream is thus carrying on a long tradition.

There are obvious benefits to having a common code within a scientific discipline, and there are good empirical reasons for thinking that the intelligent opportunism highlighted by this specific code plays a key role in much of economic life. But the cost of an increasingly elaborate code is that it induces theorists to design models, not to persuade people that this is how in reality an economic system works, but simply to show that they can 'capture' certain aspects of a phenomenon without violating the code. If there were compelling reasons for thinking that only models which adhere to the code offer plausible accounts of how economies function, there would be no point to this criticism. But just the opposite seems to be the case. For the quintessential Keynesian problem is to account for how, and how well, existing economic systems co-ordinate the activities of different transactors, whereas the neo-Walrasian assumption of mutual compatibility of plans presumes that most of this co-ordination problem is solved automatically by an unspecified and unanalysed mechanism. In actual economies the reconciliation of independently conceived plans is a costly activity involving mechanisms and institutions (money, markets, firms and so on) whose very existence is hard to comprehend in a neo-Walrasian framework.[4] Explaining how an ideal economy might exhibit some of the apparent symptoms of co-ordination problems, even if those problems and the mechanisms for resolving them did not exist, can be an exciting intellectual challenge, but it contributes nothing to an explanation of how real economic systems deal with them.

Keynes himself seems not to have appreciated the inappropriateness of equilibrium methods as a tool for analysing co-ordination problems; otherwise he would not have used them in his theory of effective demand. He rationalized his approach on the grounds that it allowed him to finesse unimportant technicalities of market adjustment, that it was impossible to define a determinate time period for all the processes involved, and that in any event the domain of uncertainty was chiefly that of long-run forecasts. But uncertainty is likely to prevail in any context, short- or long-run, where there is a problem of co-ordination, where the variables that people are trying to forecast are influenced by other people's unobservable attempts to forecast them, and where these influences are mediated by a complex macroeconomic system that no one can claim to comprehend. The context of reconciling aggregate demand and supply is a case in point. If we wish to understand how people's intelligent opportunism is manifested in such situations, we need to come to grips with how they adjust to circumstances they do not fully understand, not with how they would operate under rational expectations. The confusion sown by Keynes's neglect of this point in Chapter 3 is amply described by Clower (Chapter 3 in this volume).

The implications of uncertainty go beyond adaptive versus rational expectations, and involve the very foundations of decision-making. People are simply not in a position to act according to conventional decision theory if they cannot attach numerical probabilities to all possible consequences of their decisions. As Keynes argued, they tend to cope by falling back on custom and convention. They also devise institutions to insulate themselves from having to rely upon necessarily unreliable forecasts. While it is in fact possible to tease the neo-Walrasian code into describing behaviour that appears in some respects as if it came from blind conformity to custom and convention, as the recently popular theory of herding behaviour (Banerjee 1992; Bikhchandani *et al.* 1992) has shown, nevertheless a code that insists on modelling all choice as if it were made by rational anticipation of the consequences is an awkward tool, to say the least, for describing mechanisms that exist because of the impossibility of such anticipation. Moreover, the likelihood that almost any convention or custom can thus be 'rationalized' (perhaps even the neo-Walrasian code itself) makes one wonder what purpose is served by the effort. In any event, adherence to the code is no substitute for taking into account actual conventions and institutions as we find them. Failure to do this has in many cases distorted mainstream Keynesian economics by leading it to over-emphasize the importance of expectations instead of focusing on mechanisms that allow people to circumvent the problem of forming expectations.

In short, the limitation to rational expectations equilibria, while perhaps it helps to reduce the dissonance between Keynesian and neo-Walrasian ideas, also makes it unnecessarily difficult for contemporary mainstream Keynesian economists to deal directly and productively with their central problem. It would be more natural and direct to follow an approach suggested by behavioural or evolutionary economics: that is, to treat customs, conventions, institutions and forecasting schemes not as wild animals to be captured in a rational expectations model, but as mere state variables whose initial conditions are given by history, and whose evolution over time is governed by (possibly very random) laws of motion. Behavioural and expectational mechanisms can thus be taken as they exist, without having to torture them into conformity with an alien code, and their consequences taken into account for short-run analysis. The evolution of these mechanisms over time, under the influence of people learning from mistakes, inventing new mechanisms and eliminating mechanisms ill-suited to the historical context, can then play a central role in the observable dynamic behaviour of the economy, much as it does in Hicksian temporary equilibrium theory, but without the temporary equilibrium. The rest of this chapter illustrates how such an approach might help to overcome some of the limitations of mainstream Keynesian economics in dealing with three separate issues: instability problems; depressions; and inflation.

INSTABILITY PROBLEMS

The incompleteness of Keynesian rational expectations models is exemplified by various instability problems that seem mysteriously to have disappeared from the macroeconomics literature. Their disappearance illustrates the slippery nature of scientific progress alluded to above. The process of transforming ideas to make them conform with the neo-Walrasian code often sheds new light on them, but it also obscures those aspects which cannot easily be made to conform. One of those aspects is the possibility that an economy's adjustment mechanisms will not succeed in bringing it to a position of equilibrium, a possibility that has always constituted a weak point of neo-Walrasian theory. The literature on the stability of competitive equilibrium that flourished in the 1950s and 1960s raised but never managed to answer the stability question. When theorists discovered what a messy problem they had on their hands they just dropped it.

The recent revival of interest in adaptive and evolutionary macroeconomics has begun to re-examine the stability issue. It is interesting that the leaders of this revival have typically been not mainstream Keynesians, who ought to have a vested interest in the co-ordination and stability issues involved,[5] but new classical economists such as Lucas (1986) and Sargent (1993). As Sargent's use of the term 'bounded rationality'[6] suggests, this literature contains the seeds of a behavioural macroeconomics not confined to the neo-Walrasian code. Until now it has been interested mainly in selecting among multiple rational expectations equilibria, by asking which of them might be the asymptote of an adjustment process taking place in metatime. But the same methods can also be employed to study the real-time dynamics of economies under the assumption that uncertainty is important for more than transient adjustments. Thus, even in the context of models with unique equilibria, we can ask whether the economy's adjustment processes will tend over time to seek out co-ordinated states or to destabilize them, and whether some policy regimes or circumstances are more conducive to stability than others.

It turns out that some of the instability problems that have arisen over the course of the development of macroeconomics, and which have faded away with the passage of time, constitute examples where any plausible real-time adjustment mechanism would destabilize the unique rational expectations equilibrium. The present section presents two such examples: Wicksell's cumulative process and Harrod's knife-edge. In both cases, the approach I am advocating reveals problems that have been hidden by the neo-Walrasian code.

Consider first Wicksell's cumulative process. As reconstructed by Friedman (1968), this was once considered a powerful argument against a monetary policy aimed at strict control over the level of nominal interest rates. The argument was that unless the monetary authority knew the exact value of the natural rate of interest (the rate at which aggregate demand would just equal full-employment output), the nominal rate of interest would almost certainly be set too low or too high, giving rise to an accelerating inflation in the first case or accelerating deflation in the second. But the argument never found expression in rational expectations models. Sargent and Wallace (1975) showed that the price level would be indeterminate under an interest-pegging monetary policy, but indeterminacy is not the same as instability,[7] and in any event McCallum (1986) showed, not just in new classical models but also in new Keynesian models with nominal price stickiness, that this indeterminacy could be overcome by supplementing the interest peg with an announcement of the associated time path of the money supply. Meanwhile, a diverse set of authors (for example Barro 1989; Woodford 1990) produced rational expectations models implying that policies aimed at controlling interest rates were in many ways more conducive to stability than policies aimed at controlling nominal aggregates.

The following simple model illustrates how Friedman's argument can be cast in terms of the instability of a unique rational expectations equilibrium under any plausible learning mechanism.[8] First, assume that the (log of the) price level p_t adjusts according to an expectations-adjusted Phillips curve:

$$\Delta p_t = f(y_t) + \pi_t, f(0) = 0, f'(\ ) > 0 \tag{15.1}$$

where y_t is the level of 'aggregate excess demand', measured perhaps by the excess of aggregate demand over the level of capacity output, and π_t is the universally[9] expected rate of inflation. Next, assume that aggregate excess demand depends upon the real rate of interest, according to a decreasing function. Given that the monetary authority is pegging the nominal rate of interest, this makes excess demand an increasing function of expected inflation:

$$y_t = g(\pi_t), g'(\ ) > 0 \tag{15.2}$$

From (15.1) and (15.2) we find that the forecast error on the rate of inflation is an *increasing* function of the expected rate of inflation:

$$\Delta p_t - \pi_t = h(\pi_t), h'(\ ) > 0 \tag{15.3}$$

where $h \equiv f \circ g$.

There is only one value of the expected rate of inflation consistent with rational expectations, namely the solution π^* to $h(\pi) = 0$, but almost any learning mechanism that people employed would render this equilibrium unstable because, according to (15.3), every time people made a mistake by forecasting a rate of inflation greater than π^*, the actual rate of inflation would exceed the expected rate, and the desire to correct this forecast error would induce them to raise the expected rate even further away from its unique equilibrium value. The actual rate of inflation would again rise by more than the expected rate, and the result would be an explosive rise in both actual and expected inflation.

A true believer in the neo-Walrasian code will of course dismiss this argument as being based on an *ad hoc* departure from rational expectations – if people had rational expectations they would never make forecast errors in the first place, and no instability would arise. The fact that any attack on the foundations of a rational-expectations argument must be based on some other expectational assumption implies, however, that such a defence is impenetrable to all criticism. The defence amounts to saying: 'I'll see it when I believe it.'

Even more open-minded economists, however, tend to react with scepticism to such an instability argument – perhaps some simple adaptive mechanism would not converge to equilibrium, but that just means people will abandon the mechanism and try another; if that one does not work, they will keep trying new ones until they hit on one that does. Such scepticism, however, does not constitute a stability proof. Instead, it just underscores the point that a convincing argument will have to give full scope to people's intelligent opportunism.

With this in mind, suppose that people start with no understanding of the actual mechanism that generates inflation, that they begin with some guess π_0 as to what inflation will be in period 0, and they try to learn from the only information available to them – namely, the history of inflation under the current monetary regime – according to a sequence of learning rules:

$$\pi_t = F_t(\Delta p_0, \Delta p_1, \ldots \Delta p_{t-1}); \quad t = 1, 2, \ldots \tag{15.4}$$

Then (15.3) and (15.4), together with the historically give initial condition π_0, constitute a dynamical system determining the evolution of actual and expected inflation forever. To be perfectly general about the nature of the learning process, the only assumption we need make concerning the sequence of rules $\{F_t\}$ is that when people are faced with a rate of inflation that has always risen, and has always been higher than estimated, they will raise their expectation. Given this minimal condition, it can be shown (Howitt 1992) that whenever the initial guess π_0 exceeds the equilibrium value π^*, then the actual rate of inflation will forever exceed the expected rate, and both will rise monotonically.

Thus, although the issue of which specific rule or sequence of rules will be followed can only be addressed empirically, the example of Wicksell's cumulative process shows how a behavioural approach of taking expectations as given in the short run and allowing them to evolve over time can at least detect instability and characterize real-time dynamics, in situations where rational expectations equilibrium analysis is of no use. A second example is that of Harrod's (1939, 1948) knife-edge. Harrod was concerned, as was Domar (1946, 1947) with the question of how to ensure sufficient effective demand for the increased productive potential created by economic growth to be fully utilized, rather than become excess capacity and cause unemployment. It was a question of co-ordinating the expectations of investors with the yet-unarticulated future demands of savers. As long as the marginal propensity to consume was less than unity, business firms would somehow have to see it as in their interests to increase their investment outlays each year, and by just the right amount. Harrod rightly perceived that this brought into question the stability of equilibrium. Under his assumptions, if at any time entrepreneurs learned they had overestimated the growth of final sales, they would scale back their collective investment outlays, and the subsequent multiplier effects of this cutback would cause actual sales to fall even further below the anticipated level. A vicious circle would be created, whereby shortfalls in investment demand would feed on themselves in cumulative fashion. Thus, what Harrod called the 'warranted' growth path was a knife-edge of instability.

Most of what mainstream Keynesians know of this knife-edge comes from the Solow–Swan[10] representation of the Harrod–Domar model, the knife-edge property of which was derived from an extreme and unrealistic assumption of fixed factor proportions. But Harrod himself always (1959, for example) maintained that this fixed-proportions model was a caricature of his theory. Writers such as Eisner (1958) objected to this neoclassical representation, and maintained that the real problem raised by Harrod and Domar was obscured by the 'neoclassical resurgence'. Despite these protests, the instability problem at the heart of Harrod's original analysis gradually disappeared from the literature.

Mainstream macroeconomics is now beginning to deal with some of the adjustment and co-ordination problems created by economic growth. But a contribution by Fazzari (1985) shows clearly that conventional models of rational expectations equilibrium cannot deal with the Harrod knife-edge problem because, as the above description suggests, it is another example of instability of a unique rational expectations equilibrium under learning. Fazzari's analysis is built on two key relationships. First, suppose that the actual growth of output depends positively upon the growth of investment, as in a textbook Keynesian model of national income determination:

$$\Delta y_t = \phi\ (\Delta i_t),\ \phi' > 0 \qquad\qquad (15.5)$$

where i and y are logs of investment and output. Second, suppose that the growth in investment depends positively upon g, the expected rate of growth of output, as in an accelerator mechanism:[11]

$$\Delta i_t = \psi\ (g_t),\ \psi' > 0 \qquad\qquad (15.6)$$

Then the forecast error on economic growth will be a function of the expected growth rate:

$$\Delta y_t - g_t = \xi(g_t), \tag{15.7}$$

where $\xi \equiv \phi \circ \psi - g_t$.

If $\phi' \cdot \psi' > 1$, then the forecast error will be an increasing function of the expected growth rate. In this case there will be at most one rational expectations equilibrium g^*, which is Harrod's warranted rate of growth, but this equilibrium will be unstable under the same conditions on learning as in the previous example, and for the same reason. That is, if entrepreneurs expected a rate less than g^* they would find that they were overestimating growth, and a cumulative fall in both expected and actual growth would ensue.

Although these models are too crude to represent more than a caricature of any actual economy, the instability problems they reveal are likely to be present in a wide variety of more complete and sophisticated models.[12] This analysis suggests that Wicksell's cumulative process, Harrod's knife-edge instability, and probably many other manifestations of macroeconomic instability, instead of being outdated relics of pre-rational-expectations thinking, are in fact serious co-ordination problems which rational expectations models have obscured rather than clarified. An approach that takes expectations as given and allows for them to evolve over time at least makes it possible to recognize these problems. Perhaps it would also make it possible to ask what other sorts of policies are subject to cumulative processes, and to diagnose and prescribe policy remedies for knife-edge problems like Harrod's. Policy prescription, however, is likely to require a more detailed account of expectational mechanisms and their evolution than is provided in the above account, for reasons that are best explained in terms of the next example.

DEPRESSIONS

One of the more interesting contributions of contemporary mainstream Keynesianism has been to develop models of what Cooper and John (1988) call 'coordination failures'. These models show how an economy might get stuck in a situation of 'subnormal activity', to use an expression of Keynes. They imply that in any given historical setting, defined by tastes, technology and endowments, there can exist more than one situation of rational expectations equilibrium, each one corresponding to a different level of economic activity and a different level of unemployment. A prolonged depression can be interpreted, according to this theory, as a period in which the economy has come to rest in a low-level equilibrium.

The key ingredient underlying multiplicity is 'strategic complementarity', the idea that a higher level of activity on the part of one group of actors in the economy will raise others' perceived inducement to act. Strategic complementarity is roughly synonymous with synergy, positive feedback

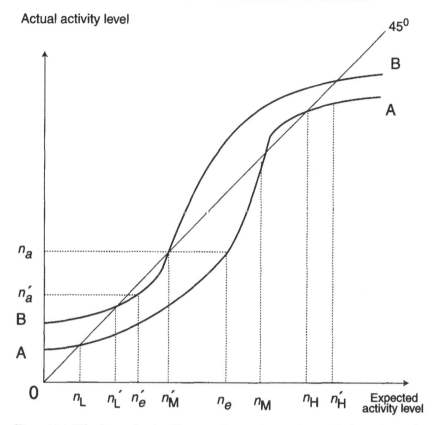

Figure 15.1 Whether a shock will cure a depression or deepen it depends on the structure of beliefs

or deviation-amplification. It is exemplified by textbook descriptions of the Keynesian multiplier process. A marginal propensity to spend of less than unity prevents the usual multiplier process from generating multiple equilibria, but the co-ordination failure literature has found other sources, most notably aggregate demand externalities in imperfectly competitive output markets and thin-market externalities in the transaction process, which are subject to no such limitation.

The typical situation is illustrated in Figure 15.1. Suppose that the actual level of an individual's economic activity could somehow be given one-dimensional representation (in terms of investment demand or effort put into the transactions process or employment, for example). Strategic complementarity makes the representative individual's choice of activity level depend positively upon the expected average of others' levels, according to the reaction curve AA in Figure 15.1 (ignore curve BB for now). According to this reaction curve there are three different rational expectations equilibria,

247

n_L, n_M and n_H. That is, each of these three numbers has the property that if everyone in the economy believed that the average activity level was going to equal that number, they would find that their beliefs were confirmed by experience. The theory asserts that the average activity level must equal one of these numbers, because any other level could only be observed if people had expectations that were inconsistent with the structure of the economy. A persistent situation of subnormal activity can accordingly be represented as a move from the high-level equilibrium n_H to the low-level equilibrium n_L.

This 'theory', sketchy though it is, captures the logical essence of more elaborate theories of co-ordination failure. It also illustrates three main weaknesses of such theories. First, although the argument is supposed to be about co-ordination failures, the hypothesis of rational expectations assumes that a remarkable amount of co-ordination takes place automatically. This would be anomalous even if there were just one equilibrium. But when there are several, the hypothesis places even more demands on people's ability to co-ordinate, for they must also somehow anticipate which of the many possible equilibrium actions will be taken by the others.

Second, because the theory yields multiple equilibria, it is at best incomplete; it cannot determine what it was constructed to determine: the level of activity. Indeed, the problem is greater than it might seem at first glance, because the model will have not just the three equilibria shown but also a huge number of other equilibria, in which people condition their expectations on extraneous random variables. For every random variable one can think of whose realization is known to everyone before they choose their activity levels, and for every mapping from that random variable into the set $\{n_L, n_M, n_H\}$ there will exist a rational expectations equilibrium in which the realization of that variable determines which level of activity will exist, according to that mapping. That is, any such mapping has the property that if everyone believed that it was going to determine the average activity level, their beliefs would be confirmed by experience.

Third, and most important for present purposes, the model cannot predict, even qualitatively, how the economy will respond to variations in exogenous variables or policy instruments that affect the position of the reaction curve AA. Conventional comparative-statics techniques would indicate that if the economy was initially in a high-level equilibrium n_H, for example, then a positive shock that shifted the reaction curve to BB would raise activity, to n'_H. But by the same argument, if it was in the middle equilibrium n_M, for example, where the reaction curve has a slope of more than unity, a positive shock would *reduce* activity (from n_M to n'_M). Formally, the variable that shifts the reaction function could be the random variable defining the equilibrium, as in the previous paragraph's discussion. Since any mapping into $\{n_L, n_M, n_H\}$ provides a rational expectations equilibrium, it seems that almost any qualitative response is possible.

In particular, even if the equilibrium never occurs at a point where the reaction curve has a slope of greater than unity, it might exhibit what I call 'perverse rational expectations': it might map a positive shock into n'_L and a negative shock into n_H. In such cases an otherwise stimulative policy will have a depressing effect simply because prevailing opinion thinks it will be bad for the economy. That is, if the prevailing opinion is that activity will equal n_H when there is no stimulative policy in place but will fall to n'_L if a stimulative policy is applied, then that is in fact what will happen, because such an opinion constitutes a rational expectation.

This result echoes Keynes's warning that 'economic prosperity is excessively dependent on a political and social atmosphere which is congenial to the average business man' (*G.T.*: 162), and shows how an extreme form of dependence is compatible with rational expectations equilibrium. But it does not rule out non-perverse rational expectations equilibria, such as those that map positive and negative shocks into n'_H and n_H respectively. In short, we just cannot predict whether a given shock will remedy a depression or provoke one, unless we know precisely what expectational scheme people are using. Just knowing that the scheme is rational does not help, because there are so many different schemes that are equally rational. This is the sense in which rational-expectations theories provide a seriously incomplete account of the logic of depression.

The general principles of evolution and learning used in the previous section can remedy some of this incompleteness. Suppose, to begin with, that there is no shock to the economy for a long period of time, that people start with arbitrary beliefs concerning what activity level others will adopt, and that they attempt to learn through experience. Then almost any learning scheme will rule out asymptotic convergence to the equilibrium n_M where there is a 'negative multiplier' because the reaction curve has more than a unit slope. In the neighbourhood of such an equilibrium a small change in expected activity away from n_M will produce an even greater change in actual activity, leading people to revise their forecasts even further in the same direction. As in the examples studied in the previous section, this will tend to drive both the actual and the expected activity levels away from such an equilibrium.[13] A similar result obtains if we relax the assumption that AA stays put. Specifically, I have shown elsewhere (Howitt, 1990a) that the same reasoning rules out convergence of a simple learning model to any equilibrium that maps even a single realization of a random variable into an associated equilibrium where the reaction curve has more than a unit slope.

Ruling out equilibria with negative multipliers does not, however, go far in solving the incompleteness problem. It deals only with long-run convergence, which is of little use in understanding short-run situations or non-recurrent phenomena. Furthermore, it does not rule out the possibility of perverse rational expectations, of self-fulfilling beliefs to the effect that stimulative policies will actually create a depression. In order to deal with these issues we need to go further into the details of expectations and their evolution by looking at empirical data on expectational schemes. We need, in other words, to borrow from Keynes, who used his own insights and experience of actual behaviour in financial markets to characterize the way people form beliefs. We can then proceed to analyse the effects of shocks, taking those expectational schemes into account not just for purposes of checking the stability of equilibrium but for predicting real-time behaviour without any necessary reference to the concept of equilibrium.

Taking expectational schemes as given runs into the problem that data on expectations are notoriously unreliable, and the schemes themselves are likely to shift in response to innovations in applied economic theory and in response to various policy actions that change incentives. But this does not distinguish expectational schemes from other analytical constructs which macroeconomists routinely take as given, such as aggregate production functions. Surely the growth of technical knowledge underlying the evolution of production relations is no more predictable or more structurally stable than the growth of economic knowledge (or opinion) underlying expectational schemes. Moreover, unlike production functions, expectational schemes are often the subject of widely reported discussion and analysis.

Thus there is often a prevailing opinion in various markets that governs the way expectations are formed and that can be observed directly. This is especially true in financial markets, where from time to time everyone is clearly obsessed with the weekly statistics on M1 growth, the size of government deficits, the outcome of regularly scheduled meetings of monetary-policy committees, the next release of inflation statistics, or the apparent willingness of central authorities to permit a currency depreciation. This opinion might or might not conform to the requirements of rational expectations. All we can learn from rational-expectations theory is that it is not likely to persist indefinitely if it does not conform. In the short run it is given historically, and we are almost certain to err in our analysis of policy changes if we ignore it.

Although the method of basing macroeconomic analysis on such direct observation is almost never used by academic economists,[14] it is becoming increasingly common, at least implicitly, in the best journalistic anlayses of monetary and fiscal policy in small open economies, particularly those with a large outstanding stock of government debt, where the question always arises as to how speculators will interpret any particular policy action. In Canada, for example, we often read the opinion that a policy of expenditure cuts on the part of the federal government will serve to stimulate the level of economic activity, because of the favourable expectational effect on foreign investors' demands for Canadian debt instruments. The argument is that this expectational effect will lead to lower interest rates, and hence to a more than compensatory rise in private demand for goods and services.

250

While this argument is of course debatable on several points, it can be discussed intelligently only by taking into account the actual prevailing state of opinion, rational or otherwise.

The reason why few academic papers try to take prevailing opinion into account is probably that following the will-o'-the-wisp of popular fads is regarded as a trivial pursuit for someone seeking a deep understanding of how a modern economy functions. If this is the way it functions, however, then this is the way it should be modelled. And if it seems almost impossible to predict the whims of fashionable opinion, surely the best we can do is to admit that the problem of macroeconomic stabilization policy is extraordinarily difficult and that any analysis of it is fraught with uncertainty.

Moreover, there are grounds for thinking that we can say at least something useful about the evolution of expectational schemes, on the basis of simple principles of adaptation and evolution. For even though there is clearly a big random element in the evolution of conventional wisdom, there is also a systematic component. The displacement of Keynesian by monetarist ideas in the conventional wisdom of financial markets in the 1970s, for example, surely had something to do with the fact that people were learning from the experience of rising monetary expansion and rising inflation. Likewise, the reason why market-watchers in the United States suddenly stopped paying attention to weekly M1 reports in October 1982 surely had something to do with the fact that the Federal Reserve System at that time abandoned the free-reserve targeting which had led them to react strongly to their own mistakes in forecasting M1.

Intelligent opportunism can account for such changes in prevailing opinion without implying rational expectations. We can use theories of learning and evolution to gain some insight into how expectational schemes are likely to change as time passes, and hence to understand how the effects of policy will vary over time. We may or may not find a tendency to converge to rational expectations equilibrium in tranquil times, but the apparent stability of conventional wisdom in the face of contradictory evidence warns us not to expect much insight into real-time dynamics from asymptotic convergence results. Furthermore, while simple schemes like (15.4) may be sufficient to reveal serious instability problems, the kaleidoscopic nature of fashionable opinion suggests that a large random component needs to be added.

In the specific case of Figure 15.1, for example, we could model prevailing opinion as the representative actor's beliefs concerning the relationship between the policy shock and the activity level that will prevail. Suppose for simplicity that there are just two settings for the policy instrument, those underlying the curves AA (contractionary) and BB (expansionary). Suppose that direct observation revealed a prevailing opinion consisting of two corresponding numbers, n_e and n_e'. Then inspection of Figure 15.1 shows that activity would indeed be reduced by a move to an expansionary policy setting, although not by as much as is generally thought, since $n'_e - n_e < n'_a - n_a < 0$.

In this case we could also say that if there were no fundamental change in the way expectations are formed, and if the evolution of prevailing opinion were guided only by the attempt to correct forecast errors, then ultimately the expansionary policy-setting would result in higher activity, because under either policy the fact that people are going to be over-estimating employment will probably result in convergence to the low-level equilibrium, and because $n'_L > n_L$. The long-run analysis would be quite different, however, if prevailing opinion were characterized initially by a value $n_e > n_M$, in which case adaptation of expectations would tend to amplify the expansionary effect of the contractionary policy. In any event, how fast and by what route the long-run outcome would come about would depend upon the precise details of the process by which prevailing opinion is revised in the light of expectational errors, about which we have had little to say, and the long-term analysis must be taken as provisional, as subject to revision if people take the failure of their forecasts and the appearance of a new trend in monetary theory as signals to switch to a radically different expectational scheme, one that depends, for example, upon an extraneous random variable.

Implicit in this mode of analysis is the idea that, at least in the absence of radical innovations, we the economic modellers can predict the bias in people's forecasts. Such hubris is certainly grounds for scepticism, but the silliness of assuming rational expectations in a world that no one understands would be even stronger grounds. Unquantifiable uncertainty should make us wary of any predictions; but if anything at all is to be said about the likely consequences of policy actions, there is no avoiding predictions. Of course, this raises the separate issue of whether the policy analyst's model is any better than that implicit in conventional forecasting schemes, an issue on which nothing can be said *a priori*. It also raises the question of whether there is not sometimes a way to avoid having to rely upon necessarily unreliable forecasts in a world of uncertainty, a question that I address in the next section.

INFLATION

The modern rational-expectations literature seems to have reached a consensus to the effect that the cost of inflation is relatively minor, especially in comparison with the cost of reducing inflation. The one possible exception relates to distortions in capital markets created by the interaction between inflation and a non-indexed tax system, distortions for which tax reform is generally seen as the appropriate remedy rather than inflation reduction (Fischer 1981). Even the most distinctively Keynesian branch of the literature, where menu-costs play a major role (for example Bénabou 1988, 1992), contains nothing to challenge that consensus, according to which inflation, rather than being the machine gun of the proletariate, is a mere tax on loose change.

The inability of mainstream Keynesians to say anything deeper than this about the costs and consequences of inflation is one price they have paid for adopting the neo-Walrasian code. For the conceptual framework of neo-Walrasian analysis abstracts from the transactions costs and the related market institutions that underlie the use of money. Since inflation is just, by definition, the process by which the value of money changes, it would be astounding to find that it had a significant real effect in an imaginary world where money has no real role to play in the first place. The most prominent exceptions to the consensus among modern Keynesians are Okun and Leijonhufvud (Okun 1975; Leijonhufvud 1981; Heymann and Leijonhufvud 1995), both of whom argue that inflation impairs the functioning of various institutions. It is no accident that of all the articles reproduced in the Mankiw–Romer collection, Okun's is the least influenced by the neo-Walrasian code.

If inflation is one of the topics least susceptible to neo-Walrasian analysis, it is also one of the most susceptible to Keynes's ideas concerning long-term expectations. For the uncertainty attached to predictions of the price-level thirty years hence must be at least as great as that attached to predicting the returns to an investment thirty years hence. In the latter case tastes and technology applicable to a particular set of markets must be predicted, but in the former it is the behaviour of an entire economic system, and of the political process that will govern its monetary policy in the future that must be predicted. As Leijonhufvud (1981: 264) put it, laying plans contingent on inflation in a world of fiat money is like playing chess with an umpire who may suddenly announce: 'From now on bishops move like rooks and *vice versa* . . . and I'll be back with more later.'

Keynes argued that uncertainty induces people to rely on custom and convention rather than rational calculation. This is especially true when it comes to inflation. As Paul Davidson (1989: 15–17) has argued, the uses of money as a unit of account and standard of deferred payment are institutions through which people cope with uncertainty without having to rely upon necessarily imperfect predictions of the future. In a money-using economy, firms and households are concerned not just with their 'real' economic profits, but also with their cash flow, for no matter what happens to the value of money they can at least stay out of the bankruptcy court as long as inflow exceeds outflow. Historical cost accounting helps firms to keep track of their cash flow better than would an indexed system; and nominal, non-indexed debt contracts allow them to insulate their cash flow from unpredictable fluctuations in the price level, especially in a world where their customers demand some assurance of predictable nominal prices. Controlling real cash flow would be the ideal objective if it were possible, but controlling nominal cash flow, with the aid of such devices as nominal debt and historical cost accounting, is at least a useful objective and has the advantage of being reasonably attainable.

Of course we could easily imagine worlds in which people reckoned, fixed contracts and kept records in some unit other than the medium of exchange, but that is not the world of modern advanced economies, in which nominal conventions and institutions are deeply imbedded. It is only by taking such conventions and institutions as given that we can begin to understand how inflation impairs the functioning of an economic system. They are based on the implicit premise that money is an unchanging measure of value, and thus constitute examples of Keynes's theory that people act according to the conventional belief that the present situation will continue unchanged; in this case, that the price level will continue unchanged. The institutions work best, therefore, when the price level does in fact continue unchanged. For then the instruments that make cash flow relatively manageable also tend to make real profitability manageable. One of the biggest costs of inflation is to undermine these and many other commercial, financial and accounting practices that are similarly predicated on money as an invariant measure of value. None of this cost is visible from the perspective of rational-expectations theory, which necessarily assumes away the unquantifiable uncertainty underlying the institutions.[15]

Consider the institution of nominal debt. Although partial indexation clauses are sometimes found in other contracts, especially in the labour market, money is the universal standard of deferred payment in pure debt contracts, even in periods of very high inflation. The non-indexation of debt is an embarrassing anomaly for rational-expectations theories, which cannot explain why people should voluntarily enter into unwanted gambles on the price level each time they borrow or lend, when they clearly have the option of avoiding that gamble by indexing the debt contract to the price level. Moreover, the omission from conventional theory of a rationale for nominal debt leads to a misleading analysis of the costs of inflation. For the theory suggests that even if we take the absence of indexation as exogenously given, a higher average level of inflation should not disrupt financial markets, because people can anticipate higher inflation by raising the nominal interest rates correspondingly. Even if the tax treatment of interest is not indexed, there should be a tax-adjusted Fisher effect (Darby 1975) of greater than unity that leaves borrower and lender in the same *ex ante* expected position. Thus, although there might be transitory problems when inflation changes unexpectedly, and although an increase in the variance of inflation might disrupt financial markets, an increase in the average level of inflation should not be a source of financial disruption.

The problem with this view is that it flies in the face of empirical evidence to the effect that even in the long run interest rates do not adjust fully to inflation. Fisher himself (1896) estimated that the adjustment of interest rates to inflation took many years to work itself out, and that even in the long run it was only partial; and the bulk of the empirical work on the subject since Fisher supports his conclusion.[16] The conventional view is also contradicted by the apparent tendency of long-term debt markets to dry out when inflation rises, and by the apparent increase in the share of GNP accounted for by financial activities when inflation rises.[17]

This evidence would be much less surprising if we accepted that nominal debt is a means for people to manage their cash flow in the face of incalculable price-level uncertainty. During periods of stability, or at least of mean-reversion, in the price level, they can be reasonably confident that the objective of managing cash flow does not conflict drastically with that of maximizing real income, and thus they are content to act as if they believed the conventional fiction that money is an invariant standard of value. When an economy has entered a prolonged period of inflation they begin to lose faith in that convention. They must now face an uncertainty which they had been willing to ignore in the past. The cost of maintaining a predictable cash flow is thereby increased, but not by any calculable amount. Instead, the cost takes the form of the anxiety of knowing that established routines for entering into long-term inter-temporal commitments are no longer reliable and have to be changed, with uncertain consequences. The most common reaction to this cost is to avoid entering into new long-term commitments. This is how inflation undermines one of the central institutions of a money-using economy, and it helps to account for why long-term bond markets tend to become inactive when inflation rises.

The fact that lenders and borrowers can see in what direction the conventional fiction is being falsified means that nominal interest rates will indeed rise, as in conventional theory. Otherwise the perceived cost of borrowing would obviously be much less affected by the experience of persistent inflation than would the perceived cost of lending, and the result would be an excess demand for loanable funds. But there is no objective probability distribution of inflation whose central location has just shifted up, for which a point-for-point rise in nominal interest rates would just compensate both borrowers and lenders. Instead, a conventional belief has been undermined without having been replaced by anything equivalent. The effect on interest rates will be as if there had been a perceived increase in the variance of inflation along with an increase in the expected value.

Thus what it takes for 'full adjustment' to inflation is not the realization that the mean of a distribution has shifted, but the replacement of an institution that is central to the functioning of a money economy. The standard question of what would happen if inflation were to remain indefinitely at 10 per cent instead of zero is a highly misleading one; for it presumes that inflation would follow a deterministic, and hence predictable, path, which in fact it does not. Even if by chance inflation were to stay at exactly 10 per cent year after year for ten years, which it never has in any economy of record, there would still be huge uncertainty as to what it will be thirty years down the road. And people would still know that there was an incalculable cost to managing their cash flow, one which they would be willing to ignore if they had some assurance of the stability of the price level, but which they cannot ignore when the price level has been rising steadily at 10 per cent per year.

While the rise in nominal interest rates and the loss of confidence in the value of money drive borrowers out of long-term debt markets, the last to leave will be the most foolish, reckless and unscrupulous, and those most willing to deal not on the basis of long-term forecasts, which are rendered more uncertain by the rise in inflation, but on their superior ability to anticipate the sentiment of the market. In Keynes's terms, speculation will tend to prevail over enterprise. Those borrowers who obtain financing on favourable terms are less likely to be those with the best economic prospects and more likely to be those whose current profitability, artificially enhanced by an inflationary regime with imperfect adjustment of interest rates, has won the favour of conventional financial wisdom. The resulting misallocation of capital may not be apparent until the inflation has been brought under control, but its likely effect is a reduction in the overall efficiency of the economic system, a cost that goes well beyond the shoe-leather cost of conventional theory.

Even after inflation has been brought under control, its effects on financial markets are likely to be felt for a long time, because lenders will not be foolish enough to go right back to acting according to a conventional fiction that has proved so costly. Meanwhile, other conventions will have formed to govern beliefs in long-term debt markets. Right now (late 1994), for example, the conventional belief appears to be that any sign of inflationary pressure is going to send long rates back to the peak levels attained in the mid-1980s, a belief that continues to hamper recovery in industrial countries. There is perhaps no more sound basis for this convention than for that of money as an unchanging measure of value. But that does not stop the convention from having a significant and lasting effect on long-term interest rates.

Historical cost accounting is another institution based on the fiction of money as an unchanging measure of value. As with nominal debt, inflation undermines the institution without providing any alternative. Thus, despite frequent arguments in favour of inflation-adjusted accounting standards, it has not proved possible, even in countries undergoing hyperinflation, to adopt them. Yet it is well known that historical cost accounting induces large distortions into firms' income statements and balance sheets. Most notably, the inclusion of all nominal interest costs, instead of just real interest costs, will cause many companies' real profits to be understated to a degree that rises as inflation increases the gap between nominal and real interest rates, whereas the use of book values rather than actual replacement of inventories and depreciable capital will tend to overstate profits to a degree that also increases with the rate of inflation.

As inflation rises, these accounting distortions impair the efficient allocation of resources in at least two separate ways: one is through the fact that tax liabilities must be calculated on the basis of existing accounting conventions, not on the basis of non-existing ones. Thus a higher rate of inflation will drive a bigger wedge between the before- and after-tax rates of return in the case of inventory- and depreciable capital-intensive companies and sectors, and a smaller wedge in the case of highly levered companies and sectors. In principle, many have argued that this reallocative effect of capital could be compensated for by changes in the tax code, but in practice no country has succeeded in finding such an inflation-neutral system, probably because it would require firms to abandon historical cost accounting, the only accounting system by which they know how to record and manage their cash flow.

There is another effect that goes beyond the tax system and brings more of Keynes's ideas on uncertainty and expectations into play. That is, even if there were no interaction between inflation and the tax system, historical cost accounting is one of the principal channels through which information about the relative profitability of different enterprises is transmitted in the economy. Higher inflation tends to degrade the quality of the signals that potential investors receive through conventional accounts. For unless all the details underlying those accounting measures are known, it is hard to distinguish how much of a firm's measured profits and assets are real and how much are illusory effects of nominal accounting in a world of inflation.[18]

This connection between inflation and the quality of accounting information seems to me to be one of the biggest aspects of the costs of inflation. For, as Keynes repeatedly emphasized, the most salient bit of information on which to base expectations of future profitability is usually current profitability. When the quality of even that bit of information is degraded, because of a rise in the level of inflation, the effects on capital markets will be as if there had been an increase in the variability of the future rate of inflation working through a system of nominal contracts. In either case a potential investor will be faced with a prospective rate of return that is now more uncertain. This is not just idiosyncratic risk of the sort that could be diversified away in a frictionless world of no transaction costs. For the same effects will be tending to make the overall rate of return to a fully diversified portfolio more uncertain.

Thus the degradation of signals generated by historical cost accounting tends to amplify and add to the distortions that inflation generates when it undermines nominal debt. Many of the companies and sectors that appear to be most profitable under an inflationary regime, and which therefore are granted credit under the most favourable terms, turn out not to be so profitable when their accounts cease to be distorted by inflation. And the tendency for speculation to grow at the expense of enterprise is enhanced when information on fundamentals gets weaker. This same degradation of signals also helps to account for the tendency, alluded to above, for inflation to induce more resources to be put into the transactions process rather than the production process, since when publicly available signals about profitability become weaker, the relative advantage to those with superior private information becomes correspondingly greater. From this point of view it is not surprising that such a flurry of financial and speculative innovation took place in the inflationary period of the 1980s. Of course, the cost of those financial innovations consisted of all the real innovations that would otherwise have taken place had this entrepreneurial talent not been diverted from more socially useful activities.

In short, I believe that Keynes's ideas on uncertainty, and on how people cope with it by resorting to custom and convention rather than to rational calculation, help to shed light on a subject that mainstream Keynesian economics has obscured by its adherence to the neo-Walrasian code. The problem in this case is not that mainstream Keynesians have used rational rather than adaptive expectations, but that they have been led to over-emphasize the role of expectations. For inflation is not something on whose probability distribution people routinely make long-term plans. Instead, it is something that undermines the institutions that permit people to act without having to face the impossible problem of calculating the incalculable. The behavioural approach that I have proposed has at least the advantage of taking these institutions into account.

CONCLUSION

Not long ago I predicted that the success of Keynesian economists in expressing their ideas according the neoclassical principles of equilibrium and rationality would serve as the springboard for a new Keynesian recovery (Howitt 1986). My optimism then was based on the emerging work on co-ordination failures and on 'sunspot', or 'animal spirits', equilibria, which I argued captured the central arguments of *The General Theory* in terms of rational expectations equilibria. I still think that work contains valuable insights, and that it has a prophylactic use against anti-Keynesian propaganda. But I now see this and other work based on rational expectations as seriously incomplete, and in some cases misleading, because it evades a vital connection between co-ordination issues, on the one hand, and Keynes's views on expectations and uncertainty, on the other: a connection which even Keynes failed to appreciate. I have tried to argue here that a more straightforward behavioural approach to expectations and decision-making under uncertainty offers some hope of sorting out that connection. We are still, however, a long way from understanding how the co-ordination mechanisms of actual economies function.

NOTES

* Useful comments from Geoff Harcourt and David Laidler are gratefully acknowledged.

1 Keynes's views on expectations, uncertainty and rational behaviour have been the subject of much recent scholarly research, of which an excellent sample is to be found in O'Donnell (1991c).

2 See Howitt (1995) for a critique of the way in which this code has influenced contemporary monetary theory.

3 See Clower (1975a) for an elaboration of this point.

4 For a fuller account of what is missing from the neo-Walrasian research programme, see Clower (1993a).

5 As with all sweeping generalizations, there are exceptions. Phelps, for example was a leader in recognizing the importance of disequilibrium learning for understanding co-ordination problems (Frydman and Phelps 1983). Also, what might be called the French school of Keynesian economics has long advocated the use of non-rational expectations (see, for example, the expectational analyses of Benassy 1986; and Grandmont and Laroque 1986).

6 The term originates with Herbert Simon.

7 See Laidler (1983) for an elaboration of this distinction and for notes on the history of related ideas.

8 The idea of seeing Wicksell's cumulative process as non-convergence to rational expectations was proposed by Cottrell (1989).

9 I show in Howitt (1992) that the substance, if not the simplicity, of the argument is unaffected if people have diverse expectations, an assumption that Keynes would surely have insisted upon.

10 Solow (1956) and Swan (1956).

11 The usual accelerator story would imply a term in g_{t-1} on the RHS of (15.6). As Fazzari observes, the inclusion of this term would not rescue stability, although it would make the model a little more involved.

12 I have shown in Howitt (1992) that Wicksell's cumulative process also arises in the context of a cash-in-advance model with flexible prices and a distributional channel of 'forced saving' through which monetary policy affects the rate of interest in the short run. Fazzari (1982) has shown that Harrod's knife-edge problem also arises in a much more general setting than the one described above.

13 This result can be demonstrated formally using almost any of the methods proposed in the literature on adaptive belief formation, such as those of Grandmont and Laroque (1986) and Moore (1993).

14 There are exceptions: for example, Frankel and Froot (1991).

15 Another institution that allows firms to manage their cash flow without trying to make impossible calculations and predictions is mark-up pricing, which, as Harcourt (1959) showed, can interact with historical cost accounting to make the economy react quite differently to a rise in inflation than if firms based their prices on correctly measured replacement costs.

16 See Fried and Howitt (1983) for references to the modern literature.
17 See Kleiman (1989) for evidence on the Israeli experience.
18 Indeed, even in the absence of inflation, accounts that base depreciation on historical rather than replacement cost may give signals of profitability that are impossible to interpret, as Harcourt (1965) argues.

16

THE THEORY OF VALUE, EXPECTATIONS AND CHAPTER 17 OF *THE GENERAL THEORY**

J.A. Kregel writing as J.M. Keynes

INTRODUCTION

The first edition of this book was directed to my fellow economists. At that time it was reasonable to presume that they would be sufficiently familiar with my prior work that a few brief references would be sufficient to indicate the extent to which it was incorporated in the present book. With the passage of time this presumption is no longer true; indeed, despite precise indications in the text and in footnotes, few readers of the original edition seem to have recognized the genesis of certain important innovations, such as user costs, in my earlier *Treatise on Money* (1930a, b). This problem was particularly acute in Chapter 17, which built on the interest rate parity theorem first set out in my *Tract on Monetary Reform* (1923), and on an extension of what I had called the 'short-period' theory of prices in Volume II of the *Treatise on Money* (1930b).

Although I alerted readers of the first edition to what I considered to be the important differences with respect to the *Treatise on Money*, they could only be appreciated by those familiar with my earlier work, and I was perhaps remiss in failing to stress sufficiently the continuity that remained. For example, in the Preface (page vii) I noted that:

> The relation between this book and my *Treatise on Money* . . . is probably clearer to myself than it will be to others; and what in my own mind is a natural evolution in a line of thought which I have been pursuing for several years, may sometimes strike the reader as a confusing change of view.

I went on to summarize 'the general relationship between the two books', noting that in the first:

> I failed to deal thoroughly with the effects of *changes* in the level of output. My so-called 'fundamental equations' were an instantaneous picture, taken on the assumption of a given output. They attempted to show how, assuming given output, forces could develop which

involved a profit-disequilibrium, and thus required a change in the level of output. But the dynamic development . . . was left incomplete and extremely confused. This book, on the other hand, has evolved into what is primarily a study of the forces which determine changes in the scale of output and employment as a whole. . . . A monetary economy . . . is essentially one in which changing views about the future are capable of influencing the quantity of employment and not merely its direction. But our method of analysing the economic behaviour of the present under the influence of changing ideas about the future is one which depends on the interaction of supply and demand, and is in this way linked up with our fundamental theory of value.

Although this seems a clear enough indication that my main purpose was a dynamic theory driven by the impact of the future upon present decisions, and that this impact was linked to the role played by money in the economy, most economists have chosen to interpret my theory in terms of a static equilibrium of the economy described in terms of real output and expenditure with little if any reference to the impact of the future on the present. For example, they seem to have overlooked statements such as 'to-day's employment can be correctly described as being governed by to-day's expectations taken in conjunction with to-day's capital equipment' (*G.T.*: 50) given that 'It is by reason of the existence of durable equipment that the economic future is linked to the present' (*G.T.*: 146) and that this linkage could be represented by 'the introduction of the concepts of user costs and the marginal efficiency of capital' (ibid.). Such a position required a major change from my earlier analysis, which I noted as follows:

> Whilst liquidity-preference due to the speculative-motive corresponds to what in my *Treatise on Money* I called 'the state of bearishness', it is by no means the same thing. For 'bearishness' is there defined as the functional relationship, not between the rate of interest (or price of debts) and the quantity of money, but between the price of assets and debts, taken together, and the quantity of money. This treatment, however, involved a confusion between results due to a change in the rate of interest and those due to a change in the schedule of the marginal efficiency of capital . . .
>
> (*G.T.*: 173)

Since I presumed that readers of the *Treatise on Money* would be familiar with the theory of bearishness, I also presumed it would be obvious that the basic change and innovation in the new book involved, first, the limitation of this theory to the explanation of the rate of interest (or the price of financial assets), thereby making the supply and demand for saving and investment redundant; but more importantly, the creation of a separate, independent theory to explain the return to capital assets, which I called the marginal efficiency of capital.

The first difference created the possibility of adopting Richard Kahn's multiplier analysis to explain the equality of savings and investment and served to reinforce the role of liquidity preference, or 'bearishness', in determining the rate of interest. The second was the result of carrying to its logical conclusions the realization that there was no general, theoretical basis for a relation between the physical output produced by physical capital assets and the return obtained by the entrepreneur operating the equipment and selling the output produced. Although this realization was not revolutionary – it had already appeared in Irving Fisher's rate of return over cost[1] and I was able to cite passages from Marshall's *Principles* which also make the point – other writers, aside from Marx and a few ignored heretics, had failed to draw its full implications for economic theory.

My own position was based on prior work[2] which convinced me that Marx had been correct when he argued that the capitalist is only interested in his monetary return. The operation of capital goods could thus be profitable, even without being productive in the sense of producing a large amount of physical product. Of course, once one sees the point there is no more reason to believe that capital earns a return because it is productive than because of some other physical (or even metaphysical) attribute, such as being 'smelly'. The point was that there was no identifiable relationship between the difference between money costs and money receipts, and the physical conditions which characterize the production process.[3]

This rejection of a natural, or physically determined, rate of return such as Wicksell's natural rate, which had played a role in my *Treatise on Money* analysis of the relation between saving and investment, meant that the explanation of the investment decision and the role of 'bearishness' had to be reconsidered. But rejecting the natural rate of interest also meant that a single explanation could no longer explain both the rate of interest and the return on capital assets (or the prices of both assets and debts). I thus restricted 'bearishness' to the determination of the prices of financial assets in the form of 'liquidity preference', and developed the marginal efficiency of capital for capital goods. I subsequently discovered that this approach was similar to the theories of a number of earlier writers such as Veblen and Myrdal, as well as Schumpeter whom I had used as an authority for my analysis of investment in the *Treatise on Money*. I believe that the novelty of my own presentation of this line of thought lies in the introduction of the concept of user costs into supply prices, in particular of capital goods, and thus its inclusion in the calculation of the marginal efficiency of capital.

What I did not stress sufficiently was that my attempt to remedy my 'incomplete and confused' description of dynamics was built on the earlier attempt to enunciate a theory of short-period prices to complement what could be considered as the 'normal prices' which emerged from the 'fundamental equations' of the *Treatise on Money*. This was particularly true of the idea of user costs, which was meant to introduce the impact of future expectations into the dynamic structure of *The General Theory*.

THE GENESIS OF THE DYNAMICS OF *THE GENERAL THEORY* IN THE SHORT-PERIOD THEORY OF PRICES

Since most readers have failed to recognize both the continuity and the importance of user costs I shall try to make this more explicit. It is useful to start with the fundamental equations of the *Treatise on Money*. They represented a departure from the quantity theory tradition by explaining the equilibrium (or normal) prices of 'available goods' by unit costs (primarily wages, but including 'normal' remuneration of entrepreneurs). They were equilibrium prices in the sense that no one had any incentive to change the contractual cost relations upon which they were based. This applies to quantities produced, as well as to prices and wages.

Any divergence from normal conditions was represented by windfall profits or losses; the divergence of prices from normal is an expression of aggregate disequilibrium between demand and supply for 'available output', or equivalently, between savings and investment representing demand and supply conditions for 'unavailable output'. This was represented in the second term of the fundamental equation. Windfall profits or losses would be reflected in undesired decreases or increases in stocks of unsold goods; any attempt to adjust production would then reveal deficient or excess productive capacity. In such conditions normal prices would no longer rule, and attempts would take place to renegotiate contracts concerning both prices and quantities to determine a new set of normal prices and quantities. It is in this sense that the theory dealt with a given level of output.

The most important question which was left unanswered was whether the price and quantity adjustments which would be set in motion by the disequilibrium would automatically eliminate the imbalance without changing the level of output and employment. It was clearly beyond the scope of the fundamental equations to predict the results of these changes and my discussion of these aspects of adjustment was contained in a short section on the 'short-period theory of prices' in Volume II. The idea was to indicate how disequilibrium in the form of excess (or deficient) stocks and productive capacity would influence the movement of prices and quantities with respect to the normal flow supply prices and quantities embodied in the 'fundamental equations'. Given the period in which the book was written, it was natural to deal with conditions of generalized excess supply, although the theory was not restricted to that case.

In simple terms, the idea is that excess stocks will cause prices to fall below their 'normal' levels; if this creates expectations of further reductions in prices, the actual behaviour of prices will shift from being determined by the 'fundamentals' of costs of production, to the short-period conditions of stock supplies in which production costs become irrelevant because supply is dominated by decisions to sell from existing stocks. This change in the factors determining prices is roughly similar to Marshall's distinction between market prices and long-period prices, but the distinction is not analytical or temporal, it is determined by actual supply conditions and expectations.

In conditions of excess stocks, prices will continue to fall as long as producers believe they can minimize losses by selling today at a higher price than they expect tomorrow. Thus prices will continue to fall until they reach a level which convinces entrepreneurs to reduce production and to hold existing stocks on the expectation that a competetive return may be made by selling them at a better price at a later date. The movement of short-period prices will then be determined by the relation between current prices and the expected future prices. For convenience I assumed that the expectation of future prices was of a recovery to the 'normal' prices given by the fundamental equations, so that 'a mere change in expectations is capable of producing an oscillation of the same kind as a cyclical movement . . . which I discussed in my *Treatise on Money*' (*G.T.*: 49).

Thus a fall in prices would only come to a halt when it was sufficient to convince a speculator that he could earn a competitive return by buying existing stocks at the reduced current, or spot, price and holding them for sale at the normal future or forward price. Crucial to the calculation of this return is the length of time expected to elapse until restoration of normal conditions, as well as the costs of holding the stocks, which would include warehousing, insurance and financing costs given by the rate of interest. Also, any changes in the rate of current production and consumption of output will change the expectation of the holding period. In general, I concluded that the higher is the rate of interest, or other components of carrying costs, the longer is the time to recovery, the larger is the size of stocks relative to normal demand, the lower is the reduction in production with respect to price and the lower is the expansion in demand in response to the fall in price, the greater is the fall in the current price which will be required to induce the expectation of a market rate of return from holding excess stocks. All this I set out in a neat little formula, $pq = xy$, where q is the proportionate reduction in normal output due to the fall in price, x is the cost of carry as a proportion of the expected normal price, y is the time period until the return to normal conditions, and p is the proportionate fall in the spot price relative to the expected future price. These are the factors which will determine both the depth and the length of the cyclical downturn, as well as the behaviour of prices. Of course, the cyclical evolution of prices may itself bring about changes in the factors which determine 'normal' prices and quantities; this is what I failed to work out fully. None the less, for analytical purposes it is useful to start by keeping the two arguments separate by assuming given expectations and thus an expectation of a return to 'normal' conditions. This is what might be called static or stationary conditions, which stop short of the 'shifting' equilibrium which represents the dynamics of *The General Theory*.[4]

The idea of 'user costs' followed directly from this analysis. Since stocks which are being held are expected to yield a return equal to the difference between their current or 'spot' price and the expected normal, or 'forward', price, a decision to 'use' them, either as an imput in production or by selling them at the current spot price, will lead to the loss of this expected future gain. The 'user cost' associated with using stocks today is thus the present value of the expected net future return which could be realized by waiting to sell at the expected normal price.

THE PRESENTATION OF EFFECTIVE DEMAND IN TERMS OF SPOT AND FORWARD PRICES

In my attempt to break away from the quantity theory of money in the *Treatise on Money* I shifted the focal point of the analysis to the effective decision-makers in the economy, to the 'effort of producers or to the expenditure of consumers' (1930a: 120). The realization that there was no theoretical relation between real returns and profitability thus led me to define the 'efforts of producers' as

> whether it is expected to *pay* a firm in possession of capital equipment to spend money on incurring variable costs: i.e. whether the result of spending money on employment and of selling the output is expected to result in a larger net sum of money at the end of the accounting period than if the money had been retained. Other criteria, such as the relation between the real output which a given employment will yield and the disutility or real cost of that employment, or the relation between the real wages of a given employment and the amount of its marginal output, are not appropriate to the actual nature of business decisions in a world in which prices are subject to change during an accounting period, such changes being themselves a function *inter alia* of the amount of investment during the period.
>
> (*C.W.* XXIX: 66)

But it was clearly insufficient to suggest that entrepreneurs would be satisfied simply by recovering their money sums committed; they would seek the highest possible returns available by committing their funds in any way, not only for production of output.

I put the idea in the last 1933 draft of *The General Theory* as follows:

> The employment of the factors of production to increase output involves the entrepreneur in the disbursement, not of product, but

266

of money. The choice before him in deciding whether or not to offer employment is a choice between using money in this way or in some other way or not using it at all. . . . The only question before him is to choose . . . that way which will yield the largest profit in terms of money. It must be remembered that future prices, in so far as they are anticipated, are already reflected in current prices, after allowing for the various considerations of carrying costs and of opportunities of production in the meantime which relate the spot and forward prices of a given commodity.[5] Thus we must suppose that the spot and forward price structure has already brought into equilibrium the relative advantages, as estimated by the holder, of holding money and other existing forms of wealth. Thus if the advantage in terms of money of using money to start up a productive process increases, this will stimulate entrepreneurs to offer more employment. . . . For the entrepreneur is guided, not by the amount of product he will gain, but by the alternative opportunities for using money having regard to the spot and forward price structure taken as a whole.

(*C.W.* XXIX: 82–3)

Now, define the per unit cost associated with producing output as the current supply price, or spot price, of that output, and the present value of the net sum received per unit of output as its demand or forward price. Then the 'actual nature of the business decision', which determines the 'effort of producers', will be described by the comparison of the spot and expected forward prices. If this is positive, and as a proportion of the initial expenditure represents a return greater than the interest promised by the 'alternative opportunities for using money' (or the costs of borrowing the money expended), then production will proceed and output and employment will be created.

I extended this basic idea of comparing spot and forward prices for an individual commodity, derived from the short-period pricing formula, to the actual sums expended and the sums expected to be received by each entrepreneur relative to the amount of employment created. Given the number of entrepreneurs in the economy, it was thus possible to derive a similar relation for the economy as a whole, which became the 'Aggregate Supply Price' and 'Aggregate Demand Price' functions of Chapter 3 of *The General Theory*. The point at which the aggregate supply price and demand price functions intersect represents the equality of the rate of return from engaging in production and the 'alternative uses of money' represented by the rate of interest. Employment, and the output produced, could then be described as being determined at the 'point' of effective demand representing the intersection of the two functions.

The explanation that I attempted to give in Books III and IV[6] of the determinants of Aggregate Demand Prices in terms of the decision to consume and invest should then be understood as a discussion of the determinants of forward or futures prices. The formal presentation of the question of 'whether it is expected to *pay* a firm in possession of capital equipment to spend money on incurring variable costs' set out in Chapter 3 of *The General Theory* thus starts with the precise definition of the amount of money spent on 'the employment of a given volume of labour by an entrepreneur' as 'the amounts which he pays out to the factors of production for their current services' and 'the amounts he pays out to other entrepreneurs for what he has to purchase from them' plus 'the sacrifice which he incurs by employing the equipment instead of leaving it idle, which we shall call the user cost of the employment in question' (*G.T.*: 23). User cost thus plays a central role in determining variable costs. As a result, the difference between the expected sales and the sum of costs paid to factors, plus user costs, is what it is expected to 'pay' a firm to operate the equipment: 'in a given situation of technique, resources and factor cost per unit of employment, the amount of employment, both in each individual firm and industry and in the aggregate, depends on the amount of proceeds which the entrepreneurs expect to receive from the corresponding output'.

The reason for these rather complicated definitions of aggregate or national income (which most readers have chosen to ignore) was to make clear the role of future expectations through user costs and aggregate demand prices. If A = aggregate sales proceeds, F = factor costs and U = user cost, then the sum of entrepreneurs' incomes will be the difference between gross receipts and costs of production: $A - (F + U)$. From this it follows that the total income for the economy, Y, is composed of factor incomes, which are given by entrepreneurs' factor costs, F, plus entrepreneurs' income or $Y = F + [A - (F + U)] = A - U$. Defining A' as entrepreneurs' acquisitions of output from other entrepreneurs, the value of consumption expenditures can be defined as $A - A'$, while investment will be $Y - (A - A')$ or $I = (A - U) - (A - A') = A' - U$. Entrepreneurs can only be expected to commit money to engage in production if they expect to recover their outlays. In the aggregate this is $F + A' - U = F + I$, which is defined as aggregate supply price.

Entrepreneurs will then have to determine whether the proceeds that they expect to receive from selling the output, or the aggregate demand price, meets or exceeds the aggregate supply price. The aggregate demand price will be composed of the sum of D_1, the proportion of the aggregate outlays (i.e. a proportion of $F + A' - U$) which entrepreneurs expect to earn from the public's expenditures on consumption, and D_2, the amount which entrepreneurs are expected to devote to new investment expenditures. Note that both amounts are net of user costs. Equality of aggregate supply and demand price, defined as the point of effective demand, is then where $F + I (= A' - U) = D_1 + D_2$. It will thus 'pay' entrepreneurs to increase expenditures of money to hire factors of production in order to increase output whenever 'demand price' is greater than 'supply price', for in such conditions current costs of production are below the expected future price (the price of the futures contract) so producers can 'go full steam ahead' on the expectation of selling their output in the future at a profit equal to the difference between the current spot or aggregate supply price and the expected futures or aggregate demand price. This incentive will only be exhausted when the two prices have come into equality, which is the 'point of effective demand' and short-period equilibrium.

The determinants of this equality will depend on the proportion of $F + A' - U$ which consumers choose to spend as D_1 and determines firms' receipts from sales of consumption goods to the public. This proportion is given by what I called the 'propensity to consume'.[7] It will also depend on D_2, which is determined by the inducement to invest, and in particular on the second set of changes introduced in the book, the marginal efficiency of capital and user costs. In order for the equality between aggregate demand and aggregate supply price to occur at any particular level of employment, investment expenditures given by D_2 must make up for any divergence between income and consumption expenditures given by the difference between D_1 and $F + A' - U$. If it does not automatically do so, the level of output and employment will change. Hence the enunciation of the factors leading to changes in the level of output.

It is important to notice that both aggregate supply and demand prices are net of user costs, so it might appear that they may be eliminated. However, this would not be appropriate for analysis of the decisions of individual producers, since user costs are the equivalent of carrying costs in the short-period price analysis. It would thus be possible to convert the difference between expected prices (aggregate or unit) and prime costs of production into a relation between the spot price of existing goods, flow supply prices and forward (or expected demand) prices. As long as the costs of production of new goods are less than the costs of carry of existing goods it will pay producers to sign contracts to supply goods at the expected future demand price and to go ahead and incur costs of using capital equipment to produce them. This is the condition which will allow entrepreneurs to end up with more 'money than they started with'. Note that expectations of future prices enter both the supply and the demand side, for they will detemine the size of user costs, a component of marginal prime costs, and the expected future net receipts which are discounted to obtain demand prices. User costs will thus play a role in determining individual prices as well as the general price level.

Thus, the relation between spot and forward prices and the role of user costs in determining this relation based on the short-period pricing relation formed the basis for the presentation of effective demand on the aggregate level in Chapter 3. This is also the case for my 'new' explanation of the inducement to invest in Chapters 11 and 12, and the discussion of the rate of interest in Chapter 13 in relation to the estimation of D_2.

THE MARGINAL EFFICIENCY OF CAPITAL AND USER COSTS

Readers will recall that the *Treatise on Money* contained no 'fundamental equation' for the prices of capital goods. In discussions of the book I was criticized for this asymmetrical approach to the determination of the prices of available and non-available output by both Richard Kahn and Piero Sraffa. They suggested that since both are produced goods, consistency required that costs of production should determine both the prices of consumption and capital goods. While this may be the case for newly produced capital goods under normal conditions, they clearly differ from consumption goods in that they are long-lived and will survive into conditions which had not been foreseen, and thus may no longer be normal. From this point of view, the pricing of capital goods corresponds more closely to my short-period pricing theory, for since they are long-lived durable goods, old capital goods represent the equivalent of stocks which compete with newly produced goods.[8] As noted above: 'It is by reason of the existence of durable equipment that the economic future is linked to the present' (*G.T.*: 146).

Given the impact of the future on the present, current costs of production will no longer be relevant to the supply price of existing capital goods. The definition of effective demand given above requires the specification of the costs incurred by entrepreneurs in undertaking production. The costs incurred in the use of existing capital goods thus cannot be ignored. User costs provide the solution to this problem by defining the cost of using existing capital goods as the difference between the cost of holding them idle (i.e. the cost of keeping them in good productive condition plus interest charges) and the expected net return from using them to produce in the future. The rate of discount which equates the expected stream of future returns to the cost of producing new capital goods thus has to compete with the rate of discount which equates the expected stream of future returns to the supply prices of existing capital goods as determined by user costs. Just as in my short-period theory, if the prime cost of using existing capital is below the flow supply price for newly produced goods because their prices are expected to continue to fall, no one will demand new investment goods and investment expenditures included in $A' - U$ will be reduced.[9]

Thus my response to the criticisms of my *Treatise on Money* explanation of the prices of capital goods involved the introduction of future conditions for capital goods prices, which enter the supply prices of capital via user costs, and the expectations of conditions for output prices which determined expected future net receipts from operating the capital goods. As I noted, it is the correction of supply prices, rather than the specification of expected future profits, which represents the innovation. This explains why I wanted to emphasize the role of changes in marginal efficiency as being independent of the influence of liquidity preference and the rate of interest. For this reason Chapter 12 attempted to give 'full weight to the importance of the influence of short-period changes in the state of long-term expectations as distinct from changes in the rate of interest'.

Looked at from this perspective, the key to recovery is to produce conditions in which current spot prices stand in relation to future prices such that it again becomes more profitable to purchase newly produced goods rather than existing goods (i.e. 'backwardation' exists in the market). My short-period price analysis suggested that the easiest way to do this would be to reduce the rate of interest (to reduce the carrying costs) and to increase demand for existing stocks, i.e. by monetary expansion or by government expenditures.

There were two obstacles in the way of taking such action to promote recovery, the 'Treasury view', which opposed government expenditures, and the Bank of England's perceived unwillingness to reduce interest rates because of the fear of jeopardizing the foreign balance. My experience on the Macmillan Committee indicated to me that these two impediments were similar in nature. It there emerged that the 'Treasury view' was not, as commonly supposed, that government investment 'crowds out' private investment because investible resources, in the form of the supply of saving, are given; but rather, that government investments are inefficient because they represent the use of resources in projects which earn returns that are lower than competitive market rates of return. In short, government investment to support demand was the equivalent of subsidizing investment and thus a distortion of the free market allocation of resources.

But there is a fallacy in this argument. Consider government investment in a project yielding a 4 per cent return when the Bank rate is 6 per cent. 'It is not true that the money going into the four per cent investment is going otherwise into a six per cent investment; for six per cent does not represent what an alternative investment is yielding, it represents the rate that has to be enforced by the banking system to prevent us from lending abroad more than we can finance by our trade balance' (*C.W.* XX: 146). In short, the alternative was not investment projects offering a 6 per cent return, but the Bank of England offering that rate in order to stop capital flowing out of the country in an amount that exceeded the positive balance on current account. Further, since the current balance was primarily determined by relative wage costs, Bank rate did not even represent the returns which could be earned by investing abroad. Thus, far from the government subsidizing capital investment, it was the Bank of England that was subsidizing the purchase of financial assets. It was the Bank that was crowding out productive investment.

In this case, it was the requirements of foreign balance which produced a rate of interest that competed with domestic investment. But this explanation of the impediments to recovery by relaxing monetary policy was directly linked to the assumption of an open economy operating under the gold standard. In *The General Theory* I reconsidered this position, for it may have implied that a closed system, or even an open system with flexible exchange rates, might achieve full employment if the monetary authority set the rate of interest at the level at which investment took off full-employment saving.

In developing *The General Theory* I worked out the concept of a 'monetary economy' in which individual decisions concerning the disposition of liquid assets expressed in 'liquidity preference' could exercise an impact on interest rates which was as difficult to overcome as that represented by the necessity for the central bank to defend the foreign exchanges. This brought the formulation of the 'Monetary Production Economy' and the idea of effective demand formulated in terms of conditions of backwardation in the relation between spot and forward prices. In simple terms, not only would existing capital goods compete with new investment expenditures, financial assets would too. Since the return on existing capital goods was given by user costs, the supply price of financial assets would also be given by user costs, i.e. by a relation between spot and expected future prices.

I was thus able to avoid the contorted discussions of the determinants of the rate of interest found in the works of my contemporaries, and in logical conformity with the definition of aggregate demand and supply prices and the marginal efficiency of capital to define the rate of interest on money as 'nothing more than the percentage excess of a sum of money contracted for forward delivery, e.g. a year hence, over what we may call the "spot" or cash price of the sum thus contracted for forward delivery' (*G.T.*: 222). It is for this reason that I have on various occasions referred to the liquidity premium on money as its 'marginal efficiency' or of the rate of interest as measuring its 'user cost', for this is the return which is forgone by retaining wealth in liquid form. This then became the 'alternative employment' (rather than Bank rate) which competed against the use of the entrepreneur's money to produce output and offer employment.

CHAPTER 17 AS A 'GENERAL' THEORY OF SPOT AND FORWARD PRICES

As we have seen above, the specification of aggregate demand and supply was derived from the decisions of individual entrepreneurs to initiate production. Having applied this spot-forward price framework to the general decisions to purchase capital goods and non-liquid financial assets, it seemed reasonable to provide a general presentation, which I attempted in Chapter 17. I thought this would make it easier to see the role of money in producing the impact of future expectations on present decisions.[10] To do this I went back to my *Tract on Monetary Reform* and applied the interest rate parity theorem, substituting possible investment expenditures for the decisions to make investments denominated in the currencies of foreign countries. Just as an international investor must keep his accounts in one currency, and compare his returns from investments in foreign currencies to the rate of interest he earns on that currency, I argued that entrepreneurs would decide 'whether it is expected to *pay* . . . to spend money on incurring variable costs' to provide employment by keeping these accounts in terms of money. Thus the returns available on investments in other types of real or financial assets would have to compete with the return available on money.

In simple terms, if the relative prices of all alternative investments are expected to be stable, the equivalent of international interest rate parity is the equality between the liquidity premium attached to money as given by its marginal efficiency or rate of return, and the marginal efficiencies representing the rates of return available on the various possible investment alternatives. Just as international investors will adjust their portfolios of international currencies until there are no arbitrage gains to be made, investors will adjust their investments until they cannot increase their aggregate return by an alternative composition of investments.

Although I pointed out in Chapter 17 that any durable or producible good can be analysed by the method of spot and forward prices which I had already employed in the definition of the rate of interest on money and the rate of return to capital, so that it was formally the same as the analysis of the interest rate parity theorem, none of my readers seem to have taken these indications seriously. It is thus possible to envisage spot and forward prices for every durable commodity in the economy, including specific types of capital goods, which will determine its rate of return or marginal efficiency, as well as for every financial asset which will determine its rate of interest.

In an open economy under the gold standard the Bank of England was constrained to keep the rate of interest high enough to prevent capital outflows exceeding the current account balance, given British wages, productivity and prices. This was the rate of return which all other investments had to match. If the return on domestic investment is 4 per cent, the return to investment abroad is 5 per cent, and Bank rate is 6 per cent, the Bank succeeds in limiting capital outflows, but only by redirecting entrepreneurs' funds into financial assets rather than capital investments, which causes a reduction in D_2. But if the level of interest rates required to bring balance on foreign account is sufficiently high, it may produce conditions of contango, the opposite of backwardation, and bring even the use of existing capital goods for production to a halt, producing a fall in F and a decline in D_1. At some proportionate fall in prices and restriction of output the expected rate of return from buying excess stocks and holding them until recovery will reach that available on financial assets so that prices stabilize. This would be what I defined in my Macmillan testimony as a 'spurious equilibrium', for although the rates of return on all alternative uses for entrepreneurs' funds are uniform, there is unused potential productive capacity which is not being used and there are idle workers available who would be willing to work for current levels of wages. In such conditions there is no incentive for entrepreneurs to commit new funds to produce additional output and provide employment, nor is there anything to stop an increase in national income and employment, except the level of the rate of interest.

It was thus British bank rate which set the standard that British investors had to meet in assessing the returns available on investments in diverse national currencies. In equilibrium the returns to be earned from holding any foreign asset denominated in foreign currency would be the same; yet this did not imply that the various national interest rates were identical. This difference was resolved by means of the adjustment of the premium or discount of the forward relative to the spot price of the various foreign currencies. Given one dominant international rate of interest, such as sterling Bank rate, the relative spot and forward prices will be determined so as to equalize the advantage of any individual currency, irrespective of its absolute rate of interest.

Chapter 17 thus follows my decision to separate liquidity preference and marginal efficiency by substituting the rate of return (or user cost or marginal efficiency) on money (or liquidity) for British bank rate, and by substituting the rate of return (or marginal efficiency) of every available durable good for the interest rates on foreign assets measured in terms of their own home currency. I called these latter rates their 'own-rates of own-return' because, just as with foreign interest rates, they were expressed in terms of themselves.[11]

This became the conceptual equivalent of what might be considered a 'real' or 'natural' rate of interest. For wheat, it would be the difference between the kernels of wheat planted and those harvested as a proportion of those planted. A 10 per cent 'own-rate of own-return' with reference to wheat was then eleven kernels of gross return for every ten advanced. This can equivalently be expressed as the forward or demand price of wheat relative to the spot or supply price, measured in terms of wheat.[12] Just as in the international system, equilibrium would occur when the relative advantages of all types of investment, in holding existing goods, in operating existing capital goods, in building new capital goods, in lending to businessmen and so forth, had reached equality.

However, the calculation of this equilibrium position, just as in the international case, has to be undertaken in terms of a single currency or durable good, which is money, so that while entrepreneurs would look at 'own-rates of own-return', they would only be interested in those which will 'yield the largest profit in terms of money' so that it could be compared to 'the alternative opportunities for using money having regard to the spot and forward price structure taken as a whole'.

Following my simple definition of the rate of interest, money takes a spot price equal to unity and an own-return given by the difference between its spot and forward price. For other durables, their return will be given by their own-rate of own-return, for example the wheat rate of interest, which has to be converted into a return comparable to money just as foreign investment returns have to be translated into a domestic return by the difference between spot and forward discounts or premiums in terms of money. The total return to holding wheat or any other investment will then be composed of two elements: the sum of the expected appreciation or depreciation of wheat in terms of money (the equivalent of the forward discount or premium) and the own-rate of own-return measured in terms of itself. I represented the first term by a, which may be defined as the forward money price of wheat less the spot money price of wheat as a proportion of the spot price. The 'own-rate of own-return', defined as the forward price of, for example, wheat in terms of wheat less the spot price as a proportion of the spot price, was presented in terms of three component characteristics: q, the real or natural return of productive goods; c, the carrying costs involved in investments which involve the holding of goods in the expectation of better future prices; and l, the user cost of liquidity or the liquidity premium.

For money, just as for the domestic currency, the value of $a = 0$, since it always buys the same amount of itself. Its return is given by l, its liquidity premium, while it has no other carrying cost or 'real' return from increasing production since it cannot be produced. For capital goods, on the other hand, the primary return is given by q, while for commodities held on speculation they will have high values of c.

The equilibrium of the system is given by equality between the return on money, i, and the value of $a \pm (q - c + l)$ for every other activity in the economy (which may include consumption).[13] Just as it was the Bank of England that could determine the profitability of investing at home and abroad and in domestic assets (capital equipment) or debts (domestic Treasury bonds) because of its role in the international gold standard, in Chapter 17 it is the user cost of money as envisaged by households, firms and banks, relative to the decision of the central bank to create money, that determines the equilibrium which is produced. Aside from this formal generalization of the previous analysis of the book, the remainder of Chapter 17 explains why the rate of interest on money may behave differently from that of other assets and debts, and why this distinguishes the role of money assets from all others in setting the point of effective demand.

J.A. KREGEL

THE ROLE OF MONEY AND CHAPTER 17

I could have retained my Macmillan Committee analysis and explained the peculiarity of the behaviour of the money rate of interest by the necessity of the Bank of England to fix bank rate at the level which assured international equilibrium. However, there are more fundamental factors in a monetary economy which will prevent market forces from automatically producing a rate of interest compatible with full employment equilibrium.

I again approached the problem as an extension of the short-period pricing theory. The general thrust of that theory was to enquire as to the possibility for short-period changes in spot relative to forward prices to provide sufficient incentives in the form of expected returns to produce changes in demand or supply which would change output levels so as to bring returns on all available investment opportunities into equality.

It was thus natural to ask the same question with respect to money. Would changes in the demand for money produce changes in the forward price of money relative to the spot price which would increase the incentive to produce money? For an economy based on what I called 'Representative money' in the *Treatise on Money* (1930a. 6ff.), I concluded that the answer was no. Since representative money is not created by entrepreneurs deciding to produce it in relation to its relative rate of return, an increase in the demand for money will not automatically increase its supply, no matter how much its forward price and relative yield changes. This became one of the 'essential properties' of money, a low or negligible 'elasticity of production'.

But if it was possible for an increase in demand to drive up the return on money without generating an increase in supply, was it possible that some alternative source of liquidity might be produced which could substitute for money? Representative money differs from other durable assets in that it has a negligible cost of carry, c, and no q, so that its entire return comes from its liquidity premium. Alternative assets that might substitute for money in this respect will usually have carrying costs that are a positive function of the demand for them because of storage, insurance and financing costs, so their returns will eventually be driven below that on money. This became the 'essential property' of the low or negligible 'elasticity of substitution' for money and is linked to the fact that the carrying cost on money is negligible and independent of demand.[14] These two factors taken together suggested that there is no reason for the supply of money to respond automatically to demand and thus that its return may move independently of the level of demand and output. The result is that there will be no automatic tendency for the return on money to fall so as to increase the attractiveness of using money to initiate the production of new output and create employment.

I was thus able to conclude that it was not a malfunction in the operation of the price mechanism, but rather the nature of money in a monetary production economy which impeded the fall in the rate of interest to the level which produced full employment. Even if expansion occurred in other sectors, this would eventually run into the limit given by the liquidity premium on money.

This, however, left the question of whether active policy might not be able to expand the money supply sufficiently to bring about the rate of interest required to achieve full employment. However, if an increase in the supply of money simply caused a matching increase in the demand for money, this would prevent the decline in the rate of interest required to increase output to the full employment level. Indeed, I concluded that this might well occur if there is a generalized expectation that the prices of other assets will be lower in the future, such that individuals choose to sell assets in exchange for money.

The decision to hold money rather than to use it is determined by the relation between its liquidity premium and the returns available on other assets. If money is 'used' today to buy investment goods or consumption goods, or to buy financial assets (which includes bank lending to either households or entrepreneurs) in order to gain a return, this means that money cannot be 'used' at some future date. The 'user cost' of money will then be the present value of the potential future gain forgone by parting with money today. This will depend on the forward prices of investment goods, consumption goods and financial assets. With respect to other financial assets the user cost of money is the forgone gain that could have been achieved by waiting to purchase financial assets at lower prices and earning higher interest rates.

If 'using' money is defined as becoming 'illiquid', then the user cost of money measures the premium which is required to convince holders of money to become illiquid. Just as spot prices have to fall sufficiently relative to expected future prices to convince people to hold excess supplies rather than sell them, in the case of money, spot asset prices have to fall relative to expected future prices to convince them to hold financial assets rather than money.

However, if an expansion in the supply of money has driven current spot prices above expected future rates, then the user cost of money may rise above the current rate of interest and the demand for money will rise, offsetting the fall in rates. Indeed, the rise in prices may reach a position in which the increase in demand just offsets the expansion in supply, blocking any further reduction in the rate of interest. This will occur when the annual percentage decline in price given by the difference between the current spot price and the expected future price is equal to the square of the current rate of interest on consols. In this case the expected capital loss from holding the non-monetary financial asset offsets the year's interest return.[15] It is for this reason that the interest rate will be primarily determined by what people expect future asset prices (or interest rates) to be, and changes in the money supply may not have a direct impact on interest rates. This is the basis of Hick's and Robertson's criticism of my theory of interest as being held up by its own bootstraps.[16]

HOW THE NEW APPROACH CHANGED MY POLICY POSITIONS

Thus, even if the Bank of England could overcome the constraints of the gold standard (or structural changes in wages and productivity could be introduced which would reduce the required capital inflows), my own view was that 'it seems likely that the fluctuations in the market estimation of the marginal efficiency of different types of capital . . . will be too great to be offset by any practicable changes in the rate of interest' (G.T.: 164). This shows the importance of eliminating the 'confusion between results due to a change in the rate of interest and those due to a change in the schedule of the marginal efficiency of capital' (G.T.: 173). It also led me to the necessity of 'the State . . . taking an ever greater responsibility for directly organising investment' because I was 'sceptical of the success of a merely monetary policy directed towards influencing the rate of interest [in] continuously stimulating the appropriate volume of investment' (G.T.: 164).

Despite these very precise indications, presentations of my theory have continued to restrict discussion of marginal efficiency and investment to an inverse monotonic relation between investment expenditures and the rate of interest, and have restricted their concerns to the appropriate fine-tuning of monetary policy to influence investment through this channel.

It also shows the importance of the break between the rate of interest and the real return to capital. As soon as I could show that the return on money given by the liquidity premium (l) on money would be determined by different factors than the return to other assets (q, c) I could argue that the automatic operation of the competitive price mechanism could not guarantee that changes in relative prices of assets (representing, say, an adjustment of demand and supply which shifts the investor from a declining to an expanding sector, such as discussed by Pigou) would necessarily bring about an adjustment in their relative returns so as to produce a progressive shift in labour and capital resources among productive uses without changing the level of employment; for as long as money's return was independent of this process, any funds released from declining sectors would be committed to investment in money or other financial assets which would not provide an offsetting change in output or in employment. I could thus argue that a

> monetary economy . . . is essentially one in which changing views about the future are capable of influencing the quantity of employment and not merely its direction. But our method of analysing the economic

behaviour of the present under the influence of changing ideas about the future is one which depends on the interaction of supply and demand, and is in this way linked up with our fundamental theory of value.

$$(G.T.: vii)$$

Professor Pigou had argued that the operation of relative prices would bring about shifts in investment and employment across different industries (bring changes in the 'direction' of employment), but that the overall level of output and employment would remain unchanged. It was for this reason that I attempted to couch the entire theory in terms of the short-period theory of spot and forward prices determining the relative rates of return that direct expenditures to different types of investment. Those who have failed to grasp the importance of my approach to price theory and the role of user cost in providing a vehicle to introduce the influence of the future on the present have failed to grasp the basic shift in emphasis, not only with respect to my previous work, but with reference to all of what I called 'classical theory'.

NOTES

* *Advertisement to the reader*: As this is a 'second edition' of *The General Theory*, I have composed this chapter as Keynes might have written it. It is *not* the result of another discovery in an attic at Tilton, and J.M. Keynes declines all responsibility for it. I have benefited from comments on numerous earlier versions from G.C. Harcourt, L.R. Wray, A.J. Cornford and the members of the MURST (40 per cent) Research Group directed by Mario Tonveronachi, all of whom also decline responsibility.

1 It is for this reason that I identified Fisher as my great grandparent (cf. 'Alternative Theories of the Rate of Interest', *C.W.* XIII: 202, n.2) antecedent to Hawtrey, in my treatment of money as a 'real' factor, rather than physical productivity, in determining the return to capital. It is to be hoped that this exposition will indicate that, despite divergences in other areas, there is no difference between Fisher and me on this point of definition.

2 For example, in 1914 I noted that the 'destruction of paper values' caused by the collapse of stock prices was independent of any change in the ability of capital goods to produce real output: 'With a . . . fall in the value of securities, we learn not, as with the destruction of Liège or Louvain, of a loss in the world's real wealth, but only of the financial world's extreme urgency for money . . . We experience, therefore, a sudden and violent change in our relative valuation of present and future income' (*C.W.* VIII: 268).

3 I had included these points more explicitly in early drafts. Compare the last draft of 1933: 'An entrepreneur is interested, not in the amount of product, but in the amount of *money* which will fall to his share. He will increase his output if by doing so he expects to increase his money profit, even though this profit represents a smaller quantity of product than before' (*C.W.* XXIX: 82).

4 This approach also played an important role in the transition to the new book. During my university lectures in 1932 I used it to investigate the question of whether an automatic adjustment of the system to full employment might take

place by means of such short-period adjustments of the prices of capital and labour in conditions of excess supply, noting that 'in the case of a machine, we assume that when it is in over-supply those of its utility-giving powers which evaporate with time will accept anything rather than go to waste. Consequently its short-period supply price is equal to the discounted long-period price of those of its qualities which will "keep", and drops like a stone, as soon as it is in oversupply, from its long-period price to the equivalent of the extra depreciation involved in using it over not using it. . . . Now suppose that the short-period supply price of labour was just like that of a machine . . . Prime cost would be next door to zero. There could be much more violent changes in relative prices without affecting output . . . Thus if we assume that the short-period supply price of labour is determined on the same principles as that of machines under free competition and that prime cost (in terms of money) is next door to zero, it follows that there will be no unemployment in the short period any more than in the long. Indeed the short period will not be so very unlike the long. . . .' This would have been the explanation of traditional theory, in which price adjustments are sufficient to eliminate any excess of demand or supply. However, I believe that this represents an inappropriate assumption concerning the behaviour of labour, since 'We cannot assume that a labourer regards any reward as better than none, *or that he will be worked whenever the value of his service is greater than the excess of his "running cost" over his cost on a "care-and-maintenance" basis.* We have to remember, on the contrary, (a) that there is a disutility in work, and also (b) that, unlike a machine, he can often insist on a care-and-maintenance basis of cost, *even when his value if in work would be greater than the excess of his running cost over what he costs the community on a care-and-maintenance basis.* Accordingly whilst the short-period supply price of a machine is almost vertical, the short-period supply price of labour is nearly horizontal; – prime cost being arrived at by combining these two supply curves. . . . The net advantages of different employments of capital and labour will be unequal in the short period, whereas they will be equal in the long period. This will be the only important difference' (*C.W.* XXIX: 51–2, emphasis added).

5 Here I added a note directing the reader to the theory of short-period prices in Chapter 29 of the *Treatise on Money.*

6 This material had been Chapter 1: 'The Differential of Consumption and Capital Goods' of Book III: 'The Determination of Price' in the 1932 table of contents.

7 Since the decision to consume was determined primarily by the expectation of future income of households, it also reflected the impact of the future on the present. However, it was excessively difficult to present this relation in terms of current and expected prices and thus the decisions of entrepreneurs became the dominant of the two equal factors which had motivated equilibrium in the *Treatise on Money.*

8 Just as newly produced capital goods will have to compete with more technically efficient capital goods produced in the future.

9 This is the condition which I described as 'backwardation' in the *Treatise on Money* (and which has gained a place in the financial literature on futures prices). In normal conditions of balanced supply and demand this will occur when prices for future delivery are driven below current spot prices because long hedgers seeking cover dominate short hedgers and speculators. In conditions of slump this requires that the prime costs (user costs of operating) of existing equipment be greater than the prime cost of producing new capital goods so that, given the expectation of the recovery of prices, it is cheaper to

order new capacity for future delivery than to buy existing capital goods to hold until future recovery. In the language of the futures market, flow supply prices are below futures prices which are below spot prices, so the most profitable action is to sell capital goods futures, hedging by producing them for sale at maturity rather than buying them spot.

10 Readers who followed the discussions of the book immediately after its publication will note that I myself found it easier to employ these terms in debating with my critics. Thus I used the framework of Chapter 17 either implicitly or explicitly in a series of *Economic Journal* exchanges in 1937, in my contribution to Irving Fisher's *Festschrift* and in my *Quarterly Journal of Economics* reply to Jacob Viner's review (all reprinted in *C.W.* XIV). Even I sometimes underestimated the implications of this approach, and it was Mr Hugh Townshend who astutely reminded me of some of the implications when I was backsliding into previous modes of thought (cf. some of his correspondence in *C.W.* XXIX: 236ff. and his article in the 1937 *Economic Journal*).

11 Although interest rates are pure numbers, and thus can be compared, a 10 per cent return on a dollar asset, compared to 10 per cent on sterling, yields US dollars, not sterling, and thus the two rates are not comparable. They thus express 'own' rates in that they give returns in terms of their own unit of account.

12 Piero Sraffa (1932a) had already employed the same concept under the name of commodity rates in his critique of Hayek's idea of neutral monetary policy. It is a straightforward application of techniques applied in futures markets for commodities and currencies in which we both were involved, so it is difficult to determine who was responsible for their application to questions of theory.

13 Recall that these relations can all be rewritten in terms of the appropriate spot and forward prices, e.g. $i = [F(t, T) - S(t)]/S(t)$, where F and S are the forward and spot prices of money as in my formal definition of the rate of interest on money. Equivalently, $a = [F_{w,m}(t, T) - S_{w,m}(t)]/S_{w,m}(t)$ representing the forward and spot prices of wheat in terms of money, and $q = [F_{w,w}(t, T) - S_{w,w}(t)]/S_{w,w}(t)$, representing the forward and spot prices of wheat in terms of wheat.

14 I had originally discussed these matters in rudimentary form in Part V of a draft of Chapter 2, entitled 'The Distinction Between a Co-operative and an Entrepreneur Economy', in the provisional table of contents for 1933 (cf. *C.W.* XXIX: 85–7).

15 This is the 'square rule' which I gave in Chapter 15 (*G.T.*: 202) and is the basis for the 'liquidity trap': 'For example, if the rate of interest on long-term debt is 4 per cent., it is preferable to sacrifice liquidity unless on a balance of probabilities it is feared that the long-term rate of interest may rise by faster than by 4 per cent. of itself per annum, i.e. by an amount greater than 0.16 per cent. per annum.' If this were the case, then the capital loss on holding a consol would exceed the annual interest. Thus user costs (measuring the liquidity premium) of using money to buy assets at current prices, instead of waiting to buy at lower expected future prices, would be greater than the interest return earned from buying them today; a rational investor should thus hold any increase in money balances in liquid form. Although the reinvestment of future interest receipts at the higher expected future rates would eventually offset the expected capital loss (often called the duration point), the time required is longer the lower is the current rate of interest. It thus follows that the conditions associated with the liquidity trap are more likely the lower is the current rate of interest, although they can occur at virtually any level because the evaluation of user costs and, what is the same thing, the expected future

value of interest rates will depend crucially on recent experience of the volatility of interest rates. The higher the volatility of interest rates, the higher the 'balance of probabilities' that the rate of interest will rise by its square and thus the higher the level of rates at which the liquidity trap may become operative. (The experienced investor will note that the square relation holds precisely for consols (perpetual bonds) and approximately for finite maturities. He or she will also have noted the affinity with the concept of duration which has recently become popular as a measure of the volatility of bond prices.)

16 I believe these critics failed to understand the full implications of the fact that the forces determining physical productivity (reflected in q) have no direct role in determining the money returns earned from holding or operating assets. It is interesting to note that the interest rate parity theorem has never been criticized as relying on bootstraps.

17

OWN-RATES OF INTEREST AND THEIR RELEVANCE FOR THE EXISTENCE OF UNDEREMPLOYMENT EQUILIBRIUM POSITIONS*

Ingo Barens and Volker Caspari

I did not feel able to argue passionately about chapter seventeen, either for or against it.

Eric Ambler (1985: 136)

We should not be writing this essay if Alvin Hansen's verdict that Chapter 17 of *The General Theory* is 'simply a detour' and 'that not much would have been lost had it not been written' (Hansen 1953: 155, 159)[1] had been taken seriously. But regardless of the validity of Hansen's judgement, it is an indisputable fact that over the years numerous writers have tried to elaborate on the analytical meaning and theoretical importance of this 'confused and most confusing' (Pigou 1936: 125) or 'mysterious chapter' (Robinson 1961b: 596), about which Keynes himself conceded: 'I admit the obscurity of this chapter' (C.W. XIV: 519).[2]

We shall not try to solve the enigma of the 'Monetary Theory of Production'.[3] Our aim is simple: to summarize Keynes's arguments concerning the notion of own-rates of interest and systematize the different problems confronting his attempt to construct a 'new' Theory of Interest and Money.

In the first section of the chapter, relying on the writings of Irving Fisher, we clarify the definition of the own-rate of interest and its relation to the definition of the own-rate of interest in terms of money. The following section deals with pre-*General Theory* discussions of the notions of own-rates of interest in the writings of Friedrich von Hayek, Pierro Sraffa and Keynes himself. The third section summarizes the main arguments of Chapter 17 of *The General Theory* together with related post-*General Theory* material. The fourth section addresses some central problems concerning the use made by Keynes of the concept of own rates of interest. In the last section we draw some conclusions concerning the future role of own-rates of interest in further developments of Keynesian economics.

* * *

In the recent literature, particularly in Post-Keynesian writings, different definitions of own-rates of interest and own-rates of money interest are presented.[4] Therefore, it is useful to start by introducing the technical terms that are used in this chapter.

In Chapter 17 of *The General Theory*, transactions over time are the object of Keynes's analysis. In such an inter-temporal economy, the system of relative prices may be expressed in two different ways: either as *discounted* or as *undiscounted* prices.

In an economy with complete future markets, the standard of value is only used in the first period, because all contracts are made and paid for in this base period, but delivery of goods is carried out in future periods. Following Kuenne (1977: 619), we call this Arrow–Debreu world 'a constant-numéraire economy'. In Keynes's economics there are no complete future markets. Therefore, not all payments can be made in the base period but have to be made at the respective dates of delivery. From this it follows that changes in the value of the numéraire between periods become essential. Again following Kuenne (1977: 627), we call this economy 'a current-numéraire economy'.

In order to clarify this point, consider a simple economy over three periods with three commodities a, b and m, where commodity m is used as the standard of value. We then have the following money prices:

$$\Pi_{a1}, \Pi_{b1}, \Pi_{m1}$$
$$\Pi a_2, \Pi b_2, \Pi m_2$$
$$\Pi_{a3}, \Pi_{b3}, \Pi_{m3}.$$

In a constant-numéraire economy the following relative prices have to be determined:

$$\Pi_{a1}/\Pi_{m1}, \Pi_{b1}/\Pi_{m1}, \Pi_{m1}/\Pi_{m1}(= 1)$$
$$\Pi_{a2}/\Pi_{m1}, \Pi_{b2}/\Pi_{m1}, \Pi_{m2}/\Pi_{m1}$$
$$\Pi_{a3}/\Pi_{m1}, \Pi_{b3}/\Pi_{m1}, \Pi_{m3}/\Pi_{m1}$$

Following Malinvaud (1972: 232), these relative prices are called *discounted* prices.

In a current-numéraire economy the following relative prices have to be determined:

$$\Pi_{a1}/\Pi_{m1}, \Pi_{b1}/\Pi_{m1}, \Pi_{m1}/\Pi_{m1} (= 1)$$
$$\Pi_{a2}/\Pi_{m2}, \Pi_{b2}/\Pi_{m2}, \Pi_{m2}/\Pi_{m2} (= 1)$$
$$\Pi_{a3}/\Pi_{m3}, \Pi_{b3}/\Pi_{m3}, \Pi_{m3}/\Pi_{m3} (= 1)$$

Again following Malinvaud (1972: 233), these relative prices are called *undiscounted* prices.

We define the *discounted relative* price of commodity a in period t as

$$p'_{at} = \Pi_{at}/\Pi_{m1}, \text{ for all } t$$

and the *undiscounted* relative price of commodity a in period t as

$$p_{at} = \Pi_{at}/\Pi_{mt}, \text{ for all } t.$$

From this it follows that:

$$p'_{a2}/p'_{a1} = (\Pi_{a2}/\Pi_{m1})/(\Pi_{a1}/\Pi_{m1}) = \Pi_{a2}/\Pi_{a1}$$

and

$$p_{a2}/p_{a1} = (\Pi_{a2}/\Pi_{m2})/(\Pi_{a1}/\Pi_{m1}) = (\Pi_{a2}/\Pi_{a1})*(\Pi_{m1}/\Pi_{m2})$$

In the constant-numéraire economy, the value of the standard cancels out, whereas in the current-numéraire economy the change in the value of the standard becomes essential for the definition of the change of relative prices over time. Because, as will be seen, Keynes argues within a current-numéraire economy, the prices relevant to his analysis are undiscounted relative prices.

In this context, spot and forward prices may be defined (see Richter 1990: 170). The spot price of commodity a is the price, in terms of money, payable today for delivery today. The forward price of commodity a is the price, in terms of money, payable tomorrow for delivery tomorrow.[5] Note that both are defined in terms of undiscounted prices.[6]

To clarify the notion of own-rate of interest three fundamental notions have to be defined:[7]

- the own-rate of interest of a commodity;[8]
- the own-rate of interest of a commodity *in terms of the standard of value* (numéraire), i.e. the money commodity;[9]
- the rate of appreciation or depreciation of a price of a commodity *in terms of the standard of value*.

The own-rate of interest of a commodity is defined as the ratio of a definite quantity of a commodity, say wheat, available at a future date ($t + 1$), exchanged against a definite quantity of the same commodity at date (t) (Fisher 1896: 8ff.).

$$(1 + \rho_{w,t}) = \frac{x_{w,t+1}}{x_{w,t}} \tag{17.1}$$

The own-rate of interest of a commodity may also be expressed in terms of discounted prices. The ratio of discounted prices (of a given commodity) at two different dates is the inverse of the ratio just defined. An exchange of equivalents requires:

$$\frac{x_{w,t+1}}{x_{w,t}} = \frac{p'_{w,t}}{p'_{w,t+1}} \tag{17.2}$$

with $p'_{w,t}$ the discounted price of wheat in t.

If we use undiscounted prices instead of discounted prices, the own-rate of interest of wheat *in terms of money* may be defined as:

$$(1 + i_{w,t}) = \frac{x_{w,t+1} \cdot p_{w,t+1}}{x_{w,t} \cdot P_{w,t}} = (1 + \rho_{w,t})(1 + \delta_{w,t}) \tag{17.3}$$

with

$$(1 + \delta_{w,t}) = \frac{p_{w,t+1}}{p_{w,t}}, \tag{17.4}$$

the gross rate of change in the relative price of wheat in terms of money between (t) and $(t + 1)$.[10]

Using equation (17.3) we may express the own-rate of interest of wheat *in terms of itself* – its own-rate of own-interest – as

$$(1 + \rho_{w,t}) = \frac{(1 + i_{w,t})}{(1 + \delta_{w,t})} \tag{17.5}$$

In addition, we have to define the own-rate of interest of the commodity chosen as the standard of value, i.e. money:

$$(1 + \rho_{m,t}) = \frac{x_{m,t+1}}{x_{m,t}} \tag{17.6}$$

By way of analogy, the own-rate of interest of money in terms of money may be expressed as

$$(1 + i_{m,t}) = \frac{x_{m,t+1} \cdot p_{m,t+1}}{x_{m,t} \cdot p_{m,t}} = (1 + \rho_{m,t})(1 + \delta_{m,t}) \tag{17.7}$$

with

$$(1 + \delta_{m,t}) = \frac{p_{m,t+1}}{p_{m,t}} \tag{17.8}$$

the gross rate of change in the relative price of money between (t) and $(t + 1)$, necessarily equal to 1 in a current-numéraire economy.

From this follows immediately:

$$(1 + \rho_{m,t}) = (1 + i_{m,t}) \equiv (1 + i_t), \tag{17.9}$$

which means that, for the commodity serving as the standard of value, its own-rate of interest is equal to the own-rate of interest in terms of the standard of value, i.e. the own-rate of interest on money is necessarily equal to the money rate of interest (i_t)

In the example given above, the constant-numéraire economy has six different own-rates of interest and in addition the current-numéraire economy has four rates of appreciation together with four own-rates in terms of money.

286

Up to now, we have only stated that the own-rate of interest of a commodity is defined as the ratio of quantities of this commodity available at different dates. Now we have to see how these quantities are determined. Sraffa describes the determination of the commodity rate of interest of cotton in the following manner:

> Loans are currently made in the present world in terms of every commodity for which there is a forward market. When a cotton spinner borrows a sum of money for three months and uses the proceeds to purchase spot, a quantity of raw cotton which he simultaneously sells three months forward, he is actually 'borrowing cotton' for that period. The rate of interest he pays, per hundred bales of cotton, is the number of bales that can be purchased with the following sum of money: the interest on the money required to buy spot 100 bales, plus the excess (or minus the deficiency) of the spot over the forward prices of the 100 bales.
>
> (Sraffa 1932a: 50)

Keynes gives the following numerical example in terms of money and wheat:

> Let us suppose that the spot price of wheat is £100 per 100 quarters, that the price of the 'future' contract for wheat for delivery a year hence is £107 per 100 quarters, and that the money-rate of interest is 5 per cent; what is the wheat-rate of interest? £100 spot will buy £105 for forward delivery, and £105 for forward delivery will buy (105/107)100 (= 98) quarters for forward delivery. Alternatively £100 spot will buy 100 quarters of wheat for spot delivery. Thus 100 quarters of wheat for spot delivery will buy 98 quarters for forward delivery. It follows that the wheat-rate of interest is *minus* 2 per cent. per annum.
>
> (*G.T.*: 223)

Thus Keynes takes as given (a) the spot price of wheat, (b) the forward price of wheat, and (c) the money rate of interest. From these he derives the own-rate of wheat (the wheat-rate of interest) by calculating the respective quantities of wheat. The quantity of wheat at date (t) is determined as

$$x_{w,t} = \frac{£100}{£1} = \frac{M_t}{p_{w,t}}, \tag{17.10}$$

while the quantity of wheat at date ($t + 1$) is determined as

$$x_{w,t+1} = \frac{£105}{£1.07} = \frac{M_{t+1}}{p_{w,t+1}} = \frac{M_t(1 + i)}{p_{w,t+1}}. \tag{17.11}$$

We then get the own-rate of interest of wheat as:[11]

$$(1 + \rho_{w;t}) = \frac{x_{w;t+1}}{x_{w;t}} = \frac{M_t(1 + i)}{p_{w;t+1}} \frac{p_{w;t}}{M_t} = \frac{(1 + i)}{(1 + \delta_{w;t})}. \tag{17.12}$$

The wheat-rate of interest is the money rate of interest *expressed in quantities of wheat* (Lerner 1952: 174, 180).[12] Therefore the wheat-rate of interest *in terms of money* is *necessarily* equal to the money rate of interest:

$$(1 + i) = (1 + \rho_{w;t})(1 + \delta_{w;t}) \tag{17.13}$$

Furthermore, *if* the price of the commodity, in terms of which the rate of interest on money is expressed, *does not change* over time ($\delta_{w;t} = 0$), its own-rate of interest will be equal to the money rate of interest.

* * *

Hayek, who, together with Lindahl, introduced inter-temporal equilibrium analysis,[13] in his *Prices and Production* (Hayek 1931) tried to combine this new apparatus with the Wicksellian explanation of the business cycle. This theory focuses on the spread between the market rate of interest on money loans and the natural rate of interest, determined by the equilibrium of demand for capital (investment) and supply of capital (saving).[14] Following Wicksell, Hayek held the view that this divergence of rates could only occur in a monetary economy.

A well-defined and unique real (own) rate of interest exists only in a one-commodity world. But, as Sraffa argued in his review of *Prices and Production*,[15] in a world of heterogeneous (capital) goods there 'may exist as many "natural" rates as there are commodities'.[16] Therefore, it is not obvious which of these own-rates should be regarded as *the* natural rate. It therefore makes no sense to speak of eliminating the divergence between the rate of interest on money loans and *the* natural rate of interest. A unique own-rate of interest, which equals the loan rate, only exists in a long-period equilibrium (i.e. when market prices equal costs of production) (Sraffa 1932a: 50). The core of Sraffa's argument can be summarized as follows:

1 There are as many commodity rates of interest as there are commodities.
2 If spot and forward prices coincide, all own-rates of interest are equal to one another and to the money rate of interest (ibid.). In this long-period equilibrium, the market expects constant prices over time.
3 But spot and forward prices need not coincide in any moment of time, which implies that the own-rates of interest will differ from one another and from the money rate of interest. Diverging own-rates of interest do not preclude the clearing of spot markets, but since the forward price diverges from the spot price, the market will expect changes in output and, therefore, changes in the relation of future supply and demand.

* * *

In Chapter 17 of *The General Theory*, Keynes made use of this notion of commodity or own rates of interest[17] in his attempt to refute the marginalist theory of the long-period position towards which the economic system is gravitating. While marginalist economists saw the economic system as always tending to a full employment equilibrium (given the flexibility of prices and money-wages), in 1934 Keynes – in the course of working out the implications of his *Treatise on Money* – had come to reject the idea that 'the existing economic system is, in the long run, a self-adjusting system, though with creaks and groans and jerks, and interrupted by time lags, outside interference and mistakes' (*C.W.* XIII: 486–7).

In contrast to this marginalist doctrine he had arrived at the conclusion that the long-period position or centre of gravitation might, and in general would, entail under-employment.[18] The cause of such long-period positions with less than full employment was the essential influence that money, or more precisely, the impact the money rate of interest had on the working of the economic system. He had 'come to believe that interest – or, rather, too high a rate of interest – is the "villain of the piece"' (*C.W.* XXIX: 16).

Adhering to the analytical framework used by Sraffa in his critique of Hayek, in Chapter 17 Keynes analysed *why* the money rate of interest is decisive in determining the long-period equilibrium position of the economy:

> It seems . . . that the *rate of interest on money* plays a peculiar part in setting a limit to the level of employment . . . That this should be so, is, at first sight, most perplexing. It is natural to enquire wherein the peculiarity of money lies as distinct from other assets, whether it is only money which has a rate of interest and what would happen in a non-monetary economy. Until we have answered the questions, the full significance of our theory will not be clear.
>
> (*G.T.*: 222)

Using the notion of own-rates, Keynes gave a negative answer to the second question (*G.T.*: 222–3). Agreeing with Sraffa's conclusion, but via a different route, he abandoned the Wicksellian concept of a unique natural rate. Instead, he focused on the money rate of interest. But since 'the money-rate of interest has no uniqueness compared with other rates of interest' (*G.T.*: 225), Keynes was now obliged to clarify the peculiarity of the money rate of interest and to specify the reasons giving rise to this peculiarity.

If there is one own-rate of interest that is relatively 'sticky', i.e. that 'is fixed (or declines more slowly as output increases than does any other commodity's rate of interest)' (*G.T.*: 228), this rate of interest sets a limit to the profitable production of commodities. The peculiarity of the money rate of interest seems to lie in its relative stickiness. Because of this stickiness, it is the money rate of interest that becomes 'essential' for the determination of the equilibrium position of output and employment. Therefore, Keynes tried to isolate conditions that lead to this stickiness. In a fiat money economy, he discovers these conditions in the 'essential properties of money':[19]

1 money has 'a zero, or at any rate a very small, elasticity of production' (*G.T.*: 230);[20]
2 money has 'an elasticity of substitution equal, or nearly equal, to zero' (*G.T.*: 231);[21]
3 money has 'low (or negligible) carrying-costs' (ibid.), its liquidity premium therefore exceeds its carrying cost, resulting in a positive money rate of interest which shows (almost) neglible reactions to changes in the money-wage rate via a real balance effect (*G.T.*: 231–4).[22]

Before we enter upon a description of the adjustment process of the own-rates of interest to the money rate of interest under these conditions, some further definitions must be introduced. Keynes distinguishes three components of the own-rate of interest of assets:

- a (physical) yield q;
- a carrying cost c;
- a liquidity premium l.

If we consider the own rate of interest in terms of money, an additional term has to be taken into account, namely the (expected) appreciation (or depreciation) in terms of the standard of value δ. Thus the own-rate of interest *in terms of money* of any commodity i, according to Keynes, can be written as:

$$i_{i,t} = \rho_{i,t} + \delta_{i,t} \equiv q_i - c_i + l_i + \delta_{i,t}.^{23} \qquad (17.14)$$

Keynes introduces three types of assets, according to the different components of the own-rate of interest these assets typically possess (*G.T.*: 226–9). In the case of durable capital goods (e.g. houses), the own-rate of interest is dominated by their (physical) yield q_1. The own-rate of interest of idle capital and liquid goods (e.g. wheat) is dominated by the carrying cost c_2, whereas the own-rate of interest of money is dominated by its liquidity premium l_3.[24] Therefore, the different own-rates of interest *in terms of money* are $(q_1 + \delta_1)$ in the case of houses, $(-c_2 + \delta_2)$ in the case of wheat and l_3 in the case of money.[25]

Keynes considers an arbitrage equilibrium, which he himself characterizes as follows:

> in equilibrium the demand-prices of houses and wheat in terms of money will be such that there is nothing to choose in the way of

advantage between the alternatives; – i.e. $a_1 + q_1$, $a_2 - c_2$ and l_3 will be equal.

$$(G.T.: 227\text{–}8)$$

As a result of arbitrage, the own-rates of interest in terms of money are equalized. According to Keynes, this determines demand prices for all assets. Within the Marshallian tradition it is well known that a difference between demand and supply price is the cause of quantity reactions; for example, if the demand price is higher than the supply price, the output of the commodity under consideration will be increased. The reason for this expansion of output lies in the surplus profits which emerge from the market clearing price (= demand price) being higher than costs of production (= normal supply price).

Keynes introduces the concepts of spot (or cash price) and forward price (G.T.: 223f.) and of 'present money-price' and 'expected future price' (G.T.: 228). Spot and present money-price can be treated as synonymous, while forward prices only exist in forward markets. If forward markets do not exist, agents have to form expectations concerning the future prices of commodities ('expected future price').

Apparently, Keynes interprets the spot or present price as a demand price and the foward or expected future price as a 'normal supply-price' (G.T.: 228; see also Kaldor 1960: 69; Huth 1989: 184). Keynes then discusses the divergence of own rates of interest as an exercise in Marshallian stability analysis.

Arbitrage equilibrium establishes a vector of spot and demand prices causing expansion of output of those commodities which have a forward/expected future price below their demand price. For these commodities the δs will be negative. Therefore, their own-rates of interest in terms of themselves will be higher than the own-rate of interest of money (see above, equation (17.3)). Keynes takes the marginal efficiency of capital of such a commodity as synonymous with its own-rate of interest, as is especially clear in his contribution to the Fisher *Festschrift* (Keynes 1937d). He then describes the adjustment in terms of a comparison of the marginal efficiency of capital and the rate of interest. A situation characterized by the spot price of a commodity exceeding its forward price corresponds with the marginal efficiency of this commodity being higher than the rate of interest (G.T.: 228).

As he already had shown in earlier parts of *The General Theory* (Chapter 11), investment, that is the production of capital assets, will be pushed to the point where the marginal efficiency of capital becomes equal to the rate of interest, i.e. demand prices are equal to supply prices (Keynes 1937d: 102). Pushing investment beyond this point will not be profitable unless the money rate of interest falls.

In terms of own-rates of interest, the argument is that all own rates of interest have fallen into line with the own-rate of money. Now, the question arises: why do they adjust to the money rate of interest and not to any other own-rate of interest? The reason for this, according to Keynes, is to be found in the 'essential properties of money'. Because money cannot be produced privately (its first essential property), that is because of its 'controlled scarcity', its stock and therefore its own-rate of interest cannot be influenced by endogenous economic forces. Furthermore, money will not be substituted for (second essential property). Finally, the own-rate of interest determined by the exogenous stock of money will stay constant because of its low (or negligible) carrying-costs (third essential property). Thus, even if the real value of money balances can be influenced by the economic system, there may be something like a lower bound to the own-rate of interest on money, that is, the 'liquidity trap'.[26]

In fact, Keynes's argument is very simple: every commodity has an own-rate of interest that is a decreasing function of its quantity; the quantity of money is exogenously given, therefore its own-rate of interest is exogenously given – and constant, because money has no carrying-costs. The money rate of interest thus determined may be too high for the achievement of full employment.

From this there arises another fundamental question: why should the liquidity premium – considered as a reservation rate of interest – be strictly positive? 'Why should anyone outside a lunatic asylum wish to use money as a store of wealth?'(C.W. XIV: 115–16). Keynes gives two answers. The first points to the uncertainty of future values of the rate of interest:

> There is . . . a necessary condition failing which the existence of a liquidity-preference for money as a means of holding wealth could not exist. This necessary condition is the existence of *uncertainty* as to the future of the rate of interest . . .
>
> (G.T.: 168)

The second answer points towards the uncertainty of the future in general:

> partly on reasonable and partly on instinctive grounds, our desire to hold money as a store of wealth is a barometer of the degree of distrust of our own calculations and conventions concerning the future . . . The possession of actual money lulls our disquietude; and the premium which we require to make us part with money is the measure of the degree of our disquietude.
>
> (C.W. XIV: 116)

Holding money means sacrificing the possibility of receiving interest by lending money: 'The rate of interest is, if you like, the *price* of hoards in the sense that it measures the pecuniary sacrifice which the holder of a hoard thinks it worth while to suffer in preferring it to other claims and assets having an equal present value' (C.W. XIV: 214). But nobody would be prepared to pay this price, 'unless the possession of cash served some purpose, i.e. had some efficiency' (*C.W.* XIV: 101).

In the face of an uncertain future money becomes productive, it 'may offer a potential convenience or service' (*G.T.*: 226).[27] His answer exposes Keynes as an adherent of a productivity theory of interest.[28, 29] 'I regard the rate of interest as being the marginal efficiency (or productivity) of money measured in terms of itself' (*C.W.* XIV: 92).

*   *   *

So far, we have paraphrased Keynes' own line of reasoning. We now discuss his analysis of the link between money and unemployment. We distinguish three questions: a problem concerning Keynes's use of own-rates of interest; the relation between own-rates of interest and the marginal efficiency of capital; and finally, we discuss the problem of a strictly positive liquidity premium, which constitutes the lower bound for the own-rate of interest on money.

There exists a fundamental problem with Keynes's use of the concept of own-rates. To elucidate this problem, it is useful to recall the logical status of own-rates of interest in general equilibrium theory. In this theory own-rates of interest only play a passive and actually irrelevant role. For own-rates of interest follow directly from the system of inter-temporal prices, which means that as soon as these prices are determined, the own-rates of interest are implicitly determined as well. So we can easily calculate own-rates, but this exercise yields no additional information whatsoever.

Keynes, however, used the concept of own-rates of interest as if he had a theory to determine the own-rates of interest and so could then deduce prices (or price movements) from this information. But as Keynes did not provide such a theory, he is not able to infer demand prices from the own-rates of interest.[30] This means that the concept of own-rates is not a suitable analytical framework with which to develop his message about money as the cause of unemployment. It therefore has to be discarded.

This raises the question: did Keynes really understand Sraffa's critique of the Wicksell–Hayek approach? Sraffa's argument was meant to be destructive of the notion of a unique natural rate of interest (Harcourt 1983: 82, 1990: 37; Huth 1989: 174). Sraffa did not provide – did not want to and did not need to – an alternative theory of the rate of interest. That is, he did not address the two fundamental questions: (a) why are interest rates positive? and (b) what determines the level of the rate of interest?

Keynes had also called into question the notion of a unique natural rate of interest, because in 'arguing out the *Treatise on Money*' he had pointed to the possibility of multiple under-employment equilibria, each corresponding to a different 'natural rate of interest' (see *C.W.* XIII: 479; *C.W.* XIV: 431; *C.W.* XXIX: 54–7, 91–2; *G.T.*: 191, 242–3). Therefore, he must have been very receptive to Sraffa's criticism, which we can see mirrored in the first part of Chapter 17 of *The General Theory* (*G.T.*: 222–5). But there are two crucial differences in the arguments of Sraffa and Keynes:

1 Sraffa's argument, as already mentioned, had a critical thrust, whereas Keynes's had a constructive intention, i.e. he aimed at the formulation of an alternative to the orthodox theory of output and employment.
2 Sraffa simply uncovered a contradiction between the implications of Hayek's theory and the monetary rule that Hayek wanted to establish. This rule aimed at keeping the rate of interest on money loans in line with the equilibrium (natural) rate of interest, i.e. that value of the rate of interest which keeps money neutral.[31] But in disequilibrium there is no unique natural rate of interest. So to which of these natural rates should the money rate be adjusted by the central bank? A pragmatic view could hold that an average 'natural' rate should be constructed. But such an average would be as arbitrary as any price level, and, moreover, had been discarded by Hayek as a possible monetary target just because of its arbitrariness (Sraffa 1932b: 251).[32]

In this context, Sraffa therefore did not have to bother about an alternative theory of the rate of interest. Keynes, however, wanted to supply such an alternative. In providing an alternative theory, Keynes moulded Sraffa's critical argument into a positive one.[33] If multiple equilibria are possible, we might, as a thought experiment, try to reverse the causal relation between the money rate and the different 'natural' rates (own-rates of interest).[34] But if there is nothing special about the different own-rates, what is so special about the money rate of interest? It was this question that prompted Keynes's search for the 'essential properties of money'.

We turn now to the relation between own-rates of interest and the marginal efficiency of capital. Having introduced the concepts of own-rates of interest and discussed the conditions of an arbitrage equilibrium, Keynes linked this analysis to the concept of marginal efficiency of capital, which he had introduced earlier in *The General Theory*. In arbitrage equilibrium all own-rates of interest in terms of money are equal to the money rate of interest. In this situation the δs will have taken definite values which will in general be different from zero. Concerning these δs, Keynes argues as follows:

> Now those assets of which the normal supply-price is less than the demand-price will be newly produced; and these will be those assets of which the marginal efficiency of capital would be greater (on the basis of their normal supply price) than the rate of interest (both being measured in the same standard of value whatever it is).
>
> (*G.T.*: 228)

Although Keynes did not analyse the relation between the own-rates and the marginal efficiency of capital, he states a systematic behaviour of marginal efficiencies of capital and own-rates. But from the extract above, we may easily infer his arguments. There, Keynes describes a situation in which the marginal efficiency of capital lies above the money rate of interest. This in turn implies that the δs are negative; that is, the own-rates of own-interest are above the money rate of interest as well. This can easily be shown. Arbitrage equilibrium implies:

$$(1 + \rho_{i,t}) \, (1 + \delta_{i,t}) = (1 + i_t), \tag{17.15}$$

with

$$(1 + \delta_{i,t}) = \frac{p_{i,t+1}}{p_{i,t}} = \frac{p_i^s}{p_i^d}. \tag{17.16}$$

Now, in a simple one-period case (see Keynes's numerical example) $p_i^s = Q_{i,t+1}/(1 + m_{i,t})$, where $Q_{i,t+1}$ are the quasi-rents of a capital good that is completely used up in one period accruing during the period and $m_{i,t}$ is the internal rate of return (marginal efficiency of capital) which makes the receipts equal to the normal supply-price (p_i^s). Since the demand price is $Q_{i,t+1}/(1 + i)$, where i is the money rate of interest, the arbitrage condition may be rewritten as:

$$(1 + \rho_{i,t}) \quad \frac{Q_{i,t+1}/(1 + m_{i,t})}{Q_{i,t+1}/(1 + i)} = (1 + i). \tag{17.17}$$

This reduces to

$$(1 + \rho_{i,t}) = (1 + m_{i,t}).$$

The marginal efficiency of any commodity is equal to its own-rate of interest in terms of itself (see Champernowne 1964: 195; Huth 1989: 183–5). Thus Keynes's verbal account of the relation between own-rates of interest, marginal efficiencies of capital and the money rate of interest is confirmed.

However, at the same time this result shows that the concept of own-rates of interest is redundant for Keynes's purpose. His central argument about the money rate of interest being a barrier to full employment can be deployed in terms of the marginal efficiency of capital, as Keynes himself did in other parts of *The General Theory*.[35] In doing so, no important information is lost. This should come as no surprise, since it makes no essential difference whether we describe a given economic situation in terms of relative prices or in terms of rates of return.

But this *in itself* does not imply that Keynes's central argument about money's role in the causation of unemployment has to be discarded as well.[36] We shall now clarify the question whether Keynes has been success-ful in demonstrating that money, the money-rate of interest, can set a limit to production below full employment.

Arguing within the framework of own-rates of interest did not, as Chapter 17 clearly shows, save Keynes from the necessity of relying on the liquidity trap. Keynes does recognize that even though money cannot be privately produced, 'nevertheless an assumption that its effective supply is rigidly fixed would be inaccurate' (G.T.: 232). Reductions of the money-wage will result in an increase in the effective supply of money, and it is 'not possible to dispute on purely theoretical grounds that this reaction might be capable of allowing an adequate decline in the money rate of interest' (ibid.).

Thus, even if the nominal quantity of money is exogenously given, its real quantity, the volume of real balances or – in Keynes's own words – the effective supply of money, is endogenous because it depends on the level of money-wages.[37] If money-wages fall in the presence of unemployment, then the money rate of interest will fall as well, resulting in a higher level of production and employment. This *indirect* effect of falling money-wages will tend to establish full employment.

Keynes draws the evident conclusion (although he rather hides it in the appendix to Chapter 14 of *The General Theory*): that if

> money-wages are assumed to fall without limit in the face of involuntary unemployment through a futile competition for employment between the unemployed labourers, there will, it is true, be only two possible long-period positions – full employment and the level of employment corresponding to the rate of interest at which liquidity-preference becomes absolute (in the event of this being less than full employment). Assuming flexible money-wages, the quantity as such is, indeed, nugatory in the long period . . .
>
> (G.T.: 191)[38]

The 'futile competition for employment between the unemployed labourers' turns out to be not so futile after all. Reductions in money-wages can, even if in an indirect manner, establish full employment: unemployment is caused either by rigid money-wages *or* the liquidity trap (*or* feedback effects of falling money-wages on the schedule of marginal efficiency of capital and the schedule of liquidity-preference).[39,40]

With this result Keynes's 'simple argument' breaks down: having started with the idea that the money rate of interest is a decreasing function of the *quantity of money*, after analysing the effects of reductions in money-wages Keynes has to admit that it is a decreasing function of the *effective supply of money*, and, resting his case on the liquidity trap – 'the most fundamental consideration in this context' (G.T.: 233) – he in fact argues that the money rate of interest is no longer a function of the *effective supply of money* but is exogenously given (see Modigliani 1944: 74–5; Ono 1994: 165).[41]

* * *

We have shown that Keynes's attempt to refute, on the basis of his analysis of own-rates of interest, the marginalist idea of the self-adjusting property of the economic system, that its centre of gravitation entails full employment, was not successful.

Own-rates of interest are implied by the system of relative prices and therefore cannot be taken to be exogenous. Own-rates of interest are redundant, because every relevant statement about the influence of the money rate of interest on the level of production and employment can be made in terms of the marginal efficiency of capital. Finally, money, or the money rate of interest – whether conceived as the own-rate of interest on money or not – can only act as a barrier to full employment in so far as the liquidity trap comes into play.[42]

But this is not the end of the story and a final remark is in order. It is Keynes's approach to the problem of unemployment *as such* that is redundant. Its central feature was the conviction that a money-rate of interest compatible with full employment does exist. Therefore,

> in the absence of money and in the absence – we must of course, also suppose – of any other commodity with the assumed characteristics of money, the rates of interest would only reach equilibrium when there is full employment.

> (*G.T.*: 235)

Having granted this possibility, Keynes could only aim to show that an economic system left to its own devices would be unable to attain the level of the money-rate of interest that would result in full employment (see Eatwell 1983b: 108).

As the results of the capital theory controversy have shown, this approach is misguided: the interest-elastic investment function, the real wage-elastic labour demand function and its mirror-image, the price-elastic supply function, that form the basis of Keynes's analysis of how monetary factors prevent the attainment of the full employment level of the money rate of interest, in general, do not exist (see Garegnani 1979; Schefold 1995b: 73). Keynes's analysis in terms of own-rates of interest becomes indefensible (Harcourt 1983: 83).[43] Furthermore, as soon as the marginalist theory is shown to be invalid, it no longer makes sense to search for 'essential properties of interest and money' blocking the road to the full employment equilibrium determined by this theory. Therefore, Keynes's analysis in Chapter 17 becomes redundant.

There remains one line of reasoning aiming to show that Keynes's schedule of marginal efficiency of capital is not based on marginalist premises[44] and that, therefore, the critique of marginalist theory of capital is irrelevant for Keynes's theory. According to this view, investment projects (capital goods) may be ranked in decreasing order of their prospective profitability, and investment may then be undertaken up to the point at which the marginal efficiency of the last project is equal to (or just higher than) the money rate of interest. The investment demand schedule arrived at by ranking investment projects in this manner does not depend on the inverse monotonic relation between capital intensity and the rate of profit of the marginalist theory of capital.[45]

This interpretation of the schedule of marginal efficiency of capital hinges on the assumption that the prospective yield of investment projects (capital goods) are *independent* of the money rate of interest. But this assumption is untenable.[46] Garegnani has shown that, in general, the required independence cannot be proven.[47] Furthermore, it has been shown that in systems with fixed capital goods the prices of newly invested capital goods measured in terms of the wage unit will rise with the rate of interest (or profits) because in some periods their future yield may increase more than the rate of interest (see Schefold 1980: 161, 1987: 1033, 1995a: 18; Caspari 1989: 193–5). Thus the prospective yield is *not* independent of the rate of interest and the ranking of investment projects (capital goods), in general, will change with changes in the money rate of interest, and the resulting schedule of marginal efficiency of capital cannot be interpreted as an investment *demand* curve (Caspari 1989: 195).[48]

Taking all these arguments into account, the conclusion cannot be resisted that in Chapter 17 Keynes gave an invalid answer to the wrong question and that his analysis carried out within the framework of own-rates of interest is not only a detour but a cul de sac.[49]

NOTES

* We are grateful for useful comments and criticisms on an earlier draft from G.C. Harcourt, T. Huth, H. Klausinger and H.D. Kurz. The usual disclaimer applies.
1 For a similar statement, see Jöhr (1937: 657).
2 After the publication of *The General Theory*, Chapter 17 was hailed enthusiastically by Townshend (1937), but soon a more sceptical assessment took over: see Lerner (1952), Hansen (1953) and Kaldor (1960). After that, the analytical framework of Chapter 17 was seldom discussed in the 1960s and 1970s; see, for instance, Conard (1959); Robinson (1961b); Lerner (1962); Champernowne (1964); Turvey (1965); Ambrosi (1976); Davidson (1972); Minsky (1975). It is only since the 1980s that Chapter 17 has received more attention; see, for instance, Bliss (1987); Chick (1983); Cottrell and Lawlor (1991); Cowen and Kroszner (1994); de Gijsel and Haslinger (1988); Deleplace (1987); Eatwell (1987); Garretsen (1992); Harcourt (1981, 1983); Harcourt and O'Shaughnessy (1985); Heering (1991, 1993); Huth (1989); Jäggi (1986); Klausinger (1991, 1993); Kregel (1980, 1982, 1983a, 1984, 1985a, 1988); Lawlor (1994b); Lawlor and Horn (1992); MacLachlan (1993a,b); Majewski (1988); Mongiovi (1990); Nell (1983); Panico (1985, 1988a); Rogers (1989, 1994); Runde (1994a); Rymes (1980). See also Keynes's discussions of the concept of own-rates with

Champernowne (*C.W.* XIV: 60–6); Hicks (ibid: 72–83), Reddaway (ibid.: 66–70) and Robertson (*C.W.* XIII: 508–19).

3 On the 'Monetary Theory of Production', see Barens (1987, 1990).

4 See, for instance, Kregel (1983a: 60); Rogers (1989: 208); Mongiovi (1990: 149); Majewski (1988: 103).

5 Although Sraffa (1932a) and Keynes (1936) do not give definitions of spot and forward prices, the context of their arguments makes it clear that both use these terms according to the definitions in the text. In the *Treatise on Money*, Keynes defines the forward price as follows: 'The "forward" price is for delivery *and payment* at the future date' (*C.W.* VI: 127, n.2; Keynes's italics).

6 In inter-temporal general equilibrium theory all contracts are made in the first period of the planning horizon. Although delivery is contracted for in the future, payment is made in the first period. So prices in inter-temporal general equilibrium theory are discounted prices.

7 Actually, these definitions should have been well known within our discipline since Fisher (1896); that is, for 100 years! The clarity and lucidity of Fisher's exposition of the relation between these three concept has never been surpassed. See also Tobin (1987: 372).

8 This term was introduced by Keynes (*G.T.*: 223). Fisher (1896) – who, contrary to Keynes's assertion in *The General Theory* (*G.T.*: 223, n.1), was the first to introduce this concept (but see Dorfman *et al.* (1958: 317, n.2), who suggest an even earlier origin) – gave no specific name to it. In Fisher (1930: 42) the term *rates of interest in terms of goods* is used. Sraffa (1932a: 59) called it the *commodity rate of interest*; and Kaldor (1960: 59) called it the *own-rate of own-interest*.

9 Kaldor (ibid.: 59) called this rate the *own-rate of money-interest*.

10 Fisher (1896: 10, n.5) calls this the 'ratio of appreciation'.

11 See Fisher (1896: 10); Eatwell (1987: 786); and Kurz (1995a: 100).

12 According to Sraffa's determination of the cotton-rate of interest, we would have for the interest payment on the money loan in terms of wheat:

$$\frac{i \cdot x_{w,t} \, p_{w,t}}{p_{w,t+1}};$$

for the 'excess (or minus the deficiency) of the spot over the forward prices' in terms of wheat:

$$\frac{x_{w,t}(p_{w,t} - p_{w,t+1})}{p_{w,t+1}};$$

and for the cotton-rate of interest:

$$\rho = \frac{(1 + i) \cdot x_{w,t} \, p_{w,t} + x_{w,t} \, p_{w,t+1}}{p_{w,t+1}} \cdot \frac{1}{x_{w,t}}$$

$$= (1 + i)\frac{p_{w,t}}{p_{w,t+1}} - 1 = \frac{(1 + i)}{(1 + \delta_{w,t})} - 1.$$

13 Hayek (1928); and Lindahl (1929), revised version published as Part III of Lindahl (1939: 271–350).

14 Wicksell's natural rate of interest measures the percentage premium on present goods over future goods of the same kind, cf. Wicksell (1936: 103).

15 On the Hayek–Sraffa debate (Hayek 1932 and Sraffa 1932a,b), see, for example, Desai (1982); Klausinger (1991); Lachmann (1986b); Lawlor and Horn (1992); Lévy (1991); McCloughry (1982); Milgate (1979); Mongiovi (1990); Tutin (1988); and especially Kurz (1995a,b).

16 Sraffa (1932a: 50). This had already been pointed out by Fisher (1907: 84): 'There are . . . just as many rates of interest as there are forms of goods diverging in value.' Cf. also Fisher (1930: 42). On the question whether Sraffa was acquainted with the work of Fisher, see Schefold (1991: 21, n.2). Although, in *The General Theory*, Keynes refers to Sraffa, it may be the case that the notion of commodity rates of interest was suggested to Sraffa by Keynes's *Tract on Monetary Reform*, which Sraffa had translated into Italian; see Keynes (1925); see also note 17 below.

17 As Kregel (1982, 1984) has pointed out, the germs of the concept of own-rates may be found in the interest parity theorem that Keynes expounded in the Reconstruction Supplement of the *Manchester Guardian Commercial* of 20 April 1922; cf. Keynes (1922); this material was included in Keynes (1923: 94–115); see also Huth (1989: 180–2); and Rogers (1989: 204–5).

18 For an early interpretation of *The General Theory* from the perspective of long-period positions see Robinson (1936); recently the validity of a long-period interpretation of *The General Theory* has been the subject of an extensive debate; see, for example, Amadeo (1989, 1992); Asimakopulos (1983a, 1985, 1988, 1989); Bharadwaj (1983); Bhattacharjea (1987); Cardim de Carvalho (1990); Eatwell (1983a,b); Eatwell and Milgate (1983b); Garegnani (1988); Hansson (1985); Harcourt and O'Shaughnessy (1985); Kregel (1983b); Kurz (1983); Lim (1990); O'Shaughnessy (1983, 1984); and Rogers (1989, 1994). For a discussion of the role of long-period positions (centres of gravitation) in Keynes's critique of the marginalist notion of self-adjustment, see Barens (1987: 39–54).

19 As the drafts of *The General Theory* show, in the course of the transition from the *Treatise on Money* to *The General Theory* Keynes tried to isolate 'essential properties of money' from two different perspectives, see Barens (1987, 1988).

20 In fact, Keynes refers to the elasticity of employment, not to an elasticity of production in any modern understanding of this term; see Klausinger (1991, 1993) for a critical discussion of Keynes's use of the elasticity of production. What Keynes obviously has in mind is not that the quantity of fiat money produced is independent of the input of resources but simply that fiat money cannot be produced by entrepreneurs as is the case with other commodities. This comes out very clearly in his discussion of the employment effects of digging up bottles filled with bank notes and buried in abandoned coal mines (*G.T.*: 129).

21 See Garretsen (1992: 145ff.) and Heering (1991: 152ff.) for a careful analysis of the elasticity of substitution.

22 Fisher (1930: 40–1) had already stressed the importance of negligible carrying-costs for a strictly positive money rate of interest. See also Keynes's remarks on Gesell (*G.T.*: 356).

23 It should be pointed out, as have several writers, that equation (17.14) only gives an approximization; as can be seen from equation (17.3), the correct expression for any own-rate of interest *in terms of money* is (cf. Fisher 1896: 9):

$$i_{i,t} = \rho_{i,t} + \delta_i + \rho_{i,t} \cdot \delta_i$$

Marshall (1895: 674) gives a correct calculation of the money rate of interest in terms of goods in general; see also Marshall (1920: 594). Cf. Fisher (1896: 9, n.3) for a comment on the 3rd edition of Marshall's *Principles*. Conard (1959: 122) – as well as Rogers (1989: 209) and Lawlor (1994b: 57ff), both following Conard – calculate the own-rate *in terms of money* by adding an 'adjustment factor' *a* to the own-rate of interest:

$$i_{i,t} = \rho_{i,t} + a_i.$$

As can easily be shown, a is an unfortunate mixture of price and quantity relations, because a obviously must be:

$$a_i = \delta_i \, (1 + \rho_{i,t})$$

Contrary to the assertion made by Conard (1959: 122, n.3 and 135), this adjustment factor is not the a used by Keynes, which is simply the 'percentage appreciation (or depreciation)' of a commodity in terms of money ($G.T.$: 227).

24 Here Keynes stands Sraffa's argument on its head in so far as he obviously considers the own-rates to be *exogenous* functions of the stocks of commodities; see Keynes ($C.W.$ XIV: 78); Turvey (1965: 165); and Bliss (1987). Thus they have the same logical status as utility functions have in neoclassical theory (Heering 1991: 153).

25 Note that by setting $\delta_3 = 0$, Keynes is arguing within the framework of a current-numéraire economy.

26 If there are other commodities which have these properties as well, then, according to Keynes, their own-rates of interest could lead to the same consequences. Keynes ($G.T.$: 241) refers to land as a possible example.

27 See Fisher (1907: 212, 1930: 216) for a similar argument.

28 See Keynes ($C.W.$ XIV: 101), where he speaks of the marginal *efficiency* of money; Ambrosi (1976: 6); and Robertson in Keynes ($C.W.$ XIII: 509).

29 But although the notion of a commodity rate of interest suggests consideration of time preference, this hint is not taken up by Keynes. On the relationship between the rate of time preference and own-rates of interest, see Ono (1994: 25).

30 Here it is most revealing that in his numerical example Keynes explicitly takes as given the spot and forward prices of wheat together with the rate of interest on a money loan (in addition, he implicitly takes as given the spot and forward price of money). Later on in Chapter 17, Keynes gives a quite different meaning to the notion of own-rate of interest (see note 24 above).

31 Neutral money is defined as a situation in which the equilibrium solutions in a barter economy and monetary economy coincide.

32 'for *any* composite commodity arbitrarily selected there is a corresponding rate that will equalise the purchasing power, in terms of that composite commodity, of the money saved and of the additional money borrowed for investment' (Sraffa 1932a: 51). In stressing the intimate link between the average price level and the average 'natural' rate of interest (in terms of a composite commodity), Sraffa points to the fact that changes in relative prices and own-rates of interest are just two sides of the same coin.

33 As Kurz (1995b: n.31) points out, 'Sraffa, as we know from his yet unpublished papers, did not think highly of Keynes's argument. His main criticism was that the benefits involved in *holding* a commodity (including money) have no relation to its own-rate of interest, and that no properties of that commodity – apart from an expected price change – have any relation to the difference between its rate and other rates' (emphasis in original).

34 In a draft of the future *General Theory* Keynes stated explicitly that 'this book . . . turns mainly on developing a new theory of relationship between the marginal efficiency of capital and the rate of interest' ($C.W.$ XIV: 362); see also Keynes ($G.T.$: 242–3) and Keynes ($C.W.$ XIV: 123).

35 See, for instance, Keynes ($G.T.$: 31, 204, 219–20, 375). The result shown in equation (17.18) may be the reason why in 1937 Keynes, in his contribution to the Fisher *Festschrift*, abstained from using the concept of own-rates of interest

altogether and instead used exclusively the concept of marginal efficiency; see Keynes (*C.W.* XIV).

36 See, for instance, Panico (1985, 1988a, 1988b) for an analysis of the role that the concept of own-rates of interest may play in a theory of distribution and prices. Interestingly enough, Panico only deals with own-rates of interest in terms of money (Panico 1985: 40, n.1).

37 Even if money's elasticity of production is zero, the 'elasticity of supply of liquidity is not zero but *unity*' Lerner (1952: 185).

38 See also Keynes (*G.T.*: 233, 253, 303–4, 308–9); see Friedman (1974: 173–4) for a fairly complete listing of relevant passages in *The General Theory*.

39 This had already been pointed by, for instance, Friedman (1974: 154). It is interesting to note that in the most recent attempt at a reconstruction of Keynes's Theory of a Monetary Economy, the possibility of under-employment equilibrium is explicitly linked to the existence of the liquidity trap; see Ono (1994: 48, 61f, 165f).

40 In Chapter 17, Keynes points to the stickiness of wages as the cause for the reluctance of the money rate of interest to fall at all (*G.T.*: 232) and to the liquidity trap as the cause for its reluctance to fall adequately if money-wages were flexible (*G.T.*: 233). This argument implies that, in the absence of the liquidity trap, unemployment can only be explained by rigid money-wages; see also *G.T.*: 253. But at the same time, he stresses the possibility that flexible money-wages would make things worse because they would result in violent instability of the price level (and by implication of employment and production) (*G.T.*: 232, 253, 269–71, 304). We shall not enter into a discussion of the validity of this claim – a growing literature lends force to it, see De Long and Summers (1986); Caskey and Fazzari (1987, 1988); Howitt (1988); Blanchard and Fischer (1989); Fazzari and Caskey (1989); Amadeo (1992); Brown (1992); Flaschel and Franke (1992); Tobin (1993, 1994); and Flaschel (1994) – instead we only refer to the fact that the need for stable money-wages in order to avoid instability of prices and output bears no relevance to the question of whether Keynes's analysis of the monetary causes of unemployment based on the notion of own-rates of interest is valid or not.

41 At this stage, Keynes becomes utterly defensive: he is only able to point out that money-wage reductions can establish full employment only through their 'roundabout repercussions' (*G.T.*: 257), i.e. 'monetary management by the trade unions' suffering from the same limitation as monetary policy proper (*G.T.*: 266–7), and by arguing that no 'classical economist' ever mentioned their indirect influence on employment, see, for instance, Keynes (*G.T.*: 266–7; and esp. *C.W.* XXIV: 272–3). Curiously, in the draft chapters of *The General Theory*, he seems to have considered the indirect influence of money-wages on the money rate of interest as part of the 'traditional doctrine', see Keynes (*C.W.* XIII: 389, 395–6) – here Keynes hints at the possibility of the liquidity trap as well – and *C.W.* XXIX: 56).

42 And, of course, taking the Pigou effect into account on a strictly theoretical level, i.e. neglecting its empirical relevance, strips the liquidity trap of its importance, leaving only rigid money-wages as the cause of unemployment.

43 The money rate of interest can only restrain the production of commodities because, according to Keynes (*G.T.*: 228), increase in their stocks will decrease their marginal efficiency (or own-rate of interest). Keynes (*G.T.*: 136) gives two reasons for this decrease: the prospective yield will fall (long-period influence) and the supply price will rise (short-period influence), and both reasons rely on

the results of marginalist theory; see Eatwell (1983b; 118–23) and Asimakopulos (1971, 1985) for a critical discussion.

44 It may be noted that this argument contrasts with Keynes's own position: on
the one hand, he saw his schedule of marginal efficiency of capital as a variant
of traditional theory (*G.T.*: 139–41) and, on the other hand, made it abundantly
clear that he considered marginalist theory as being basically correct; see
Keynes (*G.T.*: xxi, 16, 17, 112, 243–4, 339–40, 378, 379; *C.W.* XIII: 411,
489; *C.W.* XXIX: 89, 118; and esp. *C.W.* XIV: 85–8), where Keynes repeats his
argument in *The General Theory* that in conditions of full employment his theory
merges with 'orthodox theory'.

45 This argument was first made by Pasinetti (1974: 37, 43) and is taken up by, for
example, Rogers (1989: 170, 202, 216, 229) and Lawlor (1994b: 84). See also
Pasinetti, Chapter 13 in this volume.

46 Keynes (*G.T.*: 143) himself saw the possibility of the *dependence* of prospective
yield on the money rate of interest: 'It is worth noting that an expectation of a
future fall in the rate of interest will have the effect of *lowering* the schedule of
marginal efficiency of capital.'

47 See Garegnani (1979: 66, 78); in addition see Ackley (1961: 472, n.6; 1978:
619–26), whose compelling analysis highlights the impossibility of deriving an
interest-elastic investment demand schedule without having recourse to the
marginalist principle of factor substitution.

48 Of course, it could be argued that it is the (long-period) *expectation* of yield that
is relevant in the construction of the schedule of marginal efficiency of capital.
But this amounts either to assuming a certain state of expectations to be
exogenously given or a confrontation with the problem that, sooner or later,
expectations have to adapt to market outcomes, in which case the arguments
just referred to come into effect.

Restricting the schedule of marginal efficiency of capital to the short period
(see Pasinetti on the marginal efficiency of investment, Chapter 13 in the
present volume), one may circumvent capital-theoretic fallacies. But in this
case the question arises: how appropriate is it to deal with capital from a rent-
theoretic perspective, if the object of analysis is capitalism, i.e. market economies characterized by accumulation of capital?

49 But see, for instance, Panico (1985, 1988a, 1988b) for an analysis of the role
that the concept of own-rates of interest may play in a theory of distribution
and prices. Interestingly enough, Panico only deals with own-rates of interest in
terms of money (Panico 1985: 40, n.1).

18

KEYNES'S MONETARY THEORY OF VALUE AND MODERN BANKING*

Colin Rogers and T.K. Rymes

INTRODUCTION

The liquidity premium attached to money permeated the development of Keynes's monetary theory of value, culminating in its appearance in Chapter 17 of *The General Theory* and the famous 1937 *Quarterly Journal of Economics* article. Liquidity,[1] inherent in private and collective monetary arrangements, is a consequence of one of the social conventions that permit rational action in an uncertain world. By an uncertain world, we mean one in which the knowledge which we must have in order to know fully, if stochastically, the consequences of our acts is in principle unattainable (O'Donnell 1989, 1990a; Runde 1994a; Rymes 1994).

In the real world, liquidity provides conventional refuge from Keynesian uncertainty for which individuals are prepared to pay. With such uncertainty liquidity premiums attach to all durable assets to varying degrees dependent on their characteristics and historical circumstance. Modern monetary systems, however, provide the institutional framework and conventions which, under most circumstances, attribute to the debits and credits of the payments system the greatest liquidity premiums. Equilibria in Keynes's monetary theory, after *The General Theory*, are monetary in the sense that such premiums are embedded in all relative prices.[2]

After *The General Theory*, there could be no such thing, outside imaginary or Robinson Crusoe worlds, as real equilibria, dependent only on preferences, technology and endowments, independent of monetary phenomena. To Keynes, money was not something exogenous (e.g. Marshall's shells) nor neutral (Friedman's costless fiat money) but rather money services, including the services of liquidity, which are produced by private *and* central banks, that is, by people acting privately and collectively. Inter-temporal rates of substitution (preferences) between consumption flows are not equated solely to inter-temporal rates of transformation (technology and endowments), but are, inescapably in a world in which knowledge cannot be complete, affected by the states of beliefs on the part of individuals acting as consumers, producers, bankers and central bankers; that is, by liquidity preference which reflects the set of conventional expectations that individuals rationally hold in an uncertain world.

Recent developments to deregulate banking systems and the advent of computer-controlled electronic banking facilities have led to a forceful reapplication of orthodox value theory to monetary analysis. This application is associated, in particular, with Fischer Black (1970), Eugene Fama (1980) and Robert Hall (1983) (the BFH view, for short). Those monetary theorists (sometimes described as exponents of the new monetary economics) who adopt the BFH view see modern banking as providing a system of debits and credits metering the shifting allocation of real resources among private agents. On this basis, they reject liquidity preference theory and any useful role for central banks. For example, Yeager, an exponent of the BFH system, claims that:

> One advantage of the BFH system is that it avoids monetary disequilibria by accommodating supplies of liquid assets, including media of exchange, to the demand for them, at a nearly stable price level corresponding to the multi-commodity definition of the valun [the Yeager unit] . . . Through the direct accommodation of supplies of money and other assets to the demands for them the BFH system avoids the problems alluded to by Keynes in his Chapter 17.
>
> . . . Individuals can keep their options open by holding liquid assets without impairing capital formation in particular and economic activity in general.
>
> (Yeager 1989: 374-5)

We challenge the BFH analysis of modern banking by outlining the relevance of the concept of liquidity and the implications of liquidity preference to modern banking systems. We argue, on the basis of a sensible interpretation of the BFH banking world 'without money', that liquidity, liquidity preference and the functions of the central bank are essential properties of any modern banking system. Modern monetary economies cannot operate without liquidity, and monetary economics cannot be written without recognizing the role of liquidity and Keynes's concept of liquidity preference.

In the next section we deal with conceptual issues: then we provide a sketch of Keynes's monetary theory of value. The penultimate section outlines some properties of what we call a pure Keynesian banking system, and is followed by our conclusions.

THE MEANING OF MONEY AND MODERN BANKING

It is widely acknowledged that banking systems have evolved to the stage where the vision of a 'cashless' payments system is almost a reality. It is this impression which has led monetary theorists like Black and Fama to the conclusion that a modern banking system is nothing more than an accounting system. Fama (1980; emphasis added) argues that: 'An accounting system works through bookkeeping entries, debits and credits, which do not require any physical medium or *the concept of money.* . . . the banking system is best understood without the mischief introduced by *the concept of money.*'

In a similar vein Fischer Black (1970) argues that, because in modern banking systems, money (cash?) is effectively redundant, there is no role for the quantity theory of money or the liquidity preference theory of the rate of interest. In Black's view, there is no 'money' in a modern banking system. The Black–Fama vision, together with a contribution by Hall (1982), constitutes the BFH system.[3] It has been championed in the literature by Greenfield and Yeager (1983) in particular.

What, then, do we make of the claim that monetary and banking theory is best understood without the mischief introduced by the concept of money? An answer to this question is complicated by the fact that exponents of the BFH system, such as Greenfield and Yeager (1983, 1986, 1989), take up positions at odds with the theoretical perspective of Black and Fama, and ultimately endorse Irving Fisher's (1920) proposal to stabilize the dollar. Nevertheless, despite its confused state the debate serves to confirm that the 'real' vision underlying classical monetary theory remains as pervasive today as it was at the time of *The General Theory* (see, for instance, Selgin and White 1994).

A number of issues may be dealt with briefly. First, there is the relationship between the Walrasian general equilibrium system and the BFH analysis. Second is the relationship, if any, between the Walrasian general equilibrium system and a cashless payments system. The third, and substantive, issue concerns the properties of modern banking systems as they evolve towards a 'cashless' payments basis.

We clear away some false trails. First, both Black and Fama claim that the medium-of-exchange function of money is redundant in an economy with a sophisticated accounting system of exchange. Consequently, the *concept* is no longer relevant in such a system. For example, the quotation from Fama presented above claims that the *concept* of money is not required in a cashless payments system.

Reflection will confirm that even if a medium of exchange is not required in a world with a sophisticated electronic accounting system, it does not follow that the *concept* of money is thereby redundant or that media of exchange no longer exist (Niehans 1978: ch. 7). Leaping to such a conclusion involves a simple confusion between the concept of money and its physical manifestation. Even if money evolves to the stage where cash is replaced by a sophisticated accounting system, money as a tangible thing still exists. A system of book-entries is as tangible a medium of exchange as gold, a dollar bill or a cheque.

At a less trivial level, the BFH system conflates the existence of a sophisticated accounting system with the existence of a Walrasian auction. This aspect of the BFH system has drawn comment from McCallum (1985), White (1984) and Hoover (1988), among others. Their observations reveal that much of what BFH have in mind makes sense in a world of the Walrasian auction. However, it is well known that such a world is non-monetary (Hahn 1965, 1973, 1984). Consequently, as McCallum (1985: 18–19) observes, Fama (1980) on some occasions misuses his system by applying the standard results of real Walrasian general equilibrium theory to questions of monetary economics. In similar fashion, Hoover (1988) suggests that Fama solves the problem of reconciling monetary and real value theory by abolishing money. White (1986: 852) makes the same charge against Greenfield and Yeager. On reflection these observations are not surprising because, in effect, Fama is simply applying the irrelevance propositions derived from the application of real Walrasian general equilibrium models in the finance literature (Trautwein 1993). In such a world the Modigliani–Miller theorem holds and there is no analytical distinction between debt and equity; hence the habit of exponents of the BFH system of treating bank deposits as equity and banks as mutual funds.

All this is, of course, rather academic as the properties of real general equilibrium theory cannot be used to adjudicate questions of monetary theory.[4] As Laidler (1990b: 106) puts it, the Walrasian auction is an alternative to the social institution of money; and, for a recent assessment of the challenges facing attempts to integrate money and Walrasian general equilibrium theory, see Hellwig (1993).

These objections to the BFH system are not regarded as substantive by Greenfield and Yeager, who claim to have a much more 'operational' interpretation of it. They see their version as directly applicable and capable of implementation in any existing modern economy.[5] For example, Greenfield and Yeager (1983: 302, fn. 1) interpret the BFH system as descriptive of 'how an unregulated financial system would operate'. Also, in response to criticism by White (1984), they explicitly reject the Walrasian real general equilibrium framework as the context in which their proposals are to be evaluated. Greenfield and Yeager (1986: 848); respond:

> But we see in the unit's [i.e. the valun] operationality more than just the calculations of Walras' auctioneer. We use the term 'operational' only after having satisfied ourselves that in the course of honest-to-good-ness market activity, the unit denominating privately issued notes would pose no threat of prying itself loose from its commodity-bundle definition.

Central to the Greenfield and Yeager 'operational' version of the BFH scheme is the notion of indirect redeemability, that is, the idea that bank notes (preferably competitively supplied) are redeemable at banks for a 'redemption asset' (Greenfield and Yeager suggest gold or Treasury bills) which is sufficient to buy the composite commodity bundle which defines the unit of account. Unfortunately, as Schnadt and Whittaker (1993) demonstrate, the Greenfield–Yeager 'operational' version of the BFH scheme is not operational. It fails because it contains no mechanism for reversing the rising prices of commodities once it is set in motion. Some scheme for inflation-proofing the 'monetary' system! Despite these setbacks Greenfield and Yeager assert that their scheme is, for all practical purposes, the same as that suggested by Fisher (1920). Fisher's scheme is at least operational (Schnadt and Whittaker 1993), but it raises questions of general indexation that are beyond the scope of this chapter (see Greenfield *et al.* 1995; Schnadt and Whittaker 1995).

This brings us to the third and more fundamental question: the role and properties of money in a modern banking system. Starting from first principles, in its broadest sense, what is accepted as money is a convention, and this convention has, historically, been expressed in a wide variety of ways. The Austrian explanation is that what evolves as money emerges spontaneously as the solution to the co-ordination problem posed by barter (White 1984, 1986, 1987; Wärneryd 1990). The essence of the Mengerian story is that the acquisition of highly saleable goods not for their consumption but for their value in indirect exchange is individually rational. Moreover, once the convention is established, individual action cannot undermine it. What is important here is that individuals cannot dominate the choice of medium of exchange because what is generally accepted as the medium of exchange is dependent on the actions of others. To change conventions requires some social action.

In these respects a modern banking system has much in common with some older monetary systems. Keynes (1930a, b) and, more recently, Friedman (1992: ch. 1) commented on the monetary system of the island of Yap in Micronesia to illustrate the conventional nature of money. On the island of Yap, stone money operated as an accounting system but not as a medium of exchange. The transfer of title to the stones was recognized by the community without any need for physical transfer.[6] In any event, one of the stones was irretrievably lost at the bottom of the ocean and had not been seen for years. Nevertheless, on the basis of eye-witness accounts it was accepted by all as a truly fine stone and as part of the money supply in the sense that title to parts of this stone were accepted in exchange for goods. This highlights the point that money need not be defined in terms of a physical medium of exchange.[7] In this respect a modern banking system of the type imagined by BFH and based only on bookkeeping entries, inevitably also provides a means of payment. Only if the banks refuse to acknowledge debits and credits does the system fail and must recourse be made to some physical means of payment.

Accepting that even ancient banking systems operated on a cashless basis, does this then render modern cashless payments systems immune to the problems associated with liquidity preference? The answer is no, for several reasons. To begin with, in a bookkeeping system, and so long as the existing conventions and monetary institutions are maintained, individuals with credit balances can defer incurring debits against those balances even though those with debit balances are desperate for them to do so. The problems with money attributed to the existence of liquidity preference arise because credits are also a store of value. Once title to money is transferred, either physically or by electronic transfer, the owner of that title can express his preference for liquidity by refraining from incurring debits against his title; that is, by doing nothing. Consequently, liquidity preference is not a characteristic of monetary systems based only on some physical medium of exchange but exists also in a monetary system based on electronic bookkeeping and underwritten by a central bank. In short, liquidity preference would continue to exist in any practical version of the BFH world without 'money'.

In addition, the existence of an electronic bookkeeping system does not imply the existence of a Walrasian auction. And without a Walrasian auction, some means of payment or transactions recording is necessary. Thus in the absence of a Walrasian auction, in a world of stochastic certainty the BFH world of bookkeeping entries will be subject to liquidity preference because even the modern world of electronic banking is a monetary system. In such a monetary system what counts as money, be it a deposit or an overdraft, is valued independently of its physical characteristics because *it is money*. As Hoover (1988: 104–5) and Friedman (1992: 10) remind us, the value of a monetized commodity is governed largely by its monetary use, and money is valued largely because it is already valued; that is, the monetary convention imparts value to the monetary commodity because everyone will accept the monetary commodity in exchange.

Furthermore, a world without a Walrasian auction is where irreducible uncertainty exists (O'Donnell 1989, 1990a; Runde 1994a; Rymes 1994). Not only is a medium of exchange or means of payment useful in such a world, but when doubt arises, holders of credit and debit balances may decide to wait and see, rather than running them down or increasing them further; that is, they express their preference for liquidity, or for no change, as solace against the unknown. Money, whatever form it takes, also acts as a store of value.

As long as a vehicle for the expression of liquidity preference exists the automatic attainment of the full employment of resources cannot be guaranteed. That is why Greenfield and Yeager and BFH seek to eliminate money. What BFH obscure by implicit reliance on the Walrasian auction is that liquidity preference attaches to the title to the means of payment or transactions in whatever forms that may take. The rate of interest, as a barometer of liquidity preference, then emerges as a central element in

Keynes's analysis of unemployment (Rogers 1989, 1994). Yeager (1989) is quite correct to be concerned.

KEYNES'S INTER-TEMPORAL VALUE THEORY

To arrive at Keynes's monetary theory of value, we first set out the main characteristics of neoclassical inter-temporal real value theory. In other words, we first set out the Marshallian or real inter-temporal theory of value employed by Keynes in the *Treatise on Money* and then we derive the inter-temporal monetary theory of value underpinning *The General Theory*. We shall, for illumination, refer in our analysis to economic theory important to the development of Keynes's ideas.

Neoclassical own-rates of interest

From the simple one-commodity optimum neoclassical 'monetary' growth model, with 'real' fiat money services treated as an input in inter-temporal technological relationships, the temporary equilibria 'real' rates of return on capital and 'real' flat money will be:

$$q_k(k,m) - \delta_k = n + n' + \rho - \dot{U}_c/U_c = q_m(k,m) - \delta_m + i - p \quad (18.1)$$

where q_k and q_m are the gross marginal physical products of the services of 'capital' and real money balances (q_k and $q_m > 0$, $q_{km} = q_{mk} > 0$, q_{kk} and $q_{mm} < 0$) all expressed in Harrod units, δ_k and δ_m are the carrying costs of capital and money (e.g. the rate of decay of the capital stock, service charges or user costs levied by the monetary authority for the use of fiat money balances (δ_k and δ_m are treated as constant but are expressible more generally as a function of the intensity of use of services of 'capital' and money), $n + n'$ equals the rate of growth of Harrod agents, in terms of their numbers and the increasing productivity of the services of working and waiting they provide, or in terms, that is, of Harrod units, and ρ is the rate of time preference (again, all taken as exogenous), i is the nominal rate of interest the authority pays on fiat balances, p is the rationally expected rate of change in the money price level, P, and $\dot{U}_c/U_c$ is the time rate of change in the marginal utility of consumption of the representative Harrodian.[8]

Since $\dot{U}_c/U_c$ can be written as $U_{cc}\dot{c}/U_c$ and, if we define μ as $\dfrac{U_{cc}c}{U_c}$,

then we can write:

$$q_k(k,m) - \delta_k = n + n' + \rho - \mu \dot{C}/C = q_m(k,m) - \delta_m + i - p \quad (18.2)$$

so that the equilibrium relations exhibit the Keynes–Ramsey rule (Blanchard and Fischer 1989: 41) that consumption increases, remains constant or decreases, depending on whether the marginal product of capital (net of population growth) exceeds, is equal to or is less than the rate of time preference. Sometimes μ is interpreted as a co-efficient of risk aversion but it is simply the elasticity of substitution among inter-temporal consumption streams (Lucas 1988b; Weil 1990). Both Marshall and Fisher distinguished between nominal and real interest rates and certainly Keynes thoroughly discussed the inverse relationship between desired 'real' money balances and the expected rate of inflation in his *Tract on Monetary Reform*.

Our representation of Keynes's own-rates entails inclusion of his discussion of the effects of expected rates of inflation on the demand for 'real' balances as a factor determining the spot price of goods. Certainly, his discussion of the German inflation would suggest that Keynes, like Marshall, was well aware of the quantity theory aphorism: that the monetary authority determines the nominal money supply and the general public determines the 'real' money supply.[9]

One further point in the *Tract on Monetary Reform* merits attention. While it can be said that Sraffa's critique of Hayek supplied Keynes with the raw materials for Chapter 17, it can also be argued that Keynes already had the relationships in his *Tract* in his discussion of the relationship between spot and forward rates of exchange. In Keynes's arithmetic, if spot and forward prices diverge, there need be no neutral or natural or unique own-rate of interest. Sraffa's point, in his critical overview of Hayek's inter-temporal value theory, that there are multiple own-rates, was implicit in Keynes's work in the *Tract* to the effect that, for currencies, if forward and spot exchange rates diverged, own-rates of interest on different monies would also diverge and there would be no unique real rate of interest (Kregel 1983a; Rogers 1989).[10]

Keynes's own-rates of interest

How does Keynes's own-rates of interest framework in Chapter 17 of *The General Theory* differ from the neoclassical interpretation? The immediate connection with Keynes's Chapter 17 may be seen by rewriting the relationships for the steady-state conditions, $\dot{U}_c/U_c = 0$[11] as:

$$q_k(k,m) - \delta_k = q_m(k,m) - \delta_m + i - p \tag{18.3}$$

where, translating to Keynes's language and notation, $q_k(k,m) = q_k$ is the own-rate of interest on commodities, $\delta_k = c$ the user or carrying cost associated with k, $\delta_m = c_m$ is the user or carrying cost of money, and $q_m(k_m) = q_m$ is the own-rate of interest on money. Expression (18.3) includes the possibility that interest is earned by the means of payment; for example, interest earned by fiat money holdings in the form of reserves held with central banks. If we ignore that possiblility and set the carrying cost, $c_m = 0$ and let $p = a$ be the expected rate of change in the money price of the commodity, then:

$$q - c = q_m - a \tag{18.4}$$

where the net commodity own-rate of return on commodities equals the net commodity own-rate of return on money. Though all commodities would carry some liquidity premiums, we assume them to be zero in a fiat money monetary system. Thus, expression (18.4) would appear as:

$$q - c = q_m - a + l_m \tag{18.5}$$

Once the banking system has evolved beyond the use of gold and then fiat money to what we call a pure Keynesian system (outlined below), the laws of production have little significant impact on the own-rate of return on money (the ownership of title to deposits and overdraft arrangements provided by the banking system) and the liquidity premium plays the dominant role in establishing the own-rate of return on money. There is in Keynes's monetary system no market mechanism that will induce the liquidity premium automatically to be such that full employment results.

In Keynes's world, where $q_m = 0$, expression (18.5) appears as:

$$q - c + a = l_m \tag{18.6}$$

and the money net rate of return on commodities equals the money net rate of return on money. The latter, in a pure Keynesian banking system, is a function of the liquidity premium which attaches to the means of payment even if the monetary system operates in terms of an electronic transfer of funds. The world of debits and credits is still subject to the force of liquidity preference, the principle of effective demand is operative and the liquidity preference theory of the rate of interest plays a central role in the determination of employment and output.

This analysis can be used to shed further light on the BFH argument. It seeks to eliminate l_m by schemes which reinstate commodity money and the loanable funds theory of the rate of interest. For example, Yeager's vision of the BFH world is one in which entrepreneurs wish to invest only in real capital goods. Other individuals may wish to express their preference for liquidity by holding liquid assets, but then the 'resources set free from current consumption by people who instead prefer holding highly liquid assets are conveyed to investors who will use them for real capital formation' (Yeager 1989: 374). Yeager simply begs the question by reasserting the loanable funds theory of the rate of interest. In Yeager's world, Say's Law holds because expressions of liquidity preference are treated as formally equivalent to shifts in the saving function and all saving is invested. In this world there is no limit to the profitable expansion of output; Keynes's principle of effective demand does not apply (Rogers 1989).

A PURE KEYNESIAN MONETARY SYSTEM

What was money in Keynes? In his *Treatise on Money* Keynes dealt with a world in which money essentially was fiat (gold he considered a barbarous relic) and had two components: notes issued by the monetary authority; and reserves that private banks held with the central bank (part of the monetary authority). Private money was essentially bank deposits. In *The General Theory* money was bank deposits (and in his *Treatise on Money* at least two kinds, demand (personal and business) and savings) (Miller 1984; Freedman 1993). However, in *The General Theory* Keynes (*G.T.*: 247) treated money as one of the 'givens' and pushed the technical monetary details into the background on the understanding that he had written on them in his *Treatise*.[12]

A developed financial system of the type examined by Keynes in the *Treatise on Money* and taken for granted in *The General Theory* has properties which distinguish it from the system imagined by BFH. To get some insight into these properties we outline a modern version of Keynes's (1930a, b) 'cashless' monetary system.

Starting from Keynes's work in his *Treatise on Money*, we argue that the convention of money as shells or stones has evolved to a monetary system where inter-temporal transactions among private agents (firms and households acting privately and collectively) are executed through banks in a system of debits (overdrafts) and credits (deposits). Similarly, such transactions among banks are executed through a clearing house or central bank in a system of debits (negative settlement balances) and credits (positive settlement balances).[13]

Furthermore, it is a system which rests not only on the convention of money but on other conventions in financial markets. These conventions have no objective basis and are a source of both stability and instability (Darity and Horn 1993). They provide stability in the face of everyday shocks by providing an anchor to expectations. However, because they have no objective basis they can become a source of instability when credibility is lost in a crisis. In such a banking system there is no fixed stock of money; it is not the particulars of some outside money but rather the services of the banks, the clearing arrangements and the management of conventions by the monetary authority which impart stability and liquidity to modern monetary economies. Keynes provides a description of such a monetary system:[14]

> If we suppose a closed banking system, which has no relations with the outside world, in a country where all payments are made by cheque and no cash is used, and if we assume further that banks do not find it necessary in such circumstances to hold any cash reserves but settle interbank indebtedness by transfer of other assets, it is evident that there is no limit to the amount of bank money which banks can create *provided that they move forward in step*.
>
> (Keynes 1930a: 26, *C.W.* V: 23; original emphasis)

313

Keynes goes on to suggest that such a banking system would have inherent nominal indeterminacy but is controllable by the central bank. We describe such an arrangement as a pure Keynesian banking system.

In a pure banking equilibrium, although some banks will experience negative and others positive settlement balances, the net position of all banks and the desired position of each bank with the central bank will be zero. In such an eqilibrium, though some private agents who are running deficits will be reducing deposits or augmenting overdrafts, so that on balance overdrafts will appear, others who are running surpluses will be reducing overdrafts or augmenting deposits so that on balance deposits will exist. Overdrafts will equal deposits among non-bank transactors. Negative settlement balances will equal positive settlement balances with the central bank. There will be no 'real balance effect' nor any outside or inside 'money' appearing as part of the wealth of the economy.

The central bank takes on a role in addition to that of a clearing house by underwriting the purchasing power of money and managing conventional beliefs in the financial markets. That is, the central bank will behave in such a way that beliefs in the stability of the nominal and real value of deposits and overdrafts will be preserved (*C.T.*: 204) By their very nature such beliefs can only be changed in a systematic fashion by collective action, in this case by augmented government authority and the central bank. However, because the system is potentially indeterminate, the central bank must stand ready to stem any contagious movements in nominal magnitudes. Any contagion ends, indeed will not get underway, when private individuals realize that the nominal and real value of their deposits and overdrafts with the banks are secure.

Two key properties of a pure Keynesian banking system require further elaboration. First, banks and individuals try to maintain constant the nominal value of overdrafts and deposits. Second, the central bank acts to underwrite the nominal and real stability of the system. In this respect the maintenance of price stability has important consequences for the liquidity premium that attaches to money.

Banks are those financial institutions whose overdrafts and deposits are held constant in nominal terms. While other financial intermediaries' deposits and overdrafts can be used for intermediation purposes, an additional gain is acquired by the individuals and banks, by virtue of the fact that the nominal value of the overdrafts and deposits and negative and positive settlement balances are changing only because of known interest rates and service charges and their initiated debits and credits. The constancy of the nominal values of banks' overdrafts and deposits is the signal characteristic of the inter-temporal transactions services supplied by banks (Chant 1992).

Another key feature of a pure Keynesian banking system is the existence of a central bank which acts, more or less imperfectly, to stabilize the aggregate price level. By so acting it augments (attempts to underwrite) the liquidity services provided by the banking system in a world without outside money. As Wicksell noted long ago, in such a world there is no 'real' external anchor on the aggregate price level. It is also Keynes's world in which liquidity preference plays a major role in the determination of intertemporal prices.

The maintenance of nominal and corresponding 'real' values is the responsibility of the central bank[15] because this function cannot be performed to the same extent by the private banks. The activity of the central bank is the public provision of relatively stable nominal and 'real' magnitudes. Stability of the price level adds to the flow of liquidity which private individuals obtain from overdrafts and deposits, whose stable nominal value is brought about by the combined activities of the banks and the central bank, and whose stable 'real value' is brought about primarily by the central bank. This activity adds to the ability of the banks to produce intertemporal transaction arrangements, by means of overdrafts and deposits, and consequently Keynesian liquidity will be part of the inter-temporal marginal rates of transformations and substitutions among inter-temporal consumption streams, since the output of banks, reflecting Keynesian liquidity, is the provision of inter-temporal transactions services.

Stabilization of nominal and 'real' magnitudes does not mean some fixed outside money, real or fiat, because the system has advanced to the point where such contrivances no longer exist because they are unnecessary. (Some economists concentrate on the 'halfway house' of endogenous money; see Sheila Dow, Chapter 28 in Volume 2 of this work.) No outside money exists in modern monetary systems; there are merely systems of overdrafts, deposits, negative and positive settlement balances through which inter-temporal transactions are executed. There is, however, a costly central bank, one of whose functions is to stabilize the aggregate price level so as to keep also the real value of debits and credits as constant as possible. This activity has the public-good effect of increasing the liquidity associated with the overdrafts and deposits supplied by the banking system. The central bank not only directly affects the liquidity services supplied by the banks, for which prices can be found, i.e. the service charges levied by the banks, but also indirectly affects the liquidity services supplied by the banks by preserving overall nominal magnitudes and the general level of prices. The maintenance of the aggregate nominal and real values is a *pure public good*. The immediate question which arises is: how is that service priced?

Maintenance of the nominal values of the banks' overdrafts and deposits could be done, for deposits at least, by deposit insurance. The premiums for the deposit insurance would appear as part of the service charges that the depositors of banks would pay and would be part of the service charges the banks would in turn pay to the central bank, if the deposit insurance was also run by the central bank or the authorities in general. Such contractual arrangements set up the usual moral-hazard problem, and that endemic problem is resolved by the usual appropriate prudential regulations established not just for banking but for every activity subject to opportunistic behaviour. Lender of last resort activities by the central bank encounter similar difficulties, and it is sometimes argued that the lender of last resort problem is overcome if the central bank is willing to accomodate negative settlement balances at penalty or Bagehot level interest rates.

Thus, although some of the services of the central bank can be priced, for example, the routine debiting and crediting of banks' transactions through it, deposit insurance and the like, *the maintenance of overall nominal and 'real' magnitudes, which contributes to the liquidity yield of bank deposits and overdrafts, cannot be priced.*[16] As Keynes (*G.T.*: 226) put it, there is nothing to show for this liquidity. Yet liquidity premiums are embedded in the value of the services of settlement balances and the services, through overdrafts and deposits, of the banks. It is through these instruments that the central bank exercises its control over aggregate nominal and 'real' magnitudes. Thus the yields on all other assets and liabilities must reflect that they are not as immediately privy to the provision of liquidity by the central bank. Rates of return on capital goods might therefore stand above rates of return on overdrafts and deposits because the latter have greater liquidity premiums.

Liquidity premiums, then, which may arise in a Keynesian economy where the public-good aspects of the services of the central bank are necessary for the most efficient method of determining aggregate nominal and 'real' magnitudes, are always embedded in all rates of return and therefore all prices.[17] A Keynesian equilibrium is therefore always different from a classical or new classical equilibrium, because the latter equilibria are always fundamentally non-monetary whereas the Keynesian equilibria are more general, having all the attributes of the latter but having also the liquidity premiums associated with the private and collective determination of nominal and 'real' magnitudes.

The essence of Keynes's monetary equilibrium then is not that there exists some fiat money, for which in new classical economics there is no accounting except as a legal restriction designed to raise revenue, but rather that there exist private and collective arrangements to increase the liquidity of debits and credits of inter-temporal transactions systems which result in a greater output of the economy at large. Keynes, expressing sympathy with monetary heretics, wrote that:

> Credit is the pavement along which production travels; and the banks, if they know their duty, would provide the transport facilities to just the extent that is required in order that the productive powers of the community can be employed to their full capacity.[18]
>
> (*C.W.* VI: 197)

The collective arrangements are those which banks *privately* enter when they form clearing arrangements such as clearing houses, for which service prices can be established. Importantly, the wider collective arrangements are involved in the central bank acting ultimately, in fact if not in letter, as a department of monetary affairs as part of the modern, democratic, political collective arrangements for the control of nominal and 'real' economic magnitudes.

Applying these ideas we argue, ignoring risk, that for the alteration of consumption streams through the banking system, Keynes's own rates as set out in equations (18.1)–(18.6) on overdrafts and on deposits will be $R_0 + \partial C/\partial(O/P) = i_o - p + \delta_B$ and $R_D = \partial C/\partial(D/P) - \delta_B + i_D - p$ respectively, where $\partial C/\partial(O/P)$ and $\partial C/\partial(D/P)$ are the values of the marginal products, expressed in terms of consumption goods, of the inter-temporal transactions services supplied by the banks through overdrafts and deposits, δ_B are the carrying costs or service charges associated with the provision of banking services, and R_0 and R_D are the equal real rates of return earned competitively on overdrafts and deposits. In equilibrium, overdrafts associated with deficit positions must earn $n + n' + \rho - \dot{U}_c/U_c$ and if $R_0 = i_0 - p$, i.e. if banks charge the going rate of return on overdrafts, then $\partial C/\partial(O/P) = \delta_B$, or the value of the marginal product of banking services obtained through overdrafts will equal the carrying cost, service charge rate or user fee. Similarly, deposits must earn the going rate of return and the equivalence of the value of the marginal product of banking services must equal the service charge rate. The service charges reflect the liquidity services which the banks privately provide.

If overdrafters and depositors, however, *believe* that the liquidity of the transactions service provided by the banks is augmented by the central bank, then we *can* write:

$$R_0 + \frac{\partial C}{\partial(O/P)} + l_0 = i_0 - p + \delta_B \text{ and } R_D = \frac{\partial C}{\partial(D/P)} + l_D - \delta_B + i_D - p,$$

where l_0 and l_D are Keynes's Chapter 17 liquidity premiums associated with such overdrafts and deposits. A difficulty then emerges. If $l_0 = l_D = l$, then if all real interest rates are the same, the service charges will be such that

$$\frac{\partial C}{\partial(O/P)} + l = \delta_B = \frac{\partial C}{\partial(D/P)} + l$$

so that banks are able to 'price' for the liquidity services they provide. If the own rates are re-expressed as:

$$\frac{\partial C}{\partial(O/P)} + l_0 = i_0 - p - R_0 + \delta_B \text{ and } R_D - (i_D - p) = \frac{\partial C}{\partial(D/P)} + l_D - \delta_B$$

and if $i_0 - p - R_0 < 0$ and $R_D - (i_D - p) > 0$, it is said banks 'price' for their service partly through a spread in interest rates.[19] There is, however, another explanation.[20]

Consider the own-rates on negative and positive settlement balances of the banks with the central bank:

$$R_{Dr} + \partial \; \frac{(O + D)}{P} \; / \partial \; (\frac{Dr}{P}) + l_H = i_{Dr} - p + \delta_H$$

and

$$R_{Cr} = \partial \; \frac{(O + D)}{P} \; / \partial \; (\frac{Cr}{P}) + l_H + i_{Cr} - p - \delta_H$$

where again

$$\partial \; \frac{(O + D)}{P} \; / \partial \; (\frac{Dr}{P}) \quad \text{and} \quad \partial \; \frac{(O + D)}{P} \; / \partial \; \frac{Cr}{P}$$

are the gross marginal physical products of the inter-temporal transaction services, from the negative and positive settlement balances, supplied by the central bank. With the introduction of the explicit liquidity premiums into these equations, an argument can then be made that a spread in interest rates with the central bank will arise, which will be carried over into the spread in bank rates charged by banks on overdrafts and deposits, because it is the only way, consistent with its lender of last resort activities, in which the central bank can 'price' for the liquidity that it provides to banks.

It can also be argued that the liquidity of central bank services will enhance the value of the marginal product of those services and that then the banks will use more of them. As a consequence there is a liquidity enhancement in the marginal product of such services.[21] Such services, which appear simultaneously as the outputs of the central bank and as inputs in the transactions technology used by banks, will be seen to be higher in response to the liquidity-enhancement effect. The marginal products of all the services as measured will be the same, but the amount of them and the output of the economy will all be higher.

Thus, the greater the liquidity services of the central bank, the higher will be the amount of negative and positive settlement balance positions and of overdrafts and deposits of the banks, with their services being priced partly in spreads. The prices of bank services and interest rates would all retain their efficiency requirements in traditional terms, as earlier set out in the formation of neoclassical own-rates of interest, but would also all reflect indirectly the Keynesian liquidity effect. When the central bank provides smaller liquidity services, banks and agents will use inter-temporal transactions services less, the observed amounts of bank settlement balances and of overdrafts and deposits will be less, and the output of the economy will also be lower.

It is also possible to extend the argument by allowing the provision of liquidity services by the central bank to be treated as part of the determination of the Harrodian rate of technical progress. Thus, the greater the services of liquidity supplied by central banks, then, other things being equal, the steady-state rates of return $n + n' + \rho$ will all have higher n's. Thus, there will be no steady-state rate of growth or real rates of return independent of the beliefs of private agents in the ability of the central bank to enhance the liquidity of the inter-temporal transactions technology.

Our discussion of the Keynesian banking system provides some additional insights. In particular, two characteristics of what Keynes called money in Chapter 17 have always puzzled scholars The puzzles vanish if by money Keynes did not mean currency or reserves but rather the social convention involved in the provisional liquidity by the central banks. Money, Keynes said, has low elasticities of substitution and production. If by 'money' we mean, for instance, non-interest-bearing fiat currency, then there are many other kinds of 'money' which are highly substitutable for fiat currency. Similarly, if we assume that by money Keynes meant reserves or high-powered money and draw a distinction between nominal and 'real' money balances, as Keynes himself did in the *Treatise on Money*,[22] then for a change in the level of what Keynes called the cash balance standard of prices, the elasticity of production of 'real' money balances may be large even if the elasticity of production of fiat money balances is zero. Once it is realized that Keynes was talking about money as a convention and its attached liquidity, then his contentions about how the private banks may not be able to compete effectively with the central bank in the maintenance of the convention make sense. Indeed, if the liquidity that Keynes describes arises from the fact that the central bank alone determines nominal magnitudes in a private banking world where they are otherwise indeterminate, then in this sense Keynes's elasticities are indeed zero.

CONCLUSION

After *The General Theory*, Keynesian equilibria always reflect conventional responses to incomplete knowledge. Monetary arrangements, where they are privately and collectively designed to reduce the effects of uncertainty on the inter-temporal transactions system, will always be involved in the determination of interest rates and prices. They will always reflect the conventional provision of liquidity by central banks. Keynes's equilibria are always monetary.

The set of monetary values which hold in Keynesian equilibria will be determined by preferences, endowments, technology *and conventions*

(Lawson 1993; Littleboy 1990). The convention (there are many) which Keynes extensively studied was the liquidity services embedded in the outputs of banks and central banks. These *always* play a role in Keynes's equilibria. By contrast, the set of real values which hold in orthodox equilibria are determined by preferences, endowments and technology. That the convention of money plays no role in orthodox equilibria is illustrated by (a) neutrality propositions in monetary economics, including the 'real balance' argument to the effect that economic systems will tend to gravitate to full Walrasian equilibria determined by 'real' variables; (b) full Ricardian equilibria, where money plays no role; and (c) super-non-neutrality propositions with respect to the supposed optimum provisions of the services associated with the supposed existence of fiat money balances.

In our view there is no meaning to the question of whether Keynesian monetary values will gravitate to orthodox neoclassical or neo-Ricardian equilibrium values because, within the latter, there is no role for the social convention of liquidity and, fundamentally, because Keynesian inter-temporal equilibria are always characterized by liquidity premiums arising in his world because the consequences of human behaviour cannot in principle ever be completely known.

To challenge one famous interpretation of Keynes, then, it is not rewarding to see Keynesian equilibria as short-run phenomena on their way, no matter how slowly, theoretically and practically, to full Walrasian inter-temporal equilibria.[23] The set of inter-temporal monetary values which characterize Keynesian equilibria cannot be found in the set of traditional 'real' inter-temporal values. To challenge another view of Keynes, a common complaint about him as a theorist is that he was prone to construct his theories to match his policy predilections (Meltzer 1988). Keynes *was* concerned with monetary policy and, more importantly, with the connection between monetary policy and the monetary theory of value.[24] Because knowledge is always incomplete, not just in practice but in principle, in Keynes's view, inter-temporal constraints are not locked away in the fundamentals but must also incorporate the use of conventions as solutions to the problem of the conduct of rational action in the face of incompletable knowledge. While there are other conventions, liquidity and the conventions associated with monetary institutions received particular attention from Keynes. He broke from the quantity theory of money to study the demand and supply of liquidity; that is, he studied the value-theoretic outcomes of the conventional beliefs on which his monetary equilibria rest.

NOTES

* We are grateful for comments from Paul Dalziel, Charles Goodhart, Penny Neal, John Whittaker and colleagues of the Department of Economics at Carleton, Deakin, Macquarie and Adelaide, and the Post Keynesian monetary workshop held at University College London. Professor Rymes records his special indebtedness to Dr Jack Galbraith. We would like in particular to thank Geoff Harcourt for his comments on earlier drafts of this chapter. The usual disclaimer applies.

1 The concept of liquidity has been extensively dealt with by Hahn (1973), Lewis (1990) and Lucas (1990), but each adopts a perspective different from that adopted here.

2 Townshend (1937) was one of the few to notice that Keynes's analysis required the rejection of orthodox value theory, based as it is on the assumptions of given preferences, endowments and complete, if costly, stochastic knowledge. In Keynes's monetary economy all inter-temporal prices are functions as well of liquidity preference. See also Boulding (1944); Chick (1987); Wray (1991).

3 Hall's (1982) contribution to the BFH system need not detain us. He proposes to separate the medium of exchange and the unit of account functions of money. Although this idea is championed by Greenfield and Yeager, among others, the scheme ignores some fundamental properties of monetary systems. See Niehans (1978); McCallum (1985).

4 The central point to remember is that money is always an inessential addition to a general equilibrium model based on a Walrasian auction (Hahn 1965, 1984). What this means is that 'money' can always be added to the model but the conclusions which result from the model are isomorphic with the results of the real Walrasian general equilibrium system of perfect barter. The inessential nature of money should therefore be distinguished from the concept of the neutrality of money. Many examples of the neutrality of money are presented in the context of Walrasian general equilibrium systems, e.g. Patinkin (1965, 1989), but these demonstrations are worthless guides to the neutrality or otherwise of money in a monetary economy. Conclusions derived on the basis of models to which money is an inessential addition are exercises in pure logic only. This conclusion applies with particular force to Fama (1980), Black (1970) and Wallace (1983).

5 When discussing BFH, Wärneryd (1990: 265) notes that: 'It is apparent from the context that it [BFH] is meant seriously as a statement about reality – not just about Walrasian general equilibrium (Hahn 1965) models.'

6 Friedman's (1992: 4–5) quotation from William Henry Furness III, *The Island of Stone Money* (London, 1910), is most apt: '[A] noteworthy feature of this stone currency . . . is that it is not necessary for its owner to reduce it to possession. After concluding a bargain which involves the price of *fei* too large to be conveniently moved, its new owner is quite content to accept the bare acknowledgement of ownership and without so much as a mark to indicate the exchange, the coin remains undisturbed on the former owner's premises.'

7 As pointed out above, Black's characterization of a world without money as a world in which a physical medium of exchange does not exist is far too simplistic. Leyland Yeager (1989) seems to realize this point when he omits the term 'cashless' from his discussion and acknowledges that cash and what he calls 'liquid assets' may exist in the BFH system.

8 The relationships are derived from the standard problem of

$$\max{}_c W = \int_0^\infty U(c_t)e^{-pt}dt$$

subject to

$$q(k,m) - \delta\,k - \delta_m m - (n + n')\,k - (n+n')\,m + (i - p)\,m \pm x - \dot{k} - \dot{m} = c$$

where all variables are measured in terms of Harrod agents and where $\pm x$ are the lump sum taxes-transfers *said* to be available to the monetary authority, with initial conditions on k and the nominal stock of fiat money, and the transversality conditions.

9 Keynes's (1923) discussion about how developments in spot foreign exchange markets affected German expectations of net domestic inflation rates and demand for 'real' Marks is a classic study of how 'real' money balances are affected by expected rates of inflation. Though Keynes discussed the maximum inflation tax rate the authorities should follow, he did not set out the welfare loss under the Marshallian demand curve for 'real' balances associated with the inflation tax, though it is implicit in the discussion in his *Tract*.

10 For a review of the Sraffa–Hayek exchange within the context of Keynes's Chapter 17, see Lawlor (1994b) and Rogers (1994).

11 If we interpret the steady state as Marshall's long period then the manner in which Keynes set out the own-rates in Chapter 17 adds force to the argument that there he was setting out his *General Theory* in the Marshallian market, short- and long-period frameworks of analysis.

12 By 'given', Keynes (*G.T.*: 245) meant that he was not, in the context of *The General Theory*, considering the consequences of changes in variables treated as 'given'; that is, 'given' does not mean fixed.

13 Though circulating currency is still a liability of the central bank, its extent is determined entirely by demand. A system of overdrafts and deposits, which reflects the divergent uses by individuals of the inter-temporal transaction services provided by banks, and a system of positive and negative settlement balances of banks with the central bank, which reflects the divergent uses by banks (and individuals indirectly) of the inter-temporal transaction services provided by the central bank, reflects essentially what exists in Canada today (Bank of Canada 1991). A stock of money in the traditional sense is not to be found.

14 We note that this is a cashless system different from the one imagined by BFH.

15 For a recent discussion of the role of the central bank in providing liquidity, see Goodhart (1993).

16 For an account of Keynes's liquidity premium as not capable of being priced, see Cowen and Kroszner (1994).

17 Private arrangements must have always something exogenous, something like gold, for the determination of aggregate nominal magnitudes. 'Outside' constructions are, however, inefficient, e.g. earn no interest, and will come to be supplanted. Public-choice theory seems to suggest that central banks might inflate, which make the efficiency comparisons problematical: a subject for another paper.

18 We are indebted to Melody Abbott for this reference.

19 See UN (1993) for this standard interpretation of the 'pricing' of banking services.

20 Some attribute spreads to default risks (see Goldschlager and Baxter 1994) but insurable risks should be 'priced' by the service charges.

21 Some authors have treated the introduction of money into the neoclassical optimum non-monetary growth model as a form of technical progress (Purvis 1971). It is, however, not 'money' but the provision of liquidity which enhances

technological progress, not in the Solovian but in the more basic Harrodian sense (Cas and Rymes 1991).

22 Keynes does not in the *Treatise on Money* use the 'real balance effect' in Patinkin's sense of being one of the determinants of the level of real output, since Keynes's basic question there was the determination of the level of prices.

23 Despite the obvious difficulties of interpreting an interpreter, we consider this to be a correct paraphrase of Patinkin's interpretation of Keynes (Patinkin 1965, 1989: Intro.). Yet while it is clear that Patinkin pays full cognisance to Keynes's position that perfectly flexible money wages and prices might not take the economic system out of Keynesian unemployment equilibria via 'real' balance effects, he does not integrate that admission into the synthesis of monetary and value theory for which he is renowned.

24 Even in interpretations of Marshall, we find the contradiction that, in Cambridge monetary economics, theory should and can be separated from policy. In setting out Marshall's monetary theory, Laidler (1990a: 61–2) writes: 'That it has been possible to get so far without mentioning the policy concerns of his own day is surely in and of itself convincing evidence that, in Marshall's hands, monetary economics took on the characteristics of a mature branch of economic science'; and then, admitting Marshall's interest in policy, none the less goes on to say that Marshall's 'supply and demand theory of the price level undermined, once and for all, the powerful idea that, in the long run, a commodity based currency would provide the means of determining the price level independently of the human arrangements involved in the operations of the monetary system' (71).

19

THE GENERAL THEORY

Existence of a monetary long-period
unemployment equilibrium*

Colin Rogers

The theory of interest is, I think, the central point in his scheme. He
departs from old orthodoxy in holding that *the failure of the system to move
to a position of full activity is not primarily due to friction, rigidity, immobility or to
phenomena essentially connected with the trade cycle.* If a certain level of interest
is established, which is inconsistent with full employment, no flexibility
or mobility in the other parts of the system will get the system to move
to full activity.

(Harrod 1947: 69–70; emphasis added)[1]

INTRODUCTION

The quotation from Harrod is a perceptive and accurate summary of *The
General Theory*.[2] Two issues are highlighted by this summary: (a) *The General
Theory* is not primarily concerned with issues of the trade cycle but rather
with the persistence and durability of unemployment; and (b) the behaviour
of the rate of interest is a fundamental cause of that unemployment.[3] The
two elements are interdependent, but this chapter deals largely with the
question of unemployment equilibrium. In *The General Theory* (*G.T.*: 249–50)
Keynes was attempting to provide a theoretical explanation for the fact that
the economy seemed to be 'capable of remaining in a chronic condition of
sub-normal activity for a considerable period without any marked tendency
either towards recovery or towards complete collapse . . . an intermediate
situation which is neither desperate nor satisfactory is our normal lot'. It is
argued in this chapter that the relevant theoretical equilibrium concept for
an analysis of such a situation is that of Marshallian *long-period* equilibrium.

By contrast, the dominant interpretation of *The General Theory*, an assessment on which the vast majority agrees, is that Keynes failed to demonstrate the existence of an unemployment equilibrium, let alone a long-
period unemployment equilibrium. Keynes, it is usually asserted, restricted
his theoretical analysis to short-period equilibrium or disequilibrium adjust-

ment (Asimakopulos 1989; Milgate 1987: 42). On this view unemployment is a *transitory* disequilibrium dynamic phenomenon. This view is embraced by the majority of Keynesians and it may be one of the few issues on which most Keynesian schools agree (Asimakopulos 1989, 1991; Patinkin 1965, 1990). However, as Harrod stresses, *The General Theory* is *not* essentially concerned with issues relating to the trade cycle or short-period equilibrium. Rather, the fundamental theoretical contribution of *The General Theory* is the analysis of what determines the normal level of activity around which business cycle fluctuations occur.[4] The latter is a minority position proposed by Hansson (1985), Rogers (1989) and O'Donnell (1989), and it is this view that is presented in this chapter.

It is my contention that Keynesians of all shades make a fatal strategic error by failing to examine the long-period equilibrium arguments of *The General Theory* because it leaves them unable to offer an effective alternative to the classical vision.[5] In particular, the short-period or disequilibrium interpretation of *The General Theory* makes it impossible to challenge the core theoretical propositions of classical economics such as Say's Law and the quantity theory of money. This point should be obvious, because classical economists have always acknowledged that Say's Law and the quantity theory are long-period equilibrium propositions that need not hold over the business cycle or in short-period equilibrium. Consequently, to present another theory of short-period equilibrium, even a general one, would offer no fundamental challenge to the classical position. Thus, although *The General Theory* does contain a general theory of the business cycle, the more fundamental point is that it is also a theory that explains why the normal level of activity of a *laissez-faire* economy is consistent with unemployment. Unlike Marshall, in Keynes's *General Theory* the normal level of activity may be consistent with unemployment.

The theoretical basis of Keynes's claim to have demonstrated the existence of a long-period unemployment equilibrium must be assessed, first, in the context of what he called 'statical economics'; that is, in the context of the static model of *The General Theory* identified by Kregel (1976). The analysis of long-period unemployment equilibrium is undertaken first in an abstract model as a purely logical exercise. In the hands of a Marshallian analyst, this abstract analysis nevertheless provides an essential insight into the dynamic workings of the real economy. The abstract analysis underlying Keyne's claim to have demonstrated the existence of an unemployment equilibrium has, however, never been widely understood, because it rests on several, until recently, neglected aspects of *The General Theory*; namely: Keynes's use of Marshallian microeconomic foundations and the Marshallian *method of analysis*;[6] (b) the integration of monetary and real (or value) theory;[7] and (c) Keynes's general theory of rational behaviour in the face of irreducible uncertainty. These issues highlight the complexity of the analysis underlying Keynes's position, and that, no doubt, partly explains the difficulty in reaching any consensus on *The General Theory*. The analysis is interdisciplinary and complex in a way that is certainly foreign to later generations of economists who lacked Keynes's Marshallian and philosophical background.[8] However, to understand *The General Theory*, it is necessary to take account of all of these dimensions in a systematic way. As Harcourt (1987a) and O'Donnell (1991a: 3) suggest, to understand Keynes 'the economist' it is necessary to know something about Keynes 'the philosopher'.

This chapter presents the case for Keynes's claim to have demonstrated the existence of a long-period unemployment equilibrium in static analysis by drawing on recent developments in these three areas. In the spirit of the advice provided by O'Donnell (1991), the analysis is based on the multidimensional character of *The General Theory*. Keynes's brand of Marshallian aggregate economics provides a suitable vehicle for reconciling all the elements of Keynes's analysis in a systematic fashion. From the perspective of Keynes's analysis of rational behaviour, his treatment of expectations and uncertainty is compatible with his use of Marshallian statics; in particular, with his logical analysis of the existence of long-period unemployment equilibrium. These issues have troubled many Keynesians who cannot see how the existence of uncertainty (not just risk) can be reconciled with the use of static equilibrium tools.[9] However, as Keynes (*G.T.*: xxiii) put it in the preface to *The General Theory*, the ideas that he expressed so laboriously are extremely simple and should be obvious. The difficulty for many modern Keynesians, to which the past sixty years provides ample testimony, is in escaping from the modern (Walrasian) ideas.

The remainder of the chapter is arranged as follows. The next section outlines Keynes's Marshallian method. The objective is to establish the properties and role of static economics and to consider the relationship between abstraction and realtiy and between statics and dynamics in Marshallian analysis. Keynes's treatment of rational behaviour and the role of conventions or rules of thumb in facilitating rational decision-making in a world characterized by irreducible uncertainty is dealt with on pp. 330–4. These ideas are crucial to an understanding of liquidity preference theory. A statement is presented in the subsequent section of the static model of *The General Theory*. The objective is to highlight the implications of Keynes's liquidity preference theory of the rate of interest. It is shown that the liquidity preference theory is a necessary element in the operation of the principle of effective demand; and the principle of effective demand replaces Say's Law as the determinant of employment and output in a monetary economy.

KEYNES'S MARSHALLIAN METHOD

It is now generally acknowledged that Keynes was a Marshallian and not a Walrasian general equilibrium theorist. As numerous commentators have suggested, Keynes into Walrasian general equilibrium theory will not go.[10] Thus, although Keynes proposed an aggregate general equilibrium scheme, his analysis is not Walrasian: it is an extension of Marshall's method to analyse the behaviour of economic aggregates. Marshallian analysis has both static and dynamic dimensions. Moreover, as Marshall (1920: 304, n.2) explained, statics is part of dynamics and the static analysis should precede the dynamics. For Marshall, and Keynes, it was necessary to proceed by isolating issues one at a time before attempting to examine their interaction. The method has been discussed extensively by Kregel (1976) and Hoover (1988).

Kregel (1976) explains how the static model is just one element of the analytical structure presented in *The General Theory*. It is nevertheless a central element in the message of *The General Theory*, for it is in the context of the static model that the implications of Keynes's general theory of rational choice and the integration of monetary and value theory are most obvious and most easily contrasted with classical static analysis. Friedman, as an exponent of the Marshallian method, argues, quite rightly in my view, that it is false to characterize Marshallian economics as dealing only with partial equilibrium (Hoover 1988: 218–20). Friedman suggests that Walras and Marshall conceived of economic theory differently, and from the Marshallian perspective Walrasian general equilibrium theory cannot be applied as a tool because its practical application requires too-comprehensive a specification to produce a manageable analysis. Hoover describes this view as the 'Cournot problem'.[11]

The static model of *The General Theory* represents one step in Keynes's Marshallian response to the Cournot problem. As such it is the statement of Keynes's analysis that is most easily compared with static classical theory. It also provides a simple illustration of Keynes's claim to have produced a general theory in the context of which the classical results emerge as special cases (Rogers 1989). The debate is a theoretical one in which the models are compared at the same level of abstraction in the context of what Keynes called 'statical equilibrium economics'.

As Park (1994: 249) reminds us, Marshall's analytical scheme consists of four periods: the market period, the short period, the long period, and secular changes in normal values. The short and long periods deal with the determination of normal prices in periods of time extending from a few months to a year (short period) to several years (long period). The study of secular changes deals with changes in normal values that extend over very many years (Marshall 1920: 314–15). Furthermore, the study of normal prices in the first three periods is the domain of statical analysis. Statical analysis is, in turn, an element of and an aid to dynamic analysis.

Marshall explains these issues in the following terms. Starting with the statical method and the role of the *ceteris paribus* clause:

The element of time is a chief cause of those difficulties in economic investigations that make it necessary for man [sic] with his limited powers to go step by step; breaking up a complex question, studying one bit at a time, at last combining his partial solutions into a more or less complete solution of the whole riddle. In breaking it up he segregates those disturbing causes, whose wanderings happen to be inconvenient, for the time in a pound called Caeteris Paribus . . . the existence of other tendencies is not denied, but their disturbing effect is neglected for a time. The more the issue is thus narrowed, the more exactly it can be handled; but also the less closely does it correspond to real life. Each exact and firm handling of a narrow issue, however, helps towards treating broader issues, in which the narrow issue is contained, more exactly than would otherwise have been possible . . .

In a stationary state all the conditions of production and consumption are at rest; *but less violent assumptions are made by what is, not quite accurately, called the statical method.* By that method we fix our minds on some central point: we suppose it for the time to be reduced to a stationary state; we then study . . . the forces that affect things by which it is surrounded, and any tendency there may be to equilibrium of these forces.

Marshall (1920: 304, 306; emphasis added)

In the *Principles*, Marshall goes on to defend the statical equilibrim method against the charge that the real world is continually in a state of flux so the use of equilibrium concepts, particularly long-period equilibrium, is a futile exercise:

But an answer may be given here to the objection that since 'the economic world is subject to continual changes, and is becoming more complex . . . the longer the run the more hopeless the rectification' [correspondence between theory and reality]; so to speak of that position which value tends to reach in the long run is to treat 'variables as constants' (Devas, *Political Economy*, Book VI. Ch. v). It is true we do treat variables provisionally as constants. But it is also true that *this is the only method by which science has ever made any great progress in dealing with complex and changeful matter, whether in the physical or moral world.*

(Marshall 1920: 315, n.1; emphasis added)

Keynes was steeped in this Marshallian method and he applied and extended it in *The General Theory*. He differed fundamentally from Marshall on the treatment of monetary theory and on the theory of the rate of interest in particular. But he retained the Marshallian analytical method:

The object of our analysis is . . . to provide ourselves with an organised and orderly method of thinking out particular problems; and, *after we have reached a provisional conclusion by isolating the complicating factors one by one, we have then to go back on ourselves and allow, as well as we can, for the probable interaction of the factors among themselves.*

(*G.T.*: 297; emphasis added)

Seen from this perspective, the role of the static model of *The General Theory* falls into place. The statical model is a provisional, but essential, first step in the analysis of an extremely complex phenomenon. Keynes's treatment of money-wages as constant for the first eighteen chapters of *The General Theory* and his description of long-period equilibrium are illustrations of the Marshallian method at work:

If we suppose a state of expectation to continue for a sufficient length of time for the effect on employment to have worked itself out so completely that there is , , , no piece of employment going on which would not have taken place if the new state of expectation had always existed, the steady level of employment thus attained may be called the long-period employment corresponding to that state of expectation. It follows that, although expectation may change so frequently that the actual level of employment has never had time to reach the long-period employment corresponding to the existing state of expectation, nevertheless, every state of expectation has its definite corresponding level of long-period employment.

(*G.T.*: 48)

It should be stressed that both Marshall and Keynes highlight the importance of the statical method *because* of the complexity of actual events and not because they believe that the real world is stationary. Marshall explicitly states that long-period equilibrium in static analysis is not the same thing as a real-world stationary state. In addition, they both acknowledge that the data are likely to change, but nowhere propose that recognition of this fact suggests that the static equilibrium analysis should be abandoned; quite the contrary. Thus when Keynes (*C.W.* XXIX: 222) states that: 'I should, I think, be prepared to argue, that, in a world ruled by uncertainty with an uncertain future linked to an actual present, a final position, such as one deals with in static economics, does not properly exist', he is simply restating the obvious to any Marshallian-trained economist. He is not suggesting that the statical equilibrium method should be abandoned.

If anything, what Marshall and Keynes *do* suggest is that static equilibrium analysis is an essential prerequisite for dynamic analysis. The dynamic analysis of Chapter 19, which follows the static analysis of the first eighteen chapters in *The General Theory*, is an illustration of the Marshallian method at work. Those Keynesians concerned with the dynamic and indeterminate aspects of *The General Theory* would do well to heed this point.[12] In particular Harcourt and Sardoni (1994: 137–41) stress that, for Keynes, abstract models dealt with demonstrative certainty and that, once a model had been chosen, its construction and development was to be carried out in complete separation from reality, in a purely logical context. Reality enters the picture because Keynes's models are open in the sense that they cannot usefully be applied without some historical input. For this, some 'safe generalisations from experience' are required and demonstrative certainty gives way to probability relations (ibid: 139). These two dimensions to Keynes's analysis are distinct, and confusion results if they are conflated. This chapter deals with the abstract statical model in a purely logical context because it is in this context that Keynes proposes to demonstrate the existence of a long-period unemployment equilibrium.

RATIONAL BEHAVIOUR, UNCERTAINTY AND LIQUIDITY PREFERENCE

Much work has now been done to uncover the relationship between Keynes's earlier work on probablity and his treatment of expectations in *The General Theory*. The *tour de force* in this area is undoubtedly O'Donnell's (1989) comprehensive study of Keynes's economics, politics and philosophy.[13] Of particular significance for this chapter is the realization that Keynes developed and applied a general theory of rational behaviour in a world characterized by the entire spectrum of risk and irreducible uncertainty. In such a world, agents are inevitably forced to make decisions in situations where they simply have no way of independently establishing the objective nature of the situation. Agents must still form expectations when the route via mathematical expectation is not available. Thus, as O'Donnell puts it:

> expectation is the key concept in the GT, not probability. Keynes's approach to behaviour under uncertainty was expectational, but neither purely probabilistic nor purely non-probabilistic. He accepted probabilities when they were available, and irreducible uncertainty when they were not; and even when probabilities were available there was little guarantee of their numericality. (O'Donnell 1989: 265)

Faced with irreducible uncertainty, agents form expectations and they do this by relying on rules of thumb or conventions. As Keynes (C.W. XIV: 214, quoted by Carabelli 1988: 224) explained it: 'We tend, therefore, to substitute for the knowledge which is unattainable certain conventions . . . This is how we act in practice.' Behaviour in terms of conventions is rational; it is only in the absence of knowledge *and* conventions that behaviour depends on whim or 'animal spirits'. Only when reason has reached its limit is it rational to resort to such a-rational action[14]. O'Donnell (1990a: 256–7) explains the situation as follows:

indeterminacy does not entail irrationality. That is, the defeat of strong rationality does not imply the defeat of all forms of rationality; agents do not lose their capacity for rationality just because they are deprived of the preconditions necessary for the successful performance of strong rationality. They will adapt to the new circumstances and develop different strategies and responses. Such strategies I collectively group under the heading of weak rationality. Examples include the acceptance of social conventions, customs, moral duties and rules of thumb, the following of better informed opinion and even allowing arbitrary procedures such as pure caprice to coin tossing to decide issues.

The existence of irreducible uncertainty does not therefore imply that Keynes's analysis is necessarily indeterminate (Hansson 1985; Rogers 1989; Rotheim 1993). The role of conventions and stable long-term expectations, and hence weakly rational beliefs about the normal rate of interest, play a central role in Keynes's static presentation of liquidity preference theory.

A comprehensive assessment of the relationship between Keynes's notion of uncertainty and his concept of liquidity preference has been made by Runde (1994a). Applying what he calls Keynes's two-tier theory of rational belief, Runde identifies two dimensions to liquidity preference. Keynes's theory of belief has *probability*, a measure of the belief in some conclusion given a body of evidence, as the first level, and *weight*, a measure of the completeness of the evidence on which the belief is to be based, as the second level.[15] This distinction is important for isolating an important dimension of liquidity preference theory often neglected in the literature. Liquidity preference theory embodies both tiers of rational belief but, as Runde (1994a) explains, both the Tobin (1958) and Subjective Expected Utility (SEU) approaches deal only with the probability elements of liquidity preference and thereby preclude the investor from learning anything not imagined when the initial choice was made and which would necessitate a portfolio adjustment. In other words, those elements of liquidity preference influenced by the weight or reliability of evidence, and which are concerned with the ability to dissolve a position without loss, are excluded by the probabilistic approach to liquidity preference theory. Similarly, Runde (1994a) also points out that treating uncertainty as the polar opposite of risk excludes some elements of liquidity preference and Keynes's theory of rational behaviour. If risk is defined as a stituation in which probabilities are known and uncertainty as an amorphous state where probabilities cannot be determined, then Keynes's concept of weight is usually (but unnecessarily) excluded and, along with it, an important element of liquidity preference theory.

How do agents act when they know they don't know but believe that more information will be available if they wait? Keynes's more general theory of rational behaviour can deal with this situation and, as Runde (1994a: 140) indicates, general liquidity preference theory can be formalized, contrary to the extreme claims made by some Keynesians. That is to say, the existence of uncertainty does not imply that equilibrium theory should be abandoned (Lawson 1985a; Hansson 1985; Rogers 1989; Rotheim 1993). In the context of the static model, the existence of conventions plays a role in increasing the weight in support of individuals' beliefs about monetary policy in general and the normal rate of interest in particular. But, of course, weight is never absolute, and Keynes's notion of long-period equilibrium does not imply a real-world stationary state.

Darity and Horn (1993) provide a recent assessment of the role of conventions in *The General Theory* from the perspective that the adoption of conventions makes coping with uncertainty tractable (see also, Harcourt 1987a; Littleboy 1990; Lawson 1993). How particular conventions arise and persist in particular historical situations is a complex matter which need not detain us here. Analysis of the formation of conventions can, however, be given a formal treatment along game-theoretic lines. For example, Wärneryd (1990) applies this approach to show how a common medium of exchange evolves as an equilibrium solution to a non-co-operative game. Mutual self-interest leads to the use of a common medium of exchange because it is in everyone's self-interest to quote prices and accept payment in this medium of exchange so long as virtually everyone else does the same. Individuals have a strong incentive to accept the convention once it is established and, once established, the convention cannot be displaced by unilateral action. In this sense money acquires the characteristics of a convention that reduces the uncertainty surrounding multilateral and inter-temporal trade. A monetary economy is, by definiton, an economy characterized by irreducible uncertainty and, as such, an analysis of conventions is required to make sense of rational behaviour. In other words, the analysis of conventions should be an essential element of monetary theory. Keynes's treatment of the concept of the normal rate of interest should be interpreted from this perspective: as an existing convention as to what constitutes the safe rate of interest.

The point to be made here is that the existence of conventions in financial markets in general, and that relating to the normal rate of interest in particular, is an essential element of Keynes's analytical scheme. As Darity and Horn (1993: 33) stress, Keynes was not commited to any particular set of conventions. However, the existence of some conventions is essential to Keynes's analysis (Lawlor 1994b). Furthermore, the existence and persistence of conventions is both a source of stability and a potential cause of instability.

Conventions impart stability when they are durable. In particular, durable conventions provide the anchor in terms of which inelastic expectations (in the Hicksian sense) play a stabilizing role (Rogers 1989, Rappaport 1992). However, because conventions are just conventions they may not be durable. The source of stability then becomes a cause of instability when the convention collapses (Harcourt 1987a; Rogers 1989, 1990; Darity and Horn 1993: 34). Thus, when conventions collapse the outcome may, in principle, be totally unpredictable. Shackle (1974) aptly described this idea under the heading of *Keynesian Kaleidics*. Nevertheless, as O'Donnell (1989: 257) stresses, conventions are generally not in a state of perpetual and unpredictable agitation. If they were, economic theory would be impossible. As Keynes (*G.T.*: 162) puts it: 'We should not conclude from this that everything depends on waves of irrational psychology. On the contrary, the state of long-term expectation is often steady'. Furthermore, governments and monetary authorities have a role to play in generating and maintaining conventions and in facilitating the transition from one convention to another when that is deemed necessary (*G.T.*: 204; Rogers 1989; Darity and Horn 1993).

A crucial theoretical innovation introduced by Keynes was the concept of the normal rate of interest as an existing convention. The introduction of the concept of the normal rate of interest and the given state of long-term expectations was Keynes's response to his rejection of the natural rate of interest of classical theory. In addition, the existence of a convention as to the normal rate of interest meant that the normal rate of interest could be treated as part of the data (one of the independent variables) in the static model. This led to the well-known charge by Robertson (1966), Hicks (1939) and Garegnani (1978) that Keynes leaves an essential element of his theory unexplained. If by 'unexplained' it is meant that the rate of interest is not an endogenous variable in the static model, then the charge is true but misses the point. As explained above, a central theoretical claim of *The General Theory* is that the rate of interest cannot be determined as an endogenous variable in the classical manner, that is, by the market forces of productivity and thrift. Recognition of this fact provided the motivation for Keynes's replacement of the classical theory of the natural rate of interest with the *explanation* of the normal rate of interest as a conventional phenomenon.[16] It is Keynes's contention that to explain the rate of interest it is necessary to know something about the existing conventions in financial markets and the standing of the monetary authority in the eyes of the public. It is from this perspective that we should interpret Keynes's (*G.T.*: 204) remarks to the effect that:

> It might be more accurate, perhaps, to say that the rate of interest is a highly conventional, rather than a highly psychological, phenomenon. For, its actual value is largely governed by the prevailing view as to what its value is expected to be. Any level of interest which is accepted with sufficient conviction as likely to be durable will be durable; subject, of

course, in a changing society to fluctuations for all kinds of reasons round the expected normal.

KEYNES'S LOGICAL ANALYSIS OF LONG-PERIOD UNEMPLOYMENT EQUILIBRIUM

Following the Marshallian method, Keynes attempts to isolate the important factors and examine them in isolation in a static context, as a logical exercise, before allowing for their interaction in his dynamic analysis. An essential first step in this endeavour is to set up a static equilibrium model with a number of 'variables treated as constants' so as to examine the *existence* and nature of equilibrium. In conducting this exercise Keynes is effectively asking the questions: under what conditions will equilibrium exist? and will that equilibrium necessarily imply full employment of labour? In the Marshallian tradition, use of the unqualified term 'equilibrium' in Keynes's static, purely logical, analysis means long-period equilibrium. This does not preclude an analysis of short-period equilibrium but such an exercise is not central to Keynes's message. For that the logical exercise in the context of the static model is an essential first step in demonstrating how the principle of effective demand replaces Say's Law.

One of the central theoretical innovations in Keynes's monetary economy is the absence of a market in which the forces of productivity and thrift determine the natural rate of interest, as claimed, for example, by Wicksell and Robertson (Kregel 1983a; Rogers 1989). In other words, the classical capital market is abandoned by Keynes in *The General Theory* and consequently there is no unique natural or real rate of interest consistent with full employment that acts as a natural attractor for the money rate of interest in a *laissez-faire* financial system. The money rate of interest, as determined by other forces, may then determine long-period equilibrium with unemployment. The liquidity preference theory of the rate of interest provides the framework within which these forces may be analysed and is therefore central to Keynes's principle of effective demand.[17]

The principle of effective demand is usually presented in the literature as the idea that it is changes in income rather than prices and interest rates that bring about equilibrium in Keynes's system (Amadeo 1989: 1). This is correct as far as it goes but it does not go far enough: it begs the central question of what determines the equilibrium position. That is, what determines the point of effective demand? In other words, stating the principle of effective demand in terms of income adjustment is incomplete because it begs the question on existence.[18]

A more general statement of the principle of effective demand, to be contrasted with Say's Law, is something like the following. In a *laissez-faire* economy, the 'normal' money rate of interest may place a limit on the profitable production of capital goods before full employment of labour has been achieved, even in the long run. By contrast, Say's Law, the idea that supply creates its own demand, implies that there is no limit to the profitable production of capital goods until full employment has been achieved in the long run (Chick 1983). For Say's Law to hold there must then be some mechanism that adjusts the money rate of interest to the optimum level where the optimal level is the level of the rate of interest which generates the investment necessary to ensure full employment, even if the marginal propensity to consume is less than one.[19] The classical or loanable funds theory provides such a mechanism, with the natural rate of interest generated by the forces of productivity and thrift (saving and investment) in a capital market acting as an automatic attractor for the money rate of interest in long-period equilibrium.

This central role played by the rate of interest explains the importance of Keynes's rejection of the classical theory of interest. For example, in the preparation of *The General Theory* he identified the classical theory of the rate of interest as a 'fatal flaw' in the classical scheme:

> There is, I am convinced, a fatal flaw in that part of orthodox reasoning which deals with the theory of what determines the level of effective demand and the volume of aggregate employment; that flaw being largely due to the failure of the classical doctrine to develop a satisfactory theory of the rate of interest.
>
> (*C.W.* XIII: 489)

While in *The General Theory* Keynes makes numerous references to the key role of the rate of interest, he also explicitly rejects the Wicksellian concept of a unique natural rate:

> In my *Treatise on Money* I defined what purported to be a unique rate of interest which I labelled the natural rate of interest . . . I had, however, overlooked the fact that in any given society there is, on this definition, a different natural rate of interest for each hypothetical level of employment. And, similarly, for every rate of interest there is a level of employment for which that rate is the 'natural' rate, in the sense that the system will be in equilibrium with that rate of interest and that level of employment.
>
> (*G.T.*: 242)

As stressed above, this point is particularly significant because failure of the concept of the natural rate of interest is a necessary condition for the refutation of Say's Law. Introduction of liquidity preference theory allows a dominant role for the money rate of interest and a reversal of classical causality between the money and natural rates of interest (Kregel 1983a; Rogers 1989). Classical theory then appears as a special case. Liquidity preference theory is therefore an essential element of the principle of effective demand. Replacing the loanable funds theory with the liquidity preference theory allows the general principle of effective demand (outlined above, pp. 334–5) to replace Say's Law as the determinant of the volume of aggregate employment in a monetary economy. Also, the analysis ceases to be real and becomes monetary (Rogers 1989). As Harrod (1947: 69–70) put it: 'given the complex of forces affecting liquidity preference, such and such is the rate of interest that will naturally and . . . permanently obtain. Yet that rate of interest may be inconsistent with the full activity of the system.'

Having established these points, the Marshallian method – the provisional treatment of 'variables as constants' – can be applied to present the static model of *The General Theory*. Darity and Horn (1993: 33) summarize the method as follows:

> The state of long-term expectation at a particular moment is determined by the conventions that prevail at that moment. This means that Kregel's (1976) strategy of treating long-term expectation as given in a comparative statics context is eminently legitimate – given by the convention, that is.

The central points made by Keynes can be illustrated in a static context using the aggregate demand and supply framework suggested in *The General Theory* and adapted from the version developed by Dillard (1948) and Davidson (1978, 1994), among others. The version presented here differs from the usual statement of the model in that it deals with long-period equilibrium (see Figure 19.1). The two curves are drawn in nominal income–employment space.[20] The Z curve represents long-period aggregate supply and the D curve long-period aggregate demand, given the state of long-term expectation, the money-wage and the normal rate of interest. Aggregate demand, in a closed *laissez-faire* economy, consists of two main components: consumption and investment. The slope of the D curve reflects the fact that for stability the D curve must cut the Z curve from above. As interpreted in this chapter, the Z curve is an aggregate long-period supply curve in the sense that it records the nominal returns which produce, in aggregate, only normal profits for entrepreneurs. Each point on the Z curve is associated with a different capital stock. Following the Marshallian method, the two curves are held in place by treating some variables as constants, and I draw particular attention to the money-wage and the state of long-term expectations.

In addition, the marginal efficiency of capital, the propensity to consume and the capital stock are treated as given when examining the existence of equilibrium in the static analysis. In this regard a common misperception of *The General Theory* is that as Keynes treats the capital stock as given he is by definition dealing *only* with the short-period equilibrium. Two points of clarification are offered here. First, from the perspective of the existence of long-period equilibrium it must be the case that the capital stock has

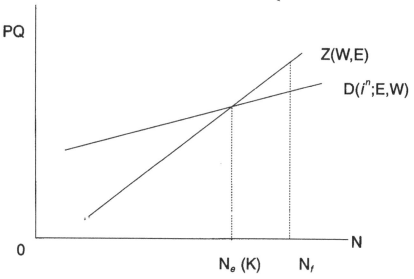

Figure 19.1 Keynes's long-period unemployment equilibrium

adjusted itself to the point of effective demand. As Hansson (1985: 334) explains, Keynes's notion of long-period equilibrium is 'based on the fact that every piece of existing capital equipment is the result of previous long term expectations which have actually been fulfilled'. The long-period employment position described by Keynes (*G.T.*: 48) therefore refers to a situation where the system, including the capital stock, has adjusted to the point of effective demand and such a position is consistent with his description that 'the existing quality and quantity of available equipment' is given (*G.T.*: 245). In all Marshallian long-period equilibria the capital stock is always given in this sense. Technological progress may well disturb long-period equilibrium but consideration of that possibility belongs to the realm of Marshall's fourth 'period' – the analysis of secular changes. Perhaps confusion has arisen because a long-period equilibrium is always a short-period equilibrium but the converse is not true. Second, it is then not the case in Keynes's system that the capital stock can be treated as an exogenous variable in the modern sense of the term. If anything, the capital stock is endogenous in Keynes's system as it responds to the forces which determine the point of effective demand.

Of particular significance is the fact that the point of effective demand determines a level of employment beyond which it is not profitable to expand aggregate production of capital goods because demand prices fall below long-period supply prices. That is, losses will be incurred in the production of capital goods if an attempt is made to increase employment beyond N_e. *Ceteris paribus*, any attempt to expand output beyond the point of effective demand will involve capital goods producers in losses as demand prices fall below long-period supply prices. All this is explained by Keynes's general theory of asset demand in Chapter 17 of *The General Theory* (Kregel 1983a; Rogers 1989; Lawlor 1994b)). Clearly, in this situation, Say's Law is broken because supply does not create its own demand, because attempts to increase supply beyond the point of effective demand would, *ceteris paribus*, involve losses for capital goods producers.

The essence of the principle of effective demand is, of course, that the point of effective demand need not coincide with the full employment of labour. This can happen because the forces of productivity and thrift do not determine the normal rate of interest. As illustrated in Figure 19.1, the forces of the system have established a long-period equilibrium in which capital goods producers in aggregate earn normal profits but in which unemployment exists and will persist, *ceteris paribus*, for as long as the normal rate of interest, in particular, remains unchanged. In the absence of 'the' natural rate of interest some explanation of the normal rate of interest is required. The essence of liquidity preference theory in the static model is the role played by the conventions that establish a durable belief in an inappropriate normal rate of interest. As Harrod (1947: 69 70) went on to explain after the quotation presented at the head of this chapter, such a 'normal' rate may be durable, and in a certain sense, in a free system is inevitable. In the absence of a classical capital market, why should the normal rate correspond with the optimum rate except by chance? In Keynes's words:

> But it [the rate of interest] may fluctuate for decades about a level too high for full employment; – particularly if it is the prevailing opinion that the rate of interest is self-adjusting so that the level established by convention is thought to be rooted in objective grounds much stronger than convention, the failure of employment to attain an optimum level being in no way associated, in the minds either of the public or of authority, with the prevalence of an inappropriate range of rates of interest.
>
> (*G.T.*: 204)

This is a central message of *The General Theory*.

It is clear from the above discussion that the existence of a long-period equilibrium in statical economics rests on the assumption of given long-term expectations, E, and money-wages, W, in particular. But it should also be clear that this does not mean that these are the cause of unemployment in Keynes's scheme. In Keynes's static model these variables must be treated as given to isolate any equilibrium position, be it a full-employment or an unemployment equilibrium. Keynes differs from the classics in his view that a statical model of a *laissez-faire* economy may produce multiple long-period equilibria (in the sense that the D and Z curves need not automatically intersect at full employment) once it is realized that the concept of automatic adjustment to the unique natural (or optimum) rate of interest consistent with full employment is untenable, even in the long run. When the unique and optimal natural rate falls away, the point of effective demand may be consistent with long-period equilibrium at less than full employment. The static model of *The General Theory* was intended to make this simple but fundamental theoretical point.

The static analysis also suggests that sticky money-wages and inelastic expectations play a role in stabilizing the economy. The question of money-wage flexibility belongs to dynamics in Keynes's scheme, and, following the Marshallian method, questions relating to the dynamic behaviour of the system are to be examined only when the static model had been set up. The discussion of money-wage cuts in Chapter 19 is a clear example of this method where dynamic issues raised by the flexibility of money-wages are addressed from the perspective of the impact that these changes have on the point of effective demand derived in the static analysis. The well-known conclusion is that sticky wages contribute to the stability of the system. But consideration of these dynamic issues is possible only after the principle of effective demand has been isolated as a logical exercise in the context of Keynes's static model. The same is true of the analysis of changing expectations and the stabilizing role of inelastic expectations (Rappaport 1992). The question of the stability or persistence of the long-period equilibrium is, however, beyond the scope of this chapter.

CONCLUDING REMARKS

This chapter attempts to isolate the essential message of *The General Theory* in the belief that the message is, as Keynes suggested, relatively straightforward. Simply put it is this: there is no way in which the forces of the system in a *laissez-faire* economy ensure that the point of effective demand coincides with the full employment of labour either in the short *or the long period*. Belief in the existence of such forces may leave resources lying idle for decades because of the failure to recognize that the point of effective demand may establish a *long-period* unemployment equilibrium. Both Keynes and Harrod state that the rate of interest plays a central role in producing that result. But that is another story.

NOTES

* I am indebted to Geoff Harcourt and Rod O'Donnell for helpful comments. The usual disclaimer applies.
1 It is well known that Harrod did not accept this revolutionary claim by Keynes. Harrod consistently argued that Keynes was raising too much dust and attempted to persuade him, with some success, to temper his revolutionary claims

(Milgate 1977; Kregel 1981; Panico 1987, 1988a). A continuation of the quotation reveals that Harrod describes the claim as relating to a 'minor flaw' in the classical analysis! An evaluation of this interpretation and Harrod's influence on Keynes is beyond the scope of this chapter but evidently Harrod never accepted the revolutionary claims made in *The General Theory* (Harrod 1947: 70). All that is claimed here is that Harrod provides a correct statement of Keynes's claim. Certainly, Keynes (*C.W.* XII: 552; emphasis added), in his correspondence with Harrod, makes his intentions clear: 'I cannot but think, however, that you would feel rather differently about the chapter if I were able to convince you that *the classical theory of the rate of interest has to be discarded in toto, and is incapable of rehabilitation in any shape or form.*'

2 Michael Lawlor (1994b: 40–2) raises the relevant questions about Harrod's statement but, in my view, ultimately falls into the too narrow short-period perspective of Keynes (Rogers 1994).

3 See also Keynes (*G.T.*: 222). Numerous economists have noted that Keynes identifies an inappropriate rate of interest as the ultimate cause of unemployment. See, for example, Leijonhufvud (1968: 181), and the discussion in Bhattacharjea (1987) who points out that there are numerous references to an interest rate barrier to full employment in *The General Theory* and that Friedman (1972: appendix 1) provides a compilation. However, Friedman (1972: 169), like most other commentators at the time, incorrectly treats these references as descriptions of absolute liquidity preference, that is, as references to the liquidity trap.

4 I am aware that it is no longer fashionable to separate trend and cycle but the distinction seems to be inherent in Keynes's vision.

5 The demise of Keynes's analysis in the context of the neoclassical synthesis is the most obvious example. Gaynor (1992) is another recent example. The importance of a long-period equlibrium analysis is a point that has been made consistently by the so-called neo-Ricardians, Garegnani (1978–9), Eatwell (1983b) and Milgate (1982). However, the perspective adopted here follows the liquidity preference route to the analysis of effective demand sketched by Kregel (1983a). For the distinction between this approach and the neo-Ricardian position, see Garegnani (1983). A recent discussion of the two approaches is presented by Dutt and Amadeo (1990a). The difficulty for the neo-Ricardian position arises from Keynes's general theory of rational behaviour and his analysis of conventions and expectations that does not integrate well with the real Sraffian foundations.

6 Attempting to interpret Keynes from a Walrasian perspective obviously hasn't helped.

7 Townshend (1937) was one of the few to pay any attention to this issue, but see also Boulding (1944); Rotheim (1981); and Wray (1991).

8 Samuelson (1947a: 146) acknowledges that he did not understand *The General Theory* until after he had seen the formal models presented by Meade, Lange, Hicks and Harrod.

9 Examples of this concern are found in the work of Robinson (1974, 1980), Shackle (1974) and Asimakopulos (1991). Seen from a Marshallian perspective the tension between uncertainty and equilibrium in *The General Theory* is resolved. However, Robinson (1980: 226) explicitly rejects the Marshallian method.

10 Patinkin (1965, 1989) has, over the years, made the most valiant attempt to interpret Keynes from a Walrasian perspective. Unfortunately, the Walrasian framework is a special case totally unsuited to dealing with Keynes's treatment

of rational behaviour and the role of money. Hence it is not surprising that the logic of the Walrasian position forces Patinkin to the conclusion that Keynes's claim about the existence of an unemployment equilibrium is unfounded. From a Walrasian perspective unemployment is inevitably a disequilibrium phenomenon.

11 Hoover (1988: 219) quotes Cournot: 'It seems, therefore, as if, for a complete and rigorous solution of the problems relative to some parts of the economic system, it were indispensable to take the entire system into consideration. But this would surpass the powers of mathematical analysis and of our practical methods of calculation, even if the values of all the constants could be assigned to them numerically.' Existence of proofs for the Walrasian general equilibrium system solve the problem in principle for imaginary economies. However, see Kirman (1989). Real business-cycle (RBC) theorists are now attempting a practical solution using computing capability beyond anything Cournot could have imagined. In any event, RBC analysts ignore Hahn's (1980) opinion that Walrasian general equilibrium theory is not descriptive.

12 As noted earlier, Marshall (1920: 304,n.2) considered statics to be a provisional but essential branch of dynamics. Some authors, for example Asimakopulos (1989, 1991), Lim (1990) and Cardim de Carvalho (1990, 1992), argue that Keynes denied the usefulness of long-period positions in *The General Theory* on the grounds that the data will change before long-period equilibrium is attained. As I have argued elsewhere, in the case of Asimakopulos and Carvalho these interpretations offer a flawed version of Marshall's method (Rogers 1990, 1993). These authors argue that the use of short-period equilibrium concepts is acceptable on the grounds that the concept of short-period equilibrium 'corresponds' more closely to the real-world situation in which agents make decisions. However, Marshallian static equilibrium analysis cannot be truncated at short-period equilibrium in this manner. Short-period equilibrium is a logical construct and part of an economic model whose implications must be examined independently of reality. In that context, once short-period equilibrium has been embraced the use of long-period equilibrium cannot be avoided. The debate about the role of long-period equilibrium in *The General Theory* has also been distorted by the view that Sraffa provides a better analytical foundation for *The General Theory* than Marshall (see Bhattacharjea 1987 or Dutt and Amadeo 1990a for a discussion of this issue).

13 Other important contributions have been made in Lawson (1985a, 1993); Carabelli (1988); Bateman and Davis (1991); Gerrard and Hillard (1992); and Darity and Horn (1993), to name a few.

14 O'Donnell (1989: 265) and Darity and Horn (1993) argue convincingly that Keynes's treatment of rational expectations includes the modern concept of the same idea as a special case.

15 The concept of weight is itself capable of further analysis (Runde 1990).

16 Maclachlan (1993a) provides a sensible counter to the view that the solution to a set of simultaneous equations constitutes an 'explanation' or a theory of the rate of interest.

17 Milgate (1977) and Panico (1987, 1988a) demonstrate convincingly that liquidity preference theory is part of the positive element of *The General Theory.*

18 For a more comprehensive discussion of this issue see Rogers (1995).

19 Davidson (1994: 22–8) seems to suggest that a sufficient condition for the failure of Say's Law is a marginal propensity to spend of less than one so that the D and Z curves do not coincide. Keynes (*G.T.*: 25–6) provides the basis for this interpretation. However, the coincindence of the D and Z curves is a

sufficient but *not a necessary condition* for Say's Law. A necessary condition for the validity of Say's Law is the classical or loanable funds theory of the rate of interest. Say's Law holds even when the D and Z curves do not coincide so long as the point of effective demand automatically coincides with full employment in long-period equilibrium. The classical theory of the rate of interest ensures that result. A general attack on Say's Law requires an attack on the necessary condition as well.

20 There is no reason why the curves should be linear. They are drawn so for convenience only.

20

THE CLASSICAL THEORY OF THE RATE OF INTEREST

M.S. Lawlor

A REVISION OF CHAPTER 14 OF *THE GENERAL THEORY*[1]
M.S. Lawlor writing as J.M. Keynes

I

As was noted at the beginning of *The General Theory*, the relationship of this work to the tradition of economics that has dominated the literature since Ricardo is difficult and controversial. The difficulty lies in the struggle to salvage and utilize what is valuable and relevant in that tradition while redirecting our attention to a different problem than has hitherto been the object of economic theory, namely, the determination of the level of output and employment of the economic system as a whole. The controversy is due to the need to delineate sharply the differences from this traditional doctrine that thereby arise in our own theory. A thin line is thus trodden by such an exercise, leaving open the distinct possibility that many readers, ingrained in old habits of thought, find that they fluctuate between a belief that I am quite wrong and a belief that I am saying nothing new. Since the publication of *The General Theory* it has become apparent to me that this is indeed a common reaction. Nowhere is this confusion more evident than in disputes about my doctrine of interest. Thus I have endeavoured in five publications since *The General Theory* (Keynes, 1937a, b, d, 1938c, 1939d) to clarify my message concerning the relationship between interest, investment and money. In what follows I shall attempt to incorporate that debate into this chapter.

What is the Classical Theory of Interest? It is something in which all economists have been trained and which they have accepted without much reserve until the debates over the great slump brought the issue into controversial focus. Yet it is difficult to state it precisely or to find an account of it in the leading texts of the modern classical school. Reaction to the first edition of this book has convinced me, however, that the economics community shares a strong set of largely unexamined preconceptions regarding the theory of interest.[2] These preconceptions, which perhaps can be best summed up as the belief in the fundamentally non-monetary character of the rate of interest, have deep roots in the traditional orthodoxy of our subject, roots which continue to sustain even the most recent crisis-inspired theories of interest. It is for this reason that interest has continued to be discussed in a framework wholly unsuitable for use in a theory of output as a whole. As I shall argue below, the classical framework for interest rate determination involves us in logical error whenever we consider the question of changes in employment. However, as will also be shown, there is still much of value in the superstructure of this traditional theory. With a proper attention to the clearness and generality of the premises of the classical tradition, especially as it applies to the study of the forces which determine changes in the scale of output as a whole, a more general theory of the rate of interest can be constructed.

Despite differences in technique and in questions addressed, a surprisingly strong degree of unanimity has been expressed amongst economists since Ricardo and down to our own time concerning the fundamental framework in which interest is to be considered. This unanimity concerns not the proximate determinants of interest nor the description of the process by which such a rate is brought about. These have been considered to be technical details of changing monetary and financial institutions, not fundamental to the theory. In essence, the classical tradition has regarded the rate of interest as the factor which brings the demand for investment and the willingness to save into equilibrium with one another. Investment represents the demand for investable resources and saving represents the supply, whilst the rate of interest is the 'price' of investable resources at which the two are equated. Just as the price of a commodity is necessarily fixed at that point where the demand for it is equal to the supply, so the rate of interest necessarily comes to rest under the play of market forces at the point where the amount of investment at that rate of interest is equal to the amount of saving at that rate.

Furthermore, and confirming the non-monetary character of this tradition, the interest rate so determined is conceived in the classical tradition as a *real* phenomenon. This is the ground for ignoring the workings of the financial system in constructing such a theory,[3] since whatever the money rate of interest, it will conform in all instances to the rate of return established by the more fundamental forces in the *natural* equilibrium. In its modern form, the foundations of this supply and demand relation (for 'capital', 'waiting' or 'loan funds') are then found in the traditional doctrines of the declining marginal productivity of investment and the marginal disutility of saving.

The above is not to be found in Marshall's *Principles* in so many words. Yet his theory seems to be this, and it is what I myself was brought up on and what I taught for many years to others. As an example the reader is urged to consider the discussion in Book IV, Chaper II, section 4 in the *Principles*. Though that discussion is notably Marshallian in its hedging and qualifications, finally in the last paragraph he states: 'Interest, being the price paid for the use of capital in any market, tends toward an equilibrium level such that the aggregate demand for capital on that market at that rate of interest, is equal to the aggregate stock forthcoming there at that rate.' Other writers of Marshall's generation could be quoted to the same effect, including Professor Cassel (*Nature and Necessity of Interest*), Professor Carver (*Distribution of Wealth*, ch. vi), Sir Alfred Flux (*Economic Principles*, p. 95), Professor Taussig (*Principles*, II 29) and Walras (Appendix I (III) of his *Eléments d'économie pure*).

Taking a longer view, and dispensing with the marginal apparatus, much of the same view can be found in Ricardo, who is adamant about the non-monetary nature of interest. The following from his *Principles of Political Economy* (page 511) puts the substance of Ricardo's theory of the rate of interest:

> The interest of money is not regulated by the rate at which the Bank will lend, whether it be 5, 3 or 2 per cent, but by the rate of profit which can be made by the employment of capital, and which is totally independent of the quantity of or of the value of money. Whether the Bank lent one million, ten millions, or a hundred millions, they would not permanently alter the market rate of interest; they would alter only the value of the money which they thus issued. In one case, ten or twenty times more money might be required to carry on the same business than what might be required in the other. The applications to the Bank for money, then, depend on the comparison between the rate of profits that may be made by the employment of it, and the rate at which they are willing to lend it. If they charge less than the market rate of interest, there is no amount of money which they might not lend; – if they charge more than that rate, none but spendthrifts and prodigals would be found to borrow of them.

There are many methods by which one could contrast this tradition with that which we have just put forward in Book IV. I shall confine myself to the following. First, we may treat the question of 'the' rate of interest from the highly aggregative standpoint of one schedule each for savings and for investment. As this is common ground upon which much of such discussion currently runs, we may in this manner simply convey the logical difficulty the classical doctrine runs up against once the principle of effective demand has been recognized. Second, we move to a more abstract plane which considers the question of interest in its most general and essential form. From this standpoint we can more readily see the fundamental extension I propose for the theory of interest and the degree to which *The General Theory* transcends and subsumes the Euclidian interest rate theory of the classical tradition. We shall then reserve for the last section a consideration of the contemporary disequilibrium 'natural-rate' theories of interest which have so dominated recent discussion.

II

To address the question of the rate of interest within a highly aggregative framework, let us begin with matters on which we are agreed. In Marshall's time it was a given assumption of the Classical School proper that aggregate savings and aggregate investment are necessarily equal. Indeed, most members of the Classical School carried this belief much too far; since they held that every act of increased saving by an individual necessarily brings into existence a corresponding act of increased investment. Nor is there any material difference, relevant in this context, between my schedule of the marginal efficiency of capital or investment-demand schedule and the demand curve for capital contemplated by some of the classical writers referenced above. When we come to the propensity to consume and its corollary, the propensity to save, we are nearer a difference of opinion, owing to the emphasis which they have placed on the influence of the rate of interest on the propensity to save. But they would, presumably, not wish to deny that the level of income also has an important influence on the amount saved; whilst I, for my part, would not deny that the rate of interest may perhaps have an influence on the amount saved *out of a given income*. All these points of agreement can be summed up in a proposition which the Classical School would accept and I should not dispute; namely, that if the level of income is assumed to be given, we can infer that the current rate of interest must lie at the point where the demand curve for capital corresponding to different rates of interest cuts the curve of the amount saved out of the given income corresponding to different rates of interest.

But this is the point at which definite error creeps into the classical theory. If the Classical School merely inferred from the above proposition that, given the demand curve for capital and the influence of changes in the rate of interest on the readiness to save out of given incomes, the level of income and the rate of interest must be uniquely correlated, there would be nothing to quarrel with. Moreover, this proposition would lead naturally to another proposition which embodies an important truth; namely, that if the rate of interest is given as well as the demand curve for capital and the influence of the rate of interest on the readiness to save out of given levels of income, the level of income must be the factor which brings the amount saved to equality with the amount invested. But, in fact, the classical theory does not merely neglect the influence of changes in the level of income, it involves formal error.

For the classical theory, as can be seen from the above, assumes that it can then proceed to consider the effect on the rate of interest of, for example, a shift in the demand curve for capital, without abandoning or modifying its assumption as to the amount of the given income out of which the savings are to be made. The (presumed) independent determinants of the classical theory of the rate of interest are the demand curve for capital and the influence of the rate of interest on the amount saved out of a given income; and when, for example, the demand curve for capital shifts, the new rate of interest, according to this theory, is given by the point of intersection between the new demand curve for capital and the curve relating the rate of interest to the amounts which will be saved out of the *given income*. The classical theory of the rate of interest seems to suppose that, if the demand curve for capital shifts, or if the curve relating the rate of interest to the amounts saved out of a given income shifts, or if both these curves shift, the new rate of interest will be given by the point of intersection of the new positions of the two curves. But this is a nonsense theory. For the two curves are not, in general, independent. If either of them shifts, then, in general, income will change; with the result that the whole schematism based on the assumption of a given income breaks down. The problem is that the classical theory has not been alive to the relevance of changes in the level of income or the possibility of the level of income being actually a function of the rate of investment.

The above can be simply illustrated as follows. Let investment demand be represented by the function I: $I = I(r)$, where r is the rate of interest. Let savings be represented by the function S: $S = S(r, Y)$. If we define equilibrium as the condition $I = S$, we have three equations for the determination of the four unknowns, I, S, Y, r. Already we are one equation short. But the difficulty is further compounded if, as shown above by our analysis of the consumption function and the propensity to consume, income itself is a function of the level investment. Then it appears that the two functions are not even independent of each other. In general, when investment demand shifts (for example, due to a change in long-term expectations) so will income, and if income shifts so will the saving function describing saving in relation to the rate of interest. But the above functions do not contain enough *data* to tell us what the new value of income will be. If, however, we introduce the state of liquidity-preference and the quantity of money and these between them tell us that the rate of interest is r_1, then the whole system becomes determinate.

Thus the functions used by the classical theory, namely, the response of investment and the response of the amount saved out of a given income to changes in the rate of interest, do not furnish material for a theory of the rate of interest; but they could be used to tell us what the level of income will be, given (from some other source) the rate of interest; and alternatively, what the rate of interest will have to be, if the level of income is to be maintained at a given figure (for example, as in the classical case it is assumed always to be at the level corresponding to full employment).

Now as I have said elsewhere, this mistake in the classical approach, while baldly evident once we take seriously the possibility of changes in investment as a cause of changes in output, is also closely linked to the classical view of what interest at bottom is. The mistake originates, so to speak, from regarding interest as the reward for waiting as such, instead of as the reward for not-hoarding; just as the rates of return on loans or investments involving different degrees of risk are quite properly regarded as the reward, not of waiting as such, but of running the risk. There is, in truth, no sharp line between these and the so-called 'pure' rate of interest, all of them being the reward for running the risk of uncertainty of one kind or another. Only in the event of money being used solely for transactions and never as a store of value, would a different theory become appropriate. Which brings us to our second characterization of the relationship between *The General Theory* and the classicals as concerns the question of interest.

III

The aggregation in the preceding discussion is a convenient abstraction, valuable so long as it is used with the knowledge that it masks a more complex reality in ways that do not distort the essential properties of interest and money. In reality, of course, we need to account for the vast complex of interest rates on every different type of asset and on the interdependencies between them. Moving to that more fundamental plane, perhaps the following is a useful way of indicating the precise points of departure of the theory of the rate of interest expounded above (Chapters 11–17) from what I take to be the orthodox theory. Once again, it is useful to begin with the areas of agreement. I submit that the following four propositions, although they may be unfamiliar in form, are not inconsistent with the orthodox theory, and that theory has no reason, so far as I am aware, to reject them.

1 Interest on money *means* precisely what the books on arithmetic say that it means; that is to say, it is simply the premium obtainable on current cash over deferred cash, so that it measures the marginal preference (for the community as a whole) for holding cash in hand over cash for deferred delivery. No one would pay this premium unless the possession of cash served some purpose, i.e. had some efficiency. Thus we can conveniently say that interest on money measures the marginal efficiency of money measured in terms of itself as a unit.
2 Money is not peculiar in having a marginal efficiency measured in terms of itself. Surplus stocks of commodities in excess of requirements and other capital assets representing surplus capacity may, indeed, have a negative marginal efficiency in terms of themselves, but normally capital assets of all kinds have a positive marginal efficiency measured in terms

of themselves. If we know the relation between the present and expected prices of an asset in terms of money we can convert the measure of its marginal efficiency in terms of money by means of a formula which I have given above (*G.T.*: 227).

3 The effort to obtain the best advantage from the possession of wealth will set up a tendency for capital assets to exchange, in equilibrium, at values proportionate to their marginal efficiencies in terms of a common unit. That is to say, if r is the money rate of interest (i.e. r is the marginal efficiency of money in terms of itself) and if y is the marginal efficiency of a capital asset A in terms of money, then A will exchange in terms of money at a price such as to make $y = r$.

4 If the demand price of our capital asset A thus determined is not less than its replacement cost, new investment in A will take place, the scale of such investment depending on the capacity available for the production of A, i.e. on its elasticity of supply, and on the rate at which y, its marginal efficiency, declines as the amount of investment in A increases. At a scale of new investment at which the marginal cost of producing A is equal to its demand price as above, we have a position of equilibrium. Thus the price system resulting from the relationships between the marginal efficiencies of different capital assets including money, measured in terms of a common unit, determines the aggregate rate of investment.

These propositions are not, I think, inconsistent with the orthodox theory, or in any way open to doubt. They establish that relative prices (and, under the influence of prices, the scale of output) move until the marginal efficiencies of all kinds of assets are equal when measured in a common unit; and consequently that the marginal efficiency of captial is equal to the rate of interest. *But they tell us nothing as to the forces which determine what this common level of marginal efficiency will tend to be. It is when we proceed to this further discussion that my argument diverges from the orthodox argument.*

Put shortly, the orthodox theory maintains that the forces which determine the common value of the marginal efficiency of various assets are independent of money, which has, so to speak, no autonomous influence, and that prices move until the marginal efficiency of money, i.e. the rate of interest, falls into line with the common value of the marginal efficiency of other assets as determined by other forces. My theory, on the other hand, maintains that this is a special case and that over a wide range of possible cases almost the opposite is true: namely, that the marginal efficiency of money is determined by forces partly appropriate to itself, and that prices move until the marginal efficiency of other assets falls into line with the rate of interest.

Let me proceed to give the further propostitions, which, I suggest, the orthodox theory requires:

5 The marginal efficiency of money in terms of itself has the peculiarity that it is independent of its quantity. In this respect it differs from other capital assets. This is a consequence of the quantity theory of money strictly stated. Thus, unless we import considerations from outside, the money rate of interest is indeterminate, for the demand schedule for money is a function solely of its supply. Nevertheless, a determinate value for r can be derived from the condition that the value of an asset A, of which the marginal efficiency in terms of money is y, must be such that $y = r$. For, provided that we know the scale of investment, we know y and the value of A, and hence we can deduce r. In other words, the rate of interest depends on the marginal efficiency of capital assets other than money. This must, however, be supplemented by another proposition; for it requires that we should already know the scale of investment. This further proposition is as follows.

6 The scale of investment will not reach its equilibrium level until the point is reached at which the elasticity of supply of output as a whole has fallen to zero.

Hence the final synthesis of this theory. The equilibrium rate of aggregate investment, corresponding to the level of output for a further increase in which the elasticity of supply is zero, depends on the readiness of the public to save. But this in turn depends on the rate of interest. Thus for each level of the rate of interest we have a given quantity of saving. This quantity of saving determines the scale of investment. The scale of investment settles the marginal efficiency of capital, to which the rate of interest must be equal. Our system is therefore determinate. To each possible value of the rate of interest there corresponds a given volume of saving; and to each possible value of the marginal efficiency of capital there corresponds a given volume of investment. Now the rate of interest and the marginal efficiency of captial must be equal. Thus the position of equilibrium is given by that common value of the rate of interest and of the marginal efficiency of capital at which the saving determined by the former is equal to the investment determined by the latter.[4]

Now my departure from the orthodox theory takes place, as I have said, at propositions 5 and 6, for which I substitute:

5* The marginal efficiency of money in terms of itself is, in general, a function of its quantity (though not of its quantity alone), just as in the case of other captial assets.

6* Aggregate investment may reach its equilibrium rate under proposition 4 above, before the elasticity of supply of output as a whole has fallen to zero.

Before we examine the grounds for substituting 5* and 6* for 5 and 6, let us stop for a moment to consider more fully the meaning and the practical implications of the special postulates of the orthodox theory.

Let us begin with proposition 5. So far as the active circulation is concerned, it is sufficiently correct as a first approximation to regard the demand for money as proportionate to the effective demand, i.e. to the level of money income; which amounts to saying that the income velocity of the active circulation is independent of the quantity of money. This is, I say, only a first approximation because the demand for money in the active circulation is also to some extent a function of the rate of interest, since a higher rate of interest may lead to a more economical use of active balances, though this only means that the active balances are partially under the same influence as the inactive balances. But we also require the postulate that the amount of the inactive balances is independent of the rate of interest. I do not see, however, how this can be the case, except in conditions of long-period equilibrium, by which I mean a state of expectation which is both definite and constant and has lasted long enough for there to be no hangover from a previous state of expectation.

In ordinary conditions, on the other hand, this postulate would have awkward consequences quite incompatible with experience. It would mean, for example, that 'open-market operations' by a central bank would have no effect, other than momentary, on the rate of interest, the price of bonds remaining the same whatever quantity of them the central bank may buy or sell; the effect of the central bank's action on prices being such as to modify the demand for money to just the same extent as that by which the central bank was altering the supply of money.

Let us now turn to proposition 6. A zero elasticity of supply for output as a whole means that an increase of demand in terms of money will lead to no change in output; that is to say, prices will rise in the same proportion as the money demand rises. Inflation will have no effect on output or employment, but only on prices. This is what I mean by saying that the orthodox theory of the rate of interest involves a strict interpretation of the quantity theory of money, namely that P changes in the same proportion as M. This does not, of course, mean that T and V in the equation $PT = MV$ are irrevocably fixed; but the above, in conjunction with proposition 5, does mean that T and V are neither of them a function of M and that they do not change merely as a result of inflation in the quantity of money. Otherwise interpreted, a zero elasticity of supply for output as a whole involves a zero elasticity of supply for employment, i.e. there is, in my terminology, full employment. Indeed, the condition in which the elasticity of supply for output as a whole is zero is, I now think, the most convenient criterion for defining full employment.

It seems, therefore, that the orthodox theory requires (a) that there should be a state of definite and constant expectation, and (b) that there should be a state of full employment. These limitations mean that it is a particular theory applicable only to certain conditions; and this is my justification for calling my own theory a *general theory*, of which the orthodox theory is a limiting case.

If I am right, the orthodox theory is wholly inapplicable to such problems as those of unemployment and the trade cycle, or, indeed, to any of the day-to-day problems of ordinary life. Nevertheless, it is often in fact applied to such problems. The postulates which it requires, not having been stated, have escaped notice, with the result that deep-seated inconsistencies have been introduced into economic thought. The orthodox theory of the rate of interest properly belongs to a different stage of economic assumptions and abstractions from that in which any of us are thinking today. For the rate of interest and the marginal efficiency of capital are particularly concerned with the *indefinite* character of actual expectations; they sum up the effect on men's market decisions of all sorts of vague doubts and fluctuating states of confidence and courage. They belong, that is to say, to a state of our theory where we are no longer assuming a definite and calculable future. The orthodox theory, on the other hand, is concerned with a simplified world where there is always full employment, and where doubt and fluctuations of confidence are ruled out, so that there is no occasion to hold inactive balances, and prices must be constantly at a level which, merely to satisfy the transactions motive and without leaving any surplus to be absorbed by the precautionary and speculative motives, causes the whole stock of money to be worth a rate of interest equal to the marginal efficiency of capital which corresponds to full employment. The orthodox theory is, for example, particularly applicable to the stationary state. For in such conditions, not only is proposition 5 valid for the same reasons that apply in the case of the long period; but the stock of capital being fixed and new investment being zero, the marginal efficiency of capital must depend on the amount of this given stock and prices must be at a level which equates the amount of money, demanded for active balances at a rate of interest equal to this fixed marginal efficiency of capital, to the fixed supply of money in existence.

There is one other comment worth making in the context. It leads to considerable difficulties to regard the marginal efficiency of money as wholly different in character from the marginal efficiency of other assets. Equilibrium requires, as we have seen above (proposition 3), that the prices of different kinds of assets measured in the same unit must move until their marginal efficiencies measured in that unit are equal. But if the marginal efficiency of money in terms of itself is always equal to the marginal efficiency of other assets, irrespective of the price of the latter, the whole price system in terms of money becomes indeterminate. It is the elements of elasticity (a) in the desire to hold inactive balances, and (b) in the supply of output as a whole, which permit a reasonable measure of stability in prices. If these elasticities are zero there is a necessity for the whole body of prices and wages to respond immediately to every change in the quantity of money. This assumes a state of affairs very different from that in which we live. For the two elasticities named above are highly characteristic of the real world; and the assumption that both of them are zero assumes away three-quarters of the problems in which we are interested.

IV

The theory of the rate of interest which prevailed before (let us say) 1914 regarded it as the factor which ensured equality between savings and investment. It was never suggested that saving and investment could be unequal. This idea arose with certain inter-war theories. As I myself was part of this tradition and was greatly influenced by the versions of it proposed by Mr Hawtrey and Mr Robertson,[5] I feel I can say with authority that the trend in this line of thought was an attempt to bridge the gap between the theory of value and the theory of money we found in the Classical School proper. In retrospect, however, I feel that this resulted in the worst muddles of all. For what the neoclassical school proposed as a means of analysing the monetary influence on the rate of interest (and so, it was then hoped, the mystery of the trade cycle) was that there must be *two* sources of supply to meet the investment-demand schedule; namely, savings proper, which are the savings dealt with by the Classical School, *plus* the sum made available by any increase in the quantity of money (this being balanced by some species of levy on the public, called 'forced saving' or the like). This leads on to the idea that there is a 'natural' or 'neutral' or 'equilibrium' rate of interest; namely, that rate of interest which equates investment to classical saving proper without any addition from 'forced saving'; and finally to what, assuming this was the right track to begin with, is the most obvious solution of all; namely, that if the quantity of money could only be kept *constant* in all circumstances, none of these complications would arise, since the evils supposed to result from the supposed excess of investment over saving proper would cease to be possible.

After *The General Theory* was published, I found to my surprise that, rather than having to defend my arguments against the classical theory, the major theoretical debates I was engaged in were with a group of these neoclassical economists who expressed themselves as agreeing with me in abandoning the classical theory of the rate of interest, but who complained that my analysis of interest as the reward for not parting with liquidity was in fact identical to their own theory of interest. The alternative theory held by Professor Ohlin and his group of Swedish economists, by Mr Robertson and Mr Hicks, and probably by many others, makes the rate of interest depend, to put it briefly, on the demand and supply of *credit* or, alternatively (meaning the same thing), of *loans*, at different rates of interest. Some of these writers believe that my theory is on the whole the same as theirs and mainly amounts to expressing it in a somewhat different way. Nevertheless,

353

the theories are, I believe, radically opposed to one another. I was sufficiently alarmed by the possibility of a concealed difference of opinion leading to a mistaken identification of my view with this tradition to initiate a debate and bring the issue into the open. As the topic is one I consider of great importance and because the subsequent exchanges seem to have led to widespread interest and confusion, I think it worthwhile giving my account in a summary fashion here.

My differences from the loanable funds school can be grouped under two related headings: one, the general lack of any mechanism in this theory for the analysis of the influence of changes in interest on output; and two, the failure to grasp what I consider the essentially monetary character of the rate of interest which distinguishes my theory from the confusion exhibited by the neoclassical identification of the supply of 'credit' or 'finance' with saving.

To begin with the first, it is my contention that, despite protestations to the contrary, the neoclassical school, after long and complicated digression, ends in the same camp as the Classicals by identifying interest as the factor which balances (or *not* in their case, this being the distinction of the neoclassical school) saving and investment. That is to say, though the analysis of savings is couched in terms of the financial realities of a monetary economy in the form of its substitution of bank loans, credit, etc., for the old classical reliance on such psychic concepts as 'waiting' or 'time preference', it is still a framework in which the 'market' for these instruments co-ordinates saving and investment. As I have said above, the initial novelty of my position lies in my maintaining that it is not the rate of interest but the level of incomes which ensures equality between saving and investment. But this novelty is coupled with the conservative approach of maintaining the traditional notions of income, saving and investment (on which, though I have tried to be a little more precise, I do not think I differ substantially from Marshall). On my theory saving and investment, though activities conducted by different groups for different reasons, will in fact be brought into co-ordination with one another by the causal sequence of the adjustment of saving to changes in investment, for reasons sufficiently clear, elaborated on above. To this way of thinking the loanable funds conflation of savings with credit and the consequent reliance on the *quantity* of available saving-cum-financing to determine the level of investment is anathema. Saving is determined by the current level of activity, which is in turn a function of the current willingness of business to invest and the public to save and consume. Saving cannot be an impediment to investment and in fact will always be forthcoming in exactly the amount needed for the current scale of investment.

The arguments which led up to this conclusion are independent of my subsequent theory of interest, and in fact I reached it before I had reached the latter theory. But the result of it was to leave the rate of interest in the air. If the rate of interest is not determined by saving and investment in the same way in which price is determined by supply and demand, how is it determined? What I now think to be the true explanation has just been reviewed. The resulting theory, whether right or wrong, is exceedingly simple, namely, that the rate of interest on a loan of a given quality and maturity has to be established at the level which, in the opinion of those who have the opportunity of choice – i.e. of wealth-holders – equalizes the attractions of holding idle cash and of holding the loan. It would be true to say that this by itself does not carry us very far. But it gives us firm and intelligible ground from which to proceed. The loanable funds approach, being a hotch-potch between a theory of saving and a theory of the loan market, provides no such intelligible ground. It does not treat our question of the determination of income, and only adds confusion to the analysis of asset markets.

Finally, to look at the matter from a different standpoint, consider the detailed phenomena most often brought up by the writers in the debate over the loanable funds theories; namely, 'hoarding' and the distinction between *ex ante* and *ex post* magnitudes of saving and investment. If we mean by 'hoarding' the holding of idle balances, then my theory of the rate of interest might be expressed by saying that the rate of interest serves to equate the demand and supply of hoards – that is, it must be sufficiently high to *offset* an increased propensity to hoard relative to the supply of idle balances available. The function of the rate of interest is to modify the money prices of other capital assets in such a way as to equalize the attraction of holding them and of holding cash. This has nothing whatever to do with current saving or new investment. There can never be available for additional hoards a surplus of current saving over and above what is represented by current investment. Moreover, no amount of anxiety by the public to increase their hoards can affect the amount of hoarding, which depends on the willingness of the banks to acquire (or dispose of) additional assets beyond what is required to offset changes in the active balances. If the banks stand firm, an increased propensity to hoard raises the rate of interest, and thereby lowers the prices of capital assets other than cash, until people give up the idea of selling them or of refraining from buying them in order to increase their hoards. The rate of interest is, if you like, the *price* of hoards in the sense that it measures the pecuniary sacrifices which the holder of a hoard thinks it worthwhile to suffer in preferring it to other claims and assets with an equal present value.

I emphasize these obvious matters to clear our minds of the idea that the quantity of hoards depends in any way on what people are doing with their savings, or that there is any connection between idle balances and the conception (meaningless on my definitions) of idle savings. Both these notions are found in the writings of some of the loanable funds theorists (e.g. Hawtrey, *Capital and Employment*). They are associated with the same deep-seated obsession we described above, associating idle balances not with the actions of the banks in fixing the supply of cash, nor with the attitude of the public towards the comparative attractions of cash and of other assets, but with some aspects of current saving. They thus err in placing too much emphasis on the quantity of money actually hoarded, and ignore the emphasis I seek to place on the rate of interest as the inducement *not* to hoard.

Lastly, I shall deal with the notions of *ex ante* versus *ex post* magnitudes of saving and investment. This ingredient in the loanable funds theory is emphasized by Professor Ohlin and the Swedish school and was also the subject of much debate after *The General Theory* was published. Lest I sound too negative a note in my discussion of the neoclassical school, let me add that this debate alerted me to an additional factor concerning the *ex ante* character of investment decisions that I had previously overlooked in my formulation of the portmanteau function relating the demand for money to the rate of interest. I have accordingly made amends above in my discussion of the 'finance motive' and the role played by the press of new investment, in a period of rising levels of activity, in altering the rate of interest. But I must emphasize that this In no way undermineo, but rather buttresses, my basic theory. The changes in scale of investment activity will operate on the rate of interest through the channel of increasing the demand for available liquidity services. As always in the case of the liquidity preference theory, the banking system's willingness to increase the available quantity of money will work in conjunction with the total demand for liquid balances to determine the degree to which this will alter the rate of interest. But this 'revolving fund of finance', as I have called it, once it has reached a level consistent with the new level of investment demand does not constitute a change in the level of saving or alter the necessary identity of eventual saving with the level of investment so enabled (or not) by this adjustment of the credit market to a new level of activity.

Thus *ex ante* investment is a valuable and genuine phenomenon, inasmuch as investment decisions have to be taken and credit or 'finance' provided well in advance of the actual purchase of *ex post* investment; though the amount of the preliminary credit demanded is not necessarily equal to the amount of investment which is projected. But once again this is not an embarrassment for our theory but a sensible refinement of it. What is an embarrassment is the Swedish attempt to construct a parallel argument for saving. First of all, there is no sensible meaning I can find to attach to *ex ante* saving. Individuals have no necessity to decide, contemporaneously with the investment decisions of the entrepreneurs, how much of their future income they are going to save. To begin with, they do not know what their incomes are going to be. But even if they form some preliminary opinion on the matter, in the first place, they are under no necessity to make a definite decision (as the investors have to do); in the second place, they do not make it at the same time; and in the third place, they most undoubtedly do not, as a rule, deplete their existing cash well ahead of their receiving the incomes out of which they propose to save, so as to oblige the investors with 'finance' at the date when the latter require to be arranging it. Finally, even if they were prepared to borrow against their prospective saving, additional cash could not become available in this way except as a result of a change in banking policy. Surely nothing is more certain than that the credit or 'finance' required by *ex ante* investment is not supplied by *ex ante* saving. The *ex ante* saver has no cash, but it is cash which the *ex ante* investor requires.

The point remains, however, that the transition from a lower to a higher scale of activity involves an increased demand for liquid resources which cannot be met without a rise in the rate of interest, unless the banks are ready to lend more cash or the rest of the public to release more cash at the existing rate of interest. If there is no change in the liquidity position, the public can save *ex ante* and *ex post* and *ex* anything else until they are blue in the face, without alleviating the problem in the least – unless, indeed, the result of their efforts is to lower the scale of activity to what it was before.

This means that, in general, banks hold the key position in the transition from a lower to a higher scale of activity. If they refuse to relax, the growing congestion of the short-term loan market or of the new issue market, as the case may be, will inhibit the improvement, no matter how thrifty the public propose to be out of their future incomes. On the other hand, there will always be exactly enough *ex post* saving to take up the *ex post* investment and so release the finance which the latter had been previously employing. The investment market can become congested through shortage of cash. It can never become congested through shortage of saving – short of full employment. This is the most fundamental of my conclusions within this field.

KEYNES, CLASSICALS AND NEOCLASSICALS ON THE RATE OF INTEREST: A RETROSPECTIVE VIEW
M.S. Lawlor writing as himself

In the preceding revision of Chapter 14 of *The General Theory* I was guided by my belief that Keynes had, in fact, indicated how he would have rewritten this chapter. Much of his professional energy from 1937 to 1939 (Keynes 1937a, b, c, d, 1938c, 1939d) was spent debating in print on the topic of the relationship between his theory of the rate of interest and that of his predecessors and contemporaries. Thus in the rewrite I used as many of his own words and included as many of his own concerns on that topic as possible, while still maintaining a thematic and narrative unity. The result is an interpolation of the original chapter (and its appendix), six published articles (Keynes, 1937a, b, c, d, 1938c, 1939d), the draft editions of *The General Theory* (*Collected Writings* XIV; hereafter *C.W.*) and the extensive correspondence surrounding this issue. The relevant correspondence is principally that between Keynes and R.F. Harrod, J.R. Hicks, Ralph Hawtrey, D.H. Robertson and Bertil Ohlin, but also includes his exchange with Hugh Townshend and some advice he sought from Joan Robinson and R.F. Kahn on these matters, all of which is contained in the *Collected Writings* (*C.W.* XIV, XXIX). My best guess is that the final product consists of about 75 per cent Keynes's own words and 25 per cent mine.

As these debates make clear, it was not possible for Keynes to treat his theory of the rate of interest independently of the rest of *The General Theory*. In each article he used much other material, especially from the various parts of Book IV, 'The Inducement to Invest', in distinguishing his views on interest, money and investment from those of his opponents (and sometimes from those of his supporters). For this reason, I suggest that were this rewritten chapter to be embodied in a true second edition of *The General Theory* it should be placed at the end of Book IV, perhaps as Chapter 18, not in the middle as it stands in the original. This is particularly so in the light of the extensive use made in it of the material introduced in Chapter 17 of *The General Theory* concerning the own-rates of interest. The references in the rewrite to matters dealt with 'above' (such as the 'finance motive' and the 'own-rate' on money) presuppose this ordering.

I have purposely avoided quotations marks with regard to Keynes's own words and have kept formal references and footnotes to a minimum, thereby staying as close as possible to Keynes's own style. Students of Keynes will no doubt be able to detect, more or less, the sources of the various parts of the chapter, and – hopefully not as frequently – the points at which my attempts to emulate his style highlight by comparison his own elegant phrasing. More importantly, for readers without the time or inclination to pore over the extensive, detailed and complex puzzle presented by the original documents, I hope I have provided a clear and concise statement of the issue as Keynes saw it.

In the rest of the space available to me I wish to comment on certain aspects of Keynes's placement of his interest rate theory in relation to the economics of his time and before. Two issues will be raised. First, was Keynes 'fair' and/or accurate in his historical account of the classical (and 'neoclassical') theory of the rate of interest? Second, what is the personal element in Keynes's view of the literature of his own time and place, and how does this personal context help us to understand his theory of interest – that part of *The General Theory* which, above all else, still remains controversial, if not downright mysterious to economists sixty years later?

Keynes as a historian and polemicist on the rate of interest

[H]e belonged securely to that school of Cambridge economists of whom it has been said that they preferred making things up to looking things up.[6]

An undeniable sense that one takes away from reading the articles and correspondence surrounding Keynes's attempts to defend and distinguish his interest rate theory is that he had little patience for detailed exegesis of the type that today occupies historians of economics. It was not that he was ungenerous in attribution, as we can see from his numerous attempts to dredge up the underworld in which he thought the principle of effective demand had eked out a furtive existence since Ricardo's time. But it must be said that in his drive to set out a persuasive account of his own view and how it departed from what he considered the conventional view, he was prone to rely on straw men. Moreover, the straw man who represented the classical position on interest – 'a composite Aunt Sally of uncertain age', as D.H. Robertson complained – was actually fabricated from a very few selected straws. Most of these consisted of the views that Keynes himself had previously believed and little else. Any history wider than his own reading and education remained uncharted territory. Alternatively, such literature as did, in his retrospective view of 1936, move his thought process forward was brought to the foreground and emphasized as it fitted into his narrative. After *The General Theory*, he went to great and over-generous lengths to reply, either privately or in print, to almost anyone who took the trouble to write to him on topics concerning the book.[7] But on matters historical, as we can see from the *Collected Writings*, Keynes most often just threw up his hands in ignorance. At times it is almost comical to read his beseeching requests to others (e.g. D.H. Robertson, Bertil Ohlin) to 'look things up' for him and provide the perfect quotation to capture the supposed antecedents of *The General Theory* in a neglected 'Classical' (e.g. Marshall, Wicksell). Nevertheless, Keynes did realize the rhetorical value of historical argument, and as I shall argue below, his lack of attention to detail was frequently compensated by a tremendous intuitive sense of the dominant theme and implicit presuppositions of the existing literature. Importantly, it was on these terms that he staked his innovations and departures from the classical theory of interest.

What we find, then, in Chapter 14 is a retrospective self-analysis on Keynes's part. Implicitly, it is a record of how and why he came to doubt the received teachings of Marshall and D.H. Robertson, to use the two most important icons of the Classical and Neoclassical Schools to which he was reacting. As in psychoanalysis, his memory colours the account with the context (Marshall's and Robertson's texts) and emotions (bewilderment and dissatisfaction with classical analysis applied to the question of income determination) of his experience and memories. For the subject of such an analysis the most important task is to weave these elements of fact and psyche into a coherent story of progress and resolution. The former underlying neurosis must be resolved to go forward. Looked at in this manner, it should be no surprise that Chapter 14 is not a clear historical account of the orthodox tradition in interest rate theory since Ricardo (the

'Classicals') and the then contemporary inter-war business-cycle literature (his 'Neoclassicals'). Instead, it is best viewed as a personal case study of intellectual disease and healing.

We could assess this record using the historian's criteria. As such, the account is barely sustainable as an undergraduate thesis. One of the many criticisms that could justly be levied against it in this respect is its scandalous disregard of Irving Fisher. Surely no one figure of Keynes's formative years so dominated the discussion of the two strands of classical analysis that he correctly identifies in this chapter as Irving Fisher did. It was Fisher's formulation in the *The Rate of Interest* (1907) that provided the most complete English-language theoretical treatment of the underlying forces of productivity and thrift in the static classical model (as Wicksell was in the German-speaking world). Futhermore, Fisher's application of the loanable funds approach to disequilibrium 'transition periods' in *The Purchasing Power of Money* (1911), ranks with, if not above, the neoclassical writers Keynes does deal with, such as Robertson, Hawtrey and Pigou. Surely this is what Keynes was getting at in his belated and only cursorily modified view of 1937 (included in the rewrite above) where he identified Fisher, in a well-known footnote, as 'the great grandparent who first influenced me strongly towards regarding money as a "real" factor'. But note that this footnote is the only reference to Fisher's work in the article from which it is drawn – which was a contribution to Irving Fisher's *Festschrift*. Of course, Keynes did refer in *The General Theory* to Fisher on the notion of the real and nominal rates and as the originator of the marginal efficiency of capital concept. But still it seems strange that he should be left entirely out of the chapter on the 'Classical Theory of the Rate of Interest'. Strange, that is, unless it was not Fisher's formulation that had a personal impact on Keynes's own thinking. One suspects that, as in the disdainful attitude Keynes had displayed in his review of Fisher in 1911 ('it is all in Marshall'), the Cambridge insularity that Ohlin was to complain of with regard to the Swedes was at work in this instance as well.

But that same excuse cannot reconcile a further oddity that arises from viewing this chapter as a piece of doctrinal history: how could Keynes have neglected to mention any of Marshall's monetary work except that of the *Principles?* It was Keynes after all, starting in that early review of Fisher and continuing in his memorial essay on Marshall, who stressed the critical importance of Marshall's unpublished essays and memoranda to the teaching of monetary theory in Cambridge during and after Marshall's tenure. Yet the text and appendix entry on Marshall in Chapter 14 analyse only his vague and strictly non-monetary discussion in the *Principles*. A review of these chapters shows Keynes to be largely correct in his opinion that '"Interest" has really no business to turn up at all in Marshall's *Principles of Economics*, – it belongs to another branch of the subject' (*G.T.*: 189). But the puzzling point is that there is much more of Marshall on the cognate topics of interest and money that Keynes never mentions here. One item from this material is especially valuable to a proper history of Cambridge interest and monetary theory as it lays out the basic analytical vision of that school up to and including Keynes of *The General Theory*.[8] Marshall's unpublished 1871 'Essay on Money' is the bedrock from which emanates Keynes's analytical treatment of asset markets in general and, in particular, the method of presenting the essential properties of interest and money both in *The General Theory* and in his later defence of it (Lawlor 1994b). It is from here, for instance, that he derives the important method of stating the terms of a general asset market equilibrium (as in section III above).

So why did Keynes leave all this out of Chapter 14? Could it be that he felt that such a recognition of continuity would rob his theory of its self-proclaimed revolutionary status? (Could Marshall be the economics father-figure whose power must be overcome for Keynes to become his own man?) Perhaps, but this is a topic for psycho-biography. We need not take the issue much further than to say that we have here uncovered such a deep presupposition of the Marshallian method of monetary analysis that even Keynes's long struggle to escape did not, and as I hope to show did not need to, bring it to the surface. Explicit evidence for this view can be found in the material from which I drew the revised edition of the this chapter. How else are we to make sense of Keynes's view that he can use the own-rates equilibrium analysis of Chapter 17 of *The General Theory* as a framework in which both the classical and Keynesian theories of interest can be depicted (see section III above)? My contention is that this Marshallian conception – essentially, that the stocks of existing assets are traded until the prices satisfy the marginal preferences of buyers who are each at all times marginally balancing their own portfolio of assets due to their preferences and the services the assets render – was used by Keynes as a *metatheoretical* construct, common to any account of the essential properties of interest and money. This is one way to interpret the irritation he often displayed in the post-*General Theory* debates on interest:

> To speak of the 'liquidity-preference theory' of the rate of interest is, indeed, to dignify it too much. It is like speaking of the 'professorship theory' of Ohlin or the 'civil servant theory' of Hawtry. *I am simply stating what it is, the significant theories on the subject being subsequent. And in stating what it is, I follow the books on arithmetic and accept the accuracy of what is taught in preparatory schools.*
>
> (Keynes 1937a: 215, empahasis added)

Keynes and the classical theory of interest: a Sraffian perspective

This still does not make Keynes much of a historian of economics, but it does help us to understand the now forgotten pedigree on which much of

Keynes's post-*General Theory* defence of his interest rate theory was conducted. As can be readily seen in 'The Theory of the Rate of Interest' (Keynes 1937d), 'The General Theory of Employment' (1937c) and to a lesser extent in 'Alternative Theories of the Rate of Interest' (1937a), Keynes employed the analysis of the own-rates of interest as the framework for distinguishing his interest rate theory from the classicals and neoclassicals. Moreover, he did so in a little-noticed two-stage process. All theories of the rate of interest are expected to obey the metatheoretical stock equilibrium that Keynes received from Marshall. The special assumptions of each – for example, the extent that the equilibrium is dependent on monetary forces – determine the second question of what level this equilibrium will settle at. For the Classicals, money neutrality and the quantity theory ensure that this equilibrium will only be established where the level of investment is driven to its full employment quantity. For Keynes, the peculiar characteristics of money as an asset will ensure that money 'rules the roost' in this respect. Looked at from another standpoint, says Keynes, this depends on the expectational environment assumed to be ruling in each theory. A long-period classical setting has no need for money as the system has fully adjusted the capital stock to the given and unchanging conditions of productivity and thrift. In Keynes's world, an uncertain future endows the expectations of investors and asset holders with a monetary cast that can hang up the level of investment short of full employment.

But to return to the issue of Keynes's Chapter 14 as a personal recounting of his struggle to escape orthodox thought: another interesting historical angle is suggested by his use of the own-rates framework to depict his differences with the Classicals. In a then widely regarded and now much debated[9] review of Hayek's *Prices and Production* in 1932, Piero Sraffa (1932a) had also used this 'own-rates' conception, along with some basic Marshallian price theory to criticize and analyse Hayek and the Wicksellian tradition in monetary economics. As his first footnote in Chapter 17 indicates, Keynes felt some debt to Piero Sraffa's review of Hayek in 1932 in formulating his ideas on the essential properties of interest and money. Two rather general points from Sraffa's review are worth mentioning at this juncture for the light they shed on the setting in which Keynes's theory of the rate of interest was introduced in 1936.

First, Sraffa had complained that Hayek and 'all modern writers on money' were establishing a tradition of 'unintelligibility', by which he seemed to mean that they constructed theories that could not answer the questions they asked of them; or, alternatively, that they drew policy conclusions that their theories in fact could not logically support. In the case of Hayek's particular argument, he had shown how on its own assumptions his forced savings theory was rendered unintelligible as an explanation of the supposedly monetary causes of the trade cycle. Also, the framework of spot and future prices implicit in the move from the Marshallian short to long periods, was shown by Sraffa to be incompatible with the traditional use of the 'natural rate'/'money rate' distinction. To use Keynes's terms, above, this meant that old classical price theory was incompatible with neoclassical monetary theory. In essence this involved Sraffa showing that commodity rates (later dubbed own-rates by Keynes) 'naturally' diverge outside the steady state and so there can be no unique 'real' benchmark to which the money rate must conform. Second, and more important than these internal critiques, Sraffa made it quite clear that all modern theories of money – what Keynes in Chapter 14 called neoclassical theories – were doomed by a self-contradictory use of a method which Sraffa, following Hayek, termed 'the method of neutral money'. The description by Keynes in paragraph 1 of section IV in the above rewrite corresponds almost exactly with this general approach. Its basic flaw, as Sraffa saw it, consisted of an inadequate attempt to introduce the true properties of money into the analogue money system to which the real system was then compared. Notably, his view of Hayek's strict character-ization of money as a neutral medium of exchange was that it missed the essential manner in which a monetary and a non-monetary economy differed. To Sraffa, a truly monetary economy was distinguished by the fact that money was the social contrivance for fixing concrete relationships, contracts, debts, and so on between people, not just by the existence of an efficient accounting scheme between things. But though highly critical of Hayek, and by implication the whole tradition of 'neoclassical' monetary theory (including Keynes of the *Treatise on Money*, one supposes), Sraffa also suggested that a truly useful application of this method could be worked out. By his account this would involve specifying two economies which were identical in all respects, except that the various monetary elements in one were absent in the other. Start each in equilibrium, and shock the systems similarly. The true value of the method of neutral money would lie in the comparison of the effects of this shock in the two systems.

Now consider the defence Keynes makes above of his interest rate theory in the light of these comments. Implicitly, we could use Sraffa's criticism to frame the debate between Keynes and the Classics. Marshall's (1871) (and Keynes's Chapter 17) asset market equilibrium is the metatheoretical setting for the initial equilibria of both systems. For Keynes (see above, and Chapter 17 of *The General Theory*) the non-monetary econ-omy has no asset valued for anything other than its productivity and carrying costs. In this system money is purely an accounting mechanism used for exchange purposes.[10] To Keynes, this must also mean that the future is certain and unchanging.[11]

Sraffa's criticism had dealt with attempts to answer the Wicksellian question of the relationship between monetary policy and the price level. But the introduction of Keynes's question of employment and output

363

determination raises other problems not considered by Sraffa. Since money is neutral in the non-monetary system (by definition), the productivity of capital, along with the carrying cost of assets due to depreciation and the rate of saving out of a given income, are the only margins on which we can depend to determine the rate of interest (see Rogers and Rymes, Chapter 18 in this volume). Yet it is not possible to use the calculus along these margins unless they are opposed against some constraint – for example, Wicksell fixed the aggregate stock of capital; Fisher fixed the production possibilities frontier; and modern general equilibrium theorists fix endowments to each agent. Hence Keynes's claim that the classical theory is not just indeterminate without a given income, but must assume *full employment income*. We can only define the relevant margins of the classical theory if income has already been pushed to the point where the efficient allocation of resources determines the marginal productivity of the capital assets in conjunction with the level of saving out of full employment income. Sraffa's criticism that the natural-rate doctrine was unintelligible here arises in a slightly altered form. Sraffa, operating on the terrain of long-period classical analysis, had pointed out that for each composite price level there exists a different composite 'natural' rate, which when used as the object of monetary policy would stabilize that price level. Keynes's claim is that each of these 'natural' rates is only natural for a given level income. But there is no method, in a non-monetary system, to determine any of these rates short of full employment. And in the monetary economy, as Keynes showed in Chapter 21 of *The General Theory*, changes in output do impact on prices, but in a vastly more complex way than is assumed by the simple quantity theory. Evidently things are much worse for neoclassical 'loanable funds' theory than even Sraffa had shown, but for the same reason: a neglect of the essential properties of money. Hence the neoclassical theory is the worst muddle of all: a disequilibrium theory of interest and the trade cycle (and so employment) in which the only equilibrium defined is full employment saving equals investment.

Nevertheless, let the analogue monetary system be distinguished from the 'real' system by the addition to the asset collection of a good which people are willing to pay to hold, which has no explicit yield, and which earns a liquidity premium in excess of its carrying cost. For convenience let this correspond to the existence of stocks of idle money which yield no return, have no carrying costs and which are valued purely for the potential convenience or security they offer the holders in terms of ease of disposing of them – in short, money. The value of this potential convenience (a term used both by Marshall in 1871 for transactions balances and by Keynes for liquidity in general in Chapter 17) of the liquid asset is measured by the premium which must be payed to persuade a holder to give up this service by lending. This premium is what we – along with the arithmetic books – call the rate of interest on money. In 1936, Keynes added this liquidity convenience to those of productivity and carrying cost as one of the fundamental forces determining asset demand in his view of a monetary economy (Townshend 1937). For him, such a preference and such a premium could only exist in the presence of an uncertain future. In so doing he suggested a third margin along which the rate of interest is determined.

Now to Sraffa's suggested experiment. Let each system start off in full employment equilibrium (the non-monetary system appears to leave no other choice). Investment demand declines as the perceived yield on productive assets falls. In the non-monetary economy this will require a lower level of interest, less investment and saving, and more consumption, if the economy is to maintain full employment. Transitional problems aside, this requires that saving adjusts automatically, to increase consumption as investment projects are curtailed. With no mechanism to determine output, the theory must assume a jump to the new natural rate. Money's neutrality ensures it will not get in the way.[12]

Things are not necessarily as smooth in the monetary case. A number of possibilties present themselves. With expectations, the state of liquidity preference and the stock of money unchanged, the marginal efficiency of capital must be brought into line with the rate of interest on money. As Keynes says above (p. 349), this will occur via a fall in the price of capital assets until their new expected returns, discounted at the going rate of interest, equal their prices again; that is, the marginal efficiencies of capital and money are the same. If nothing else happens this will reduce the level of investment, and income will shrink to bring saving into line. Mitigating factors due to the real balance effect, the release of transactions balances and the reduction in the 'finance' demand for cash could all increase the effective money stock, reduce the rate of interest and cushion the fall in investment and output. Keynes, of course, sees these forces as insufficiently powerful in practice to correct the situation. Alternatively, the maintenance of full employment could be accomplished by an increase in the money supply, expectations again remaining unchanged (which Keynes also seems to think unlikely).

Other possibilities are suggested by the various ways in which the expectations might react to the initial fall. At one extreme all holders of idle balances could immediately and correctly speculate on the new 'natural' rate as the convention against which to compare the current money rate.[13] The interest rate adjusts downward automatically and forestalls the fall in investment without a change in the money supply. Furthermore, each of the expectations scenarios we could imagine is complicated by the possible extra cash that might be released, and by the possibility of the interest sensitivity of the demand for transactions balances. Obviously, the possible permutations of these effects are uncountable.

This experiment, however, appears to be intelligible in Sraffa's sense of capable of definition, if not of measurement and testing. We can show what the sequence of events will lead to with the theory of income and employment. The monetary and the non-monetary system are determinate but yield different experimental results. We have evidently escaped what Sraffa termed the 'essential confusion' of neoclassical models: 'the belief that the divergence of rates is a characteristic of a money economy . . . implied by the very terminology adopted, which identifies the "actual" with the "money" rate and the "equilibrium" with the "natural" ' (Sraffa 1932a: 49). Both systems have an equilibrium. Only one has money, though, and that is the only one that exhibits the possibility of less-than-full employment.

Conclusion

To summarize, I believe Keynes did accurately go to the heart of the matter when he characterized the classical theory of the rate of interest as incoherent outside full employment. I also find that he was essentially correct in his criticism of the neoclassical disequilibrium loanable funds tradition. Such theories are uneasy crosses between a strictly non-monetary analysis and a tentative, and ultimately abortive, recognition of the vast changes wrought by the introduction of money into economic theory. Keynes cannot be relied upon as a historian of economic ideas in the strict sense. But the many interesting issues which analysis of his case brings to light make his personal account of intellectual struggle worth preserving.

NOTES

1 This revision is designed to be placed at the end of Book IV, 'The Inducement to Invest'. Barring other alterations in chapter ordering, this would make it Chapter 18. Also, the original appendix to Chapter 14 has been removed, part of its content having been incorporated into the body of this revision.
2 See Robertson (1937); Ohlin (1937a,b); Viner (1936); and Keynes (1937a).
3 However, see below in my discussion of the more recent disequilibrium theories of interest, how these monetary factors are now brought in as a disturbing factor that upsets the 'natural' equilibrium described by the old classicals.
4 Notice that this case corresponds to the full employment equilibrium of the more aggregate description of the system above, p. 348.
5 I should also single out Professor Irving Fisher as the real pioneer in this regard. He embodies the historical transition I have in mind in one person in the evolution from a properly classical account of saving and investment in his *The Rate of Interest* (1907), to his neoclassical account of 'transitions periods' in his *Purchasing Power of Money* (1911). That is to say, in so far as I am concerned, I find looking back that it was Professor Fisher who first influenced me strongly towards regarding money as a 'real' factor.
6 Lekachman (1964b: x).
7 This is even more evident in the files associated with this period in the unpublished Keynes papers, which are filled with correspondence, some quite

inane. Each has attached to it a respectful reply by Keynes.

8 For a full account see Lawlor (1994a).
9 See Lawlor and Horn (1992) for a detailed exegesis of the 'Sraffa-Hayek Exchange', and Lawlor (1994b) for an extended interpretation of the own-rates framework and Keynesian theory.
10 Note the distinction from what Sraffa saw as Hayek's approach, where one system was barter and one was endowed with a medium of exchange. To Sraffa both of these were essentially non-monetary systems.
11 Strictly speaking, this would be a stationary state and as such would escape Sraffa's stricture on the non-uniqueness of the natural rate.
12 It is of course just these transitional problems that the 'neoclassical' theories such as Wicksell's, Fisher's, Robertson's, Hawtrey's and Hayek's were all about, as is the case with the modern loanable funds approach. The difference Keynes is trying to establish here from that view is based on the following criticisms: (a) the loanable-fund theories illigitimately define money and so the money rate of interest; (b) the loanable funds theory can never say what output and employment are outside of equilibrium (i.e. full employment). One supposes that a methodological question would inevitably arise in this context, and it did: the superiority of disequilibrium versus equilibrium theorizing and the conse-quent issue of the definition of a particular state of the system as being in 'equilibrium'. These are the terms on which the debate of the 1950s and 1960s was waged over 'liquidity preference' versus 'loanable funds' theories of the rate of interest (see Johnson 1951; Leijonhufvud 1981). I am suggesting here that there was another road leading out of this debate that was little noticed at the time, and only later taken by some Post-Keynesians in the 1970s and 1980s.
13 Allin Cottrell and I (Cottrell and Lawlor 1991) explore exactly this possibility in our critique of Leijonhufvud's view that the liquidity preference theory makes such a smooth (classical) transition impossible.

Books V and VI

MONEY-WAGES AND PRICES: SHORT NOTES SUGGESTED BY *THE GENERAL THEORY*

21

KEYNESIAN BUSINESS CYCLE THEORY

Marc Jarsulic

INTRODUCTION

The 'Notes on the Trade Cycle' in Chapter 22 of *The General Theory* are a subtle mixture of theory, observation and policy prescription. They show Keynes at his best, explaining why capitalist economies exhibit persistent fluctuations, and devising ways to limit those fluctuations. The theoretical explanation he offers is in marked contrast to the accounts which dominate professional discourse today. He views cycles as the outcome of fluctuations in aggregate demand; and he views these fluctuations in demand as an outcome of investment decisions which must be made in ignorance about the future. At the same time, he suggests that institutional change, which is not the same thing as countercyclical demand management, can be used to modify the business cycle.

It will be the argument of this chapter that Keynes's perspective finds important and useful development in two superficially disparate places. The first is in the theoretical literature on 'endogenous' cycles. There is a family tree running from *The General Theory*, through the work of theorists such as Kaldor and Goodwin, and to the work of several contemporary macro-economists. They have shown that persistent, self-sustaining and irregular oscillations can be rigorously and convincingly analysed in an aggregate demand framework. The second site where Keynes's ideas are echoed and developed is in the work of institutionally oriented macroeconomists. These economists have paid attention to the decline of the post-war 'Golden Age', and are able to offer explanations for the post-1970s trans-formations in advanced economies that are striking and extraordinarily insightful. Taken together, these two development of Keynes's ideas pro-vide a view of cyclical behaviour that is both scientifically interesting and of some policy relevance.

KEYNES ON THE TRADE CYCLE

To explain the existence of sustained involuntary unemployment, Keynes had introduced an analysis of investment demand based on a theory of real-world expectations. Future returns on long-lived projects are not knowable. Nor is there any truly sound way to divine a probability distribution of future economic outcomes. Instead, businessmen must make their best guess and take their chances. Animal spirits rule where economic rationality is allegedly the determining factor.

Given this view of investment, there is an obvious point of departure for business cycle theory. Significant fluctuations of investment demand, working through the multiplier, will cause significant fluctuations in employment. However, the realities of business cycle behaviour raise some important theoretical questions. Cycles are called cycles because there are significant timing regularities involved. Burns and Mitchell, whose empirical work remains an important benchmark in the subject, summarize these regularities in a succinct fashion:

> Business cycles are a type of fluctuation found in the aggregate economic activity of nations that organize their work mainly in business enterprises: a cycle consists of expansions occuring at about the same time in many economic activities, followed by similarly general recessions, contractions and revivals which merge into the expansion phase of the next cycle; the sequence of changes is recurrent but not periodic; in duration business cycles vary from more than one year to ten or twelve years; they are not divisible into shorter cycles of similar character with amplitude approximating their own.
>
> (Burns and Mitchell 1946: 1)

To explain these regularities with the apparatus of *The General Theory*, two important theoretical questions must be addressed. First, if profit expectations are not solidly grounded, why do we not observe erratic fluctuations of investment and output? Business cycles are characterized by sustained expansions and contractions, during which large numbers of economic variables, including investment, exhibit strong co-movement. Second, what brings expansions and contractions to an end? Although expansions and contractions vary in length, there are discernible turning points, which investment exhibits along with other variables.

Keynes's answers to these questions are connected. Expansions take place because expectations of future profitability are high enough to sustain significant rates of investment. Increasing investment increases output and realized profits, validating the positive expectations. The forces of demand 'at first gather force and have a cumulative effect on one another but gradually lose their strength until at a certain point they tend to be replaced by forces operating in the other direction' (Keynes 1936: 314; hereafter *G.T.*). It is excessive optimism over a sustained period of time which creates a ceiling for the expansion and causes self-reinforcing downward movement:

The later stages of the boom are characterised by optimistic expectations as to the future yield of capital-goods sufficiently strong to offset their growing abundance and their rising costs of production and, probably, a rise in the rate of interest also. It is of the nature of organised investment markets, under the influence of purchasers largely ignorant of what they are buying and of speculators who are more concerned with forecasting the next shift of market sentiment than with a reasonable estimate of the future yield of capital-assets, that, when disillusion falls upon an over-optimistic and over-bought market, it should fall with sudden and even catastrophic force.

(*G.T.*: 315–16)

After the collapse of expected profits and therefore investment demand, output and realized profits also fall. It is then 'not so easy to revive the marginal efficiency of capital, determined, as it is by the uncontrollable and disobedient psychology of the business world. It is the return of confidence, to speak in ordinary language, which is so insusceptible to control in an economy of individualistic capitalism' (*G.T.*: 317).

In order to restore investment demand, something must happen to raise profit expectations. Keynes suggests that this will happen as capital becomes relatively scarcer over time, and demand increases relative to capacity. Over time, existing fixed capital will depreciate or be made obsolescent; inventories of finished goods will be depleted; and stocks of working capital will be exhausted (*G.T.*: 317–18, 331). These processes will raise the profits of existing capital goods and translate into higher profit expectations. Since these processes can take years, the contraction can take years.

Thus, from Keynes's point of view, cycles are created by the ordinary functioning of the economic system. Because of the realities of expectation formation, investment demand generates oscillations. Exuberant animal spirits create expansions; caution and pessimism require that slow-developing economic changes must take place before attitudes about the future can become positive again. However, it was his conviction that investment had never really approached the point of eliminating long-term scarcity in productive capacity. Hence, there was social gain to eliminating fluctuations caused by variations in expected profitability. His proposed solution is to sustain demand, and thereby sustain realized profits and business confidence. The aim was to moderate what is, by the market's own measure of profitability, an irrational cycle:

Whilst aiming at a socially controlled rate of investment with a view to a progressive decline in the marginal efficiency of capital, I should support at the same time all sorts of policies for increasing the propensity to consume. For it is unlikely that full employment can be maintained, whatever we may do about investment, with the existing propensity to consume.

(*G.T.*: 325)

It seems inadequate to read Keynes as focusing exclusively on discretionary policy in the ordinary sense of fiscal and monetary interventions to alter fluctuations as they develop. The emphasis is on sustaining steady demand, rather than reacting to cyclical fluctuations with policy manoeuvres. Income redistribution to sustain consumption demand is a fundamental institutional change, as is an overall social target for investment demand. Of course, these sorts of institutional change demand much political and social effort to implement. Keynes's struggles to implement such change, reflected in his work to influence the reconstruction of post-war international economic institutions, is consistent with this part of his theory.

EMPIRICAL RELEVANCE OF KEYNES'S THEORY OF THE CYCLE

At this point it is reasonable to ask how closely Keynes's cycle theory fits the facts. His characterization of investment timing and variability is quite accurate for the US economy before and after the Second World War. Investment demand, whether for producers' durable equipment, non-residential structures or inventories, is closely procyclical. Turning points in these categories closely match NBER cyclical turning points (Zarnowitz 1992: 94). Also, investment exhibits much greater variability over the cycle than either GNP or consumption. This can be seen from the cycle amplitudes displayed in Table 21.1.

Keynes's belief that investment and output have positive feedback on one another is also consistent with substantial empirical research. Perhaps the longest-lasting econometric investment hypothesis is the accelerator. It continues to be part of empirical research on investment. Direct tests of his conjectures about profit expectations would of course be difficult. However, the recently developed econometric literature on financial constraints (e.g. Fazzari and Mott 1986; Fazzari *et al.* 1988) and the older literature on macroeconometric investment functions (Abel and Blanchard 1986; Clarke 1979; Kopke 1985) indicates that *realized* profitability is a statistically significant determinant of investment, even after accelerator effects are taken into account. Indeed, a striking if prima facie argument for the importance of profitiability can be made using Figure 21.1. The figure shows the close correlation between capital stock growth and the profit rate (lagged two years) in the US non-financial corporate sector.

In fact, it is possible to make an empirical case for the deterioration of profitability during US business cycle expansions. There has been substantial empirical work pointing toward a non-linear relationship between profit

374

Table 21.1 Amplitudes of national income accounts: expenditures

	Average, 4 cycles 1921–38		Average, 4 cycles 1949–70		Average, 3 cycles 1970–82	
	Expansion	Contraction	Expansion	Contraction	Expansion	Contraction
GNP (50)	21.2	−16.4	17.9	−1.5	12.1	−3.5
Consumption						
Total (231)	15.0	−9.9	16.6	1.0	10.4	−0.7
Non-durables (238)	16.4	−11.4	14.2	0.7	6.9	−0.4
Durables (233)	31.0	−27.0	24.1	−5.9	20.8	−5.0
Services (239)	14.4	−6.4	18.0	2.9	10.7	2.1
Investment						
Gross Private Domestic (241)	55.4	−49.3	23.5	−9.5	29.8	−28.0
Equipment (88)	46.0	−39.4	29.8	−12.0	24.0	−12.8
Non-residential structures (87)	30.6	−32.9	18.4	−0.4	17.7	−9.9
Residential structures (89)	33.9	−22.0	6.9	3.0	16.9	−18.4

Source: Sherman (1991: 41)
Note: The numbers in parentheses indicate the series number from the *Business Conditions Digest*. These series are fully described by number in US Department of Commerce, Bureau of Economic Analysis. *Handbook of Cyclical Indicators: A supplement to the Business Conditions Digest*, 1984 edition, Washington, D.C.: US Government Printing Office. Note that all expansion amplitudes are for stages 1 to 5 and all contraction amplitudes are for stages 5 to 9, except for total consumption in 1970–82, which declined in stages 5 to 7.

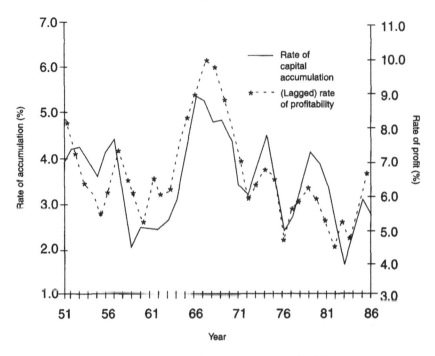

Figure 21.1 Profitability and accumulation in the US economy
Source: Bowles *et al.* (1989: 110)

rate, defined as the ratio of profit to capital stock, and capacity utilization in the US macroeconomy. Business cycle and econometric research (Boddy and Crotty 1975; Weisskopf 1979; Hahnel and Sherman 1982; Bowles *et al.* 1989) shows that the non-financial corporate business (NFCB) profit rate rises during the early stages of a business cycle expansion, declines during the later stages of the expansion, and continues to decline during the contraction. The evidence suggests that the early expansion can be characterized by an increasing profit share and increasing capacity utilization; that the contraction is characterized by declining profit share and utilization; and that the late expansion decline in profitability is explained largely by a declining profit share. Hahnel and Sherman's reference-cycle analysis indicates that declines in the profit share always begin well before declines in utilization.

Hence it might be concluded that, in the case of the United States, Keynes's claims about investment and profit expectations can be given a meaningful empirical reformulation. Since profits are non-linearly related to utilization, and since there is evidence that declining profits have a negative effect on investment, it is reasonable to say that investment demand produces non-linear feedbacks. At low rates of utilization the feedback will be positive, since output and profitability are both increasing. But at higher levels of utilization, profitability begins to fall, and the feedback can become negative. Thus the decline in *realized* profits during an expansion can help to bring the expansion to an end.[1]

DEVELOPMENTS OF KEYNESIAN CYCLE THEORY

After the publication of *The General Theory*, and with the rise of modelling as a common language in the discipline, economists attempted to represent Keynes's ideas on business cycles in a variety of mathematical forms. Many used macroeconometric models, which rely on linear-stochastic equations. By doing so they tied themselves to a dynamical framework which is quite limited.

The linear-stochastic account of business cycles has its origin in Slutsky's (1927) work. Using random numbers generated by a Russian lottery, he produced a synthesized time series. He then constructed a variety of rather complicated weighted moving averages of these random numbers. When these moving averages were plotted, they showed a strong similarity to cyclical economic time series. This similarity, perhaps as much as the accompanying analytical results on cyclicality, captured the interest of economists who wanted to explain business fluctuations.

In fact, Slutsky had implicitly created a ready-made analytical framework. If an aggregate economic variable x can be explained by a linear difference equation as simple as $x_t = \alpha x_{t-1} + \varepsilon_t$, where ε_t is a random variable, then a Slutsky-like process can be produced. Recursive substitution of the equation into itself will produce a moving average of εs, hence a rudimentary cyclical series. To bear adequate similarity to an economic time series, serial correlation of the εs would also be required.

In this one-dimensional example, and in linear models of higher dimension, theorists are forced to choose parameter values which correspond to local stability. If they do not, shocks would produce explosive behaviour everywhere around the equilibrium. Linear models can produce oscillations, but the range of parameter values which do so are implausibly narrow. Thus linear cycle models are stable equilibrium systems subject to perturbations.

The stochastic account of economic dynamics was exploited and developed by Tinbergen, Frisch and Klein. The family of macroeconometric models which descended from Klein and Goldberger (1955) was for a long time considered state-of-the-art in Keynesian cycle theory. The demonstration by Adelman and Adelman (1959) that the cyclical dynamics of Klein and Goldberger derived from exogenous shocks was not considered a devastating criticism. However, it vividly illustrated that although such models had damped multiplier–accelerator dynamics, they lacked an endogenous economic account of business cycle behaviour.

For a variety of reasons, Keynesian macroeconometrics has fallen out of favour. It was displaced briefly by the 'new monetarist' cycle theory advanced by Lucas (1975). However, empirical implausibility (Barro 1980; Gordon 1982; Mishkin 1982) and problems of internal consistency (Tobin 1980a; Dore 1993: 57–75) caused the new monetarist cycle theory to be abandoned rather quickly. For the moment its place has been taken by so-called 'real' business cycle theory (e.g. Long and Ploesser 1983), a theory not without its neoclassical critics (e.g. Summers 1986; Mankiw 1989). Although new monetarist and real business cycle theorists wish to dismiss Keynesian ideas, their accounts of cycles remain qualitatively indistinguishable from their Keynesian macroeconometric brethren. All rely on the linear-stochastic mechanism to explain observed dynamics.

All varieties of the linear-stochastic account of business cycles have some distinct weaknesses. The shocks to the aggregate economy, which are the source of cyclical dynamics in these models, have received scant attention. No one has compiled a convincing list of 'big' events, affecting entire economies at the same time, which are frequent and large enough to cause cycles. Nor has anyone explained why a large number of small shock events, which may well affect individuals and firms, should not wash out in the aggregate, as the law of large numbers suggests they should. Also, multi-period serial correlation of shocks is necessary to make linear stochastic models behave believably, and there is rarely a convincing economic explanation for this serial correlation. In addition, there is evidence of asymmetry in business cycles (Blatt 1980; Neftci 1984; Sichel 1991; Zarnowitz 1992: 256–9). Such asymmetry is not explicable by a linear system, no matter how complicated the serial correlation of the stochastic terms.

There is, however, a substantial tradition in Keynesian business cycle theory which avoids the limitations of stochastic theory and is conceptually closer to *The General Theory*. Its point of departure is Harrod (1939). It was Harrod's argument that investment behaviour should be self-reinforcing, and that this would produce instability in any aggregate demand system. To a crude first approximation, his dynamic argument for a closed economy can be represented as a one-dimensional differential equation. Let s be the marginal propensity to save, v the desired marginal and average output–capital ratio, K the real capital stock, and g the rate of growth of the capital stock. The actual output–capital ratio will be $Y/K = I/sK = g/s$. When $Y/K = 1/v$, firms will be happy with the rate of investment. When the output–capital ratio exceed $1/v$, there will be a desire to increase capacity, so g will rise; when the output–capital ratio is lower than $1/v$, g will be adjusted downward. Hence the adjustment mechanism can be simply written as $\dot{g} = \alpha \, (g/s - 1/v)$, $\alpha > 0$. This is an unstable system, explosive in both the upward and downward directions.

Now Harrod recognized that economies do not explode in the upward direction without limit. So he suggested that labour force growth would provide an upper ceiling to growth. In fact, the existence of this ceiling may cause an ultimate contraction in output. That is, if n is the rate of labour force growth and $n/s < 1/v$, g can increase above $1/v$ during the expansion, and then be forced below that value by labour constraints. However, it was immediately clear to some Keynesians that the language of linear dynamical systems was inadequate to the tasks that Harrod was trying to accomplish.

Kaldor (1940) saw this limitation very quickly, and produced a synthesis of Harrod and Kalecki which introduced non-linear methods into Keynesian cyclical analysis. Like Harrod, he assumed that the accelerator-type effects on investment would produce unstable equilibria at intermediate levels of output. Like Kalecki (1937b), he assumed that financial constraints and changes in income distribution would provide a ceiling to the growth of demand, and that autonomous investment would prevent a collapse of demand. The resulting trade cycle model, although somewhat sparsely specified, has rich dynamics, and it has proved to be of lasting influence. Much subsequent theoretical and empirical work has used its basic formulation.

For purposes of exposition, consider a model developed by Goodwin (1951). In a closed economy, let aggregate real consumption be determined by $C = a + b\,Y$, and real income by the equilibrium condition $Y = C + \dot{K}$. Here C is real consumption, Y is real NNP, K is the real capital stock, $\dot{K} = dK/dt$ is the rate of investment, and $A > 0, 1 > c > 0$. Dynamics are introduced by an investment function of the form

$$\dot{K} = \begin{cases} \kappa_1 > 0, & K < K^* \\ 0, & K = K^* \\ \kappa_2 < 0, & K > K^* \end{cases}$$

where $K^* = \lambda\,Y$ is the desired capital stock, $\lambda > 0$, a constant. Hence income moves according to $Y = (a + \dot{K})/(1 - c)$, which produces a crude cycle. Macroeconomic equilibrium is unstable because investment shifts radically, from κ_1 to κ_2. The maximum rate of investment, κ_1, is given by the capacity of the capital goods industry; the minimum rate, κ_2, by the rate of depreciation. Hence the floors and ceilings to demand are in this case provided by somewhat unreasonable assumptions. It is doubtful that the capacity of any sector of advanced economies reaches full capacity outside of wartime. And for the US non-financial corporate business sector, at least, capital stock growth was not negative except in wartime and the Great Depression.

The resulting cycle in Y and K is illustrated in Figure 21.2. The fact that investment rates and the desired capital stock are bounded prevents global instability and provides turning points. Goodwin makes the model more realistic by assuming that investment is determined by a non-linear accelerator term of the form $\dot{K} = h + F(\dot{Y}(t - \theta))$, where $F(\dot{Y}(t - \theta))$ is a smooth, cubic-like replacement of the jump assumption of the first model. The introduction of this non-linearity also preserves the floors and ceilings.

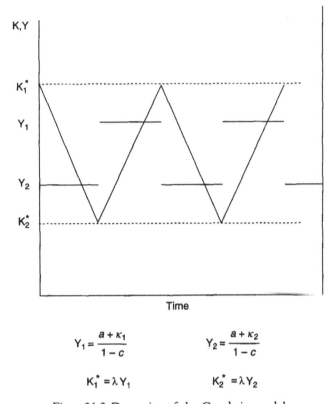

$$Y_1 = \frac{a + \kappa_1}{1 - c} \qquad\qquad Y_2 = \frac{a + \kappa_2}{1 - c}$$

$$K_1^* = \lambda Y_1 \qquad\qquad K_2^* = \lambda Y_2$$

Figure 21.2 Dynamics of the Goodwin model

Together with the assumption that multipliers are not instantaneous, this changes the model to $e\dot{Y} + (1 - b)Y - F(\dot{Y}(t - \theta)) = b + a$. This equation then produces a limit cycle in Y and $\dot{Y}$.

Models from the Goodwin–Kaldor family, which are based on versions of the multiplier–accelerator mechanism, are instructive. They show that the positive feedbacks generated by aggregate demand, represented by an investment accelerator, can easily produce unstable aggregate equilibria under economically reasonable assumptions. When the dynamics of the system are constrained by non-linearities, which in the Goodwin case stand for 'floors' and 'ceilings' to investment demand, self-sustaining cycles are the outcome. Thus the models suggest that empirically reasonable depictions of economic behaviour can produce, independent of external 'shocks', at least part of business cycle dynamics.

Because of the apparent reasonableness of the accelerator hypothesis, and because of the obvious need to provide specific and economically reasonable explanations of the upper and lower limits to aggregate demand, a large number of authors have explored Goodwin–Kaldor models. Various specifications of investment functions, time lags and non-linearities have been examined, and their effects on stability and cyclical behaviour studied for consistency and economic relevance (e.g. Hicks 1950; Minsky 1959; Chang and Smyth 1971; Torre 1977; Schinasi 1981; van der Ploeg 1983; Ricci and Vellupillai 1988; DiMatteo *et al.* 1989; Skott 1989)

More recently, financial factors have been integrated into non-linear Keynesian models. When interest rates or liquidity constraints are allowed to affect investment decisions, there are many instances in which endogenous cycles result (e.g. Hudson 1957; Day and Shaefer 1985, 1987; Foley 1986, 1987, 1988; Jarsulic 1989; Franke and Semmler 1991). In these theoretical models, instability usually results from multiplier–accelerator sources; and interest rate and liquidity changes tend to provide the upper and lower cyclical turning points through their effects on investment demand. Income distribution has also been included in Keynesian cycle analysis to explain both (e.g. Rose 1967; Foley 1986, 1987, 1988).

While these models show how aspects of Keynes's ideas can be captured and extended in non-linear dynamic models, they have an important limitation. The cyclical behaviour they produce is asymptotically periodic. Unless the models are perturbed by outside forces – which would put them on a level with the linear-stochastic models which they seek to displace – they are too regular in their behaviour. Until recently, this was counted as a significant weakness in this approach to business cycles. However, recent developments in the mathematics of non-linear dynamics have changed matters. The discovery that simple, deterministic non-linear systems are capable of producing extremely complex dynamics has filtered into the economics profession. Economists interested in explaining business cycles have realized that endogenous explanations of quasi-periodic behaviour may have been lurking in the background of previous theoretical work.

The technical characteristics of chaotic behaviour are quite easy to understand and have potentially important implications for economic analysis. A major defining characteristic of chaotic dynamical systems is the so-called 'sensitive dependence on initial conditions'. Formally, this means that for any point on an attractor, there is another arbitrarily close which will separate exponentially over time. It implies that any error about the initial state of the dynamical system will cumulate as an attempt is made to forecast the trajectory of the dynamical system. The same problem will be caused by any computational errors made in forecasting. Since everyone in the economic world does make measurement errors, and since computational capacity is always limited, sensitive dependence implies unpredictability about dynamical paths. Even if the deterministic structure of a chaotic economic system is known with complete certainty, a failure to specify perfectly initial conditions or to make error-free computations will mean significant errors of forecast.

A second characteristic of chaotic dynamical systems is the existence of orbits of arbitrarily high period. Thus, although there is unpredictability, some of the dynamics involve infinitely complicated regularities. A third characteristic of chaos is the existence of dense orbit, which means that dynamical behaviour of the system cannot be confined to any disjointed subsets in the domain. Among other things, this implies that no orbit can be stable, an additional complication of dynamics (Wiggins 1990: 420–44).

Thus it is possible that simple, deterministic non-linear economic models can produce time series behaviour which is dynamically complex, not-quite-periodic and extraordinarily resistant to prediction. This sounds like the business cycle behaviour with which empirical economists are concerned, and which Keynes was trying to explain. Non-linear Keynesian macroeconomic models can in many cases be shown to produce dynamical complexity. This has been done analytically and by means of computer simulation by several authors (e.g. Dana and Malgrange 1983; Day and Shaefer 1985, 1987; Lorenz 1987; Goodwin 1990; Jarsulic 1993a, b).

To illustrate the ease with which complexity can arise in an empirically reasonable context, consider an example taken from Jarsulic (1993a), which has a close family resemblence to the work of Goodwin. In a closed economy let aggregate demand consist of investment and consumption. The equilibrium condition in the goods market can be written in intensive form as $Y_t/K_{t-1} = I_t/K_{t-1} + C_t/K_{t-1}$, where Y_t is real GDP, K_{t-1} is real beginning-of-period capital stock, I_t is real investment demand, and C_t is real consumption demand. Assuming that consumption is proportional to current income the equilibrium condition then can be written as:

$$u_t = g_t/s$$

where $u_t = Y_t/K_{t-1}$; $g_t = [K_t/K_{t-1}] - 1$; and $s = 1 - c$, where $1 > c > 0$ is the marginal and average propensity to consume. For purposes of the model, it is assumed that capacity output is proportional to (beginning-of-period) capital stock. This allows utilization to be identified with the output–capital ratio. Investment demand is a function of past profitability:

$$g_t = \sigma\pi_{t-1}$$

where π_t is the aggregate rate of profit, defined as the flow of profits divided by the beginning-of-period capital stock, and σ is a positive constant.

The empirical work on profitability and the business cycle cited earlier suggests that a non-linear relationship between profitibility and utilization – in which as the capacity utilization rises, the profit rate first rises and then falls – is a reasonable stylized fact about the US macroeconomy. This relationship can be represented most conveniently as the piecewise linear function:

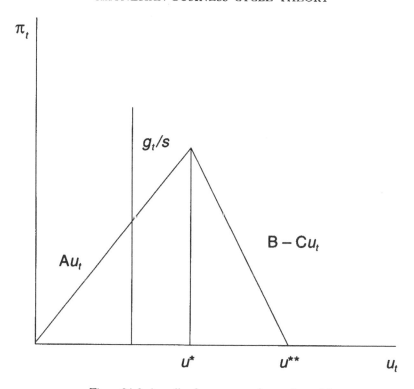

Figure 21.3 A stylized aggregate demand model

$$\pi_t = \begin{cases} Au_t & 0 \le u_t \le u^* \\ B - Cu_t & u^* \le u_t \le u^{**} \end{cases}$$

where A, B and C are positive constants; u^* is the utilization rate at which the profit rate begins to decline; and $u^{**} = B/C$ is the upper bound to the output–capital ratio. This function is shown in Figure 21.3.

Combining these three relationships gives a first-order difference equation:

$$\pi_t = F(\pi_{t-1}) = \begin{cases} \gamma \pi_{t-1} & 0 \le \pi_{t-1} \le \pi^* \\ \psi - \phi \pi_{t-1} & \pi^* \le \pi_{t-1} \le \pi^{**} \end{cases}$$

where $\gamma = A\sigma/s$, $\psi = B/s$, $\phi = C\sigma/s$; and where $\pi^* = \psi/\phi$ and $\pi^{**} = \psi/(\gamma + \phi)$. This is represented in Figure 21.4. As long as $(1 + \gamma/\phi) > \gamma$, the system will produce only positive values of π if the initial value is positive and less than ψ/ϕ. Note that the upper and lower bounds for the growth rate have an economic explanation, and are not dependent on physical capacity limits nor on exogenously given components of demand.[2]

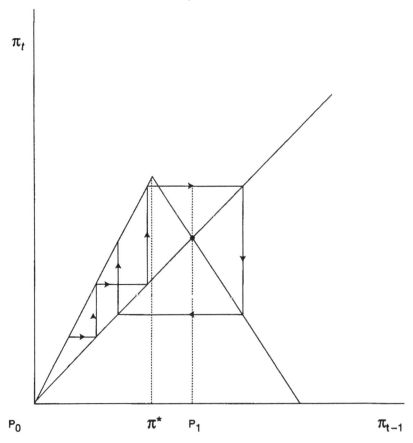

Figure 21.4 Endogenous dynamics of the demand model

When P_1 is unstable, which can easily occur for economically plausible parameter values, complicated and self-sustaining fluctutations can occur. This can be seen from Figure 21.4. A contraction from peak profitability can last at most one period, but it is possible for expansions to last more than one period. This bias is consistent with the observed tendency for expansions to last longer than contractions in the post-war US business cycle. Moreover, for plausible parameter values, it can be shown that chaotic trajectories can result. Thus self-sustaining, irregular and asymmetric cyclical behaviour is easily produced by an empirically grounded aggregate demand model.

The presence of strictly chaotic behaviour in macroeconomic data is at present controversial, although the presence of non-linearity is less so (cf. Appendix). Hence it is too much to say that observed cycle behaviour is in fact the outcome of chaotic economic processes. However, this and similiar modelling exercises imply that endogenous explanations of observed cycle behaviour are respectable competitors for the currently more popular linear-stochastic models. They are capable of representing qualitative aspects of cyclical economic time series – such as the combination of asymmetry and aperiodicity – at least as successfully as their stochastic counterparts.

It also is worth noting that the possibility of chaotic economic behaviour raises important issues for non-Keynesian accounts of expectation formation. The existence of sensitive dependence means unpredictability in the face of measurement error. Even when the underlying economic mechanism is perfectly known, errors will cumulate and forecasted trajectories will diverge from actual trajectories. Since it is unlikely that anyone could assert error-free measurement and expect to be taken seriously, it is not clear how any account of expectation formation could claim that expectations are in the long run mostly correct. In the presence of sufficient non-linearity, where equilibria are locally unstable and there is no centre of gravitation, an error in measurement cannot be treated as an insignificant displacement from a well-known rest point. Chaos-inducing non-linearities appear to make the notion of perfect foresight a self-contradictory one.

Hence, to the extent that economic chaos exists, the Keynesian view of the difficulty of expectation formation receives a new source of support. Even when economic actors are assumed to have the unreasonably complete economic knowledge which contemporary theory pretends they have, measurement and computational difficulties still eliminate their ability to know the future.

In summary, numerous theorists have been able to develop and extend the business cycle theory of *The General Theory*. Keynes's insights about the instability of aggregate demand, the self-reinforcing nature of changes in aggregate demand, the importance of profitability to investment and the endogenous nature of the cycle behaviour have proved to be empirically relevant and a source of theoretical innovation. What remains to be considered are his views about the importance of institutional structure for the nature of business cycles.

THE INSTITUTIONAL FOUNDATIONS OF CYCLICAL TRANSFORMATION

After the Second World War, US business cycle behaviour exhibited two significant sets of changes. From 1945, expansions lengthened and contractions shortened, as can be seen in in Table 21.2. Moreover, the variability of investment demand was reduced, which is evident from the reduction of investment amplitude after 1945 (Table 21.1). During the period 1945–73 there were also historically anomalous increases in GDP and productivity growth rates. After 1973, there was a dramatic end to

Table 21.2 Duration of business cycles in the United States by selected sub-periods, 1846–1982

Period (1)	Number of business cycles covered (2)	Duration in months[a] Expansions Mean (3)	SD (4)	Contractions Mean (5)	SD (6)	Business cycles Mean (7)	SD (8)	Percentage of time in contraction[b] All (9)	Peacetime[c] (10)
All cycles									
1846–85	8	32	16	27	18	59	28	45	46
1885–1912	8	23	5	17	5	40	4	42	42
1912–45	8	33	24	17	12	51	20	34	47
1945–82	8	45	28	11	4	56	27	20	25
Excluding marginal recessions[c]									
1846–85	7	39	21	28	19	68	38	42	
1885–1912	6	36	21	18	5	53	21		33
Summary									
1846–1945	24	30	17	20	13	50	21	41	
1846–1945[c]	21	36	21	21	14	57	27	37	
1846–1982	32	33	21	18	12	51	22	35	
Peacetime cycles[d]									
1846–1982	27	28	13	19	12	46	18		41
1846–1982[c]	24	33	18	19	13	52	25		37

Source: Moore and Zarnowitz (1986: 524)

Notes

[a] Based on the monthly NBER reference dates, except for the two earliest cycles dated in calendar years (troughs: 1846 and 1848; peaks: 1847 and 1853). Mean = mean duration; SD = standard deviation, in months. Col. (3) + col. (5) = col. (7), except for rounding.

[b] Months of business cycle contractions divided by total months covered, times 100.

[c] The following phases designated as contractions in the NBER chronology are treated as retardations rather than recessions and included, along with the preceding and following phases, in long expansions: 6/1869–12/1870; 3/1887–4/1888; 6/1899–12/1900.

[d] Excludes five wartime cycles (trough–peak–trough dates) associated with the Civil War (6/1861–4/1865–12/1867); First World War (12/1914–8/1918–3/1919); Second World War (6/1938–2/1945–10/1945); Korean War (10/1949–7/1953–5/1954); and Vietnam War (2/1961–12/1969–11/1970).

Table 21.3 Post-war economic performance in six major industrial countries (average annual percentage growth rates)

	Average unemployment				Consumer prices			Real GDP			Real GDP per person-hour	
	1952–64	1965–73	1973–9	1980–3	1950–73	1973–9	1979–83	1950–73	1973–9	1979–83	1950–73	1973–81
US	5.0	4.5	6.5	8.4	2.7	8.2	8.2	2.2	1.9	0.7	2.6	1.1
UK	2.5	3.2	4.6	9.0	4.6	15.4	10.7	2.5	1.3	0.4	3.1	2.9
France	1.7	2.4	4.2	7.6	5.0	10.7	12.1	4.1	2.6	1.1	5.1	3.0
Germany	2.7	0.8	3.1	5.7	2.7	4.7	5.1	5.0	2.6	0.5	6.0	3.7
Italy	5.9	3.4	6.0	8.6	3.9	16.3	17.5	4.8	2.0	0.6	5.8	2.5[a]
Japan	1.9	1.3	1.8	2.3	5.2	10.0	4.3	8.4	3.0	3.9	8.0	3.1

	Non-residential fixed capital stock[b]		Non-residential fixed capital stock per person-hour		Volume of exports		
	1950–73	1973–9	1950–73	1973–8	1950–73	1973–9	1979–83
US	4.0	3.0	2.9	1.8	6.3	4.9	−1.6
UK	3.9	3.2	4.0	4.3	3.9	4.7	−0.1
France	4.5	4.5	4.5	5.3	8.2	6.1	2.3
Germany	6.1	4.1	6.1	6.3	12.4	4.7	4.1
Italy	5.1[b]	4.2[c]	5.4	6.3	11.7	7.1	1.2
Japan	9.2[d]	6.2[d]	7.6	6.8	15.4	7.6	10.2

Source: Marglin and Schor (1990: 47)

Notes:

a 1973–9

b Averaged gross and net except where stated

c Gross stock only

d Average of gross stock for whole economy and net stock for private sector only.

these two decades of rapid expansion (Table 21.3). Growth rates fell off, and have yet to recover. While the transformation of cycle lengths appears to persist, the amplitudes of investment fluctuations increased during the 1970s and 1980s. Similar phenomena can be observed across advanced market economies.

Keynesian economists (e.g. Marglin and Schor 1990, cf. especially the essay by Hughes *et al.*) have produced explanations of these striking transformations of economic performances in productivity and GDP growth rates.[3] They emphasize that institutional coherence and stability are necessary to maintaining high levels of aggregate demand. The 'Golden Age' period is depicted as one in which the institutional framework of advanced market economies were simultaneously rearranged in a new and effective fashion. While a review of this extended literature would be a difficult task, a brief summary of some of the main elements of the Keynesian view can give an indication of the line of argument. In this view, the period 1945–73 was distinguished by (a) a stable international financial and trade regime, under the direction of the US; (b) an expansion of state spending relative to GDP, providing a stable source of demand; (c) a general commitment to using fiscal and monetary policy to maintain demand and full employment; (d) roughly proportional growth of real wages and productivity, which sustained consumer demand, helped to stabilize price increases, and encouraged capital accumulation by guaranteeing a roughly stable profit rate. These and other institutional changes acted to sustain overall demand, keep unemployment rates low, and stimulated the remarkable burst of productivity growth witnessed during the period. The motivation for these extensive changes was a widespread recognition that a return to pre-war economic disorganization could spell the end to capitalism. As the historian Eric Hobsbawm (1994: 272–3) has observed:

> for a variety of reasons, the politicians, officials and even many of the businessmen of the post-war West were convinced that a return to laissez-faire and the unreconstructed free market were out of the question. Certain policy objectives – full employment, the containment of communism, the modernization of lagging or declining and ruined economies – had absolute priority and justified the strongest government presence. Even regimes dedicated to economic and political liberalism now could, and had to, run their economies in ways which would once have been rejected as 'socialist'. After all, that is how Britain and even the USA had run their war-economies. The future lay with the 'mixed economy'. Though there were moments when the old orthodoxies of fiscal rectitude, stable currencies and stable prices still counted, even these were no longer absolutely compelling. Since 1933 the scarecrows of inflation and deficit finance no longer kept the birds away from the economic fields, but the crops still seemed to grow.

The 'Golden Age' ended as each of these institutional constants dissolved in the 1970s. The fixed exchange rate system of Bretton Woods was abandoned, and world financial markets were allowed to become quite volatile. The ascent of monetarist polices, which began with Whitlam, Thatcher and Volker, signalled an attack on aspects of the state sector spending, and an unwillingness to use fiscal and monetary policy in the pursuit of employment targets. Finally, generalized problems with profitability affected investment growth and further reduced government willingness to sustain demand. The disintegration of these institutions is then part of a complex account of the post-1973 declines in productivity and GDP growth, and the general disorganization of the advanced market economies.

If we accept Keynes's points that market economies are never stable and that aggregate demand can fail, then an institutional structure to limit the effects of instability and sustain demand becomes crucial. Those Keynesians who have applied these ideas to the explanation of growth and cycles before, during and after the 'Golden Age' have made a potentially important theoretical and practical contribution. By offering a framework for understanding a set of extraordinarily important events, they have suggested how useful changes might be made.[4]

CONCLUSIONS

It is evident that Keynes thought that good economics is never static, neither in its view of economic phenomena, nor in its conclusions. The object of analysis is a dynamical system which produces growth, cycles, crises and sharp qualitative change. He clearly believed that macroeconomic theory must explain how these behaviours fit together; and that serious theory must pay attention to changes in the underlying behaviours of these systems. Those who have developed the Keynesian account of economic dynamics have worked along these lines. The stream of non-linear growth and cycle theory, which descends from the initial efforts of Kaldor and Goodwin, integrates human agency, imperfect foresight, and financial and distributional constraints to explain instability and cyclical behaviour. It can be used to show that the not-quite-periodic aspects of cycles can be given an economic explanation. The historically specific work of Keynesian institutionalists offers significant insight into the major changes in economic performance through which we are all living. Together they present an economic explanation of growth and cycles, and indicate that institutional changes may influence them. This is a theoretical position which has much to offer in an economic world with increasingly discouraging dynamics.

APPENDIX

Attempts to test for the presence of chaotic behaviour in economic data have drawn on a variety of techniques developed by scientists. Sensitive dependence can be identified by the presence of a positive Lyapunov exponent. This measure can be calculated using simple algorithms and a single time series, and does not require any knowledge of the underlying dynamical system (Wolf 1986). Accurate estimation requires runs of data several thousand observations long. Since chaotic processes often (but *not* always) operate on sets which have a fractal (i.e non-integer) dimension, it is also common practice to try to estimate the dimension of the dynamical system producing the time series. A fractal estimate is counted as evidence for chaos. This too can be done using easily implemented algorithms (Grassberger and Proccaccia 1983), and also requires long runs of data for accuracy (cf. Jarsulic 1993a). In addition, since chaotic systems sometimes (but *not* always) exhibit spectral densities which appear to be white noise, spectral densities are sometimes calculated.

Unfortunately for economic researchers, many economic time series have lengths which range from inadequate to just barely sufficient for these tests. At times economists have behaved as if these data limitations could be ignored. Attempts have been made to estimate set dimension for GNP (Brock 1986; Frank and Stegnos 1989; Mullineux *et al.* 1993), work stoppages (Sayers 1987) and monetary aggregates (Barnett and Chen 1988; Chen 1993). Since the series from macroeconomic aggregates are short, it is unreasonable to expect any firm conclusions. The conclusion of Ramsey *et al.* (1990), who review the dimension estimates of Barnett and Chen, Sayers, and Scheinkman and Lebaron – that there is little evidence for chaotic behaviour, but some for non-linearity, in the data considered – is hardly surprising. When time series are longer, the dimension results are more believable and have in some cases been more in line with chaos. Frank and Stegnos (1989) find strong evidence of fractal dimension in gold and silver returns; DeCoster *et al.* (1992) believe that their dimension results for commodities futures prices indicate non-linearity; and Yang and Brorsen (1993) also find evidence of non-linearity in dimension estimate for different futures prices. Positive Lyapunov exponents, more closely connected to the definition of chaos, have been estimated for monetary aggregates (Barnett and Chen 1988).

Since economists have put so much emphasis on dimension estimates, it should be emphasized that drawing conclusions about the existence of non-linearity and chaos on the basis of dimension alone is a problematic procedure. The definition of chaos does not include any notion of a fractal dimension; and as Grassberger and Proccaccia pointed out, not every chaotic system has a fractal dimension. Some economists have also used the BDS statistic (Brock *et al.* 1991), which utilizes estimates of correlation dimension and which is actually a test for stochastic dependence against the null hypothesis of stochastic independence, as a device for discriminating between stochastic and chaotic systems. Its usefulness as a test for non-linearity or chaos is controversial (Barnett and Hinich 1993).

On the basis of the empirical work done so far, there is insufficient evidence to draw firm conclusions about the presence or absence of chaos in economic data. However, when time series ae sufficiently long, tests seem to point in the direction of non-linearity and chaos. As in the case of deductive theorizing, progress in the empirical study of economic time series will very likely have to wait for discoveries by scientists and mathematicians. Something along the line of bootstrapping may be necessary to overcome the shortness of macroeconomic time series in which there is so much interest.

NOTES

1 Note that this observed relationship between the profit rate and utilization is more complex than the one often assumed in theoretical macroeconomic models in the Post-Keynesian tradition. Kalecki (1971b: 78–92) and Robinson (1962b), for example, assume that the realized rate of profit is proportional to the output–capital ratio. The data suggest a non-linear relationship between these two variables. The implications of this non-linearity are explored on pp. 381–85.

2 Provided that $\gamma > 1$, there will be two equilibrium points in this system, one zero and one positive, as can be seen in Figure 21.3. The eigenvalue of $F(\pi_{t-1})$ at P_0 is γ, and at P_1 it is $-\phi$. P_0 is unstable if $\gamma > 1$. P_1 will be unstable if $\phi > 1$, which will be more likely the stronger is the tendency of profits to decline, the larger is the multiplier and the stronger is the investment response to profitability.

3 Although the text emphasizes the contribution of Hughes *et al.*, there are other economists who have worked along similar lines. Kalecki (1971b: 165–83), Cornwall (1977, 1990), Aglietta (1979), and Bowles *et al.*, (1986), have all made contributions with a strong family resemblance to work discussed in the text.

4 It is useful to compare the demand-oriented explanation of the 'Golden Age' transformations of the cycle to those offered by 'real business cycle' proponents. In their influential macroeconomics textbook, for example, Blanchard and Fischer (1989: 8) write of the trend behaviour of the US macroeconomy:

> A useful way of approaching the issue is to think of the economy as being affected by two types of shocks. Some shocks have permanent effects on output – we shall call them permanent shocks. Prime candidates are improvements in productivity or increases in the labor force. Some shocks have transitory effects, effects on output that disappear over time; they may include bad crops, temporary increases in government spending, changes in the money [supply].We may then think of the trend as that part of output that is due to permanent shocks . . .

Although they try to identify permanent and transitory shocks by econometric means, there is no attempt to explain what economic events these shocks can be said to represent. Later, they admit (Blanchard and Fischer 1989: 28) that there is 'little direct evidence on such shocks and how they propagate'. In the main, real business cycle theorists seem forced to take a position of studied agnosticism on an economic issue of significant practical importance.

22

NOTES ON THE TRADE CYCLE AND SOCIAL PHILOSOPHY IN A POST-KEYNESIAN WORLD*

John Cornwall

THE COMPATIBILITY OF CAPITALISM AND DEMOCRACY

The revolutionary message of *The General Theory* was that capitalism is not a self-regulating system in which aggregate demand automatically adjusts to aggregate supply. To Keynes, recognition of this fundamental truth was the essential first step in a programme for preserving capitalism and democracy, as its acceptance would direct attention to the task of developing full employment policies.[1] Events of the inter-war period had raised doubts about the compatability of capitalism and democracy. On the one hand, it was widely believed that the economic consequences of universal suffrage was that the state would replace capitalism with socialism in the interests of 'distributional fairness'. During this same period, these events also fostered a belief that democracy was doomed. The political consequence of capitalism was the authoritarian state, as capitalists, in an effort to preserve power, would use their superior power to end democracy before suffrage had become widespread. To Keynes, neither the decay of capitalism nor democracy was inevitable, provided labour was fully employed and capitalists could retain control over the production process. Under these conditions capitalism would gain political acceptability and with general acceptance there would be no need for the conservative forces to oppose democracy. Given the circumstances of the time, Keynes believed monetary policy to be incapable of generating the necessary level of aggregate demand; fiscal policy would be required. To the political and economic establishment, this constituted a new and highly suspect economic role for the state. Keynes himself envisaged this expanded role as a limited one. Government policies would not replace the market system but would work through it, allowing the free play of decentralized decision-making and the pursuit of self-interest to regulate markets as it had in the past. Nevertheless, while the new economic role was strictly limited, it was absolutely essential. The achievement of full employment was seen 'as the only practicable means of avoiding the destruction of existing economic forms

393

in their entirety and as the condition of the successful functioning of individual initiative' (*G.T.*: 380).

While the initial opposition to his views was strong, Keynes foresaw a rapid acceptance of his ideas; in particular, fiscal policy would be accepted in a manner similar to dentistry. A temporary rise in unemployment would be attended to by public-spirited fiscal authorities much as a sore tooth would be treated by the dentist.

THE POST-WAR RECORD

The economic record of the first two decades following the Second World War reconversion period supported Keynes's belief in the importance of full employment in securing the general acceptance of both capitalism and democracy. Although it is not clear to what extent fiscal policy, or merely a commitment to employ stimulative fiscal policy if needed, was responsible, a prolonged 'quasi boom' (to use Keynes's expression) took place in most developed capitalist economies. Moreover, unexpected and prolonged growth generated not only growing profits and real wages, but also the tax revenues needed to finance increased economic demands on the state, including programmes that greatly reduced potential distributional conflicts. The economic consequence was not 'socialism' but a more limited yet still important state intervention to bolster welfare state capitalism; the political consequence was a shift in the distribution of political power to labour, accompanied by a greater acceptance of capitalism on the part of the trade unions.

Events of the late 1960s to early 1970s marked an end to this 'Golden Age' and a reappraisal of Keynes's economic role of the state. A common charge was that Keynes's vision of economic policy was at best naive in at least two important senses. First, basic to the Keynesian argument in support of interventionist policies was the assumption that policy-makers in performing their duties would forgo the personal gains made possible by their privileged positions.[2] In contrast, public-choice theorists argued that the authorities are primarily motivated by a desire to be re-elected, and would therefore be forced to accede to excessive demands on the state, promising pressure groups programmes and rewards that could not be realized. The inevitable result would be widespread disillusionment, undermining both democracy and capitalism.

A related criticism of a 'dentistry' view of policy concerned its naivety in assuming that the achievement of full employment would not entail sacrificing other desirable economic goals. For example, even if the fiscal instruments were set at a level just sufficient to generate the required level of aggregate demand, the likelihood of serious inflation was overlooked by Keynes. According to these critics, the economic consequences of democ-

Table 22.1 Average standardized unemployment rates (U) and rates of inflation ($\dot{p}$) for eighteen OECD economies, selected periods (%)

	1960–73	1974–9	1980–3	1984–90	1991–2
U	2.3	4.1	6.3	7.0	7.8
$\dot{p}$	4.5	9.9	9.7	6.5	3.6

Sources: OECD, *Economic Outlook,* June 1992: tables 50, R18, R19, and December 1993: tables A15, A18 and A19; OECD, *Historical Statistics, 1960–90,* Paris, 1992: table 8.11; R. Layard *et al.,* *Unemployment: Macroeconomic performance and the labour market,* Oxford: Oxford University Press, 1991: table A3

racy are an 'overloaded' economy prone to adverse side-effects such as serious inflation.

Events of the 1970s and 1980s, especially the inflation record, are often cited as evidence of the correctness of this critique. Table 22.1 gives annual average rates of inflation and unemployment in 18 OECD countries for four sub-periods beginning in the 1960s.[3] The upward trend in inflation rates until the 1980s is pronounced, illustrating the alleged propensity of the Keynesian state to overload itself with demands far in excess of the ability to supply them. However, this rise of inflation rates did not mark the beginning of a long period of *accelerating* inflation as implied by the overload thesis. Rather, since the mid-1970s the priority of the state has been to reduce inflation through restrictive aggregate demand policies. This is reflected in Table 22.1 by the sharp and prolonged rise in unemployment rates beginning in the second half of the 1970s, a record that Keynes would have characterized as a permanent 'semi-slump'.

AN APPRAISAL OF KEYNES'S VIEWS

Considering events of the past half-century, what can be said in support of Keynes's views? First, Keynes was correct in arguing that there is no automatic tendency for capitalism to perform even close to some kind of full employment equilibrium, as the record of the past three-quarters of a century makes clear. This is especially true of the Anglo–American economies. Over the period 1920–93, but excluding the Second World War years and the immediate post-war recovery period, unemployment rates in Canada, in the United Kingdom and in the United States averaged a little less than 7 per cent and exceeded 6 per cent in approximately one year out of two.[4] These are unemployment rates characterized by widespread involuntary unemployment.

Second, the economic programme of *The General Theory* was incomplete; it failed to consider the potential inflationary side-effects of full employment policies.[5] To be sure, there were no automatic full employment tendencies as Keynes asserted, but if the full employment goal were achieved (for whatever reason), events of more recent times have shown it to be incompatible with politically acceptable rates of inflation.

Third, as of this writing (July 1995), Keynes's belief that capitalism and democracy could only be reconciled through full employment has not been borne out. Since the mid-1970s the trend has been a rise in unemployment in the OECD economies, yet there has been no strong movement by the electorate to replace capitalism or democracy. The economic consequences of democracy have not led to socialism or to an overloaded economy but to restrictive aggregate demand policies, high unemployment and less state intervention in the economy. However we choose to appraise the economic role played by governments today, it is vastly different from that proposed in *The General Theory* and the extended role that emerged during the 'Golden Age' period.

These last two paragraphs are not offered in order to detract from the great insights of *The General Theory* or from Keynes's unique and important role in advancing economics. What Keynes could not have foreseen were the radical and rapid institutional changes about to unfold. In retrospect, events since *The General Theory* have taught us that the Great Depression was not unique in the following sense. Because of an evolving institutional framework, capitalist economies can periodically perform poorly because of an inability of policy-makers to articulate and implement new macroeconomic policies that 'fit' the latest stage of institutional development. The remainder of the chapter takes up the institutional causes of today's serious macroeconomic malfunction, and the continued failure to implement policies that can bring recovery in the OECD economies.

MACROECONOMIC POLICIES AND PERFORMANCE

The post-war performance of capitalism since the mid-1970s raises several basic questions, all of which Keynes would be concerned with were he to rewrite *The General Theory* today. There have been occasional public statements by policy-makers admitting that the real aim of policy over approximately the past two decades has been simply to reduce the power of labour by increasing unemployment. However, the official reason given for the restrictive aggregate demand policies has been that this is the only way to recreate something like the macroeconomic record of the 'Golden Age' era. The professed goals of the recovery programme have been not merely to achieve low inflation but also to permit an eventual return to low unemployment if not to full employment.

The key assumption underlying this policy scenario is that the authorities can alter the behaviour of market participants in such a way as to reduce inflationary tendencies at low unemployment rates 'once and for all'. However, it must be done indirectly by first creating high unemployment, i.e. the short-term pain, as the means to the long-term gain of low inflation and low unemployment.

The most serious attempt to outline the rationale of the strategy – one that has been highly influential in government circles – was the so-called McCracken Report, which offered an explanation and a cure for the Great Inflation from the late 1960s to the early 1970s. According to the report, provided the pain of high unemployment was allowed to persist long enough, inflation would no longer be a serious problem and the restrictive policies could be followed by 'a sustained expansion, initially less rapid than would otherwise be desirable during which memories of recent inflation should fade, and confidence in rising sales and employment be restored' (OECD 1978: 276).

As Table 22.1 and other data reveal, these policies have actually been associated with a most unsatisfactory macroeconomic performance, including low growth, high unemployment, rising inequalities of income, a rising incidence of poverty and, until recently, politically unacceptable rates of inflation. Whatever the intentions of the programme, then, the first important question to consider is to what extent the economic policies of the last two decades contributed to the deterioration in performance.

Consider first whether the restrictive policies have succeeded in their aims. Since the announced strategy of the policy was to achieve low unemployment *and* low inflation by first restricting demand and deliberately driving up unemployment rates, the optimistic predictions of the McCracken Report nicely summarize the test of success or failure. The test is not whether the policy can reduce inflation, but rather, what happens if and when the authorities decide to restimulate the economy (or even to allow a boom to develop). The policy will have failed in its own terms if attempts to restimulate the economy lead to unacceptably high rates of inflation before involuntary unemployment has been appreciably reduced. Unfortunately, advocates of restrictive policies either do not bother to consider this issue or refuse to let others in on their views. Even more unfortunately, the evidence supports the position that restrictive aggregate demand policies have failed this test.

Table 22.2 tracks the unemployment–inflation records of the G7 and two of its members from 1979 to 1992.[6] Restrictive aggregate demand policies successfully reduced inflation in roughly the first half of the 1980s to rates experienced in the 1950s, but at a great cost in terms of unemployment. Unemployment rates averaged 7.3, 11.2 and 8.0 per cent in the G7, the United Kingdom and the United States, respectively, over the 1980–6 period.

More critical, in 1987 unemployment dropped below these rates, and although unemployment was still high by post-war standards, inflation rates accelerated. Moreover, even though average unemployment rates in the G7 fell only a little over 1 per cent further by 1990, inflation rates continued to

Table 22.2 Unemployment and inflation rates for the G7, the United Kingdom and the United States, 1979–92 (%)

		1979[a]	*1980–3*[a]	*1984*	*1985*	*1986*	*1987*	*1988*	*1989*	*1990*	*1991*	*1992*
G7	U	4.9	6.9	7.3	7.2	7.1	6.7	6.1	5.7	5.6	6.3	6.9
	p	9.8	8.5	4.7	4.0	2.1	2.9	3.4	4.5	5.0	4.3	3.0
USA	U	5.8	8.4	7.4	7.1	6.9	6.1	5.4	5.2	5.4	6.6	7.3
	p	11.3	8.3	4.3	3.5	1.9	3.7	4.1	4.8	5.4	4.2	3.0
UK	U	5.0	10.0	11.7	11.2	11.2	10.3	8.6	7.1	6.8	8.9	9.9
	p	13.4	10.8	5.0	6.1	3.4	4.1	4.9	7.8	9.5	5.9	3.7

Sources: OECD, *Historical Statistics, 1960–90*, Paris, 1992: table 8.11; OECD, *Economic Outlook*, June 1992: tables 50 and R18, and December 1993: tables A15 and A19.
Note: [a] annual average

rise between 1987 and the recession that began in 1990. The worsening of the inflation problem can be seen in another way. Inflation rates in the G7 averaged 2.9 per cent in the 1960–8 period, the same as the 1987 G7 average shown in Table 22.2. However, the average G7 unemployment rate in the earlier period was only 2.8 per cent compared to 6.7 per cent in 1987.

Table 22.1 portrays the failure of restrictive policies from a longer-run perspective. From the 1960–73 period until 1984–90 there was an upward drift in average unemployment rates throughout the OECD, with inflation rates on average rising from the 1960s to the 1970s and then falling about half-way back to their pre-1974 levels in the 1980s. Only after the onset of the 1990 downturn did inflation fall back to the levels of the 'Golden Age' period. Note that this required not just a further rise in average unemployment rates to almost 8 per cent in 1991–2, but a thirteen-year period of depressed labour markets from 1980 to 1992 during which unemployment rates for the group averaged almost 7 per cent.[7]

What Tables 22.1 and 22.2 suggest, in spite of efforts to rid capitalism permanently of the inflation problem, is that these economies have developed an increased inflationary bias. Rates of inflation that in the early postwar period were associated with relatively low rates of unemployment are now associated with much higher rates of unemployment. A corollary of this worsening inflation–unemployment trade-off is that full employment now leads to higher and politically more unacceptable rates of inflation.

The question raised at the beginning of this section was whether the restrictive policies of the last two decades bear any responsibility for the poor macroeconomic performance of the period. Certainly these policies have failed in their aim of simultaneously achieving low unemployment *and* low inflation, and have not achieved much success in controlling inflation until the 1990s. Periods of 'success' in reducing inflation have been at the cost of high unemployment, often followed by periods of accelerating inflation. Moreover, these same policies are a source of other dimensions of unsatisfactory macroeconomic performance of recent times. Not only have they led to increased unemployment and poverty, they have also contributed to the decline in productivity growth rates.[8]

The imposition of these failed policies can be traced to an assumed inability to contain inflation in any way other than by increasing unemployment. The remaining key questions, therefore, are: why has inflation become a more serious problem than it was in the 'Golden Age'? and is there some way to contain inflation other than high unemployment? A first step to answering these questions is to understand that the causes of the greater inflation problems are to a large extent rooted in the 'Golden Age' itself.

INSTITUTIONAL DEVELOPMENTS IN THE LABOUR MARKET DURING THE 'GOLDEN AGE'

To understand why capitalism has become so inflation prone, it must first be recognized that important institutional changes have occurred since *The General Theory*, generating *potentially* stronger inflationary pressures everywhere at all rates of unemployment, but especially at full employment. These changes are nowhere more apparent than in the labour market.[9] In particular, the consolidation of union power and the spread of the welfare state during the period following the Second World War led to a shift in the relative economic and political power of labour, allowing labour to introduce and enforce 'fairness' considerations in wage settlements.[10] Fairness came to be defined in terms of the growth of real wages and the protection of relative wages. Simplifying somewhat, during this period one or other of two types of labour market strategies was adopted by labour (and agreed to by the other principal actors) to institutionalize fairness in the labour markets of the OECD economies. Depending upon the strategy chosen, the potential inflationary bias either was or was not contained and, as a consequence, full employment was or was not consistent with low and politically acceptable rates of wage and therefore price inflation.

The first strategy can be called a 'market power strategy'. In this strategy, wage settlements were the result of an unrestricted collective bargaining process between labour and management. There was only a weak or inconsistent effort by either, or by any third party, to bring wage settlements into line with some common interest or national goal such as wage and price stability. One of the purposes of collective bargaining was to determine a fair real wage and a fair relative wage through negotiations over the money wage, with the cost of living and wage settlements elsewhere being the key considerations.

Since labour's market power increased when unemployment fell, this strategy generated the familiar negative short-run relationship between rates of unemployment and money wage inflation, that is, the Phillips curve. More than that, as the record of these economies shows, full employment was not consistent with politically acceptable rates of inflation. Policy-induced high unemployment became the only means available for containing the inflationary bias in these economies. The economies in which a market-power strategy best describes the policy adopted in the 1960–73 period were Canada, Ireland, Italy and the United States. The United Kingdom can also be included although with less confidence.[11]

In contrast, during the 'Golden Age' a 'social bargain strategy' was adopted in various forms in the majority of the developed OECD economies. The concluded social bargain involved efforts to modify labour's behaviour directly by offering rewards for 'good' behaviour in order to restrain inflation, rather than indirectly by first deliberately driving up unemployment through policy. This allowed these economies to operate at rates of unemployment of $1\frac{1}{2}$ per cent on average without suffering from relatively high rates of inflation.[12]

In these economies labour accepted the need for money-wage restraint in the interests of the national goals of wage and price stability and international competitiveness. In return, labour was given full employment and, depending upon the country, other rewards such as generous welfare benefits, rising real wages as a result of the growing productivity associated with full employment, and more congenial industrial relations. Labour was also assigned a role in developing, implementing and monitoring the social bargain and in organizing the workplace, at least as a junior partner. The social bargain was the instrument for restraining inflation, thereby permitting high employment.

The success of social bargain strategies is brought out clearly in Table 22.3. The average inflation and unemployment rates of a sample of eighteen OECD economies during the 1960–73 period are shown, together with the averages for the thirteen countries that adopted a social-bargain strategy and for the five that adopted a market-power strategy. While inflation rates varied only modestly between the two groups, average unemployment rates were almost three times higher in the economies that sought to control inflation by creating unemployment.

In spite of the large unemployment differences between the two groups, the average unemployment rate in the eighteen OECD economies during

Table 22.3 Average rates of unemployment (U) and inflation ($\dot{p}$) for eighteen OECD economies and in two sub-groups, 1960–73 (all figures %)

Total	Social-bargain group	Market-power group
$U_{18} = 2.3$	$U_{13} = 1.5$	$U_5 = 4.3$
$\dot{p}_{18} = 4.5$	$\dot{p}_{13} = 4.7$	$\dot{p}_5 = 4.1$

Source: R. Layard *et al.*, *Unemployment: Macroeconomic performance and the labour market*, Oxford: Oxford University Press, 1991: Table A3

this period was one-third of the average rate of unemployment of 6.9 per cent for the 1980–92 period. In understanding what has gone wrong since, the important issue is why so many economies were relieved of any constraint on their aggregate demand policies during the early period.

For most of the 1960–73 period a relatively fixed exchange rate system prevailed, forcing inflation discipline on the various countries. This led the authorities to target a rate of domestic inflation similar to that of their principal trading partners, especially the United States. Because of the success of their social bargains (and favourable movements in the terms of trade), such targets were more or less achieved and were consistent with full employment in the overwhelming majority of the countries.[13]

The rapid expansion of exports throughout the OECD also played a key role in the ability and willingness of the authorities to keep unemployment rates low as it relieved most economies of a payments constraint. For this group as a whole, the balance of payments showed a small deficit, with the deficits of the smaller economies slightly exceeding the surpluses of the larger economies over the period. In most of the deficit economies, the size of the deficit relative to output was small and their export growth was substantial. This facilitated both the willingness of international lenders to finance the deficits and the borrowing countries' willingness to accumulate foreign debt.

Outside the United States, growth in exports was also aided by periods of an overpriced dollar, but more fundamental influences were at work. The 'late start' in industrialization outside the United States generated a large productivity bonus through an ability to borrow technology (largely from the United States). This led to superior productivity and cost performances and enhanced export success in these economies. By generating rapid growth in real wages, rapid productivity growth also fostered success of the social bargain by reducing labour's efforts to improve conditions through excessive money-wage demands.

The causal connections between productivity growth and product improvement also contributed to the rapid growth of exports. For example, high rates of productivity growth generate rapid growth of profits and cash flows, allowing greater expenditures on product improvement and marketing. In addition, once superior product quality had been established, growing demand led to accelerated productivity growth because of dynamic scale economies.

All things considered, most economies were free during this period to pursue a relatively independent aggregate demand policy because they were relieved of both serious payments constraints and unacceptable inflation problems.[14] The result was a stable low unemployment and low inflation equilibrium. If devaluations of the currency were necessary to handle a 'fundamental disequilibrium', they could be successfully targeted because of restrictions on capital flows and co-ordinated efforts to prevent misalignments of exchange rates. The breakdown of the Bretton Woods agreement, as well as other shocks and certain structural changes in the late 1960s to early 1970s marked the end of this phase of low inflation and unemployment, rapid growth of productivity and exports and relief from an aggregate demand constraint. Inflation had become a more serious problem.

THE RISING INFLATIONARY BIAS

From a level hovering around 10 million workers throughout the 1960–73 period, unemployment rose steadily throughout the OECD to a post-war high of 31.1 million in 1983; it then declined to 24.5 million by 1990. Since 1990 unemployment has resumed its upward trend, surpassing the previous highs of the early 1980s to reach 33.9 million in 1993. Forecasts for 1994, 1995 and 1996 are 35.0, 33.9 and 33.3 million unemployed, respectively.[15] Notwithstanding the decline in unemployment during the 1980s, levels of unemployment have had a strong upward trend for the past three decades with little evidence of any significant reversal in the short to medium term. Underlying this rising unemployment trend has been the response of the authorities to the worsening inflationary bias. Most OECD economies by the 1990s face a less-favourable trade-off between inflation and unemployment, including a more unacceptable rate of inflation at full employment, as discussed briefly on p. 398 above.

The greater inflationary bias in the OECD economies can be attributed to one or more of three institutional changes (depending upon the economy). First, in several economies a greater inflationary bias can be attributed to the breakdown in social bargains towards the end of the 'Golden Age' period. For various reasons, by the second half of the 1960s labour ended its commitment to a social-bargain strategy and opted for a market-power strategy in its efforts to achieve fairness in many economies, thereby expanding the number of economies subject to an inflationary bias.[16]

Second, the prolonged period of policy-induced high unemployment since the mid-1970s has induced new forms of hysteresis in the labour markets of these economies. By the 1990s labour had come to believe that *when labour market conditions improve*, money wage demands must be sufficient to generate a 'catch-up' in real wages, which had failed to grow at anything like the rates experienced during the 1950s and 1960s. In addition, the prevailing view among labour by the 1990s is that it has had to bear the main cost of fighting inflation, and that accelerated money-wage demands are a means of redressing the balance when labour markets tighten. These hysteretic effects operate with special force under low unemployment conditions.[17] Unfortunately for labour, this source of increased inflationary bias has only strengthened the resolve of the authorities to push unemployment rates even higher in order to control inflation.

Third, the breakdown of the Bretton Woods Agreement initiated a radical change in the international monetary system. Along with the replacement of a fixed but adjustable exchange rate system by a relatively flexible exchange rate system, the 1970s ushered in a period of increasing deregulation of international capital movements. Under the new regime the inflation costs are increased in any economy in which pursuit of the low unemployment goal involves depreciation of the currency.[18] In this case, the response of managers of large, mobile capital funds to unilateral reflationary policies acts to worsen the inflation–unemployment trade-off both directly and by interacting with the internal institutional changes just discussed. Together these three institutional changes guaranteed high unemployment almost everywhere in the OECD. This is seen most clearly by considering the impact on a country's external balance and inflation and unemployment rates when a full employment policy is implemented unilaterally in a highly interdependent mass unemployment environment.

UNILATERAL DEPRECIATION AND STIMULATION

Any attempt by an individual country to return to full employment (or merely to maintain relatively low unemployment) while others apply restrictive aggregate demand policies, requires policies to stimulate exports or curtail imports or both. The traditional policy instrument for achieving this result is the exchange rate. Unfortunately, depreciation has become an ineffective instrument for correcting the balance of payments difficulties *if at the same time strong additional efforts are made to stimulate aggregate demand.* Equally unfortunately, in this policy context it has relatively large inflation effects. At least two difficulties stand in the way of achieving external balance and strong growth in real aggregate demand when a depreciation of the exchange rate is part of the recovery programme: real wage resistance, and speculative capital outflows, problems that have become more acute since the early 1970s.[19]

Whether a reduction of the exchange rate is intended as the sole instrument for achieving external balance and providing the necessary aggregate demand stimulus for attaining full employment or, more likely, is supplemented by stimulative fiscal and monetary policies, the programme will not achieve either goal if it leads to serious real wage resistance. Depreciation will lead to a decline in real wages, and in response labour can be expected to press for higher money wage increases in order to protect real wages. The extent of labour's resistance will vary depending upon the size of the decline in real wages and upon how much labour markets tighten while the stimulating aggregate demand policies are in effect. If unemployment is reduced significantly, serious wage (and therefore price) inflation will result. In the extreme case, the resulting wage–price spiral can lead to the real exchange rate returning to its previous level. Even allowing for some reduction in the real exchange rate, the inflation effects will be larger than in the 1960–73 period for those countries in which social bargains have been abandoned and hysteretic effects have developed. The impact on inflation in these cases will be large enough to force the authorities to reverse full employment policy long before that goal has been reached.

Second, whether or not internal changes have themselves increased the inflationary bias, any country that wishes to reflate unilaterally can expect to run into serious difficulties in controlling the extent of the depreciation of its exchange rate. The dramatic increase in the free movement of international capital since the 1970s allows speculators to play a dominating role in exchange rate movements. This is especially true with the full employment programme being considered. Even in the absence of real wage resistance, the more 'credible' and persistent is the full employment policy, the greater and more prolonged will be the speculation against the currency because of the impact of the policy on expected and actual rates of inflation. If real wage resistance occurs as well as speculative attacks against the currency, the two will interact to magnify the unfavourable effects on the exchange rate, inflation and real wages. In both instances, developments will force the abandonment of the programme.

Events since the 1970s also indicate that speculators respond to changes in aggregate demand policies in a way that generates an asymmetry in the ability of the authorities to achieve macro policy goals. As discussed, stimulative aggregate demand policies generate 'capital flight' and a depreciation of the exchange rate as long as such policies persist. Sooner or later the inflationary impact forces a reversal of the aggregate demand policy. The international response to Mitterrand's policies in the early 1980s is a case in point. In contrast, restrictive aggregate demand policies are reinforced by the market.

THE HIGH UNEMPLOYMENT EQUILIBRIUM TRAP

The institutional changes that have given rise to a greater inflationary bias have serious implications for the 1990s. Acting individually, most economies are unable to pursue full employment policies without generating unacceptable rates of inflation. As a result, under existing institutional arrangements, most OECD economies are caught in a high unemployment equilibrium trap.

To clarify these points it is helpful to assign each OECD economy to one of three groups, depending upon whether or not it is subject to an inflationary bias and, if it is, for what reason. First, there are those economies which experience (or where the authorities anticipate) unacceptably high or even accelerating rates of inflation under full employment conditions because labour has adopted a market-power strategy. Aggregate demand policies will be constrained in these economies whether or not the rest of

404

the OECD economies are at full employment because of their existing institutional framework. The breakdown of the social bargains beginning in the late 1960s has greatly enlarged this group.

There is a second group of economies which could realize full employment with acceptable rates of inflation (they would be pursuing a social-bargain strategy) *if full employment policies were adopted by the first group of economies* because under these conditions they would be spared the adverse effects of depreciation. Because the first group has in fact adopted high unemployment policies, their high unemployment is exported to the second group as reduced demand for the latter's exports. Acting alone in an effort to return to full employment, none of the second group is able to offset the adverse effects of stimulative demand policies on its payments position through manipulation of the exchange rate. Such policies, however, do lead to unacceptably high rates of inflation, as was made clear in the previous section.

Obviously, economies of the first group are trapped in a high unemployment state, but so are members of the second group. A strong inflationary bias amongst the first group of economies leads not only to high unemployment in their economies but to an inflationary bias and mass unemployment throughout most of the capitalist world. Simplifying somewhat, the interdependence of trade forces high unemployment upon the second group of economies; the free movement of international capital ensures that they will be trapped there. Together these two groups comprise the vast majority of the OECD economies. The remaining small third group is made up of those able to realize full employment or near full employment with manageable payments positions and acceptable rates of inflation despite depressed economic conditions elsewhere. The continued success of a social bargan strategy and a strong payments position at full employment, which greatly reduces the dangers of disruptive speculation against their currencies, are the underlying explanations. By 1994 only Japan and Switzerland could be considered to satisfy these conditions, and even in these two cases unemployment rates had risen above their 'Golden Age' levels.

The emphasis on two sources of depressed aggregate demand policies is clearly a simplification of current conditions in which the full employment goal has been so widely sacrificed. Nevertheless, nothing essential is overlooked by modelling OECD economic conditions using a dual explanation of widespread restrictive aggregate demand policies nor in considering what must be done to correct matters. What is being stressed is the overwhelming strain that a widespread slump and free capital movements under a flexible exchange rate system put on some economies that, under more fortunate circumstances, could perform satisfactorily.[20]

MACROECONOMIC POLICY AS RADICAL SURGERY

As discussed above (pp. 396–9), policies of the last two decades must be considered a failure. Until innovative policies are devised and implemented to bring about major institutional changes, only a few OECD economies will be able to maintain low unemployment rates. Unfortunately, to explain why economic conditions have deteriorated so badly is one thing; to propose a programme for recovery in unemployment that offers some chance of being adopted is another matter.

Writing in the 1930s, Keynes saw the solution to the mass unemployment as essentially an 'educational' problem. The problem was to dislodge deeply rooted but false and harmful economic beliefs, for example that capitalism is self-regulating and budget deficits are intrinsically evil. Once achieved, the fiscal authorities could proceed to reflate the economy with little fear of this causing unacceptable inflation.

The analysis of the causes of the mass unemployment since the early 1970s clearly indicates that macroeconomic policy in the 1990s will not be like dentistry, something Keynes would have been the first to recognize were he to rewrite *The General Theory* today. The much-altered institutional framework of the post-war period has greatly increased the obstacles to recovery and greatly complicated the policy-makers' tasks. Further policy-induced changes in institutions are required before the usual macroeconomic policy instruments, such as aggregate demand and exchange rate policies, can be implemented. These changes will be very difficult to achieve.

The restrictive aggregate demand policies since the mid-1970s that have led to mass unemployment were responses to increased inflationary pressures beginning in the late 1960s and early 1970s. These pressures were traced to common institutional changes within a large number of OECD economies and to a radical change in the international monetary framework that affected all of them. Any programme for recovery in unemployment must therefore start with measures to greatly reduce inflationary pressures by altering these institutions. In very general terms, a programme for full recovery requires the co-ordination of monetary and fiscal policies by the OECD economies and policies that lead to a co-operative solution of a serious malfunction within most of these economies.

CO-ORDINATION POLICIES FOR RECOVERY

A popular argument put forward during the Bretton Woods era was that, with flexible exchange rates, external balance would be generated automatically by market forces. This was alleged to be an improvement over the adjustable-peg system in that it freed up monetary and fiscal policy to serve as alternative instruments for achieving internal balance, for example, an unemployment target. In fact, flexible exchange rates in a world of unregulated capital movements have led to serious adverse side-effects. Under the Bretton Woods system of fixed but adjustable exchange rates, speculation usually acted to contain otherwise disruptive movements in exchange rates. In contrast, the progressive deregulation of capital movements in a flexible exchange rate system has led to a marked increase in speculative capital flows and to disruptive and highly volatile movements of nominal and real exchange rates. The greater uncertainty this has engendered has adversely affected international trade. As already noted, these developments have also greatly increased the inflationary bias in the developed capitalist world, thereby forcing economies into a high-equilibrium unemployment trap. Reducing the volatility of exchange rates and the size of speculative international capital flows is an essential step in improving macroeconomic performance. A highly simplified outline of the kind of co-ordination policies required is as follows.[21] It is stated in rather bold terms in order to make more apparent the tremendous difficulties in implementing this part of the recovery programme.

The assignment of policy instruments compared to the flexible exchange rate regime is radically altered. A 'sustainable' balance of payments over some medium-term horizon would be the external target, achieved by an agreed-upon fixed but adjustable system of real exchange rates, the so-called intermediate targets.[22] Among the various monetary policy instruments employed to keep the exchange rates aligned are announcement effects (that is, credibility), co-ordinated central bank intervention in the foreign exchange markets, and adjustments in interest rates when necessary to prevent the deviation of exchange rates from their target levels. In addition a 'Tobin tax' would be adopted whereby all foreign exchange transactions would be subject to a uniform tax in all countries.[23] The aim would be to make short-term financial round trips into another currency unprofitable and thus, as Keynes put it, 'to mitigate the predominance of speculation over enterprise'. By greatly reducing the amount of speculative foreign exchange transactions, the volatility of exchange rates would be reduced and the ability of central banks to intervene effectively would be revived.[24]

Internal balance, an unemployment target in this chapter, would be achieved through co-ordinated fiscal policies that target levels of aggregate demand and therefore unemployment rates across the OECD economies. However, even assuming that under this fixed exchange rate system every OECD economy introduces the agreed-upon stimulative fiscal policy, there are other difficulties. To focus attention, assume that the goal of each country is to return to the unemployment rates of the 1960–73 period. Since fiscal as well as monetary policies are co-ordinated, payments difficulties will be reduced but not necessarily absent as there could be serious payments imbalances initially that must be handled. Disregard this possibility and assume a system of real exchange rates such that in each country the 1960–73 average rate of unemployment coincides with the rate of unemployment at which external balance is achieved in that country. Also assume that any minor (permitted) adjustments in exchange rates can be handled and that capital flight is no longer a serious problem anywhere in the OECD.

Unfortunately, even under these favourable conditions the OECD boom would be short-lived, as inflation would rise to unacceptable rates before full employment was achieved in those economies in which labour pursues a market-power strategy. Since this labour market strategy prevails today in most of the OECD economies, the reimposition of restrictive aggregate demand policies almost everywhere can be anticipated. The fact of the matter is that a sustained co-ordinated restimulation of aggregate demand is necessary for a full employment recovery but it is not sufficient. The reintroduction of social bargains is also a necessary condition for an escape from the high unemployment equilibrium trap since it will reduce, if not eliminate, the unacceptable inflationary effects of the breakdown of the earlier bargains discussed above (pp. 402–3).[25]

A CO-OPERATIVE SOLUTION

Autonomy, neutrality and the social bargain

The successful social bargains of the 'Golden Age' period differed among economies because of differences, for example, in the distribution of economic and political power, the structure of the industrial relations systems and the extent of the welfare state. However, they had important similarities. In all cases a chief aim was to reduce unemployment rates to a minimum. Success of the bargain therefore depended upon the ability to achieve a politically acceptable rate of inflation at this low unemployment rate, otherwise the unemployment goal would have had to be sacrificed. The key to success in controlling inflation were conditions in the labour market; restraining price inflation necessitated restraining the growth of money-wages, and this required a general acceptance by labour of the fairness of the bargain. Hence the need for rewards to labour as part of the social bargain to induce it to accept a policy of money-wage restraint.

The success of a social bargain required its acceptance by capital as well, and this too required positive incentives since full employment strengthened the relative economic and political power of labour. Fortunately, the implementation of social bargains during this period was a solution to a positive-sum game, as the benefits were widely spread over different economic groups, full employment for labour, relative price stability for the owners of financial assets and greater profits and more rapidly expanding markets for entrepreneurial capital. To put the point in other terms, with respect to their benefits, social bargains were 'neutral'. Their acceptance and success can be partly attributed to the fact that the programmes were structured in this way.

But social bargains were structured so that not only were the economic benefits widely spread but also so that widespread participation in the formulation, implementation and monitoring of the social bargain was assured.[26] Equally important, once implemented their continued success required a minimum of partisan political interference. For example, attempts to alter the distribution of benefits without consultation with the affected groups were considered unfair and unpatriotic and were resisted, as they might lead one or more of the 'partners' to withdraw support. The ability and willingness to resist pressure from special-interest groups conferred, in effect, autonomous powers upon those responsible for the success of the programmes.

The intended aims of the co-ordination policies are little different from those put forth by Keynes in his writings: for example, greater stability in exchange rates and exchange rate operations limited to financing trade and long-term investment. With regard to Keynes's attitude today towards social bargains and the political autonomy of its administrators, we can only speculate. Certainly, the Keynes of *The General Theory* favoured a *laissez-faire* policy with respect to the market system, once full employment was realized. But Keynes was writing before capitalism had experienced a period of prolonged, widespread full employment, rapidly rising living standards, the spread of the welfare state, the rise of egalitarianism and the decline of political and economic deference. In short, *The General Theory* outlined a recovery policy for a stage of capitalism prior to the development of a serious inflationary bias.

Certainly, an economist of Keynes's abilities would have been aware of the profound effect that institutional changes such as these would have on inflationary pressures at low unemployment rates and the radical nature of policies needed to solve simultaneously the inflation and unemployment problems. The question is: would Keynes under today's changed circumstances have chosen to sacrifice the low unemployment goal in his programme in order to maintain a strictly *laissez-faire* policy towards markets?

We know that in Keynes's view necessary conditions for government intervention were an inability of the private sector to provide the needed correctives for macroeconomic malfunctions and an ability of proposed policies to generate widespread benefits. Furthermore, Keynes was also concerned that policy decisions would remain in the hands of 'an intellectual aristocracy' capable of resisting partisan demands that might, if satisfied, overload the economy. Without using the expression, his concern was that policy-makers should retain enough 'autonomy' to ensure that policies operated in the general interest. As discussed, the social bargains of the 'Golden Age' did meet Keynes's conditions for intervention; achieving full employment with acceptable rates of inflation could not be left simply to the market but required a social bargain: bargains were neutral in their effects in the sense used here, and they were institutionalized to a degree that provided the autonomy needed for success throughout most of the 'Golden Age'. Social bargains can still fulfil these conditions today. If it is necessary to speculate on the matter, it seems likely that if Keynes were to rewrite *The General Theory*, a social bargain would be a key part of his programme.

Autonomy, neutrality and an 'independent' central bank

This conclusion is given added force by recalling the effects of the policies used to combat inflation over the past two decades. Over most of the period since the mid-1970s, restrictive monetary policies have been assigned the task of reducing inflation rates significantly. More recently, the fiscal authorities have shifted policies so as to reinforce restrictive monetary measures. As argued in earlier pages, these policies have failed to bring low inflation and low unemployment; they have led to mass unemployment.

This is but to say that the effects of restrictive policies managed by an 'independent' central bank (or by the fiscal authorities) entailed much more than merely reduction of inflation rates.[27] These were also policies of high unemployment and a reduction of labour's economic and political power; they were political choices. Certainly, whatever the long-run intentions of the policy-makers, labour interpreted these policies as highly partisan, enacted for the benefit of those least harmed by the resulting unemployment and those who benefit most by reduced inflation.

The actual 'success' of restrictive policies in increasing unemployment and their failure to bring about the long-run gain of both low inflation and low unemployment has only strengthened the view that the monetary authorities especially have been, and still are in fact, acting on behalf of special interests today.[28] Keynes would have correctly understood the long-run effects of such policies under current conditions. Surely, rather than accept policies that in effect benefit special groups and which lead to prolonged mass unemployment, he would have assigned a key role in a recovery programme to an autonomous body representing the broader interests of society.

RECAPITULATION AND CODA

Contrary to the received wisdom, capitalism is not a self-regulating system. Rather, it is a system capable of generating institutional changes as part of its normal evolution that lead to lengthy periods of poor as well as of superior performance. Superior macroeconomic performance requires a good institutional–policy fit, that is an institutional framework which enables the authorities to implement economic policies that can achieve the desired macroeconomic goals.

The earlier message was that during the 'Golden Age' of capitalism, low rates of unemployment prevailed widely throughout OECD economies because there was no constraint forcing the authorities to restrict aggregate demand to something less than its full employment level. This had two aspects. First, the existence of the fixed exchange rate system forced an inflation discipline on the OECD economies to which most responded successfully, even though unemployment rates were pushed to a minimum. The critical condition was the implementation of a social bargain strategy that restrained inflation at full employment.

Furthermore, aggregate demand was not seriously held back by a payments constraint. Leaving aside the United Kingdom and the United States, a sustainable balance of payments position was possible at full employment in most economies. This was largely traceable to superior productivity, cost and export performance, ultimately due to borrowing technology from the industrial leader(s). If situations arose in which devaluation became necessary to correct payments disequilibria, restrictions on international capital flows and co-ordinated efforts by central banks and international agencies were able to provide the needed currency realignments.

By the 1970s matters began to unravel and by the 1980s unfavourable effects of the new institutional order were becoming clear. In place of social bargains, labour was increasingly prone to employ market-power strategies in collective bargaining. By the 1980s the Bretton Woods fixed but adjustable exchange rate system was long gone and the trend towards decontrol of capital movements had accelerated. These 'unfriendly' institutions were sufficient to establish a framework in which the escalating inflation costs forced the abandonment of full employment goals almost everywhere. Policy-induced institutional changes were required for recovery then and they still are today.

The core of a recovery programme discussed here involves the co-ordination of monetary and fiscal policies throughout the OECD and the widespread adoption of a second generation of social bargains. Until this is achieved, the strong inflationary bias throughout the OECD will remain and inflation will be controlled by continued mass unemployment. The likelihood of the necessary policies being accepted, let alone implemented, in the near future is slight. The introduction of a tax on foreign exchange transactions is more likely and would certainly be a step towards recovery.[29] Even here the obstacles to implementation are formidable.

As the number of years of mass unemployment accumulates, the failure of current policies will become more widely recognized. Even so, this cannot be relied upon to generate a new set of attitudes towards the role of government in recovery. Unless a convincing alternative programme that can lead to recovery is available and its message widely disseminated, the mere recognition of the failure of past policies will lead only to resignation and cynicism at best. Meanwhile the policy agenda will become more cluttered with recovery programmes advocating a continued or even a greater reliance on 'market forces', even though such policies have been responsible for the deterioration in economic conditions in the past.

There is an even worse scenario looming on the horizon. It is true that two decades of mass unemployment have not led to the demise of capitalism or democracy; rather, the outcome can be better described as an increased tolerance of a high unemployment equilibrium trap. But even if unemployment rates do not rise further, the signs point to a worsening in political, social and economic conditions. Conditions of prolonged and high unemployment lead to a labour force with a high proportion of workers increasingly accustomed to unemployment, especially the long-term kind. The cumulative effect is an erosion of the work ethic as those unemployed develop life-styles that downplay the importance of legitimate work. While collecting whatever benefits society offers the unemployed, they will learn to supplement their incomes by joining the underground and underworld economies.

Periods of prolonged economic slack also lead to slow growth of markets and profits and demands by business for greater 'flexibility' in work arrangements, a trend presently accelerated by growing competition from the newly industrialized countries and increased globalization. An alternative and more appropriate expression for these demands is 'social dumping', the replacement of relatively high-wage, full-time workers by low-paid, part-time or casual workers with reduced non-pecuniary job benefits, such as reduced pensions and poorer safety and health conditions.[30]

As is readily admitted, breaking out of the high unemployment equilibrium trap requires overcoming enormous obstacles. A programme for recovery of the type presented here will never be implemented until a much different political and economic climate has first been created. In this new ideological climate, policy-induced institutional changes must be seen as essential, and therefore, acceptable *in principle* by the political leaders.

For economists, the main task is to formulate a recovery programme for the 1990s. Just as in the 1930s, this task can be subdivided into two basic parts: developing a new research agenda and undertaking an 'educational' mission (to paraphrase Keynes). Developing the new research agenda involves a massive effort to understand the changes in the structure of capitalism since the 1930s and the manner in which a post-*General Theory* form of capitalism works. Only then can the politically acceptable set of policies for recovery be worked out. But recovery also requires a massive educational effort by the economics profession. The political leaders must be convinced that present attitudes about the role of the state, the workings of a modern capitalist system and the consequences of current policies are

412

helping to create a nineteenth-century version of capitalism, a condition defined by exaggerated inequalities, widespread and growing poverty and crime, and an absence of civility, trust and social cohesiveness. We can only hope for the best.

NOTES

* This work was supported by a grant from the Social Sciences and Humanities Research Council of Canada. I should also like to thank Wendy Cornwall, Sheila Dow, David Felix, Robert Heilbroner, William Milberg, Tony Thirlwall and the two editors of this collection for their helpful comments.

1 Increasingly the full employment rate of unemployment has become confused with the unemployment rate at which the inflation rate is constant, i.e. the non-accelerating inflation rate of unemployment (NAIRU). The key defining feature of full employment is the absence of involuntary unemployment; even staunch believers in the NAIRU now recognize that a large component of the unemployment at the NAIRU is involuntary.

2 Harrod in his biography of Keynes refers to Keynes's belief 'that the government of Britain was and would continue to be in the hands of an intellectual aristocracy using the method of persuasion' (see Harrod 1963: 192–3).

3 The eighteen countries covered exclude the less-developed and very small OECD economies, namely Greece, Iceland, Luxembourg, Mexico, Portugal, Spain and Turkey.

4 Cornwall (1994: table 12.1); and OECD (1994a: Annex table 21).

5 Keynes's writings in the 1940s indicated a concern with potential inflation problems even at relatively high rates of unemployment.

6 The unemployment–inflation pattern for most OECD economies is very similar.

7 While the figures in Table 22.1 are averages, the pattern was very similar in each of the eighteen countries.

8 Governments have also contributed to the deterioration in economic conditions of large numbers of people by cutting back on state welfare programmes in response to declining tax revenues.

9 Naturally it would be expected that if institutional changes in the labour market have led to potentially stronger wage inflationary pressures, these potential pressures would be passed through to prices.

10 The role of fairness in wage settlements was popularized by Hicks (see Hicks 1974).

11 See Cornwall (1994: ch. 5) for a more detailed treatment.

12 The term 'social bargain' is used throughout the text rather than 'incomes policy'. The latter term is often associated with policies in which the authorities unilaterally impose money-wage norms on labour. The term 'social bargain' is meant to suggest programmes in which the wage norms were the outcome of consultation and agreement with labour.

13 Such results are predicted by the 'Scandinavian' model of inflation. For the earliest study, see Aukurst (1970).

14 The United Kingdom was a noticeable exception, and the authorities were forced to apply restrictive aggregate demand policies beginning in the second half of the 1960s.

15 See OECD, *Labour Force Statistics*, various issues; and OECD (1994b).

16 See Flanagan *et al.* (1983). The text deliberately ignores a series of adverse

shocks that affected inflation rates in the early 1970s and also the early 1980s in order to concentrate on the important structural changes in the labour market.

17 See Cornwall (1994: 169 and references cited) for additional hysteretic effects of restrictive aggregate demand policies.

18 Greater interdependence of trade is taken up in the next section.

19 Assuming infinite supply elasticities, if the sum of the price elasticities for a country's exports and imports is less than one in absolute value, a depreciation of the currency, even if it leads to a decline in the real exchange rate, will lead to a deterioration of the trade position. This also will lead to a reversal of a full employment policy.

20 Large budget deficits and national-debt–GDP ratios have reinforced restrictive aggregate demand policies in many economies. A co-ordinated programme of aggregate demand stimulation in the OECD is essential for relief from this constraint as much of the deficit and debt problems can be traced in large measure to depressed world demand conditions.

21 For a full description of most of the key points, see Miller and Williamson (1987). Among other things, Miller and Williamson give attention to exchange rate zones, the special problems raised by existing imbalances, lags, uncertainties and intermediate targets.

22 External balance is defined as a 'current account surplus or deficit equal to the underlying capital flows over the cycle, given that the country is pursuing "internal balance" as best it can' (ibid.: 11).

23 Tobin (1978); Felix (1994).

24 See Felix (1994).

25 An alternative programme limited to the EC economies is to adopt the fiscal criteria of the Maastricht Treaty which place limits on both government debt and fiscal deficits. Unless these criteria are satisfied, entrance to the EMU is denied and penalties are imposed on those inside who violate the criteria. Under present fiscal conditions, most EC members would fail to meet these stringent criteria, and in order to do so would be forced to adopt highly restrictive fiscal policies, thereby intensifying the already severe recessions in the EC economics (see Buiter *et al.*: 1993).

26 In Japan the social bargain generated widespread economic benefits but labour's participation in administering the bargain was largely confined to shop-floor activities.

27 Much of the argument in favour of greater autonomy or independence for central blanks assumes incorrectly that this would lead to a more intense fight against inflation without adversely affecting output and employment (see Treasury and Civil Service Select Committee 1993).

28 On BBC2 television in June 1992, Professor Alan Budd, chief economic advisor to the Conservative government at the time, offered the opinion that the restrictive aggregate demand policies of the 1980s might have been simply to shift the distribution of power and income to capital and to create a reserve army of labour (see the column by 'Pendennis' in the *Observer*, 21 June 1992).

29 The references in note 23.

30 Reduced job security for the employed labour force has obvious adverse aggregate demand effects as well.

23

UNDERCONSUMPTION

J.E. King

PART I
J.E. King writing as J.M. Keynes

The mercantilist theories described by Professor Heckscher were directed, in substance, to the constituent of effective demand which depends on the sufficiency of the inducement to invest. It is no new thing, however, to ascribe the evils of unemployment to the insufficiency of the other constituent, namely, the insufficiency of the propensity to consume. But this alternative explanation of the economic evils of the day – equally unpopular with the classical economists – played a much smaller part in sixteenth- and seventeenth-century thinking and has only gathered force in comparatively recent times.

Though complaints of underconsumption were a very subsidiary aspect of mercantilist thought, Professor Heckscher quotes a number of examples of what he calls 'the deep-rooted belief in the utility of luxury and the evil of thrift. Thrift, in fact, was regarded as the cause of unemployment, and for two reasons: in the first place, because real income was believed to diminish by the amount of money which did not enter into exchange, and secondly, because saving was believed to withdraw money from circulation.'[1] Barbon wrote in 1690 that 'Prodigality is a vice that is prejudicial to the Man, but not to trade.' . . . Covetousness is a Vice, prejudicial both to Man and Trade.'[2] In 1695 Cary argued that if everybody spent more, all would obtain larger incomes 'and might then live more plentifully'.[3]

But it was by Bernard Mandeville's *Fable of the Bees* that Barbon's opinion was mainly popularized, a book convicted as a nuisance by the grand jury of Middlesex in 1723, which stands out in the history of the moral sciences for its scandalous reputation. The text of the *Fable of the Bees* is an allegorical poem, 'The Grumbling Hive, or Knaves turned honest', in which is set forth the appalling plight of a prosperous community in which all the citizens suddenly take it into their heads to abandon luxurious living, and the state to cut down armaments, in the interests of Saving.

And what is the result?

Now mind the glorious Hive, and see
How Honesty and Trade agree:
The Shew is gone, it thins apace;
And looks with quite another Face,
For 'twas not only they that went,
By whom vast sums were yearly spent;
But Multitudes that lived on them,
Were daily forc'd to do the same.
In vain to other Trades they'd fly;
All were o'er-stocked accordingly.
The price of Land and Houses falls;
Mirac'lous Palaces whose Walls,
Like those of Thebes, were rais'd by Play,
Are to be let . . .
The Building Trade is quite destroy'd,
Artificers are not employ'd;
No limner for his Art is fam'd,
Stone-cutters, Carvers are not nam'd.

And the Moral? That frugality might be a public vice, and prodigality a social virtue. No wonder that such sentiments called down the opprobrium of two centuries of moralists and economists who felt much more virtuous in possession of their austere doctrine that no sound remedy for unemployment was discoverable except in the utmost of thrift and economy both by the individual and by the State.

The doctrine did not reappear in respectable circles for another century, until in the later phase of Malthus the notion of the insufficiency of effective demand takes a definite place as a scientific explanation of unemployment. Since I have already dealt with this somewhat fully in my essay on Malthus,[4] it will be sufficient if I note here that Ricardo was stone-deaf to what Malthus was saying. The last echo of the controversy is to be found in John Stuart Mill's discussion of his Wages-Fund Theory,[5] which in his own mind played a vital part in his rejection of the later phase of Malthus, amidst the discussions of which he had, of course, been brought up. Mill's successors rejected his Wages-Fund Theory but overlooked the fact that Mill's refutation of Malthus depended on it. Their method was to dismiss the problem from the corpus of Economics not by solving it but by not mentioning it. It altogether disappeared from controversy. Mr Cairncross, searching recently for traces of it amongst the minor Victorians,[6] has found even less, perhaps, than might have been expected.[7]

Thus the great puzzle of Effective Demand with which Malthus had wrestled vanished from economic literature. You will not find it mentioned even once in the whole works of Marshall, Edgeworth and Professor Pigou, from whose hands the classical theory has received its most mature embodiment. It could only live on furtively, below the surface, in the underworld of Karl Marx and his followers.[8]

It is easy to conceive of a community in which the factors of production are rewarded by dividing up in agreed proportions the actual output of their co-operative efforts. This is the simplest case of a society in which the presuppositions of the classical theory are fulfilled. But they would also be fulfilled in a society of the type in which we actually live, where the starting up of productive processes largely depends on a class of entrepreneurs who hire the factors of production for money and look to their recoupment from selling the output for money, provided that the whole of the current incomes of the factors of production are necessarily spent, directly or indirectly, on purchasing their own current output from the entrepreneurs.

The first type of society we shall call a *real-wage* or *co-operative economy.* The second type, in which the factors are hired by entrepreneurs for money but where there is a mechanism of some kind to ensure that the exchange value of the money income of each factor is always equal in the aggregate to the proportion of current output which would have been the factor's share in a co-operative economy, we shall call a *neutral entrepreneur economy*, or a *neutral economy* for short. The third type, of which the second is a limiting case, in which the entrepreneurs hire the factors for money but without such a mechanism as the above, we shall call a *money-wage* or *entrepreneur economy.* It is obvious on these definitions that it is in an entrepreneur economy that we live today.

The law of production in an entrepreneur economy can be stated as follows. A process of production will not be started up, unless the money proceeds expected from the sale of the output are at least equal to the money costs which could be avoided by not starting up the process.

The distinction between a co-operative economy and an entrepreneur economy bears some relation to a pregnant observation made by Karl Marx – though the subsequent use to which he put this observation was not entirely satisfactory. He pointed out that the nature of production in the actual world is not, as economists seem often to suppose, a case of $C - M - C'$, i.e. of exchanging commodity (or effort) for money in order to obtain another commodity (or effort). That may be the standpoint of the private consumer. But it is not the attitude of *business*, which is a case of $M - C - M'$, i.e. of parting with money for commodity (or effort) in order to obtain more money.[9]

The excess of M' over M is the source of Marx's *surplus value.* It is a curiosity in the history of economic theory that the heretics of the past hundred years who have, in one shape or another, opposed the formula $M - C - M'$ to the classical formula $C - M - C'$, have tended to believe *either* that M' must always and necessarily exceed M *or* that M must always and necessarily exceed M', according as they were living in a period in which the one or the other predominated in actual experience. Marx and those who believe in the necessarily exploitative character of the capitalist system, assert the inevitable excess of M'; whilst Hobson, or Foster and Catchings, or Major Douglas, who believe in its inherent tendency towards deflation and under-employment, assert the inevitable excess of M. Marx, however, was approaching the intermediate truth when he added that the continuous excess of M' would be inevitably interrupted by a series of crises, gradually increasing in intensity, or entrepreneur bankruptcy and under-employment, during which, presumably, M must be in excess. Mrs Robinson has drawn my attention to several passages in which Marx attributes crises to restrictions on the consuming power of society.[10] My own argument, if it is accepted, should at least serve to effect a reconciliation between the followers of Marx and those of Major Douglas, leaving the classical economists still high and dry in the belief that M and M' are always equal!

After Marx, theories of underconsumption hibernated until the appearance in 1889 of *The Physiology of Industry*, by A.F. Mummery and J.A. Hobson, the first and most significant of many volumes in which for nearly fifty years Mr Hobson has flung himself with unflagging, but almost unavailing, ardour and courage against the ranks of orthodoxy. Though it is so completely forgotten today, the publication of this book marks, in a sense, the beginning of an epoch in economic thought.[11] Hobson and Mummery point out in their preface the nature of the conclusions which they attack:

Saving enriches and spending impoverishes the community along with the individual, and it may be generally defined as an assertion that the effective love of money is the root of all economic good. Not merely does it enrich the thrifty individual himself, but it raises wages, gives work to the unemployed, and scatters blessings on every side. . . . Economic critics have ventured to attack the theory in detail, but they have shrunk appalled from touching its main conclusions. Our purpose is to show that these conclusions are not tenable, that an undue exercise of the habit of saving is possible, and that such undue exercise impoverishes the Community, throws labourers out of work, drives down wages, and spreads that gloom and prostration through the commercial world which is known as Depression in Trade. . . .

The object of production is to provide 'utilities and conveniences' for consumers, and the process is a continuous one from the first handling of the raw material to the moment when it is finally consumed as a utility or a convenience. The only use of Capital being to aid the production of these utilities and conveniences, the total used will necessarily vary with the total of utilities and conveniences daily or weekly consumed. Now saving, while it increases the existing aggregate of Capital, simultaneously reduces the quantity of utilities and conveniences consumed; any undue exercise of this habit must, therefore, cause an accumulation of Capital in excess of that which is required for use, and this excess will exist in the form of general over-production.[12]

This is the first explicit statement of the fact that capital is brought into existence, not by the propensity to save, but in response to the demand resulting from actual and prospective consumption. I formerly believed Hobson and Mummery to be mistaken in supposing that it is a case of excessive saving causing the *actual* accumulation of capital in excess of what is required, and that this is, in fact, a secondary evil which only occurs through mistakes of foresight; whereas the primary evil is a propensity to save in conditions of full employment more than the equivalent of the addition to capital which is required, thus preventing full employment except when there is a mistake of foresight. I suggested, in addition, that their theory failed of completeness, essentially on account of their having no independent theory of the rate of interest; with the result that Mr Hobson laid too much emphasis on underconsumption leading to over-investment, in the sense of unprofitable investment, instead of explaining that a relatively weak propensity to consume helps to cause unemployment by requiring and *not* receiving the accompaniment of a compensating volume of new investment, which, even if it may sometimes occur temporarily through errors of optimism, is in general prevented from happening at all by the prospective profit falling below the standard set by the rate of interest.[13]

This, however, is much too harsh a judgement. In his later books Mr Hobson has clarified his argument in such a way as to render it entirely consistent with the general theory which I am proposing here. As he writes in his recent (and most engaging) *Confessions of an Economic Heretic*:

> I hope that the later statement of my over-saving heresy has made clear the right distinction between over-saving and over-investment. A nation, like an individual, may save any proportion of his income he likes [*sic*] without causing excess of investment or depression of trade, provided it can find an adequate internal or external market for the increase of capital goods or consumption goods into which his savings go. So long as savings continue to be employed in paying workers to produce more capital goods, in plant and materials, either for home use or for export, there is no over-saving in the proper sense of the term. *It is only when some of the current savings cannot find a profitable investment*, owing to the failure of consumer markets (home or external) to keep pace with the increase of producing power, that depression and unemployment set in. Part of the recent savings lies idle in banks waiting for an opportunity for investment, and the decline of profit which underproduction brings about causes a reduction in the rate of savings and in the proportion of the aggregate income which is saved.[14]

Evidently Hobson had never wished to suggest that over-investment could be 'absolute' in the sense that it was independent of the rate of return expected by entrepreneurs to accrue to new investments. It was always implicit in his writings that the marginal efficiency of capital would fall once a certain definite ratio of capital to consumption expenditure was surpassed. Hobson's argument differs from my own merely by relating the marginal efficiency to this ratio, rather than to the level of current investment expenditure; and a case can certainly be made for his view of the matter.

This reformulation of Mr Hobson's theory predates the publication of my own by some years, having been rendered explicit in an article as early as 1932.[15] He deserves further credit for his early discovery that savings depend on the level of income much more than on the rate of interest, and his recognition that this severely damages the classical theory of output and employment. Hobson and Mummery were not totally clear on this question,[16] but the defects in their exposition were rectified by Mr Hobson at precisely the time when I was struggling to emancipate myself from the classical doctrine:

> What may be termed 'bourgeois saving', directed consciously to make some definite provision for the future income of the saver or his family, will probably be larger when interest is high, for an increased amount of 'sacrifice' will yield larger results at such a time. But here, as in working-class savings, the amount saved will depend much more upon the rates of salaries, wages and other incomes than upon the rate of interest offered for new savings . . . taking the saving process as a whole, the 'price law' is inoperative. There is no ascertainable relation between the price of saving and the supply.[17]

It is but a short step from this to the concepts of the marginal propensity to consume (and to save), and the multiplier.

Since the great war there has been a spate of even more heretical theories of underconsumption, of which those of Major Douglas are the most famous. The strength of Major Douglas's advocacy has, of course, largely depended on orthodoxy having no valid reply to much of his destructive criticism. On the other hand, the detail of his diagnosis, in particular the so-called A + B theorem, includes much mere mystification, as Mr Frank Ramsay demonstrated some years ago.[18] If Major Douglas had limited his B-items to the financial provisions made by entrepreneurs to which no current expenditure on replacement and renewals corresponds, he would be nearer the truth. But even in that case it is necessary to allow for the possibility of these provisions being offset by new investment in other directions as well as by increased expenditure on consumption. Major Douglas is entitled to claim, as against some of his orthodox adversaries, that he at least has not been wholly oblivious of the outstanding problem of our economic system. Yet he has scarcely established an equal claim to rank – a private, perhaps, but not a major in the brave army of heretics – with Mandeville, Malthus, Gesell and Hobson, who, following their intuitions, have preferred to see the truth obscurely and imperfectly rather than to maintain error, reached indeed with clearness and consistency and by easy logic but on hypotheses inappropriate to the facts.

It is now time to draw some general conclusions about these important schools of thought, which all maintain, from various points of view, that the chronic tendency of contemporary societies to underemployment is to be traced to underconsumption; that is to say, to social practices and to a distribution of wealth and income which result in a propensity to consume which is unduly low.

In existing conditions – or, at least, in the conditions which existed until lately – where the volume of investment is unplanned and uncontrolled, subject to the vagaries of the marginal efficiency of capital as determined by the private judgement of individuals ignorant or speculative, and to a long-term rate of interest which seldom or never falls below a conventional level, these schools of thought are, as guides to practical policy, undoubtedly in the right. For in such conditions there is no other means of raising the average level of employment to a more satisfactory level. If it is impracticable materially to increase investment, obviously there is no means of securing a higher level of employment except by increasing consumption.

Practically I differ from these schools of thought only in thinking that they may lay a little too much emphasis on increased consumption at a time when there is still much social advantage to be obtained from increased investment. Theoretically, however, they are open to the criticism of neglecting the fact that there are *two* ways to expand output. Even if we were to decide that it would be better to increase capital more slowly and to concentrate effort on increasing consumption, we must decide this with open eyes after considering well the alternative. I am myself impressed by the great social advantages of increasing the stock of capital until it ceases to be scarce. But this is a practical judgement, not a theoretical imperative.

Moreover, I should readily concede that the wisest course is to advance on both fronts at once. Whilst aiming at a socially controlled rate of investment with a view to a progressive decline in the marginal efficiency of capital, I should support at the same time all sorts of policies for increasing the propensity to consume. For it is unlikely that full employment can be maintained, whatever we may do about investment, with the existing propensity to consume. There is room, therefore, for both policies to operate together; to promote investment and, at the same time, to promote consumption, not merely to the level which with the existing propensity to consume would correspond to the increased investment, but to a higher level still.

If, to take round figures for the purpose of illustration, the average level of output of today is 15 per cent below what it would be with continuous full employment, and if 10 per cent of this output represents net investment and 90 per cent of it consumption; if, furthermore, net investment would have to rise by 50 per cent in order to secure full employment with the existing propensity to consume, so that with full employment output would rise from 100 to 115, consumption from 90 to 100 and net investment from 10 to 15, then we might aim, perhaps, at so modifying the propensity to consume that with full employment consumption would rise from 90 to 103 and net investment from 10 to 12. Precisely how this might be achieved is the subject of the following chapter, which deals with questions of social philosophy.

PART II
J.E. King writing as himself

The chapter on underconsumption

The final chapters of the *General Theory* were written late in the day, and apparently in some haste. Peter Clarke concludes that 'Keynes did not seriously begin his study of Hobson's writings until the summer of 1935, by which time the preceding twenty-two chapters of his book, with their full exposition of the theory of effective demand, had already been set up in proof' (Clarke 1990: 112). He sent the last three chapters to Joan Robinson for her comments as late as September, when they were still 'completely unrevised' (*C.W.* XIII: 650). As Keynes had told Roy Harrod a week earlier:

> What I want is to do justice to schools of thought which the classicals have treated as imbecile for the last hundred years and, above all, to show that I am not really being so great an innovator, except as against the classical school, but have important predecessors and am returning to an age-long tradition of common sense. . . . I should certainly like to reduce the space given to the mercantilists, but feel that I must give chapter and verse.
>
> (Ibid.: 552)

Harrod's reaction was most unfavourable: 'Mercantilist chapter. I appreciate what you say about returning to age-long tradition of common sense. But the common sense was embodied in a hopelessly confused notion of economic system as a whole. I think you are inclined to rationalise isolated pieces of common sense too much, and to suggest that they were part of a coherent system of thought' (Ibid.: 555). Robinson tried to reassure him: 'I hope you won't let Roy intimidate you about [Chapter 23]. I think it is very enjoyable to read. I don't think you have overstated matters at all' (Ibid.: 651).

There is no evidence that after the publication of his book Keynes gave much thought to underconsumption theory, or indeed to questions of doctrinal history more generally. Thus we can only speculate as to how he might have revised Chapter 23 for a second edition. It is probably unobjectionable to infer that he would have abbreviated those sections dealing with the mercantilists; after all, he had told Harrod as much.

I have assumed also that Keynes would have gathered together at the end of the book those isolated remarks on the history of effective demand found on earlier pages in the first edition. More controversially, I have required him to do justice to both Hobson and Marx, his two most illustrious predecessors in this area of thought, disregarding the opinions of those commentators who feel that no significant injustice had been done (on Hobson, compare Clarke 1990 with King 1994a; on Marx, Barens 1990 with Rotheim 1981). The revised chapter therefore consists of a drastically shortened version of the Chapter 23 of the first edition (taken from pages 358–62); the famous reference to the disappearance of effective demand from the economic literature (from page 32); a long extract from the discarded 1933 draft of *The General Theory* in which Keynes draws heavily on Marx, thereby meeting one of the principal Marxian objections to his analysis by rendering it historically and socially specific (*C.W.* XXIX: 77–82); and a much more generous tribute to Hobson, modifying the highly critical remarks in the first edition (cf. *G.T.*: 364–70). The chapter concludes with Keynes's comments on the policy implications of underconsumption theory, and the rare numerical example, from Chapter 22 (*G.T.*: 324–6).

Underconsumption theory since 1936

In the very year in which *The General Theory* appeared, major progress was made in underconsumption theory in a far-off land of which Keynes could have known very little. Otto Bauer, the leader of the Austrian socialist party, who had been exiled to Prague after the Dollfuss putsch, was renowned for his treatise on the Marxian theory of nationalism and for a stinging (if ultimately unsuccessful) critique of Rosa Luxemburg's *Accumulation of Capital* (Orzech and Groll 1991). In 1936 Bauer published a formalization of arguments that were commonplace among his contemporaries, whether social democrats like Natalie Moszkowska or Stalinists such as Eugen Varga (Howard and King 1992: 13–18). His model is designed to show that a crisis of underconsumption is the inevitable outcome of a shift in the distribution of income from wages to profits, which makes consumption lag behind the growth of income and actual productive capacity run ahead of what is required.

Bauer begins with the 'classical' savings assumption that the propensity to save of the capitalist class is positive, while that of the workers is insignificantly different from zero. Thus an increase in the profit share – in Marxian terms, a rising rate of exploitation – increases the average saving ratio. Assuming that all saving is invested, this leads to a faster rate of growth of actual productive capacity. But the required rate of increase in capacity depends, Bauer argues, upon the growth of consumption, the relation between them being determined by what would soon be known as the accelerator, or in Bauer's words by a coefficient 'which depends on the prevailing degree of development of technology' (Bauer 1936: 351).

This model had very little impact on English-speaking economists, with one important exception. Paul Sweezy was an early American exponent of Keynesian economics, but he also had an unparalleled knowledge of the continental literature on Marxian political economy. In his *Theory of Capitalist Development*, published in 1942 but based on lectures that he had given at Harvard in previous years, Sweezy paid extensive tribute to Bauer's analysis, a version of which he set out in an appendix. The two critical assumptions are, first, that the wage bill rises with investment, but less rapidly; and, second, that a constant proportion must be maintained between the capital stock and the output of consumer goods. Sweezy then writes a condition for dynamic macroeconomic equilibrium, setting the required rate of increase in the capital stock (given by the 'factor of proportionality' between capital and consumption) equal to the actual rate of increase (which depends on the saving behaviour of the capitalists and the distribution of income between profits and wages). He argues that a contradiction arises, unless the rate of growth of output is increasing: the required rate of growth of capital must decline, while the actual rate increases. The consequent crises of underconsumption, he concludes, will be most severe in 'old' capitalist countries where output growth is least likely to accelerate (Sweezy 1942: 186–9).

This was a classic underconsumption model, requiring a constant relationship between consumption and the capital stock and making the further assumption (troubling to more orthodox Keynesians) that all saving was always and automatically invested. There were serious difficulties with the Bauer–Sweezy model, although it was not until 1960 that a formal critique became available, when the distinguished mathematical economist Nicholas Georgescu-Roegen demonstrated that Sweezy's formulation contained mathematical errors, in particular a lack of dimensional homogeneity. After reformulating the model to eliminate these errors, Georgescu-Roegen proved that a capitalist system may grow at a decreasing rate almost indefinitely without breaking down as a result of underconsumption (Georgescu-Roegen 1960).

Sweezy himself had concluded, somewhat ambiguously, that 'Bauer's highly interesting suggestions are essentially correct though they are not presented quite accurately and they do not bring out with sufficient clarity the connection between underconsumption and the basic characteristics of capitalist production' (Sweezy 1942: 186); he subsequently made no attempt to rebut Georgescu-Roegen's criticisms. His own analysis of the forces leading to stagnation in contemporary capitalism owed as much to Keynes, and to Alvin Hansen, as it did to Bauer, emphasizing the weakness of the incentive to invest no less than the dangers of over-saving. The influence of the underconsumptionists was, however, very evident in the *Theory of Capitalist Development*, especially where Sweezy discusses the expansionary implications of faulty investments, population growth, wasteful and unproductive consumption, and state expenditure, all of which add to effective demand without also expanding productive capacity. He argued, however, that these forces were weakening: 'on the whole there seems to be little doubt that the resistance to underconsumption is on the decline in the chief centers of world population' (Ibid.: 234). Only a huge increase in consumption expenditure by the state could offset this tendency, Sweezy maintained, and this would be associated with fascism and imperialist warfare rather than the liberal democratic capitalism anticipated by Keynes.

There was a certain irony in the fact that two Marxists had made the most significant advance in underconsumption theory since the publication of Hobson's and Mummery's *Physiology of Industry* in 1889. Was not Marx noted for his scathing, often abusive, criticism of Malthus? Had he not advanced the apparently decisive objection that the rate of exploitation fell at the peak of the boom, so that the theory was empirically false? Did he not insist that the production of surplus value was a more basic problem than its realization, describing as 'vulgar' those economists who took the opposite position? Considerations such as these induced Keynes, on more than one occasion, to dismiss Marx as a 'Ricardian' who supported Say's Law and denied the principle of effective demand (Howard and King 1992: 91–3). At first they even confused Joan Robinson, who found Keynes's view of Marx confirmed by the popularizing work of John Strachey (Robinson 1937: 246–55).

But there was another side to this story. Underconsumptionist arguments had played a prominent role in the early socialist literature which had influenced Marx; Sismondi, Owen and Bray helped to condition his thinking on the 'realisation problem' (King 1981, 1983). There are many passages in both *Capital* and *Theories of Surplus Value* where Marx shows himself to be sympathetic to underconsumptionist arguments, and subsequent socialist writers turned it into the cornerstone of their theories of crisis and (in some cases) of imperialism. Although she was only dimly aware of this literature, Robinson was soon led by her reading of Marx to reinterpret his macroeconomics in a much more favourable light:

> demand for the product of the consumption-good industries is restricted – the workers cannot consume, and the capitalists will not. The consumption-good industries therefore present a narrow field for investment, and the capital-good industries in turn suffer from restricted

demand. Here at last Say's Law is overthrown, and Marx appears to foreshadow the modern theory of effective demand.

(Robinson 1941: 248; cf. Robinson 1942, ch. VIII)

This was written under the influence of Michal Kalecki, whose work forms an important bridge between Marx and Keynes. Although he was never in any strict sense an underconsumption theorist, Kalecki's identification of what he termed 'the tragedy of investment' links him closely with that tradition. Investment expenditure adds both to effective demand and to productive capacity, he argued. Its implications for the realization of profits were therefore no simple matter; depression could result from overinvestment (and thus from underconsumption) as readily as from underinvestment (Kalecki 1939b: 138–9). Kalecki's most distinguished disciple, Josef Steindl, took these insights and applied them to the twentieth-century economic history of the United States. As the American economy matured, Steindl maintained, competition increasingly gave way to monopoly and profit margins grew. The resulting shift in the distribution of income led to stagnation as consumption failed to keep pace with the growth of the capital stock and the degree of capacity utilization declined. The Great Depression was no aberration, but rather an inevitable episode in the history of monopoly capitalism (Steindl 1952).

Similar ideas, much less rigorously expressed, were put forward by J.K. Galbraith in his best-selling book, *The Great Crash* (1955). They also profoundly affected the approach to capitalist crisis of later Marxian writers on both sides of the Atlantic, the French 'regulation school' (Aglietta 1979) no less than the US theorists of the 'social structure of accumulation' (Gordon *et al.* 1983). There was, of course, an obvious and quite fundamental problem. If underconsumption had been responsible for the catastrophe of the 1930s, why had it not recurred in the post-war period? Perhaps capitalism had changed after 1945, with the introduction of the welfare state and the emergence of large and powerful trade unions, in such a way that mass consumption had expanded at the same rate as production. Underconsumption could then be viewed as a historically specific phenomenon, which had been overcome by the adaptation of institutions and policies in what came to be known as the 'Fordist' phase of capitalist development (Henry Ford's high-wage strategy had been motivated, at least in part, by his fear of underconsumption). When Fordist capitalism ran into difficulties of its own, at the beginning of the 1970s, it was because wages were running ahead of productivity growth, not lagging behind. Very crudely put, overconsumption rather than underconsumption lay behind the profit squeeze (Howard and King 1992: ch. 16).

This perspective failed to convince either Paul Sweezy or his collaborator Paul Baran, who had refined Sweezy's analysis and extended it to underdeveloped economies in a very important article in the *Manchester School* and in his book *The Political Economy of Growth* (Baran 1952, 1957). Nine years later there appeared the most influential underconsumptionist text of the post-war period, *Monopoly Capital* (Baran and Sweezy 1966). At the level of the individual corporation Baran and Sweezy invoked orthodox neoclassical price theory – the Fellner model of joint profit maximization by tacitly colluding oligopolists – to establish a tendency for profit margins to rise. For the whole economy they propounded a 'law of the rising surplus', according to which potential output grew faster than the necessary costs of producing it. Thus underconsumption was an immanent tendency of monopoly capital, its stagnation-inducing consequences being evaded only (and precariously) by the massive expansion of wasteful expenditures by the private sector and by the civilian and military branches of the state. Twenty-five years later, Sweezy was still loyal to this underconsumptionist vision of modern capitalism (Sweezy 1991; cf. J.B. Foster 1986).

In its way *The Political Economy of Growth* was no less important than *Monopoly Capital*. The notion that the economic progress of backward areas was impeded by deficient consuming power – the so-called 'vicious circle of poverty' – was fundamental to the development literature of the 1950s and 1960s, and was by no means confined to Marxian theorists. One quasi-Marxian variant was, however, particularly significant. In his book, *Unequal Exchange*, Arghiri Emmanuel (1972) attributed underconsumption in the Third World to the exploitation of poor primary producers by rich manufacturing nations, which turned the terms of trade against low-wage producers and, by impoverishing them, blocked development at the periphery of the world economy. As had been the case in much of the classical Marxian literature, in the work of Emmanuel underconsumption and imperialism were intimately connected.

All of this, of course, was remote indeed from the contemporary mainstream of 'Keynesian' macroeconomics. Yet there were two points at which underconsumption theory impinged on more orthodox analysis. One was in the theory of economic growth, and the other in the aggregate supply and demand formulation of Keynes's system. The first has already been alluded to: there is a clear relationship between Otto Bauer's 'technical coefficient' linking consumption and the capital stock, and the accelerator mechanism which underpins the Harrod growth model. Harrod was reluctant to accept the analogy, though his respect for J.A. Hobson is well-known (Clarke 1990: 112, n. 48). Domar, on the other hand, was quite explicit in acknowledging his debt to Kalecki, to underconsumptionists like Foster and Catchings, and above all to Hobson:

> Keynes analyzed what happened when savings (of the preceding period) are not invested. . . . Hobson, on the other hand, went a step further and stated the problem in this form: suppose savings are invested. Will the new plants be able to dispose of their products?

Such a statement of the problem was not at all, as Keynes thought, a mistake. It was a statement of a different, and possibly also a deeper problem.

(Domar 1947: 52)

Hobson, Domar asserts, 'was fully armed with the σ effect of investment, and he saw that it could be answered only by growth' (ibid.: 52). Here the coefficient σ is 'the potential social average productivity of investment' (ibid.: 39), or the inverse of the average capital–output ratio. It indicates the increase in the productive capacity of the economy that is associated with a given increase in the capital stock. 'Hobson's weakness', Domar concluded, 'lay in a poor perception of the multiplier effect and his analysis lacked rigour in general. But the problem to which he addressed himself is just as alive today as it was fifty and twenty years ago' (ibid.: 52). Thus underconsumption theory had been vindicated, in effect, by the generalization of *The General Theory* to the long period.

In 1956 the future Post-Keynesian Sidney Weintraub demonstrated that it might also be relevant to the short period. Weintraub based his macroeconomic theory of wages on the aggregate supply and demand analysis sketched by Keynes in Chapter 3. An increase in the general level of money wages, Weintraub noted, would affect both aggregate demand and aggregate supply. By raising costs of production, it would shift the aggregate supply curve upwards to the left, tending to reduce employment; by increasing consumption on the part of wage-earners, it might also shift the aggregate demand curve upwards to the right, tending to raise the level of employment. The net effect would depend on the relative strength of these two forces. Weintraub distinguished three cases: the classical, where employment falls as money-wages rise; the Keynesian, where shifts in aggregate supply and demand curves cancel each other out and leave employment unchanged; and the underconsumptionist, where employment increases (Weintraub 1956: 839–42).

For a number of reasons Weintraub was unimpressed by the practical likelihood of underconsumption (ibid.: 842–6). Later Post-Keynesian writers have, however, been more favourably disposed towards it (Rowthorn 1981; Lavoie 1992: ch. 5). While no Post-Keynesian would insist, with Hobson, Bauer and Sweezy, that underconsumption is *the* key to the contradictions of advanced capitalist economies, most would accept it as a contingent possibility, depending, perhaps, on the relative sensitivity of consumption and investment expenditures to changes in the wage level (King and Regan 1988: 85–6). If little has been added analytically in recent years, there has been an increasing understanding of the historical evolution of underconsumption theory (Bleaney 1976; Costabile and Rowthorn 1985; Schneider 1987). It is, however, only in the Post-Keynesian and Marxian camps that these ideas have any credibility whatsoever. For those New

Classical and 'New Keynesian' theorists who think about it at all, under-consumption remains, as it was for Keynes's 'classical economists', a pathetic and inconsequential heresy.

NOTES

1 Heckscher 1931: ii. 208.
2 Quoted in ibid.: 291.
3 Quoted in ibid.: 209.
4 Keynes (1933d: 139–42).
5 J.S. Mill, *Political Economy*, Book I, ch. v. There is a most important and penetrating discussion of this aspect of Mill's theory in Mummery and Hobson (1889: 38ff), and, in particular, of his doctrine (which Marshall, in his very unsatisfactory discussion of the Wages-Fund Theory, endeavoured to explain away) that 'a demand for commodities is not a demand for labour'.
6 Alec Cairncross, 'The Victorians and Investment', *Economic History*, 1936.
7 Fullarton's tract *On the Regulation of Currencies* (1844) is the most interesting of his references.
8 In the first edition of this book I bracketed Marx with Silvio Gesell and Major Douglas. Discussions with Mr Dobb and, especially, with Mrs Robinson have convinced me that this did him much less than justice. What follows is taken from an early draft of *The General Theory*, where I was, I now think correctly, more inclined to see Marx as an important pioneer of anti-Ricardian thinking on these questions [*C.W.* XXIX: 77–82].
9 Cf. McCracken (1933: 46), where this part of Marx's theory is cited in relation to modern theory.
10 For example: 'The last cause of all real crises always remains the poverty and restricted consumption of the masses as compared to the tendency of capitalist production to develop the productive forces in such a way that only the absolute power of consumption of the entire society would be their limit' (Marx, *Capital*, vol. III: 568, C.H. Kerr & Co., cf. ibid.: 286–7).
11 J.M. Robertson's *The Fallacy of Saving*, published in 1892, supported the heresy of Mummery and Hobson. But it is not a book of much value or significance, being entirely lacking in the penetrating intuitions of *The Physiology of Industry*.
12 Mummery and Hobson (1889: iii–v).
13 *G.T.*: 367–70.
14 Hobson (1938: 192–3), emphasis added.
15 Hobson (1932b: 53): cf. (1934: 443).
16 Mummery and Hobson (1889: 130–2).
17 Hobson (1932a: 29–30); cf. Hobson (1934: 443).
18 Ramsey (1922).

24

KEYNES'S 'CONCLUDING NOTES'

Robert Skidelsky writing as J.M. Keynes

The General Theory has suffered the fate of all books, revolutionary in their time. It is now an unread 'classic'. I set out to produce a 'theory of output as a whole', the absence of which I identified as the main gap in classical economics. The need to treat output as the variable to be explained arose because of the tendency of capitalist economies to experience prolonged periods of sub-normal activity. But there is nothing in my theory formally inconsistent with the view that capitalist economies may spontaneously experience long periods of satisfactory employment on average, in which case no special measures of government intervention are necessarily called for. For this reason, my 'general theory' is more properly regarded, like Marshall's *Principles*, as an 'organum of thought', a framework for thinking about aggregate problems, a statement of logical possibility, rather than as a proof that unmananged capitalist economies are inevitably demand-constrained. What I was asserting is that the limiting case when involuntary unemployment is absent cannot be the general case in an economy where contracts, or debts, are fixed in money terms, and economic agents are free to refrain from spending.

Without an understanding of these points it is impossible to arrive at a correct appreciation of the social philosophy to which my *General Theory* pointed. As I tried to make clear in Chapter 24, my aim in filling the gaps in the classical theory was not to supersede the market economy by a system of central planning but 'to indicate the nature of the environment which the free play of economic forces requires if it is to realise the full potentialities of production'. Hayek's economics were frightfully muddled; but I agreed with the moral and philosophical position he adopted in his *Road to Serfdom*. I wish I had lived long enough to write a companion volume to *The General Theory* on political and social theory. It is amazing how much I actually did manage to write about the science of politics – going back to my undergraduate essay on Burke – without having the leisure to assemble these writings into an extended argument. As I still lack leisure – my services are in continuous demand in this place – I shall content myself with elaborating some passages in my 'Concluding Notes' which, on re-reading, I find may have given rise to misunderstanding, as well as modifying some things I wrote in the light of the experience of government behaviour since my death.

At the outset of my 'Concluding Notes' I identified 'the outstanding faults of the economic society in which we live' as its 'failure to provide for full employment and its arbitrary and inequitable distribution of wealth and incomes'.[1] Having been properly educated, I understood perfectly well the difference between equity, which is a principle of justice, implying that reward should be proportioned to effort and ability, and equality, which may not be equitable if effort or ability is unequal. A careful student of my writings will notice that I typically use 'inequitable' and 'unjust' in connection with changes in the value of money, which, owing to the fixity of contracts and uncertainty of expectation, inflict 'windfall' gains and losses on large sections of the community.[2] From this fact I concluded that a stable value of money is necessary for the survival of capitalism as a social system. At no time was my economic theory based on the proposition that the long-run distribution of wealth and incomes in capitalist societies was unjust; still less that the struggle for distributional shares was the major cause of the malfunctioning of the capitalist system. It is true that I endorsed John Stuart Mill's view that inherited wealth rewards no current contribution to the growth of wealth and that therefore heavy death duties may be justified. But the scale of taxes on both wealth and incomes will always need to be judged by a set of considerations which go beyond equity alone.

One implication of my *General Theory* is that, in conditions of heavy unemployment, a decrease in the propensity to save would, other things being equal, increase rather than diminish the inducement to invest. A policy directed towards maintaining a low rate of interest would itself result in an increase in the average propensity to consume. But such an aim would also furnish a justification for measures of taxation to redistribute wealth and income from those with a high to those with a low propensity to save. However, I emphasized that experience alone would show how far the process of redistribution could go without diminishing the inducement to invest, as well as efficiency and freedom. Taking all these factors into account, I rejected the socialist goal of equalizing wealth and incomes, but concluded none the less that the capitalist game could be played for 'lower stakes'.[3] How much lower will always remain a matter of judgement. In particular, wise and prudent statesmanship will need to take into consideration the effects of redistributionary policies on the marginal efficiency of capital.

I was wrong to suggest that 'the demand for capital' might be satiated 'within one or two generations'. In saying this I greatly underestimated the power of economic progress itself to stimulate new wants. At the same time, I was not unaware that it is always possible to recreate conditions of capital scarcity by destroying the accumulated stock of capital goods, as happened in the Second World War; and such is mankind's fear of leisure that I have no confidence that this method will not be employed many more times on the road to general abundance. I warned further that the rate of capital accumulation could be slowed down by 'an excessive change [increase] in the aggregate propensity to consume (including the State)'.[4] My own theory would have justified an increase in thriftiness, on the part of both the individual and the state, to maintain a sufficient rate of investment in the post-1945 conditions of full employment. Instead, the vast expansion of state consumption and transfer payments which started in the 1960s was, I believe, a major cause of the slowing down of the rate of capital accumulation from the 1970s onwards.

It follows as a matter of logic that a genuine state of capital abundance would 'mean the euthanasia of the rentier'.[5] However, it must not be supposed that I advocated a policy of rapid capital accumulation in order to bring this about. Rather, I saw it as a by-product of policies whose aim was to create conditions of general abundance as quickly as possible, bringing man – as I explained in my essay *Economic Possibilities for our Grand-children* – as quickly as possible to face 'his real, his permanent problem – how to use his freedom from pressing economic cares . . . to live wisely and agreeably and well'.[6] Paradoxically, the great cultural achievements of aristocratic and bourgeois civilization depended precisely on land and capital being scarce; and in particular, on the power of the owner of capital to keep capital artificially scarce by demanding a rate of interest which slowed down its accumulation. The problem was to maintain and extend the achievements of the rentier class while pursuing policies which both required and brought about a progressive fall in the long-term rate of interest. It should not have been impossible to use the proceeds of a wise scheme of taxation to endow, on a lavish scale, centres of learning and the arts, on the model of Cambridge and Oxford, which would have progressively extended the circle of civilization. In practice, this has been done only to a very limited extent. The munificence of mediaeval rulers contrasts favourably not just with the penny-pinching attitudes of the nineteenth-century Treasury, but with the improvidence of the twentieth-century welfare state, which has crowded out many of the civilizing state expenditures that I envisaged.

Nothing I wrote has been subject to more misinterpretation than the sentence: 'I conceive . . . that a somewhat comprehensive socialisation of investment will prove the only means of securing an approximation to full employment.'[7] This was widely understood as a call for the State to take over the accumulation function from the private sector by methods which included the nationalization of industry. It was supported by the alleged interest-inelasticity of investment – a doctrine I was also supposed to uphold, despite the fact that all my theoretical writings, including *The*

General Theory, were directed to the problem of securing a reduction in the rate of interest.

It is true that on two occasions – in 1929 and in 1933– I advocated programmes of loan-financed public works in circumstances where, for one reason or another, it was impossible to secure a rate of interest consistent with a full employment level of investment.[8] But such proposals were not justified by the alleged interest-inelasticity of investment; and carried no implication that the state should assume responsibility for the community's investment as a permanent system. Indeed, even in the depth of depression, when the case for a programme of loan-financed public works was strongest, I was always alert to the effects of public borrowing on interest rates and urged conservative budgets at times of financial crisis.[9]

Let me, then, recall, my full doctrine from the 'Concluding Notes', before reminding the reader of the contexts in which I used the words 'State' and 'socialisation':

> Only experience can show how far the common will, embodied in the policy of the State, ought to be directed to increasing and supplement-ing the inducement to invest. . . . It seems unlikely that the influence of banking policy on the rate of interest will be sufficient by itself to determine an optimum rate of investment. I conceive, therefore, that a somewhat comprehensive socialisation of investment will prove the only means of securing an approximation to full employment; though this need not exclude all manner of compromises and devices by which public authority will co-operate with private initiative . . . It is not the ownership of the instruments of production which it is important for the State to assume. If the State is able to determine the aggregate amount of resources devoted to augmenting the instruments and the basic rate of reward to those who own them, it will have accomplished all that is necessary. Moreover, the necessary measures of socialisation can be introduced gradually and without a break in the general tradi-tions of society.[10]

Two points from the quotation above are in need of emphasis. The first is my view that 'only experience will show' how big a role public investment policy will need to play in securing a full employment level of aggregate demand. We can add here a sentence from Chapter 12 of *The General Theory*: 'Only experience . . . can show how far management of the rate of interest is capable of continuously stimulating the appropriate volume of invest-ment.'[11] The second is my emphasis on the 'gradual' character of the 'necessary measures of socialisation'. The meaning of the first observation is self-evident. It was intended as a warning against the mechanical applica-tion of the same policy to widely differing circumstances. To understand the force of the second remark, the reader will need to have some acquain-tance with other writings of mine.

Let me explain that I never used the term 'State' as a synonym for the 'government of the day', or even to refer to those institutions which are conventionally located in the 'public sector'; nor by 'socialisation' did I mean the transfer of property ownership, by Act of Parliament, from private individuals to the government. By the 'State' I meant a network of institutions whose stake in the proper functioning of the economy and society was so deep and extensive that their corporate actions were not determined by motives of short-term profit maximization; and by 'the socialisation of investment' I meant the growth in the share of aggregate investment controlled by such institutions. These conceptions of the 'State' and 'socialisation' are well brought out in a letter I wrote to *The Times* on 25 March 1925:

> So far from wishing to diminish the authority of the Bank of England I regard that great institution as a heaven-sent gift, ideally suited to be the instrument of the reforms I advocate. We have here a semi-independent corporation *within the state*, with immense prestige and historical tradition, not in fact working for private profit, with no interest whatever except the public good, yet detached from the wayward influence of politics . . . The Bank of England is a type of that *socialism* of the future which is in accord with the British instincts of government, and which – perhaps one may hope – our Commonwealth is evolving within its womb. The Universities are another example of the semi-independent institutions divested of private interest which I have in mind. *The state* is generally sterile and creates little. New forms and modes spring from the fruitful minds of individuals. But when a corporation, devised by private resources, has reached a certain age and a certain size, it *socialises* itself, or falls into decay.[12]

My notion here of privately owned, but public-spirited, organization cuts across the conventional division between the public and private sectors. The state includes bodies which are legally private, but which in the course of their evolution have come to acquire a sense of public responsibility. In so far as politicians seek the public good they are part of the state; in so far as they pursue their private interests through politics they are no different from profit-maximizing firms.

All this may sound strange to the modern reader. But my language has its roots in a mediaeval past, when property was invested with both private and public functions. In the capitalist era, property escaped from vassalage to become fully 'privatized', with its public functions taken over by the modern 'State'. I was suggesting that this tendency was now reversing itself. The State was no longer rigidly separated from private property and private enterprise; rather, the two spheres were merging in hybrid forms.

In my essay 'The End of *Laissez-faire*', in my contributions to the Liberal

Industrial Enquiry of 1927–8, and in other of my writings, I trace the 'socialisation' of the economy from the decline of family firms and the emergence of joint-stock companies in the nineteenth century to the rise of large-scale business corporations under the nominal control of anonymous shareholders but in fact run by salaried managers whose motives more closely approximate to those of public servants than of profit-maximizing entrepreneurs.[13] 'Time and the Joint Stock Company and the Civil Service have silently brought the salaried class into power', I wrote in 1934.[14] I pointed to the fact that various types of socialized, semi-socialized and other state-regulated enterprises – of which building, transport and public utilities were the chief example – already controlled two-thirds of the capital stock of the country.[15] I pointed to the 'smallness of the part [in investment] which purely private enterprise now plays', and how, if the State could control the aggregate investment of 'public and semi-public bodies', it could 'safely leave industry to raise what funds it needs as and when it chooses'.[16] In *Britain's Industrial Future* I proposed that the investment funds of the public utilities should be pooled, and segregated into a 'capital budget' to be spent under the direction of a national investment board. Such a board would be able to influence or control the spending of one-fifth of annual national savings, using it to finance new capital expenditure by public bodies as well as to make advances for new capital improvements to railways, or even to private companies. By such mechanisms, which involved new patterns of co-operation between legally private and public concerns, 'an era of rapid progress in equipping the country with all the material adjuncts of modern civilisation might be inaugurated, which would rival the great Railway Age of the nineteenth century'.[17] The culmination of this train of thought was a wartime Treasury Note I wrote in 1943 which sums up accurately what I believed to be the possibilities of stabilization in the light of this evolution:

> If two-thirds or three-quarters of total investment is carried out or can be influenced by public or semi-public bodies, a long-term programme of a stable character should be capable of reducing the potential range of fluctuation to much narrower limits than formerly, when a smaller volume of investment was under public control and when even this part tended to follow, rather than correct, fluctuations of investment in the strictly private sector . . . The main task should be to *prevent* large fluctuations by a stable long-term programme. If this is successful it should not be too difficult to offset small fluctuations by expediting or retarding some items in this long-term programme.[18]

The correct meaning of my investment philosophy should, at any rate, be clear. I was frankly sceptical about the ability of monetary policy alone to maintain continuous full employment in view of the large fluctuations in the marginal efficiency of capital. I conceived that the higher the share of 'socialized' investment in the total, the stabler, other things being equal, economies would be at a high level of employment. I believed that the evolution of modern capitalism was tending to enlarge the share of 'socialised' investment in the total, and that policy should take advantage of this fact by maintaining a sizeable core of stable investment across the business cycle. I concluded, though, that only experience would show what the share of State-controlled or State-influenced investment in the total would need to be, and how best to build on the evolutionary 'socialisation of investment' taking place. Once again it is necessary to remind the reader of the distinction between my 'general theory' as a logic of possibilities and the particular applications of it which can be made in different circumstances according to different sets of realistic assumptions.

How, then, might I wish to modify my investment doctrine in the light of experience since my departure? I feel I would now wish to do so in two respects. First, the thesis that capital was 'socialising' itself depended very heavily on the observed fact of growing industrial concentration, itself driven, in part, by the advantages which existing technology conferred on large-scale production. I believe that advantages of this kind were still to be secured till the end of the 1960s; I am no longer convinced that this is the case. The new computer and information technology has decreased the advantages of economies of scale, bringing the benefits of automation within reach of specialists as well as mass producers. There is now firm evidence of a de-concentration of industry and services, and with it a 'de-socialisation' of production. This has, of course, been encouraged by policy, but I have little doubt that it also reflected a technologically driven trend which may have been caused by rising labour and energy costs. I do not believe that a State-led investment policy can, in present circumstances, draw much support from the spontaneous evolution of the capitalist system. In particular, necessary restraints on individual initiative and enterprise, such as the prevention of unlimited capital movements, are much more difficult to organize today than they were in the aftermath of the Great Depression and Second World War, when international capital markets were virtually moribund.

A second modification of my views is prompted by the actual experience of extensive State involvement in industrial policy since the Second World War. When I wrote that the State was 'in a positon to calculate the marginal efficiency of capital-goods on long views and on the basis of the general social advantage'[19] I believed, and to some extent still do believe, that this was technically correct. But I seriously underestimated the extent to which state spending policies would be determined by political and sectional interests – a consideration which overshadows the fact that they need not be, and in fact are not, subject to the same volatility as private investment decisions. That is to say, the loss in economic efficiency produced by misguided State investment policies has come to outweigh the gain in stability; and since such policies have also been associated with acute financing problems, the gain in stability ultimately turned out to be chimerical. State-managed economies, after a long period of success, became as volatile as the unmanaged economies of my day.

It is easy to point to the technical flaw in the budget accounts which contributed to producing this outcome. There was a lack of the clear demarcation between the current account and capital budgets which I had proposed in 1928 and again in 1933.[20] When I talked about the desirability of increasing the volume of State-controlled or State-influenced investment I had in mind investments which, while undertaken for prospective social advantage, would nevertheless yield a positive commercial return, even though this need not be equal to that required by private investors.[21] My scheme of fiscal policy required the government's 'normal' budget to be balanced over the cycle, with the government incurring debt in the downswing and repaying debt out of taxation to check the boom.[22] Over the cycle, that is, the government's normal expenditure, including expenditure on non-revenue-yielding capital works, would be financed entirely from taxation. At the same time, the State – using the term in the extended sense I have outlined above – would borrow for capital works which yielded a cash return to service debt interest, just like a private firm, to the extent necessary to stabilize investment. Furthermore, I agreed with Mr Colin Clark in 1945 that there was 'sound empirical evidence' for his proposition that rates of taxation in excess of 25 per cent of net national income generated inflationary pressures.[23] In retrospect it is obvious that the 'bonds of revenue' were loosened somewhat by the war. But I was sure that there was a safe upper limit to taxation, and was indeed working on this problem when I died.

Post-war budgetary policy, carried out in my name, did not stick to my principles. There was always a considerble amount of public borrowing to finance both current consumption and non-revenue-yielding investments, even though statistically measured unemployment was negligible; and by the mid-1970s the British government was taking 40 per cent of the national income in taxation. In reality, technical weaknesses in the control of public expenditure reflected underlying political pressures which I had hoped to exclude, and which recent public-choice theory has illuminated. In the light of its suggestive, if far from conclusive, findings I would now wish to limit drastically the discretionary element in economic policy-making, which experience shows exercises a depressing effect on business expectations; and I would support a reduction of public spending to within limits which can be financed without generating inflationary pressures and other inefficiencies. For the fact remains that public finance can be used for stabilization purposes only if business opinion regards it as sound. Conceptions of what is economically sound must, in turn, be based on cogent economic analysis, not on fleeting political calculation.

The restoration of a sound condition in the public finances is thus a *sine qua non* for the resumption of policies which aim to stabilize employment at a high level (the misuse of my concept of 'full employment' deserves a chapter on its own). I see no need to modify my statement that 'if nations can learn to provide themselves with full employment by their domestic policy . . . there need be no important economic forces calculated to set the interest of one country against that of its neighbours'.[24] Experience of the 1930s showed that 'beggar-my-neighbour' policies are the fruit of inadequate domestic demand. The biggest threat to free trade at present comes from heavy unemployment in Europe, and the *general* sense of insecurity provoked by the re-emergence of a largely unmanaged global capitalist market economy. It would be tragic if the vast opportunities for the expansion of trade and investment opened up by the welcome collapse of Bolshevism were to be aborted by the increased insecurity generated by a triumphant capitalism.

A greater degree of economic stability in the short run is thus a necessary condition of long-run expectations favourable to peace and prosperity. A decentralized capitalist system remains the most powerful instrument for realizing the abundance which is the true end of economic activity. It is also the best safeguard for individual liberty and variety of life. But I doubt whether it can guarantee either the moral or material conditions for its own survival. Each age will need to work out the division of responsibility between the individual and the State appropriate for the conditions of its time. The general rule is that the State should not do those things which individuals are capable of doing, and do them a little better or a little worse, but do necessary things which will not be done at all unless the State does them. The State's job is not to direct the labours of society to a predetermined end but to fill the gaps in the market and voluntary provision of goods and services necessary for a good life for all. What these gaps are, by what means they might be filled – these are matters for the living to decide, in the light of their reason and experience.

NOTES

All references to Keynes's published writings are to *The Collected Writings of John Maynard Keynes* (Keynes 1971–89), hereafter abbreviated to *C.W.*

1 *C.W.* VII: 372.
2 For example, in *C.W.* IX: 306.
3 *C.W.* VII: 374.
4 Ibid.: 375.
5 Ibid.: 376.
6 *C.W.* IX: 328.
7 *C.W.* VII: 378.
8 In 'Can Lloyd George Do It?' (with Hubert Henderson), 1929 (*C.W.* IX: 86–125); and 'The Means to Prosperity', 1933 (ibid.: 335–66).

9 As, for example, to the Swedish banker, Marcus Wallenberg on 12 April 1933; in the Keynes Papers, King's College, Cambridge, File L/33.

10 *C.W.* VII: 377–8.

11 Ibid.: 164.

12 *C.W.* XIX: 347; emphasis added.

13 See *C.W.* IX: 289.

14 *C.W.* XXVIII: 32.

15 *C.W.* XIX: 696.

16 *C.W.* XXI: 135.

17 Keynes (1928: 114).

18 *C.W.* XXVII: 322.

19 *C.W.* VII: 164.

20 Keynes (1928: 112); *C.W.* IX: 348n.

21 *C.W.* XXI: 394–5.

22 Ibid.: 390.

23 *C.W.* XXVII: 414; see also Colin Clark's 'Memories of J.M. Keynes', unpublished ms., pp.14–15. The reference is to Clark (1945).

24 *C.W.* VII: 382.

BIBLIOGRAPHY

Abbot, E.A. (1884) *Flatland: A Romance of Many Dimensions*, New York: Dover.

Abel, A. and Blanchard, O. (1986) 'The present value of profits and cyclical movements in investment', *Econometrica* 54: 249–73.

Ackley, G. (1961) *Macroeconomic Theory*, New York: Macmillan.

—— (1978) *Macroeconomics: Theory and Policy*, New York: Macmillan.

Adelman, I. (1991) 'Long term economic development', Working Paper no. 589, California Agricultural Station.

—— and Adelman, F. (1959) 'The dynamic properties of the Klein–Golberger model', *Econometrica* 27: 596–625.

Agazzi, E. (ed.) (1991) *The Problem of Reductionism in Science*, Dordrecht: Kluwer.

Aglietta, M. (1979) *Theory of Capitalist Regulation*, London: New Left Books.

Alston, W. (1964) *Dimensions of Meaning*, Englewood Cliffs, N.J.: Prentice Hall.

Amadeo, E.J. (1989) *Keynes's Principle of Effective Demand*, Aldershot, Hants: Edward Elgar.

—— (1992) 'Equilibrium unemployment in Keynes's *General Theory*: some recent debates', *Contributions to Political Economy* 11: 1–14.

—— (1994) 'Changes in output in Keynes's *Treatise on Money*', in J. Davis (ed.) *The State of Interpretation of Keynes*, Norwell, Mass.: Kluwer.

Ambler, E. (1985) *Here Lies: An Autobiography*, London: Weidenfeld & Nicolson.

Ambromovitz, M. *et al.* (eds.) (1958) *The Allocation of Resources: Essays in Honour of B.F. Haley*, Stanford, Calif: Stanford University Press.

Ambrose, A. (1979) *Wittgenstein's Lectures, Cambridge, 1932–35*, Oxford: Blackwell.

Ambrosi, G.M. (1976) 'Das Keynessche Portfoliomodell', *Diskussionsbeiträge des Fachbereichs*, Wirtschaftswissenschaften der Universität Konstanz.

Ancott, J. (ed.) (1983) *Analysing the Structure of Econometric Models*, New York: Martinus Nijhoff.

Andrews, P.W.S. and Brunner, E. (1975) *Studies in Pricing*, London: Macmillan.

Arestis, P. (ed.) (1988) *Contemporary Issues in Money and Banking*, London: Macmillan.

—— (1992) *The Post-Keynesian Approach to Economics*, Aldershot, Hants: Edward Elgar.

—— (ed.) (1993) *Money and Banking: Issues for the Twenty-first Century*, London: Macmillan.

—— and Chick, V. (eds) (1992) *Recent Developments in Post Keynesian Economics*, Aldershot, Hants: Edward Elgar.

—— and Dow, S.C. (eds) (1986) *On Money, Method and Keynes*, London: Macmillan.

—— and Howells, P. (forthcoming) 'Theoretical reflections on endogenous money: the problem with "convenience lending"', *Cambridge Journal of Economics*.

440

Arestis, P. and Marshall, M. (eds) (1995) *The Political Economy of Full Employment, Conservatism, Corporatism, and Institutional Change*, Aldershot, Hants: Edward Elgar.

—— and Sawyer, M. (eds) (1994) *The Elgar Companion to Radical Political Economy*, Aldershot, Hants: Edward Elgar.

Arrow, K.J. (1958) 'Toward a theory of price adjustment', in M. Abramovitz *et al.* (eds) *The Allocation of Economic Resources: Essays in Honour of B.F. Haley*, Stanford, Calif: Stanford University Press.

—— and Debreu, G. (1954) 'Existence of an equilibrium for a competitive economy', *Econometrica* 22: 265–90.

—— and Hahn, F.H. (1971) *General Competitive Analysis*, San Francisco: Holden-Day.

—— and Hurwicz, L. (1958) 'On the stability of competitive equilibrium', *Econometrica* 26: 522–52.

Aschauer, D. (1989) 'Is public expenditure productive?', *Journal of Monetary Economics* 24: 177–200.

Asimakopulos, A. (1971) 'The determination of investment in Keynes' model', *Canadian Journal of Economics* 4: 382–8.

—— (1977) 'Profits and investment: a Kaleckian approach', in G.C. Harcourt (ed.) *The Microeconomic Foundations of Macroeconomics*, London: Macmillan.

—— (1983a) 'The role of the short period: comment on Bharadwaj', in J.A. Kregel (ed.) *Distribution, Effective Demand and Internatonal Economic Relations*, London: Macmillan.

—— (1983b) 'Kalecki and Keynes on finance, investment and savings', *Cambridge Journal of Economics* 7: 221–33.

—— (1985) 'Keynes and Sraffa: visions and perspectives', *Political Economy* 1: 33–50.

—— (1988) 'Reply to Garegnani's comment', *Political Economy* 4: 259–62.

—— (1989) 'The nature and role of equilibrium in Keynes's *General Theory*', *Australian Economic Papers* 28: 16–28.

—— (1991) *Keynes's* General Theory *and Accumulation*, Cambridge: Cambridge University Press.

Aukurst, O. (1970) 'PRIM I: a model of the price and income distribution mechanism of an open economy', *Review of Income and Wealth* 16: 51–78.

Backhouse, R. (ed.) (1994) *New Perspectives on Economic Methodology*, London: Routledge.

Banerjee, A.V. (1992) 'A simple model of herd behaviour', *Quarterly Journal of Economics* 107: 797–807.

Bank of Canada (1991) 'The implementation of monetary policy in a system with zero reserve requirements', Discussion Paper 3, 6 Sept.

Baran, P.A. (1952) 'On the political economy of backwardness', *Manchester School of Economic and Social Studies* 20: 66–84.

—— (1957) *The Political Economy of Growth*, New York: Monthly Review Press.

—— and Sweezy, P.M. (1966) *Monopoly Capital*, New York: Monthly Review Press.

Baranzini, M. (ed.) (1982) *Advances in Economic Theory*, Oxford: Blackwell.

—— and Scazzieri, R. (eds) (1986) *Foundations of Economics: Structure of Inquiry and Economic Theory*, Oxford: Blackwell.

Barens, I. (1987) 'Geld und Unterbeschäftigung. John Maynard Keynes' Kritik der Selbstregulierungsvorstellung', *Volkswirtschaftliche Schriften*, Heft 368, Berlin: Duncker & Humblot.

—— (1988) 'Die (doppelte) Rolle des Geldes bei Keynes', in H. Hagemann and O. Steiger (eds) *Keynes'* General Theory *nach fünfzig Jahren*, Volkswirtschaftliche Schriften Heft 384, Berlin: Duncker & Humblot.

Barens, I. (1989) 'From the "banana parable" to the principle of effective demand: some reflections on the origin, development and structure of Keynes' *General Theory*', in D.A. Walker (ed.) *Perspectives on the History of Economic Thought*, Vol II, Aldershot, Hants: Edward Elgar.

—— (1990) 'The rise and fall of the "entrepreneur economy": some remarks on Keynes's taxonomy of economics', in D.E. Moggridge (ed.) *Perspectives on the History of Economic Thought*, Vol. IV: *Keynes, Macroeconomics and Method*, Aldershot, Hants: Edward Elgar.

Barnett, W.A. and Chen, P. (1988) 'The aggregation–theoretical monetary aggregates are chaotic and have strange attractors: an econometric interpretation of mathematical chaos', in W. Barnett, R. Ernst and W. Halbert (eds) *Dynamic Econometric Modelling*, Cambridge: Cambridge University Press.

Barnett, W.A. and Hinich, M. (1993) 'Has chaos been discovered with economic data?', in P. Chen and R. Day (eds) *Nonlinear Dynamics and Evolutionary Economics*, Oxford: Oxford University Press.

Barnett, W.A. and Singleton, K.J. (eds) (1986) *New Approaches to Monetary Economics: Proceedings of the Second International Symposium in Economic Theory and Econometrics*, Cambridge: Cambridge University Press.

Barrère, A. (ed.) (1988) *The Foundations of Keynesian Analysis*, Proceedings of a Conference held at the University of Paris I-Panthéon-Sorbonne, London: Macmillan.

Barro, R.J. (1978a) 'Unanticipated money, output, and the price level in the United States', *Journal of Political Economy* 86: 22–51.

—— (1978b) *The Impact of Social Security on Private Saving: Evidence from US Time Series*, Washington, D.C.: American Enterprise Institute.

—— (1980) 'A capital market in an equilibrium business cycle model', *Econometrica* 48: 1393–417.

—— (1989) 'Interest-rate targeting', *Journal of Monetary Economics* 23: 3–30.

—— (1994) 'The aggregate supply/aggregate demand model', *Eastern Economic Journal* 20 (1): 1–6.

—— and Gordon, D.B. (1983a) 'A positive theory of monetary policy in a natural rate model', *Journal of Political Economy* 91: 589–610.

—— and —— (1983b) 'Rules, discretion and reputation in a model of monetary policy', *Journal of Monetary Economics* 12: 101–21.

—— and Grilli, V. (1994) *European Macroeconomics*, Basingstoke, Hants: Macmillan.

—— and Grossman, H. (1976) *Money, Employment and Inflation*, Cambridge: Cambridge University Press.

Bartholomew, J. (1993) 'Least-squares learning and the stability of equilibria with externalities', *Review of Economic Studies* 60: 197–208.

Bateman, B.W. (1987) 'Keynes's changing conception of probability', *Economics and Philosophy* 3: 97–120.

—— (1990a) 'Keynes, induction and econometrics', *History of Political Economy* 22: 359–79.

—— (1990b) 'The elusive logical relation', in D.E. Moggridge (ed.) *Perspectives in the History of Economic Thought, Vol. IV, Keynes, Macroeconomics and Method*, Aldershot, Hants: Edward Elgar.

—— (1991) 'Das Maynard Keynes Problem', *Cambridge Journal of Economics* 15: 101–11.

—— (1994) 'Keynes uncertain revolution', unpublished book manuscript.

—— and Davis, J.B. (eds) (1991) *Keynes and Philosophy: Essays on the Origin of Keynes's Thought*, Aldershot, Hants: Edward Elgar.

Bauer, O. (1936) *Zwischen zwei Weltkriegen?*, Bratislava: Prager.

Bauer, P. (1945) 'Notes on Cost', *Economica* 12: 90–100.

Baumol, W.J. (1971) 'On the behavioural theory of the firm', in R. Marris and A. Wood (eds) *The Corporate Economy*, Cambridge, Mass.: Harvard University Press.

Baumol, W.J. (1977) 'Say's (at least) eight laws, or what Say and James Mill may really have meant', *Economica* 44: 145–61.

Bean, C.R. (1984) *The Estimation of 'Surprise' Models and the 'Surprise' Consumption Function*, Discussion Paper no. 191, London: London School of Economics: Centre for Labour Economics.

Beckerman, W. (ed.) (1986) *Wage Rigidity and Unemployment*, Baltimore, Md.: Johns Hopkins University Press.

Behrens, R. (1985) 'What Keynes knew about Marx', *Studi Economici* 26: 3–14.

Bell, D. and Kristol, I. (eds) (1981) *The Crisis in Economic Theory*, New York: Basic Books.

Bénabou, R. (1988) 'Search, price setting and inflation', *Review of Economic Studies* 55: 353–76.

—— (1992) 'Inflation and efficiency in search markets', *Review of Economic Studies* 59: 299–329.

Benassy, J. (1986) *Macroeconomics: An Introduction to the Non-Walrasian Approach*, London: Harcourt Brace Jovanovich.

Beranek, W. and Timberlake, R.H. (1987) 'The liquidity trap theory: a critique', *Southern Economic Journal* 54: 387–96.

Berg, L. (1994) 'Household savings and debts: the experience of the Nordic countries', *Oxford Review of Economic Policy* 10: 42–53.

Berle, A.A. and Means, G.C. (1932) *The Modern Corporation and Private Property*, New York: Macmillan.

Bernanke, B. (1981) 'Bankruptcy, liquidity and recession', *American Economic Review* 71: 155–9.

—— (1983) 'Irreversibility, uncertainty and cyclical investment', *Quarterly Journal of Economics* 98: 85–106.

Beveridge, W.H. (1936a) 'Employment theory and the facts of unemployment', unpublished MS. Held at British Library of Political and Economic Science, London.

—— (1936b) 'Supplementary notes on Keynes', unpublished MS. Held at British Library of Political and Economic Science, London.

Bhaduri, A. (1986) *Macroeconomics: The Dynamics of Commodity Production*, London: Macmillan.

—— (1996) 'Economic growth and the theory of capital: an evaluation of Joan Robinson's contribution', in C. Marcuzzo, L. Pasinetti and A. Roncaglia (eds) *The Economics of Joan Robinson*, London: Routledge, 200–6.

—— and Robinson, J. (1980) 'Accumulation and exploitation: an analysis in the tradition of Marx, Sraffa and Kalecki', *Cambridge Journal of Economics* 4: 103–15.

Bharadwaj, K. (1983) 'On effective demand: certain recent critiques', in J.A. Kregel (ed.) *Distribution, Effective Demand and International Economic Relations*, London: Macmillan.

Bhaskar, R. (1978) *A Realist Theory of Science*, Hemel Hempstead, Herts.: Harvester Press.

—— (1979) *The Possibility of Naturalism*, Hemel Hempstead, Herts.: Harvester Press.

—— (1986) *Scientific Realism and Human Emancipation*, London: Verso.

—— (1989) *Reclaiming Reality: A Critical Introduction to Contemporary Philosophy*, London: Verso.

Bhattacharjea, A. (1987) 'Keynes and the long-period theory of employment: a note', *Cambridge Journal of Economics* 11: 275–84.

Bikhchandani, S., Hirshleifer, D. and Welch, I. (1992) 'A theory of fads, fashion, custom and cultural change as informational cascades', *Journal of Political Economy* 100: 992–1026.

Black, F. (1970) 'Banking and interest rates in a world without money: the effects of uncontrolled banking', *Journal of Bank Research* 1: 8–20.

—— (1976) 'The dividend puzzle', *Journal of Portfolio Management* 2: 5–8.

—— (1987) *Business Cycles and Equilibrium*, Oxford: Blackwell.

Black, M. (1949) *Language and Philosophy: Studies in Method*, Ithica, N.Y.: Cornell University Press.

Blanchard, O. (1987) *Aggregate and Individual Price Adjustments*, Brookings Papers on Economic Activity no. 1, Washington, D.C.: Brookings Institution.

—— and Fischer, S. (1989) *Lectures on Macroeconomics*, Cambridge, Mass.: MIT Press.

—— and Kiyotaki, N. (1987) 'Monopolistic competition and aggregate demand', *American Economic Review* 77: 647–68.

Blatt, J. (1980) 'On the Frisch model of business cycles', *Oxford Economic Papers* 32: 467–79.

Blaug, M. (1980) *The Methodology of Economics*, Cambridge: Cambridge University Press.

Bleaney, M. (1976) *Underconsumption Theories: A History and Critical Analysis*, London: Lawrence & Wishart.

Blinder, A.S. (1976) 'Intergenerational transfers and life cycle consumption', *American Economic Review* 66: 87–93.

Bliss, C.J. (1987) 'Equal rates of profit', in J. Eatwell, M. Milgate and P. Newman (eds) *The New Palgrave: A Dictionary of Economics*, vol. 2, London: Macmillan.

Blundell, R. (1991) 'Consumer behaviour: theory and empirical evidence – a survey', in A.J. Oswald (ed.) *Surveys in Economics*, vol. II., Oxford: Blackwell, for the Royal Economic Society.

Boddy, R. and Crotty, J. (1975) 'Class conflict and macro policy: the political business cycle', *Review of Radical Political Economics*, Spring.

Boehm, S., Frowen, S. and Pheby, J. (eds) (1993) *Economics as the Art of Thought: Essays in Memory of G.L.S. Shackle*, London: Routledge.

Boitani, A. and Rodano, G. (eds) (1995) *Relazioni Pericolose. L'avventura dell'economia nella cultura contempporanea*, Bari: Laterza.

Boserup, M. (1969) 'A note on the prehistory of the Kahn multiplier', *Economic Journal* 79: 667–9.

Boskin, M. (1988) 'Consumption, saving and fiscal policy', *American Economic Review* 78: 401–7.

—— (ed.) (1979) *Economics and Human Welfare: Essays in Honour of Tibor Scitovsky*, New York: Academic Press.

Boulding, K. (1944) 'A liquidity preference theory of market prices', *Economica* 11: 55–63.

Bowles, S., Gordon, D. and Weisskopf, T. (1986) *Beyond the Wasteland*, New York: Anchor Press.

——, —— and —— (1989) 'Business ascendancy and economic impasse: a structural retrospective on conservative economics', *Journal of Economic Perspectives* 3: 107–34.

Bradford, W. (1993) 'Words and deeds: Keynes's "spectrum of appropriate languages" and the formation of macroeconomic theory and policy', University of Cambridge, mimeo.

Brady, M.E. (1993) 'J.M. Keynes's theoretical approach to decision-making under conditions of risk and uncertainty', *British Journal for the Philosophy of Science* 43, forthcoming.

—— and Lee, H.B. (1989a) 'Dynamics of choice behaviour: the logical relation between linear objective probability and nonlinear subjective probability', *Psychological Reports* 64: 91–7.

Brady, M.E. and Lee, H.B. (1989b) 'Is there an Ellsberg–Fellner paradox? A note on its resolution', *Psychological Reports* 64: 1087–90.

Brainard, W.C. and Tobin, J. (1968) 'Pitfalls in financial model building', *American Economic Review* 58: 99–122.

Braithwaite, R.B. (ed.) (1931) *The Foundations of Mathematics*, London: Routledge & Kegan Paul.

Branson, W.H. and Klevorick, A.K. (1969) 'Money illusion and the aggregate consumption function', *American Economic Review* 59: 832–43.

Brennan, G. and Waterman, A.M.C. (eds) (1994) *Economics and Religion: Are They Distinct?*, Boston, Mass.: Kluwer.

Brenner, Y.S., Reinders, J.P.G. and Spithoven, A.H.G.M. (eds) (1988) *The Theory of Income and Wealth Distribution*, Brighton: Wheatsheaf.

Brigham, E.F. and Gordon, M.J. (1968) 'Leverage, dividend policy and the cost of capital', *Journal of Finance* 23: 85–103.

Brock, W. (1986) 'Distinguishing random and deterministic systems', *Journal of Economic Theory* 40: 168–96.

——, Hsieh, D. and LeBaron, B. (1991) *Nonlinear Dynamics, Chaos and Instability*, Cambridge, Mass.: MIT Press.

Brothwell, J. (1975) 'A simple Keynesian's response to Leijonhufvud', *Bulletin of Economic Research* 27: 3–21.

—— (1983) 'Wages and employment: a reply to Maynard and Rose', *Journal of Post Keynesian Economics* 6: 101–4.

—— (1986) '*The General Theory* after fifty years: why are we not all Keynesians now?', *Journal of Post Keynesian Economics* 8: 531–47.

Brown, A.J. (1958) 'Inflation and the British Economy', *Economic Journal* 66: 449–63.

—— assisted by Jane Darby (1985) *World Inflation since 1950*, Cambridge: Cambridge University Press, for National Institute of Economic and Social Research.

Brown, C. (1992) 'Commodity money, credit money and the real balance effect', *Journal of Post Keynesian Economics* 15: 99–107.

Brunner, K. and Meltzer, A.H. (eds) (1976) *The Phillips Curve and Labour Markets*, Carnegie–Rochester Conference Series on Public Policy, vol. 1, Amsterdam: North-Holland.

—— and —— (1981) *The Costs and Consequences of Inflation*, Carnegie–Rochester Conference Series on Public Policy, Amsterdam: North-Holland.

Bruno, M. and Sachs, J.O. (1985) *Economics of Worldwide Stagflation*, Oxford: Blackwell.

Bryant, J. and Wallace, N. (1980) 'A suggestion for further simplifying the theory of money', Minneapolis: Federal Reserve Bank of Minneapolis and University of Minnesota, MS.

Buiter, W., Corsetti, G. and Roubini, N. (1993) 'Excessive deficits: sense and nonsense in the treaty of Maastricht', *Economic Policy* 16: 57–100.

Burch, S.W. and Werneke, D. (1975) 'The stock of consumer durables, inflation and personal saving decisions', *Review of Economics and Statistics* 57: 141–54.

Burda, M. and Wyplosz, C. (1993) *Macroeconomics: A European Text*, Oxford: Oxford University Press.

Burmeister, E. (1980) *Capital Theory and Dynamics*, Cambridge: Cambridge University Press.

Burns, A. and Mitchell, W. (1946) *Measuring Business Cycles*, New York: National Bureau of Economic Research.

Bush, J. (1994) 'Inflation obsession blinds policy makers to other ills', *The Times*, 25 August.

Bushaw, D.W. and Clower, R.W. (1957) *Introduction to Mathematical Economics*, Homewood, Ill.: Irwin.

Cagan, P. (1956) 'The monetary dynamics of hyperinflation', in M. Friedman (ed.) *Studies in the Quantity Theory of Money*, Chicago, Ill.: Chicago University Press.

Cairncross, Sir A. (1985) *Years of Recovery: British Economic Policy, 1945–51*, London: Methuen.

—— and Cairncross, F. (eds) (1992) *The Legacy of the Golden Age: The 1960s and their Consequences*, London: Routledge.

Campbell, J.Y. and Mankiw, N.G. (1989) 'Consumption, income and interest rates: reinterpreting the time series evidence', *NBER Macroeconomics Annual* 4: 185–216.

Capra, F. (1983) *The Turning Point*, London: Flamingo.

Carabelli, A. (1988) *On Keynes's Method*, London: Macmillan.

—— (1992) 'Organic interdependence and Keynes's choice of units in the *General Theory*', in B. Gerrard and J. Hillard (eds) *Philosophy and Economics of J.M. Keynes*, Aldershot, Hants: Edward Elgar.

Caravale, G.A. (ed.) (1991) *Marx and Modern Economic Analysis*, 2 vols, Aldershot, Hants: Edward Elgar.

Cardim de Carvahlo, F.J. (1990) 'Keynes and the long period', *Cambridge Journal of Economics* 14: 277–90.

—— (1992) *Mr Keynes and the Post Keynesians: Principles of Macroeconomics for a Monetary Production Economy*, Aldershot, Hants: Edward Elgar.

Cas, A. and Rymes, T.K. (1991) *On Concepts and Measures of Multifactor Productivity in Canada, 1961–80*, Cambridge: Cambridge University Press.

Caskey, J. and Fazzari, S. (1987) 'Aggregate demand contractions with nominal debt commitments: is wage flexibility stabilizing?', *Economic Enquiry* 25: 583–97.

—— and —— (1988) 'Price flexibility and macroeconomic stability: an empirical simulation analysis', Working Paper, St Louis, Mo.: Washington University, Department of Economics.

Caspari, V. (1989) 'Walras, Marshall, Keynes. Zum Verhältnis von Mikro- und Makroökonomie', *Volkswirtschaftliche Schriften*, Heft 387, Berlin: Duncker & Humblot.

Cassel, G. (1937) 'Mr Keynes' *General Theory*', *International Labour Review* 36: 437–45.

Chamberlain, T. and Gordon, M.J. (1989) 'Liquidity, profitability and long-run survival: theory and evidence on business investment', *Journal of Post Keynesian Economics* 11: 589–610.

Chamberlin, E. (1933) *The Theory of Monopolistic Competition*, Cambridge, Mass.: Harvard University Press.

Champernowne, D.G. (1964) 'Expectations and the links between the economic future and the present', in R. Lekachmann (ed.) *Keynes' General Theory: Reports of Three Decades*, New York: St Martin's Press.

Chang, W. and Smyth, D. (1971) 'The existence and persistence of cycles in a non-linear model: Kaldor's 1940 model re-examined', *Review of Economic Studies* 38: 37–44.

Chant, J. (1992) 'The new theory of financial intermediation', in K. Dowd and M.K. Lewis (eds) *Current Issues in Financial and Monetary Economics*, London: Macmillan.

Chapple, S. (1991) 'Did Kalecki get there first? The race for the *General Theory*', *History of Political Economy* 23: 243–61.

Chen, P. (1993) 'Searching for economic chaos: a challenge to econometric practice', in P. Chen and R. Day (eds) *Nonlinear Dynamics and Evolutionary Economics*, Cambridge: Cambridge University Press.

Chick, V. (1978) 'The nature of the Keynesian revolution', *Australian Economic Papers* 17: 1–20; reprinted in P. Arestis and S.C. Dow (eds) *On Money, Method and Keynes: Selected Essays*, London: Macmillan, 1992.

—— (1983) *Macroeconomics after Keynes: A Reconsideration of the* General Theory, London: Philip Allan and MIT Press.

—— (1984) 'Monetary increases and their consequences: streams, backwaters and floods', in A. Ingham and A.M. Ulph (eds) *Demand, Equilibrium and Trade: Essays in Honour of I.F. Pearce*, London: Macmillan; reprinted in P. Arestis and S.C. Dow (eds) *On Money, Method and Keynes, Selected Essays*, London: Macmillan, 1992.

—— (1986) 'The evolution of the banking system and the theory of saving, investment and interest', *Economics et sociétés* 20: 111–26 (Monnaie et production 3); reprinted in P. Arestis and S.C. Dow (eds) *On Money, Method and Keynes, Selected Essays*, London: Macmillan, 1992.

—— (1987) 'Hugh Townshend', in J. Eatwell, M. Milgate and P. Newman (eds) *The New Palgrave: A Dictionary of Economics*, Vol. IV, London: Macmillan.

—— (1988) 'Sources of finance, recent changes in bank behaviour and the theory of investment and interest', in P. Arestis (ed.) *Contemporary Issues in Money and Banking*, London: Macmillan.

—— (1993a) 'Sources of finance, recent changes in bank behaviour and the theory of investment and interest', in P. Arestis (ed.) *Money and Banking: Issues for the Twenty-first Century*, London: Macmillan.

—— (1993b) 'The evolution of the banking system and the theory of monetary policy', in S.F. Frowen (ed.) *Monetary Theory and Monetary Policy: New Tracks for the 1990s*, London: Macmillan.

—— (forthcoming) 'Keynes-inspired contributions of Post-Keynesian economics', in V. Chick (ed.) *Keynes and the Post Keynesians*, London: Macmillan.

Chirinko, R.S. (1993) 'Business fixed investment spending: modelling strategies, empirical results and policy implications', *Journal of Economic Literature* 31: 1875–1911.

Church, K.B., Smith, P.N. and Wallis, K.F. (1994) 'Econometric evaluation of consumers' expenditure equations', *Oxford Review of Economic Policy* 10: 71–85.

Clark, C. (1945) 'Public finance and changes in the value of money', *Economic Journal* 55: 371–89.

Clarke, P. (1979) 'Investment in the 1970s: theory, performance and prediction', *Brookings Papers in Economic Activity* 1: 73–113.

—— (1988) *The Keynesian Revolution in the Making, 1924–36*, Oxford: Clarendon Press.

—— (1990) 'Hobson and Keynes as economic heretics', in M. Freeden (ed.) *Reappraising J.A. Hobson*, London: Unwin Hyman.

Clower, R.W. (1955) 'Competition, monopoly and the theory of price', *Pakistan Economic Journal* 5: 219–26.

—— (1960) 'Keynes and the Classics: a dynamic perspective', *Quarterly Journal of Economics* 74: 318–23.

—— (1965) 'The Keynesian counter-revolution: a theoretical appraisal', in F.H. Hahn and F.P.R. Brechling (eds) *The Theory of Interest Rates*, London: Macmillan.

—— (1967) 'A reconsideration of the microfoundations of monetary theory', *Western Economic Journal* 6: 1–33.

—— (1975a) 'Reflections on the Keynesian perplex', *Zeitschrift für Nationalökonomie* 35: 1–24.

Clower, R.W. (1975b) 'The obscurantist approach to economics: Keynes on Shackle', *Eastern Economic Journal* 2: 99–101.

—— (1977) 'The anatomy of monetary theory', *American Economic Review* 67: 206–12.

—— (1989) 'Keynes's *General Theory*: the Marshall connection', in D.A. Walker (ed.) *Perspectives in the History of Economic Thought*, Vol. II, Upleadon, Glos.: Edward Elgar.

—— (1990) 'Keynes's *General Theory*: a contemporary perspective', *Greek Economic Review* 12 (suppl.): 73–84.

—— (1991) 'Ohlin and *The General Theory*', in L. Jonung (ed.) *The Stockholm School of Economics Revisited*, New York: Cambridge University Press.

—— (1993a) 'Towards a reconstruction of economics', address to the annual meeting of the Canadian Economic Association, Ottawa, 5 June.

—— (1993b) 'The fingers of the invisible hand', mimeo.

—— (1993c) 'On truth in teaching macroeconomics', mimeo.

—— and Due, J.F. (1972) *Microeconomics*, Homewood, Ill.: Irwin.

—— and Leijonhufvud, A. (1975) in D.A. Walker (ed.) *Money and Markets*, Cambridge: Cambridge University Press, 1985.

—— and —— (1975) 'The coordination of economic activities: a Keynesian perspective', *American Economic Review* 65: 182–8.

Coates, J. (1990) 'Ordinary language economics: Keynes and the Cambridge philosophers', Cambridge University, unpublished PhD thesis.

—— (1996) *The Claims of Common Sense: Cambridge Philosophy and the Social Sciences*, Cambridge: Cambridge University Press.

Coddington, A. (1976) 'Keynesian economics: the search for first principles', *Journal of Economic Literature* 14: 1258–73.

—— (1982) 'Deficient foresight: a troublesome theme in Keynesian economics', *American Economic Review* 72: 480–7.

—— (1983) *Keynesian Economics: The Search for First Principles*, London: George Allen & Unwin.

Coen, R.M. (1971) 'The effect of cash flow on the speed of adjustment', in G. Fromm (ed.) *Tax Incentives and Capital Spending*, Washington, D.C.: The Brookings Institution.

Cohen, A.J. and Smithin, J. (eds) (1995) *Money, Financial Institutions and Macroeconomics*, Dordrecht: Kluwer.

Conard, J.W. (1959) *An Introduction to the Theory of Interest*, Berkeley, Calif.: University of California Press.

Conniffe, D. (1992) 'Keynes on probability and statistical inference and the links to Fisher', *Cambridge Journal of Economics* 16: 475–89.

Cooley, T.F., LeRoy, S.F. and Raymon, N. (1984) 'Econometric policy evaluation: a note', *American Economic Review* 74: 467–70.

Cooper, R. and John, A. (1988) 'Coordinating coordination failures in Keynesian models', *Quarterly Journal of Economics* 103: 441–63.

Cornwall, J. (1977) *Modern Capitalism: Its Growth and Transformation*, Oxford: Blackwell.

—— (1990) *The Theory of Economic Breakdown*, Armonk, N.Y.: M.E. Sharpe.

—— (1994) *Economic Breakdown and Recovery: Theory and Policy*, Armonk, N.Y.: M.E. Sharpe.

Cornwell, J. (ed.) (1995) *Nature's Imagination: The Frontiers of Scientific Vision*, Oxford: Oxford Press.

Costabile, L. and Rowthorn, R. (1985) 'Malthus's theory of wages and growth', *Economic Journal* 95: 418–37.

Cottrell, A. (1989) 'Price expectations and equilibrium when the interest rate is pegged', *Scottish Journal of Political Economy* 36: 125–40.

—— (1993) 'Keynes's theory of probability and its relevance to his economics: three theses', *Economics and Philosophy* 9: 25–51.

—— (1994) 'Keynes's vision and tactics', in J. Davis (ed.) *The State of Interpretation of Keynes*, New York: Kluwer.

—— and Lawlor, M.S. (1991) '"Natural rate" mutations: Keynes, Leijonhuvfud and the Wicksell connection', *History of Political Economy* 23: 625–43.

Cournot, A. (1838) *Recherches sur les principes mathématique de la théorie de la richesse*, English trans. N. Bacon and I. Fisher *Researches into the Mathematical Principles of the Theory of Wealth*, London: Macmillan, 1929.

Coveney, P. and Highfield, R. (1990) *Arrow of Time*, New York: Ballantine.

Cowen, T. and Krosszner, R. (1994) 'Money's marketability premium and the microfoundations of Keynes's theory of money and interest', *Cambridge Journal of Economics* 18: 379–90.

Crawley, K. (ed.) (1986) *The Collected Scientific Papers of Paul A. Samuelson*, Vol. 5, Cambridge, Mass., and London: MIT Press.

Cross, R. (1982) 'The Duhem–Quine thesis, Lakatos, and the appraisal of theories in macroeconomics', *Economic Journal* 92: 320–40.

Curtis, M. (1938) 'Saving and savings', *Quarterly Journal of Economics* 53: 623–6.

Cyert, R. and March, J. (1963) *A Behavioural Theory of the Firm*, Englewood Cliffs, N.J.: Prentice Hall.

Daly, V. and Hadjimatheou, G. (1981) 'Stochastic implications of the life-cycle–permanent-income hypothesis: evidence for the UK economy', *Journal of Political Economy* 89: 596–9.

Dalziel, P. (1996) 'The Keynesian miltiplier, liquidity preference and endogenous money', *Journal of Post Keynesian Economics* 18: 311–31.

Dana, R. and Malgrange, P. (1983) 'The dynamics of a discrete version of a growth cycle model', in J. Ancott (ed.) *Analysing the Structure of Econometric Models*, New York: Martinus Nijhoff.

Darby, M.R. (1975) 'The financial and tax effects of monetary policy on interest rates', *Economic Enquiry* 13: 266–76.

Dardi, M. (1994) 'Kahn's theory of liquidity preference and monetary policy', *Cambridge Journal of Economics* 18: 91–107.

Darhendorf, R. (1995) *LSE: A History of the London School of Economics and Political Science, 1895–1995*, Oxford: Oxford University Press.

Darity, W., Jr (1985) 'On involuntary unemployment and increasing returns', *Journal of Post Keynesian Economics* 7: 363–73.

—— and Goldsmith, A.H. (1995) 'Mr. Keynes, the New Keynesians and the concept of full employment', in P. Wells (ed.) *Post Keynesian Economic Theory*, Boston, Mass.: Kluwer, 73–94.

—— and Horn, B.L. (1983) 'Involuntary unemployment reconsidered', *Southern Economic Journal* 49: 717–33.

—— and —— (1993) 'Rational expectations, rational belief and Keyne's *General Theory*', in W.J. Samuels and J. Biddle (eds) *Research in the History of Economic Thought and Methodology*, Greenwich, Conn. and London: JAI Press.

Dasgupta, P., Hart, O. and Maskin, E. (eds) (1992) *Economic Analysis of Markets and Games: Essays in Honour of Frank Hahn*, Cambridge, Mass.: MIT Press.

Davidson, J.E.H., Hendry, D.F., Srba, F. and Yeo, S. (1978) 'Econometric modelling of the aggregate time-series relationship between consumers' expenditure and income in the United Kingdom', *Economic Journal* 80 (September): 661–92.

Davidson, P. (1963) 'Public problems of the domestic crude oil history', *American Economic Review* 53: 85–108.

—— (1967) 'A Keynesian view of Patinkin's theory of employment', *Economic Journal* 77: 559–78.

—— (1972) *Money and the Real World*, London: Macmillan.

—— (1977) 'Money and general equilibrium', *Economie appliquée* 30: 542–63.

—— (1978) *Money and the Real World*, 2nd edn, London: Macmillan.

—— (1980) 'The dual faceted nature of the Keynesian revolution', *Journal of Post Keynesian Economics* 2: 291–313.

—— (1981) 'Post Keynesian economics: solving the crisis in economic theory', in D. Bell and I. Kristol (eds) *The Crisis in Economic Theory*, New York: Basic Books.

—— (1983) 'The marginal product is not the demand curve for labour and Lucas's labour supply function is not the supply of labour in the real world', *Journal of Post Keynesian Economics* 6: 105–17.

—— (1984) 'Reviving Keynes's revolution', *Journal of Post Keynesian Economics* 6: 561–75.

—— (1986) 'Finance, funding, saving and investment', *Journal of Post Keynesian Economics* 9: 101–11.

—— (1987) 'User cost', in J. Eatwell, M. Milgate and P. Newman (eds) *The New Palgrave: A Dictionary of Economics*, Vol. 4, London: Macmillan.

—— (1987 8) 'A modest set of proposals for resolving the international debt problem', *Journal of Post Keynesian Economics* 10: 323–38.

—— (1988) 'Endogenous money, the production process, and inflation analysis', *Economie appliquée* 41: 151–69.

—— (1989) 'Keynes and money', in R. Hill (ed.) *Keynes, Money and Monetarism: The Eighth Keynes Seminar*, held at the University of Kent at Canterbury, London: Macmillan.

—— (1991) 'Is probability theory relevant for uncertainty? A Post Keynesian perspective', *Journal of Economic Perspectives* 5: 129–44.

—— (1994) *Post Keynesian Macroeconomic Theory*, Aldershot, Hants: Edward Elgar.

—— and Smolensky, E. (1964) *Aggregate Supply and Demand Analysis*, New York: Harper & Row.

Davis, E.G. (1980) 'The correspondence between R.G. Hawtrey and J.M. Keynes on the *Treatise*: the genesis of output adjustment models', *Canadian Journal of Economics* 13: 716–24.

Davis, J.B. (1994a) *Keynes's Philosophical Development*, Cambridge: Cambridge University Press.

—— (ed.) (1994b) *The State of Interpretation of Keynes*, Norwell, Mass.: Kluwer.

—— (1996) 'Convergence in Keynes and Wittgenstein's later views', forthcoming in *European Journal of the History of Economic Thought*.

Davis, J.R. and Casey, F.J., Jr (1977) 'Keynes's misquotation of Mill', *Economic Journal* 87: 329–30.

Day, R. and Shaefer, W. (1985) 'Keynesian chaos, *Journal of Macroeconomics* 7: 277–95.

—— and —— (1987) 'Ergodic fluctuations in deterministic models', *Journal of Economic Behaviour and Organisation* 8: 339–61.

Deaton, A. (1978) 'Involuntary saving through unanticipated inflation', *American Economic Review* 68: 899–910.

—— (ed.) (1980) *Essays in the Theory and Measurement of Consumers' Behaviour*, Cambridge: Cambridge University Press.

—— (1992) *Understanding Consumption*, Oxford: Clarendon Press.

Debreu, G. (1959) *Theory of Value: An Axiomatic Analysis of Economic Equilibrium*,

Cowles Foundation Monograph no. 17, New Haven, Conn.: Yale University Press.

DeCoster, G., Labys, W. and Mitchell, D. (1992) 'Evidence of chaos in commodity futures prices', *Journal of Futures Markets* 12: 291–305.

de Gijsel, P. and Haslinger, F. (1988) 'Keynes' monetäre Begründung unfreiwilliger Arbeitslosigkeit. Anmerkungen zum 17. Kapitel der *General Theory*', in H. Hagemann and O. Steiger (eds) *Keynes' General Theory nach fünfzig Jahren, Volkswirtschaftliche*, Heft 384, Berlin: Duncker & Humblot.

Deleplace, G. (1987) 'Ajustement de marché et "taux d'intérêt spécifiques" chez Keynes et Sraffa', *Cahiers d'economie politique* (La 'Théorie Générale' de J.M. Keynes: un cinquantenaire), 214–15: 75–97.

DelMonte, A. (ed.) (1992) *Recent Developments in the Theory of Industrial Organisation*, London: Macmillan.

De Long, J.B. and Summers, L.H. (1986) 'Is increased price flexibility stabilizing?', *American Economic Review* 76: 1031–44.

De Marchi, N. and Morgan, M. (eds) (1994) 'Higgling: transactors and their markets in the history of economics', *History of Political Economy* 26 (suppl.): 184–225.

Desai, M. (1982) 'The task of monetary theory: the Hayek–Sraffa debate in a modern perspective', in M. Baranzini (ed.) *Advances in Economic Theory*, Oxford: Blackwell.

Dillard, D. (1948) *The Economics of John Maynard Keynes: The Theory of a Monetary Economy*, New York: Prentice Hall.

Dilworth, C. (ed.) (1992) *Intelligibility in Science*, special issue of *Poznan Studies in the Philosophy of the Sciences* 2: 319–54.

Dimand, R. (1988) *The Origins of the Keynesian Revolution*, Aldershot, Hants: Edward Elgar.

DiMatteo, M., Goodwin, R. and Vercelli, A. (eds) (1989) *Technological and Social Factors in Long Term Fluctuations*, New York: Springer Verlag.

Dirks, F.C. (1938) 'Retail sales and labor income', *Review of Economic Statistics* 20: 128–34.

Dirlam, J.B., Kaplan, A.D.H. and Lanzillotti, R.F. (1958) *Pricing in Big Business: A Case Approach*, Washington, D.C.: Brookings Institution.

Dixit, A. (1976) *The Theory of Equilibrium Growth*, London: Oxford University Press.

Dixon, H. (1987) 'A simple model of imperfect competition with Walrasian features', *Oxford Economic Papers* 39: 134–60.

Domar, E.D. (1946) 'Capital expansion, rate of growth and employment', *Econometrica* 14: 137–47.

—— (1947) 'Expansion and employment', *American Economic Review* 37: 34–55.

Dore, M. (1993) *The Macroeconomics of Business Cycles*, Oxford: Blackwell.

Dorfman, R., Samuelson, P.A. and Solow, R.M. (1958) *Linear Programming and Economic Analysis*, New York: McGraw-Hill.

Dow, A.C. and Dow, S.C. (1989) 'Endogenous money creation and idle balances', in J. Pheby (ed.) *New Directions in Post Keynesian Economics*, Aldershot, Hants: Edward Elgar.

Dow, J.C.R. and Saville, I.D. (1990) *A Critique of Monetary Policy: Theory and British Experience*, 2nd edn, Oxford: Oxford University Press.

Dow, S.C. (1985) *Macroeconomic Thought: A Methodological Approach*, Oxford: Blackwell.

—— (1990) 'Beyond dualism', *Cambridge Journal of Economics* 14: 143–58.

—— (1993) *Money and the Economic Process*, Aldershot, Hants: Edward Elgar.

Dow, S.C. (forthcoming) 'Knowledge, information and credit creation', in R.J. Rotheim (ed.) *New Keynesian Economics: A Post Keynesian Alternative*, London: Routledge.

—— and Hillard, J. (eds) (1995) *Keynes, Knowledge and Uncertainty*, Aldershot, Hants: Edward Elgar.

Dowd, K. and Lewis, M.K. (eds) (1992) *Current Issues in Financial and Monetary Economics*, London: Macmillan.

Downward, P. (1994) 'A reappraisal of case study evidence on business pricing: neoclassical and Post Keynesian perspectives', *British Review of Economic Issues* 16: 23–44.

Dreze, J. (1975) 'The existence of an exchange equilibrium under price rigidities', *International Economic Review* 16: 301–20.

Dunlop, J.T. (1938) 'The movement of real and money wage rates', *Economic Journal* 48: 413–34.

Dutt, A.K. (1986–7) 'Wage rigidity', *Journal of Post Keynesian Economics* 9: 279–90.

—— (1987) 'Keynes with a perfectly competitive goods market', *Australian Economic Papers* 26: 275–93.

—— (1992) 'Keynes, market forms and competition', in B. Gerrard and J. Hillard (eds) *The Philosophy and Economics of J.M. Keynes*, Aldershot: Edward Elgar.

—— and Amadeo, E.J. (1990a) *Keynes's Third Alternative? The Neo-Ricardian Keynesians and the Post Keynesians*, Aldershot: Edward Elgar.

—— and —— (1990b) 'Keynes's dichotomy and wage-rigidity Keynesianism', in D.E. Moggridge (ed.) *Perspectives in the History of Economic Thought*, Vol. 14, Aldershot, Hants: Edward Elgar.

Dybvig, P.H. and Ross, S.A. (1987) 'Arbitrage', in J. Eatwell, M. Milgate and P. Newman (eds) *The New Palgrave: A Dictionary of Economics*, Vol. 1, London: Macmillan.

Eatwell, J. (1983a) 'The long period theory of employment', *Cambridge Journal of Economics* 7: 269–85.

—— (1983b) 'Theories of value, output and employment', in J. Eatwell and M. Milgate (eds) *Keynes's Economics and the Theory of Value and Distribution*, London: Duckworth.

—— (1987) 'Own-rates of interest', in J. Eatwell, M. Milgate and P. Newman (eds) *The New Palgrave: A Dictionary of Economics*, Vol. 3, London: Macmillan.

—— and Milgate, M. (eds) (1983a) *Keynes' Economics and the Theory of Value and Distribution*, London: Duckworth.

—— and —— (1983b) 'Unemployment and the market mechanism', in J. Eatwell and M. Milgate (eds) *Keynes' Economics and the Theory of Value and Distribution*, London: Duckworth.

——, —— and Newman, P. (eds) (1987) *The New Palgrave: A Dictionary of Economics*, 4 vols, London: Macmillan.

Eckstein, O. (ed.) (1972) *The Econometrics of Price Determination*, Washington, D.C.: Board of Governors of the Federal Reserve System.

Edgeworth, F.Y. (1925) *Selected Papers in Political Economy*, London: Macmillan.

Eichner, A.S. (1976) *The Megacorp and Oligopoly*, Cambridge, Mass.: MIT Press.

Eisner, R. (1953) 'Guaranteed growth of income', *Econometrica* 21: 169–71.

—— (1958) 'On growth models and the neo-classical resurgence', *Economic Journal* 68: 707–21.

—— (1960) 'A distributed lag investment function', *Econometrica* 28: 1–29.

—— (1967) 'A permanent income theory for investment', *American Economic Review* 57: 363–90.

—— (1978) *Factors in Business Investment*, Cambridge, Mass.: Ballinger, for National Bureau of Economic Research.

452

Eisner, R. (1986) *How Real is the Federal Deficit?*, New York: The Free Press.

—— (1989) *The Total Incomes System of Accounts*, Chicago, Ill.: University of Chicago Press.

—— (1993a) 'US national saving and budget deficits', in G. Epstein and H. Gintis (eds) *The Political Economy of Investment, Saving and Finance: A Global Perspective*, A project of the World Institute for Development and Economic Research (WIDER), Helsinki: United Nations University.

—— (1993b) 'Sense and nonsense about budget deficits', *Harvard Business Review* 71: 99–111.

—— (1994a) 'Real government saving and the future', *Journal of Economic Behavior and Business Organisation* 23: 170–1.

—— (1994b) 'National saving and budget deficits', *Review of Economics and Statistics* 76: 181–6.

—— (1994c) *The Misunderstood Economy: What Counts and How to Count It*, Boston, Mass.: Harvard Business School Press.

—— (1996) 'US national saving and budget deficits', in G.A. Epstein and H. Gintis, *Macroeconomic Policy after the Conservative Era*, Cambridge: Cambridge University Press, 109–42.

—— and Chirinko, R.S. (1983) 'Tax policy and investment in major US macroeconomic econometric models', *Journal of Public Economics* 20: 139–66.

—— and Nadiri, M.I. (1968) 'Investment behavior and neo-classical theory', *Review of Economics and Statistics* 50: 369–82.

—— and —— (1970) 'Neoclassical theory of investment behaviour: a comment', *Review of Economics and Statistics* 52: 216–22.

—— and Pieper, P.J. (1984) 'A new view of the federal debt and budget deficits', *American Economic Review* 74: 11–29.

—— and Strotz, R.H. (1963) 'Determinants of business investment', in Commission on Money and Credits, *Impacts of Monetary Policy*, Englewood Cliffs, N.J.: Prentice Hall.

Ellsberg, D. (1961) 'Risk, ambiguity and the Savage axioms', *Quarterly Journal of Economics* 75: 643–69.

Elton, E.J. and Gruber, M.J. (1991) *Modern Portfolio Theory and Investment Analysis*, New York: John Wiley.

Emmanuel, A. (1972) *Unequal Exchange*, London: New Left Books.

Employment Policy, Cmd 6527 (1944), London: HMSO.

Epstein, G. and Gintis, H. (eds) (1993) *The Political Economy of Investment, Saving and Finance: A Global Perspective*, a project of the World Institute for Development and Economic Research (WIDER), Helsinki: United Nations University.

Erdos, P. (1977) 'A contribution to the criticism of Keynes and Keynesianism', in J. Schwartz (ed.) *The Subtle Anatomy of Capitalism*, Santa Monica, Calif.: Goodyear.

Eshag, E. (1963) *From Marshall to Keynes: An Essay on the Monetary Theory of the Cambridge School*, Oxford: Blackwell.

Fair, R.C. (1994) *Testing Macroeconomic Models*, Cambridge, Mass.: Harvard University Press.

Fama, E.F. (1978) 'The effects of a firm's investment and financing decisions on the welfare of its security holders', *American Economic Review* 68: 272–84.

—— (1980) 'Banking in the theory of finance', *Journal of Monetary Economics* 6: 39–57.

Favereau, O. (1988) 'Probability and uncertainty: "after all, Keynes was right"', *Economica* 10: 133–67.

Fazzari, S.M. (1982) 'The microeconomic dynamics of output and employment', Stanford University, unpublished PhD thesis.

Fazzari, S.M. (1985) 'Keynes, Harrod and the rational expectations revolution', *Journal of Post Keynesian Economics* 8: 66–80.

—— and Caskey, J. (1989) 'Debt commitments and aggregate demand: a critique of the neoclassical synthesis and policy', in W. Semmler (ed.) *Financial Dynamics and Business Cycles: New Perspectives*, Armonk, N.Y.: M.E. Sharpe.

—— and Mott, T. (1986) 'The investment theories of Kalecki and Keynes: an empirical study of firm data, 1970–82', *Journal of Post Keynesian Economics* 9: 141–206.

—— Hubbard, R.G. and Peterson, B.C. (1988) 'Financing constraints and corporate investment', *Brookings Papers on Economic Activity*, April: 141–95.

Feiwel, G.R. (ed.) (1985) *Issues in Contemporary Macroeconomics and Distribution*, London: Macmillan.

Felix, D. (1994) 'The Tobin tax proposal: background, issues and prospects', Working Paper no. 191, St. Louis, Mo.: Washington University.

Fender, J. (1981) *Understanding Keynes: An Analysis of* The General Theory, Brighton: Wheatsheaf.

Ferber, R. (1953) *A Study of Aggregate Consumption Functions*, New York: National Bureau of Economic Research.

—— (1966) 'Research in household behaviour', in *Surveys of Economic Theory*, Vol. III: *Resource Allocation*, London: Macmillan, for American Economic Association and the Royal Economic Society.

—— (1973) 'Consumer economics: a survey', *Journal of Economic Literature* 11: 1303–342.

Fetter, F.W. (1977) 'Lenin, Keynes and inflation', *Economica* 44: 77–80.

Fewings, D. (1979) *Corporate Growth and Common Stock Risk*, Greenwich, Conn.: JAI Press.

Finer, S.E. (1966) *Vilfredo Pareto: Sociological Writings*, London: Pall Mall Press.

Fischer, S. (1977) 'Long-term contracts, rational expectations, and the optimal money supply rule', *Journal of Political Economy* 85: 191–206.

—— (1981) 'Toward an understanding of the costs of inflation: II', in K. Brunner and A. Meltzer (eds) *The Costs and Consequences of Inflation*, Carnegie-Rochester Conference Series on Public Policy, Amsterdam: North-Holland.

Fisher, I. (1896) 'Appreciation and interest', *American Economic Association Publications* 3(11): 331–442.

—— (1907) *The Rate of Interest: Its Nature, Determination and Relation to Economic Phenomena*, New York: Macmillan.

—— (1911) *The Purchasing Power of Money*, New York: Macmillan.

—— (1920) *Stabilizing the Dollar*, New York: Macmillan.

—— (1930) *The Theory of Interest*, reprinted New York: Augustus M. Kelley, 1965.

Fitzgibbons, A. (1988) *Keynes's Vision: A New Political Economy*, Oxford: Clarendon Press.

Flanagan, R., Soskice, D. and Ulman, L (1983) *Unionism, Economic Stabilization and Incomes Policies: European Experience*, Washington, D.C.: Brookings Institution.

Flaschel, P. (1994) 'The stability of models of monetary growth with adaptive expectations or myopic perfect foresight', in W. Semmler (ed.) *Business Cycles: Theory and Empirical Methods*, London: Kluwer.

—— and Franke, R. (1992) 'Instability and price flexibility in generalized Tobin–Sargent models', Discussion Paper no. 259, Bielefeld: Universität Bielefeld.

Flavin, M. (1981) 'The adjustment of consumption to changing expectations about future income', *Journal of Political Economy* 89: 974–1007.

Foley, D. (1986) 'Stabilisation policy in a nonlinear business cycle model', in W. Semmler (ed.) *Competition, Instability and Nonlinear Cycles*, Berlin: Springer-Verlag.

Foley, D. (1987) 'Liquidity–profit rate cycles in a capitalist economy', *Journal of Economic Behaviour and Organisations* 8: 363–76.

—— (1988) 'Endogenous financial-production cycles', in W. Barnett, J. Geweke and K. Shell (eds) *Economic Complexity: Chaos, Sunspots, Bubbles and Nonlinearity*, Cambridge: Cambridge University Press.

Foster, G.P. (1986) 'The endogeneity of money and Keynes's *General Theory*', *Journal of Economic Issues* 20: 953–68.

Foster, J.B. (1986) *The Theory of Monopoly Capitalism: An Elaboration of Marxian Political Economy*, New York: Monthly Review Press.

Frank, M. and Stegnos, T. (1988) 'Some evidence concerning macroeconomic chaos', *Journal of Monetary Economics* 22: 423–38.

—— and —— (1989) 'Measuring the strangeness of gold and silver rates of return', *Review of Economic Studies* 56: 533–67.

Franke, R. and Semmler, W. (1991) 'Debt-financing of firms, stability and cycles in a dynamical macroeconomic growth model', in W. Semmler (ed.) *Financial Dynamics and Business Cycles*, Armonk, N.Y.: M.E. Sharpe.

Frankel, J.A. and Froot, K. (1991) 'Exchange rate forecasting techniques, survey data, and implications for the foreign exchange market', Working Paper in Economics 91–158, Berkely, Calif.: University of California.

Freeden, M. (ed.) (1990) *Reappraising J.A. Hobson*, London: Unwin Hyman.

Freedman, C. (1993) 'In defence of footnotes – a clarification of a misunderstanding of Keynes's definition of money', *Cambridge Journal of Economics* 16: 241–4.

Freimer, M. and Gordon, M.J. (1965) 'Why bankers ration credit', *Quarterly Journal of Economics* 79: 397–416.

Fried, J.S. and Howitt, P. (1983) 'The effects of inflation on real interest rates', *American Economic Review* 73: 968–80.

Friedman, B.M. and Hahn, F.H. (eds) (1990) *Handbook of Monetary Economics*, Amsterdam: North-Holland.

Friedman, M. (1953) 'The methodology of positive economics', in *Essays in Positive Economics*, Chicago, Ill.: University of Chicago Press.

—— (1956) *Studies in the Quantity Theory of Money*, Chicago, Ill.: Chicago University Press.

—— (1957) *A Theory of the Consumption Function*. Princeton, N.J.: Princeton University Press.

—— (1968) 'The role of monetary policy', *American Economic Review* 58: 1–17.

—— (1972) 'Comments on the critics', *Journal of Political Economy* 80: 906–50.

—— (1974) 'Comments on the critics', in R.J. Gordon (ed.) *Milton Friedman's Monetary Framework: A Debate with his Critics*, Chicago: University of Chicago Press.

—— (1992) *Money Mischief*, New York: Harcourt Brace Jovanovich.

—— and Meiselman, D. (1963) 'The relative stability of monetary velocity and the investment multiplier in the United States, 1897–1958', in Commission on Money and Credit, *Stabilization Policies*, Englewood Cliffs, N.J.: Prentice Hall.

Frisch, R. (1933) 'Propagation problems and impulse problems in dynamic economics', in *Essays in Honour of Gustav Cassel*, London: Allen & Unwin.

Fromm, G. (ed.) (1971) *Tax Incentives and Capital Spending*, Washington, D.C.: Brookings Institution.

Frowen, S.F. (ed.) (1993) *Monetary Theory and Monetary Policy: New Tracks for the 1990s*, London: Macmillan.

Frydman, R. and Phelps, E.S. (eds) (1983) *Individual Forecasting and Aggregate Outcomes: 'Rational Expectations' Examined*, New York: Cambridge University Press.

BIBLIOGRAPHY

Furness, W.H. (1910) *The Island of Stone Money: Uap and the Carolines*, Philadelphia and London: J.B. Lippincott.

Galbraith, J.K. (1955) *The Great Crash 1929*, London: Hamish Hamilton.

—— (1975) *Money: Whence it Came, Where it Went*, London: André Deutsch.

Gardener, E.P.M. (1988) 'Innovation and new structural frontiers in banking', in P. Arestis (ed.) *Contemporary Issues in Money and Banking*, London: Macmillan.

Garegnani, P. (1978–9) 'Notes on consumption, investment and effective demand', 2 parts, *Cambridge Journal of Economics* 2: 335–53; 3: 63–82.

—— (1983) 'Two routes to effective demand', in J.A. Kregel (ed.) *Distribution, Effective Demand and International Economic Relations*, London: Macmillan.

—— (1988) 'Actual and normal magnitudes: a comment on Asimakopulos', *Political Economy, Studies in the Surplus Approach* 4: 251–8.

Garretsen, H. (1992) *Keynes, Coordination and Beyond: The Development of Macroeconomics and Monetary Theory since 1945*, Aldershot, Hants: Edward Elgar.

Garrison, R. (1985) 'Intertemporal coordination and the invisible hand: an Austrian perspective on the Keynesian vision', *History of Political Economy* 17: 309–19.

—— (1987) 'Full employment and intertemporal coordination: a rejoinder', *History of Political Economy* 19: 335–41

Gaynor, W.B. (1992) 'The transformation of the natural rate of interest into *The General Theory*'s state of long-term expectations', *Cambridge Journal of Economics* 16: 55–68.

Georgescu-Roegen, N. (1960) 'Mathematical proofs of the breakdown of capitalism', *Econometrica* 28: 225–43.

Gerrard, B. (1990) 'On matters methodological in economics', *Journal of Economic Surveys* 4: 197–219.

—— (1992) 'From *A Treatise in Probability* to *The General Theory*: continuity or change in Keynes's thought?', in B. Gerrard and J.V. Hillard (eds) *The Philosophy and Economics of J.M. Keynes*, Aldershot, Hants: Edward Elgar.

—— (1993) 'Book review', *Economic Analysis and Policy* 23: 94–5.

—— (1994a) 'Beyond rational expectations: a constructive interpretation of Keynes's analysis of behaviour under uncertainty', *Economic Journal* 104: 327–37.

—— (1994b) 'Animal spirits', in P. Arestis and M. Sawyer (eds) *The Elgar Companion to Radical Political Economy*, Aldershot, Hants: Edward Elgar.

—— (1995) 'Keynes, the Keynesians and the Classics: a suggested interpretation', *Economic Journal* 105: 445–58.

—— and Hillard, J. (1992) *The Philosophy and Economics of J.M. Keynes*, Aldershot, Hants: Edward Elgar.

Giblin, L.F. (1930) *Australia 1930*, Melbourne: Melbourne University Press.

Giddens, A. (1984) *The Constitution of Society*, Cambridge: Polity Press.

Gilboy, E. (1938) 'The propensity to consume', *Quarterly Journal of Economics* 53: 120–40.

—— (1939) 'The propensity to consume: reply', *Quarterly Journal of Economics* 53: 633–8.

Gillies, D.A. (1988) 'Keynes as a methodologist', *British Journal for the Philosophy of Science* 39: 117–29.

—— (1991) 'Intersubjective probability and confirmation theory', *British Journal for the Philosophy of Science* 42: 513–33.

Goldschlager, L.M. and Baxter, R. (1994) 'The loans standard model of credit money', *Journal of Post Keynesian Economics* 16: 453–77.

Goodhart, C.A.E. (1989) 'Has Moore become too horizontal?', *Journal of Post Keynesian Economics* 12: 29–34.

—— (1990) 'Dennis Robertson and the real business cycle theory: a centenary lecture', London: London School of Economics Finance Markets Group; reprinted in J. Presley (ed.) *Essays on Robertsonian Economics*, Basingstoke, Hants: Macmillan, 1992.

Goodhart, C.A.E. (1993) 'Can we improve the structure of financial systems?', *European Economic Review* 37: 269–91.

Goodwin, R. (1951) 'The non-linear accelerator and the persistence of business cycles', *Econometrica* 19: 1–17.

—— (1990) *Chaotic Economic Dynamics*, Oxford: Oxford University Press.

Gordon, D.M., Weisskopf, T.E. and Bowles, S. (1983) 'Long swings and the non-reproductive cycle', *American Economic Review*, 73(2): Papers and Proceedings 152–7.

Gordon, M.J. (1962) *The Investment, Financing and Valuation of the Corporation*, Homewood, Ill.: Irwin.

—— (1994) *Finance, Investment and Macroeconomics: The Neoclassical and a Post Keynesian Solution*, Aldershot, Hants: Edward Elgar.

—— and Gould, L.I. (1978) 'The cost of equity capital: a reconsideration', *Journal of Finance* 33: 849–61.

—— and Kwan, C.C. (1979) 'Debt maturity, default risk and capital structure', *Journal of Banking and Finance* 3: 313–29.

Gordon, R. (1982) 'Price inertia and policy ineffectiveness in the United States, 1890–1980', *Journal of Political Economy* 90: 1087–1117.

—— (ed.) (1986) *The American Business Cycle*, Chicago, Ill.: Chicago University Press.

—— (1990) 'What is the New-Keynesian economics?', *Journal of Economic Literature* 28: 1115–71.

Gossling, W.F. (1969) 'A note on user cost', *Manchester School of Economic and Social Studies* 37: 259–61.

Grandmont, J. and Laroque, G. (1986) 'Stability of cycles and expectations', *Journal of Economic Theory* 40: 138–51.

Grassberger, P. and Proccaccia, I. (1983) 'Characterisation of strange attractors', *Physical Review Letters* 50: 346–9.

Grassl, W. and Smith, B. (eds) (1986) *Austrian Economics: Historical and Philosophical Background*, New York: New York University Press.

Graziani, A. (1984) 'The debate on Keynes's finance motive', *Economic Notes of Monte dei Paschi di Siena* 1: 5–33.

Greenfield, R. and Yeager, L. (1983) 'A laissez-faire approach to monetary stability', *Journal of Money, Credit and Banking* 15: 302–15.

—— and —— (1986) 'Competitive payments systems: comment', *American Economic Review* 76: 848–9.

—— and —— (1989) 'Can monetary disequilibrium be eliminated?', *Cato Journal* 9: 405–21.

——, Woolsey, W.W. and Yeager, L.B. (1995) 'Is direct convertibility impossible?', *Journal of Money, Credit and Banking* 27: 293–7.

Groenewegen, P. (1995) *A Soaring Eagle: Alfred Marshall, 1842–1924*, Aldershot, Hants: Edward Elgar.

Grossman, S.J. and Stiglitz, J.E. (1980) 'On the impossibility of informationally efficient markets', *American Economic Review* 66: 246–53.

Gunning, P. (1985) 'Causes of unemployment: the Austrian perspective', *History of Political Economy* 17: 223–44.

Gurley, J.G. and Shaw, E.S. (1960) *Money in a Theory of Finance*, Washington, D.C.: Brookings Institution.

Guthrie, W. (1993) 'Book review', *Southern Economic Journal* 59: 546–7.

Haavelmo, T. (1958) 'What can static equilibrium models tell us?', *Economic Enquiry* 12: 27–34.

Haberler, G. (1941) *Prosperity and Depression*, New York: McGraw-Hill.

Hadamard, J. (1898) 'Les surfaces à courbures opposées et leur lignes géodésiques', *Journal de mathématiques pures et appliquées* 4: 27–73.

Hadjimatheou, G. (1987) *Consumer Economics after Keynes: Theory and Evidence of the Consumption Function*, London: Wheatsheaf.

Hagemann, H. and Steiger, O. (eds) (1988) *Keynes's General Theory after Fifty Years*, Berlin: Duncker & Humblot.

Hahn, F.H. (1965) 'On some problems of proving the existence of equilibrium in a monetary economy', in F.H. Hahn and F.P.R. Brechling (eds) *The Theory of Interest Rates*, London: Macmillan.

—— (1973) 'On the foundation of monetary theory', in M. Parkin (ed.) *Essays in Modern Economics*, London: Longman; reprinted in F.H. Hahn, *Equilibrium and Macroeconomics*, Oxford: Blackwell, 1984.

—— (1980) 'General equilibrium theory', *Public Interest* 58 (special issue): 123–8.

—— (1982) *Money and Inflation*, Oxford: Blackwell.

—— (1984) *Equilibrium and Macroeconomics*, Oxford: Blackwell.

—— (1985) *Money, Growth and Stability*, Oxford: Blackwell.

—— (1988) 'Liquidity', *Handbook of Monetary Economics*, II, Amsterdam: North Holland Press.

—— (ed.) (1989) *The Economics of Missing Markets, Information, and Games*, Oxford: Clarendon Press.

—— (1991) 'The next hundred years', *Economic Journal* 101: 47–50.

—— (1992a) 'Reflections', *Royal Economic Society Newsletter* no. 77: 5.

—— (1992b) 'Answer to Backhouse: Yes', *Royal Economic Society Newsletter* no. 78: 5.

—— and Brechling, F.P.R. (eds) (1965) *The Theory of the Rate of Interest*, London: Macmillan.

—— and Solow, R.M. (1986) 'Is wage flexibility a good thing?', in W. Beckerman (ed.) *Wage Rigidity and Unemployment*, Baltimore, Md.: Johns Hopkins University Press.

—— and —— (1996) *A Critical Essay on Modern Macroeconomic Theory*, Oxford: Blackwell.

Hahnel, R. and Sherman, H. (1982) 'The rate of profit over the business cycle', *Cambridge Journal of Economics* 6: 185–94.

Hall, R. and Hitch, C. (1939) 'Price theory and business behaviour', *Oxford Economic Papers* 2: 12–45.

Hall, R.E. (1978) 'Stochastic implications of the life-cycle–permanent-income hypothesis: theory and evidence', *Journal of Political Economy* 86: 971–87.

—— (1982) 'Explorations in the gold standard and related policies for stabilizing the dollar', in R.E. Hall (ed.) *Inflation: Cause and Effects*, Chicago, Ill.: University of Chicago Press.

—— (1983) 'Optimal fiduciary monetary systems', *Journal of Monetary Economics* 12: 33.

Hamouda, O.F. and Smithin, J.N. (eds) (1988) *Keynes and Public Policy after Fifty Years*, Vol. 2: *Theories and Method*, Aldershot, Hants: Edward Elgar.

Hansen, A.H. (1938) *Full Recovery or Stagnation?*, New York: W.W. Norton.

—— (1953) *A Guide to Keynes*, New York: McGraw-Hill.

Hansen, L.P. and Sargent, T.J. (1980) 'Estimating and formulating dynamic linear rational expectations models', reprinted in R. Lucas and T. Sargent (eds) *Rational Expectations and Econometric Practice*, London: George Allen & Unwin, 1981.

Hansson, B. (1985) 'Keynes's notion of equilibrium in *The General Theory*', *Journal of Post Keynesian Economics* 7: 332–41.

Harcourt, G.C. (1959) 'Pricing policies and inflation', *Economic Record* 35: 133–6; reprinted in P. Kerr (ed.) *The Social Science Imperialists: Selected Essays*, London: Routledge, 1982.

—— (1965) 'The accountant in a golden age', *Oxford Economic Papers* 17: 66–80; reprinted in C. Sardoni (ed.) *On Political Economists and Modern Political Economy: Selected Essays of G.C. Harcourt*, London: Routledge, 1992.

—— (1972) *Some Cambridge Controversies in the Theory of Capital*, London: Cambridge University Press.

—— (1976) 'The Cambridge controversies: old ways and new horizons – or dead end?', *Oxford Economic Papers* 28: 25–65; reprinted in C. Sardoni (ed.) *On Political Economists and Modern Political Economy: Selected Essays of G.C. Harcourt*, London: Routledge, 1992.

—— (ed.) (1977) *The Microeconomic Foundations of Macroeconomics*, London: Macmillan.

—— (1981) 'Marshall, Sraffa and Keynes: incompatible bedfellows?', *Eastern Economic Journal* 5: 39–50; reprinted in C. Sardoni (ed.) *On Political Economists and Modern Political Economy: Selected Essays of G.C. Harcourt*, London: Routledge, 1992.

—— (1982) *The Social Science Imperialists: Selected Essays*, ed. P. Kerr, London: Routledge.

—— (1983) 'Keynes' college bursar view of investment: comment on Kregel', in J.A. Kregel (ed.) *Distribution, Effective Demand and International Economic Relations*, London: Macmillan.

—— (1984) 'Reflections on the development of economics as a discipline', *History of Political Economy* 16: 489–517; reprinted in C. Sardoni (ed.) *On Political Economists and Modern Political Economy: Selected Essays of G.C. Harcourt*, London: Routledge, 1992.

—— (ed.) (1985) *Keynes and his Contemporaries: The Sixth and Centennial Keynes Seminar held at the University of Kent at Canterbury (1983)*, London: Macmillan.

—— (1987a) 'The legacy of Keynes: theoretical models and unfinished business', in D.A. Reese (ed.) *The Legacy of Keynes: Nobel Conference XXII*, San Francisco, Calif.: Harper & Row, 1–22; reprinted in C. Sardoni (ed.) *On Political Economists and Modern Political Economy: Selected Essays of G.C. Harcourt*, London: Routledge, 1992.

—— (1987b) 'Bastard Keynesianism', in J. Eatwell, M. Milgate and P. Newman (eds) *The New Palgrave: A Dictionary of Economics*, Vol. 1, London: Macmillan.

—— (1990) 'On the contributions of Joan Robinson and Pierro Sraffa to economic theory', in M. Berg (ed.) *Political Economy in the Twentieth Century*, London: Philip Allan; reprinted in C. Sardoni (ed.) *On Political Economists and Modern Political Economy: Selected Essays of G.C. Harcourt*, London: Routledge, 1992.

—— (1992) 'Introduction', in C. Sardoni (ed.) *On Political Economists and Modern Political Economy: Selected Essays of G.C. Harcourt*, London: Routledge.

—— (1993) *Post-Keynesian Essays in Biography: Portraits of Twentieth Century Political Economists*, London: Macmillan.

—— (1994a) 'Kahn and Keynes and the making of *The General Theory*', *Cambridge Journal of Economics* 18: 11–23.

—— (1994b) 'The structure of Tom Asimakopulos's later writings', in G.C. Harcourt, A. Roncaglia and R. Rowley (eds) *Income and Employment in Theory and Practice*, London: Macmillan.

—— and Kenyon, P. (1976) 'Pricing and the investment decision', *Kyklos* 29:

449–77; reprinted in C. Sardoni (ed.) *On Political Economists and Modern Political Economy: Selected Essays of G.C. Harcourt*, London: Routledge, 1992.

Harcourt, G.C. and O'Shaughnessy, T.J. (1985) 'Keynes's unemployment equilibrium: some insights from Joan Robinson, Piero Sraffa and Richard Kahn', in G.C. Harcourt (ed.) *Keynes and his Contemporaries*, London: Macmillan.

—— and Sardoni, C. (1994) 'Keynes's vision: method, analysis and "tactics"', in J.B. Davis (ed.) *The State of Interpretation of Keynes*, Dordrecht: Kluwer.

——, Karmel, P.H. and Wallace, R.H. (1967) *Economic Activity*, Cambridge: Cambridge University Press.

——, Roncaglia, A. and Rowley, R. (eds) (1994) *Income and Employment in Theory and Practice*, London: Macmillan.

Harcourt, W. and Sardoni, C. (trs) (1993) 'Piero Sraffa: "Monetary Inflation in Italy during and after the war"', *Cambridge Journal of Economics*, 17: 7–26.

Harris, S.E. (ed.) (1947) *The New Economics: Keynes's Influence on Theory and Policy*, New York: Alfred A. Knopf.

Harrod, R.F. (1937) 'Mr Keynes and traditional theory', *Econometrica* 5: 74–146.

—— (1939) 'An essay in dynamic theory', *Economic Journal* 49: 14–33.

—— (1947) 'Keynes, the economist', in S.E. Harris (ed.) *The New Economics: Keynes's Influence on Theory and Policy*, New York: Alfred A. Knopf.

—— (1948) *Towards a Dynamic Economics*, London: Macmillan.

—— (1951) *The Life of John Maynard Keynes*, London: Macmillan; 2nd edn, 1963.

—— (1959) 'Domar and dynamic economics', *Economic Journal* 69: 451–64.

—— (1963) *The Life of John Maynard Keynes*, London: Macmillan.

Hart, O. (1982) 'A model of imperfect competition with Keynesian features', *Quarterly Journal of Economics* 97: 109–38.

Hassard, J. (ed.) (1990) *Sociology of Time*, London: Macmillan.

Hawtrey, R.G. (1937a) *Capital and Employment*, London: Longmans.

—— (1937b) 'Alternative theories of the rate of interest', *Economic Journal* 47: 436–43.

—— (1952) *Capital and Employment*, 2nd edn, London: Longmans.

Hayek, F.A. von (1928) 'Das intertemporale Gleichgewichtssystem der Preise und die Bewegung des "Geldwerts"', *Weltwirtschaftliches Archiv* 28: 33–79.

—— (1931) *Prices and Production*, London: Routledge.

—— (1932) 'Money and capital: a reply', *Economic Journal* 42: 237–49.

—— (1941) *The Pure Theory of Capital*, Chicago, Ill.: University of Chicago Press.

—— (1978) *New Studies in Philosophy, Politics, Economics and the History of Ideas*, London: Routledge & Kegan Paul.

Hébert, R.F. (1987) 'Isnard, Achylles Nicolas', in J. Eatwell, M. Milgate and P. Newman (eds) *The New Palgrave: A Dictionary of Economics*, Vol. 2, London: Macmillan.

Heckscher, E.F. (1931) *Merkatilsmen*, 2 vols, Stockholm: P.A. Norstedt; authorized trans. Mendel Shapiro, as *Mercantilism*, London: Allen & Unwin, 1935; rev. edn. New York: Macmillan, London: Allen & Unwin, 1955.

Heering, W. (1991) 'Geld, Liquiditätsprämie und Kapitalgüternachfrage. Studien zur entscheidungstheoretischen Fundierung einer Monetären Theorie der Produktion', in *Studien zur monetären Ökonomie*, Vol. 10, Regensburg: Transfer Verlag.

—— (1993) 'Analytische Aspekte einer Monetären Theorie des Outputs', in H.J. Stadermann and O. Steiger (eds) *Der Stand und die Nächste Zukunft der Geldforschung*. Festschrift für Hajo Riese zum 60. Geburtstag, Volkswirtschaftliche Schrifen Heft 424, Belrin: Dincker & Humblot.

Hegeland, H. (1954) *The Multiplier Theory*, reprinted New York: A.M. Kelley, 1966.

Heller, W. (ed.) (1986) *Essays in Honor of Kenneth Arrow*, Vol. 2, Cambridge: Cambridge University Press.

—— and Starr, R.M. (1979) 'Capital market imperfection, the consumption function and the effectiveness of fiscal policy', *Quarterly Journal of Economics* 93: 455–63.

Hellwig, F.M. (1993) 'The challenge of monetary theory', *European Economic Review* 37: 215–42.

Hempel, C.G. (1939) 'Vagueness and logic', *Philosophy of Science* 6: 178.

—— (1965) *Aspects of Scientific Explanation*, New York: Free Press.

Hendry, D.F. (1983) 'Econometric modelling: the consumption function in retrospect', *Scottish Journal of Political Economy* 30: 193–220.

—— (1994) 'HUS revisited', *Oxford Review of Economic Policy* 10: 86–106.

—— and von Ungern-Sternberg, T. (1980) 'Liquidity and inflation effects on consumers' expenditure', in A.S. Deaton (ed.) *Essays in the Theory and Measurement of Consumers' Behaviour*, Cambridge: Cambridge University Press.

——, Muellbauer, J. and Murphy, A. (1990) 'The econometrics of DHSY', in J.D. Hey and D. Winch (eds) *A Century of Economics: 100 Years of the Royal Economic Society and the* Economic Journal, Oxford: Blackwell.

Hey, J.D. and Winch, D. (eds) (1990) *A Century of Economics: 100 Years of the Royal Economic Society and the* Economic Journal, Oxford: Blackwell.

Heymann, D. and Leijonhuvfud, A. (1995) *High Inflation*, Oxford: Clarendon Press.

Hicks, J.R. (1936) 'Mr Keynes's theory of employment', *Economic Journal* 46: 138–252.

—— (1937) 'Mr Keynes and the "Classics": a suggested interpretation', *Econometrica* 5: 147–59.

—— (1939) *Value and Capital*, Oxford: Oxford University Press.

—— (1950) *A Contribution to the Theory of the Trade Cycle*, Oxford: Oxford University Press.

—— (1965) *Capital and Growth*, Oxford: Oxford University Press.

—— (1967) *Critical Essays in Monetary Theory*, Oxford: Clarendon Press.

—— (1974) *The Crisis in Keynesian Economics*, New York: Basic Books.

—— (1982) *Money, Interest and Wages*, Oxford: Blackwell.

Hill, R. (ed.) (1987) *Keynes, Money and Monetarism: The Eighth Keynes Seminar held at the University of Kent at Canterbury*, London: Macmillan.

Hobsbawm, E. (1994) *The Age of Extremes*, London: Michael Joseph.

Hobson, J.A. (1932a) *From Capitalism to Socialism*, London: Hogarth Press.

—— (1932b) 'The world's economic crisis', *The Nation*, 20 July: 53.

—— (1934) 'Under-production and under-consumption', *New Statesman and Nation*, 24 March: 443.

—— (1938) *Confessions of an Economic Heretic*, with an introd. by M. Freeden, Brighton: Harvester Press, 1976.

Holden, A. (ed.) (1986) *Chaos*, Princeton, N.J.: Princeton University Press.

Holden, G.R. (1938a) 'Mr Keynes' consumption function and the time preference postulate', *Quarterly Journal of Economics* 52: 281–96.

—— (1938b) 'Rejoinder', *Quarterly Journal of Economics* 52: 709–12.

Hoover, K. (1988) *The New Classical Macroeconomics*, Oxford: Blackwell.

Howard, D.H. (1978) 'Personal saving behavior and the rate of inflation', *Review of Economics and Statistics* 60: 547–54.

Howard, M.C. and King, J.E. (1992) *A History of Marxian Economics*, Vol. II: *1929–90*, London: Macmillan.

Howitt, P. (1978) 'The limits to stability of a full-employment equilibrium', *Scandinavian Journal of Economics* 80: 265–82.

Howitt, P. (1986) 'The Keynesian recovery', *Canadian Journal of Economics* 19: 626–41.

—— (1988) 'Wage flexibility and employment', in O.F. Hamouda and J.N. Smithin (eds) *Keynes and Public Policy after Fifty Years*, Vol. 2: *Theories and Method*, Aldershot, Hants: Edward Elgar.

—— (1990a) 'Deterministic outcomes with multiple equilibria', unpublished.

—— (1990b) *The Keynesian Recovery, and Other Essays*, Ann Arbor, Mich.: University of Michigan Press.

—— (1992) 'Interest rate control and nonconvergence to rational expectations', *Journal of Political Economy* 100: 776–800.

—— (1995) 'Cash in advance, microfoundations in retreat', in K. Velupillai (ed.) *Inflation, Institutions and Information*, London: Macmillan.

—— and McAfee, R.P. (1992) 'Animal spirits', *American Economic Review* 82: 493–505.

Howrey, E.P. and Hymans, S.H. (1978) 'The measurement and determination of loanable-funds saving', *Brookings Papers on Economic Activity*, 655–85.

Hudson, H. (1957) 'A model of the trade cycle', *Economic Record* 33: 378–89.

Huth, T. (1989) *Kapital und Gleichgewicht. Zur Kontrovere zwischen neoKlassischer und neoricardianischer Theorie des allgemeinen Gleichgewichts*, Marburg: Metropolis-Verlag.

Hutt, W.H. (1974) *A Rehabilitation of Say's Law*, Athens: Ohio University Press.

Hymans, S.H. (1970) 'Consumption: new data and old puzzles', *Brookings Papers on Economic Activity* 117–26.

Ingham, A. and Ulph, A.M. (eds) (1984) *Demand, Equilibrium and Trade: Essays in Honour of I.F. Pearce*, London: Macmillan.

Ingrao, B. and Israel, G. (1990) *The Invisible Hand: Economic Equilibrium in the History of Science*, Cambridge, Mass.: MIT Press.

Jaffe, W. (1956) *English Translation of Walras'* Elements, London: Allen & Unwin.

Jäggi, C.M. (1986) *Die Makroökonomik von J.M. Keynes*, Berlin: Springer Verlag.

Jarsulic, M. (ed.) (1985) *Money and Macro Policy*, Boston, Mass.: Kluwer-Nijhof.

—— (1989) 'Endogenous money and credit cycles', *Journal of Post Keynesian Economics* 12: 35–48.

—— (1993a) 'A nonlinear model of the pure growth cycle', *Journal of Economic Behaviour and Organisation* 22: 133–51.

—— (1993b) 'Complex dynamics in a Keynesian growth cycle model', *Metroeconomica* 44: 43–64.

Johnson, H.J. (1951) 'Some Cambridge controversies in monetary theory', *Review of Economic Studies* 19: 90–104.

Jöhr, W.A. (1937) ' "Verbrauchsneigung" und "Liquiditätsvorliebe". Eine Auseinandersetzung mit J.M. Keynes', *Jahrbücher für Nationalökonomie und Statistik*, 146: 641–62.

Jones, R. and Ostroy, J.M. (1984) 'Flexibility and uncertainty', *Review of Economic Studies* 51: 13–32.

Jonung, L. (ed.) (1991) *The Stockholm School of Economics Revisited*, New York: Cambridge University Press.

Jorgensen, D.W. (1963) 'Capital theory and investment behaviour', *American Economic Review* 53(May): 247–59.

—— and Siebert, C.D. (1968) 'A comparison of alternative theories of investment behaviour', *American Economic Review* 58: 681–712.

—— and Stephenson, J.A. (1967) 'Investment behavior in US manufacturing', *Econometrica* 35: 169–220.

Juster, F.T. and Taylor, L.D. (1975) 'Towards a theory of saving behavior', *American Economic Review* 65(May): 203–9.

Juster, F.T. and Wachtel, P. (1972) 'Inflation and the consumer', *Brookings Papers on Economic Activity* 71–121.

Kahn, R.F. (1929) 'The economics of the short period', Fellowship Dissertation, King's College, Cambridge; 1st English edn, London: Macmillan, 1989.

—— (1931) 'The relation of home investment to unemployment', *Economic Journal* 41: 173–98.

—— (1959) 'Exercises in the analysis of growth', *Oxford Economic Papers* 2: 143–56.

—— (1971) 'Notes on the rate of interest and the growth of firms'; reprinted in R.F. Kahn, *Selected Essays on Employment and Growth*, Cambridge: Cambridge University Press. 1972: 208–32.

—— (1972) *Selected Essays on Employment and Growth*, Cambridge: Cambridge University Press.

—— (1984) *The Making of Keynes's 'General Theory'*, Cambridge: Cambridge University Press.

Kaldor, N. (1939–40) 'Speculation and economic stability', *Review of Economic Studies* 7. 1–27.

—— (1955–6) 'Alternative theories of distribution', *Review of Economic Studies* 23: 83–100.

—— (1957) 'A model of economic growth', *Economic Journal* 67: 591–624.

—— (1960) 'Keynes's theory of own-rates of interest', in N. Kaldor (ed.) *Essays on Economic Stability and Growth*, London: Duckworth.

—— (1966) 'Macroeconomic theory and income distribution', *Review of Economic Studies* 33: 309–19.

—— (1970) 'The new monetarism', *Lloyds Bank Review* April: 1–18.

—— (1980) 'Monetary policy in the United Kingdom', in *Memoranda on Monetary Policy: Evidence to the Treasury and Civil Service Committee*, London: HMSO.

—— (1982) *The Scourge of Monetarism*, Oxford: Oxford University Press.

—— (1983a) 'Keynesian economics after fifty years', in D. Worswick and J. Trevithick (eds) *Keynes and the Modern World*, Cambridge: Cambridge University Press.

—— (1983b) 'Limitations of *The General Theory*', in F. Targetti and A. Thirlwall (eds) *Further Essays on Economic Theory and Policy*, London: Duckworth.

—— and Mirrlees, J. (1962) 'A new model of economic growth', *Review of Economic Studies* 29: 174–92.

Kalecki, M. (1933) 'Essays on the business cycle theory'; reprinted in J. Osiatynski (ed.) *Collected Works of Michal Kalecki*, Vol. I: *Capitalism: Business Cycles and Full Employment*, Oxford: Clarendon Press.

—— (1936) 'Some remarks on Keynes's theory'; reprinted in J. Osiatynski (ed.) *Collected Works of Michal Kalecki*, Vol. I: *Capitalism: Business Cycles and Full Employment*, Oxford: Clarendon Press, 1960.

—— (1937a) 'The principle of increasing risk', *Economica* 4: 440–7; reprinted in J. Osiatynski (ed.) *Collected Works of Michal Kalecki*, Vol. I: *Capitalism: Business Cycles and Full Employment*, Oxford: Clarendon Press.

—— (1937b) 'A theory of the business cycle', *Review of Economic Studies* 4: 77–97.

—— (1938) 'The determinants of the distribution of the national income', *Econometrica* 6: 97–112.

—— (1939a) 'Money and real wages, Part I (theory)'; translated from the Polish in M. Kalecki, *Studies in the Theory of Business Cycles, 1933–39*, Oxford: Blackwell, 1969.

—— (1939b) *Essays in the Theory of Economic Fluctuations*, London: George Allen & Unwin.

—— (1943) *Studies in Economic Fluctuations*, London: George Allen & Unwin.

Kalecki, M. (1944) 'Professor Pigou on "The Classical Stationary State": a comment', *Economic Journal* 54: 131–2.

—— (1954) *Theory of Economic Dynamics*, New York: Rinehart.

—— (1968) 'Trend and business cycle reconsidered', *Economic Journal* 78: 263–76.

—— (1969) *Studies in the Theory of Business Cycles, 1933–1939*, Oxford: Blackwell.

—— (1971a) 'Class struggle and distribution of national income', *Kyklos* 24: 1–9; reprinted in M. Kalecki, *Selected Essays on the Dynamics of The Capitalist Economy (1933–70)*, Cambridge: Cambridge University Press.

—— (1971b) *Selected Essays on the Dynamics of the Capitalist Economy (1933–70)*, Cambridge: Cambridge University Press.

—— (1990) 'Three systems', in J. Osiatynski (ed.) *Collected Works of Michal Kalecki*, Vol. I, Oxford: Clarendon Press.

—— (1991) *Collected Works of Michal Kalecki*, Vol. II: *Capitalism: Economic Dynamics*, ed. J. Osiatynski Oxford: Clarendon Press.

Kelsey, D. and Quiggin, J. (1992) 'Theories of choice under ignorance and uncertainty', *Journal of Economic Surveys* 6: 133–53.

Keynes, J.M. (1904) 'Ethics in relation to conduct', unpublished mimeo, King's College Library, Cambridge University.

—— (1919) *The Economic Consequences of the Peace*, London: Macmillan; *C.W.* II.

—— (1921) *A Treatise on Probability*, London: Macmillan; *C.W.* VIII.

—— (1922) 'The forward market in foreign exchanges', *Manchester Guardian Commercial* (Reconstruction Supplement) 20 April: 11–18.

—— (1923) *A Tract on Monetary Reform*, London: Macmillan; *C.W.* IV.

—— (1925) *La Riforma Monetaria*, Italian trans. P. Sraffa, Milan: Fratelli Treves Editori.

—— (1926) *The End of Laissez-faire*, Edinburgh: Neill; *C.W.* IX: 272–94.

—— (1928) *Britain's Industrial Future: Being the Report of the Liberal Industrial Inquiry*, Ernest Benn.

—— (1930a) *A Treatise on Money: The Pure Theory of Money*, London: Macmillan; *C.W.* V.

—— (1930b) *A Treatise on Money: The Applied Theory of Money*, London: Macmillan; *C.W.* VI.

—— (1933a) 'A monetary theory of production' in *Der Stand und die nächste Zukunft der Konjunkturforschung: Festschrift für Arthur Spiethoff*, reprinted in *C.W.* XIII: 408–11.

—— (1933b) *The Means to Prosperity*, London: Macmillan; *C.W.* IX: 335–66.

—— (1933c) Letter to Marcus Wallenburg, Keynes Papers, King's College, Cambridge, File L/33.

—— (1933d) *Essays and Sketches in Biography*, London: Macmillan.

—— (1934) 'Poverty in plenty: is the economic system self-adjusting?', *The Listener*, 21 Nov: 850–1; *C.W.* XIII: 485–92.

—— (1936) *The General Theory of Employment, Interest and Money*, London: Macmillan; *C.W.* VII.

—— (1937a) 'Alternative theories of the rate of interest', *Economic Journal* 47: 241–52; *C.W.* XIV: 201–15.

—— (1937b) 'The "ex ante" theory of the rate of interest', *Economic Journal* 47: 663–9; *C.W.* XIV: 215–26.

—— (1937c) 'The General Theory of Employment', *Quarterly Journal of Economics* 51: 209–23; *C.W.* XIV: 109–23.

—— (1937d) 'The theory of the rate of interest', in A.D. Gayer (ed.) *The Lessons of Monetary Experience: Essays in Honour of Irving Fisher*, reprinted in *Readings in the Theory of Income Distribution*, Philadelphia, Pa: Blakiston, 1946; *C.W.* XIV: 101–8.

Keynes, J.M. (1938a) 'Mr Keynes' consumption function: reply', *Quarterly Journal of Economics* 52: 708–9; *C.W.* XIV: 268–70.

—— (1938b) 'Mr Keynes' consumption function: further note', *Quarterly Journal of Economics* 53: 160; *C.W.* XIV: 268–70.

—— (1938c) 'D.H. Robertson on Mr Keynes and "finance": a comment', *Economic Journal* 48: 318–22; *C.W.* XIV: 229–33.

—— (1939a) 'Mr Keynes on the distribution of incomes and "propensity to consume": a reply', *Review of Economic Statistics* 21: 129; *C.W.* XIV: 270–1.

—— (1939b) 'Professor Tinberg's method', *Economic Journal* 49: 558–68; *C.W.* XIV: 306–18.

—— (1939c) 'Relative movements of real wages and output', *Economic Journal* 49: 34–51; *C.W.* VII: 394–412.

—— (1939d) 'The process of capital formation', *Economic Journal* 49: 569–74; *C.W.* XIV: 278–85.

—— (1940a) '[On a method of statistical business-cycle research] Comment', *Economic Journal* 50: 154–6; *C.W.* XIV: 318–20.

—— (1940b) *How to Pay for the War*, London: Macmillan; *C.W.* IX: 367–439.

—— (1971–89) *The Collected Writings of John Maynard Keynes [C.W.]* ed. D.E. Moggridge, Vols I–XXX, London: Macmillan.

—— (1971) *A Tract on Monetary Reform*, in *The Collected Writings of John Maynard Keynes* Vol. IV, London: Macmillan.

—— (1972a) *Essays in Persuasion*, in *The Collected Writings of John Maynard Keynes*, Vol. IX, London: Macmillan.

—— (1972b) *Essays in Biography*, in *The Collected Writings of John Maynard Keynes*, Vol. X, London: Macmillan.

—— (1973a) *The General Theory of Employment, Interest and Money* in *The Collected Writings of John Maynard Keynes*, Vol. VII, London: Macmillan.

—— (1973b) *A Treatise on Probability*, in *The Collected Writings of John Maynard Keynes*, Vol. VIII, London: Macmillan.

—— (1973c) *The General Theory and After. Part I: Preparation*, in *The Collected Writings of John Maynard Keynes*, Vol. XIII, London: Macmillan.

—— (1973d) *The General Theory and After. Part II: Defence and Development*, in *The Collected Writings of John Maynard Keynes*, Vol. XIV, London: Macmillan.

—— (1979) *The General Theory and After: A Supplement*, in *The Collected Writings of John Maynard Keynes*, Vol. XXIX, London: Macmillan.

—— (1980) *Activities, 1940–46*, in *The Collected Writings of John Maynard Keynes*, Vol. XXVII, London: Macmillan.

—— (1981) *Activities, 1929–31: Rethinking Employment and Unemployment Policies*, in *The Collected Writings of John Maynard Keynes*, Vol. XX, London: Macmillan.

—— (1983a) *Economic Articles and Correspondence – Academic*, in *The Collected Writings of John Maynard Keynes*, Vol. XI, London: Macmillan.

—— (1983b) *Economic Articles and Correspondence: Investment and Editorial*, in *The Collected Writings of John Maynard Keynes*, Vol. XII, London: Macmillan.

—— and Henderson, H. (1929) 'Can Lloyd George do it?', in *The Collected Writings of John Maynard Keynes*, Vol. IX, London: Macmillan.

King, J.E. (1981) 'Perish commerce! Free trade and underconsumption in early British radical economics', *Australian Economic Papers* 20: 235–57.

—— (1983) 'Utopian or scientific? A reconsideration of the Ricardian socialists', *History of Political Economy* 15: 345–73.

—— (1994a) 'J.A. Hobson's macroeconomics: the last ten years (1930–40)', in J. Pheby (ed.) *Free-thought in Economics and Politics*, London: Macmillan.

King, J.E. (1994b) 'Aggregate supply and demand analysis since Keynes: a partial history', *Journal of Post Keynesian Economics* 17: 3–31.

—— (ed.) (1996) *An Alternative Macroeconomic Theory: The Kaleckian Model and Post-Keynesian Economics*, Boston, Mass.: Kluwer.

—— and Regan, P. (1988) 'Recent trends in labour's share', in Y.S. Brenner, J.P.G. Reinders and A.H.G.M. Spithoven (eds) *The Theory of Income and Wealth Distribution*, Brighton: Wheatsheaf.

Kirman, A. (1989) 'The intrinsic limits of modern economic theory: the emperor has no clothes', *Economic Journal* 99 (suppl.): 126–39.

—— (1992) 'Whom or what does the representative individual represent?', *Journal of Economic Perspectives* 6: 117–36.

Kiyotaki, N. and Blanchard, O. (1987) 'Monopolistic competition and the effects of aggregate demand', *American Economic Review* 77: 647–67.

Klamer, A. (1984) *The New Classical Macroeconomics: Conversations with the New Classical Economists and their Opponents*, Brighton: Harvester.

Klausinger, H. (1991) *Theorien der Geldwirtschaft. Von Hayek und Keynes zu neueren Ansätzen*, Volkswirtschaftliche Schriften Heft 407, Berlin: Duncker & Humblot.

—— (1993) 'Keynes und die Postkeynsianer zur Produktionselastizität des Geldes – Eine Kritik', in H.J. Stadermann and O. Steiger (eds) *Der Stand und die nächste Zukunft der Geldforschung. Festschrift für Hajo Riese zum 60. Geburtstag*, Volkswirtschaftliche Schriften Heft 424, Berlin: Duncker & Humblot.

Kleiman, E. (1989) 'The cost of inflation', Working Paper, Jerusalem: Hebrew University.

Klein, L. (1947) *The Keynesian Revolution*, New York: Macmillan.

—— (1950) *Economic Fluctuations in the United States, 1921–41*, New York: John Wiley.

—— and Goldberger, A. (1955) *An Econometric Model of the United States, 1929–52*, Amsterdam: North-Holland.

Knight, F.H. (1921) *Risk, Uncertainty and Profit*, Chicago, Ill.: Chicago University Press.

—— (1937) 'Underemployment and Mr Keynes' revolution in economic theory', *Canadian Journal of Economics and Political Science* 3: 100–23.

Kopke, R. (1985) 'The determinants of investment spending', *New England Economic Review* July/Aug: 19–35.

Koslowski, P. (ed.) (1985) *Economics and Philosophy*, Tubingen: Siebeck.

Kregel, J.A. (1976) 'Economic methodology in the face of uncertainty: the modelling methods of Keynes and the Post-Keynesians', *Economic Journal* 86: 209–25.

—— (1980) 'Markets and institutions as features of a capitalist production system', *Journal of Post Keynesian Economics* 3: 32–48.

—— (1981) 'On distinguishing between alternative methods of approach to the demand for output as a whole', *Australian Economic Papers* 20: 63–71.

—— (1982) 'Money, expectations and relative prices in Keynes' monetary equilibrium', *Economie appliquée* 35: 449–65.

—— (1983a) 'Effective demand: origins and development of the notion', in J.A. Kregel (ed.) *Distribution, Effective Demand and International Economic Relations*, London: Macmillan.

—— (1983b) 'The microfoundations of the "Generalisation of *The General Theory*" and "bastard Keynesianism": Keynes' theory of employment in the long and short period', *Cambridge Journal of Economics* 7: 343–61.

—— (1983c) 'Budget deficits, stabilisation policy and liquidity preference: Keynes's post-war policy proposals', in F. Vicarelli (ed.) *Keynes's Relevance Today*, London: Macmillan.

Kregel, J.A. (ed.) (1983d) *Distribution, Effective Demand and International Economic Relations*, London: Macmillan.

—— (1984) 'Expectations and rationality within a capitalist framework', in E.J. Nell (ed.) *Free Market Conservatism: A Critique of Theory and Practice*, London: Allen & Unwin.

—— (1984–5) 'Constraints on output and employment', *Journal of Post Keynesian Economics* 7: 139–52

—— (1985a) 'Hamlet without the prince: Cambridge macroeconomics without money', *American Economic Review* 75: 133–9.

—— (1985b) 'Harrod and Keynes: increasing returns, the theory of employment and dynamic economics', in G.C. Harcourt (ed.) *Keynes and his Contemporaries: The Sixth and Centennial Keynes Seminar held at the University of Kent at Canterbury, 1983*, London: Macmillan, 66–88.

—— (1988) 'The multiplier and liquidity preference: two sides of the theory of demand', in A. Barrère (ed.) *The Foundations of Keynesian Analysis*, proceedings of a conference held at the University of Paris I-Panthéon-Sorbonne, London: Macmillan.

—— (1994) 'Causality and real time in Asimakopulos's approach to saving and investment in the theory of distribution', in G.C. Harcourt, A. Roncaglia and R. Rowley (eds) *Income and Employment in Theory and Practice*, London: Macmillan.

Kreps, D.M. (1992) 'Static choice and the presence of unforeseen contingencies', in P. Dasgupta, O. Hart and E. Maskin (eds) *Economic Analysis of Markets and Games: Essays in Honour of Frank Hahn*, Cambridge, Mass.: MIT Press.

Kriesler, P. (1987) *Kalecki's Microanalysis: The Development of Kalecki's Analysis of Pricing and Distribution*, Cambridge: Cambridge University Press.

—— (1988a) 'Keynes and Kalecki on method', School of Economics Discussion Paper 88/14, University of New South Wales.

—— (1988b) 'The methods of Keynes and Kalecki', in H. Hagemann and O. Steiger (eds) *Keynes's General Theory after Fifty Years*, Berlin: Duncker & Humblot.

—— (1996) 'Microfoundations: a Kaleckian perspective', in J. King (ed.) *An Alternative Macroeconomic Theory: The Kaleckian Model and Post-Keynesian Economics*, Boston, Mass.: Kluwer.

—— and McFarlane, B. (1993) 'Michael Kalecki on capitalism', *Cambridge Journal of Economics* 17: 215–35.

Kuenne, R.E. (1977) 'Money, capital and interest in intertemporal general equilibrium theory', *Economie appliquée* 30: 617–38.

Kuhn, T.S. (1953) *The Copernican Revolution*, New York: Vintage Books.

—— (1962) *The Structure of Scientific Revolutions*, Chicago, Ill.: University of Chicago Press.

Kurihara, K.K. (ed.) (1954) *Post Keynesian Economics*, London: Allen & Unwin.

—— (1956) *Introduction to Keynesian Dynamics*, London: Allen & Unwin.

Kurz, H.D. (1983) 'What is wrong with Keynesian economics? Comment on Bharadwaj', in J.A. Kregel (ed.) *Distribution, Effective Demand and International Economic Relations*, London: Macmillan.

—— (1995a) 'Über "natürliche" und "künstliche" Störungen des allgemeinen wirtschaftlichen Gleichgewichts: Friedrich August Hayeks monetäre Überinvestitionstheorie in *Preise und Produktion*', in *Vademecum zu einem Klassiker der Marktkoordination*, Düsseldorf: Verlag Wirtschaft und Finanzen.

—— (1995b) 'The Hayek–Keynes–Sraffa controversy reconsidered', University of Graz, unpublished MS.

Kydland, F.E. and Prescott, E.C. (1977) 'Rules rather than discretion: the inconsistency of optimal plans', *Journal of Political Economy* 85: 473–91.

Kydland, F.E. and Prescott, E.C. (1982) 'Time to build and aggregate fluctuations', *Econometrica* 50: 1345–69.

Lachmann, L.M. (1986a) *The Market as an Economic Process*, Oxford: Blackwell.

—— (1986b) 'Austrian theory under fire: the Hayek–Sraffa duel in retrospect', in W. Grassl and B. Smith (eds) *Austrian Economics: Historical and Philosophical Background*, New York: New York University Press.

Laidler, D. (1983) 'Misconceptions about the real bills doctrine and the quantity theory: a comment on Sargent and Wallace', Research Report no. 8314 University of Western Ontario, Dept of Economics.

—— (1990a) 'Alfred Marshall and the development of monetary economics', in J.K. Whitaker (ed.) *Centenary Essays on Alfred Marshall*, Cambridge: Cambridge University Press, 44–78.

—— (1990b) *Taking Money Seriously*, London: Philip Allan.

Lange, O. (1938a) 'The rate of interest and the optimal propensity to consume', *Economica* NS 5: 12–32.

—— (1938b) 'Saving in process analysis', *Quarterly Journal of Economics* 53: 620–2.

—— (1942) 'Say's Law: a restatement and criticism', in O. Lange, F. McIntyre and T.O. Yntema (eds) *Studies iin Mathematical Economics and Econometrics, in Memory of Henry Schultz*, Chicago, Ill.: University of Chicago Press.

——, McIntyre, F. and Yntema, T. (eds) (1942) *Studies in Mathematical Economics and Econometrics, in Memory of Henry Schultz*, Chicago, Ill.: University of Chicago Press.

Latsis, S.J. (ed.) (1976) *Method and Appraisal in Economics*, Cambridge: Cambridge University Press.

Lavoie, M. (1985) 'Credit and money: the dynamic circuit, overdraft economics, and Post-Keynesian economics', in M. Jarsulic (ed.) *Money and Macro Policy*, Boston, Mass.: Kluwer-Nijhof.

—— (1992) *Foundations of Post Keynesian Economic Analysis*, Aldershot, Hants: Edward Elgar.

Lawlor, M.S. (1994a) 'The historical context of Keynes's views on financial markets', in N. de Marchi and M. Morgan (eds) *Higgling: Transactors and Their Markets in the History of Economics* (History of Political Economy series, Vol. 26, suppl.), Durham, N.C.: Duke University Press, 184–225.

—— (1994b) 'The own-rates framework as an interpretation on *The General Theory*: a suggestion for complicaitng the Keynesian theory of money', in J.B. Davis (ed.) *The State of Interpretation of Keynes*, Dordrecht: Kluwer.

—— and Horn, B.L. (1992) 'Notes on the Sraffa–Hayek exchange', *Review of Political Economy* 4: 317–40.

——, Darity, W., Jr and Horn, B.L. (1987) 'Was Keynes a chapter two Keynesian?', *Journal of Post Keynesian Economics* 10: 516–28.

Lawson, T. (1985a) 'Uncertainty and economic analysis', *Economic Journal* 95: 909–27.

—— (1985b) 'Keynes, prediction and econometrics', in T. Lawson and H. Peseran (eds) *Keynes' Economics: Methodological Issues*, London: Croom Helm.

—— (1987) 'The relative/absolute nature of knowledge and economic analysis', *Economic Journal* 97: 951–70.

—— (1989) 'Realism and instrumentalism in the development of econometrics', *Oxford Economic Papers* 41: 236–58.

—— (1990a) 'Review of *Keynes: Philosophy, Economics and Politics*', *Economic Journal* 100: 987–9.

—— (1990b) 'Realism, closed systems and expectations', International School of Economic Research workshop paper: presented at Certosa di Pontignani, Siena, Italy.

468

Lawson, T. (1991) 'Keynes and the analysis of rational behaviour', in R.M. O'Donnell (ed.) *Keynes as the Philosopher Economist*, London: Macmillan.

—— (1993) 'Keynes and convention', *Review of Social Economy* 51: 174–200.

—— (1994a) 'Why are so many economists opposed to methodology?', *Journal of Economic Methodology* 1: 105–33.

—— (1994b) 'A realist theory for economics', in R. Backhouse (ed.) *New Perspectives on Economic Methodology*, London: Routledge.

—— (1994c) 'Critical realism and the analysis of choice, explanation and change', *Advances in Austrian Economics* 1: 3–30.

—— (1995a) 'A realist perspective on contemporary economic theory', *Journal of Economic Issues* 29: 1.

—— (1995b) 'Economics and expectations', in S.C. Dow and J. Hillard (eds) *Keynes, Knowledge and Uncertainty*, Cheltenham, Glos.: Edward Elgar.

—— and Pesaran, H. (eds) (1985) *Keynes' Economics: Methodological Issues*, London: Croom Helm.

Le Corbeiller, Ph. (1933) 'Les systèmes autoentretenus et les oscillations de relaxation', *Econometrica* 1: 28–32.

Leijonhufvud, A. (1968) *On Keynesian Economics and the Economics of Keynes: A Study in Monetary Theory*, London: Oxford University Press.

—— (1969) *Keynes and the Classics: Two Lectures on Keynes' Contribution to Economic Theory*, London: Institute of Economic Affairs.

—— (1981) *Information and Coordination: Essays in Macroeconomic Theory*, New York: Oxford University Press.

—— (1983a) 'Book review', *Journal of Economic Literature* 21: 107–10.

—— (1983b) 'Keynesianism, monetarism and rational expectations: some reflections and conjectures', in R. Frydman and E.S. Phelps (eds) *Individual Forecasting and Aggregate Outcomes*, Cambridge: Cambridge University Press.

—— (1983c) 'What would Keynes have thought of rational expectations?', in D. Worswick and J. Trevithick (eds) *Keynes and the Real World*, Cambridge: Cambridge University Press.

—— (1983d) 'Constitutional constraints on the monetary powers of government', *Economia della Scelte Pubbliche* 2: 87–100.

—— (1984) 'Hicks on time and money', *Oxford Economic Papers* 36 (suppl.): 26–46.

—— (1985) 'Ideology and analysis in macroeconomics', in P. Koslowski (ed.) *Economics and Philosophy*, Tubingen: Siebeck.

—— (1992) 'Keynesian economics: past confusions, future prospects', in A. Vercelli and N. Dimitri (eds) *Macroeconomics: A Survey of Research Strategies*, London: Oxford University Press.

Lekachman, R. (ed.) (1964a) *Keynes' General Theory: Reports of Three Decades*, London: Macmillan.

—— (1964b) *Keynes and the Classics*, Boston, Mass.: D.C. Heath.

Leontief, W. (1954) 'Mathematics in economics', *Bulletin of the American Mathematical Society* 60: 215–33.

Lerner, A.P. (1934) 'The concept of monopoly and the measurement of monopoly power', *Review of Economic Studies*, 1(2): 157–75.

—— (1943) 'User cost and prime user cost', *American Economic Review*, 33: 131–2.

—— (1944) *The Economics of Control: Principles of Welfare Economics*, New York: Augustus M. Kelley.

—— (1952) 'The essential properties of interest and money', *Quarterly Journal of Economics* 66: 172–93.

—— (1962) 'Own-rates and the liquidity trap', *Economic Journal* 72: 449–52.

LeRoy, S.F. (1994) 'On policy regimes', in K.D. Hoover (ed.) *Macroeconometrics: Developments, Tensions, Prospects*, Dordrecht: Kluwer.

—— and Singell, Larry D. Jr (1987) 'Knight on risk and uncertainty', *Journal of Political Economy* 95(2): 394–406.

Lévy, P. (1991) 'Keynes aprés Sraffa et Hayek: les origins trompeuses du chapitre 17 de la *Théorie Général*. Commentaire sur Gary Mongiovi', *Economie appliquée* 44: 153–9.

Lewis, D. (1969) *Convention: A Philosophical Study*, Cambridge, Mass.: Harvard University Press.

Lewis, M.K. (1990) 'Liquidity', in John Creedy (ed.) *Foundations of Economic Thought*, Oxford: Blackwell.

Lewis, W.A. (1949) *Overhead Costs*, London: Unwin University Books.

Lim, S.K. (1990) 'Keynes's long-period theory of employment: the evidence against', *The Manchester School of Economic and Social Studies* 58: 66–73.

Lindahl, E. (1929) 'Prisbildningspoblements uppläggning från kapitalteoretisk synpunkt', *Economisk tidskrift* 31: 31–81.

—— (1939) *Studies in the Theory of Money and Capital*, New York: Rhinehart.

Lipsey, R.G. (1972) 'The foundations of the theory of national income: an analysis of some fundamental errors', in M. Peston and B.A. Corry (eds) *Essays in Honour of Lord Robbins*, London: Weidenfeld & Nicolson.

—— and Stone Tice, H. (eds) (1989) *The Measurement of Saving, Investment and Wealth*, Chicago, Ill.: University of Chicago Press.

Lipton, P. (1991) *Inference to the Best Explanation*, London: Routledge.

Littleboy, B. (1990) *On Interpreting Keynes: A Study in Reconciliation*, London: Routledge.

—— (1994) 'The foregotten common sense of Keynes', *WISER* (Whitlam Institute for Social and Economic Research) 2: 29–32.

Long, J. and Ploesser, C. (1983) 'Real business cycles', *Journal of Political Economy* 91: 39–69.

Lorenz, H.W. (1987) 'Strange attractors in a multisectoral business cycle model', *Journal of Economic Behaviour and Organisation* 8: 397–411.

Lubell, H. (1947) 'Effects of redistribution of income on consumers' expenditure', *American Economic Review* 37: 157–70.

Lucas, R.E., Jr (1972a) 'Econometric testing of the natural rate hypothesis', in O. Eckstein (ed.) *The Econometrics of Price Determination*, Washington, D.C.: Board of Governors of the Federal Reserve System, 50–9.

—— (1972b) 'Expectations and the neutrality of money', *Journal of Economic Theory* 4: 103–24.

—— (1973) 'Some international evidence on output–inflation tradeoffs', *American Economic Review* 63: 326–34.

—— (1975) 'An equilibrium model of the business cycle', *Journal of Political Economy* 83: 1113–34.

—— (1976) 'Econometric policy evaluation: a critique', in K. Brunner and A.H. Meltzer (eds) *The Phillips Curve and Labour Markets*, Carnegie-Rochester Conference Series on Public Policy, Vol. 1, Amsterdam: North-Holland, 19–46.

—— (1977) 'Understanding business cycles', in Karl Brunner and Alan H. Meltzer (eds) *Stabilization of the Domestic and International Economy*, Carnegie-Rochester Conference Series on Public Policy, Vol. 5, Amsterdam: North-Holland; reprinted in Robert E. Lucas, Jr, *Studies in Business-Cycle Theory*, Oxford: Blackwell, 1981: 215–39.

—— (1980) 'Two illustrations of the quantity theory of money', *American Economic Review* 80: 1005–14.

Lucas, R.E., Jr (1981) *Studies in Business Cycle Theory*, Oxford: Blackwell.

—— (1986) 'Adaptive behaviour and economic theory', *Journal of Business* 59: 401–26.

—— (1987) *Models of Business Cycles*, Oxford: Blackwell.

—— (1988a) 'Money demand in the United States: a quantitative review', *Carnegie-Rochester Series on Public Policy* 29: 137–68.

—— (1988b) 'On the mechanics of economic development', *Journal of Monetary Economics* 22 (July): 3–42.

—— (1990) 'Liquidity and interest rates', *Journal of Monetary Theory* 50: 237–64.

—— and Sargent, T.J., Jr (1979) 'After Keynesian macroeconomics', *Federal Reserve Bank of Minneapolis Review* Spring: 1–16; reprinted in R.E. Lucas, Jr and T.J. Sargent, Jr, *Rational Expectations and Econometric Practice*, London: George Allen & Unwin, 1981: 295–319.

—— and —— (1981) *Rational Expectations and Econometric Practice*, London: George Allen & Unwin.

Lutz, F. and Hague, D.C. (eds) (1961) *The Theory of Capital*, London: Macmillan.

—— and Lutz, V. (1951) *The Theory of Investment of the Firm*, New York: Greenwood Press.

Luxemburg, R. (1963) *The Accumulation of Capital*, London: Routledge & Kegan Paul.

McCallum, B.T. (1985) 'Bank deregulation, accounting systems of exchange and the unit of account: a critical review', *Carnegie-Rochester Conference Series on Public Policy* 23: 13–46.

—— (1986) 'Some real issues concerning interest rate pegging, price level determinacy, and the real bills doctrine', *Journal of Monetary Economics* 17: 135–60.

McCloskey, D.N. (1983) 'The rhetoric of economics', *Journal of Economic Literature* 21: 481–517.

—— (1986) *The Rhetoric of Economics*, Brighton, Wheatsheaf.

McCloughry, R. (1982) 'Neutrality and monetary equilibrium: a note on Desai', in M. Baranzini (ed.) *Advances in Economic Theory*, Oxford: Blackwell.

McCracken, H.L. (1933) *Value Theory and Business Cycles*, New York: Falcon Press.

MacDougall, G.D.A. (1936) 'The definition of prime and supplementary costs', *Economic Journal* 46: 4430–61.

McKinnon, R.I. (1990) 'Interest rate volatility and exchange rate risk: new rules for a common monetary standard', *Contemporary Policy Studies* 8: 10.

Maclachlan, F.C. (1993a) *Keynes's General Theory of Interest: A Reconsideration*, London: Routledge.

—— (1993b) 'Austrian and Post Keynesian interest rate theory: some unexpected parallels', in G. Mongiovi and C. Rühl (eds) *Macroeconomic Theory: Diversity and Convergence*, Aldershot, Hants: Edward Elgar.

Madan, D.P. and Owings, J.C. (1988) 'Decision theory with complex uncertainties', *Synthese* 75: 25–44.

Maddison, A. (1964) *Economic Growth in the West*, London: Allen & Unwin, for the 20th Century Fund.

—— (1982) *Phases of Capitalist Development*, Oxford: Oxford University Press.

Majewski, R. (1988) 'The Hayek challenge and the origins of Chapter 17 of Keynes' *General Theory*', in H. Hagemann and O. Steiger (eds) *Keynes'* General Theory *nach fünfzig Jahren*, Volkswirtschaftliche Schriften Heft 384, Berlin: Duncker & Humblot.

Mäki, U. (1992) 'On the method of isolation in economics', in C. Dilworth (ed.) *Intelligibility in Science*, special issue of *Poznań Studies in the Philosophy of the Sciences* 2: 319–54.

Makowski, L. (1989) 'Keynes' liquidity preference theory: a suggested reinterpretation', in F.H. Hahn (ed.) *The Economics of Missing Markets, Information, and Games*, Oxford: Clarendon Press.

Malinvaud, E. (1972) *Lectures on Microeconomic Theory*, Amsterdam: North Holland.

—— (1977) *The Theory of Unemployment Reconsidered*, Oxford: Blackwell.

—— (1980) *Profitability and Unemployment*, Cambridge: Cambridge University Press.

Mankiw, N. (1985) 'Small menu costs and large business cycles: a macroeconomic model of monopoly', *Quarterly Journal of Economics* 100: 529–39.

—— (1988) 'Imperfect competition and the Keynesian cross', *Economics Letters*, 26: 7–13.

—— (1989) 'Real business cycles: a New Keynesian perspective', *Journal of Economic Perspectives* 3: 79–90.

—— (1992) 'The reincarnation of Keynesian economics', *European Economic Review* 36: 559–65.

—— and Romer, D. (eds) (1991) *New Keynesian Economics*, Cambridge, Mass.: MIT Press.

—— and Shapiro, M.D. (1985) 'Trends, random walks and tests of the permanent income hypothesis', *Journal of Monetary Economics*, 16 (June): 165–74.

Marcuzzo, M. (1994) 'R.F. Kahn and imperfect competition', *Cambridge Journal of Economics* 18: 25–39.

——, Pasinetti, L. and Roneaglia, A. (eds) (1996) *The Economics of Joan Robinson*, London: Routledge.

Marglin, S. and Schor, J. (1990) *The Golden Age of Capitalism*, Oxford: Oxford University Press.

Margolit, A. (1976) 'Vagueness in vogue', *Synthese* 33: 211–21.

Marris, R. (1964) *The Economic Theory of Managerial Capitalism*, London: Macmillan.

—— (1972) 'Why economics needs a theory of the firm', special issue of *Economic Journal* 82: 321–52.

—— (1991) *Reconstructing Keynesian Economics with Imperfect Competition*, Aldershot, Hants: Edward Elgar.

—— (1992) 'R.F. Kahn's fellowship dissertation: a missing link in the history of economic thought', *Economic Journal* 102: 1235–43.

—— and Mueller, D. (1980) 'The corporation and competition', *Journal of Economic Literature* 18: 32–63.

—— and Wood, A. (eds) (1971) *The Corporate Economy*, Cambridge, Mass.: Harvard University Press.

Marschak, J. (1939) 'Personal and collective budget functions', *Review of Economic Statistics* 21: 69–74.

—— (1942) 'Economic interdependence and statistical analysis', in O. Lange (ed.) *Studies in Mathematical Economics and Econometrics*, Chicago, Ill.: University of Chicago Press.

Marshall, A. (1871) 'Money', reprinted in J. Whittaker (ed.) *The Early Writings of Alfred Marshall*, 2 vols, London: Macmillan, 1975.

—— (1889) *The Pure Theory of Foreign Trade: Domestic Values*, reprinted London: London School of Economics, 1930.

—— (1895) *Principles of Economics*, 3rd edn, London: Macmillan.

—— (1920) *Principles of Economics*, 8th edn, London: Macmillan.

Marx, K. (1904) *A Contribution to the Critique of Political Economy*, trans from 2nd German edn by N.I. Stone, Chicago, Ill.: Charles H. Kerr.

—— (1954) *Capital*, Book I, Moscow: Progress Publishers.

—— (1956) *Capital*, Book II, Moscow: Progress Publishers.

—— (1959) *Capital*, Book III, Moscow: Progress Publishers.

Marx, K. (1968) *Theories of Surplus-Value*, Part II, Moscow: Progress Publishers.

Matthews, R.C.O. (1991) 'Animal spirits', in J.G.T. Meeks (ed.) *Thoughtful Economic Man: Essays on Rationality, Moral Rules and Benevolence*, Cambridge: Cambridge University Press.

Meade, J.E. (1975) 'The Keynesian revolution', in M. Keynes (ed.) *Essays on John Maynard Keynes*, Cambridge: Cambridge University Press.

—— (1993) 'The relation of Mr Meade's relation to Kahn's multiplier', *Economic Journal* 103: 664–5.

Meek, R.L. (1967) 'The place of Keynes in the history of economic thought', in *Economics, Ideology and Other Essays*, London: Chapman & Hall.

Meeks, J.G.T. (1991a) 'Keynes on the rationality of decision procedures under uncertainty: the investment decision', in J.G.T. Meeks (ed.) *Thoughtful Economic Man: Essays on Rationality, Moral Rules and Benevolence*, Cambridge: Cambridge University Press.

—— (ed.) (1991b) *Thoughtful Economic Man: Essays on Rationality, Moral Rules and Benevolence*, Cambridge: Cambridge University Press.

Meltzer, A.H. (1988) *Keynes's Monetary Theory: A Different Interpretation*, Cambridge: Cambridge University Press.

Merton, R.C. (ed.) (1972) *The Collected Scientific Papers of Paul A. Samuelson*, Vol. 3, Cambridge, Mass., and London: MIT Press.

—— and Samuelson, P.A. (1974) 'Fallacy of the log-normal approximation to optimal portfolio decision making over many periods', *Journal of Financial Economies* 1: 67–94.

Metzler, L.A. (1943) 'Effects of income distribution', *Review of Economic Statistics* 25: 49–57.

—— *et al.* (1948) *Income, Employment and Public Policy: Essays in Honor of Alvin H. Hansen*, New York: W.W. Norton.

Meyer, J.R. and Kuh, E. (1957) *The Investment Decision: An Empirical Study*, Cambridge, Mass.: Harvard University Press.

Milgate, M. (1977) 'Keynes on the "Classical" theory of interest', *Cambridge Journal of Economics* 1: 307–15.

—— (1979) 'On the origin of the notion of "intertemporal equilibrium"', *Economica* 46: 1–10.

—— (1982) *Capital and Employment: A Study of Keynes's Economics*, London: Academic Press.

—— (1987) 'Keynes' *General Theory*', in J. Eatwell, M. Milgate and P. Newman (eds) *The New Palgrave: A Dictionary of Economics*, Vol. 2, London: Macmillan.

Millar, J.R. (1972) 'The social accounting basis of Keynes' aggregate supply functions', *Economic Journal* 82: 600–11.

Miller, E.M. (1984) 'Bank deposits in the monetary theory of Keynes', *Journal of Money, Credit and Banking* 16: 242–6.

Miller, M.H. (1988) 'The Modigliani–Miller propositions after thirty years', *Journal of Economic Perspectives* 2: 99–120.

—— and Modigliani, F. (1961) 'Dividend policy, growth, and the valuation of shares', *Journal of Business* 34: 411–33.

—— and —— (1966) 'Some estimates of the cost of capital to the electric utility industry, 1954–57', *American Economic Review* 56: 333–91.

Miller, M. and Williamson, J. (1987) *Targets and Indicators: A Blueprint for the International Coordination of Economic Policy*, Washington, D.C.: Institute for International Economics.

Mini, P. V. (1991) *Keynes: Bloomsbury and the General Theory*, New York: St Martins Press.

Minsky, H. (1959) 'A linear model of cyclical growth', *Review of Economics and Statistics* 41: 133–45.

—— (1975) *John Maynard Keynes*, New York: Columbia University Press.

—— (1976) *John Maynard Keynes*, London: Macmillan.

—— (1978) 'The financial instability hypothesis: a restatement', *Thames Papers in Political Economy*, Autumn.

—— (1982) *Inflation, Recession and Economic Policy*, Brighton: Wheatsheaf.

Mishkin, F.S. (1976) 'Illiquidity, consumer durable expenditure and monetary policy', *American Economic Review* 66: 642–54.

—— (1977) 'What depressed the consumer? The household balance sheet and the 1973–75 recession', *Brookings Papers in Economic Activity* 1: 123–64.

—— (1982) 'Does anticipated monetary policy matter? An econometric investigation', *Journal of Political Economy* 82: 22–51.

Mittermaier, K.H.M. (1986) 'The hand behind the invisible hand: dogmatic and pragmatic views on free markets and the state of economic theory', unpublished PhD dissertation, University of Witwatersrand.

Modigliani, F. (1944) 'Liquidity preference and the theory of interest and money', *Econometrica* 12: 45–88.

—— (1949) 'Fluctuations in the saving ratio: a problem in economic forecasting', *Social Research* 14: 413–20.

—— (1975) 'The life cycle hypothesis of saving twenty years later', in M. Parkin and A.R. Nobay (eds) *Contemporary Issues in Economics*, Manchester: Manchester University Press.

—— (1977) 'The monetarist controversy; or, should we forsake stabilisation policies?', *American Economic Review* 67: 1–19.

—— and Ando, A. (1957) 'Tests of the life-cycle hypothesis of savings', *Bulletin of the Oxford Institute of Economics and Statistics* 19: 99–124.

—— and Brumberg, R. (1954) 'Utility analysis and the consumption function: an interpretation of cross-section data', in K.K. Kurihara (ed.) *Post-Keynesian Economics*, London: Allen & Unwin.

—— and Miller, M.H. (1958) 'The cost of capital, corporation finance, and the theory of investment', *American Economic Review* 48: 261–97.

—— and —— (1963) 'Corporate income taxes and the cost of capital: a correction', *American Economic Review* 53: 433–43.

—— and Steindel, C. (1977) 'Is a tax rebate an effective tool for stabilization policy?', *Brookings Papers on Economic Activity* 1: 175–203.

Moggridge, D.E. (ed.) (1990) *Perspectives in the History of Economic Thought: Keynes, Macroeconomics and Method*, Aldershot, Hants: Edward Elgar.

—— (1992) *Maynard Keynes: An Economists's Biography*, London: Routledge.

Mongiovi, G. (1990) 'Keynes, Sraffa and Hayek: on the origins of Chapter 17 of the *General Theory*', *Economie appliquée* 43: 131–56.

—— and Rühl, C. (eds) (1993) *Keynes' General Theory nach fünfzig Jahren*, Berlin: Duncker & Humblot.

Moore, Basil J. (1988) *Horizontalists and Verticalists: The Macroeconomics of Credit Money*, Cambridge: Cambridge University Press.

—— (1994) 'The demise of the Keynesian multiplier: a reply to Cottrell', *Journal of Post Keynesian Economics* 17: 121–34.

Moore, G.E. (1903) *Principia Ethica*, Cambridge: Cambridge University Press.

Moore, G.E. and Zarnowitz, V. (1986) 'Major changes in cyclical behaviour', in R. Gordon (ed.) *The American Business Cycle*, Chicago: Chicago University Press.

Morgan, D.P. (1991) 'New evidence firms are financially constrained', *Federal Reserve Bank of Kansas City Quarterly Review* 76: 5.

Morishima, M. (1992) *Capital and Credit: A New Formulation of General Equilibrium Theory*, Cambridge: Cambridge University Press.

Mott, T. (1985–6) 'Towards a Post-Keynesian formulation of liquidity preference', *Journal of Post Keynesian Economics* 8: 222–32.

Muellbauer, J. (1983) 'Surprises in the consumption function', *Economic Journal Conference Papers* 93: 34–49.

—— (1994) 'The assessment: consumer expenditure', *Oxford Review of Economic Policy* 10: 1–41.

Mullineux, A., Dickinson, D. and Peng, W. (1993) *Business Cycles*, Oxford: Blackwell.

Mummery, A.F. and Hobson, J.A. (1889) *The Physiology of Industry*, reprinted New York: Augustus M. Kelley, 1989.

Muth, J.F. (1960) 'Optimal properties of exponentially weighted forecasts', *Journal of the American Statistical Association* 29: 299–306.

—— (1961) 'Rational expectations and the theory of price movements', *Econometrica* 29: 315–35.

Nagatani, H. and Crowley, K. (eds) (1977) *The Collected Scientific Papers of Paul A. Samuelson*, Vol. 4, Cambridge, Mass., and London: MIT Press.

Nash, J.F. (1951) 'Non-cooperative games', *Annals of Mathematics* 54: 286–95.

Neftci, S. (1984) 'Are economic time series asymmetric over the business cycle?', *Journal of Political Economy* 92: 307–28.

Negishi, T. (1979) *Microeconomic Foundations of Keynesian Macroeconomics*, Amsterdam: North-Holland.

Nell, E.J. (1983) 'Keynes after Sraffa: the essential properties of Keynes' theory of interest and money: comment on Kregel', in J.A. Kregel (ed.) *Distribution, Effective Demand and International Economic Relations*, London: Macmillan.

—— (ed.) (1984) *Free Market Conservatism: A Critique of Theory and Practice*, London: Allen & Unwin.

Neumann, J. von and Morgenstern, O. (1944) *Theory of Games and Economic Behaviour*, Princeton, N.J.: Princeton University Press.

Ng, Y.K. (1980) 'Macroeconomics with non-perfect competition', *Economic Journal* 90: 479–92.

—— (1986) *Mesoeconomics*, Brighton: Wheatsheaf.

Nickell, S. and Layard, R. (1985) 'The causes of British unemployment', *National Institute Economic Review* 111: 62–85.

Niehans, J. (1978) *The Theory of Money*, Baltimore, Md: Johns Hopkins University Press.

Nikaido, H. (1975) *Monopolistic Competition and Effective Demand*, Princeton, N.J.: Princeton University Press.

O'Donnell, R. (1982) *Keynes: Philosophy and Economics: An Approach to Rationality and Uncertainty*, PhD dissertation, University of Cambridge.

—— (1989) *Keynes: Philosophy, Economics and Politics. The Philosophical Foundations of Keynes's Thought and their Influence on his Economics and Politics*, London: Macmillan.

—— (1990a) 'An overview of probability, expectations, uncertainty and rationality in Keynes's conceptual framework', *Review of Political Economy* 2: 253–66.

—— (1990b) 'Keynes on mathematics: philosophical foundations and economic applications', *Cambridge Journal of Economics* 14: 29–47.

—— (1990c) 'Continuity in Keynes's conception of probability', in D.E. Moggridge (ed.) *Perpsectives in the History of Economic Thought: Keynes, Macroeconomics and Method*, Aldershot, Hants: Edward Elgar.

O'Donnell, R. (1991a) 'Keynes on probability, expectations and uncertainty', in R.M. O'Donnell (ed.) *Keynes as Philosopher-Economist*, London: Macmillan.

—— (1991b) 'Keynes on mathematical economics and econometrics: some new evidence', Research Paper 344, School of Economic and Financial Studies, Macquarie University.

—— (ed.) (1991c) *Keynes as Philosopher-Economist*, London: Macmillan.

—— (1992) 'The unwritten books and papers of J.M. Keynes', *History of Political Economy* 24: 767–817.

—— (1995a) 'A supplementary edition of J.M. Keynes's writings: rationale, nature and significance', *History of Economics Review* 23, Winter: 61–73.

—— (1995b) 'The genesis of the only diagram in *The General Theory*', Macquarie Economics Research Papers, Macquarie University.

OECD (1978) *Towards Full Employment and Price Stability*, Paris: OECD.

—— (1994a) *Economic Outlook*, Paris: OECD.

—— (1994b) *Labour Force Statistics*, Paris: OECD.

Ohlin, B.G. (1937a) 'Some notes on the Stockholm theory of savings and instrument, Parts I and II', *Economic Journal* 47: 53–69, 221–40.

—— (1937b) 'Alternative theories of the rate of interest', *Economic Journal* 47: 423–7.

Okun, A. (1975) 'Inflation: its mechanics and welfare costs', *Brooking Papers on Economic Activity* 2: 366–73.

—— (1981) *Prices and Quantities*, Princeton, N.J.: Princeton University Press.

Ono, Y. (1994) *Money, Interest and Stagnation*, Oxford: Clarendon Press.

Orcutt, G.H. and Roy, A.D. (1949) *A Bibliography of the Consumption Function*, Cambridge: Department of Applied Economics, mimeo.

Orléan, A. (1989) 'Mimetic contagion and speculative bubbles', *Theory and Decision* 27: 63–92.

Orzech, Z.B. and Groll, S. (1991) 'Otto Bauer's business cycle theory: an integration of Marxian elements', *History of Political Economy* 23: 745–63.

O'Shaughnessy, T.J. (1983) 'On a long-period interpretation of the principle of effective demand', unpublished PhD dissertation, King's College, Cambridge.

—— (1984) 'Short-period and long-period interpretations of the principle of effective demand', Jesus College, Cambridge, mimeo.

Osiatynski, J. (ed.) (1990) *Collected Works of Michael Kalecki*. Vol. 1: *Capitalism: Business Cycles and Full Employment*, Oxford: Clarendon Press.

Panico, C. (1985) 'Market forces and the relationship between the rate of interest and the rate of profits', *Contributions to Political Economy* 4: 37–60.

—— (1987) 'The evolution of Keynes's thought on the rate of interest', *Contributions to Political Economy* 6: 53–61.

—— (1988a) *Interest and Profit in the Theories of Value and Distribution*, London: Macmillan.

—— (1988b) 'Sraffa on money and banking', *Cambridge Journal of Economics* 12: 7–28.

Park, M.S. (1994) 'Long period', in P. Arestis and M. Sawyer (eds) *The Elgar Companion to Radical Political Economy*, Aldershot, Hants: Edward Elgar.

Parkin, M. (1990) *Economics*, Reading, Mass.: Addison-Wesley.

—— and Nobay, A.R. (eds) (1975) *Contemporary Issues in Economics*, Manchester: Manchester University Press.

Pasinetti, L.L. (1962) 'Rate of profit and income distribution in relation to economic growth', *Review of Economic Studies* 29: 267–79.

—— (ed.) (1974) *Growth and Income Distribution: Essays in Economic Theory*, Cambridge: Cambridge University Press.

Pasinetti, L.L. (ed.) (1980) *Essays in the Theory of Joint Production,* New York: Columbia UniversityPress.

—— (1981) *Structural Change and Economic Growth: A Theoretical Essay on the Dynamics of the Wealth of Nations,* Cambridge: Cambridge University Press.

—— (1986) 'Theory of value: a source of alternative paradigms in economic analysis', in M. Baranzini and R. Scazzieri (eds) *Foundations of Economics: Structure of Inquiry and Economic Theory,* Oxford: Blackwell.

—— (1993) *'Structural Economic Dynamics: A Theory of the Economic Consequnce of Human Learning,* Cambridge: Cambridge University Press.

—— *et al.* (1966) 'Symposium on "Paradoxes in Capital Theory"', *Quarterly Journal of Economics* 80: 503–83.

Patinkin, D. (1965) *Money, Interest and Prices: An Integration of Monetary and Value Theory,* New York: Harper & Row.

—— (1972a) 'Interest', in D. Patinkin (ed.) *Studies in Monetary Economics,* New York: Harper & Row.

—— (ed.) (1972b) *Studies in Monetary Economics,* New York: Harper & Row.

—— (1976a) *Keynes's Monetary Thought: A Study of its Development,* Durham, N.C.: Duke University Press.

—— (1976b) 'Keynes and econometrics: on the interaction between the macro-economics revolutions of the interwar period', *Econometrica* 44: 1091–1123.

—— (1978) 'Keynes' misquotation of Mill', *Economic Journal* 88: 341–2.

—— (1982) *Anticipations of* The General Theory?, Chicago, Ill.: University of Chicago Press.

—— (1989) *Money, Interest and Prices,* abridged 2nd edn, Cambridge, Mass.: MIT Press.

—— (1990) 'On different interpretations of *The General Theory', Journal of Monetary Economics* 26: 205–43.

Peston, M. and Corry, B.A. (eds) (1972) *Essays in Honour of Lord Robbins,* London: Weidenfeld & Nicolson.

Pheby, J. (ed.) (1989) *New Directions in Post Keynesian Economics,* Aldershot, Hants: Edward Elgar.

—— (ed.) (1994) *Free-thought in Economics and Politics,* London: Macmillan.

Phelps, E.S. (1967) 'Phillips curves, expectations of inflation and optimal unem-ployment over time', *Economica* 34: 254–81.

—— and Taylor, J.B. (1977) 'Stabilizing powers of monetary policy under rational expectations', *Journal of Political Economy* 85: 163–90.

Phillips, A.W.H. (1958) 'The relationship between unemployment and the rate of change of money wages in the United Kingdom, 1861–1957', *Economica* NS 25: 283–99.

Phillips, H. (1924) 'The theory of social economy, by Gustav Cassel', *Economic Journal* 34: 235–41.

Pigou, A.G. (1936) 'Mr J.M. Keynes' *General Theory of Employment, Interest and Money', Economica* 3: 115–32.

Pindyck, R.S. (1991) 'Irreversibility, uncertainty and investment', *Journal of Economic Literature* 29: 1110–48.

Pissarides, C.A. (1978) 'Liquidity considerations in the theory of consumption', *Quarterly Journal of Economics* 92: 279–96.

Pollin, R. (1991) 'Two theories of money supply endogeneity: some empirical evidence', *Journal of Post Keynesian Economics* 13: 366–96.

Ponsard, C. (1985) 'Fuzzy sets in economics: foundation of soft decision theory', *Management Decision Support Systems* 83.

Prendennis (1992) *Observer,* 21 June.

Presley, J. (ed.) (1992) *Essays in Robertsonian Economics*, Basingstoke, Hants: Macmillan.

Purvis, D. (1971) 'Introducing useful money into a growth model', *Canadian Journal of Economics* 4 (August): 374–81.

Quine, W. (1960) *Word and Object*, Cambridge, Mass.: MIT Press.

—— (1981) *Theories and Things*, Cambridge, Mass.: Belknap Press.

—— (1987) *Quiddities*, Cambridge, Mass.: Belknap Press.

Ramsey, F.P. (1922) 'The Douglas proposals', *Cambridge Magazine* 10: 74–6.

—— (1926) 'Truth and probability', reprinted in R.B. Braithwaite (ed.) *The Foundations of Mathematics*, London: Routledge & Kegan Paul, 1931.

—— (1978) *Foundations of Mathematics*, London: Routledge & Kegan Paul.

Ramsey, J., Sayers, C. and Rothman, P. (1990) 'The statistical properties of dimension calculations using small data sets: some economic applications', *International Economic Review* 31: 991–1020.

Rappaport, P. (1992) 'Meade's general theory model: stability and the role of expectations', *Journal of Money, Credit and Banking* 24: 356–69.

Reddaway, W.B. (1936) '*The General Theory of Employment, Interest and Money* [review]', *Economic Record*, 12: 28–36.

—— (1966) 'Rising prices for ever?', *Lloyds Bank Review*, July.

—— (1983) 'How useful are Keynesian ideas in the 1980s?', *Proceedings of the British Academy* 69: 263–78.

—— (1992) *Portfolio Management for Not-for-profit Institutions*, London: Institute for Public Policy Research.

Reese, D.A. (ed.) (1987) *The Legacy of Keynes*, Nobel Conference XXII, New York: Harper & Row.

Remenyi, J. (1991) *Where Credit is Due*, London: IT Publications.

Riach, P.A. (1995) 'Wage-employment determination in a Post Keynesian world', in P. Arestis and M. Marshall (eds) *The Political Economy of Full Employment: Conservatism, Corporatism, and Institutional Change*, Aldershot, Hants.: Edward Elgar.

Ricardo, D. (1951–73) *Works and Correspondence of David Ricardo*, ed. P. Sraffa and M. Dobb, 11 vols, Cambridge: Cambridge University Press.

Ricci, G. and Vellupillai, K. (eds) (1988) *Growth Cycles and Multisectoral Economics: The Goodwin Tradition*, New York: Springer-Verlag.

Richardson, D.R. (1986) 'Asimakopulos on Kalecki and Keynes on finance, saving and investment', *Cambridge Journal of Economics* 10: 191–9.

Richardson, G.B. (1990) *Information and Investment: A Study of the Working of the Competitive Economy*, 2nd edn, New York: Oxford University Press.

Richter, R. (1990) *Geldtheorie*, 2nd rev. edn, Berlin: Heidelberg.

Roberts, D.L. (1978) 'Patinkin, Keynes, and aggregate supply and demand analysis', *History of Political Economy* 10: 549–76.

Robertson, D.H. (1926) *Banking Policy and the Price Level*, New York: Augustus M. Kelley.

—— (1936) 'Some notes on Mr Keynes' *General Theory of Employment*', *Quarterly Journal of Economics*, 51: 168–91.

—— (1937) 'Alternative theories of the rate of interest', *Economic Journal* 47: 428–36.

—— (1938a) 'Mr Keynes and "finance"', *Economic Journal* 48: 314–18.

—— (1938b) 'Mr Keynes and "finance"', *Economic Journal* 48: 555–6.

—— (1957–9) *Lectures on Economic Principles*, 3 vols, London: Staples Press.

—— (1966) *Essays on Money and Interest*, London: Fontana.

Robinson, J. (1933) *The Economics of Imperfect Competition*, London: Macmillan.

Robinson, J. (1936) 'The long period theory of employment', *Zeitschrift für National-ökonomie* 7: 74–93.

—— (1937) *Essays in the Theory of Employment*, London: Macmillan.

—— (1941) 'Marx on unemployment', *Economic Journal* 51: 234–48.

—— (1942) *An Essay on Marxian Economics*, London: Macmillan.

—— (1951–79) *Collected Economic Papers* [*C.E.P.*], Oxford: Blackwell; general index published 1980.

—— (1951) 'Marx and Keynes', in *Collected Economic Papers*, Vol. I, Oxford: Blackwell.

—— (1952) 'The model of an expanding economy', reprinted in *C.E.P.* II, 2nd edn: 74–8.

—— (1953) *On Re-reading Marx*, reprinted in *C.E.P.* IV: 247–68.

—— (1956) *The Accumulation of Capital*, London: Macmillan.

—— (1960) *Collected Economic Papers*, Vol. II, Oxford: Blackwell.

—— (1961a) 'Prelude to a critique', *Oxford Economic Papers* 13: 53–8.

—— (1961b) 'Own-rates of interest', *Economic Journal* 71: 596–600.

—— (1962a) '*The General Theory* after twenty-five years', *Economic Journal* 72: 690–2.

—— (1962b) *Essays in the Theory of Economic Growth*, London: Macmillan.

—— (1964) 'Kalecki and Keynes', in *C.E.P.* III, 2nd edn: 92–9.

—— (1965) 'Piero Sraffa and the rate of exploitation', *New Left Review*, 31: 128–34; reprinted as 'A reconsideration of the theory of value', *C.E.P.* III: 173–81.

—— (1971a) *Economic Heresies*, New York: Basic Books.

—— (1971b) 'The second crisis in economic theory', in *C.E.P.* IV.

—— (ed.) (1973) *After Keynes*, Oxford: Blackwell.

—— (1974) 'History versus equilibrium', *Thames Papers in Political Economy*, reprinted in *C.E.P.* V: 48–58.

—— (1975a) *Collected Economic Papers*, Vol. II, 2nd edn, Oxford: Blackwell.

—— (1975b) *Collected Economic Papers*, Vol. III, 2nd edn, Oxford: Blackwell.

—— (1977) 'Michal Kalecki', reprinted in C.E.P. V: 184–96.

—— (1979) *Collected Economic Papers*, Vol. V, Oxford: Blackwell.

—— (1980) 'Time in economic theory', *Kyklos* 33: 219–29.

—— (1980, 1985) 'Spring cleaning', mimeo; reprinted as 'The theory of normal prices and the reconstruction of economic theory', in G.R. Feiwel (ed.) *Issues in Contemporary Macroeconomics and Distribution*, London: Macmillan, 1985: 157–65.

—— (1982) 'Shedding darkness', *Cambridge Journal of Economics* 6: 295–6.

Rogers, C. (1989) *Money, Interest and Capital*, Cambridge: Cambridge University Press.

—— (1990) 'The nature and role of equilibrium in Keynes's *General Theory*: an alternative perspective', University of Adelaide, unpublished mimeo.

—— (1993) 'Review of Cardim de Carvalho (Ferdinand J.), *Mr Keynes and The Post Keynesians*', *Economic Journal* 103: 1317.

—— (1994) 'Michael Lawlor's own-rates interpretation of *The General Theory*', in J.B. Davis (ed.) *The State of Interpretation of Keynes*, Dordrecht: Kluwer.

—— (1995) 'Post Keynesian monetary theory and the principle of effective demand', in A.J. Cohen and J. Smithin (eds) *Money, Financial Institutions and Macroeconomics*, Dordrecht: Kluwer.

Rosch, E. (1975) 'Family resemblances: studies in the internal structure of categories', *Cognitive Psychology* 7: 573–605.

Rose, H. (1967) 'On the nonlinear theory of the employment cycle', *Review of Economic Studies* 34: 153–73.

Ross, S.A. (1988) 'Comment on the Modigliani–Miller propositions', *Journal of Economic Perspectives* 2: 127–33.

Ross, S.A., Westerfield, R., Jordan, B. and Roberts, G. (eds) (1993) *Fundamentals of Corporate Finance*, Burr Ridge, Ill.: Irwin.

Rostow, W.W. (1980) *Why the Rich Get Richer and the Poor Slow Down*, Austin, Tex.: University of Texas.

Rotheim, R.J. (1981) 'Keynes's monetary theory of value (1933)', *Journal of Post Keynesian Economics* 3: 568–85.

—— (1993) 'On the indeterminacy of Keynes's monetary theory of value', *Review of Political Economy* 5: 197–216.

—— (ed.) (forthcoming) *New Keynesian Economics: A Post Keynesian Alternative*, London: Routledge.

Rousseas, S. (1986) *Post-Keynesian Monetary Economics*, Basingstoke, Hants: Macmillan.

Rowthorn, R. (1981) 'Demand, real wages and economic growth', *Thames Papers in Political Economy*, Spring.

Ruelle, D. (1991) *Chance and Chaos*, Princeton, N.J.: Princeton University Press.

Runde, J. (1990) 'Keynesian uncertainty and the weight of arguments', *Economics and Philosophy* 6: 275–92.

—— (1991) 'Keynesian uncertainty and the stability of beliefs', *Review of Political Economy* 3: 125–45.

—— (1993) 'Shackle on probability', in S. Boehm, S. Frowen and J. Pheby (eds) *Economics as the Art of Thought: Essays in Memory of G.L.S. Shackle*, London: Routledge.

—— (1994a) 'Keynesian uncertainty and liquidity preference', *Cambridge Journal of Economics* 18: 129–44.

—— (1994b) 'Keynes after Ramsey: in defence of *A Treatise on Probability*', *Studies in the History and Philosophy of Science* 25: 97–121.

—— (1994c) 'The Keynesian probability-relation: in search of a substitute', in J. Davis (ed.) *The State of Interpretation of Keynes*, Dordrecht: Kluwer.

—— (1995) 'Chances and choices: some notes on probability and belief in economic analysis', *Monist* 78: 97–121.

Russell, B. (1923) 'Vagueness', *Australasian Journal of Psychology and Philosophy* 1: 90.

Rymes, T.K. (1980) 'Sraffa and Keynes on interest rates', *Carleton Economic Papers*, Ottawa: Carleton University.

—— (1987) 'Keynes's lectures, 1932–35: notes of students', *Carleton Economics Papers*, Ottawa: Carleton University.

—— (1989a) *Keynes's Lectures, 1932–35: Notes of a Representative Student*, London: Macmillan; Ann Arbor, Mich.: University of Michigan Press.

—— (1989b) 'The theory and the measurement of the nominal output of banks, sectoral rates of saving and wealth in the national accounts', in R.G. Lipsey and H. Stone Tice (eds) *The Measurement of Saving, Investment and Wealth*, Chicago, Ill.: University of Chicago Press.

—— (1989c) 'Keynes's lectures, 1932–35: notes of students', *Carleton Economics Papers*, Ottawa: Carleton University.

—— (1994) 'Keynes and knowledge', in G. Brennan and A.M.C. Waterman (eds) *Economics and Religion: Are They Distinct?*, Boston, Mass.: Kluwer.

Salter, W.E.G. (1960) *Productivity and Technical Change*, Cambridge: Cambridge University Press; 2nd edn, with Addendum by W.B. Reddaway, 1966.

Samuels, W.J. and Biddle, J. (eds) (1993) *Research in the History of Economic Thought and Methodology*, Greenwich, Conn., and London: JAI Press.

Samuelson, P.A. (1939) 'A synthesis of the principle of acceleration and the multiplier', *Journal of Political Economy* 47: 786–97.

—— (1946) 'The General Theory', *Econometrica* 14: 187–200.

BIBLIOGRAPHY

Samuelson, P.A. (1947a) 'The General Theory (3)', in S.E. Harris (ed.) The New Economics: Keynes's Influence on Theory and Policy, New York: Alfred A. Knopf.
—— (1947b) Foundations of Economic Analysis, Cambridge, Mass.: Harvard University Press.
—— (1948) Economics: An Introductory Analysis, New York: McGraw-Hill.
—— (1966–86) The Collected Scientific Papers of Paul A. Samuelson, 5 vols, ed. J.E. Stiglitz (Vols 1 and 2, 1966), R.C. Merton (Vol. 3, 1972), H. Nagatani and K. Crowley (Vol. 4, 1977), K.Crowley (Vol. 5, 1986), Cambridge, Mass. and London: MIT Press.
—— (1983) 'Sympathy from the other Cambridge', Economist 287: 21–5.
Sardoni, C. (1981) 'Multisectoral models of balanced growth and the Marxian schemes of expanded reproduction', Australian Economic Papers 20: 383–97.
—— (1987) Marx and Keynes on Economic Recession, Brighton, Sussex: Wheatsheaf.
—— (1989) 'Some aspects of Kalecki's theory of profits: its relationship to Marx's schemes of reproduction', in M. Sebastiani (ed.) Kalecki's Relevance Today, London: Macmillan, 206–19.
—— (1991) 'Marx and Keynes: the critique of Say's Law', in G.A. Caravale (ed.) Marx and Modern Economic Analysis, Aldershot, Hants: Edward Elgar, 219–39.
—— (1992a) 'Market forms and effective demand: Keynesian results with perfect competition', Review of Political Economy 4: 377–95.
—— (ed.) (1992b) On Political Economists and Modern Political Economy: Selected Essays of G.C. Harcourt, London: Routledge.
Sargent, T.J. (1978) 'Estimation of dynamic labour demand schedules under rational expectations', in R.E. Lucas, Jr and T.J. Sargent, Jr, Rational Expectations and Econometric Practice, London: George Allen & Unwin, 429–500.
—— (1979) Macroeconomic Theory, Orlando, Fla.: Academic Press.
—— (1981) 'Interpreting economic time series', Journal of Political Economy 89: 213–48.
—— (1984) 'Autoreggressions, expectations and policy advice', American Economic Review 74: 408–15.
—— (1993) Bounded Rationality in Macroeconomics, Oxford: Clarendon Press.
—— and Wallace, N. (1973) 'Rational expectations and the dynamics of hyperinflation', International Economic Review 14: 328–50.
—— and —— (1975) '"Rational" expectations: the optimal monetary instrument and the optimal money supply rule', Journal of Political Economy 83: 241–54.
—— and —— (1976) 'Rational expectations and the theory of economic policy', Journal of Monetary Economics 2: 169–83.
Sawyer, M. (1985) The Economics of Michal Kalecki, London: Macmillan.
—— (1992a) 'The relationship between Keynes's macroeconomic analysis and theories of imperfect competition', in B. Gerrard and J. Hillard (eds) The Philosophy and Economics of J.M. Keynes, Aldershot, Hants: Edward Elgar.
—— (1992b) 'On imperfect competition and macroeconomic analysis', in A. DelMonte, Recent Developments in the Theory of Industrial Organisation, London: Macmillan.
Sayers, C. (1987) 'Diagnostic tests for nonlinearity in time series data: an application for the work stopping series', University of Houston, mimeo.
Scarf, H. (1960) 'Some examples of global instability of the competitive equilibrium', International Economic Review 1: 157–72.
Schefold, B. (1979) 'Fixes Kapital als Kuppelprodukt und die Analyse der Akkumulation bei unterschiedlichen Formen des technischen Fortschritts', in Gesellschaft, Beiträge zur Marxistischen Theorie 13, Edition Suhrkamp, Vol. 692, Frankfurt: Suhrkamp.

481

Schefold, B. (1980) 'Fixed capital as a joint product and the analysis of accumulation with different forms of technical progress', in L.L. Pasinetti (ed.) *Essays in the Theory of Joint Production*, New York: Columbia University Press.

—— (1987) 'Joint production in linear models', in J. Eatwell, M. Milgate and P. Newman (eds) *The New Palgrave: A Dictionary of Economics*, Vol. 2, London: Macmillan.

—— (1991) 'Einleitung zur Neuausgabe von Irving Fisher *The Nature of Capital and Interest*', in B. Schefold (ed.) *Irving Fisher* The Nature of Capital and Interest. *Vademecum zu einem Klassiker der Zinstheorie*, Düsseldorf: Verlag Wirtschaft und Finanzen.

—— (1995a) 'Die Relevanz der Cambridge-Theorie für die ordnungspolitische Diskussion', in B. Schefold (ed.) *Wirtschaftsstile*. Band 2: *Studien zur ökonomischen Theorie und zur Zukunft der Technik*, Frankfurt a.M.: Fischer Taschenbuch Verlag.

—— (1995b) 'Überlegungen zu einer neowalrasianischen, marshallianischen und klassischen Mikrofundierung der Theorie der effektiven Nachfrage', in B. Schefold (ed.) *Wirtschaftsstile*. Band 2: *Studien zur ökonomischen Theorie und zur Zukunft der Technik*, Frankfurt a.M.: Fischer Taschenbuch Verlag.

Scheinkman, J. and LeBaron, B. (1989) 'Nonlinear dynamics and stock returns', *Journal of Business* 62: 311–37.

Schinasi, B. (1981) 'A nonlinear dynamic model of short-run fluctuations', *Review of Economic Studies* 48: 649–56.

Schnadt, N. and Whittaker, J. (1993) 'Inflation-proof currency? The feasibility of variable commodity standards', *Journal of Money, Credit, and Banking* 25: 214–21.

—— (1995) 'Is indirect convertibility impossible?', *Journal of Money, Credit, and Banking* 27: 297–8.

Schneider, M. (1987) 'Underconsumption', in J. Eatwell, M. Milgate and P. Newman (eds) *The New Palgrave: A Dictionary of Economics*, Vol. 4, London: Macmillan.

Schumpeter, J.A. (1911) *Theorie der wirtschaftlichen Entwicklung*, Leipzig: Duncker & Humblot; English trans. in *The Theory of Economic Development*, Oxford: Oxford University Press, 1934.

—— (1936) 'Review of Keynes's *General Theory*', *Journal of the American Statistical Association* 31: 791–5.

—— (1942) *Capitalism, Socialism and Democracy*, New York: Harper & Row.

—— (1946a) 'Keynes and statistics', *Review of Economics and Statistics* 28: 194–6.

—— (1946b) 'John Maynard Keynes, 1883–1946', *American Economic Review* 36: 495–518.

—— (1954) *History of Economic Analysis*, London: Allen & Unwin.

Schwartz, J. (ed.) (1977) *The Subtle Anatomy of Capitalism*, Santa Monica, Calif.: Goodyear.

Scott, A.D. (1953) 'Notes on user cost', *Economic Journal* 63: 368–84.

Sebastiani, M. (ed.) (1989) *Kalecki's Relevance Today*, London: Macmillan.

Selgin, G.A. and White, L.H. (1994) 'How would the invisible hand handle money?', *Journal of Economic Literature* 32: 1718–49.

Semmler, W. (ed.) (1986) *Competition, Instability and Nonlinear Cycles*, New York: Springer-Verlag.

—— (1987) 'A macroeconomic limit cycle with financial perturbations', *Journal of Economic Behaviour and Organisation* 8: 469–95.

—— (ed.) (1989) *Financial Dynamics and Business Cycles: New Perspectives*, Armonk, N.Y.: Sharpe.

Shackle, G.L.S. (1951) 'Twenty years on: a survey of the theory of the multiplier', *Economic Journal* 59: 241–60.

Shackle, G.L.S. (1955) *Uncertainty in Economics and Other Reflections*, Cambridge: Cambridge University Press.

—— (1965) *A Scheme of Economic Theory*, Cambridge: Cambridge University Press.

—— (1967) *The Years of High Theory*, Cambridge: Cambridge University Press.

—— (1972) *Epistemics and Economics*, Cambridge: Cambridge University Press.

—— (1974) *Keynesian Kaleidics*, Edinburgh: Edinburgh University Press.

—— (1979) *Imagination and the Nature of Choice*, Edinburgh: Edinburgh University Press.

—— (1983) 'An interview with G.L.S. Shackle', *Austrian Economics Newsletter* 4: 1, 5–8.

Shapiro, N. (1995) 'Markets and mark-ups: Keynesian views', in S. Dow and J. Hillard (eds) *Keynes, Knowledge and Uncertainty*, Aldershot, Hants: Edward Elgar.

Shepherd, A., Turk, J.S. and Silbertson, A. (eds) (1983) *Microeconomic Efficiency and Macroeconomic Performance*, Oxford: Philip Allan.

Sherman, H. (1991) *Business Cycles*, Princeton, N.J.: Princeton University Press.

Shove, G.F. (1942) 'The place of Marshall's *Principles* in the development of economic theory', *Economic Journal* 52: 294–329.

Sichel, D. (1991) 'Business cycle duration dependence: a parametric approach', *Review of Economics and Statistics* 73: 254–60.

Simmons, G.F. (1963) *Introduction to Topology and Modern Analysis*, New York: McGraw-Hill.

Simon, H.A. (1957) *Models of Man*, New York: John Wiley.

—— (1959) 'Theories of decision making in economics and behavioural science', *American Economic Review* 49: 253–83.

—— (1976) 'From substantive to procedural rationality', in S.J. Latsis (ed.) *Method and Appraisal in Economics*, Cambridge: Cambridge University Press.

—— (1982) *Models of Bounded Rationality*, Cambridge, Mass.: MIT Press.

——, Egidi, M., Marris, R. and Viale, R. (1992) *Economics, Bounded Rationality and the Cognitive Revolution*, Aldershot, Hants: Edward Elgar.

Sims, C.A. (1982) 'Policy analysis with econometric modes', *Brookings Papers on Economic Activity* 1: 107–52.

—— (1986a) 'A rational expectations framework for short run policy analysis', in W.A. Barnett and K.J. Singleton (eds) *New Approaches to Monetary Economics: Proceedings of the Second International Symposium in Economic Theory and Econometrics*, Cambridge: Cambridge University Press.

—— (1986b) 'Are forecasting models usable for policy analysis?', *Federal Reserve Bank of Minneapolis Quarterly Review* 10: 2–15.

Skidelsky, R. (1983) *John Maynard Keynes*. Vol. I: *Hopes Betrayed, 1883–1920*, London: Macmillan.

—— (1989) 'Keynes and the state', in D. Helm (ed.) *The Economic Borders of the State*, Oxford: Oxford University Press.

—— (1992) *John Maynard Keynes*. Vol. II: *The Economist as Saviour, 1920–1937*, London: Macmillan.

—— (1995a) 'The role of ethics in Keynes's economics', in S. Brittan and A. Hamlin (eds) *Market Capitalism and Moral Values*, Aldershot, Hants: Edward Elgar.

—— (1995b) 'J.M. Keynes and the quantity theory of money', in M. Blaug *et al. The Quantity Theory of Money*, Aldershot, Hants: Edward Elgar.

Skott, P. (1989) 'Effective demand, class struggle, and economic growth', *International Economic Review* 30: 231–47.

Slutsky, E. (1927) *The Summation of Random Causes as the Source of Cyclical Processes*,

Vol. III, no. 1, Moscow: Conjuncture Institute; reprinted in *Econometrica* 5 (1937): 105–46.

Smith, A. (1776) *An Enquiry into the Nature and Causes of the Wealth of Nations*, reprinted New York: Modern Library, 1937.

Smithson, M. (1988) 'Fuzzy sets theory and the social sciences: the scope for application', *Fuzzy Sets and Systems* 26: 12–15.

Snippe, J. (1987) 'Intertemporal coordination and the economics of Keynes: comment on Garrison', *History of Political Economy* 19: 329–41.

Snower, D. (1984) 'Imperfect competition, underemployment and crowding out', *Oxford Economic Papers* 36: 177–99.

Solow, R.M. (1956) 'A contribution to the theory of economic growth', *Quarterly Journal of Economics* 70: 65–94.

—— (1957) 'Technical change and the aggregate production function', *Review of Economics and Statistics*, 39: 312–20.

—— (1984) 'Mr Hicks and the Classics', *Oxford Economic Papers* 36: 13–25.

—— (1986) 'Monopolistic competition and the multiplier', in W. Heller (ed.) *Essays in Honour of Kenneth Arrow*, Vol. 2, Cambridge: Cambridge University Press.

Sonnenschein, H. (1972) 'Market excess demand functions', *Econometrica* 40: 549–63.

—— (1987) 'Oligopoly and game theory', in J. Eatwell, M. Milgate and P. Newman (eds) *The New Palgrave: A Dictionary of Economics*, Vol. 3, London: Macmillan.

Soper, C.S. (1956) 'The supply curve in Keynesian economics', *South African Journal of Economics* 24: 1–8.

Speight, A.E.H. (1990) *Comsumption, Rational Expectations and Liquidity: Theory and Evidence*, Hemel Hempstead, Herts.: Harvester Wheatsheaf.

Springer, W.L. (1977) 'Consumer spending and the rate of inflation', *Review of Economics and Statistics* 59: 299–306.

Sraffa, P. (1932a) 'Dr Hayek on money and capital', *Economic Journal* 42: 42–53.

—— (1932b) 'A rejoinder', *Economic Journal* 42: 249–51.

—— (1960) *Production of Commodities by Means of Commodities: Prelude to a Critique of Economic Theory*, Cambridge: Cambridge University Press.

—— (1961) 'Comment', in F. Lutz and D.C. Hague (eds) *The Theory of Capital*, London: Macmillan, 305–6.

—— (1962) 'Production of commodities: a comment', *Economic Journal* 72: 477–9.

—— (1993) 'Monetary inflation in Italy during and after the war', trans. W.J. Harcourt and C. Sardoni, *Cambridge Journal of Economics* 17: 7–26.

Stadermann, H.J. and Steiger, O. (eds) (1993) *Der Stand und die nächste Zukunft der Geldforschung*, Berlin: Duncker & Humblot.

Staehle, H. (1937) 'Short-period variations in the distribution of incomes', *Review of Economic Statistics* 19: 133–43.

—— (1938) 'New considerations on the distribution of incomes and the propensity to consume (partly in reply to Mr Dirks)', *Review of Economic Statistics* 20: 134–41.

—— (1939) 'A rejoinder', *Review of Economic Statistics* 21: 129–30.

Stanners, W. (1993) 'Is low inflation an important condition for high growth?', *Cambridge Journal of Economics* 17: 79–107.

Startz, R. (1989) 'Monopolistic competition as a foundation for Keynesian macroeconomic models', *Quarterly Journal of Economics* 104: 738–52.

Steindl, J. (1952) *Maturity and Stagnation in American Capitalism*, Oxford: Blackwell.

—— (1985) 'J.M. Keynes: society and the economist', in F. Vicarelli (ed.) *Keynes's Relevance Today*, London: Macmillan.

Stiglitz, J.E. (ed.) (1966) *The Collected Scientific Papers of Paul A. Samuelson*, Vols 1 and 2, Cambridge, Mass., and London: MIT Press.

—— (1984) 'Price rigidities and market structure', *American Economic Review* 74 (proceedings): 350–5.

—— (1988) 'Why financial structure matters', *Journal of Economic Perspectives* 2: 121–6.

—— (1993) 'New and old Keynesians', *Journal of Economic Perspectives* 7: 43–4.

—— and Weiss, A. (1981) 'Credit rationing in markets with imperfect information', *American Economic Review* 71: 393–410.

Stigum, B.P. (1990) *Towards a Formal Science of Economics: The Axiomatic Method in Economics and Econometrics*, Cambridge: Mass.: MIT Press.

Stone, R. (1978) *Keynes, Political Arithmetic and Econometrics*, Proceedings of the British Academy, Vol. 64, Oxford: Oxford University Press.

—— (1991) 'The ET interview', *Econometric Theory* 7: 85–123.

—— and Stone, W.M. (1938) 'The marginal propensity to consume and the multiplier: a statistical investigation', *Review of Economic Studies* 6: 1–24.

Strachey, J. (1935) *The Nature of Capitalist Crisis*, London: Victor Gollancz.

Studart, R. (1995) *Investment Finance in Economic Development*, London: Routledge.

Suits, D.B. (1963) 'The determinants of consumer expenditure: a review of present knowledge', in *Impacts of Monetary Policy: Commission on Money and Credit*, Englewood Cliffs, N.J.: Prentice Hall.

Summers, L. (1986) 'Some skeptical observations on real business cycle theory', *Federal Reserve Bank of Minneapolis Quarterly Review* Autumn: 23–7.

Swan, T.W. (1956) 'Economic growth and capital accumulation', *Economic Record* 32: 334–61.

Sweezy, P.M. (1942) *The Theory of Capitalist Development*, New York: Oxford University Press.

—— (1963) 'The first quarter century', in R. Lekachmann (ed.) *Keynes' General Theory*, London: Macmillan.

—— (1991) '*Monopoly Capital* after twenty-five years', *Monthly Review* 43(7): 52–7.

Sylos-Labini, P. (1956) *Oligopoly and Technical Progress*; English trans. Cambridge, Mass.: Harvard University Press, 1969.

—— (1987) 'Oligopoly', in J. Eatwell, M. Milgate and P. Newman (eds) *The New Palgrave: A Dictionary of Economics*, Vol. 3, London: Macmillan.

Targetti, F. and Kinda-Hass, B. (ed. and trans.) (1982) 'Kalecki's review of Keynes' *General Theory*', *Australian Economic Papers* 21: 244–60.

—— and Thirlwall, A.P. (eds) (1983) *Further Essays on Economic Theory and Policy*, London: Duckworth.

Tarshis, L. (1939) 'Changes in real and money wages', *Economic Journal* 49: 150–4.

—— (1948) 'An exposition of Keynesian economics', *American Economic Review* 38: 261–72.

—— (1979) 'The aggregate money supply function in Keynes's *General Theory*', in M.J. Boskin (ed.) *Economics and Human Welfare: Essays in Honor of Tibor Scitovsky* New York: Academic Press.

—— (1989) 'Keynes's cooperative economy and his aggregate supply function', in J. Pheby (ed.) *New Directions in Post Keynesian Economics*, Aldershot, Hants: Edward Elgar.

Terzi, A. (1986–7) 'The independence of finance from saving: a flow of funds interpretation', *Journal of Post Keynesian Economics* 9: 188–97.

Tew, B. (1953) 'Keynesian accountancy', *Yorkshire Bulletin of Economic and Social Research* 5: 147–53.

Thirlwall, A.P. (1979) 'The balance of payments constraint as an explanation of international growth rate difference', *Banca Nazionale del Lavoro Quarterly Review* 128: 45–53.

Thomas, J.J. (1989) 'The early econometric history of the consumption function', *Oxford EconomicPapers* 41: 131–49.

—— (1992) 'Income distribution and the estimation of the consumption function: an historical analysis of the early arguments', *History of Political Economy* 24: 153–81.

Thomas, R.L. (1993) *Introductory Econometrics: Theory and Applications*, 2nd edn, London: Longman.

Thrift, N. (1990) 'The making of a capitalist time consciousness', in J. Hassard (ed.) *Sociology of Time*, London: Macmillan.

Thweatt, W.O. (1983) 'Keynes on Marx's *Das Kapital*', *History of Political Economy* 15: 617–20.

Timlin, M.F. (1942) *Keynesian Economics*, Toronto: University of Toronto Press.

Tinbergen, J. (1940) 'On a method of stastical business-cycle research: a reply', *Economic Journal* 50: 141–54.

Tirole, J. (1982) 'On the possibility of speculation under rational expectations', *Econometrica* 50: 1163–81.

Tobin, J. (1955) 'A dynamic aggregative model', *Journal of Political Economy* 63(1): 103–15.

—— (1958) 'Liquidity preference as behaviour towards risk', *Review of Economic Studies* 25: 65–86.

—— (1969) 'A general equilibrium approach to monetary theory', *Journal of Money, Credit, and Banking* 1: 15–29.

—— (1972) 'Inflation and unemployment', *American Economic Review* 62: 1–19.

—— (1975) 'Keynesian models of recession and depression', *American Economic Review* 65: 195–202.

—— (1978) 'A proposal for international monetary reform', *Eastern Economic Journal* 4: 153–9.

—— (1980a) *Asset Accumulation and Economic Activity: Reflections on Contemporary Macroeconomic Theory*, Oxford: Blackwell.

—— (1980b) 'Are New Classical models plausible enough to guide policy?', *Journal of Money, Credit, and Banking* 12: 788–99.

—— (1982) 'Money and finance in the macroeconomic process', *Journal of Money, Credit and Banking* 14: 171–204.

—— (1983) 'Comment', in J. Trevithick and D. Worswick (eds) *Keynes and the Modern World*, Cambridge: Cambridge University Press.

—— (1987) 'Fisher, Irving', in J. Eatwell, M. Milgate and P. Newman (eds) *The New Palgrave: A Dictionary of Economics*, Vol. 2, London: Macmillan.

—— (1988) 'The future of Keynesian economics', *Eastern Economic Journal* 12: 347–58.

—— (1993) 'Price flexibility and output stability: an old Keynesian view', *Journal of Economic Perspectives* 7: 45–65.

—— (1994) 'Price flexibility and output stability: an old Keynesian view', in W. Semmler (ed.) *Business Cycles: Theory and Empirical Methods*, Boston, Mass.: Kluwer Academic.

Torr, C.S.W. (1992) 'The dual role of user cost in the derivation of Keynes's aggregate supply function', *Review of Political Economy* 4: 1–17.

Torre, V. (1977) 'Existence of limit cycles and control in complete Keynesian systems by theory of bifurcations', *Econometrica* 45: 1457–66.

Townend, J.C. (1976) 'The personal saving ratio', *Bank of England Quarterly Bulletin* 16: 53–73.

Townshend, H. (1937) 'Liquidity-premium and the theory of value', *Economic Journal* 47: 157–69.

Trautwein, H.M. (1993) 'A fundamental controversy about money: Post-Keynesian and new monetary economics', in G. Mongiovi and C. Rühl (eds) *Macroeconomic Theory: Diversity and Convergence*, Aldershot, Hants: Edward Elgar.

Treasury and Civil Serviced Select Committee (1993) *The Role of the Bank of England*, Committee Reports Vols I and II, London: HMSO.

Trevithick, J. (1992) *Involuntary Unemployment: Macroeconomics from a Keynesian Perspective*, Hemel Hempstead, Herts.: Harvester Wheatsheaf.

—— (1994) 'The monetary prerequisites for the multiplier: an adumbration of the crowding-out hypothesis', *Cambridge Journal of Economics* 18: 77–90.

—— and Worswick, D. (eds) (1983) *Keynes and the Modern World*, Cambridge: Cambridge University Press.

Tuchscherer, T. (1979) 'Keynes' model and the Keynesians: a synthesis', *Journal of Post Keynesian Economics* 1: 96–109.

Turvey, R. (1965) 'Does the rate of interest rule the roost?', in F. Hahn and F.P.R. Brechling (eds) *The Theory of the Rate of Interest*, London: Macmillan.

Tutin, C. (1988) 'Intérêt et ajustement: le débat Hayek–Keynes (1931–32)', *Economie appliquée* 41: 247–87.

United Nations (UN) (1993) *System of National Accounts*, New York: UNO.

United States Bureau of Census (1959) *Statistical Abstract of the United States, 1959*, Washington, D.C.: USGPO.

van der Ploeg, F. (1983) 'Predator–prey and neoclassical models of cyclical growth', *Zeischrift für Nationalökonomie* 43: 235–56.

van Fraassen, B.C. (1989) *Laws and Symmetry*, Oxford: Clarendon Press.

Velupillai, K. (ed.) (1995) *Inflation, Institutions and Information*, London: Macmillan.

Vercelli, A. (1991) *Methodological Foundations of Macroeconomics: Keynes and Lucas*, Cambridge: Cambridge University Press.

—— (1994) 'Por una macroeconomia nao reductionista: una perspectiva de longo prazo', *Economia e Sociedade* 3: 3–19.

—— (1995a) 'Economia e fisica', in A. Boitani and G. Rodano (eds) *Relazioni Pericolose. L'avventura dell'economia nella cultura contemporanea*, Bari: Laterza.

—— (1995b) 'Coherence, meaning and responsibility in the language of economics', paper presented at the conference on 'The Language of Science' at the University of Bologna, 25–27 October 1995, forthcoming in the *Proceedings of the Conference*.

—— and Dimitri, N. (eds) (1992) *Macroeconomics: A Survey of Research Strategies*, Oxford: Oxford University Press.

Vicarelli, F. (1984) *Keynes: The Instability of Capitalism*, New York: Macmillan.

—— (ed.) (1985) *Keynes's Relevance Today*, London: Macmillan.

Viner, J. (1936) 'Mr Keynes on the causes of unemployment', *Quarterly Journal of Economics* 51: 147–67.

Walker, D.A. (1984) *Money and Markets*, Cambridge: Cambridge University Press.

—— (1987a) 'Edgeworth versus Walras on the theory of tatonnement', *Eastern Economic Journal* 13: 155–65.

—— (1987b) 'Leon Walras', in J. Eatwell, M. Milgate and P. Newman (eds) *The New Palgrave, A Dictionary of Economics*, Vol. 4, London: Macmillan.

—— (ed.) (1989) *Perspectives in the History of Economic Thought*, Vol. II, Aldershot, Hants.: Edward Elgar.

Wallace, N. (1983) 'A legal restrictions theory of the demand for money and the role of monetary policy', *Federal Reserve Bank of Minneapolis Quarterly Review*, Winter: 1–7.

BIBLIOGRAPHY

Wallis, K.F., Andrews, M.J., Bell, D.N.F., Fisher, P.G. and Whitley, J.D. (1984) *Models of the UK Economy: A Review by the ESRC Macroeconomic Modelling Bureau*, Oxford; Oxford University Press.

—, Fisher, P.G., Longbottom, J.A., Turner, D.S. and Whitley, J.D. (1986) *Models of the UK Economy: A Fourth Review by the ESRC Macroeconomic Modelling Bureau*, Oxford: Oxford University Press.

—, Andrews, M.J., Fisher, P.G., Longbottom, J.A. and Whitley, J.D. (1987) *Models of the UK Economy: A Fifth Review by the ESRC Macroeconomic Modelling Bureau*, Oxford: Oxford University Press.

Walras, L. (1874) *Elements of Pure Economics*, trans and annotated W. Jaffe, Homewood, Ill.: Richard D. Irwin, 1954.

Warming, J. (1932) 'The financing of public works: a note', *Economic Journal* 42: 492–5.

Wärneryd, K. (1989) 'Legal restrictions and the evolution of the media of exchange', *Journal of Institutional and Theoretical Economics* 145: 613–26.

—— (1990) 'Legal restrictions and monetary evolution', *Journal of Economic Behaviour and Organisation* 13: 117–24.

Weil, P. (1990) 'Nonexpected utility in macroeconomics', *Quarterly Journal of Economics* 105: 29–42.

Weinberg, S. (1995) 'Reductionism redux', *New York Review of Books* 42: 39–42.

Weintraub, R. (1979) *Microfoundations*, Cambridge: Cambridge University Press.

Weintraub, S. (1949) *Price Theory*, New York: Pitman.

—— (1956) 'A macroeconomic approach to the theory of wages', *American Economic Review* 46: 835–56.

—— (1957) 'The micro foundations of aggregate demand and supply', *Economic Journal* 67: 455–70.

Weisskopf, T. (1979) 'Marxism crisis theory and the rate of profit in the post-war US economy', *Cambridge Journal of Economics* 3: 340–77.

Wells, P. (ed.) (1995) *Post Keynesian Economic Theory*, Boston, Mass.: Kluwer.

Wennerberg, H. (1967) 'The concept of family resemblance in Wittgenstein's later philosophy', *Theoria* 33: 107–32.

Westin, R.B. (1975) 'Empirical implications of infrequent purchase behavior in a stock adjustment model', *American Economic Review* 65: 384–96.

Whitaker, J. (1975) *The Early Writings of Alfred Marshall: 1867–90*, 2 vols, New York: Free Press.

White, L. (1984) 'Competitive payments systems and the unit of account', *American Economic Review* 74: 699–712.

—— (1986) 'Competitive payments systems: reply', *American Economic Review* 76: 850–3.

—— (1987) 'Accounting for non-interest bearing currency: a critique of the legal restrictions theory of money', *Journal of Money, Credit, and Banking* 19: 448–56.

—— (1989) *Competition and Currency: Essays on Free Banking and Money*, New York: New York University Press.

Whitley, J. (1994) *A Course in Macroeconomic Modelling and Forecasting*, Hemel Hempstead, Herts.: Harvester Wheatsheaf.

Wickens, M.R. and Molana, H. (1984) 'Stochastic life cycle theory with varying interest rates and prices', *Economic Journal Conference Papers* 94: 133–47.

Wicksell, K. (1935) *Lectures on Political Economy*, 2 vols, New York: Macmillan.

—— (1936) *Interest and Prices: A Study of the Causes Regulating the Value of Money*, London: Macmillan.

Wiggins, S. (1990) *Introduction to Applied Nonlinear Dynamical Systems and Chaos*, New York: Springer-Verlag.

Williamson, J. (1987) 'Exchange rate management: the role of target zones', *American Economic Review* 77: 200–4.

Winnett, A. (1992) 'Some semantics of endogeneity', in P. Arestis and V. Chick (eds) *Recent Developments in Post Keynesian Economics*, Aldershot, Hants: Edward Elgar.

Winslow, T. (1986) 'Keynes and Freud: psychoanalysis and Keynes's account of the "animal spirits" of capitalism', *Social Research* Winter: 549–78.

Wittgenstein, L. (1921) *Tractatus Logico-philosophicus*, English trans. D. Pears and B. McGuiness, New York: Routledge & Kegan Paul, 1961.

—— (1953) *Philosophical Investigations*, Oxford: Blackwell; 2nd edn rev., 1958.

—— (1974) *Letters to Russell, Keynes and Moore*, Oxford: Blackwell.

—— (1975) *Philosophical Remarks*, trans. R. Hargreaves and R. White, Chicago, Ill.: Chicago University Press.

Wojnilower, A.M. (1980) 'The central role of credit crunches in recent financial history', *Brookings Papers on Economic Activity* 2: 277–326.

Wolf, A. (1986) 'Quantifying chaos with Lyapunov exponents', in A. Holden (ed.) *Chaos*, Princeton, N.J.: Princeton University Press.

Wood, A. (1975) *A Theory of Profits*, Cambridge: Cambridge University Press.

Woodford, M. (1990) 'The optimum quantity of money', in B.M. Friedman and F.H. Hahn (eds) *Handbook of Monetary Economics*, Amsterdam: North-Holland.

—— (1992) 'Self fulfilling expectations and fluctuations in aggregate demand', in N.G. Mankiw and D. Romer (eds) *New Keynesian Economics*, Vol. 2, Cambridge, Mass.: MIT Press.

Worswick, G.D.N. (1991) *Unemployment: A Problem of Policy*, Cambridge: Cambridge University Press, for the National Institute of Economic and Social Research.

—— and Trevithick, J. (eds) (1983) *Keynes and the Modern World*, Cambridge: Cambridge University Press.

Wray, L.R. (1990) *Money and Credit in Capitalist Economies: The Endogenous Money Approach*, Aldershot, Hants: Edward Elgar.

—— (1991) 'Boulding's balloons: a contribution to monetary theory', *Journal of Economic Issues* 25: 1–20.

Yang, R.-S. and Brorsen, W.B. (1993) 'Nonlinear dynamics of daily futures prices: conditional heteroskedasticity or chaos?', *Journal of Futures Markets* 13(2): 175–91.

Yeager, L.B. (1989) 'A competitive payments system: some objections considered', *Journal of Post Keynesian Economics* 11: 370–7.

Young, W. (1987) *Interpreting Mr Keynes: The IS–LM Enigma*, London: Polity Press.

Zadeh, L. (1973) 'Outline of a new approach to the analysis of complex systems and decision processes', *Institute of Electrical and Electronics Engineers Transactions on Systems, Man, and Cybernetics* SMC-3: 28–44.

—— (1975) 'Fuzzy logic and approximate reasoning', *Synthese* 30: 407–28.

Zarnowitz, V. (1992) *Business Cycles: Theory, History, Indicators, and Forecasting*, Chicago, Ill.: Chicago University Press.

—— and Moore, G. (1986) 'Major changes in cyclical behaviour', in R. Gordon (ed.) *The American Business Cycle*, Chicago, Ill.: Chicago University Press.

Zeitlin, I. (1967) *Marxism: A Re-examination*, New York: Van Nostrand.

Zellner, A., Huang, D.S. and Chau, L.C. (1965) 'Further analysis of the short-run consumption function with emphasis on the role of liquid assets', *Econometrica* 33: 571–81.

NAME INDEX

491

SUBJECT INDEX

Printed and bound by CPI Group (UK) Ltd, Croydon, CR0 4YY

08/05/2025

01864427-0001